AF884283

SUNAN ABU DAWUD

ENGLISH TRANSLATION WITH
EXPLANATORY NOTES

by

AḤMAD HASAN
Professor, Islamic Research Institute
Islamia University, Islamabad

Volume I (Chapters 1-518)

KITAB BHAVAN
New Delhi-110002

SUNAN ABU DAWUD (Vol. I)

KITAB BHAVAN
Publishers, Distributors, Exporters & Importers
1784, Kalan Mahal, Darya Ganj,
New Delhi - 1100 02 (India)

Phones : +91-11-23277392, 23274686
Fax : (+91-11) 23263383
Mob. ✆ : +91-11-9953098606

Website : www.kitabbhavan.net
E-mail : info@kitabbhavan.net

Reprint : 2020

ISBN-10 : 81-7151-113-9 (Set)
ISBN-13 : 978-81-7151-113-6 (Set)

ISBN-10 : 81-7151-114-7 (Vol. I)
ISBN-13 : 978-81-7151-114-3 (Vol. I)

Book Code No. : ZZZ014 (Set)
Book Code No. : S000018 (Vol. I)

Printed & Published in India by :

Moonis Ali Nasri for KITAB BHAVAN
1784, Kalan Mahal, Darya Ganj,
New Delhi - 1100 02 [India]

INTRODUCTION

Imām Abū Dāwūd

His Life and Work. His name was Sulaimān. His genealogy is as follows: Sulaimān b. al-Ash'ath b. Isḥāq b. Bashīr b. Shaddād b. 'Amr b. 'Imrān. There is some difference of opinion amongst historians about his genealogy. His great-grandfather 'Imrān is reported to have participated in the Battle of Ṣiffīn on the side of 'Alī and was martyred in the same battle.

Abū Dāwūd was born at Sijistān in 202 A.H. He belonged to Azd, a well-known Arab tribe. Hence he is called al-Azdī His native city Sijistān was a famous town in Khurāsān. It was situated in the vicinity of Makrān and Sindh opposite to Hirāt.

He heard *Ḥadīth* from about three hundred persons who were his teachers (*shuyūkh*). The eminent of them are as follows: Aḥmad b. Ḥanbal, Isḥāq b. Rāhwaih, Abū Thaur, Yaḥyā b. Ma'īn, Hishām b. 'Abd al-Malik al-Ṭayālisī, Abū Bakr b. Abī Shaibah and 'Uthmān b. Abū Shaibah. He had a large number of disciples. Here we give a few illustrious names: Abū Bakr b. Abū Dāwūd, Abū 'Alī Muḥammad b. Aḥmad b. 'Amr al-Lū'lū', Abū Sa'īd Aḥmad b. Muḥammad b. Ziyād b. Bishr, *alias* Ibn al-A'rābī, Abū Bakr Muḥammad b. Bakr b. Muḥammad b. 'Abd al-Razzāq al-Tammār al-Baṣrī, *alias* Ibn Dāsah, Abū 'Īsā al-Tirmidhī, Abū 'Abd al-Raḥmān al-Nasā'ī. Abū 'Amr Aḥmad b. Abū 'Īsā Isḥāq b Mūsā b Sa'īd al-Ramlī These are the transmitters of his *Sunan*. Some of the transmitters of his other books are: 'Abd Allah Muḥammad b. Aḥmad al-Baṣrī, Abū Bakr Aḥmad b. Sulaimān al-Najjār, Ismā'īl b. Muḥammad al-Ṣaffār.

Although Imām Abū Dāwūd was born at Sijistān, he spent the greater part of his life at Baṣrah which was a seat of learning in his day. He widely travelled throughout the world for collecting *Ḥadīth*. Many times he visited Baghdad, and also journeyed to Hejaz, Iraq Khurāsān, Egypt, Syria, al-Jazīrah, Nishapur and Iṣfahān.

Imām Abū Dāwūd had a strong memory and a penetrating mind. His retaining power was recognised by the doctors of *Ḥadīth* of his time. Alongside of his memory he was also well versed in the criticism of *Ḥadīth*. He was expert in distinguishing the sound traditions from the weak, defective, and spurious ones. Four persons are reported to have earned their name for the criticism of *Ḥadīth*: Imām al-Bukhārī. Imām Muslim, Imām Abū Dāwūd and Imām al-Nasā'ī Imām Abū Dāwūd lived during the period when the Muslim world was full of eminent scholars. He attained so much command over *Ḥadīth* that great masters of his time recognised his eminence and distinction amongst contemporary scholars of *Ḥadīth*. He was considered *Imām al-Muḥaddithīn* of his time.

Besides his expertise in *Ḥadīth* he was also a great jurist. He had keen insight in *fiqh* and *ijtihād*. Some scholars are of opinion that Imām Abū Dāwūd had the most prominent position in *fiqh* and *ijtihād* amongst the doctors of *Ḥadīth* after Imām al-Bukhārī. He was so much inclined towards jurisprudence that Abū Isḥāq al-Shīrāzī has included him alone in *Ṭabaqāt al-Fuqahā'* from amongst the authors of the six canonical collections of *Ḥadīth*. This is the reason why he has collected only legal traditions (*aḥādīth al-aḥkām*) in his *Sunan*.

There is a dispute over the school of law to which he belonged. Abū Isḥāq al-Shīrāzī considers him a Ḥanbalī jurist, for he was a disciple of Aḥmad b. Hanbal and agreed with him on a number of questions. But other scholars regard him as a Shāfi'ī jurist.

Imām Abū Dāwūd was a religious man. He led pious and ascetic life. He devoted most of his time to worship, devotion and remembrance of Allah. He renounced pleasure in worldly things. He always kept away from the company of Sulṭāns, courtiers and men of rank and dignity. Once he was asked by the Governor of Basrah to give his sons a prominent seat in the circle of *Ḥadīth*. But Imām Abū Dāwūd did not accept this request of him and replied that there was no distinction between high and low in learning *Ḥadīth* from the teacher.

Imām Abū Dāwūd died on Friday, 16 Shawwāl 275, at the age of seventy-two years. 'Abbās b. 'Abd al-Wāḥid led the funeral prayer. We do not find any details about his descendants His biographers have made a mention of the name of his son Abū Bakr b. Abū Dāwūd, who was his disciple and an eminent doctor of *Ḥadīth*.

His Works. His works are :

(1) *Kitāb al-Radd 'Alā Ahl al-Qadar*

(2) *Kitāb al-Masā'il*

(3) *Musnad Mālik*

(4) *Kitāb al-Marāsīl*

(5) *Sunan Abū Dāwūd*

Sunan Abū Dāwūd. This is one of the six canonical collections of Traditions of the Prophet (*Ṣiḥāḥ Sittah*). It contains 4800 select Traditions. Imām Abū Dāwūd completed it in Baghdad in 241 A.H. The collections of *Ḥadīth* before *Sunan Abū Dāwūd* were compiled on the pattern of the type known as *Jawāmi'* (sing. *Jāmi'*) and *Masānīd* (sing. *Musnad*). They contained traditions relating to various subjects, e.g. *ahkām* (law), *tafsīr* (exegesis), *qasas* (stories), *akhbār* (history), *mawā'iẓ* (homilies), *ādāb* (general behaviour). The distinctive quality of this book is that Imām Abū Dāwūd collected only legal traditions (*aḥkām*) in it and omitted others. In his epistle to the people of Mecca, he said: "I have collected only legal traditions in the *Sunan* (i.e. *Sunan Abū Dāwūd*). They do not include traditions relating to asceticism and merits of deeds The four thousand and eight hundred traditions contained in it relate to legal questions.

Sunan Abū Dāwūd is an important collection of *Ḥadīth*. Most of the scholars have assigned it the third position among the six collections of *Ḥadīth* after those compiled by Imām al-Bukhārī and Imām Muslim. Imām Aḥmad b. Hanbal appreciated it very much when it was presented to him after its completion. We give below a few statements of some scholars of *Ḥadīth* about the worth of this collection.

Zakariyā b. Yaḥyā al-Sājī said: "The Qur'ān is the foundation of Islam and *Sunan Abū Dāwūd* is its pillar."

Ibn al-A'rābī said: "There is no need of acquaintance of anything after acquiring the knowledge of the Qur'ān and of *Sunan Abū Dāwūd*."

Muḥammad b Makhlad said: "When Abū Dāwūd presented the *Sunan* to the people after its compilation, the scholars of *Ḥadīth* considered it a book worthy of being followed like the Qur'ān."

Al-Khaṭṭābī said: "*Sunan Abū Dāwūd* is an excellent book. No such unpralleled work has been produced so far in religious sciences. It has gained popularity among people. It has a decisive position among various classes of scholars and jurists. All have equally benefited from it The people of Iraq, Egypt, Maghrib and of most of the countries depend upon it."

Ibn al-Jawzī said: "Abū Dāwūd was an eminent doctor of *Ḥadīth* and an outstanding scholar. No one has compiled a book like his *Sunan*"

Ibn Kathīr remarked: "*Sunan Abū Dāwūd* is considered to be a famous and popular work among scholars."

Abū Dāwūd himself said: "The knowledge of any book other than it is not necessary after the Qur'ān. There is no harm if a person does not possess the knowledge of any book except of these two books"

Characteristics. (1) The most outstanding feature of this book is that it contains only legal traditions. No other book contains such a large number of traditions as it contains on law.

(2) It is a meritorious work with regard to *fiqh* and derivation of rules, for Imām Abū Dāwūd was as eminent jurist.

(3) The traditions it contains were generally followed by Companions, Successors, and their followers. It is a basic source of knowledge about the legal points of view held by Mālik, Sufyān al-Thaurī, and al-Auzā'ī. It serves as an arbiter for disagreement among jurists.

(4) It takes a special care of sound, strong, continuous and those traditions which are traced back to the Prophet (may peace be upon him). These traditions have been selected from five lakhs by Imām Abū Dāwūd. He himself said about these traditions in his *Risālah* :

"The *Sunan* contains 4800 traditions All of them are entirely or nearly sound. I have tried to the best of my knowledge and belief to transmit sound, rather most sound, traditions in this book. I always preferred those traditiions which were superior in respect of the chain of narrators. I narrate the *mursal* traditions when *musnad* and *muttaṣil* traditions are not available, for *marāsīl* are also recognised as authentic by early jurists like Mālik, al-Thaurī and al-Auzā'ī. Al-Shāfi'ī and Aḥmad b. Ḥanbal have criticised them. In my opinion, they are authentic and reliable in the absence of *musnad* and *muttaṣil* traditions, but I do not consider them as they are (i.e *musnad* and *muttaṣil*). I have not included in it any tradition which has been unanimously rejected by scholars. Similarly, I have refrained from narrating traditions from those narrators who have been rejected by doctors of *Ḥadīth*. I do not take into consideration *munkar* (unusual) and *ḍa'īf* (weak) traditions But in the absence of sound traditions on a subject I have transmitted them after describing the reasons of their weakness and rejection Where I have kept silence with regard to those traditions whose chains are not considered to be sound, they should be considered to be sound and reliable Similarly, I have taken much care of collecting in it the traditions which are well known and those which have been generally followed and practised by the people, instead of transmitting rare and obscure (*gharīb* and *shādhdh*) traditions."

At another place he has said :

"In this *Sunan* I have mentioned sound, quasi-sound and those traditions which are approximately sound. If any tradition is seriously weak, I have pointed out its weakness clearly. The traditions of which I have said nothing are genuine Some of the traditions which are not seriously weak are more sound than others."

The author of *Kashf al-Ẓunūn* has explained this statement as follows: Abū Dāwūd has classified the traditions contained in his *Sunan* into five divisions: *ṣaḥīḥ lidhātihī* (sound in itself), *ṣaḥīḥ lighairiḥī* (sound by some external reason), *ḥasan lidhatihī* (good in itself), seriously weak (*wahn shadīd*), and not seriously weak (*wahn lais bi shadīd*). If a weak tradition is reinforced by any other version, it becomes *ḥasan lighairihī*. This may be a sixth kind.

(5) Sometimes Imām Abū Dāwūd mentions many chains and many texts through one chain and one text, and gives the wordings of each tradition severally.

(6) No collection of *Ḥadīth* is free from repetition of traditions. Imām Abū Dāwūd has avoided this repetition as far as possible in his *Sunan*. He has neglected variety of chains and condensed the lengthy traditions He has repeated a tradition when something new is found in it.

(7) Besides exhaustiveness and comprehensiveness of the traditions we find an excellent order and synthesis of the material.

(8) The *Sunan* contains also a *thulāthī* (a chain comprising three narrators) tradition.

(9) The *Sunan* presents a detailed description of the names of the narrators, and of their surnames, indication of their trustworthiness or unreliability, and elucidation of the soundness and weakness of the tradition.

Four Significant Traditions of Sunan Abū Dāwūd. Abū Dāwūd has stated that this collection of traditions (i.e. the *Sunan*) contains four traditions which are sufficient for a man to follow religion. These are as follows :

(*i*) Deeds are to be judged only by intentions.

(*ii*) Part of a man's good observance of Islam is that he leaves alone what does not concern him.

(*iii*) A believer does not become a perfect believer until he likes for his brother what he likes for himself.

(*iv*) What is lawful is clear and what is unlawful is clear, but between them are certain doubtful things.

These traditions are concerned with important things of life. The first relates to the validity of deeds and rituals ; the second pertains to the precious moments of life ; the third deals with the rights of man ; and the fourth removes the doubts that arise from disagreement of the scholars.

Copies of Sunan Abū Dāwūd. Seven disciples of Imām Abū Dāwūd have transmitted the *Sunan* from him. Four of them are well known ; hence four copies of the *Sunan* have been in circulation among the people. These disciples are :

(1) Abū Bakr Muḥammad b. Bakr b. Muḥammad b. 'Abd al-Razzāq al-Tammār al-Baṣrī, *alias* Ibn Dāsah.

(2) Abū Sa'īd Aḥmad b. Muḥammad b. Ziyād b Bishr, *alias* Ibn al-A'rābī.

(3) Abū 'Alī Muḥammad b. Aḥmad b. 'Amr al-Lū'lū' al-Baṣrī.

(4) Abū 'Īsā Isḥāq b Mūsā b Sa'īd al-Ramlī.

The copy prepared by al-Lū'lū' is generally popular in this subcontinent and in most of the cities and in the east of Arabia. This is considered to be the most authentic version, for Imām Abū Dāwūd dictated it in the last part of his life in 375 A.H. Al-Mundhirī has made an abridgment of this copy and mentioned the names of the books in which the traditions contained in the *Sunan* are found. Ibn Rislān, al-'Irāqī, Ibn al-Qayyim, al-Sindhī and al-Suyūṭī have written commentaries of this copy of the *Sunan*. Al-Suyūṭī has observed that al-Lū'lū's version is the most authentic one.

The second copy was prepared by Ibn Dāsah. His version is the most perfect of all versions of the *Sunan*. It was popular in al-Maghrib. This copy is similar to the copy prepared by al-Lū'lū'. The difference between the two is of the order of chapters The copy of Ibn Dāsah contains a number of traditions which are not found in al-Lū'lū's version. Al-Khaṭṭābī, the commentator of *Sunan Abū Dāwūd*, had this copy while writing its commentary. He narrated its traditions directly from Ibn Dāsah.

The third copy of the *Sunan* was prepared by Ibn al-A'rābī. This is a defective copy, and it lacks the following chapters: Kitāb al-Fitan wa'l-Malāḥim, al-Ḥurūb, al-Khātam, half of Kitāb al-Libās, Kitab al-Wuḍū, al-Ṣalāt, and Kitāb al-Nikāḥ.

The fourth copy was composed by Ramlī. It was similar to the copy of Ibn Dāsah.

The fifth copy was made by al-'Abd. It is contained in *Aṭrāf al-Mizzi*. Ibn Ḥajar al-'Asqalānī has also mentioned it in *Fatḥ al-Bārī*.

Al-Dhahabī has also mentioned three copies, but they are obscure.

Commentaries and Annotations of Sunan Abū Dāwūd. Due to the significance of this book a large number of scholars have written its commentaries, annotations, and made its abridgments. Some of them are as follows:

(1) Al-Khaṭṭābī, Abū Sulaimān Ḥamd b. Muḥammad (d. 388 A.H.), *Ma'ālim al-Sunan*. This is the earliest and most famous commentary on the *Sunan*. It was published in Aleppo in 1351 A H

(2) Quṭb al-Dīn Abū Bakr b. Aḥmad (d 752 A H.) wrote a commentary of the *Sunan* in four volumes.

(3) Al-Nawawī, Abū Zakariyyā Muḥyī al-Dīn Yaḥyā b. Sharaf (d. 676 A H.) started writing a commentary of the *Sunan*, but he could not complete it.

(4) Ibn al-Qayyim, Muḥammad b. Abū Bakr (d. 751 A.H.), *Tahdhīb*. This commentary has been published.

(5) 'Alā' al-Dīn Mughalṭā'ī (d. 762 A.H.) started to write a commentary on the *Sunan*, but he could not complete it.

(6) Al-Maqdisī, Abū Maḥmūd Shihāb al-Dīn Aḥmad b. Muḥammad (d. 765 A.H.), *'Ujālai al-'Ālim min Kitāb al-Ma'ālim*, published in four volumes. It is an abridgment of *Ma'ālim al-Sunan*.

(7) Ibn al-Mulaqqin, Sirāj al-Dīn 'Umar b. 'Alī (d. 804 A.H.) wrote a commentary on those traditions of *Sunan Abū Dāwud* which were not found in al-Bukhārī and Muslim.

(8) Al-'Irāqī, Walī al-Dīn Aḥmad b. 'Abd al-Raḥīm, Zain al-Dīn (d. 844 A H.) started to write a comprehensive commentary of the *Sunan*, but it could not be completed.

(9) Ibn Rislān, Abū al-'Abbās Aḥmad b. Ḥusain al-Ramlī (d. 844 A.H.) wrote a comprehensive commentary of the *Sunan*.

(10) Al-'Ainī, Badr al Dīn (d 855 A H), wrote a commentary on the *Sunan*.

(11) Al-Suyūṭī, Jalāl al-Dīn, *Mirqāt al-Ṣu'ūd ilā Sunan Abī Dāwūd*.

(12) Abū al-Ḥasan al-Sindhī, *Fatḥ al-Wadūd 'alā Sunan Abī Dāwūd*.

(13) Shams al-Ḥaqq 'Aẓīmābādī, *Ghāyat al-Maqṣūd*. This was the most comprehensive commentary of the *Sunan* in 32 volumes, but only one volume could be published.

(14) Shams al-Ḥaqq 'Aẓīmābādī, *'Awn al-Ma'būd* This is an abridgment of *Ghāyat al-Maqṣūd.*

(15) Khalīl Aḥmad, *Badhl al-Majhūd fī Ḥall Sunan Abī Dāwūd* This commentary deals at length with the narrators and presents a Ḥanafī point of view.

(16) Al-Mundhirī, Zakī al-Dīn 'Abd al-'Aẓīm (d. 656 A.H.), made an abridgment of *Sunan Abū Dāwūd* and named it *al-Mujtabā.*

(17) Fakhr al-Ḥasan Gangawhī wrote annotations of the *Sunan* known as *al-Ta'līq al-Maḥmūd.*

(18) 'Allāmah Waḥīd al-Zamān translated *Sunan Abū Dāwūd* into Urdu with explanatory notes, known as *al-Hady al-Maḥmūd.*

The Translation. The accurate rendering of *Ḥadīth* into English is a very difficult task. It requires full command over both languages, Arabic and English. In addition, the translator must be well versed in the science of *Ḥadīth.* All these qualifications are essential to undertake this gigantic task. When this assignment was offered to me, I apologised owing to the lack of the requisite qualifications and my engagements. However, after much insistence by the publishers of this book I had to surrender.

The translation of *Sunan Abū Dāwūd* became easy for me by the rendering of *Ṣaḥīḥ Muslim* and *Miskhāt* into English before me. Not only did my publishers allow me, but also demanded me to borrow the translation from these two books as far as possible, and to do the translation of my own where found necessary. Hence some of the renderings in the *Sunan* agree with those of *Miskhāt* and *Ṣaḥīḥ Muslim.* The translation is, of course, mostly literal and nearer to the original Abrabic. An attempt has, however, been made to produce a translation in natural English and avoid strict adherence to the actual words in Arabic. In many places Arabic was very succinct. Hence it was necessary for me to add a few words for the sake of clarity. The definite article *al* has been retained throughout. The word *Nabī* has been translated as the "Prophet," and the word *Rasūl* as the "Apostle"

It will be noticed that some Arabic words have been translated and the translation of some words has been omitted. The reason is that there is no exact equivalent of such words in English. An attempt to translate them would be useless. For instance, these words are *rak'ah, zakāt, i'tikāf, 'umrah, ḥajj,* and others.

As per instructions of my publishers, I have added explanatory notes and brief biographical sketches of major narrators in the footnotes. In the explanatory notes I have also mentioned various points of view on a certain question. This was necessary because the traditions are sometimes contradictory about one and the same question. The jurists differ amongst themselves on the basis of these traditions. While writing the explanatory notes I have depended mostly on *'Awn al-Ma'būd* by Shams al-Haqq

'Aẓīmābādī. I have consulted other sources too where it was felt necessary.

I admit that I am not competent to undertake such a difficult and enormous job. There might be some mistakes in the rendering of the traditions into English, as to err is human and to forgive is Divine. If the readers happen to find any mistakes, they may kindly point out to the publishers, so that they may be corrected in the next edition.

I offer my humble thanks to the Almighty Allah Who helped me to complete this heavy task. I am also thankful to Sh. Muhammad Ashraf, Publisher and Bookseller, Lahore, who assigned this work to me and provided all facilities for its preparation and for publication. My thanks are also due to Professor Mazharuddin Siddiqi, and Mr Muhammad Ashraf Darr who very kindly read the manuscript, edited it, and improved the language.

Islamabad *Ahmad Hasan*
19 February 1979

Sources :

(1) Shams al-Ḥaqq 'Aẓīmābādī, *'Awn al-Ma'būd*
(2) Ḥājjī Khalīfah, *Kashf al-Ẓunūn*
(3) Ibn al-Nadīm, *al-Fihrist*
(4) Ibn Ḥajar al-'Asqalānī. *Tahdhīb al-Tahdhīb*
(5) Shāh 'Abd al-'Azīz, *Bustān al-Muḥaddithīn*
(6) Ḍiyā' al-Dīn, *Tadhkirat al-Muḥaddithīn*

SOME TERMS EXPLAINED*

Ḥadīth and Sunnah. In the context of *Ḥadīth* literature these two terms are considered to be synonymous. There is, however, a slight difference in them. The word *Sunnah* means a trodden path, a precedent, a practice and a custom. In technical sense, it is a model behaviour of the Prophet (may peace be upon him). It represents his doings and practices.

Ḥadīth originally means a news, a tale, a story, a talk or report. Technically, it denotes the report of the words, deeds, and approval or disapproval of the Prophet (may peace be upon him).

Some scholars have differentiated them in another manner. According to them, *Sunnah* is a norm, a rule of law, a principle and a pattern, whereas *Ḥadīth* is a vehicle through which this norm or law, i.e. the *Sunnah,* is conveyed. *Sunnah* is thus a behavioural concept, while *Ḥadīth* is the narration of the behaviour. Both are interlinked and sometimes identical.

Ṣaḥīḥ (sound). A faultless *ḥadīth* in which there is no weakness either in the chain (*isnād*) or in the text (*matan*).

Ḥasan (approved). A *ḥadīth* like a *ṣaḥīḥ* but for the fact that some of its narrators are found to have defective memory in comparison to the narrators of a *ṣaḥīḥ ḥadīth*. It is inferior to *ṣaḥīḥ*.

Ḍa'īf (weak). A tradition in which there is some defect either in the chain, or in proper understanding of the transmitter, or its contents contradict Islamic belief and practices.

Mutawātir (constant). A tradition reported by a large number of people at different times, so as to make it impossible for them to agree upon any falsehood.

Mashhūr (well known). A tradition handed down by at least three different reliable narrators. Another definition goes : A tradition that was originally transmitted by one person in the first generation, but later on it was widely disseminated.

Mauḍū' (spurious). A tradition which a liar fabricates and then attributes ~~it to~~ the Prophet (may peace be upon him).

Muttafaq 'Alaih (agreed upon). A tradition accepted both by Imām al-Bukhārī and by Imām Muslim, and included in their respective collections.

* Adapted from the Introduction of the English translation (by Professor 'Abd al-Ḥamīd Ṣiddīqī) of *Ṣaḥīḥ Muslim* and from that of *Mishkāt al-Maṣābīḥ* (by Dr James Robson).

Gharīb (unusual). It is applied sometimes to the text and sometimes to the chain. Thus it may refer to the only tradition known by a certain line of transmission, although the same tradition may be known by other lines; it may refer to a tradition whose text has only one transmaitter. It may also refer to a tradition which comes only from a man who is considered reliable.

Majhūl (unknown). A tradition which has been transmitted by someone in an unrecognised manner.

Mauqūf (stopped). A tradition which stops at one of the Companions and is not traced back to the Prophet (may peace be upon him).

Munkar (unusual). A tradition narrated by a weak transmitter which disagrees with what is generally reported.

Munqaṭi' (disconnected). A tradition having an *isnād* (chain) with a link missing at the beginning, middle or end.

Mursal (free from the link of the Companion). A tradition having an *isnād* (chain) where a man in the generation following that of the Prophet's Companions quotes the Prophet directly In other words, a chain where the link of a Companion is missing, and a Successor relates a tradition directly from the Prophet.

Shādhdh (rare). A tradition coming from a single transmitter and contradicting another. If the transmitter is a recognised authority, it deserves examination, but if he is not, the tradition is to be rejected.

Mu'allal (defective). A tradition which may ostensibly be sound but has some weakness not readily apparent. This may consist of pretending that a *mursal* tradition has a full *isnād*; or that a *mauqūf* tradition goes back to the Prophet ; or two traditions may be jumbled together, or there may be some misconception introduced by a transmitter.

SYSTEM OF TRANSLITERATION

ا	a	ط	ṭ
ب	b	ظ	ẓ
ت	t	ع	ʻ
ث	th	غ	gh
ج	j	ف	f
ح	h	ق	q
خ	kh	ک	k
د	d	ل	l
ذ	dh	م	m
ر	r	ن	n
ز	z	ه	h
س	s	ة	t
ش	sh	و	w
ص	ṣ	ء	’
ض	ḍ	ی	y

Vowels : short			
		َ	a
		ِ	i
		ُ	u
	long	آ	ā
		ای	ī
		آو	ū
Dipthongs		آو	au
		آی	ai

CONTENTS

I. KITĀB AL-ṬAHĀRAH (*Book of Purification*), pp. 1-101

Chapters

II. KITĀB AL-ṢALĀṬ (*Book of Prayer*), pp. 102-402

Chapters on the Details of Commencing Prayer

*A mistake has occurred in the numbering of chapters. Chapter 253 should have been chapter 252. The mistake is regretted ; it will be corrected in the next edition—*Publishers*.

Chapters on Prayer at Night

Detailed Injunctions About Ramaḍān

Chapters on Prostration While Reciting the Qur'ān

Detailed Injunctions About Witr

I. KITĀB AL-ṬAHĀRAH

[BOOK OF PURIFICATION]

Chapter 1

OBSERVING PRIVACY WHILE RELIEVING ONESELF

(1) Mughīrah b. Shu'bah reported that when the Prophet (may peace be upon him) went (outside) to relieve himself, he went to a far-off place.[1]

(2) Jābir b. 'Abd Allah reported: When the Prophet (may peace be upon him) felt the need of relieving himself, he went far off where no one could see him.

Chapter 2

ONE SHOULD SEEK SOFT GROUND FOR URINATION

(3) Abu al-Tayyāḥ reported on the authority of a *shaikh* (an old man): When 'Abd Allah b. 'Abbās came to Baṣrah, people narrated to him traditions from Abū Mūsā. Therefore Ibn 'Abbās wrote to him asking him about certain things. In reply Abū Mūsā wrote to him saying: One day I was in the company of the Apostle of Allah (may peace be upon him). He wanted to urinate. Then he came to a soft ground at the foot of a wall and urinated. He (the Prophet) then said: If any of you wants to urinate, he should look for a place (like this) for his urination.[2]

Chapter 3

WHAT SHOULD A MAN UTTER WHILE ENTERING THE PRIVY

(4) Anas b. Mālik reported: When the Apostle of Allah (may peace be upon

1. The same narrator reported a tradition recorded in *Jāmi' al-Tirmidhi* (*Kitāb al-Ṭahārah*) which explains this tradition. It says: "During a journey I accompanied the Prophet (may peace be upon him). He felt the need of relieving himself and went far away." This shows that he did so in the desert. The distance is sometimes reckoned about two miles from Mecca (*Ma'ārif al-Sunan*, I, 134).

2. Some traditions recorded in *Ṣaḥiḥ Muslim* and also reported by Abū Dāwūd indicate that defiling by urine causes punishment in the grave. Hence the Prophet (may peace be upon him) took every care to safeguard himself from the impurity of urine. If one urinates on hard or stony ground, one's clothes will naturally be defiled by the sprinkles of urine.

him) entered the toilet, he used to say (before entering) : "O Allah, I seek refuge in Thee."

This is according to the version of Ḥammād. 'Abd al-Wārith has another version : "I seek refuge in Allah from male and female devils."[3]

Explaining the variance of version Abū Dāwūd says : Shu'bah on the authority of 'Abd al-'Azīz narrated : "O Allah, I seek refuge in Thee," and sometimes he reported : "I take refuge in Allah." Wuhaib (b. Khālid) (on the authority of 'Abd al-'Azīz) narrated : One should take refuge in Allah.

(5) Another tradition on the authority of Anas has : "O Allah, I seek refuge in Thee."

Shu'bah said : Anas sometimes reported the words : "I take refuge in Allah."

(6) Zaid b. Arqam reported : The Apostle of Allah (may peace be upon him) said : These privies are frequented by the jinns and devils. So when anyone amongst you goes there, he should say : "I seek refuge in Allah from male and female devils."

Chapter 4

DISAPPROVAL OF FACING THE *QIBLAH*[4] WHILE RELIEVING ONESELF

(7) Salmān reported that it was said to him : Your Prophet teaches you everything, even about excrement. He replied : Yes. He has forbidden us to face the *qiblah* at the time of easing or urinating,[5] and cleansing with right hand, and cleansing with less than three stones, or cleansing with dung or bone.[6]

(8) Abū Hurairah reported the Apostle of Allah (may peace be upon him) as saying : I am like a father to you. When any of you goes to the privy, he should not face or turn his back towards the *qiblah*. He should not cleanse with his right hand.[7]

3. The words *al-khubth* and *al-khabā'ith* literally mean wicked and noxious things. But they have been construed as male and female devils. This tradition also refers to their presence in the lavatory.

Although the Prophet (may peace be upon him) was safe from the influence of the devil, he used to seek refuge in Allah in order to teach his followers and also to show that man requires the aid of Allah in all circumstances. It is reported that Sa'd b. 'Ubādah, a famous Companion of the Prophet (may peace be upon him), was killed by the jinn. He was found dead in the toilet (*Ma ārif al-Sunan*, I, 78).

4. The Ka'bah at Mecca, the direction towards which Muslims face at the time of prayer.

5. In order to show respect to the *qiblah*, it is desirable that we should not turn our faces towards it while answering the call of nature.

6. This shows that Islam is a total way of life. The teachings of Islam cover all the facets of human life.

7. We eat food, write and do so many other good things with our right hand, and the sense of decency and cleanliness, therefore, demands that we should avoid its use for cleansing the private parts of our body.

He (the Prophet) also commanded the Muslims to use three stones and forbade them to use dung or decayed bone.

(9) Abū Ayyūb reported that he (the Holy Prophet) said : When you go to the privy, neither turn your face nor your back towards the *qiblah* at the time of excretion or urination, but turn towards the east or the west.[8] (Abū Ayyūb said) : When we came to Syria, we found that the toilets already built there were facing the *qiblah*. We turned our faces away from them and begged pardon of Allah.

(10) Ma'qil b. Abī Ma'qil al-Asadī reported : The Apostle of Allah (may peace be upon him) has forbidden us to face the two *qiblahs* at the time of urination or excretion.[9]

(11) Marwān al-Aṣfar said : I saw Ibn 'Umar make his camel kneel down facing the *qiblah*, then he sat down urinating in its direction. So I said : Abū 'Abd al-Raḥmān, has this not been forbidden? He replied : Why not, that was forbidden only in open country ; but when there is something between you and the *qiblah* that conceals you, then there is no harm.

Chapter 5

PERMISSION TO FACE THE *QIBLAH* AT THE TIME OF RELIEVING ONESELF

(12) 'Abd Allah b. 'Umar reported : I ascended the roof of the house and saw the Apostle of Allah (may peace be upon him) sitting on two bricks facing Jerusalem (Bait al-Maqdis) for relieving himself.[10]

(13) Jābir b. 'Abd Allah reported : The Prophet of Allah (may peace be upon him) forbade us to face the *qiblah* at the time of making water. Then I saw him facing it (*qiblah*) (urinating or easing himself) one year before his death.

8. The commandment of turning towards the east or the west at the time of urination or excretion was specified for the people of Medina where the *qiblah* lay towards the south. But the places where the *qiblah* lies towards the east or the west, people should avoid turning their face or back to these directions while answering the call of nature (*'Awn al-Ma'būd*, I, 7)

9. This may be out of respect for Bait al-Maqdis as it has been the *qiblah* for Muslims for about sixteen months when the Muslims migrated to Medina. The other reason for the prohibition may be that the Prophet (may peace be upon him) intended to avoid turning his back towards the Ka'bah (Mecca), because whosoever turns his face towards Bait al-Maqdis turns his back towards the Ka'bah (*'Awn al-Ma'būd*, I, 7).

10. The apparent contradiction has been resolved by scholars of *Ḥadith*. This *ḥadith* indicates that the prohibition to face the *qiblah* or to turn one's back towards it while urinating or relieving oneself applies only when one does so in an open place, but not in a built-up area or an enclosure.

Chapter 6

HOW TO UNCOVER THE PRIVATE PARTS OF THE BODY

(14) Ibn 'Umar reported: When the Prophet (may peace be upon him) wanted to relieve himself, he would not raise his garment, until he lowered himself near the ground.

Abū Dāwūd said: This tradition has been transmitted by 'Abd al-Salām b. Ḥarb on the authority of al-A'mash from Anas b. Mālik. This chain of narrators is weak (because A'mash's hearing traditions from Anas b. Mālik is not established).

Chapter 7

DISAPPROVAL OF CONVERSATION IN THE PRIVY

(15) Abū Sa'id reported: I heard the Apostle of Allah (may peace be upon him) say: When two persons go together for relieving themselves uncovering their private parts and talking together, Allah, the Great and Majestic, becomes wrathful at this (action).[11]

Abū Dāwūd said: This tradition has been narrated only by 'Ikrimah b. 'Ammār.

Chapter 8

RETURN OF SALUTATION AT THE TIME OF URINATION

(16) Ibn 'Umar reported: A man passed by the Prophet (may peace be upon him) while he was urinating, and saluted him. The Prophet (may peace be upon him) did not return the salutation to him.

Abū Dāwūd said: It is narrated on the authority of Ibn 'Umar that the Prophet (may peace be upon him) performed *tayammum*, then he returned the salutation to the man.

(17) Muhājir b. Qunfudh reported that he came to the Prophet (may peace be upon him) while he was urinating. He saluted him. The Prophet (may peace be upon him) did not return the salutation to him until he performed ablution. He then apologised to him, saying: I disliked remembering Allah except in the state of purification.[12]

11. The Prophet (may peace be upon him) took meticulous care in showing modesty. Islam never allows immodesty and indecency in any condition.

12. Salutation is a kind of supplication and remembrance of Allah. This tradition shows that one should not offer salutation or return it while urinating. It is permissible to return the salutation after urination if one fears that the man will go away. But it is not permitted to do so while one is urinating. It is commendable to return the salutation after performing ablution or *tayammum* (*'Awn al-Ma'būd*, I, 8).

Chapter 9

ONE MAY REMEMBER ALLAH WITHOUT PURIFICATION

(18) 'Ā'ishah reported: The Apostle of Allah (may peace be upon him) used to remember Allah, the Great and Majestic, at all moments.[13]

Chapter 10

ENTERING THE PRIVY WITH A RING IN THE HAND ON WHICH IS INSCRIBED THE NAME OF ALLAH

(19) Anas reported: When the Prophet (may peace be upon him) entered the privy, he removed his ring.

Abū Dāwūd said: This is a *munkar* tradition, i.e. it contradicts the well-known version reported by reliable narrators. On the authority of Anas the well-known version says: The Prophet (may peace be upon him) had a silver ring made for him. Then he cast it off. The misunderstanding is on the part of Hammām (who is a narrator of the previous tradition mentioned in the text). This is transmitted only by Hammām.

Chapter 11

SAFEGUARDING ONESELF FROM URINE

(20) Ibn 'Abbās reported: The Prophet (may peace be upon him) passed by two graves. He said: Both (the dead) are being punished, but they are not being punished for a major (sin). One did not safeguard himself from urine. The other carried tales. He then called for a fresh twig and split it into two parts and planted one part on each grave and said: Perhaps their punishment may be mitigated as long as the twigs remain fresh.

Another version of Hannād has: "One of them did not cover himself while urinating." This version does not have the words: "He did not safeguard himself from urine."

13. Another tradition on the authority of 'Alī, recorded in *Jāmi' al-Tirmidhi*, says: The Prophet (may peace be upon him) used to teach us the Qur'ān in all conditions except when he had sexual defilement (*junub*). This indicates that one is permitted to recite the Qur'ān verbally without touching it, and to remember Allah in the state of minor defilement (when one needs only ablution and not bathing). The performance of ablution for remembering Allah is recommended (*mustaḥabb*) and not necessary.

There is, however, a difference of opinion whether one can recite the Qur'ān in a state of sexual defilement or in case of menses of a woman. The general view is that it is not permitted. It is also forbidden to remember Allah while one is in the privy or is busy in sexual intercourse (*Fatḥ al-Mulhim*. I, 498).

(21) Ibn 'Abbās also reported a tradition from the Prophet (may peace be upon him) conveying similar meaning.

The version of Jarīr has the wording: "he did not cover himself while urinating."

The version of Abū Mu'āwiyah has the wording: "he did not safeguard himself (from urine)".

(22) 'Abd al-Raḥmān b. Ḥasanah reported: I and 'Amr b. al-'Āṣ went to the Prophet (may peace be upon him). He came out with a leather shield (in his hand). He covered himself with it and urinated. Then we said: Look at him. He is urinating as a woman does. The Prophet (may peace be upon him), heard this and said: Do you not know what befell a person from amongst Banū Isrā'īl (the children of Israel)? When urine fell on them, they would cut off the place where the urine fell; but he forbade them (to do so), and was punished in his grave.

Abū Dāwūd said: One version of Abū Mūsā has the wording: "he cut off his skin".

Another version of Abū Mūsā goes: "he cut off (part of) his body."

Chapter 12

URINATING WHILE ONE IS STANDING

(23) Ḥudhaifah reported: The Apostle of Allah (may peace be upon him) came to a midden of some people and urinated while standing.[14] He then asked for water and wiped his shoes.

Abū Dāwūd said: Musaddad, a narrator, reported: I went far away from him. He then called me and I reached just near his heals.

Chapter 13

A MAN MAY URINATE IN A VESSEL AT NIGHT AND KEEP IT WITH HIM

(24) Umaimah, daughter of Ruqaiqah, reported: The Prophet (may peace be upon him) had a wooden vessel under his bed in which he would urinate at night.

14. This tradition indicates that urinating while one is standing is permissible. The Prophet (may peace be upon him) normally used to urinate in the sitting position. On this occasion he urinated standing either to show its permissibility or he did not find a suitable place for sitting. In explanation of this tradition it is also said that he did so because of severe pain which he had in his back or in his knee, according to another version. But such traditions have been considered weak. There is, however, no tradition from the Prophet (may peace be upon him) which prohibits making water while one is standing. 'Umar, 'Alī and Zaid b. Thābit are also reported to have urinated occasionally in a standing position (*Awn al-Ma'būd*, I, 10).

Chapter 14

PLACES WHERE URINATING IS PROHIBITED

(25) Abū Hurairah reported the Prophet (may peace be upon him) as saying : Be on your guard against two things which provoke cursing. They (the hearers) said : Prophet of Allah, what are these things which provoke cursing ? He said : Easing in thoroughfares (where people walk) or under the shades (of the trees) (where they take shelter and rest).

(26) Mu'ādh b. Jabal reported : The Apostle of Allah (may peace be upon him) said : Be on your guard against three things which provoke cursing : easing in the watering places and on the thoroughfares, and in the shade (of the tree).

Chapter 15

URINATING IN THE BATH

(27) 'Abd Allah b. Mughaffal reported : The Apostle of Allah (may peace be upon him) said : No one of you should make water in his bath and then wash himself there (after urination).

The version of Aḥmad has : Then performs ablution there, for evil thoughts come from it.

(28) Ibn 'Abd al-Raḥmān reported : I met a man who remained in the company of the Prophet (may peace be upon him) just as Abū Hurairah remained in his company. He then added : The Apostle of Allah (may peace be upon him) forbade that anyone amongst us should comb (his hair) every day or urinate in the place where he takes a bath.

Chapter 16

PROHIBITION TO URINATE IN A HOLE

(29) 'Abd Allah b. Sarjis reported : The Prophet (may peace be upon him) prohibited to urinate in a hole.

Qatādah (a narrator) was asked about the reason for the disapproval of urinating in a hole. He replied : It is said that these (holes) are the habitats of the jinn.

Chapter 17

WHAT A MAN SHOULD UTTER WHEN HE COMES OUT OF THE PRIVY

(30) 'Ā'ishah reported : When the Prophet (may peace be upon him) came out of

the privy, he used to say : "Grant me Thy forgiveness."

Chapter 18

DISAPPROVAL OF TOUCHING THE PENIS WITH THE RIGHT HAND WHILE PURIFYING

(31) Abū Qatādah reported : The Prophet (may peace be upon him) said : When any one of you urinates, he must not touch his penis with his right hand, and when he goes to relieve himself he must not wipe himself with his right hand (in the privy), and when he drinks, he must not drink in one breath.

(32) Ḥafṣah, wife of the Prophet (may peace be upon him), reported : The Prophet (may peace be upon him) used his right hand for taking his food and drink and used his left hand for other purposes.

(33) 'Ā'ishah reported : The Prophet (may peace be upon him) used his right hand for getting water for ablution and taking food, and his left hand for his evacuation and for anything repugnant.

(34) 'Ā'ishah also reported a tradition bearing similar meaning through another chain of transmitters.

Chapter 19

TAKING COVER AT THE TIME OF RELIEVING ONESELF

(35) Abū Hurairah reported the Prophet (may peace be upon him) as saying : If anyone applies collyrium, he should do it an odd number of times. If he does so, he has done well ; but if not, there is no harm. If anyone cleanses himself with pebbles, he should use an odd number. If he does so, he has done well ; but if not, there is no harm. If anyone eats, he should throw away what he removes with a toothpick and swallow what sticks to his tongue. If he does so, he has done well ; if not, there is no harm. If anyone goes to relieve himself, he should conceal himself, and if all he can do is to collect a heap of sand, he should sit with his back to it, for the devil makes sport with the posteriors of the children of Adam.[15] If he does so, he has done well ; but if not, there is no harm.

15. The word ***maqā'id*** (sing. ***maq'ad***) means both the lower parts of the body and the places where one sits. Both the meanings may be applicable here. The tradition means that the devil makes sport with the lower part of the body of a man, or with the place he sits for easing himself. Hence the Prophet (may peace be upon him) commanded to conceal oneself as much as possible. One should avoid easing at places where people may see him, or where the wind be blowing causing the defilement of the body or garment. All this is tantamount to the playing of the devil (***'Awn al-Ma'būd***, I, 13).

The tradition may also mean that if there is no curtain, one might be injured by some animal, or someone might laugh at him.

Chapter 20

THINGS WITH WHICH CLEANSING AFTER EASING ONESELF IS FORBIDDEN

(36) Shaibān al-Qatbānī reported that Maslamah b. Mukhallad[16] made Ruwaifi' b. Thābit[17] the governor of the lower parts (of Egypt). He added: We travelled with him from Kūm Sharīk to 'Alqamah or from 'Alqamah to Kūm Sharīk (the narrator doubts) for 'Alqām.[18] Ruwaifi' said: Any one of us would borrow a camel during the lifetime of the Prophet (may peace be upon him) from the other, on condition that he would give him half the booty, and the other half he would retain himself. Further, one of us received an arrowhead and a feather, and the other an arrowshaft as a share from the booty.[19] He then reported: The Apostle of Allah (may peace be upon him) said: You may live for a long time after I am gone, Ruwaifi', so, tell people that if anyone ties his beard[20] or wears round his neck a string to ward off the evil eye, or cleanses himself with animal dung or bone, Muḥammad has nothing to do with him.[21]

(37) This tradition has also been narrated by Abū Sālim al-Jaishānī on the authority of 'Abd Allah b. 'Amr. He narrated this tradition at the time when he besieged the fort at the gate of Alyūn.

Abū Dāwūd said: The fort of Alyūn lies at the mountain in Fuṣṭāṭ. Abū Dāwūd said: The *kunyah* (surname) of Shaibān b. Umayyah is Abū Ḥudhaifah.

(38) Jābir b. 'Abd Allah reported: The Apostle of Allah (may peace be upon him) forbade us to use a bone or dung for wiping.

(39) 'Abd Allah b. Mas'ūd reported: A deputation of the jinn came to the

16. He was a Companion of the Prophet (may peace be upon him) and was appointed governor of Egypt during the reign of Mu'āwiyah. He died in 62 H.

17. He was also a Companion of the Prophet (may peace be upon him) and lived in Egypt. Mu'āwiyah appointed him governor of Tripoli in 46 H. He was later appointed as the ruler of Barqah by Maslamah b. Mukhallad, the governor of Egypt. He died in 56 H.

18. Names of places in Egypt.

19. By this statement Ruwaifi' meant that the Muslims in the early days of Islam did not receive much booty in their wars. Even one arrow was divided between two persons. He also wanted to inform them that he had embraced Islam in the earlier days. Hence the tradition reported by him is very significant and reliable (*Badhl al-Majhūd*, I, 24).

20. People used to tie their beards for several reasons in pre-Islamic Arabia: (1) for treatment; (2) during battle; (3) to follow the customs of non-Arabs who practised it; (4) it was a custom of the Arabs to tie one small knot in the beard if a person had one wife; in case he had two wives, he tied two knots.

The Prophet (may peace be upon him) forbade such a custom of the pagan days and commanded Muslims to comb the beard instead of tying it (*Badhl al-Majhūd*, I, 24, 25).

21. The Prophet (may peace be upon him) forbade to cleanse oneself with dung because it is itself impure, and with bone which is a provision for the jinn, as Tradition 39 above indicates.

Prophet (may peace be upon him) and said: O Muḥammad, forbid your community to cleanse themselves with a bone or dung or charcoal, for in them Allah has provided sustenance for us. So the Prophet (may peace be upon him) forbade them to do so.

Chapter 21

CLEANSING WITH STONES

(40) 'Ā'ishah reported: The Apostle of Allah (may peace be upon him) said: When any of you goes to relieve himself, he should take with him three stones to cleanse himself, for they will be enough for him.

(41) Khuzaimah b. Thābit reported: The Prophet (may peace be upon him) was asked about cleansing (after relieving oneself). He said: (One should cleanse oneself) with three stones which should be free from dung. Abū Dāwūd said: A similar tradition has been narrated by Abū Usāmah and Ibn Numair from Hishām.

Chapter 22

PERFORMING ABLUTION AFTER RELIEVING ONESELF

(42) 'Ā'ishah reported: The Prophet (may peace be upon him) urinated and 'Umar was standing behind him with a jug of water. He said: What is this, Umar? He replied: Water for you to perform ablution with. He said: I have not been commanded to perform ablution every time I urinate. If I were to do so, it would become a *sunnah*.[22]

Chapter 23

CLEANSING WITH WATER AFTER RELIEVING ONESELF

(43) Anas b. Mālik reported: The Apostle of Allah (may peace be upon him) entered a park. He was accompanied by a boy who had a jug of water with him. He was the youngest of us. He placed it near the lote-tree. He (the Prophet) relieved himself. He came to us after he had cleansed himself with water.

(44) Abū Hurairah reported: The Prophet (may peace be upon him) said: The following verse was revealed in connection with the people of Qubā': "In it are men who love to be purified" (ix. 108). He (Abū Hurairah) said: They used to cleanse themselves with water after easing. So the verse was revealed in connection with them.

22. The tradition indicates that performing ablution after urination or excretion is not essential.

Chapter 24

WIPING ONE'S HAND ON THE GROUND AFTER EASING

(45) Abū Hurairah reported : When the Prophet (may peace be upon him) went to the privy, I took to him water in a small vessel or a skin, and he cleansed himself. He then wiped his hand on the ground. I then took to him another vessel and he performed ablution.

Abū Dāwūd said : The tradition transmitted by al-Aswad b. 'Āmir is more perfect.

Chapter 25

THE TOOTH-STICK[23]

(46) Abū Hurairah reported (the Prophet) as saying : Were it not that I might overburden the believers, I would order them to delay the night (*'ishā'*) prayer and use the tooth-stick at the time of every prayer.

(47) Abū Salamah b. 'Abd al-Raḥmān reported Zaid b. Khālid al-Juhanī as saying : I heard the Apostle of Allah (may peace be upon him) say : Were it not hard on my *Ummah*, I would order them to use the tooth-stick at the time of every prayer. Abū Salamah said : Zaid b. Khālid used to attend the prayers in the mosque with his tooth-stick on his ear where a clerk carries a pen, and whenever he got up for prayer he used it.

(48) 'Abd Allah b. 'Abd Allah b. 'Umar reported : Muḥammad b. Yaḥyā b. Ḥabbān asked him about the reason for Ibn 'Umar's performing ablution for every prayer, whether he was with or without ablution. 'Abd Allah b. 'Abd Allah replied : Asmā', daughter of Zaid b. al-Khaṭṭāb, reported to me that 'Abd Allah b. Ḥanẓalah b. Abī 'Āmir narrated to her that the Apostle of Allah (may peace be upon him) was earlier commanded to perform ablution for every prayer whether or not he was with ablution. When it became a burden for him, he was ordered to use tooth-stick for every prayer. As Ibn 'Umar thought that he had the strength (to perform the ablution for every prayer), he did not give up performing ablution for every prayer.

Abū Dāwūd said : Ibrāhīm b. Sa'd narrated this tradition on the authority of Muḥammad b. Isḥāq, and there he mentions the name 'Ubaid Allah b. 'Abd Allah (instead of 'Abd Allah b. 'Abd Allah b. 'Umar).

23. *Siwāk* or *miswāk* : a piece of small stick with which the teeth are rubbed and cleaned, the end being made like a brush by beating or chewing it so as to separate the fibres.

Chapter 26

HOW TO USE THE TOOTH-STICK

(49) Abū Burdah, on the authority of his father (Abū Mūsā al-Ash'arī), reported (according to the version of Musaddad) : We came to the Apostle of Allah (may peace be upon him) to provide us with a mount, and found him using the tooth-stick, its one end being at his tongue (i.e. he was rinsing his mouth).

According to the version of Sulaimān it goes : I entered upon the Prophet (may peace be upon him) who was using the tooth-stick and had it placed at one side of his tongue, producing a gurgling sound.

Abū Dāwūd said : Musaddad said that the tradition was lengthy but he shortened it.

Chapter 27

USING OTHER'S TOOTH-STICK

(50) 'Ā'ishah reported : The Apostle of Allah (may peace be upon him) was using the tooth-stick, when two men, one older than the other, were with him. A revelation came down to him about the merit of using the tooth-stick. He was asked to show proper respect and give it to the elder of the two.

Chapter 28

THE WASHING OF THE TOOTH-STICK

(51) 'Ā'ishah reported : The Prophet of Allah (may peace be upon him) was accustomed to use the tooth-stick and then give it to me to wash it. I would first use it myself, then wash it and hand it over to him.[24]

Chapter 29

USING TOOTH-STICK IS ONE OF THE CHARACTERISTICS OF *FIṬRAH* (NATURE)

(52) 'Ā'ishah reported the Apostle of Allah (may peace be upon him) as saying. Ten are the acts according to *fiṭrah*[25] (nature) : clipping the moustache, letting

24. The tradition indicates the permissibility of using the tooth-stick of one person by the other.

25. Commenting upon the word *fiṭrah* (lit. nature), Maulānā 'Abd al-Ḥamīd Ṣiddīqī says that it "stands for the Sunnah of the Apostles cf Allah, because in a ḥadīth transmitted by Abū 'Awāna, there is the word ***Sunnah*** instead of fiṭra. The conduct of the Apostle is quite close to

the beard grow,[26] using the tooth-stick, cutting the nails, washing the finger joints, plucking the hair under the arm-pits,[27] shaving the pubes, and cleansing one's private parts (after easing or urinating) with water. The narrator said : I have forgotten the tenth, but it may have been rinsing the mouth.

(53) 'Ammār b. Yāsir reported : The Apostle of Allah (may peace be upon him) said : The rinsing of the mouth and snuffing up water in the nose are acts that bear the characteristics of *fiṭrah* (nature). He then narrated a similar tradition (as reported by 'Ā'ishah), but he did not mention the words "letting the beard grow". He added the words "circumcision"[28] and "sprinkling water on the private part of the body".[29] He did not mention the words "cleansing oneself after easing".

Abū Dāwūd said : A similar tradition has been reported on the authority of Ibn 'Abbās. He mentioned only five *sunnahs* all relating to the head, one of them being parting of the hair ; it did not include wearing the beard.

Abū Dāwūd said : The tradition as reported by Ḥammād has also been transmitted by Ṭalq b. Ḥabīb, Mujāhid, and Bakr b. 'Abd Allah b. al-Muzanī as their own statement (not as a tradition from the Prophet). They did not mention the words "letting the beard grow". The version transmitted by Muḥammad b. 'Abd Allah b. Abī Maryam, Abū Salamah, and Abū Hurairah from the Prophet (may peace be upon him) mentions the words "letting the beard grow". A similar tradition has been reported by Ibrāhīm al-Nakha'ī. He mentioned the words "wearing the beard and circumcision". [30]

Chapter 30

USING THE TOOTH-STICK AFTER GETTING UP DURING THE NIGHT

(54) Ḥudhaifah reported : When the Apostle of Allah (may peace be upon him)

nature. Some of the commentators have explained this word by the religion of Islam, because it is given to man by the same Lord Who has created nature and thus there is a very close affinity between the two. Some of the scholars are of the view that fiṭra here implies the inner sense of cleanliness in a man which is a proof of his moral and mental health" (*Ṣaḥīḥ Muslim*, Eng. tr., I, 159, footnote 466).

26. So that the Muslims might be distinguished from the non-Muslims who did not trim the moustaches and shaved the beards.

27. The armpits may also be shaved, the purpose being cleanliness of the body.

28. It is an old form of minor operation in which the foreskin of the male sexual organ is cut away.

29. Sprinkling a little water on the private part of the body after ablution is designed to ward off evil notions (*'Awn al-Ma'būd*, I, 20).

30. Mark how even the minutest details have been recorded by the experts of traditions.

got up during the night (to pray),[31] he cleansed his mouth with the tooth-stick.

(55) 'Ā'ishah reported : Ablution water and tooth-stick were placed by the side of the Prophet (may peace be upon him). When he got up during the night (for prayer), he relieved himself, then he used the tooth-stick.

(56) 'Ā'ishah reported : The Prophet (may peace be upon him) did not get up after sleeping by night or by day without using the tooth-stick before performing ablution.

(57) Ibn 'Abbās said : I spent a night with the Prophet (may peace be upon him). When he woke up from his sleep (in the latter part of the night for prayer) he came to his ablution water. He took the tooth-stick and used it. He then recited the verse : "Verily in the creation of the heavens and the earth and the alternation of the night and the day are tokens (of His sovereignty) for men of understanding" (iii. 190). He recited these verses almost up to the end of the chapter or he finished the whole chapter. He then performed ablution and came to the place of prayer. He then said two *rak'ahs* of prayer. He then lay down on the bed and slept as much as Allah wished. He then got up and did the same. He then lay down and slept. He then got up and did the same. Every time he used the tooth-stick and offered two *rak'ahs* of prayer. He then offered the prayer known as *witr*.[32]

Abū Dāwūd said : Fuḍail on the authority of Ḥuṣain reported the wording : He then used the tooth-stick and performed ablution while he was reciting the verses : "Verily in the creation of the heavens and the earth . . ." until he finished the chapter.

Chapter 31

(58) Shuraiḥ (b. Hānī) said that he asked 'Ā'ishah : What did the Apostle of Allah (may peace be upon him) do first when he entered his house ? She replied : He used the tooth-stick.

Chapter 32

ABLUTION IS OBLIGATORY FOR PRAYER

(59) Abū al-Malīḥ reported : The Prophet (may peace be upon him) said : Allah does not accept charity from goods acquired by embezzlement as He does not accept prayer without purification.

(60) Abū Hurairah reported : The Apostle of Allah (may peace be upon him) said : Allah, the Exalted, does not accept the prayer of any of you when you are defiled until you perform ablution.[33]

31. This is the *tahajjud* prayer offered in the latter part of the night.

32. This is an additional prayer offered after the night prayer. There is a difference of opinion amongst scholars as to the number of its *rak'ahs*.

33. In the absence of water one is allowed to perform *tayammum*.

(61) 'Alī reported the Apostle of Allah (may peace be upon him) as saying: The key to prayer is purification;[34] its beginning is *takbīr*[35] and its end is *taslīm*.[36]

Chapter 33

A MAN MAY RENEW THE ABLUTION WITHOUT DEFILEMENT

(62) Abū Ghuṭaif al-Hudhalī reported: I was in the company of Ibn 'Umar. When the call was made for the noon (*ẓuhr*) prayer, he performed ablution and said the prayer. When the call for the afternoon (*'aṣr*) prayer was made, he again performed ablution. Thus I asked him (about the reason of performing ablution). He replied: The Apostle of Allah (may peace be upon him) said: For a man who performs ablution in

34. The Prophet (may peace be upon him) called ablution the key to prayer because defilement prevents one from saying the prayer.

Defilement is, therefore, likened to a lock set on the person who is defiled. When he performs ablution, the lock is opened. The Prophet (may peace be upon him), in another tradition, is reported to have said: The key to Paradise is prayer. The doors of Paradise are unlocked by virtuous actions, of which prayer is an essential part. Al-Nawawī said: The community is agreed upon the unlawfulness of prayer without ablution or *tayammum*. This equally applies to the obligatory and supererogatory prayers, prostration on account of the recitation of the Qur'ān or thanksgiving, and funeral prayer. Al-Sha'bī and Ibn Jarīr al-Ṭabarī are reported to have held that the funeral prayer is valid without purification (ablution). This view has been rejected by the consensus of the community. If anyone says prayer in a state of impurity deliberately without valid reason, he will be sinful. But, according to the majority opinion, he will not become an unbeliever (*kāfir*) by saying the prayer in a state of impurity. Abū Ḥanīfah, however, holds that he will become an unbeliever because of making sport with prayer (*'Awn al-Ma'būd*, I, 22).

35. *Taḥrīm* (making unlawful) and *taḥlīl* (making lawful) are two opposite terms used for the beginning and completing of the prayer. *Takbīr* means saying *Allah-u-Akbar* (Allah is the most Great). The utterance of these words in the beginning of a prayer makes all the permissible acts unlawful during prayer. The word *taḥrīm* has also been construed as entering into the prayer because it makes eating and drinking unlawful. The word may also mean to enter into the sanctity (*ḥurmah*) of the prayer.

Abū Bakr b. al-'Arabī remarks that the wordings of the tradition require that saying a *takbīr* before commencing the prayer is an essential part of it like standing, bowing and prostration Moreover, the word *takbīr* indicates that one must utter the words *Allah-u Akbar* specifically. The mention of other epithets of Allah which indicate His exaltation will not be valid. According to al-Shāfi'ī, one may say *Allah al-Akbar*. Abū Yūsuf also holds the view that a prayer will be valid if one utters *Allah al-Kabīr* (*'Awn al-Ma'būd*, I, 22).

36. *Taslīm* means saying *al-salāmu-'alaikum wa raḥmatullah* (may peace and mercy of Allah be upon you). The prayer comes to an end after the utterance of these words. And the acts prohibited during the prayer now become lawful. Hence the use of the word *taḥlīl*, meaning to make lawful. The tradition shows that it is essential to utter the words of salutation for the completion of the prayer. Abū Ḥanīfah maintains, on the basis of analogy, that any act or word which makes prayer void, such as defilement, is sufficient to complete prayer (*'Awn al-Ma'būd*, I, 22).

a state of purity, ten virtuous deeds will be recorded (in his favour).

Abū Dāwūd said: This is the tradition narrated by Musaddad, and it is more perfect.

Chapter 34

THINGS THAT POLLUTE WATER

(63) 'Abd Allah b. 'Umar said: The Prophet (may peace be upon him) was asked about water (in desert country) and what is frequented by animals and wild beasts. He replied: When there is enough water to fill two pitchers,[37] it bears no impurity.[38]

(64) 'Abd Allah b. 'Umar reported: The Messenger of Allah (may peace be upon him) was asked about water in desert. He then narrated a similar tradition (as mentioned above).

(65) 'Abd Allah b. 'Umar reported: The Apostle of Allah (may peace be upon him) said: When there is enough water to fill two pitchers, it does not become impure.

Abū Dāwūd said: Ḥammād b. Zaid has narrated this tradition on the authority of 'Āṣim (without any reference to the Prophet).

Chapter 35

ON THE WELL CALLED BUḌĀ'AH

(66) Abū Sa'īd al-Khudrī reported: People asked the Messenger of Allah (may peace be upon him): Can we perform ablution out of the well of Buḍā'ah, which is a well into which menstrual clothes, dead dogs and stinking things were thrown? He replied: Water is pure and is not defiled by anything.[39]

37. Scholars differ on the size and measurement of the pitchers mentioned in the tradition. There are nine shades of opinion about their identity. It is generally supposed that the pitchers mentioned in the tradition refer to the large size of pitchers made in Ḥajar, near Medina, known for their manufacture. According to the majority opinion, such a pitcher contains about 250 rotl (Baghdādī) of water. As such two pitchers contain approximately 500 or 600 rotl of water (about 6½ maunds). It is said that a pitcher is called *qullah* because it can be lifted by hand or by camel (*Badhl al-Majhūd*, I, 41).

38. The tradition indicates that if impurities fall into such a quantity of water, it does not become unclean. It can be used for washing and ablution. The followers of al-Shāfi'ī and the traditionists strictly follow this tradition. But the Ḥanafīs do not follow it considering it a weak *ḥadīth*.

39. The well of Buḍā'ah lay in the locality of Banū Sā'idah at Medina. Buḍā'ah is said to be the name of the owner or of the place where it is situated. The Prophet (may peace be upon him) performed ablution with its water and gave his blessings to it.

(67) Abū Sa'īd al-Khudrī reported: I heard that the people asked the Prophet of Allah (may peace be upon him): Water is brought for you from the well of Buḍā'ah. It is a well in which dead dogs, menstrual clothes and excrement of people are thrown. The Messenger of Allah (may peace be upon him) replied: Verily water is pure and is not defiled by anything.

Abū Dāwūd said: I heard Qutaibah b. Sa'īd say: I asked the person in charge of the well of Buḍā'ah about the depth of the well. He replied: At most the water reaches pubes. Then I asked: Where does it reach when its level goes down? He replied: Below the private part of the body.

Abū Dāwūd said: I measured the breadth of the well of Buḍā'ah with my sheet which I stretched over it. I then measured it with the hand. It measured six cubits in breadth. I then asked the man who opened the door of the garden for me and admitted me to it: Has the condition of this well changed from what it had originally been in the past? He replied: No. I saw that the colour of water in this well had changed.

Chapter 36

THE WATER LEFT OVER AFTER BATH IS NOT DEFILED

(68) Ibn 'Abbās reported: One of the wives[40] of the Prophet (may peace be upon him) took a bath from a large bowl. The Prophet (may peace be upon him) wanted to perform ablution or take a bath from the water left over. She said to him: O Prophet of Allah, verily I was sexually defiled. The Prophet said: Water is not defiled.[41]

Chapter 37

URINATING IN STAGNANT WATER

(69) Abū Hurairah reported: The Prophet (may peace be upon him) said: None

It is remarkable that people did not throw impurities in it deliberately. The flood of water during rain carried them into it as the well lay in its passage.

The tradition indicates that a large quantity of water is not defiled by the mixing of impurities unless its quality is changed. The well of Buḍā'ah had a large quantity of water which was not affected by these impurities (*'Awn al-Ma'būd*, I, 24).

40. The wife of the Apostle (may peace be upon him) referred to in the tradition was Maimūnah.

41. The tradition shows that things like water, garment and earth are not defiled by their association with a person who is sexually defiled. Further, the water left over after bath in the vessel can be used for purification.

amongst you should urinate in stagnant water, and then wash in it.[42]

(70) Abū Hurairah reported : The Prophet (may peace be upon him) said : None amongst you should urinate in standing water, then wash in it after sexual defilement.

Chapter 38

PERFORMING ABLUTION WITH WATER LEFT OVER AFTER A DOG HAS DRUNK OF IT

(71) Abū Hurairah reported : The Prophet (may peace be upon him) said : The purification of the utensil belonging to any one of you, after it has been licked by a dog, consists in washing it seven times, using sand in the first instance.[43]

Abū Dāwūd said : A similar tradition has been narrated by Abū Ayyūb and Ḥabīb b. al-Shahīd on the authority of Muḥammad.

(72) A similar tradition has been transmitted by Abū Hurairah through a different chain of narrators. But this version has been narrated as a statement of Abū Hurairah himself and not attributed to the Prophet (may peace be upon him). The version has the addition of the words : "If the cat licks (a utensil), it should be washed once."

(73) Abū Hurairah reported the Prophet (may peace be upon him) as saying : When a dog licks a (thing contained in a) utensil you must wash it seven times, using

42. "Water is used for ablution, washing and drinking purposes; it is, therefore, essential that it should be kept clean from all kinds of impurities. Special care should be taken in case of standing and stagnant water, because any impurity added to it would not be washed away. The Holy Prophet has, therefore, forbidden to urinate in standing water and has prohibited the Muslims to wash themselves in such water in which the people are accustomed to urinate. It may also be added that urination in flowing water is not desirable and this evil practice should be avoided.

"The second point to be noted is that if standing water is like a big lake or a pond, one can wash oneself in it even if it contains impurities, but on condition that those impurities have neither changed its colour, nor odour, nor taste. But if the water containing such impurities is small in quantity (less than 6½ maunds) it is unfit for washing or performing ablution, even if its colour, odour, or taste are unchanged" ('Abdul Ḥamīd Ṣiddīqī, Tr., *Saḥiḥ Muslim*, I, 167-68, footnote 488).

43. "The dog is one of the unclean beasts according to Islam and eating its flesh is forbidden, and its keeping in the houses as a pet is also prohibited for the Muslims. They have, however, been permitted to keep dogs for hunting, herding and watching. The food or water or the vessel which the dog licks is rendered impure. Thus such food and water should be thrown away and the vessel should be cleaned several times in order to purify it. Islam has declared the dog to be an unclean beast because its saliva has the germs of rabies in it. The writer of the article on 'Dog' in the *Encyclopaedia Britannica* says : 'It [rabies] is more common in dogs than in any other animal' (Vol. VII, p. 497). The dog is also responsible for the spread of 'Canine Plague'. The virus causing this disease is air-borne and affects the other dogs very quickly" ('Abdul Ḥamid Ṣiddīqī, Tr., *Ṣaḥīh Muslim*, I, 166, footnote 486).

earth (sand) for the seventh time.[44]

Abū Dāwūd said: This tradition has been transmitted by another chain of narrators in which there is no mention of earth.

(74) Ibn Mughaffal reported: The Messenger of Allah (may peace be upon him) ordered the killing of the dogs,[45] and then said: Why are they (people) after them (dogs)?– and then granted permission (to keep) the dog for hunting and for (the security) of the herd, and said: When the dog licks the utensil wash it seven times, and rub it with earth the eighth time.

Abū Dāwūd said: Ibn Mughaffal narrated in a similar way.

Chapter 39

THE LEFT-OVER OF A CAT

(75) Kabshah, daughter of Ka'b b. Mālik and wife of Ibn Abī Qatādah, reported: Abū Qatādah visited (me) and I poured out water for him for ablution. A cat came and drank some of it and he tilted the vessel for it until it drank some of it. Kabshah said: He saw me looking at him; he asked me: Are you surprised, my niece? I said: Yes. He then reported the Messenger of Allah (may peace be upon him) as saying: It is not unclean; it is one of those (males or females) who go round among you.[46]

44. The majority of scholars follow this tradition literally. Mālik, al-Shāfi'ī, and Aḥmad b. Ḥanbal hold that a vessel licked by a dog should be washed seven times using earth in the beginning or at the end. Abū Ḥanīfah maintains that it is sufficient to wash such a vessel, like other impurities, only three times. In his opinion washing seven times and the use of earth are not essential.

The use of earth has been mentioned in the traditions variantly: "for the first time," "for the seventh time," "for the eighth time," and "one time." Ibn Ḥajar al-'Asqalānī says that the variance indicates option in the use of earth at any time. He, however, prefers the version which mentions the wordings "for the first time".

Scholars differ on the performance of ablution with the water licked by a dog. Al-Zuhrī expresses the opinion that one can perform ablution with such a water if one has no water except the one licked by a dog. Sufyān al-Thawrī holds that one should perform both ablution and *tayammum* because the purity of such a water is doubtful and one may have misgivings in mind after performing ablution alone (*'Awn al-Ma'būd*, I, 27).

45. "The word used in the ḥadīth is *al kilāb* which means particular dogs and not all dogs. What the Holy Prophet, therefore, ordered was not the indiscriminate killing of dogs as a species, but the killing of stray dogs and those which were infected by rabies and other dangerous diseases" 'Abdul Ḥamīd Siddiqī, Tr., *Ṣaḥīḥ Muslim*, I, 167, footnote 487).

46. The tradition indicates that the left-over of the cat is not impure. Water can be used for purification. The Prophet (may peace be upon him) made a concession in this respect giving the reason that a cat frequently visits the houses like domestic servants. Hence it is not possible to avoid it. The same rule applies to the left-over of a rat and other animals frequenting the house (*'Awn al-Ma'būd*, I, 29).

(76) Dāwūd b. Ṣāliḥ b. Dīnār al-Tammār quoted his mother as saying that her mistress sent her with some pudding (*harīsah*) to 'Ā'ishah who was offering prayer. She made a sign to me to place it down. A cat came and ate some of it, but when 'Ā'ishah finished her prayer, she ate from the place where the cat had eaten. She stated : The Messenger of Allah (may peace be upon him) said : It is not unclean : it is one of those who go round among you. She added : I saw the Messenger of Allah (may peace be upon him) performing ablution from the water left over by the cat.

Chapter 40

PERMISSIBILITY OF PERFORMING ABLUTION WITH THE WATER LEFT OVER BY A WOMAN

(77) 'Ā'ishah reported : I and the Messenger of Allah (may peace be upon him) took a bath from one vessel while we were sexually defiled.[47]

47. What the tradition makes clear is that the left-over of water is not impure and can make the body clean. If a male or female uses water and some part of it is left over, there is no harm in utilising it for the purification of the body provided the person taking a bath does not sit in the tub.

"This hadīth and others like it have been the target of criticism by the hostile critics of Ḥadīth, though there is nothing noxious in it. It is a simple act of purification. These critics deliberately conjure up before the minds of people the modern system of tub bath in the glaring light of bulbs and tubes, and then try to create an opinion that is unworthy of the modesty and high sense of chastity of the Holy Prophet that such things should be attributed to him, and then jump to the conclusion that all the collections of aḥādīth are mere fabrications having no truth in them. The whole argument and the case on which it rests is fallacious and wrong. There are so many authentic aḥādīth which show that the Holy Prophet had a very keen sense of modesty.

"Secondly, although the Holy Prophet and his wives, on occasions, took a bath from one vessel, it had never been a tub bath wherein the couple could sit together and wash themselves. What they did was that they took out water from one vessel and bathed separately.

"Thirdly, the bathroom of the Holy Prophet was not illuminated with light so that his body and that of his pious wife could be visible to each other. He and his wives took bath before Tahajjud prayer, i.e. much before the dawn in pitch darkness, and, therefore, there was no question of their seeing the body of each other. [Another version of this tradition has the words : 'our hands alternated into it.' This] clearly indicates that their hands touched each other since they could not see them.

"These critics ignore the conditions under which the Holy Prophet (may peace be upon him) and his pious wives (may Allah be pleased with them) lived, and resort to indiscriminate criticism. The fact is that there was no practice of taking bath, because of sexual intercourse, in broad daylight. Every Muslim got up for tahujjud prayer and especially in the house of the Holy Prophet prayer, meditation and dhikr [remembrance of Allah] were the most common feature, and the whole family spent the latter part of the night in the remembrance of the Lord. The pious members of this sacred house, therefore, bathed themselves long before the daybreak.

"The point of importance here is that the left over of the water is not defiled, even if it is used by a person who has a sexual intercourse" ('Abdul Ḥamīd Ṣiddīqī. Tr., *Ṣaḥīḥ Muslim*, I, 185, footnote 538).

(78) 'Ā'ishah reported: My hands and the hands of the Messenger of Allah (may peace be upon him) alternated into one vessel while we performed ablution.[48]

(79) Ibn 'Umar reported: The males and females during the time of the Apostle of Allah (may peace be upon him) used to perform ablution from one vessel together.[49]

The wordings "from one vessel" occur in the version of Musaddad.

(80) 'Abd Allah b. 'Umar reported: We (men) and the women during the lifetime of the Apostle of Allah (may peace be upon him) used to perform ablution from one vessel. We all put our hands in it.

Chapter 41

PROHIBITION OF WASHING WITH THE WATER LEFT OVER BY THE MALE OR THE FEMALE

(81) Ḥumaid al-Ḥimyarī reported: I met a person who remained in the company of the Prophet (may peace be upon him) for four years as Abū Hurairah remained in his company. He reported: The Apostle of Allah (may peace be upon him) forbade that the female should wash with the water left over by the male, and that the male should wash with the left-over of the female.

The version of Musaddad adds: "That they both take the handful of water together."[50]

(82) Ḥakam b. 'Amr reported: The Prophet (may peace be upon him) forbade that the male should perform ablution with the water left over by the female.[51]

(48) Taking a bath or performing ablution by a male and a female together from one vessel is permissible in case they are husband and wife or have close relationship. This is not permissible for strangers (*Awn al-Ma'būd*, I, 30).

49. This practice was prevalent before the revelation of the Commandment of veil. The man and woman who are strangers are not allowed to take a bath or perform ablution together from one vessel. (*'Awn al-Ma'būd*, I, 30).

50. Taking a bath together from the same vessel is permissible only for the husband and wife. The tradition prohibits the strangers to do so. The use of the left-over of the water is permissible if they do not take out water together, but use it separately.

51. Al-Nawawī said: The tradition narrated by Ḥakam b. 'Amr is weak. It has been considered weak by the experts of *Ḥadīth*, especially by al-Bukhārī and other eminent traditionists.

Scholars differ on the permissibility of using the water left over by the male or female for purification. There are several viewpoints. The more correct and preferable view is that both the male and female can use the left-over of water as the traditions narrated by 'Ā'ishah indicate. Al-Nawawī thinks that at most the prohibition means that the water coming down from the limbs after washing them should not be used (*'Awn al-Ma'būd*, I, 31).

Chapter 42

PERFORMING ABLUTION WITH SEA WATER

(83) Abū Hurairah reported: A man asked the Apostle of Allah (may peace be upon him): Messenger of Allah, we travel on the sea and take a small quantity of water with us. If we use this for ablution, we would suffer from thirst. Can we perform ablution with sea water? The Messenger (may peace be upon him) replied: Its water is pure[52] and what dies in it is lawful food.[53]

Chapter 43

PERFORMING ABLUTION WITH *NABĪDH*[54]

(84) Abū Zaid quoted 'Abd Allah b. Mas'ūd as saying that on the night when the jinn listened to the Qur'ān[55] the Prophet (may peace be upon him) said: What is in your skin vessel? He said: I have some *nabidh*. He (the Holy Prophet) said: It consists of fresh dates and pure water.[56]

Sulaimān b. Dawud reported the same version of this tradition on the authority of Abū Zaid or Zaid. But Sharīk said that Ḥammād did not mention the words "night of the jinn."

(85) 'Alqamah reported: I asked 'Abd Allah b. Mas'ūd: Which of you was in the company of the Messenger of Allāh (may peace be upon him) on the night when the jinn attended him? He replied: No one of us was with him.[57]

52. The tradition indicates that the sea water is pure and can be used for the purposes of purification.

53. There is a difference of opinion on the lawfulness of all the animals that live in the sea. Mālik, al-Shāfi'ī and Aḥmad b. Ḥanbal hold that all are lawful. Abū Ḥanīfah maintains that only fish is lawful (*'Awn ul-Ma'būd*. I, 32).

54. A kind of drink prepared with dates, raisins, honey and barley by adding water to them. Sometimes it becomes an intoxicant (*'Awn al-Ma'būd*, I. 32).

55. Lit. "the night of the jinn." After the death of Abū Ṭālib the Prophet (may peace be upon him) went to al-Ṭā'if to proclaim his message. But the people there did not listen to him. Returning to Mecca he spent a night in the valley of Nakhlah where a company of the jinn listened to him reciting the Qur'ān. It is disputed whether Ibn Mas'ūd accompanied the Prophet (may peace be upon him) or not

56. Scholars differ on the legitimacy of ablution with *nabidh*. Al-Shāfi'ī, Aḥmad b. Ḥanbal and Isḥāq b. Rahwaih and the majority of the traditionists hold that it is unlawful to perform ablution with *nabidh*. Abū Ḥanīfah and Sufyān al-Thawrī hold that this is lawful in the absence of water (*'Awn al-Ma'būd*, I. 32).

57. This tradition shows that the previous tradition is weak.

It is said that the jinn called upon the Prophet (may peace be upon him) twice. On the first occasion no one accompanied him. But on the second occasion Ibn Mas'ūd might have remained in his company as reported by Ibn Abī Hātim (*'Awn al-Ma'būd*, I, 33).

(86) It is reported that 'Aṭā' did not approve of performing ablution with milk and *nabīdh* and said: *tayammum* is more to my liking (than performing ablution with milk and *nabīdh*).

(87) Abū Khaldah reported: I asked Abu'l-'Āliyah[58] whether a person who is sexually defiled and has no water with him, but he has only *nabīdh*, can wash with it? He replied in the negative.

Chapter 44

CAN A MAN OFFER PRAYER WHILE HE IS FEELING THE CALL OF NATURE?

(88) 'Urwah reported on the authority of his father that 'Abd Allah b. al-Arqam travelled for performing *Ḥajj* (pilgrimage) or *'Umrah*. He was accompanied by the people whom he led in prayer. One day when he was leading them in the dawn (*fajr*) prayer, he said to them: One of you should come forward. He then went away to relieve himself. He said: I heard the Messenger of Allah (may peace be upon him) say: When any of you feels the need of relieving himself while the congregational prayer is ready, he should go to relieve himself.[59]

(89) 'Abd Allah b. Muḥammad reported: We were in the company of 'Ā'ishah. When her food was brought in, al-Qāsim stood to say his prayer. Thereupon, 'Ā'ishah said: I heard the Messenger of Allah (may peace be upon him) say: Prayer should not be offered in the presence of meals, nor at the moment when one is struggling with two evils (i.e. when one is feeling the call of nature).

(90) Thawbān reported: The Messenger of Allah (may peace be upon him) said: Three things one is not allowed to do: supplicating Allah specifically for himself and ignoring others while leading people in prayer; if he did so, he deceived them; looking inside a house before taking permission: if he did so, it is as if he entered the house, saying prayer while one is feeling the call of nature until one eases oneself.

(91) Abū Hurairah reported: The Prophet (may peace be upon him) said: It is not permissible for a man who believes in Allah and in the Last Day that he should say the prayer while he is feeling the call of nature until he becomes light (by relieving himself).[60]

58. An eminent and noted successor (*tābi'i*).

59. This tradition shows that one should have total devotion and perfect peace of mind while offering prayer. If one does not relieve oneself before saying prayer, one cannot concentrate on it.

60. These traditions indicate that it is a disapproved practice to say the prayer while one is feeling the call of nature, or while one is feeling hungry and the food is placed before him. According to the majority of scholars this is disapproved in case there is ample time for prayer.

Then the narrator Thawr b. Yazīd transmitted a similar tradition with the following wordings: "It is not permissible for a man who believes in Allah and in the Last Day that he should lead the people in prayer but with their permission; and that he should not supplicate to Allah exclusively for himself leaving all others. If he did so, he violated the trust."

Abū Dāwūd said: This is a tradition reported by the narrators of Syria; no other person has joined them in relating this tradition.

Chapter 45

THE QUANTITY OF WATER THAT IS DESIRABLE FOR ABLUTION

(92) 'Ā'ishah reported: The Prophet (may peace be upon him) used to wash himself with a ṣā' (of water) and perform ablution with a *mudd* (of water).[61]

Abū Dāwūd said: This tradition has also been narrated by Abān on the authority of Qatādah. In this version he said: "I heard Ṣafiyah"

(93) Jābir reported: The Prophet (may peace be upon him) used to take a bath with a ṣā' (of water) and perform ablution with a mudd (of water).

(94) Ḥabīb al-Anṣārī reported: I heard 'Abbād b. Tamīm who reported on the authority of my grandmother, Umm 'Umārah,[62] saying: The Prophet (may peace be upon him) wanted to perform ablution. A vessel containing ⅔ mudd of water was brought to him.[63]

If the time is so short that if a person takes food or relieves himself, the prayer time will elapse, then he should offer the prayer immediately in the same condition. As such, no delay is allowed. Abū Sa'īd says that some Shāfi'ī scholars maintain that a man should not say the prayer in such a condition; but he should take food or relieve himself, even if the prayer time elapses. Al-Nawawī says that if one said the prayer in such a condition, although there was ample time for prayer, then he committed a disapproved act. But his prayer is valid; nevertheless, it is commendable to offer it again. Al-Qāḍī 'Iyāḍ says that, according to the Ẓāhirīs, the prayer offered in such a condition is void (*'Awn al-Ma būd*, I, 34).

61. Ṣā' is a measurement equal to four mudds. And mudd is also a standard of measurement which varies according to the place and circumstances. But it is generally equal to one bushel. The mudd of Ḥijāz contains 1⅓ rotls (about ¾ seer) of water and that of Iraq contains 2 rotls (about 1 seer) of water. The ṣā' of Ḥijāz, therefore, contains about 3 seers of water.

This tradition does not prescribe any quantity of water essential for the validity of ablution and bath. The Prophet (may peace be upon him) sometimes performed ablution and took a bath with this quantity of water and sometimes used more than this. A tradition recorded in *Ṣaḥiḥ Muslim* says: "The Prophet (may peace be upon him) took a bath from the vessel (which contained seven to eight seers, i. e. fifteen to sixteen pounds) of water." This in fact depends on circumstances (*'Awn al-Ma'būd*, I, 35).

62. Her name is Nasībah. She is the daughter of Ka'b al-Anṣārī from the tribe of al-Najjār (*'Awn al-Ma'būd*, I. 35).

63. This tradition shows that one mudd of water is not necessary for ablution

(95) Anas reported: The Prophet (may peace be upon him) performed ablution with a vessel which contained two rotls[64] (of water) and took a bath with a ṣā‘ (of water).

Abū Dāwūd said: This tradition has been narrated on the authority of Anas through a different chain. This version mentions: "He performed ablution with one makkūk."[65] It makes no mention of two rotls.

Abū Dāwūd said: This tradition has also been narrated by Yaḥyā b. Ādam from Sharīk. But this chain mentions Ibn Jabr b. ‘Atīk instead of ‘Abd Allah b. Jabr.

Abū Dāwūd said: This tradition has also been narrated by Sufyān from ‘Abd Allah b. ‘Īsā. This chain mentions the name Jabr b. ‘Abd Allah instead of ‘Abd Allah b. Jabr.

Abū Dāwūd said: I heard Aḥmad b. Ḥanbal say: One ṣā‘ measures five rotls. It was the ṣā‘ of Ibn Abī Dhi'b and also of the Prophet (may peace be upon him).

Chapter 46

EXCEEDING THE LIMITS IN ABLUTION

(96) ‘Abd Allah b. Mughaffal heard his son praying to Allah: O Allah, I ask Thee a white palace on the right of Paradise when I enter it. He said: O my sonny, ask Allah for Paradise and seek refuge in Him from Hell-Fire, for I heard the Messenger of Allah (may peace be upon him) say: In this community there will be some people who will exceed the limits in purification[66] as well as in supplication.[67]

Chapter 47

PERFORMING ABLUTION IN FULL

(97) ‘Abd Allah b. ‘Amr reported: The Messenger of Allah (may peace be upon him) saw some people (performing ablution) while their heels were dry. He then

64. A unit of weight varying from about one to about five pounds, according to locality.

65. A standard of measurement equal to mudd.

66. Extravagance in ablution and bath consists in washing the limbs more than three times and spending excessive water. Scholars are agreed upon the disapproval of spending more water in ablution and bath than the quantity necessary for purification. A tradition recorded in ***Sunan Ibn Mājah*** says: The Prophet came upon Sa‘d when he was performing ablution and asked: What is this extravagance, Sa‘d? He replied: Is there extravagance in ablution? He said: Yes, if, you are beside a flowing river (*‘Awn al-Ma‘būd*, I, 36).

67. One may exceed the limits in supplication by asking Allah unlawful things, by praying at the top of one's voice, and by rhyming (*‘Awn al-Ma‘būd*, I, 36).

said : Woe to the heels because of Hell. Perform the ablution in full.[68]

Chapter 48

PERFORMING ABLUTION WITH A BRASS VESSEL

(98) 'Ā'ishah said : I and the Messenger of Allah (may peace be upon him) used to take bath with a brass vessel.[69]

(99) This tradition has also been narrated on the authority of 'Ā'ishah through a different chain.

(100) 'Abd Allah b. Zaid said : The Messenger of Allah (may peace be upon him) came upon us. We brought water for him in a brass vessel and he performed ablution.

Chapter 49

THE UTTERANCE OF *BISMILLĀH* IN THE BEGINNING OF ABLUTION

(101) Abū Hurairah reported : The Messenger of Allah (may peace be upon him) said : The prayer of a person who does not perform ablution is not valid, and the ablution of a person who does not mention the name of Allah (in the beginning) is not valid.[70]

68. This is the abridged version of a lengthy tradition reported by Muslim. It says : 'Abd Allah b. 'Amr reported : We returned from Mecca to Medina with the Messenger of Allah (may peace be upon him) and when we came to some water on the way, some of the people were in a hurry at the time of the afternoon prayer and performed ablution hurriedly ; and when we reached them, their heels were dry, no water had touched them. The Prophet (may peace be upon him) said : Woe to (dry) heels because of Hell-Fire. Perform your ablution in full.

"When ablution is performed carelessly, some parts of the body are not properly washed, and it betrays the fact that the man is not performing his religious duty with the seriousness that it rightly deserves. In this state of carelessness it is generally the heels which are not thoroughly washed. In order to make believers fully conscious of the importance of Wuḍū' for prayer it has been stressed that it should be performed well and every part of the body that has to be washed in Wuḍū' should be carefully cleaned" ('Abdul Hamīd Siddīqī, Tr., *Sahiḥ Muslim*, I, 454, footnote 452).

69. This tradition indicates the permissibility of performing ablution with a vessel made of brass or bronze.

70. Mentioning the name of Allah means the utterance of ***Bismillāh al-Raḥmān al-Raḥim*** or ***Bismillāh wa'l-ḥamdu lillāh.*** If one forgets the utterance of ***Bismillāh*** in the beginning, he may utter in the middle the word "***Bismillāh awwalan wa ākhiran***". This tradition outwardly shows that if one does not mention the name of Allah in the beginning of ablution, it is not valid.

(102) Explaining the tradition of the Prophet (may peace be upon him) that the ablution of a person who does not mention the name of Allah is valid, Rabī'ah said: This tradition means that if a person performs ablution and takes a bath but does not have the intention to perform ablution for prayer and purify himself from sexual defilement, his ablution or bath is not valid.[71]

Chapter 50

A MAN WHO PUTS HIS HAND IN THE UTENSIL BEFORE WASHING IT

(103) Abū Hurairah reported: The Messenger of Allah (may peace be upon him) said: When anyone amongst you wakes up from sleep at night, he should not put his hand in the utensil until he has washed his hand three times, for he does not know where his hand was during the night.[72]

(104) This tradition has been reported by Abū Hurairah through another chain of transmitters. It adds: "twice or thrice." This version does not mention Abū Razīn.

(105) Abū Hurairah reported: I heard the Messenger of Allah (may peace be upon him) say: When any of you wakes up from sleep, he should not put his hand in the utensil until he washes it three times, for none of you knows where his hand remained during the night or where it went round.

Scholars differ on this point. According to one statement ascribed to Aḥmad b. Ḥanbal utterance of *Bismillāh* is a necessary condition for the validity of ablution. According to Mālik, al-Shāfi'ī and Abū Ḥanīfah, it is commendable to mention the name of Allah in the beginning of ablution. The same opinion is also attributed to Ibn Ḥanbal. Isḥāq b. Rahwaih holds that if a person forgets *tasmiyah* his ablution is valid; in case one leaves it deliberately, it is not valid.

Al-Tirmidhī and Ibn Mājah have stated that the traditions on this subject (*tasmiyah*) are not sound Aḥmad b. Ḥanbal says that the traditions on this subject are weak in respect of their chains (*'Awn al-Ma'būd*, I, 37-38).

71. The statement of Rabi'ah that purification is not valid without intention is in itself correct, but obviously this tradition does not mean so. There are other traditions which indicate the necessity of intention (*'Awn al-Ma'būd*, I, 38).

72. It is agreed upon by the scholars that one should not put one's hand in the vessel containing water after waking up from sleep by day or by night before washing his hand. But most of the scholars hold that the tradition does not mean that omission to wash one's hand renders the act strictly unlawful; it only means that it is preferable that one should wash the hand after waking up and then put it in the water. If a person puts his hand in the vessel, the water will not become impure. During the time of the Prophet (may peace be upon him) people took out water from the large bowls or utensils to perform ablution. Hence the commandment (*'Awn al-Ma'būd*, I, 38).

Chapter 51

DESCRIPTION OF THE PROPHET'S (MAY PEACE BE UPON HIM) ABLUTION

(106) Ḥumrān b. Abbān, the freed slave of 'Uthmān, said: I saw 'Uthmān b. 'Affān while he performed ablution. He poured water over his hands three times and then washed them. He then rinsed his mouth and then cleansed his nose with water (three times). He then washed his right arm up to the elbow three times, then washed his left arm in a similar manner; then wiped his head; then washed his right foot three times, then washed his left foot in a similar manner, and then said: I saw the Apostle of Allah (may peace be upon him) performing ablution like this ablution of mine. Then he (the Prophet) said: He who performs ablution like this ablution of mine and then offered two *rak'ahs* of prayer without allowing his thoughts to be distracted, Allah will pardon all his past sins.

(107) Ḥumrān said: I saw 'Uthmān b. 'Affān performing ablution. He then narrated the same tradition. In this version there is no mention of rinsing the mouth and snuffing up water. This tradition adds: "He wiped his head three times. He then washed his feet three times. He then said: I saw the Apostle of Allah (may peace be upon him) performing ablution in like manner. He (the Prophet) said: He who performs ablution less than this, it is sufficient for him.[73] The narrator did not mention prayer (in this version).

(108) 'Abd al-Raḥmān al-Taimī reported: Ibn Abī Mulaikah was asked about ablution. He said: I saw 'Uthmān b. 'Affān who was asked about ablution. He called for water. A vessel was then brought to him. He inclined it towards his right hand (poured water upon it). He then put it in the water; then he rinsed his mouth three times and cleansed his nose with water three times, and washed his face three times. He then put his hand in the water and took it out; then he wiped his head and ears, in and out only once. He then washed his feet, and said: Where are those who asked me to perform ablution? I saw the Messenger of Allah (may peace be upon him) performing ablution like that.

Abū Dāwūd said: All the sound traditions narrated by 'Uthmān indicate that the head is to be wiped once, because they mentioned (the washing of each part in) ablution three times. In their versions of tradition they mentioned the wordings: "he wiped his head." In this case they did not mention any number as they did in other cases.

(109) Abū 'Alqamah said that 'Uthman called for water and performed ablution. He then poured water with the right hand or the left hand; he then washed them up to the wrist; he then rinsed the mouth and snuffed up water three times. The

73. It is commendable to wash all the relevant parts of body three times. If a person washes once or twice, or some parts once or twice and others thrice, there will be no harm. The ablution will be valid.

narrator mentioned that 'Uthmān washed each part three times. He then wiped head and washed his feet. He said: I saw the Apostle of Allah (may peace be upon him) performing ablution as you saw me perform ablution. He then reported the tradition like that of al-Zuhrī and completed it.

(110) Shaqīq b. Salamah said: I saw 'Uthmān b. 'Affān (perform ablution). He washed his forearms three times and washed his head thrice. He then said: I saw the Messenger of Allah (may peace be upon him) doing like that.

Abū Dāwūd said: Another version says: "He performed ablution three times only.'

(111) 'Abd Khair said: 'Alī came upon us; he had already offered prayer. He called for water. We asked: What will you do with water when you have already offered prayer?—Perhaps to teach us. A utensil containing water and a wash-basin were brought (to him). He poured water from the utensil on his right hand and washed both his hands three times, rinsed the mouth, snuffed up water and cleansed the nose three times. He then rinsed the mouth and snuffed up water with the same hand by which he took water. He then washed his face three times, and washed his right hand three times and washed his left hand three times. He then put his hand in water and wiped his head once. He then washed his right foot thrice and left foot thrice, then said: If one is pleased to know the method of performing ablution of the Apostle of Allah, this is how he did it.

(112) 'Abd Khair said: 'Alī offered the dawn prayer and went to Raḥbah (a locality in Kūfah). He called for water. A boy brought him a vessel containing water and a wash-basin. He held the vessel with his right hand and poured water over his left hand. He washed both of his hands (to the wrist) three times. He then put his right hand in the vessel (to take water) and rinsed his mouth three times and snuffed up water three times. He then narrated almost the same tradition as narrated by Abū 'Awānah. He then wiped his head, both its front and back sides, once. He then narrated the tradition in like manner.

(113) Mālik b. Ghurfaṭah says: I heard 'Abd Khair say: I saw a chair was brought to 'Alī who sat on it. A vessel of water was then brought to him. He washed his hands three times; he then rinsed his mouth and snuffed up water with one handful of water. He narrated the tradition completely.

(114) Zirr b. Ḥubaish said that he heard that 'Alī was asked how the Apostle of Allah (may peace be upon him) used to perform ablution. He then narrated the tradition and said: He wiped his head so much so that drops (of water) were about to trickle down. He then washed his feet three times and said: This is how the Apostle of Allah (may peace be upon him) performed ablution.

(115) 'Abd al-Raḥmān b. Abī Lailā says: I saw 'Alī performing ablution. He washed his face three times and his hands three times and wiped his head once. Then he ('Alī) said: The Apostle of Allah (may peace be upon him) used to perform

ablution in this way.

(116) Abū Ḥayyah said: I saw 'Alī perform ablution. He (Abū Ḥayyah) then described that 'Alī went through every part of the ablution three times, i.e. he performed each detail of his ablution three times. He then wiped his head, then washed his feet up to the ankles. He then said: I wanted to show you how the Apostle of Allah (may peace be upon him) performed ablution.

(117) Ibn 'Abbās said: 'Alī b. Abī Ṭālib entered upon me after he had passed water. He then called for water for ablution. We brought to him a vessel containing water, and placed it before him. He said: O Ibn 'Abbās, may I not show you how the Apostle of Allah (may peace be upon him) used to perform ablution? I replied: Why not? He then inclined the vessel to his hand and washed it. He then put his right hand in the vessel and poured water over the other hand and washed his hands up to the wrist. He then rinsed his mouth and snuffed up water. He then put both of his hands together in the water and took out a handful of water and threw it upon the face. He then inserted both of his thumbs in the front part of the ears. He did like that twice and thrice. He then took a handful of water and poured it over his forehead and left it running down his face. He then washed his forearms up to the elbows three times. He then wiped his head and the back of his ears. He then put both of his hands together in the water and took a handful of it and threw it on his foot. He had a shoe on his foot which he twisted (or washed) by throwing water; then he washed his other foot like that. Do you wash your foot while it is in the shoe? He replied: Yes, while it is in the shoe. This question and answer were repeated thrice.

Abū Dāwūd said: The version transmitted by Ibn Juraij from Shaibah is similar to the one narrated by 'Alī. In this version Ḥajjāj reported on the authority of Ibn Juraij the wording: He wiped his head once. Ibn Wahb narrated from Ibn Juraij the wording: He wiped his head three times.

(118) 'Amr b. Yaḥyā al-Māzinī reports on the authority of his father who asked 'Abd Allah b. Zaid, the grandfather of 'Amr b. Yaḥyā al-Māzinī: Can you show me how the Messenger of Allah (may peace be upon him) performed ablution? 'Abd Allah b. Zaid replied: Yes. He called for ablution water, poured it over his hands, and washed them; then he rinsed his mouth and snuffed up water in the nose three times; then he washed his face three times and washed his forearms up to elbows twice; then he wiped his head with both hands, moving them fron tand back of the head, beginning from his forehead, and moved them to the nape; then he pulled them back to the place from where he had started (wiping); then he washed his feet.

(119) 'Abd Allah b. Ẓaid b. 'Āṣim reported this tradition saying: He rinsed his mouth and snuffed up water from one hand, doing that three times.

(120) Ḥabban b. Wāsi' reported on the authority of his father who heard 'Abd Allah b. Zaid al-'Āṣim al-Māzinī say that he saw the Messenger of Allah (may peace be upon him) performing ablution. He then described his ablution saying: He wiped

his head with water which was not what was left over after washing his hands (i.e. he wiped his head with clean water); then he washed his feet until he cleansed them.

(121) Al-Miqdām b. Ma'dīkarib al-Kindī reported: The ablution water was brought to the Messenger (may peace be upon him) and he performed ablution; he washed his hands up to wrists three times, then washed his forearms three times. He then rinsed his mouth and snuffed up water three times; then he wiped his head and ears inside and outside.

(122) Al-Miqdām b. Ma'dīkarib reported: I saw the Apostle of Allah (may peace be upon him) perform ablution. When he reached the stage of wiping his head, he placed his palms on the front of the head. Then he moved them until he reached the nape. He then returned them to the place from where he had started.

(123) Another version says: He wiped his ears inside and outside. Hishām adds: He inserted his fingers in the ear-holes.

(124) Abu'l-Azhar al-Mughīrah b. Farwah and Yazīd b. Abī Mālik reported: Mu'āwiyah performed ablution before the people, as he saw the Apostle of Allah (may peace be upon him) perform ablution. When he reached the stage of wiping his head, he took a handful of water and poured it with his left hand over the middle of his head so much so that drops of water came down or almost came down. Then he wiped (his head) from its front to its back and from its back to its front.

(125) Another version says: He performed each part of the ablution three times and washed his feet times without number.

(126) Al-Rubayyi' daughter of Mu'awwidh b. 'Afrā' said: The Messenger of Allah (may peace be upon him) used to come to us. He once said: Pour ablution water on me. She then described how the Prophet (may peace be upon him) performed ablution saying: He washed his hands up to wrists three times and washed his face three times, and rinsed his mouth and snuffed up water once. Then he washed his forearms three times and wiped his head twice beginning from the back of his head, then wiped its front. He wiped his ears outside and inside. Then he washedh is feet three times.

Abū Dāwud said: The tradition narrated by Musaddad carries the same meaning.

(127) Ibn 'Uqail reported this tradition with a slight change of wording. In his tradition he said: He rinsed his mouth three times and snuffed up water three times.

(128) Al-Rubayyi' daughter of Mu'awwidh b. 'Afrā' reported: The Messenger of Allah (may peace be upon him) performed ablution in her presence. He wiped the whole of his head from its upper to the lower part moving every side. He did not move the hair from their original position.

(129) Al-Rubayyi' daughter of Mu'awwidh b. 'Afrā' said: I saw the Messenger of Allah (may peace be upon him) performing ablution. He wiped his head front and back, his temples and his ears once.

(130) Al-Rubayyi' reported: The Prophet (may peace be upon him) wiped his head with water which was left over in his hand.

(131) Al-Rubayyi' daughter of Mu'awwidh b. 'Afrā' reported: The Prophet (may peace be upon him) performed ablution. He inserted his two fingers in the ear-holes.

(132) Ṭalḥah b. Muṣarrif reported on the authority of his father from his grandfather: I saw the Apostle of Allah (may peace be upon him) wiping his head once up to his nape.[74]

Musaddad reported: He wiped his head from front to back until he moved his hands from beneath the ears.

Abū Dāwūd said: Musaddad said: I narrated this tradition to Yaḥyā, but he called it *munkar* (rejected).

Abū Dāwūd said: I heard Aḥmad say: People thought that Ibn 'Uyainah had considered it to be *munkar* (rejected) and said: What is this chain: Ṭalḥah—his father—his grandfather?

(133) Sa'īd b. Jubair reported: Ibn 'Abbās saw the Apostle of Allah (may peace be upon him) performed ablution. He narrated the tradition which says that he (the Prophet) performed each detail of ablution three times. He wiped his head and ears once.

(134) Abū Umāmah mentioned how the Messenger of Allah (may peace be upon him) performed ablution, saying that he used to wipe the corners of his eyes, and he said that the ears are treated as part of the head.

Sulaimān b. Ḥarb said: the wording "the ears are treated as part of the head" were uttered by Abū Umāmah.

Ḥammād said: I do not know whether the phrase "the ears are treated as part of the head" was the statement of the Prophet (may peace be upon him) or of Abū Umāmah.

Chapter 52

WASHING THE LIMBS IN ABLUTION THREE TIMES

(135) 'Amr b. Shu'aib, quoting his father on the authority of his grandfather, said: A man came to the Prophet (may peace be upon him) and asked him: Messenger of Allah, how is the ablution (to be performed)? He (the Prophet) then called for water in a vessel and washed his hands up to the wrists three times, then washed his face three times, and washed his forearms three times. He then wiped his head and inserted both his index fingers in his ear-holes; he wiped the back of his ears with his thumbs and the front of his ears with the index fingers. He then washed his feet three

74. Some scholars argue in favour of the desirability of wiping the nape with the back of the fingers after wiping the head and ears on the basis of this tradition. But their argument is not correct. The wiping of the nape is not proved from any single tradition, sound or good. All the traditions narrated in support of wiping the nape are weak (*'Awn al-Ma'būd*, I, 50).

times. Then he said : This is how ablution should be performed. If anyone does more or less than this, he has done wrong and transgressed, or (said) transgressed and done wrong.[75]

Chapter 53

WASHING THE LIMBS IN ABLUTION TWICE

(136) Abū Hurairah reported: The Prophet (may peace be upon him) washed the limbs in ablution twice.

(137) 'Aṭā' b. Yasār quoting Ibn 'Abbās said: Do you like that I should show you how the Messenger of Allah (may peace be upon him) performed ablution? He then called for a vessel of water and took out a handful of water with his right hand. He then rinsed his mouth and snuffed up water. He then took out another handful of water and washed his face by both his hands together. He then took out another handful of water and washed his right hand and then washed his left hand by taking out another. He then took out some water and shook off his hand and wiped his head and ears with it. He then took out a handful of water and sprinkled it over his right foot in his shoe and wiped the upper part of the foot with his one hand, and beneath the shoe with his other hand. He then did the same with his left foot.

Chapter 54

WASHING THE LIMBS IN ABLUTION ONCE

(138) 'Aṭā' b. Yasār quoting Ibn 'Abbās said: May I not tell you how the Messenger of Allah (may peace be upon him) performed ablution? He then performed ablution washing each limb once only.

75. The washing of the limbs in ablution more than three times is undesirable. But this tradition shows that washing them less than three times, i.e. once or twice, is also undesirable, although it is already established by other traditions narrated by al-Ṭahāwī, al-Bazzār and al-Ṭabrānī and also by consensus of opinion of the scholars that the Prophet (may peace be upon him) washed the limbs in ablution sometimes once and sometimes twice. In reply to this, it has been said that the words "less than this" which occur in this version are a misunderstanding on the part of the narrator and an addition of his own. The version narrated by Aḥmad, al-Nasā'ī and Ibn Mājah have only the words "more than this." Explaining the words "less than this" some scholars take them to mean leaving to wash a certain limb or washing it imperfectly (*'Awn al-Ma'būd*, I, 52).

Chapter 55

DISTINCTION BETWEEN RINSING THE MOUTH AND SNUFFING UP WATER

(139) Ṭalḥah quoting his father on the authority of his grandfather said: I entered upon the Prophet (may peace be upon him) while he was performing ablution, and the water was running down his face and beard to his chest. I saw him rinsing his mouth and snuffing up water separately.[76]

Chapter 56

EJECTING MUCUS AFTER SNUFFING UP WATER

(140) Abū Hurairah reported: The Apostle of Allah (may peace be upon him) said: When any of you performs ablution, he should snuff up water in his nose and eject mucus.

(141) Ibn 'Abbās reported: The Messenger of Allah (may peace be upon him) said: Cleanse your nose well (after snuffing up water) twice or thrice.

(142) Laqīṭ b. Ṣabirah reported: I was the leader of the delegation of Banu'l-Muntafiq or (the narrator doubted) I was among the delegation of Banu'l-Muntafiq that came to the Messenger of Allah (may peace be upon him). When we reached the Prophet, we did not find him in his house. We found there 'Ā'ishah, the Mother of the Believers. She ordered that a dish called *Khazīrah* should be prepared for us. It was then prepared. A tray containing dates was then presented to us. (The narrator Qutaibah did not mention the word *qinā'*, tray). Then the Messenger of Allah (may peace be upon him) came. He asked: Has anything been served to you or ordered for you? We replied: Yes, Messenger of Allah. While we were sitting in the company of the Messenger of Allah (may peace be upon him) we suddenly saw that a shepherd was driving a herd of sheep to their abode. He had with him a newly-born kid that was crying. He (the Prophet) asked him: What did it deliver, O so-and-so? He replied: Female sheep. He then said: Slaughter for us in its place a sheep. Do not think that we are slaughtering it for you. We have one hundred sheep and we do not want that their number may increase. Whenever a female kid is born, we slaughter a sheep in its place. (The narrator says that the Prophet [may peace be upon him] used the word *la-taḥsabanna*, do not think). I (the narrator Laqīṭ) then said: Messenger

76. This tradition shows that the Prophet rinsed his mouth separately and snuffed up with fresh water separately. But there are also some traditions which indicate that he rinsed his mouth and snuffed with the same water. He did not take water twice. This is also permissible. Both these actions have been supported by sound traditions. The chain of the traditions which indicate separation is sounder (*'Awn al-Ma'būd*, I, 53).

of Allah, I have a wife who has something (wrong) in her tongue, i.e. she is insolent. He said : Then divorce her. I said : Messenger of Allah, she had company with me and I have children from her. He said : Then ask her (to obey you). If there is something good in her, she will do (obey) ; and do not beat your wife as you beat your slave-girl. I said : Messenger of Allah, tell me about ablution. He said : Perform ablution in full and make the fingers go through the beard and snuff up water well except when you are fasting.

(143) Laqīṭ b. Ṣabirah reported that he was the leader of Banu'l-Muntafiq (name of a tribe). He came to 'Ā'ishah. He then narrated the tradition in a similar manner. He said : The Prophet (may peace be upon him) then came shortly with rapid strides inclining forward. The narrator used the word *'aṣīdah* (name of a dish) in this version instead of *Khazīrah*.[77]

(144) The version of Ibn Juraij has the wording : "If you perform ablution, then rinse your mouth."

Chapter 57

MAKING THE WATER GO THROUGH THE BEARD BY INSERTING FINGERS

(145) Anas b. Mâlik reported : Whenever the Messenger of Allah (may peace be upon him) performed ablution, he took a handful of water, and, putting it under his chin, made it go through his beard, saying : Thus did my Lord command me.

Chapter 58

WIPING OVER THE TURBAN

(146) Thawbān reported : The Messenger of Allah (may peace be upon him) sent out an expedition. They were affected by cold. When they returned to the Messenger of Allah (may peace be upon him), he commanded them to wipe over turbans[78]

77. *Khazirah* is a dish prepared with the slices of meat by adding water and flour in the end. If such a dish is prepared only with flour, having no meat, it is called *'aṣidah* (*'Awn al-Ma'būd*, I, 55).

78. This tradition shows that wiping over the turban is sufficient, and wiping the head is not essential. Scholars differ on the question of wiping over the turban alone. Abū Bakr, 'Umar, Anas, al-Auzā'ī, Aḥmad b. Ḥanbal and Isḥāq consider it to be permissible. Others hold that wiping over the turban alone is not sufficient unless one wipes the head too. This is the view held by Sufyān al-Thawrī, Mālik b. Anas, Ibn al-Mubārak and al-Shāfi'ī. This is also the generally accepted viewpoint on this question. But it should be noted that the traditions show that the Prophet (may peace be upon him) sometimes wiped over the turban alone, sometimes wiped the head alone, and at times wiped over both the turban and the head. Hence there seems no reason to permit the one and reject the other. All the traditions on this question are well established and sound (*'Awn al-Ma'būd*, I, 56).

and stockings.

(147) Anas b. Mālik said : I saw the Messenger of Allah (may peace be upon him) perform ablution. He had a Quṭrī[79] turban. He inserted his hand beneath the turban and wiped over the forelock, and did not untie the turban.

Chapter 59

WASHING THE FOOT

(148) Al-Mustaurid b. Shaddād reported : I saw the Messenger of Allah (may peace be upon him) rubbing his toes with his little finger when he performed ablution.

Chapter 60

WIPING OVER THE SHOES

(149) Al-Mughīrah b. Shu'bah reported : I was in the company of the Messenger of Allah (may peace be upon him) in the expedition of Tabūk. He abandoned the main road before the dawn prayer, and I also did the same along with him. The Prophet (may peace be upon him) made his camel kneel down and (went to) relieve himself. He then came back and I poured water upon his hands from the skin-vessel. He then washed his hands and face. He tried to get his forearms out (of the gown), but the sleeves of the gown were too narrow, so he entered back both his hands, and brought them out from beneath the gown. He washed his forearms up to the elbows and wiped his head and wiped over his socks.[80] He then mounted (his camel) and we began to proceed until we found people offering the prayer. They brought forward 'Abd al-Raḥmān b. 'Awf who was leading them in prayer, starting it at the proper time. He had already completed a *rak'ah* of the dawn prayer. The Prophet (may peace be upon him) stood in the row side by side with other Muslims. He performed the second *rak'ah* of the prayer behind 'Abd al-Raḥmān b. 'Awf. Then 'Abd al-Raḥmān uttered salutation. The Prophet (may peace be upon him) stood to perform the remaining *rak'ah* of the prayer. The Muslims were alarmed. They began to utter

79. Quṭr is the name of a place in al-Baḥrain known for the manufacture of turbans. Quṭrī turbans are a little red in colour and bear red stripes.

80. "Islam does not prescribe rigorous rules in anything. In Wuḍū' or ablution, the concession of wiping over the socks has been granted in order to provide relief to the people. With the exception of the Khwārij and Shī'a, there is a consensus of opinion amongst the Muslims that it is permissible to wipe the socks while performing ablution without doing it any harm. Difference, if there is any, is about the nature of the socks. Imām Mālik is of the view that wiping is permitted only on leather socks. Imām Shāfi'ī deems it desirable only when a man is wearing shoes along with socks. Imām Abū Yūsuf and Imām Muḥammad consider it permissible in case of thick socks" ('Abdul Ḥamīd Ṣiddīqī, Tr. *Ṣaḥīḥ Muslim*, I, 162, footnote 479).

tasbīḥ (Subḥān Allāh) presuming that they had offered prayer before the Prophet (may peace be upon him) had done. When he uttered the salutation (i.e. finished his prayer), he said : You were right, or (he said) you did well.

(150) Al-Mughīrah b. Shu'bah said : The Messenger of Allah (may peace be upon him) performed ablution and wiped his forelock and turban. Another version says : The Messenger of Allah (may peace be upon him) wiped his socks and his forelock and his turban.

Bakr said : I heard it from Ibn al-Mughīrah.

(151) 'Urwah b. al-Mughīrah reported his father as saying : We accompanied the Apostle of Allah (may peace be upon him) to a caravan, and I had a jug of water. He went to relieve himself and came back. I came to him with the jug of water and poured upon him. He washed his hands and face. He had a tight-sleeved Syrian woollen gown. He tried to get his forearms out, but the sleeve of the gown was very narrow, so he brought his hands out from under the gown. I then bent down to take off his socks. But he said to me : Leave them, for my feet were clean when I put them in, and he only wiped over them.[81]

Yūnus said on the authority of al-Sha'bī that 'Urwah narrated this tradition from his father before him, and his father reported it from the Messenger of Allah (may peace be upon him).

(152) Al-Mughīrah b. Shu'bah said : The Messenger of Allah (may peace be upon him) lagged behind (in a journey). He then narrated this story saying : Then we came to the people. 'Abd al-Raḥmān was leading them in the dawn prayer. When he perceived the presence of the Prophet (may peace be upon him), he intended to retire. The Prophet (may peace be upon him) asked him to continue and I and the Prophet (may peace be upon him) offered one *rak'ah* of prayer behind him. When he had pronounced the salutation, the Prophet (may peace be upon him) got up and offered the *rak'ah* which had been finished before, and he made no addition to it.

Abū Dāwūd said : Abū Sa'īd al-Khudrī, Ibn al-Zubair and Ibn 'Umar hold the opinion that whoever gets an odd number of the *rak'ahs* of prayer, he should perform two prostrations on account of forgetfulness.[82]

(153) Abū 'Abd al-Raḥmān al-Sulamī said that he witnessed 'Abd al-Raḥmān b. 'Awf asking Bilāl about the ablution of the Prophet (may peace be upon him). Bilāl said : He went out to relieve himself. Then I brought water for him and he performed ablution, and wiped over his turban and socks.

81. Ablution is completed by merely wiping over the socks only when these are worn afte ablution.

82. This is the view of a group of scholars like 'Aṭā', Ṭāwūs, Mujāhid and Isḥāq. But according to the majority of the scholars, the prostration for forgetfulness at the end of the prayer is not necessary (*'Awn al-Ma'būd*, I, 59).

(154) Abū Zur'ah b. 'Amr b. Jarīr said: Jarīr urinated. He then performed ablution and wiped over the socks. He said: What can prevent me from wiping (over the socks); I saw the Messenger of Allah (doing so). They (the people) said: This (action of yours) might be valid before the revelation of Sūrat al-Mā'idah. He replied: I embraced Islam after the revelation of Sūrat al-Mā'idah.[83]

(155) Abū Buraidah, on the authority of his father, reported: Negus presented to the Messenger of Allah (may peace be upon him) two black and simple socks. He put them on; then he performed ablution and wiped over them.

Musaddad reported this tradition from Dulham b. Ṣāliḥ.

Abū Dāwūd said: This tradition has been narrated by the people of Baṣrah alone.

(156) Al-Mughīrah b. Shu'bah said: The Messenger of Allah (may peace be upon him) wiped over the socks and I said: Messenger of Allah, have you forgotten? He said: My Lord has commanded me to do this.

Chapter 61

TIME LIMIT FOR WIPING OVER THE SHOES

(157) Khuzaimah b. Thābit reported: The Prophet (may peace be upon him) said: The time limit for wiping over the socks for a resident is three days (and three nights) and for a traveller it is one day and one night.

Abū Dāwūd said: Another version adds: Had we requested him to extend (the period for wiping), he would have extended.

(158) Yaḥyā b. Ayyūb who had said prayer along with the Messenger of Allah (may peace be upon him) facing both the directions (Ka'bah and Bait al-Maqdis) asked: Messenger of Allah, may I wipe over the socks? He replied: Yes. He asked: For one day? He replied: For one day. He again asked: And for two days? He replied: For two days too. He again asked: And for three days? He replied: Yes, as long as you wish.[84]

83. "This part of the ḥadīth explains the importance of the teachings of the Holy Prophet in Islam. Had Sūrat al-Mā'ida been revealed after this act of the Holy Prophet, it was then quite logical to argue that it had been abrogated by the verse of the Qur'an (v. 7) in which washing of the feet to the ankles had been made compulsory. But as Jarīr had embraced Islam after the revelation of this verse, it implies that wiping over the socks is permitted, as the act and the word of the Holy Prophet explain the true significance of the teachings of the Qur'ān. His interpretation is divinely inspired and is, therefore, to be accepted as final in all matters. . . ." 'Abdul Ḥamīd Siddīqī, Tr. *Ṣaḥīh Muslim*. I. 163, footnote 480).

84. As indicated by Abu Dāwūd the chain of this tradition is disputed. Hence the tradition is weak. What is correct about the time limit for wiping over the socks is the tradition narrated by Shuraih b. Hānī recorded in *Ṣaḥiḥ Muslim*. It says: I asked 'Alī b. Abī Ṭālib about wiping over the

Abū Dāwūd said: Another version says: He asked him about the period until he reached the period of seven days. The Messenger of Allah (may peace be upon him) replied: Yes, as long as you wish (i.e. there is no time limit).

Abū Dāwūd said: There is a variance in the chain of narrators of this tradition. The chain is not strong.

Another chain from Yaḥyā b. Ayyūb is also disputed.

Chapter 62

WIPING OVER THE STOCKINGS

(159) Al-Mughīrah b. Shu'bah reported: The Messenger of Allah (may peace be upon him) performed ablution and wiped over the stockings and shoes.

Abū Dāwūd said: 'Abd al-Raḥmān b. Mahdī did not narrate this tradition because the familiar version from al-Mughīrah says that the Prophet (may peace be upon him) wiped over the socks.

Abū Mūsā al-Ash'arī has also reported: The Prophet (may peace be upon him) wiped over the stockings. But the chain of narrators of this traditon is neither continuous nor strong.

'Alī b. Abī Ṭālib, Ibn Mas'ūd, al-Barā' b. 'Āzib, Anas b. Mālik, Abū Umāmah, Sahl b. Sa'd and 'Amr b. Ḥuraith also wiped over the stockings.[85]

Chapter 63

(160) Aws b. Abī Aws al-Thaqafī reported: The Messenger of Allah (may peace be upon him) performed ablution and wiped over his shoes and feet.

'Abbād said: The Messenger of Allah (may peace be upon him) came to the well of a people. Musaddad did not mention the words *Mīḍāt* (a place where ablution is performed), and *Kaẓāmah* (well). Then both agreed on the wording: "He performed ablution and wiped over his shoes and feet."

shoes and he replied that the Messenger of Allah (may peace be upon him) had appointed three days and nights as the period when a traveller may do it, and one day and night as the period for one who is not travelling (is resident). A similar tradition has been recorded by al-Tirmidhī and al-Nasā'ī.

85. Scholars differ on the permissibility of wiping over the stockings. Aḥmad b. Ḥanbal, Isḥāq b. Rahwaih, 'Abd Allah b. al-Mubārak, Muḥammad b. al-Ḥasan, and Abū Yūsuf hold that wiping over the stockings is permissible, whether they are made of leather, or have leather soles, or they are only thick, having no leather sole. This is also held by Abū Ḥanīfah according to one statement ascribed to him. The opinions of the Shāfi'ī scholars are confused on this subject (*'Awn al-Ma'būd*, I, 62).

Chapter 64

HOW TO WIPE OVER THE SOCKS

(161) Al-Mughīrah b. Shu'bah reported: The Messenger of Allah (may peace be upon him) wiped over the socks.

Another version adds: "On the back (upper part) of the socks."

(162) 'Alī said: If the religion were based on opinion, it would be more important to wipe the under part of the shoe than the upper, but I have seen the Messenger of Allah (may peace be upon him) wiping over the upper part of his shoes.

(163) This tradition has been transmitted through a different chain of narrators. This version adds: "I always preferred to wash the under part of the feet until I saw the Messenger of Allah (may peace be upon him) wiping the upper part of them.

(164) A'mash transmitted this tradition saying: If religion were based on opinion, it would be more proper to wipe the under part of the feet than the upper. The Prophet (may peace be upon him) wiped over the upper part of his shoes.

The narrator Wakī' said: By feet he meant the socks.

Another version says: I saw 'Alī perform ablution and wash the upper part of his feet, and say: Had I not seen the Messenger of Allah (may peace be upon him) doing like this—and he narrated the tradition in full.

(165) Al-Mughīrah b. Shu'bah said: I poured water while the Prophet (may peace be upon him) performed ablution in the battle of Tabūk. He wiped over the upper part of the socks and their lower part.

Abū Dāwūd said: I have been told that Thawr did not hear this tradition from Rajā'.

Chapter 65

SPRINKLING WATER ON PRIVATE PARTS OF THE BODY AFTER ABLUTION

(166) Hakam b. Sufyān al-Thaqafī reported: When the Messenger of Allah (may peace be upon him) urinated, he performed ablution and sprinkled water on private parts of the body.[86]

Abū Dāwūd said: A group of scholars agreed with Sufyān upon this chain of narrators. Some have mentioned the name Sufyān b. al-Ḥakam, and others al-Ḥakam b. Sufyān.

86. Sprinkling water on the private parts of the body was practised to keep away the evil notions (*'Awn al-Ma'būd*, I, 64).

(167) A man from Thaqīf on the authority of his father reported : I saw the Messenger of Allah (may peace be upon him) urinate, and he sprinkled water on the private parts of his body.

(168) Ḥakam or Ibn al-Ḥakam on the authority of his father reported : The Prophet (may peace be upon him) urinated ; then he performed ablution and sprinkled water on the private parts of his body.

Chapter 66

WHAT A MAN SHOULD SAY AFTER ABLUTION

(169) 'Uqbah b. 'Āmir said : We served ourselves in the company of the Messenger of Allah (may peace be upon him). We tended our camels by turn. One day I had my turn to tend the camels, and I drove them in the afternoon. I found the Messenger of Allah (may peace be upon him) addressing the people. I heard him say : Anyone amongst you who performs ablution, and does it well, then he stands and offers two ***rak'ahs*** of prayer, concentrating on it with his heart and body, Paradise will be his lot by all means. I said : Ha-ha ! How fine it is ! A man in front of me said : The action (mentioned by the Prophet) earlier, O 'Uqbah, is finer than this one. I looked at him and found him to be 'Umar b. al-Khaṭṭāb. I asked him : What is that, O Abū Ḥafṣ ? He replied : He (the Prophet) had said before you came : If any one of you performs ablution, and does it well, and when he finishes the ablution, he utters the words : I bear witness that there is no deity except Allah, He has no associate, and I bear witness that Muḥammad is His Servant and His Messenger, all the eight doors of Paradise will be opened for him ; he may enter (through) any of them.

Mu'āwiyah said: Rabī'ah b. Yazīd narrated this tradition to me from Abū Idrīs on the authority of 'Uqbah b. 'Āmir.

(170) 'Uqbah b. 'Āmir al-Juhanī narrated this tradition from the Prophet (may peace be upon him) in a similar way. He did not mention about tending the camels. After the words "and he performed ablution well" he added the words : "he then raises his eyes towards the sky". He transmitted the tradition conveying the same meaning as that of Mu'āwiyah.

Chapter 67

OFFERING VARIOUS PRAYERS WITH THE SAME ABLUTION

(171) Abū Asad b. 'Amr said : I asked Anas b. Mālik about ablution. He replied : The Prophet (may peace be upon him) performed ablution for each prayer

and we offered (many) prayers with the same ablution.

(172) Buraidah on the authority of his father reported : The Messenger of Allah (may peace be upon him) performed five prayers with the same ablution on the occasion of the capture of Mecca, and he wiped over his socks. 'Umar said to him (the Prophet) : I saw you doing a thing today that you never did. He said : I did it deliberately.

Chapter 68

LEAVING ANY SPOT DRY IN ABLUTION

(173) Anas reported : A person came to the Messenger of Allah (may peace be upon him). He performed ablution and left a small part equal to the space of a nail upon his foot. The Messenger of Allah (may peace be upon him) said to him : Go back and perform ablution well.

Abū Dāwūd said : This tradition is not known through Jarīr b. Ḥāzim. It was transmitted only by Ibn Wahab.

Another version adds the wording : "Go back and perform the ablution well."

(174) Ḥasan narrated from the Prophet (may peace be upon him) a tradition conveying the same meaning as that of Qatādah.

(175) Khālid, on the authority of some Companions of the Prophet (may peace be upon him) reported : The Prophet (may peace be upon him) saw a person offering prayer, and on the back of his foot a small part equal to the space of a dirham remained unwashed ; the water did not reach it. The Prophet (may peace be upon him) commanded him to repeat the ablution and prayer.

Chapter 69

A MAN WHO IS SURE OF PURIFICATION BUT DOUBTS THAT SOMETHING HAS RENDERED IT INVALID

(176) 'Abbād b. Tamīm reported from his uncle that a person made a complaint to the Prophet (may peace be upon him) that he entertained (doubt) as if something had happened to him which had rendered his ablution invalid. He (the Prophet) said : He should not cease (to pray) unless he hears a sound or perceives a smell (of passing wind).

(177) Abū Hurairah reported : The Messenger of Allah (may peace be upon him) said : If any one of you offers prayer and feels a movement between his paddocks, but is doubtful whether or not his ablution broke, he should not cease praying unless he hears a sound or perceives a smell.

Chapter 70

ABLUTION DOES NOT BECOME VOID BY KISSING A WOMAN

(178) 'Ā'ishah reported: The Prophet (may peace be upon him) kissed me and did not perform ablution.

Abū Dāwūd said: This tradition is *Mursal* (i. e. where the link of the Companions is missing and the Successor reports from the Prophet directly). Ibrāhīm al-Taimī did not hear anything from 'Ā'ishah.

Abū Dāwūd said: Al-Firyābī and others narrated this tradition in a like manner.

(179) 'Ā'ishah reported: The Prophet (may peace be upon him) kissed one of his wives and went out for saying prayer. He did not perform ablution. 'Urwah said: I said to her: Who is she except you! Thereupon she laughed. Abu Dāwūd said: The same version has been reported through a different chain of narrators.

(180) This tradition has been transmitted through another chain of narrators on the authority of 'Ā'ishah.

Abū Dāwūd said: Yaḥyā b. Sa'īd al-Qiṭṭān said to a person: Narrate these two traditions from me, that is to say, one tradition on the authority of al-A'mash from Ḥabīb (about kissing); another through the same chain about a woman who has a prolonged flow of blood and she is asked to perform ablution for every prayer.

Yaḥyā said: Narrate from me that both these traditions are weak in respect of their chains.

Abū Dāwūd said: Al-Thawrī is reported to have said: Ḥabīb narrated this tradition to us only on the authority of 'Urwat al-Muzanī, that is, he did not narrate any tradition on the authority of 'Urwah b. al-Zubair.

Abū Dāwūd said: Ḥamzah al-Zayyāt reported a sound tradition on the authority of Habīb, from 'Urwah b. al-Zubair from 'Ā'ishah.

Chapter 71

BY TOUCHING THE PENIS ABLUTION BECOMES VOID

(181) 'Abd Allah b. Abī Bakr reported that he heard 'Urwah say: I entered upon Marwān b. al-Ḥakam. We mentioned things that render the ablution void. Marwān said: Does it become void by touching the penis? 'Urwah replied: This I do not know. Marwān said: Busrah daughter of Ṣafwān reported to me that she heard the Messenger of Allah (may peace be upon him) say: He who touches his penis should

perform ablution.[87]

Chapter 72

ABLUTION IS NOT NECESSARY AFTER TOUCHING THE PENIS

(182) Qais b. Ṭalq on the authority of his father reported: We came upon the Prophet of Allah (may peace be upon him). A man came to him: he seemed to be a bedouin. He said: Prophet of Allah, what do you think about a man who touches his penis after performing ablution? He (may peace be upon him) replied: That is only a part of his body.[88]

Abū Dāwūd said: The tradition has been transmitted through a different chain of narrators.

(183) The tradition has also been reported by Qais b. Ṭalq through a different chain of narrators. This version adds the wording: "during the prayer"

Chapter 73

PERFORMING ABLUTION AFTER EATING THE FLESH OF CAMEL

(184) Barā' b. 'Āzib reported: The Messenger of Allah (may peace be upon him) was asked about performing ablution after eating the flesh of the camel. He replied:

87. Ablution becomes void in case one touches one's penis, unwrapped. Ibn Ḥibbān recorded in his *Ṣaḥīh* a tradition from the Prophet (may peace be upon him) on the authority of Abū Hurairah. It says: "If any one of you touches the private part of his body, if there is no curtain and wrapper between them, he should perform ablution." In case one touches the penis wrapped, there is no need of performing ablution This includes both male and female, and any private part of the body.

This tradition has been followed by a large number of the Companions and scholars, e g. 'Umar, Ibn 'Umar, Abū Ayyūb al-Anṣārī. Zaid b. Khālid, Abū Ḥurairah, 'Abd Allah b. 'Amr b. al-'Āṣ, Jābir, 'Ā'ishah, Umm Ḥabībah. Busrah daughter of Ṣafwān, Sa'd b Abī Waqqāṣ and Ibn 'Abbās according to one statement, 'Urwah b. al-Zubair, Sulaimān b. Yasār, Hishām, al-Awzā'i, al-Shāfi'i, Aḥmad, Isḥāq and Mālik.

According to Abū Ḥanīfah, the ablution does not become void by touching the penis (*'Awn al-Ma'būd*, I, 71).

88. The traditionists differ on this question. Some have preferred the tradition reported by Busrah and others have adopted the one narrated by Ṭalq.

'Alī, 'Ammar b. Yāsir, Ibn Mas'ūd, Ibn 'Abbās, Ḥudhaifah b. al-Yamān 'Imrān b. al-Ḥuṣain, Abu'l-Dardā', Sa'd b. Abī Waqqāṣ, according to one statement, Sa'īd b. al-Musayyab according to one statement, Sa'īd b. Jubair, Ibrāhīm al-Nakha'ī, Rabī'ah b. Abī 'Abd al-Rahmān, Sufyān al-Thawrī, Abū Ḥanīfah, Yaḥyā b. Ma'īn, and the people of Kūfah (*'Awn al-Ma'būd*, I, 72).

Perform ablution, after eating it.[89] He was asked about performing ablution after eating mutton. He replied: Do not perform ablution after eating it. He was asked about saying prayer in places where the camels lie down. He replied: Do not offer prayer in places where the camels lie down. These are the places of Satan. He was asked about saying prayer in the sheepfolds. He replied: You may offer prayer in such places; these are the places of blessing.

Chapter 74

PERFORMING ABLUTION AFTER TOUCHING THE FLESH OF AN ANIMAL OR WASHING IT IS NOT NECESSARY

(185) Abū Sa'īd reported: The Prophet (may peace be upon him) passed by a boy who was skinning a goat. The Messenger of Allah (may peace be upon him) said: Give it up until I show you. He (the Prophet) inserted his hand between the skin and the flesh until it reached the armpit. He then went away and led the people in prayer and he did not perform ablution The version of 'Amr added that he did not touch water.

Abū Dāwūd said: This tradition has been narrated through another chain of transmitters, making no mention of Abū Sa'īd.

Chapter 75

PERFORMING ABLUTION IS NOT NECESSARY AFTER TOUCHING A CARCASE

(186) Jābir reported: The Messenger of Allah (may peace be upon him) passed

89. "There is a difference of opinion amongst the jurists about this matter. Some of the scholars of Ḥadīth are of the opinion that the eating of camel's flesh does not break the ablution, but, according to others, e.g. Aḥmad b. Ḥanbal, Isḥāq b. Rahwai and Yaḥyā and Ibn Mundar, it does break. The question naturally arises why such an exception is made for the flesh of the camel. Various reasons have been put forward for this. Maulānā Shabbīr Aḥmad deems its offensive smell to be the main cause of it. Shāh Walīullāh of Delhi has given a different view. His argument is that the eating of camel's flesh had been forbidden in the Torah and all the apostles of Banū Isrā'īl agreed on it, but it was made permissible for the followers of Muḥammad (may peace be upon him) and ablution was enjoined upon them as an expression of thankfulness to the Lord for this favour. Similarly, other scholars have given other arguments, but . . . the most convincing reason is given by Maulānā Shabbīr Aḥmad 'Uthmānī. that this order of ablution after eating the flesh of camel is one of the main phases through which new converts had to pass for learning the laws of purification. Firstly, ablution was made obligatory for everyone who ate food touched by fire. This was done in order to accustom people to this habit of purification. Later on concession was granted in this matter but it

by the market when on his return from one of the villages of 'Āliyah.[90] People accompanied him from both sides. On the way he found a dead kid with both its ears joined together. He caught hold of it by its ear. He then said: Which of you likes to take it? The narrator transmitted the tradition in full.

Chapter 76

THE PERFORMING OF ABLUTION IS NOT ESSENTIAL WHEN ONE TAKES SOMETHING COOKED WITH THE HELP OF FIRE

(187) Ibn 'Abbās said: The Messenger of Allah (may peace be upon him) took (the meat of) a (goat's) shoulder and offered prayer and did not perform ablution.[91]

(188) Al-Mughīrah b. Shu'bah said: One night I became the guest of the Prophet (may peace be upon him). He ordered that a piece of mutton be roasted, and it was roasted. He then took a knife and began to cut the meat with it for me. In the meantime Bilāl came and called him for prayer. He threw the knife and said: What happened! May his hands be smeared with earth! He then stood for offering prayer.

Al-Anbārī added: My moustaches became lengthy. He trimmed them by placing a tooth-stick; or he said: I shall trim your moustaches by placing the tooth-stick there.

(189) Ibn 'Abbās said: The Messenger of Allah (may peace be upon him) took a shoulder (of goat's meat) and after wiping his hand with a cloth on which he was sitting, he got up and prayed.

(190) Ibn 'Abbās said: The Prophet (may peace be upon him) ate a little meat from a (goat's) shoulder. He then offered prayer and did not perform ablution.

(191) Muḥammad b. al-Munkadir said: I heard Jābir b. 'Abd Allah say: I presented bread and meat to the Prophet (may peace be upon him). He ate them and called for ablution water. He performed ablution and offered the noon (*ẓuhr*) prayer. He then called for the remaining food and ate it. He then got up and prayed and did not perform ablution.

(192) Jābir said: The last practice of the Messenger of Allah (may peace be upon him) was that he did not perform ablution after taking anything that was cooked with

was ordained to continue this practice of ablution in case of camel's flesh and subsequently the full concession was given. (For detailed study see *Fatḥ al-Mulhim*, Vol. I, p. 490, and Shāh Walīullāh's *Ḥujjat Allāh al-Bāligha*, Vol. I, p. 177)" 'Abdul Ḥamid Ṣiddiqī, Tr., *Ṣaḥīḥ Muslim*, I. 198, footnote 571).

90. 'Āliyah and Awālī are the names of villages in the suburb of Medina four to eight miles distant.

91. In the early days of Islam it was essential to perform ablution if one took anything cooked with the help of fire. Later on this commandment was abrogated.

the help of fire.

Abū Dāwūd said: This is the abridgment of the former tradition.

(193) 'Ubaid b. Thumāmah al-Murādī said: 'Abd Allah b. Ḥārith b. Jaz', one of the Companions of the Prophet (may peace be upon him), came upon us in Egypt. When he was narrating traditions in the Mosque of Egypt, I heard him say: I was the seventh or the sixth person in the company of the Messenger of Allah (may peace be upon him) in the house of a person. In the meantime Bilāl came and called him for prayer. He came out and passed by a person who had his fire-pan on the fire. The Messenger of Allah (may peace be upon him) said to him: Has the food in the fire-pan been cooked? He replied: Yes, my parents be sacrificed upon you. He then took a piece out of it and continued to chew it until he uttered the first ***takbir*** (***Allāh-u-Akbar***) of the prayer. All this time I was looking at him.

Chapter 77

STRICTNESS IN PERFORMING ABLUTION AFTER EATING ANYTHING COOKED WITH THE HELP OF FIRE

(194) Abū Hurairah reported: The Messenger of Allah (may peace be upon him) said: Perform ablution after eating anything which has been cooked by fire.

(195) Abū Sufyān b Sa'īd b. al-Mughīrah reported that he entered upon Umm Ḥabībah who presented him a glass of *sawīq* (a drink prepared with flour and water) to drink. He called for water and rinsed his mouth. She said: O my cousin, don't you perform ablution? The Prophet (may peace be upon him) said: Perform ablution after eating anything cooked with fire, or he said: anything touched by fire.

Abū Dāwūd said: The version of al-Zuhrī has: O my paternal cousin.

Chapter 78

RINSING THE MOUTH AFTER DRINKING MILK

(196) 'Abd Allah b. 'Abbās said that the Prophet (may peace be upon him) drank some milk and then rinsed his mouth saying: It contains greasiness.

Chapter 79

RINSING THE MOUTH AFTER DRINKING MILK IS NOT NECESSARY

(197) Anas b. Mālik reported: The Messenger of Allah (may peace be upon

him) drank some milk and he did not rinse his mouth nor did he perform ablution, and he offered the prayer [92]

Chapter 80

PERFORMING ABLUTION IS NECESSARY BECAUSE OF BLEEDING

(198) Jābir reported : We proceeded in the company of the Messenger of Allah (may peace be upon him) for the battle of Dhāt al-Riqā'.[93] One of the Muslims killed the wife of a person from among the unbelievers. He (the husband of the woman killed) took an oath saying : I will not rest until I kill one of the Companions of Muḥammad. He went out following the footsteps of the Prophet (may peace be upon him). The Prophet (may peace be upon him) encamped at a certain place. He said : Who will keep a watch on us ? A person from the ***Muhājirīn*** (Emigrants) and another from the ***Anṣār*** (Helpers) responded. He said : Go to the mouth of the mountain-pass. When they went to the mouth of the mountain-pass the man from the ***Muhājirīn*** lay down while the man from the ***Anṣār*** stood praying. The man (enemy) came to them. When he saw the person he realised that he was the watch-man of the Muslims. He shot him with an arrow and hit the target. But he (took the arrow out and) threw it away. He (the enemy) then shot three arrows. Then he (the Muslim) bowed and prostrated and awoke his companion. When he (the enemy) perceived that they (the Muslims) had become aware of it, he ran away. When the man from the ***Muhājirīn*** saw the (man from the ***Anṣār***) bleeding, he asked him : Glory be to Allah ! Why did you not wake me up for the first time when he shot at you. He replied : I was busy in reciting a chapter of the Qur'ān. I did not like to leave it.[94]

Chapter 81

PERFORMING ABLUTION AFTER AWAKING FROM SLEEP

(199) 'Abd Allah b. 'Umar said : One night the Messenger of Allah (may peace

92. This tradition shows that it is better to rinse the mouth after drinking milk but it is not necessary.

93. This battle took place in 4 H.

94. This tradition shows that bleeding does not make ablution void : Hence the Companion continued his prayer and did not perform ablution after bleeding. Al-Shāfiʿī, Mālik, a group of the Companions and of the Successors hold that bleeding from the body other than the channels of urine and excretion does not render ablution void. The Companions used to offer their prayer in the battle while their wounds were bleeding and their garments were smeared with blood. The Prophet (may peace be upon him) never commanded them to take off their clothes or to perform ablution. The Ḥanafīs, however, hold that ablution becomes void by bleeding. They argue from other traditions from the Prophet (may peace be upon him) (*Awn al Ma'būd*, I. 78).

be upon him) was busy and he delayed the night (*'ishā'*) prayer so much so that we dosed in the mosque. We awoke, then dozed, and again awoke and again dozed. He (the Prophet) then came upon us and said : There is none except you who is waiting for prayer.[95]

(200) Anas said : The Companions during the lifetime of the Messenger of Allah (may peace be upon him) used to wait for the night prayer so much so that their heads were lowered down (by dozing). Then they offered prayer and did not perform ablution.

Abū Dāwūd said : Shu'bah on the authority of Qatādah added : We lowered down our heads (on account of dozing) in the day of the Messenger of Allah (may peace be upon him).

Abū Dāwūd said : This tradition has been narrated through a different chain of narrators.

(201) Anas b. Mālik reported : (The people) stood up for the night prayer and a man stood up and spoke forth : Apostle of Allah, I have to say something to you. He (the Prophet) entered into secret conversation with him, till the people or some of the people dozed off, and then he led them in prayer. He (Thābit al-Bunānī) did not mention ablution.

(202) Ibn 'Abbās reported: The Apostle of Allah (may peace be upon him) used to prostrate and sleep (in prostration) and produce puffing sounds (during sleep). Then he would stand and pray and would not perform ablution. I said to him: you prayed but did not perform ablution though you slept (in prostration). He replied: Ablution is necessary for one who sleeps while he is lying down. 'Uthmān and Hannād added: For when he lies down, his joints are relaxed.

Abū Dāwūd said: The statement "ablution is necessary for one who sleeps while one is lying down" is a ***Munkar*** (rejected) tradition. It has been narrated only by Yazīd Abū Khālid al-Dālānī, on the authority of Qatādah. And its earlier part has been narrated by a group (of narrators) from Ibn 'Abbās; they did not mention anything about it. He (Ibn 'Abbās) said: The Prophet (may peace be upon him) was protected (during his sleep). 'Ā'ishah reported: The Prophet (may peace be upon him) said: My eyes sleep, but my heart does not sleep. Shu'bah said: Qatādah heard from Abu'l-'Āliyah only four traditions: the tradition about Jonah son of Matthew, the tradition reported by Ibn 'Umar about prayer, the tradition stating that the judges are three, and the tradition narrated by Ibn 'Abbās saying: (This tradition) has been

95 The other versions of this tradition indicate that the Prophet (may peace be upon him) then offered prayer The Companions also prayed but did not perform ablution although they slept. This shows that ablution does not become void by dozing in a sitting posture. In dozing and half-sleeping ablution does not become void. Many other traditions indicate that ablution becomes void in case one sleeps while one is lying down or reclining on something.

narrated to me by reliable persons; 'Umar is one of them, and the most reliable of them in my opinion is 'Umar. Abu Dāwūd said: I asked Aḥmad b. Ḥanbal about the tradition narrated by Yazīd al-Dālānī. He rebuked me out of respect for him. Then he said: Yazīd al-Dālānī does not add anything to what has been narrated by the teachers of Qatādah. He did not care for this tradition (due to its weakness).

(203) 'Alī b. Abī Ṭālib reported: The Apostle of Allah (may peace be upon him) said: The eyes are the leather strap of the anus, so one who sleeps should perform ablution.

Chapter 82

A MAN WHO TREADS ON UNCLEAN PLACE

(204) Ibn Mas'ud said: We would not wash our feet after treading on something unclean,[96] nor would we hold our hair and garments (during prayer).

Abū Dāwūd said: The tradition has been reported by Ibrāhīm b. Abī Mu'āwiyah through a different chain of narrators: A'mash—Shaqīq –Masrūq –'Abd Allah (b. Mas'ud). And Hannād reported from Shaqīq, or reported on his authority saying: 'Abd Allah (b. Mas'ūd) said.

Chapter 83

ON THE BREACH OF ABLUTION DURING PRAYER

(205) 'Ali b. Ṭalq reported: The Apostle of Allah (may peace be upon him) said: When any of you breaks wind during the prayer, he should turn away and perform ablution and repeat the prayer.

Chapter 84

ON PROSTATIC FLUID (*MADHĪ*)[97]

(206) 'Alī said: My prostatic fluid flowed excessively. I used to take a bath until

96. The tradition has been interpreted in a towfold way. First, in case the Companions passed by an unclean place and their feet were smeared with dirt, they did not wash them, nor did they repeat their ablution because of being smeared with dirt Secondly if they walked on unclean place and had dust on their feet, they did not wash them particularly when the dust or dirt was dry The reason is, as other versions of this tradition indicate the dirt is removed when one goes ahead and passes by a clean place Hence it is not necessary to remove the dust or dirt when it is dry, or to wash feet or repeat ablution if one treads on an unclean place By providing such licence the Prophet (may peace be upon him) made religion easier for the people (*'Awn al-Ma'būd*, I, 82 83).

97. There are three terms in Arabic for the fluid that comes out of the sexual organ, namely, ***mani*** (semen), ***madhi*** (prostatic fluid) and ***wadi*** (fluid that comes out before or after urination). *Mani*

my back cracked (because of frequent washing). I mentioned it to the Prophet (may peace be upon him), or the fact was mentioned to him (by someone else). The Apostle of Allah (may peace be upon him) said: Do not do so. When you find prostatic fluid, wash your penis and perform ablution as you do for prayer, but when you have seminal emission, you should take a bath.[98]

(207) Al-Miqdād b. al-Aswad said that 'Alī b. Abī Ṭālib commanded him to ask the Apostle of Allah (may peace be upon him) what a man should do when he wants to have intercourse with his wife and the prostatic fluid comes out (at this moment). (He said): I am ashamed of consulting him because of the position of his daughter. Al-Miqdād said: I asked the Apostle of Allah (may peace be upon him) about it. He said: When any of you finds it, he should wash his private part, and perform ablution as he does for prayer.

(208) 'Urwah said: 'Alī b Abī Ṭālib said to al-Miqdād, and made a similar statement as above. Al-Miqdād asked him (the Prophet). The Apostle of Allah (may peace be upon him) said: He should wash his penis and testicles.

Abū Dāwūd said: The tradition has been narrated by al-Thawrī and a group of narrators from Hishām on the authority of his father from al-Miqdād, from 'Alī reporting from the Prophet (may peace be upon him).

(209) 'Urwah reported on the authority of his father a tradition from 'Alī b. Abī Ṭālib who said: I asked al-Miqdād (to consult the Prophet). He then narrated the tradition bearing the same meaning.

Abū Dāwūd said: This tradition has been reported with another chain of narrators. This version does not mention the word "testicles."

(210) Sahl b. Ḥunaif said: I felt greatly distressed by the frequent flowing of prostatic fluid. For this reason I used to take a bath very often. I asked the Apostle of Allah (may peace be upon him) about this. He replied: Ablution will be sufficient for you because of this. I asked: Apostle of Allah, what should I do if it smears my clothes. He replied: It is sufficient if you take a handful of water and sprinkle it on your clothe when you find it has smeared it.

(211) 'Abd Allah b. Sa'd al-Anṣārī said: I asked the Apostle of Allah (may peace be upon him) as to what makes it necessary to take a bath and about the (prostatic) fluid that flows after taking a bath. He replied: that is called *madhī* (prostatic fluid). It flows from every male. You should wash your private parts and testicles because of it and perform ablution as you do for prayer.

(semen) is a thick fluid that comes out after cohabitation. *Madhi* (prostatic fluid) comes out in watery form before cohabitation by kissing and hugging and other factors that precede intercourse.

98. The tradition shows that ablution is sufficient if one has prostatic fluid. Washing is not necessary. In case one has seminal emission, one should take a bath. This is the view agreed upon by al-Shāfi'ī, Aḥmad b. Ḥanbal, Abū Ḥanifah, and all other jurists (*'Awn al-Ma'būd*, I. 84).

Chapter 85

ON MUTUAL CONTACT AND EATING WITH A MENSTRUATING WOMAN

(212) Ḥarām b. Ḥakīm reported on the authority of his uncle who asked the Apostle of Allah (may peace be upon him): What is lawful for me to do with my wife when she is menstruating? He replied : What is above the waist-wrapper is lawful for you. The narrator also mentioned (the lawfulness of) eating with a woman in menstruation, and he transmitted the tradition in full.[99]

(213) Mu'ādh b. Jabal said : I asked the Apostle of Allah (may peace be upon him): What is lawful for a man to do with his wife when she is menstruating? He replied : What is above the waist-wrapper, but it is better to abstain from it, too.

Abū Dāwūd said : This (tradition) is not strong.

Chapter 86

BATHING IS OBLIGATORY AFTER SEXUAL INTERCOURSE WITHOUT SEMINAL EMISSION

(214) Ubayy b. Ka'b reported : The Apostle of Allah (may peace be upon him) made a concession in the early days of Islam on account of the paucity of clothes that one should not take a bath if one has sexual intercourse (and has no seminal emission). But later on he commanded to take a bath in such a case and prohibited its omission.[100]

(215) Ubayy b. Ka'b said : The verdict that water (bath) is necessary when there is emission given by the people (in the early days of Islam) was due to the concession granted by the Apostle of Allah in the beginning of Islam. He then commanded to take a bath (in such a case).

Abū Dāwūd said : By Abū Ghassān is meant Muhammad b. Muṭarrif.

99. Islam looks upon the menses as a natural impurity which does not pollute the whole of the woman. In many other religions such as Hinduism and Judaism a woman is segregated during the period she is menstruating. In Islam only sexual intercourse is unlawful during this period. Mutual contact and association with her is permitted.

100. In the beginning the Prophet (may peace be upon him) granted permission to the people not to take a bath if they had no ejaculation after intercourse. But later on this injunction was abrogated. Henceforth the bath became obligatory if one had sexual intercourse although one had no seminal emission.

The reason of the lack of clothes is not intelligible. Another version has the word *thabāt* meaning firmness. The Prophet (may peace be upon him) might have taken into consideration the weak faith of the early Muslims in the beginning of Islam. But with the passage of time when their faith became firm, the commandment was repealed (*'Awn al-Ma'būd*, I, 86).

(216) Abu Hurairah reported the Prophet (may peace be upon him) as saying: When anyone sits between the four parts of a woman[101] and the parts (of the male and the female) which are circumscised join together, then bath becomes obligatory.

(217) Abū Sa'īd al-Khudrī reported: The Apostle of Allah (may peace be upon him) said: Water (bath) is necessary only when there is seminal emission. And Abū Salamah followed it.[102]

Chapter 87

A PERSON WITH SEXUAL DEFILEMENT MAY REPEAT INTERCOURSE WITHOUT TAKING A BATH

(218) Anas reported: One day the Apostle of Allah (may peace be upon him) had sexual intercourse with (all) his wives with a single bath.[103]

Abū Dāwūd said: This tradition has been transmitted through another chain of narrators.

Chapter 88

DESIRABILITY OF PERFORMING ABLUTION AFTER INTERCOURSE IF ONE DESIRES TO REPEAT IT

(219) Abū Rāfi' reported: One day the Prophet (may peace be upon him) had intercourse with all his wives. He took a bath after each intercourse. I asked him: Apostle of Allah, why don't you make it a single bath? He replied: This is more purifying, better and cleaning.

Abū Dāwūd said: The tradition narrated by Anas is more sound than this tradition.

(220) Abū Sa'īd al-Khudrī reported: The Prophet (may peace be upon him) said:

101. This is a metaphor referring to the sexual intercourse. It means a man sitting within the thighs of the female for intercourse. It should be noted that bath becomes necessary on both the male and the female by the mere entry of the penis although there is no ejaculation.

102. Abū Salamah practised the previous commandment of the Prophet (may peace be upon him), presumably because he might have thought that the commandment had not been abrogated. Some of the Companions and the Successors hold that bath is not necessary if there is no seminal emission. They argue from the tradition of the Prophet (may peace be upon him) that bath is necessary only when there is seminal emission. This is also held by Dāwūd al-Zāhirī. But the majority of the jurists and scholars consider such traditions to have been abrogated. According to them the correct view is that washing is necessary whenever there is the penetration of the penis (*'Awn al-Ma'būd*. I, 86-87).

103. To provide facility to the people the Prophet (may peace be upon him) did not take a bath after every intercourse. He simply performed ablution and took a bath at the end.

When any of you has intercourse with his wife and desires to repeat it, he should perform ablution between them.[104]

Chapter 89

PERMISSIBILITY OF SLEEPING BEFORE TAKING A BATH FOR A PERSON WHO IS SEXUALLY DEFILED

(221) 'Abd Allah b. 'Umar reported : 'Umar b. al-Khaṭṭāb said to the Apostle of Allah (may peace be upon him) that he became sexually defiled at night (asking him what he should do). The Apostle of Allah (may peace be upon him) said : You should perform ablution and wash your penis and then sleep.[105]

Chapter 90

A PERSON WHO IS SEXUALLY DEFILED IS PERMITTED TO EAT ANYTHING BEFORE WASHING

(222) 'Ā'ishah reported : When the Prophet (may peace be upon him) intended to sleep while he was sexually defiled, he would perform ablution as he did for prayer.[106]

(223) This tradition has been narrated on the authority of al-Zuhrī through a different chain. It adds : If he intends to eat while he is defiled, he should wash both his hands.

Abū Dāwūd said : Ibn Wahb narrated this tradition on the authority of Yūnus. He described the fact of eating as the statement of 'Ā'ishah (not the saying of the Prophet). It has also been narrated through another chain on the authority of Ibn al-Mubārak. He narrated it from 'Urwah or Abū Salamah. Al-Awzā'ī narrated it from Yūnus on the authority of al-Zuhrī from the Prophet (may peace be upon him) as narrated by Ibn al-Mubārak.

104. Scholars differ amongst themselves on performing ablution between the two intercourses. Abū Yūsuf holds that it is not desirable. The majority of scholars are of opinion that it is desirable to perform ablution. Ibn Ḥabīb al Mālikī and Ibn Ḥazm consider it to be necessary. Another tradition reported by 'A'ishah says : The Prophet (may peace be upon him) had intercourse, then he repeated it but did not perform ablution between the two (*'Awn al-Ma'būd*, I, 88).

105. The majority of scholars hold that performing ablution after intercourse but before sleep is only desirable and not necessary.

106. In this tradition there is no mention of the permissibility of eating anything before washing. In fact, this version is an abridged form of a lengthy tradition. Another version mentions eating (*'Awn al-Ma'būd*, I, 89).

Chapter 91

DESIRABILITY OF PERFORMING ABLUTION FOR A PERSON WHO IS SEXUALLY DEFILED BEFORE EATING OR SLEEPING

(224) 'Ā'ishah reported : When the Prophet (may peace be upon him) wanted to eat or sleep, he would perform ablution. She meant that (the Prophet did so) when he was sexually defiled.

(225) 'Ammār b. Yāsir reported : The Prophet (may peace be upon him) granted permission to a person who was sexually defiled to eat or drink or sleep after performing ablution.

Abū Dāwūd said : In the chain of this tradition there is a narrator between Yaḥyā b. Ya'mūr and 'Ammār b. Yāsir. 'Alī b. Abī Ṭalib, Ibn 'Umar and 'Abd Allah b. 'Amr said : When a person who is sexually defiled wants to eat, he should perform ablution.[107]

Chapter 92

A PERSON WHO IS SEXUALLY DEFILED MAY POSTPONE WASHING

(226) Ghuḍaif b. al-Ḥārith reported : I asked 'Ā'ishah : Have you seen the Apostle of Allah (may peace be upon him) washing (because of defilement) in the beginning of the night or at the end ? She replied : Sometimes he would take a bath in the beginning of the night and sometimes at the end. Thereupon I exclaimed : Allah is most Great. All praise be to Allah Who made this matter accommodative. I again asked her : What do you think, did the Apostle of Allah (may peace be upon him) say the *witr* prayer (additional prayer after obligatory prayer at night) in the beginning of the night or at the end ? She replied : Sometimes he would say the *witr* prayer in the beginning of the night and sometimes at the end. I exclaimed : Allah is most Great. All praise be to Allah Who made the matter accommodative. Again I asked her : What do you think, did the Apostle of Allah (may peace be upon him) recite the Qur'an (in the prayer) loudly or softly ? She replied : Sometimes he would recite loudly and sometimes softly. I exclaimed . Allah is most Great. All praise be to Allah Who made the matter accommodative.

(227) 'Alī reported : The Prophet (may peace be upon him) said : Angels do not

107. The tradition means that if a man cannot take a bath after intercourse for a valid reason he is permitted to eat or drink or sleep after performing ablution only.

enter the house where there is a picture,[108] or a dog,[109] or a person who is sexually defiled.[110]

(228) 'Ā'ishah reported : The Apostle of Allah (may peace be upon him) would sleep while he was sexually defiled without touching water.

Abū Dāwūd said : Ḥasan b. 'Alī al-Wāsiṭī said that he heard Yazīd b. Hārūn say : This tradition is based on a misunderstanding, i.e. the tradition reported by Abū Isḥāq.

Chapter 93

ON RECITING THE QUR'ĀN BY A PERSON WHO IS DEFILED

(229) 'Abd Allah b. Salamah said : I, accompanied by other two persons, one from us and the other from Banū Asad, called upon 'Alī. He sent them to a certain territory (on some mission) saying : You are sturdy and vigorous people ; hence display your power for religion. He then stood and entered the toilet. He then came out and called for water and took a handful of it. Then he wiped (his hands) with it and began to recite the Qur'ān. They were surprised at this (action). Thereupon he said : The Apostle of Allah (may peace be upon him) came out from the privy and taught us the Qur'ān and took meat with us. Nothing prevented him ; or the narrator said : Nothing prevented him from (reciting) the Qur'ān except sexual defilement.[111]

108. Picture refers to a portrait of animate objects. It also applies to a statue, an idol or an image. The tradition prohibits to have the picture in the house in any form such as hanging from the wall, or erected on the floor, or made in the clothes or bed (*'Awn al-Ma'būd*, I, 90).

In modern times pictures on curtains or in the newspapers may be overlooked because of necessity.

109. The dog kept for watching agricultural fields, cattle or the house or designed for hunting is exempted from this prohibition (*'Awn al-Ma'būd*, I, 90)

110. This tradition refers to a person who is habituated to abandon the bath after intercourse, or who is extremely careless in washing after defilement, postponing it indefinitely. There is no harm if one sleeps without taking a bath and purifies himself before the dawn prayer. A number of traditions indicate that the Prophet (may peace be upon him) slept without taking a bath (*'Awn al-Ma'būd*, I. 90).

111. This tradition indicates that the reciting of the Qur'ān verbally is permissible if one has not performed ablution. This is agreed upon by the jurists But the person who is sexually defiled is not allowed to recite the Qur'ān verbally. Similarly, a menstruating woman is not permitted to recite the Qur'ān. Besides, it is not lawful for a person who has not performed ablution to touch the copy of the Qur'ān. The Prophet (may peace be upon him) is reported to have written a letter to the people of Yemen, asking them not to touch the copy of the Qur'ān without purification (ablution). It is essential to perform ablution for touching the Qur'ān (*'Awn al-Ma'būd*, I, 91).

Chapter 94

PERMISSIBILITY TO SHAKE HANDS WITH A PERSON WHO IS SEXUALLY DEFILED

(230) Ḥudhaifah reported: The Prophet (may peace be upon him) visited him and inclined towards him (for shaking hand). He said: I am sexually defiled. The Prophet (may peace be upon him) replied: A Muslim is not defiled.[112]

(231) Abū Hurairah reported: The Apostle of Allah (may peace be upon him) met me on one of the streets of Medina while I was sexually defiled. I retreated and went away. I then took a bath and came to him. He asked: Where were you, O Abū Hurairah? I replied: As I was sexually defiled, I disliked to sit in your company without purification. He exclaimed: Glory be to Allah! A Muslim is not defiled.

He (Abū Dāwūd) said: The version of this tradition reported by Bishr has the chain: Humaid reported from Bakr.

Chapter 95

A PERSON WHO IS SEXUALLY DEFILED IS PROHIBITED TO ENTER THE MOSQUE

(232) 'Ā'ishah said: The Apostle of Allah (may peace be upon him) came and saw that the doors of the houses of his Companions were facing the mosque. He said: Turn the direction of the houses from the mosque. The Prophet (may peace be upon him) then entered (the houses or the mosque), and the people did take any step in this regard hoping that some concession might be revealed. He (the Prophet) again came upon them and said: Turn the direction of these (doors) from the mosque I do not make the mosque lawful for a menstruating woman and for a person who is sexually defiled.[113]

Abū Dāwūd said: Aflat b. Khalifah is also called Fulait al-'Āmirī.

Chapter 96

ABOUT A PERSON WHO IS SEXUALLY DEFILED AND LEADS THE PEOPLE IN PRAYER IN FORGETFULNESS

(233) Abū Bakrah said: The Apostle of Allah (may peace be upon him) began to

112. The tradition shows that the whole body of a Muslim or his sweat is not polluted by sexual defilement. It is only a legal defilement and not physical. It also indicates that a Muslim remains pure in his lifetime and after his death. Hence it is permissible to associate, to eat and drink, with a person who is sexually defiled.

113. A menstruating woman and a person sexually defiled are not allowed to enter or stay in the mosque on account of its sanctity. One is, however, allowed to pass through the mosque hurriedly without staying there for long time.

lead (the people) in the dawn prayer. He then signalled with his hand: (Stay) at your places. (Then he entered his home). He then returned while drops of water were coming down from him (from his body) and he led them in prayer.[114]

(234) This tradition has been reported by Ḥammād b. Salamah through the same chain of narrators and conveying a similar meaning. This version adds in the beginning: "He uttered *takbīr* (Allāh-u akbar), and in the end: When he finished the prayer, he said: I am a human being; I was sexually defiled.

Abū Dawūd said: This tradition has been narrated by al-Zuhrī from Abū Salamah b. 'Abd al-Raḥmān on the authority of Abū Hurairah. It says: When he stood at the place of prayer, we waited for his utterance of *takbīr* (Allāh-u akbar). He went away and said: (Remain) as you were.

Another version on the authority of Muḥammad reporting from the Prophet (may peace be upon him) says: He uttered *takbīr* (Allāh-u akbar) and then made a sign to the people, meaning "sit down". He then went away and took a bath. This tradition has also been narrated through a different chain. It says: The Apostle of Allah (may peace be upon him) uttered *takbīr* (Allāh-u akbar) in a prayer.

Abū Dādūd said: Another version through a different chain says: The Prophet (may peace be upon him) uttered *takbīr* (Allāh-u akbar).

(235) Abū Hurairah reported: The prayer (in congregation) began and people stood in their rows. The Apostle of Allah (may peace be upon him) came out (from his residence). When he stood at his proper place he recalled that he did not take a bath. He then said to the people: (Remain standing) at your places. Then he returned to his house and came out upon us after taking a bath while the drops of water were coming down from his head. We were standing in the rows (of prayer). This is the version of Ibn Ḥarb. 'Ayyāsh reported in his version: We kept on waiting for him while we were standing until he came upon us after he had taken a bath.

Chapter 97

WASHING IS NECESSARY IF A MAN FINDS MOISTURE (ON HIS CLOTHES) DUE TO SEXUAL DREAM AFTER AWAKING FROM SLEEP

(236) 'Ā'ishah reported: The Prophet (may peace be upon him) was asked about a person who found moisture (on his body or clothes) but did not remember the sexual dream. He replied: He should take a bath. He was asked about a person who remembered that he had a sexual dream but did not find moisture. He replied: Bath

114. The other traditions indicate that the Prophet (may peace be upon him) was sexually defiled but he did not remember it. But when he recalled, he left the prayer and entered his house for taking a bath.

is not necessary for him. Umm Salamah then asked: Is washing necessary for a woman if she sees that (in her dream)? He replied: Yes. Women are counterpart of men.[115]

Chapter 98

PERTAINING TO A WOMAN WHO SEES WHAT A MAN SEES (IN HIS SEXUAL DREAM)

(237) 'Ā'ishah reported on the authority of Umm Sulaim al-Anṣāriyah, who was the mother of Anas b. Mālik, said: Apostle of Allah, Allah is not ashamed of truth What do you think, if a woman sees what a man sees in dream, Should she take a bath or not? The Prophet (may peace be upon him) replied: Yes, she should take a bath if she finds the liquid (vaginal secretion) 'Ā'ishah said: Then I came upon her and said to her: Woe to you! Does a woman see that (sexual dream)? In the meantime, the Apostle of Allah (may peace be upon him) came upon me and said: May your right hand be covered with dust![116] How can there be the resemblance (i.e. between the child and the mother)?[117]

Abū Dāwūd said: A similar version has been narrated by al-Zubaidī, 'Uqail, Yūnus, cousin of al-Zuhrī, Ibn Abi'l-Wazīr, on the authority of al-Zuhrī. Musāfi' al-Hajabī, like al-Zuhrī, narrated on the authority of 'Urwah from 'Ā'ishah. But Hishām b. 'Urwah narrated from 'Urwah on the authority of Zainab daughter of Abū Salamah from Umm Salamah saying. Umm Sulaim came to the Apostle of Allah (may peace be upon him).

Chapter 99

QUANTITY OF WATER SUFFICIENT FOR BATH

(238) 'Ā'ishah said: The Apostle of Allah (may peace be upon him) used to take

115. Women are like men temperamentally and physically. Hence if a woman sees what a man sees in his dream, and finds moisture after sleep, she should take a bath (*'Awn al-Ma'būd*, I, 96).

116. This is not a curse. This is a common expression of disagreement in Arabic. The Prophet (may peace be upon him) did not like the behaviour of 'Ā'ishah in discouraging Umm Sulaim from asking him the problems of cleanliness. As sexual dream was net common with women, 'Ā'ishah did not approve of its expression before the Prophet (may peace be upon him). But the Prophet (may peace be upon him) encouraged her to seek guidance from him, whatever it may be.

117. The tradition means that the offspring is created by the mixture of the semen of the male and the female (vaginal excretion). Whoever dominates, the child resembles him. The sex is determined by the domination and vigour of either of the parents. The Prophet (may peace be upon him) by this expression meant that there was nothing astonishing in the question of Umm Sulaim. Women like men, experience orgism in dream. Hence they are counterpart of men in this respect (*'Awn al-Ma'būd*, I, 96).

bath with water from a vessel[118] (which contained seven to eight seers, i.e. fifteen to sixteen pounds) because of sexual intercourse.

Abū Dāwūd said : The version narrated by Mu'ammar on the authority of al-Zuhrī has : She ('Ā'ishah) said : I and the Apostle of Allah (may peace be upon him) took a bath from a vessel which was equal to al-faraq in measurement (i.e. containing water about seven or eight seers).

Abū Dāwūd said : Ibn 'Uyainah also narrated like the version of Mālik.

Abū Dāwūd said : I heard Aḥmad b. Ḥanbal say : Al-Faraq contains sixteen rotls (of water). I also heard him say: The ṣā' of Ibn Abī Dhi'b contained 5⅓ rotls (of water) The view that a ṣā' contains eight rotls (of water) is not safe.

Abū Dāwūd said : I heard Aḥmad (b. Ḥanbal) say : Whoever gave 5⅓ rotls (measuring) with our rotl alms of *fiṭr* (*ṣadaqat al-fiṭr*), he gave in full. Thereupon he was questioned : Are the dates called *al-ṣaiḥānī* heavier (can one ṣā' of them be given as alms of *fiṭr*) ? He replied : The dates called *al-ṣaiḥānī* are good.[119] But I do not know (whether water is heavier or the dates).

Chapter 100

ON TAKING A BATH BECAUSE OF SEXUAL DEFILEMENT

(239) Jubair b. Muṭ'im reported : People made a mention of washing because of sexual defilement before the Apostle of Allah (may peace be upon him). The Apostle of Allah (may peace be upon him) said : I pour (water) on my head three times. And he made a sign with both his hands.

(240) 'Ā'ishah reported : When the Apostle of Allah (may peace be upon him) wanted to wash himself because of sexual defilement, he called for a vessel like *ḥilāb* (a vessel used for milking the camel). He then took a handful of water and began to pour it on the right side of his head and then on the left side. He then took water in both his hands together and poured it on his head.

(241) Jumai' b. 'Umair, one of the sons of Banū Taim Allah b. Tha'labah, said : Accompanied by my mother and aunt I entered upon 'Ā'ishah. One of them asked her : How did you do while taking a bath ? 'Ā'ishah replied : The Apostle of Allah

118. The text has the word *faraq*. It is a vessel of large size containing three ṣā' of water (seven to eight seers).

119. He meant that one ṣā of these dates is sufficient for alms of *fiṭr* (the alms given after the end of Ramaḍān).

There is a difference of opinion among the scholars on the measurement of ṣā'. According to the people of Ḥijāz, ṣā' contains 5⅓ rotls of water (about three seers). According to the people of Iraq, ṣā' contains eight rotls of water (about 3½ seers). Both have arguments in support of their viewpoints. The traditionists, however, emphasise that by the ṣā' which occurs in the traditions of the Prophet (may peace be upon him) is meant the ṣā' of Ḥijāz.

(may peace be upon him) performed ablution (in the beginning) as he did for prayer. He then poured (water) upon his head three times. But we poured water upon our heads five times due to plaits.

(242) 'Ā'ishah reported: When the Apostle of Allah (may peace be upon him) would take a bath because of sexual defilement, according to the version of Sulaimān, in the beginning he would pour water with his right hand (upon his left hand); and according to the version of Musaddad, he would wash both (hands) pouring water from the vessel upon his right hand. According to the agreed version, he then would wash the private part of his body. Musaddad said: She sometimes used metonymy for the private part. He would then perform ablution as he did for prayer, then put his hands in the vessel and made the water go through his hair. When he knew that water had reached the entire surface of the body and cleaned it well, he would pour water upon his head three times. If some water was left, he would pour it also upon himself.

(243) 'Ā'ishah said: When the Apostle of Allah (may peace be upon him) intended to take a bath because of sexual defilement, he would begin with his hands and wash them. Then he would wash the joints of his limbs and pour water upon them When he cleansed both his (hands), he would rub them on the wall (to make them perfectly clean with the dust). Then he would perform ablution and pour water over his head.

(244) 'Ā'ishah said: If you want, I can certainly show you the marks of the hand of the Apostle of Allah (may peace be upon him) on the wall where he took a bath because of sexual defilement.

(245) Maimūnah reported: I placed (the vessel of) water for the Prophet (may peace be upon him) to wash himself because of sexual defilement. He lowered down the vessel and poured water on his right hand. He then washed it twice or thrice. He then poured water over his private parts and washed them with his left hand. Then he put it on the ground and wiped it. He then rinsed his mouth and snuffed up water, and washed his face and hands. He then poured water over his head and body. Then he moved aside and washed his feet. I handed him a garment, but he began to shake off water from his body.[120] I mentioned it to Ibrāhīm. He said that they (Companions) did not think there was any harm in using the garment (to wipe the water), but

120. It should be noted that there is a difference of opinion about drying off water with a garment (i.e. towel, etc.) after washing and ablution. A group of scholars have disapproved of its use arguing from this tradition of the Prophet (may peace be upon him). They adduce another tradition reported by Anas which says: The Apostle of Allah (may peace be upon him) did not wipe his face with the garment after ablution, nor did Abū Bakr, 'Umar, 'Alī and Ibn Mas'ūd practise it. Others are of opinion that it is permissible to use garment for wiping water after ablution or washing. They argue from the tradition of the Prophet (may peace be upon him) by Salmān al-Fārisī, recorded by Ibn Mājah in his *Sunan*. It says that the Prophet (may peace be upon him) performed ablution and. turning his woollen cloak. he wiped his face. This view is held by al-Ḥasan b. 'Alī, Anas, 'Uthmān, Sufyān al-Thawrī and Mālik (*'Awn al-Ma'būd*, I, 101).

they disliked its use as a habit.

Abū Dāwūd said: Musaddad said: I asked 'Abd Allah b. Dāwūd whether they (the Companions) disliked to make it a habit. He replied: It (the tradition) goes in a similar way and I found it in a similar way in this book of mine.

(246) Shu'bah reported : When Ibn 'Abbās took a bath because of sexual defilement, he poured (water) over his left hand with his right hand seven times. Once he forgot how many times he had poured (water). Therefore he asked me : How many times did I pour (water) ? I do not know. He said : May you miss your mother ! What prevented you from remembering it ? He then performed ablution as he did for prayer and poured water over his skin (body). He then said : This is how the Apostle of Allah (may peace be upon him) purified (himself).

(247) 'Abd Allah b. 'Umar said : There were fifty prayers (obligatory in the beginning) ; and (in the beginning of Islam) washing seven times because of sexual defilement (was obligatory) ; and washing the urine from the cloth seven times (was obligatory). The Apostle of Allah (may peace be upon him) kept on praying to Allah until the number of prayers was reduced to five and washing because of sexual defilement was allowed only once and washing the urine from the clothe was also permitted only once.

(248) Abū Hurairah reported : The Apostle of Allah (may peace be upon him) said : There is sexual defilement under every hair ; so wash the hair and cleanse the skin.

Abū Dāwūd said : The tradition narrated by Ḥārith b. Wajīh is rejected (***munkar***). He is weak (in transmission).

(249) 'Alī reported : The Apostle of Allah (may peace be upon him) said : If anyone who is sexual defiled leaves a spot equal to the breadth of a hair without washing, such and such an amount of Hell-fire will have to be suffered for it. 'Alī said : On that account I treated my head (hair) as an enemy, meaning I cut my hair. He used to cut the hair (of his head). May Allah be pleased with him.[121]

Chapter 101

PERFORMING ABLUTION AFTER TAKING A BATH IS NOT NECESSARY

(250) 'Ā'ishah reported : The Apostle of Allah (may peace be upon him) took

121. The tradition shows that not a single spot of an hair should be left dry while taking a bath. If any spot is left from washing, the bath will not be valid. The general rule contained in this tradition applies only to men. Men should pour water very carefully so that it may reach the roots of the hair. But the plaited hair of the women, even closely bound together, are exempted from this rule. The Prophet (may peace be upon him) has granted permission to women to wash their plaited hair from above ; they need not undo them (*'Awn al-Ma'būd*, I, 102).

a bath and offered two *rak'ahs* of prayer and said the dawn prayer. I do not think he performed ablution afresh after taking a bath.[122]

Chapter 102

SHOULD A WOMAN UNDO HER PLAITED HAIR AT THE TIME OF TAKING A BATH ?

(251) Umm Salamah said : One of the Muslims asked, and Zubair reported : Umm Salamah (herself) asked : Apostle of Allah, I am a woman who keeps her hair closely plaited ; should I undo it when I wash after sexual defilement ? He replied : (No), it is enough for you to throw three handfuls over it (your head). Zubair's version has : You should pour three handfuls of water over it. Then pour water over all your body and you will be purified.[123]

(252) Umm Salamah said : A woman came to her. This is according to the version of the former tradition. I asked the Prophet (may peace be upon him) a similar question (as in the former tradition). But this version adds : "And wring out your locks after every handful of water."

(253) 'Ā'ishah said : When any of us was sexually defiled, she took three handfuls (of water) in this way, that is to say, with both hands together and poured (water) over her head. She took one handful (of water) and threw it on one side and the other on the other side.

(254) 'Ā'ishah said : We took a bath while having an adhesive substance over us (our head) in both states, namely, when wearing a robe for *Ḥajj (iḥrām)* and when wearing ordinary clothes (not meant for *Ḥajj*) [124]

(255) Shuraiḥ b. 'Ubaid said : Jubair b. Nufair gave me a verdict about the bath because of sexual defilement that Thaubān reported to them that they asked the Prophet (may peace be upon him) about it. He (the Prophet) replied : As regards man, he should undo the hair of his head and wash it until the water should reach the roots of the hair. But there is no harm if the woman does not undo it (her hair) and pour three handfuls of water over her head.

122. The tradition indicates that it is not necessary to perform ablution after taking a bath if nothing happens during or after the bath that makes the ablution void. The reason is that one already performs ablution in the beginning of the bath.

123. This tradition clearly indicates that women are allowed, as an exceptional case, to throw water over their heads while taking a bath and they need not undo their hair.

124. 'Ā'ishah aims at explaining the question of bath for women. In any condition, whether putting on special robe for *Ḥajj* or clad in ordinary clothes, it is not necessary to undo the plaited hair. She might have used some kind of substance for strengthening the plaited or for perfume.

Chapter 103

A MAN WHO IS SEXUALLY DEFILED MAY WASH HIS HEAD WITH MARSH-MALLOW

(256) 'Ā'ishah said : The Prophet (may peace be upon him) used to wash his head with marsh-mallow while he was sexually defiled. It was sufficient for him and he did not pour water upon it.

Chapter 104

FLOW OF THE FLUID BETWEEN MAN AND WOMAN

(257) On being asked about (washing) the fluid that flows between man and woman 'Ā'ishah said : The Apostle of Allah (may peace be upon him) used to take a handful of water and pour it on the fluid. Again, he would take a handful of water and pour it over the fluid.[125]

Chapter 105

EAT'NG WITH A MENSTRUATING WOMAN AND ASSOCIATION WITH HER

(258) Anas b. Mālik said: Among the Jews, when a woman menstruated, they ejected her from the house, and they did not eat with her, nor did they drink with her, nor did they associate with her in (their houses) so the Apostle of Allah (may peace be upon him) was questioned about that. Thereupon Allah revealed: "They question thee concerning menstruation. Say: It is an illness, so let women alone at such times" (ii. 222). The Apostle of Allah (may peace be upon him) then said: Associate with them in the houses and do everything except sexual intercourse. Thereupon the Jews said: This man does not want to leave anything we do without opposing us in it. Usaid b. Ḥuḍair and 'Abbād b. Bishr came and said: Apostle of Allah, the Jews are saying such and such a thing. Shall we not then have intercourse with women during menstruation? The face of the Apostle of Allah (may peace be upon him) underwent such a change that we thought he was angry with them ; but when they went out they received a gift of milk which was being brought to the Apostle of Allah (may peace be upon him), and he sent after them and gave them a drink, whereupon we thought that he was not angry with them.

125. The tradition indicates the method of purifying a cloth when it is smeared with seminal or prostatic fluid. The garment becomes pure by pouring water over it only once. The Prophet (may peace be upon him) poured water once again to cleanse it more perfectly. Washing it a second time is not necessary (*'Awn al-Ma'būd*, I, 107).

(259) 'Ā'ishah said: I would eat flesh from a bone when I was menstruating, then hand it over to the Prophet (may peace be upon him) and he would put his mouth where I had put my mouth; I would drink, then hand it over to him, and he would put his mouth (at the place) where I drank.

(260) 'Ā'ishah said: The Apostle of Allah (may peace be upon him) would recline on my lap when I was menstruating, then recite the Qur'ān.

Chapter 106

IT IS PERMISSIBLE FOR A MENSTRUATING WOMAN TO GET SOMETHING FROM THE MOSQUE

(261) 'Ā'ishah said: The Apostle of Allah (may peace be upon him) said to me: Get me the mat from the mosque. I said: I am menstruating. The Apostle of Allah (may peace be upon him) then replied: Your menstruation is not in your hand.[126]

Chapter 107

A MENSTRUATING WOMAN SHOULD NOT COMPLETE THE ABANDONED PRAYERS AFTER PURIFICATION

(262) Mu'ādhah reported: A woman asked 'Ā'ishah: Should a menstruating woman complete the prayers abandoned during the period of menses? 'Ā'ishah said: Are you a Ḥarūrīyyah?[127] During menstruation in the time of the Apostle of Allah (may peace be upon him) we would not complete (the abandoned prayers), nor were we commanded to complete them.

(263) This tradition has also been narrated through a different chain on the authority of Mu'ādhah al-'Adawīyyah from 'Ā'ishah. This version adds: We were

126. Al-Nawawī and other commentators have interpreted this tradition in a different way. The Prophet (may peace be upon him) was observing *i'tikāf* (seclusion) in the mosque. He asked 'Ā'ishah to get the mat while he was in the mosque and she was outside the mosque. She hesitated to do; hence he told her that there was no harm in getting something in the mosque with hands during periods. According to this interpretation 'Ā'ishah had not entered the mosque. As a general rule menstruating women are not allowed to enter the mosque according to another tradition of the Prophet (may peace be upon him). But it should be noted that another group of traditionists like Abū Dāwūd himself, al-Nasā'ī, al-Tirmidhī, Ibn Mājah, al-Khaṭṭābī and some other eminent scholars have interpreted this tradition literally. The author of *'Awn al-Ma'būd* says that the meaning of the tradition is obvious and there seems no reason to interpret it in a different way (I, 108).

127. The Khawārij were called Ḥarūrīyyah because of their early settlement at a place called Ḥarūrah near Kūfah. They held, against the belief of the majority of the Muslims, that a menstruating woman should complete the abandoned prayers after purification like the abandoned fasts. Their view runs counter to the generally accepted law of the *Sharī'ah*.

commanded to complete the (abandoned) fast, but were not commanded to complete the (abandoned) prayer.

Chapter 108

ON COHABITATION WITH A MENSTRUATING WOMAN

(264) Ibn 'Abbās reported: The Prophet (may peace be upon him) said about a person who had intercourse with his wife while she was menstruating: He must give one dīnār or half a dīnār in alms.[128]

Abū Dāwūd said: The correct version says so: One dīnār or half a dīnār. Shu'bah (a narrator) did not sometimes narrate this tradition as a statement of the Prophet (may peace be upon him).

(265) Ibn 'Abbās said: If one has intercourse in the beginning of the menses, (one should give) one dīnār; in case one has intercourse towards the end of the menses, then half a dīnār (should be given).

(266) Ibn 'Abbās reported the Prophet (may peace be upon him) as saying: When a man has intercourse with his wife while she is menstruating, he must give half a dīnār in alms.

Abū Dāwūd said: 'Alī b. Budhaimah reported similarly on the authority of Miqsam from the Prophet (may peace be upon him). Al-Awzā'i narrated from Yazīd b. Abī Mālik, from 'Abd al-Ḥamīd b. 'Abd al-Raḥmān from the Prophet (may peace be upon him): He ordered him to give two fifth of a dīnār in alms. But this is a chain where two narrators (Miqsam and Ibn 'Abbās) are missing.

Chapter 109

IT IS PERMISSIBLE FOR A MAN TO DO ANYTHING WITH HIS WIFE WHILE SHE IS MENSTRUATING EXCEPT SEXUAL INTERCOURSE

(267) Maimūnah said: The Prophet (may peace be upon him) would contact and embrace any of his wives while she was menstruating. She would wear the wrapper up to half the thighs or cover her knees with it.

128. To have an intercourse with one's wife during the period of menses in unlawful according to the Qur'ān. If a person does so by mistake he may give one or half a dīnār in alms. There is a difference of opinion among scholars whether the giving of alms is obligatory or not. One group holds that it is necessary to give alms, and they argue from such traditions. The other group maintains that the giving of alms is not necessary. The man who commits such a mistake should beg pardon of Allah. They argue that this tradition is a statement of Ibn 'Abbās and not of the Prophet (may peace be upon him) or the chain is broken (*'Awn al-Ma'būd*, I, 109).

(268) 'Ā'ishah said: When anyone amongst us (the wives of the Prophet) menstruated, the Apostle of Allah (may peace be upon him) asked her to tie a waist-wrapper (over her body) and then her husband lay with her, or he (Shu'bah) said: embraced her.[129]

(269) Khallās al-Hujarī reported: I heard 'Ā'ishah say: I and the Apostle of Allah (may peace be upon him) used to pass night in one (piece of) cloth (on me) while I menstruated profusely. If anything from me (i.e. blood) smeared him (i.e. his body), he would wash that spot and would not exceed it (in washing), then he would offer prayer with it.[130] If anything smeared his clothe, he would wash that place and would not exceed it; and then he offered prayer with it.

(270) 'Umarah b. Ghurāb said that his paternal aunt narrated to him that she asked 'Ā'ishah: What any if one of us menstruates and she and her husband have no bed except one? She replied: I relate to you what the Apostle of Allah (may peace be upon him) had done. One night he entered (upon me) while I was menstruating. He went to the place of his prayer, that is, to the place of prayer reserved (for this purpose) in his house. He did not return until I felt asleep heavily, and he felt pain from cold. And he said: Come near me. I said: I am menstruating. He said: Uncover your thighs. I, therefore, uncovered both of my thighs. Then he put his cheek and chest on my thighs and I lent upon he until he became warm and slept.[131]

(271) 'Ā'ishah said: When I menstruated, I left the bed and lay on the reed-mat and did not approach or come near the Apostle of Allah (may peace be upon him) until we were purified.[132]

(272) 'Ikrimah reported on the authority of one of the wives of the Prophet (may peace be upon him) saying: When the Prophet (may peace be upon him) wanted to do something (i.e. kissing, embracing) with (his) menstruating wife, he would put a garment on her private part.

(273) 'Ā'ishah said: The Apostle of Allah (may peace be upon him) would ask us in the beginning of our menstruation to tie the waist-wrapper. Then he would

129. The narrator Shu'bah is doubtful about the correct wording of the tradition. He sometimes mentions the words "lay with her" and sometimes said "embraced her".

130 The word *fihi* (in it or with it) here seems to be redundant as it does not convey any sense. This word does not occur in the version recorded by al-Baihaqī. In this version it occurs only once in the last sentence where it makes sense (*Badhl al-Majhūd*, I, 160).

131. This tradition provides sanction for lying with a menstruating woman and embracing her. Moreover, 'Ā'ishah narrated even the private matters confined to a wife and husband in order to teach the people legal injunctions about such cases. Had she not narrated the practice and the sayings of the Prophet (may peace be upon him) about these matters, the Muslims would have remained ignorant of them.

132. Al-Ṭībī says that this tradition has been abrogated. A large number of traditions permit a man to lie with a menstruating woman and to embrace her (*'Awn al-Ma'būd*, I, 110).

embrace us. And who amongst you can have as much control over his desire as the Apostle of Allah (may peace be upon him) had over his desire?

Chapter 110

PERTAINING TO THE WOMAN WHO HAS A PROLONGED FLOW OF BLOOD, AND ABOUT ONE WHO SAID THAT SHE SHOULD ABANDON PRAYER FOR THE NUMBER OF DAYS SHE USED TO MENSTRUATE

(274) Umm Salamah, the wife of the Prophet (may peace be upon him), reported: In the time of the Apostle of Allah (may peace be upon him) there was a woman who had an issue of blood. So Umm Salamah asked the Apostle of Allah (may peace be upon him) to give a decision about her. He said: She should consider the number of nights and days during which she used to menstruate each month before she was afflicted with this trouble and abandon prayer during that period each month. When those days and nights are over, she should take a bath, tie a cloth over her private parts and pray.[133]

(275) Sulaimān b. Yasār said that a man reported to him from Umm Salamah: There was a woman who had an issue of blood. And he narrated the rest of the tradition to the same effect saying: When the menstruation period is over and the time of prayer arrives, she should take a bath, as mentioned in the previous tradition.

(276) Sulaimān b. Yasār reported on the authority of a person from the Anṣār: There was a woman who had an issue of blood. He then narrated the rest of the tradition like that of al-Laith. He said: When the period of menstruation is over and the time of prayer arrives, she should take a bath. He narrated the tradition conveying the same meaning.[134]

(277) This tradition has been transmitted through the chain of narrators like that of al-Laith to the same effect. It says: She should abandon prayer considering that period (she used to menstruate). When the time of prayer approaches, she should take a bath, tie a cloth over her private parts and offer prayer.

(278) Sulaimān b. Yasār reported this narrative on the authority of Umm Salamah. This version has: He (the Prophet) said: She should abandon prayer and take a bath at the beginning of the additional period, and tie a cloth over her private parts

133. A woman who bleeds on account of some abnormality or disease and not on account of menses is called *mustaḥāḍah*. She is required to offer prayer regularly and keep fast like other women. The menstrual period extends normally from five to ten days.

134. These traditions indicate that in case bleeding exceeds the normal period of menses, the woman should not take the excess into consideration. The prolonged flow of blood might be due to some other reason. Hence she should take a bath while she is bleeding and offer the immediate prayer.

and offer prayer.

Abū Dāwūd said: Ḥammād b. Zaid on the authority of Ayyūb has pointed out the name of the woman who had a prolonged flow of blood (referred to) in this tradition to be Fāṭimah daughter of Abū Ḥubaish.

(279) 'Ā'ishah reported: Umm Ḥabībah asked the Prophet (may peace be upon him) about the blood (which flows beyond the period of menstruation). 'Ā'ishah said: I saw her wash-tub full of blood. The Apostle of Allah (may peace be upon him) said: Keep away (from prayer) equal (to the length of time) that your menses prevented you. Then wash yourself.

Abū Dāwūd said: Qutaibah mentioned the name Ja'far b. Rabī'ah in the middle of the text of the tradition for the second time (i.e. Qutaibah, being doubtful about the narrator Ja'far b. Rabī'ah, mentioned his name twice: once in the chain and again while reporting the text). 'Alī b. 'Ayyāsh and Yūnus b. Muḥammad reported it on the authority of al-Laith. They mentioned the name Ja'far b. Rabī'ah.

(280) 'Urwah b. Zubair said that Fāṭimah daughter of Abū Ḥubaish narrated to him that she asked the Apostle of Allah (may peace be upon him) and complained to him about the flowing of (her) blood. The Apostle of Allah (may peace be upon him) said to her: That is only (due to) a vein: look, when your menstruation comes, do not pray; and when your menstruation ends, wash yourself and then offer prayer during the period from one menstruation to another.

(281) 'Urwah b. al-Zubair said: Fāṭimah daughter of Abū Ḥubaish narrated to me that she asked Asmā' (daughter of Abū Bakr), or Asmā' narrated to me that Fāṭimah daughter of Abū Ḥubaish asked her to question the Apostle of Allah (may peace be upon him). He advised her to refrain (from prayer) equal to the period she refrained previously. She then should wash herself.

Abū Dāwūd said: Qatādah narrated it from 'Urwah b. al-Zubair, from Zainab daughter of Umm Salamah, that Umm Ḥabībah daughther of Jaḥsh had a prolonged flow of blood. The Prophet (may peace be upon him) commanded her to abandon prayer for the period of her menses. She then should take a bath, and offer prayer.

Abū Dāwūd said: Qatādah did not hear anything from 'Urwah. And Ibn 'Uyainah added in the tradition narrated by al- Zuhrī from 'Umrah on the authority of 'Ā'ishah. Umm Ḥabībah had a prolonged flow of blood. She asked the Prophet (may peace be upon him). He commanded her to abandon prayer during her menstrual period.

Abū Dāwūd said: This is a misunderstanding on the part of Ibn 'Uyainah. This is not found in the tradition reported by the transmitters from al-Zuhrī except that mentioned by Suhail b. Abī Ṣāliḥ. Al-Ḥumaidī also narrated this tradition from Ibn 'Uyainah, but he did not mention the words "she should abandon prayer during her menstrual period"

Qumair daughter of Masrūq reported on the authority of 'Ā'ishah: The woman who has a prolonged flow of blood should abandon prayer during her menstrual period.

'Abd al-Raḥmān b. al-Qāsim reported on the authority of his father: The Prophet (may peace be upon him) commanded her to abandon prayers equal (to the length of time) that she has her (usual) menses.

Abū Bishr Ja'far b. Abī Waḥshīyyah reported on the authority of 'Ikrimah from the Prophet (may peace be upon him) saying: Umm Ḥabībah daughter of Jaḥsh had a prolonged flow of blood; and he transmitted it like that.

Sharīk narrated from Abū al-Yaqẓān from 'Adī b. Thābit from his father on the authority of his grandfather from the Prophet (may peace be upon him): The woman suffering from a prolonged flow of blood should abandon prayer during her menstrual period; she then should wash herself and pray.

Al-'Alā' b. al-Musayyab reported from al-Ḥakam on the authority of Abū Ja'far, saying: Saudah had a prolonged flow of blood. The Prophet (may peace be upon him) commanded that when her menstruation was finished, she should take a bath and pray.

Sa'īd b. Jubair reported from 'Alī and Ibn 'Abbās: A woman suffering from a prolonged flow of blood should refrain from prayers during her menstrual period.

'Ammār, the freed slave of Banū Hāshim, and Ṭalq b. Ḥabīb narrated in a similar way. Similarly, it was reported by Ma'qil al-Khath'amī from 'Alī, al-Sha'bī also transmitted it in a similar manner from Qumair, the wife of Masrūq, on the authority of 'Ā'ishah.

Abū Dāwūd said: Al-Ḥasan, Sa'īd b. al-Musayyab, 'Aṭā', Makḥūl, Ibrāḥīm, Sāiim and al-Qāsim also hold that a woman suffering from a prolonged flow of blood should abandon prayer during her menstrual period.

Abū Dāwūd said: Qatādah did not hear anything from 'Urwah.

Chapter 111

THE WOMAN WHO HAS A PROLONGED FLOW OF BLOOD SHOULD NOT ABANDON PRAYER WHEN HER MENSTRUAL PERIOD IS FINISHED

(282) 'Urwah reported on the authority of 'Ā'ishah: Fāṭimah daughter of Abū Ḥubaish came to the Apostle of Allah (may peace be upon him) and said: I am a woman who has a prolonged flow of blood; I am never purified; should I abandon prayer? He replied: This is (due to) a vein, and not menstruation. When the menstruation begins, you should abandon prayer; when it is finished, you should wash away the blood and pray.

(283) This tradition has also been transmitted by Zuhair through a different chain of narrators, to the same effect. He said: When the menstruation begins, you should abandon prayer; when the period equal to its length of time passes, you should wash away the blood and pray.

Chapter 112

THE WOMAN SUFFERING FROM A PROLONGED FLOW OF BLOOD SHOULD ABANDON PRAYER WHEN MENSTRUATION BEGINS

(284) Bahīyyah said: I heard a woman asking 'Ā'ishah about the woman whose menses became abnormal and she had an issue of blood. The Apostle of Allah (may peace be upon him) asked me to advise her that she should consider the period during which she used to menstruate every month, when her menstruation was normal. Then she should count the days equal to the length of time (of her normal menses); then she should abandon prayer during those days or equal to that period. She should then take a bath, tie a cloth on her private parts and pray.

(285) 'Ā'ishah said: Umm Ḥabībah, daughter of Jaḥsh and sister-in-law of the Apostle of Allah (may peace be upon him), and wife of 'Abd al-Raḥmān b. 'Awf, had a prolonged flow of blood for seven years. She inquired from the Apostle of Allah (may peace be upon him) about it. The Apostle of Allah (may peace be upon him) said: This is not menstruation, but this is (due to) a vein. Therefore, wash yourself and pray.

Abū Dāwūd said: In this tradition which has been transmitted by al-Zuhrī from 'Urwah and 'Umrah on the authority of 'Ā'ishah, al-Awzā'ī added: She ('Ā'ishah) said: Umm Ḥabībah daughter of Jaḥsh and wife of 'Abd al-Raḥmān b. 'Awf had a prolonged flow of blood for seven years. The Prophet (may peace be upon him) commanded her saying: When the menstruation begins, abandon prayer; when it is finished, take a bath and pray.

Abū Dāwūd said: None of the disciples of al-Zuhrī mentioned these words except al-Awzā'ī. From al-Zuhrī it has been narrated by 'Amr b. al-Ḥārith, al-Laith, Yūnus, Ibn Abī Dhi'b, Ma'mar, Ibrāhīm b. Sa'd, Sulaimān b. Kathīr, Ibn Isḥāq and Sufyān b. 'Uyainah, they did not narrate these words.

Abū Dāwūd said: These are the words of the version reported by Hishām b. 'Urwah from his father on the authority of 'Ā'ishah.

Abū Dāwūd said: In this tradition Ibn 'Uyainah also added the words: He commanded her to abandon prayer during her menstrual period. This is a misunderstanding on the part of Ibn 'Uyainah. The version of this tradition narrated by Muḥammad b. 'Amr from al-Zuhrī has the addition similar to that made by al-Awzā'ī in his version.

(286) 'Urwah b. al-Zubair reported from Fāṭimah daughter of Abū Ḥubaish that her blood kept flowing, so the Prophet (may peace be upon him) said to her: When the blood of the menses comes, it is black blood which can be recognised; so when that comes, refrain from prayer; but when a different type of blood comes, perform ablution and pray, for it is (due only to) a vein.

Abū Dāwūd said: Ibn al-Muthannā narrated this tradition from his book on the authority of Ibn 'Adī in a similar way. Later on he transmitted it to us from his memory: Muḥammad b. 'Amr reported to us from al-Zuhrī from 'Urwah on the authority of 'Ā'ishah who said: Fāṭimah used to have her blood flowing. He then reported the tradition conveying the same meaning.

Abū Dāwūd said: Anas b. Sīrīn reported from Ibn 'Abbās about the woman who has a prolonged flow of blood. He said: If she sees thick blood, she should not pray; if she finds herself purified even for a moment, she should wash and pray.

Makḥūl said: Menses are not hidden from women. Their blood is black and thick. When it (blackness and thickness) goes away and there appears yellowness and liquidness, that is the flow of blood (from vein). She should then wash and pray.

Abū Dāwūd said: This tradition has been transmitted by Sa'īd b. al-Musayyab through a different chain of narrators, saying: The woman who has a prolonged flow of blood should abandon prayer when the menstruation begins; when it is finished, she should wash and pray.

Sumayy and others have also reported it from Sa'īd b. al-Musayyab. This version adds: She should refrain (from prayer) during her menstrual period.

Ḥammād b. Salamah has reported it similarly from Yaḥyā b. Sa'īd on the authority of Sa'id b. al-Musayyab.

Abū Dāwūd said: Yūnus has reported from al-Ḥasan: When the bleeding of a menstruating woman extends (beyond the normal period), she should refrain (from prayer), after her menses are over, for one or two days. Now she becomes the woman who has a prolonged flow of blood.

Al-Taimī reported from Qatādah: If her menstrual period is prolonged by five days, she should pray. Al-Taimī said: I kept on reducing (the number of days) until I reached two days. He said: If the period extends by two days, they will be counted from the menstrual period. When Ibn Sīrīn was questioned about it, he said: Women have better knowledge of that.

(287) Ḥamnah daughter of Jaḥsh said: My menstruation was great in quantity and severe. So I came to the Apostle of Allah (may peace be upon him) for a decision and told him. I found him in the house of my sister Zainab daughter of Jaḥsh. I said: Apostle of Allah, I am a woman who menstruates in great quantity and it is severe, so what do you think about it? It has prevented me from praying and fasting.

He said: I suggest that you should use cotton, for it absorbs the blood. She replied: It is too copious for that. He said: Then take a cloth. She replied: It is too copious for that, for my blood keeps flowing. The Apostle of Allah (may peace be upon him) said: I shall give you two commands; whichever of them you follow, that will be sufficient for you without the other, but you know it best whether you are strong enough to follow both of them. He added: This is a stroke of the devil, so observe your menses for six or seven days, Allah alone knows which it should be; then wash. And when you see that you are purified and quite clean, pray during twenty-three or twenty-four days and nights and fast, for that will be enough for you, and do so every month, just as women menstruate and are purified at the time of their menstruation and their purification. But if you are strong enough to delay the noon prayer and advance the afternoon ('aṣr) prayer, then wash and combine the noon and the afternoon prayer; to delay the sunset prayer and advance the night prayer, then wash and combine the two prayers, do so; and to wash at dawn, do so; and fast if you are able to do so.

The Apostle of Allah (may peace be upon him) said: Of the two commands this is more to my liking.

Abū Dāwūd said: 'Amr b. Thābit narrated from Ibn 'Aqīl: Ḥamnah said: Of the two commands this is the one which is more to my liking. In this version these words were not quoted as the statement of the Prophet (may peace be upon him); it gives it as a statement of Ḥamnah.

Abū Dāwūd said: 'Amr b Thābit was a Rāfiḍī. This has been said by Yaḥyā b. Ma'īn.

Abū Dāwūd said: I heard Aḥmad (b. Ḥanbal) say: I am doubtful about the tradition transmitted by Ibn 'Aqīl.

Chapter 113

REPORTS STATING THAT THE WOMAN SUFFERING FROM PROLONGED FLOW OF BLOOD SHOULD TAKE A BATH FOR EVERY PRAYER

(288) 'Ā'ishah, wife of the Prophet (may peace be upon him), said: Umm Ḥabībah daughter of Jaḥsh, sister-in-law of the Apostle of Allah (may peace be upon him) and wife of 'Abd al-Raḥmān b. 'Awf, had flow of blood for seven years. She asked the Apostle of Allah (may peace be upon him) about it. The Apostle of Allah (may peace be upon him) said: This is not menstruation but only a vein; so you should take a bath and pray. 'Ā'ishah said: She used to take a bath in a wash-tub in the apartment of her sister Zainab daughter of Jaḥsh; the redness of (her) blood dominated the water

(289) This tradition has been transmitted through a different chain of narrators. According to this version, 'Ā'ishah said: She would wash herself for every prayer.

(290) This has been narrated through a different chain of narrators by 'Ā'ishah. This version has the words: "She used to take a bath for every prayer."

Abū Dāwūd said: Al-Qāsim b. Mabrūr reported from Yūnus from Ibn Shihāb from 'Amrah from 'Ā'ishah from Umm Ḥabībah daughter of Jaḥsh. Similarly, it was reported by Ma'mar from al-Zuhrī from 'Amrah from 'Ā'ishah. Ma'mar sometimes reports from 'Amrah on the authority of Umm Ḥabībah to the same effect. Similarly, it was reported by Ibrāhīm b. Sa'd and Ibn 'Uyainah from al-Zuhrī from 'Amrah from 'Ā'ishah. Ibn 'Uyainah said in his version: He (al-Zuhrī) did not say that the Prophet (may peace be upon him) commanded her to take a bath.

It has also been transmitted by al-Awzā'ī in a similar way. In this version he said: 'Ā'ishah said: She used to take a bath for every prayer.

(291) 'Ā'ishah said: Umm Ḥabībah had a prolonged flow of blood for seven years. The Apostle of Allah (may peace be upon him) commanded her to take a bath; so she used to take a bath for every prayer.

(292) 'Ā'ishah said: Umm Ḥabībah daughter of Jaḥsh had a prolonged flow of blood during the time of the Apostle of Allah (may peace be upon him). He commanded her to take a bath for every prayer.[135] The narrator then transmitted the tradition (in full).

Abū Dāwūd said: It has also been narrated by Abū al-Walīd al-Ṭayālisī, but I did not hear him. He reported it from 'Ā'ishah through a different chain of narrators. 'Ā'ishah said: Zainab daughter of Jaḥsh had a prolonged flow of blood. The Prophet (may peace be upon him) said to her: Take a bath for every prayer. The narrator then reported the tradition (in full).

Abū Dāwūd said: The version transmitted by 'Abd al-Ṣamad from Sulaimān b Kathīr has: "Perform ablution for every prayer." This is a misunderstanding on the part of 'Abd al-Ṣamad. The correct version is the one narrated by Abū al-Walīd.

135. These traditions show that a woman having prolonged flow of blood should wash herself for every prayer. But obviously this puts a woman in a great hardship. Hence these traditions have been interpreted differently. Al-Shāfi'ī is of opinion that the Prophet (may peace be upon him) commanded Umm Ḥabībah to take a bath only once and pray. But she began to take a bath for every prayer of her own accord. There was no such command from the Prophet (may peace be upon him). Al-Mundhirī says: Al-Laith b. Sa'd said that al-Zuhrī did not mention in his report that the Prophet (may peace be upon him) had commanded Umm Ḥabībah to wash herself for every prayer In fact, she would do it herself, not complying with the command of the Prophet (may peace be upon him). Al-Baihaqī is of opinion that what is correct is the version narrated by the majority of reporters from al-Zuhrī. And it does not make a mention of the Prophet's (may peace be upon him) command to take a bath for every prayer. She used to wash of her own accord. Some of the jurists hold that the command for taking a bath at the time of every prayer was not obligatory. It was voluntary. The Prophet (may peace be upon him) only recommended to do so (*'Awn al-Ma'būd*, I, 118).

(293) Abū Salamah said: Zainab daughter of Abū Salamah reported to me that a woman had a copious flow of blood. She was the wife of 'Abd al-Raḥmān b. 'Awf. The Apostle of Allah (may peace be upon him) commanded her to take a bath at the time of every prayer, and then to pray. He reported to me that Umm Bakr told him that 'Ā'ishah said: The Apostle of Allah (may peace be upon him) said about a woman who was doubtful of her menstruation after purification that it was a vein or veins.

Abū Dāwūd said: The two commands (of which the Prophet gave option) were as follows in the version reported by Ibn 'Aqīl: He said: If you are strong enough, then take a bath for every prayer; otherwise combine the (two prayers), as al-Qāsim reported in his version. This statement was also narrated by Sa'īd b. Jubair from 'Alī and Ibn 'Abbās.

Chapter 114

THE VIEW THAT A WOMAN WHO HAS PROLONGED FLOW OF BLOOD SHOULD COMBINE THE TWO PRAYERS AND TAKE A BATH ONLY ONCE FOR THEM

(294) 'Ā'ishah said: A woman had a prolonged flow of blood in the time of the Apostle of Allah (may peace be upon him). She was commanded to advance the afternoon prayer and delay the noon prayer, and to take a bath for them only once; and to delay the sunset prayer and advance the night prayer and to take a bath only once for them; and to take a bath separately for the dawn prayer.

I (Shu'bah) asked 'Abd al-Raḥmān: (Is it) from the Prophet (may peace be upon him)? I do not report to you anything except from the Prophet (may peace be upon him).[136]

(295) 'Ā'ishah said: Sahlah daughter of Suhail had a prolonged flow of blood. She came to the Prophet (may peace be upon him). He commanded her to take a bath for every prayer. When it became hard for her, he commanded her to combine the noon and afternoon prayers with one bath and the sunset and night prayer with one bath, and to take a bath (separately) for the dawn prayer.

Abū Dāwūd said: Ibn 'Uyainah reported from 'Abd al-Raḥmān b. al-Qāsim on the authority of his father, saying: A woman had a prolonged flow of blood. She asked the Prophet (may peace be upon him). He commanded her to the same effect.

(296) Asmā' daughter of 'Umais said: I said: Apostle of Allah, Fāṭimah daughter

136. Shu'bah was doubtful about the person who gave the command to the woman to wash. Hence he asked 'Abd al-Raḥmān. But 'Abd al-Raḥmān was not aware of this fact whether the Prophet (may peace be upon him) gave her this command, or some other person (*'Awn al-Ma'būd*, I, 119).

of Abū Ḥubaish had a flow of blood for a certain period and did not pray. The Apostle of Allah (may peace be upon him) said: Glory be to Allah! This comes from the devil. She should sit in a tub, and when she sees yellowness on the top of the water, she should take a bath once for the noon and afternoon prayer, and take another bath for the sunset and night prayers, and take a bath once for the dawn prayer, and in between times she should perform ablution.[137]

Abū Dāwūd said: Mujāhid reported on the authority of Ibn 'Abbās: When bathing became hard for her, he commanded her to combine the two prayers.

Abū Dāwūd said: Ibrāhīm reported it from Ibn 'Abbās. This is also the view of Ibrāhīm al-Nakh'ī and 'Abd Allah b. Shaddād.

Chapter 115

THE VIEW THAT THE WOMAN HAVING FLOW OF BLOOD SHOULD TAKE A BATH ONCE WHEN PURIFIED FROM HER MENSES

(297) 'Adī b. Thābit reported from his father on the authority of his grandfather that the Prophet (may peace be upon him) said about the woman having a prolonged flow of blood: She should abandon prayer during her menstrual period; then she should take a bath and pray. She should perform ablution for every prayer.

Abū Dāwūd said: 'Uthmān added: She should keep fast and pray.

(298) 'Ā'ishah said: Fāṭimah daughter of Abū Ḥubaish came to the Prophet (may peace be upon him) and narrated what happened with her. He said: Then take a bath and then perform ablution for every prayer and pray.

(299) 'Ā'ishah said about the woman who has a prolonged flow of blood: She should take a bath, i.e. only once; then she should perform ablution until her next menstrual period.

(300) This tradition has also been narrated by 'Ā'ishah through a different chain of transmitters.

Abū Dāwūd said: All the traditions (on this subject) transmitted by 'Adī b. Thābit and A'mash on the authority of Ḥabīb and Ayyūb Abū al-'Alā' are weak; none of them is sound. This tradition indicates the tradition reported by al-A'mash on the authority of Ḥabīb. Ḥafṣ b. Ghayāth has narrated it from al-A'mash as a statement of the Companion, i.e. 'Ā'ishah. Ḥafṣ b. Ghayāth has rejected the tradition trans-

137. The commandment to take a bath for each prayer or to wash once for two prayers as indicated in these traditions was recommendatory and not obligatory. The generally accepted view about the washing of a woman suffering from a flow of blood only once after her menstrual period is finished until her next period begins. It is not necessary for her to wash for every prayer or for the two prayers when they are combined (*'Awn al-Ma'būd*, I, 119).

mitted by Ḥabīb as a statement (of the Prophet). And Asbāṭ also reported it as a statement of 'Ā'ishah.

Abū Dāwūd said: Ibn Dāwūd has narrated the first part of this tradition as a statement (of the Prophet), and denied that there was any mention of performing ablution for every prayer. The weakness of the tradition reported by Ḥabīb is also indicated by the fact that the version transmitted by al-Zuhrī from 'Urwah on the authority of 'Ā'ishah says that she used to wash herself for every prayer; (these words occur) in the tradition about the woman who has a flow of blood. This tradition has been reported by Abū al-Yaqẓān from 'Adī b. Thābit from his father from 'Alī, and narrated by 'Ammār, the freed slave of Banū Hāshim, from Ibn 'Abbās, and transmitted by 'Abd al-Mālik b. Maisarah, Bayān, al-Mughīrah, Firās; on the authority of al-Sha'bī, from Qumair from 'Ā'ishah, stating: You should perform ablution for every prayer. The version transmitted by Dāwūd, and 'Āṣim from al-Sha'bī from Qumair from 'Ā'ishah has the words: She should take a bath only once every day. The version reported by Hishām b. 'Urwah from his father has the words: The woman having a flow of blood should perform ablution for every prayer. All these traditions are weak except the tradition reported by Qumair and the tradition reported by 'Ammār, the freed slave of Banū Hāshim, and the tradition narrated by Hishām b. 'Urwah on the authority of his father. What is commonly known from Ibn 'Abbās is bathing (for every prayer)

Chapter 116

THE VIEW THAT THE WOMAN HAVING A FLOW OF BLOOD SHOULD TAKE A BATH AT THE TIME OF THE NOON PRAYER

(301) Sumayy, the freed slave of Abū Bakr, says that al-Qa'qā' and Zaid b. Aslam sent him to Sa'īd b. al-Musayyab to ask him as to how the woman who has a flow of blood should wash. He replied: She should wash at the time of the noon prayer (the bath will be valid from one noon prayer until the next noon prayer); and should perform ablution for every prayer. If there is excessive bleeding, she should tie a cloth over her private part.

Abū Dāwūd said: It has been narrated by Ibn 'Umar and Anas b. Mālik that she should take a bath at the time of the noon prayer (being valid) until the next noon prayer. This tradition has also been transmitted by Dāwūd and 'Āṣim from al-Sha'bī from his wife from Qumair on the authority of 'Ā'ishah, except that the version of Dāwūd has the words: "every day," and the version of 'Āṣim has the words: "at the time of noon prayer". This is the view held by Sālim b. 'Abd Allah, al-Ḥasan and 'Aṭā'.

Abū Dāwūd said : Mālik said : I think that the tradition narrated by Ibn al-Musayyab must contain the words : "from one purification to another". But it was misunderstood and the people changed it to : "from one noon prayer to another".

It has also been reported by Miswar b. 'Abd al-Malik b. Sa'īd b. 'Abd al-Raḥmān b. Yarbū', saying: "from one purification to another," but the people changed it to : "from one noon prayer to another."

Chapter 117

THE VIEW THAT THE WOMAN HAVING A FLOW OF BLOOD SHOULD TAKE A BATH ONLY ONCE EVERY DAY AND NOT AT THE TIME OF THE NOON PRAYER

(302) 'Alī said : The woman who has a prolonged flow of blood should wash herself every day when her menstrual period is over and take a woollen cloth greased with fat or oil (to tie it over the private parts).

Chapter 118

THE VIEW THAT THE WOMAN HAVING A PROLONGED FLOW OF BLOOD SHOULD WASH DURING MENSTRUAL PERIOD

(303) Muḥammad b. 'Uthmān asked al-Qāsim b. Muḥammad about the woman who has a prolonged flow of blood. He replied : She should abandon prayer during her menstrual period, then wash and pray ; then she should wash during her menstrual period.

Chapter 119

THE VIEW THAT THE WOMAN HAVING A FLOW OF BLOOD SHOULD PERFORM ABLUTION FOR EVERY PRAYER

(304) 'Urwah b al-Zubair said that Fāṭimah daughter of Abū Ḥubaish had a prolonged flow of blood. The Prophet (may peace be upon him) said to her : When the blood of the menses comes, it is black blood which can be recognised ; so when that comes, refrain from prayer, but when a different type comes, perform ablution and pray.

Abū Dāwūd said : Ibn al-Muthannā said : Ibn 'Adī narrated this tradition from his memory on the authority of 'Urwah from 'Ā'ishah.

Abū Dāwūd said: This tradition has also been transmitted by al-'Alā' b. al-Musayyab and Shu'bah from al-Ḥakam on the authority of Abū Ja'far. Al-'Alā' reported it as a statement of the Prophet (may peace be upon him), and Shu'bah as a statement of Abū Ja'far, saying: She should perform ablution for every prayer.

Chapter I20

THE VIEW THAT THE WOMAN HAVING A PROLONGED FLOW OF BLOOD SHOULD PERFORM ABLUTION ONLY WHEN IT BECOMES VOID AND NOT FOR EVERY PRAYER

(305) 'Ikrimah said: Umm Ḥabībah daughter of Jaḥsh had a prolonged flow of blood. The Prophet (may peace be upon him) commanded her to refrain (from prayer) during her menstrual period; then she should wash and pray. If she sees anything (which renders ablution void) she should perform ablution and pray.

(306) Rabī'ah held that the woman who had a prolonged flow of blood should not perform ablution for every prayer except in the case that she finds anything save bleeding that renders ablution void, then she should perform ablution.[138]

Abū Dāwūd said: This is the view held by Mālik b. Anas.

Chapter 121

THE *SHARĪ'AH* LAW ABOUT THE WOMAN WHO SEES YELLOWNESS OR BROWNNESS AFTER PURIFICATION

(307) Umm 'Aṭīyyah who took an oath of allegiance to the Prophet (may peace be upon him) said: We would not take into consideration brown and yellow (fluid) after purification.

(308) Umm 'Aṭīyyah has narrated this tradition also through a different chain of transmitters.

Abū Dāwūd said: The name of Umm al-Hudhail is Ḥafṣah daughter of Sīrīn. The name of her son was Hudhail and of his husband 'Abd al-Raḥmān.

138. This is a point of view held by Rabī'ah and Mālik b. Anas. Others hold that such a woman should wash when her menstrual period is finished and perform ablution for every prayer.

Chapter 122

THE HUSBAND IS ALLOWED TO COHABIT WITH HIS WIFE WHO HAS A PROLONGED FLOW OF BLOOD

(309) 'Ikrimah said: Umm Ḥabībah had a prolonged flow of blood; her husband used to cohabit with her.

Abū Dāwūd said: Yaḥyā b. Ma'īn has pronounced Mu'allā (a narrator of this tradition) as trustworthy. But Aḥmad b. Ḥanbal would not report (traditions) from him because he exercised personal opinion.

(310) 'Ikrimah reported Ḥamnah daughter of Jaḥsh as saying that her husband would have intercourse with her during the period she had a flow of blood.

Chapter 123

THE LAW OF *SHARĪ'AH* PERTAINING TO THE WOMAN WHO HAS A BLEEDING AFTER DELIVERY (PUERPERAL HAEMORRHAGE)

(311) Umm Salamah said: The woman having bleeding after delivery (puerperal haemorrhage) would refrain (from prayer) for forty days or forty nights; and we would anoint our faces with an aromatic herb called *wars* to remove dark spots.

(312) Al-Azdīyyah, viz. Mussah, said: I performed *Ḥajj* and came to Umm Salamah and said (to her): Mother of the believers, Samurah b. Jundub commands women to complete the prayers abandoned during their menstrual period. She said: They should not do so. The wives of the Prophet (may peace be upon him) would refrain (from prayer) for forty nights (i.e. days) during the course of bleeding after childbirth. The Prophet (may peace be upon him) would not command them to complete the prayers abandoned during the period of bleeding.[139]

Muḥammad b. Ḥātim said: The name of al-Azdīyyah is Mussah and her patronymic name is Umm Bussah.

Abū Dāwūd said: The patronymic name of Kathīr b. Ziyād is Abū Sahl.

139. According to the consensus of the Companions, the Successors and the majority of the scholars, a woman should abandon prayer and fasting only for forty days after childbirth. After purification she is not required to complete the abandoned prayers. But she should complete any fasts she may have abandoned (*'Awn al-Ma'būd*, I, 123).

Chapter 124

ON WASHING THE BLOOD OF MENSTRUATION AND BATHING AFTER IT

(313) Umayyah daughter of Abū al-Ṣalt quoted a certain woman of Banū Ghifār, whose name [140] was mentioned to me, as saying: The Apostle of Allah (may peace be upon him) made me ride behind him on the rear of the camel saddle. By Allah, the Apostle of Allah (may peace be upon him) got down in the morning. He made his camel kneel down and I came down from the back part of his saddle. There was a mark of blood on it (saddle) and that was the first menstruation that I had. I struck to the camel and felt ashamed. When the Apostle of Allah (may peace be upon him) saw what had happened with me and saw the blood, he said: Perhaps you have menstruation. I said: Yes. He then said: Set yourself right (i.e. tie some cloth to prevent bleeding), then take a vessel of water and put some salt in it, and then wash the blood from the back part of the saddle, and then return to your mount. When the Apostle of Allah (may peace be upon him) conquered Khaibar, he gave us a portion out of the booty. Whenever the woman became purified from her menses, she would put salt in water. And when she died, she left a will to put salt in water for washing her (after death).

(314) 'Ā'ishah reported: Asmā' entered upon the Apostle of Allah (may peace be upon him) and said: Apostle of Allah, how should one of us take a bath when she is purified from her menses? He said: She should take water mixed with the leaves of lote-tree; then she should perform ablution and wash her head and rub it so much so that water reaches the roots of the hair; she should then pour water upon her body. Then she should take a piece of cloth (or cotton or wool) and purify with it. She asked: Apostle of Allah, how should I purify with it? 'Ā'ishah said: I understood what he (the Prophet) said metaphorically; I, therefore, said to her: Remove the marks of blood.

(315) 'Ā'ishah made a mention of the women of the Anṣār and admired them stating that they had obliged (all Muslims). She then said: One of their women came upon the Apostle of Allah (may peace be upon him). She then reported the rest of the tradition to the same effect; but in this version she said the words: "a musk-scented piece of cloth."

Musaddad said: Abū 'Awānah used the word *firṣah* (i.e. a piece of cloth), but Abū al-Aḥwaṣ used the word *qarṣah* (i.e. a small piece of cloth).

(316) 'Ā'ishah said: Asmā' asked the Prophet (may peace be upon him) and then narrated the rest of the tradition to the same effect. He (the Prophet) said: "a musk-

140. The narrator forgot the name. Her name was Lailā. She was the wife of Abū Dharr al-Ghifārī (*'Awn al-Ma'būd*, I, 123).

scented piece of cloth." She (Asmā') said: How should I purify with it? He said: By glory to Allah! Purify with it, and he covered his face with the cloth. This version also adds: "She asked about the washing because of sexual defilement." He said: Take your water and purify yourself as best as possible. Then pour water over your head and rub it so that water reaches the roots of your hair. Then pour water over yourself. 'Ā'ishah said: The best of the women are the women of the Anṣār. Shyness would not prevent them from inquiring about religion and from acquiring deep understanding in it.

Chapter 125

TAYAMMUM[141]

(317) 'Ā'ishah reported: The Apostle of Allah (may peace be upon him) sent Usaid b. Ḥuḍair and some people with him to search the necklace lost by 'Ā'ishah. The time of prayer came and they prayed without ablution. When they returned to the Prophet (may peace be upon him) and related the fact to him, the verse concerning *tayammum* was revealed.

Ibn Nufail added: Usaid said to her: May Allah have mercy upon you! Never has there been an occasion when you were beset with an unpleasant matter but Allah made the Muslims and you come out of that.

(318) 'Ammār b. Yāsir said: They (the Companions of the Prophet) wiped with pure earth (their hands and face) to offer the dawn prayer in the company of the Apostle of Allah (may peace be upon him). They struck the ground with their palms and wiped their faces once. Then they repeated and struck the ground with their palms once again and wiped their arms completely up to the shoulders and up to the armpits with the inner side of their hands.[142]

(319) This tradition has also been reported through a different chain of narrators. This version has: The Muslims stood up and struck the earth with their palms, but did not get any earth (in their hands). He (Ibn Wahb) then narrated the rest of the tradition in like manner, but he did not mention the words "shoulders" and "armpits".

141. *Tayammum* literally means intention; legally it means wiping of hands and face with earth with the intention of purification, if one needs ablution or bath in the absence of water or if there is some other handicap. It is a substitute for ablution or bath as the case may be. Its religious sanction is established by the Qur'ān, *Sunnah*, and consensus of the community. It is peculiar with the Muslim community.

142. In the beginning when the Qur'ānic revelation came down about *tayammum*, the Companions did not know the right method and details of *tayammum*. Hence they performed it in accordance with their own opinion. The Prophet (may peace be upon him) later on explained its details. The generally accepted method of the performance of *tayammum* is to wipe the face once and to wipe the hands up to the elbows (*'Awn al-Ma'būd*, I, 125).

Ibn al-Laith said: (They) wiped above the elbows.

(320) 'Ammār b. Yāsir said: The Apostle of Allah (may peace be upon him) encamped at Ūlat al-Jaish[143] and 'Ā'ishah was in his company. Her necklace of onyx of Ẓifār[144] was broken (and fell somewhere). The people were detained to make a search for that necklace until the dawn broke. There was no water with the people. Therefore Abū Bakr became angry with her and said: You detained the people and they have no water with them. Thereupon Allah, the Exalted, sent down revelation about it to His Apostle (may peace be upon him) granting concession to purify themselves with pure earth. Then the Muslims stood up with the Apostle of Allah (may peace be upon him) and struck the ground with their hands and then they raised their hands, and did not take any earth (in their hands). Then they wiped with them their faces and hands up to the shoulders, and from their palms up to the armpits.

Ibn Yaḥyā added in his version: Ibn Shihāb said in his tradition: The people do not take this (tradition) into account.

Abū Dāwūd said: Ibn Isḥāq also reported it in a similar way. In this (version) he said on the authority of Ibn 'Abbās. He mentioned the words "two strikes" (i.e. striking the earth twice) as mentioned by Yūnus. And Ma'mar also narrated on the authority of al-Zuhrī "two strikes". And Mālik said: From al-Zuhrī from 'Ubaid Allah b. 'Abd Allah from his father on the authority of 'Ammār. Abū Uwais also reported it in a similar way on the authority of al-Zuhrī. But Ibn 'Uyainah doubted it, he sometimes said: from his father, and sometimes he said: from Ibn 'Abbās. Ibn 'Uyainah was confused in it and in his hearing from al-Zuhrī. No one has mentioned "two strikes" in this tradition except those whose names I have mentioned.

(321) Shaqīq said: While I was sitting between 'Abd Allah and Abū Mūsā, the latter said: Abū 'Abd al-Raḥmān, what do you think if a man becomes defiled (because of seminal emission) and does not find water for a month; should he not perform *tayammum*? He replied: No, even if he does not find water for a month.[145] Abū Mūsā then said: How will you do with the Qur'ānic version (about *tayammum*) in the

143. The name of a place between Mecca and Medina. It is sometimes mentioned in other versions as Dhāt al-Jaish and sometimes al-Baiḍā.

144. The name of a city on the coast of Yemen.

145. 'Abd Allah b. Mas'ūd held that a man who becomes defiled due to seminal emission should take a bath necessarily. *Tayammum* is not valid in case one needs a bath when one is defiled. In fact, in this matter he followed 'Umar b. al-Khaṭṭāb who held the same view. According to him, the Qur'ānic verses about *tayammum* meant that *tayammum* should be performed, if one needs ablution only and not bath. 'Umar was also not satisfied with the tradition narrated by 'Ammār to him. As he was himself in the company of 'Ammār during that journey, he thought that 'Ammār could not remember the tradition of the Prophet (may peace be upon him) and the incident correctly. Hence he did not change his view. The rest of the Companions and the majority of the community hold that *tayammum* is valid in both cases when one needs ablution or bath. This view is supported by a large number of the traditions of the Prophet (may peace be upon him).

chapter al-Mā'idah which says: "... and ye find not water, then go to clean, high ground" (v. 6)? 'Abd Allah (b. Mas'ūd) then said: If they (the people) are granted concession in this respect, they might perform *tayammum* with pure earth when water is cold. Abū Mūsā said: For this (reason) you forbade it ? He said: Yes. Abū Mūsā then said: Did you not hear what 'Ammār said to 'Umar? (He said): The Apostle of Allah (may peace be upon him) sent me on some errand. I had seminal emission and I did not find water. Therefore, I rolled on the ground just as an animal rolls down. I then came to the Prophet (may peace be upon him) and made a mention of that to him. He said: It would have been enough for you to do thus. Then he struck the ground with his hands and shook them off and then struck the right hand with his left hand and his left hand with his right hand (and wiped) over the hands (up to the wrist) and wiped his face. 'Abd Allah then said to him: Did you not see that 'Umar was not satisfied with the statement of 'Ammār?

(322) 'Abd al-Raḥmān b. Abzā said: While I was with 'Umar, a man came to him and said: We live at a place (where water is not found) for a month or two (what should we do, if we are sexually defiled?). 'Umar said: So far as I am concerned, I do not pray until I find water. 'Ammār said: Commander of the faithful, do you not remember when I and you were among the camels (for tending them)? There we became sexually defiled. I rolled down on the ground. We then came to the Prophet (may peace be upon him) and I mentioned that to him. He said: It was enough for you to do so. Then he struck the ground with both his hands. He then blew over them and wiped his face and both hands by means of them up to half the arms.[146] 'Umar said: 'Ammār, fear Allah. He said: Commander of the faithful, if you want, I will never narrate it. 'Umar said: Nay, by Allah, we shall turn you from that towards which you turned (i.e. you have your choice).

(323) Ibn Abzā reported on the authority of 'Ammār b. Yāsir in this tradition as saying (from the Prophet): 'Ammār, it would have been enough for you (to do) so. He then struck only one stroke on the ground with both his hands; he then struck one with the other; then he wiped his face and both arms up to half the forearms and did not reach the elbows.

Abū Dāwūd said: This is also transmitted by Wakī' from al-A'mash from Salamah b. Kuhail from 'Abd al-Raḥmān b. Abzā.

It is also transmitted through a different chain by Jarīr from al-A'mash from Salamah from Sa'īd b. 'Abd al-Raḥmān b. Abzā from his father.

146. Al-Baihaqī said : The report of Abū Mālik, a narrator, is disputed. He sometimes reports from 'Abd al-Raḥmān b. Abzā the words "up to half the arm," and sometimes from 'Ammār himself the words "(wiped) his face and both his hands (up to the wrists)". His report is, therefore, not reliable. The report of al-Ḥakam is more reliable. He mentions the wiping of the face and the hands up to the wrists (*'Awn al-Ma'būd*, I, 127).

(324) Ibn 'Abd al-Raḥmān b. Abzā reported on the authority of his father this incident from 'Ammār. He said: This would have been enough for you, and the Prophet (may peace be upon him) struck the ground with his hand. He then blew it and wiped with it his face and hands. Being doubtful Salamah said: I do not know (whether he wiped) up to the enblows or the wrists.

(325) This is transmitted by Shu'bah through a different chain of narrators. This version adds: He ('Ammār) said: He (the Prophet) then blew it and wiped with it his face and hands up to the elbows or up to the forearms. Shu'bah said: Salamah used to narrate (the words) "the hands and the face and the forearms,"; one day Manṣūr said to him: Look, what are you saying, because no one except you mentions the (word) "forearms"

(326) This is also transmitted by Ibn 'Abd al-Raḥmān b. Abzā on the authority of his father from 'Ammār. He reported the Prophet (may peace be upon him) as saying: It would have been enough for you to strike the ground with your hands and then wipe with them your face and your hands (up to the wrists). He then narrated the rest of the tradition.

Abū Dāwūd said: This is also transmitted by Shu'bah from Ḥuṣain on the authority of Abū Mālik. He said: I heard 'Ammār saying so in his speech, except that in this version he added the words: "He blew." And Ḥuṣain b. Muḥammad narrated from Shu'bah on the authority of al-Ḥakam and in this version added the words: "He (the Prophet) struck the earth with his palms and blew."

(327) 'Ammār b. Yāsir said: I asked the Prophet (may peace be upon him) about *tayammum*. He commanded me to strike only one stroke[147] (i.e. to strike the ground) for (wiping) the face and the hands.

(328) Abān said: Qatādah was asked about *tayammum* during a journey. He said: A traditionist reported to me from al-Sha'bī from 'Abd al-Raḥmān b. Abzā on the

147. There is a difference of opinion amongst the scholars as to how many times the earth should be struck with hands for wiping the face and hands. This difference is due to the variance in the versions of the tradition. The following are a few points of view:

(1) Only one stroke for wiping both the hands and the face. This is held by Aḥmad b. Ḥanbal, Isḥāq, al-Awzā'ī and the traditionists.

(2) Striking twice, namely, one stroke for wiping the face and one for wiping the hands. This is maintained by Abū Ḥanīfah, Mālik, al-Thawrī, al-Shāfi'ī, al-Laith, and by the jurists in general. It is reported to have been held by 'Alī, 'Umar, Ḥasan al-Baṣrī, al-Sha'bī and Salim b. 'Abd Allah

(3) Striking twice together for wiping the face and the hands. This is the opinion of Hasan b. Ḥayy and Ibn Abī Lailā.

(4) Striking three times each for wiping the face, the hands, and then both together. This is held by Ibn Sīrīn.

(5) Striking four times. Two strokes are for wiping the face and two for the hands. But this is not supported by any tradition (*Ma'ārif al-Sunan*, I, 477-78).

authority of 'Ammār b. Yāsir who reported the Apostle of Allah (may peace be upon him) as saying: (He should wipe) up to the elbows.[148]

Chapter 126

PERFORMING *TAYAMMUM* WHILE ONE IS AT HOME

(329) 'Umair, the freed slave of Ibn 'Abbās, said that he heard him say: I and 'Abd Allah b. Yasār, the freed slave of Maimūnah, wife of the Prophet (may peace be upon him), came and entered upon Abu'l-Juhaim b. al-Ḥārith b. al-Ṣimmat al-Anṣāri. Abū al-Juhaim said: The Apostle of Allah (may peace be upon him) came from Bīr Jamal (a place near Medina) and a man met him and saluted him. The Apostle of Allah (may peace be upon him) did not return the salutation until he came to a wall and wiped his face and hands and then returned the salutation (i.e. after performing *tayammum*).[149]

(330) Nāfi' said: Accompanied by 'Abd Allah b. 'Umar, I went to Ibn 'Abbās for a certain work. He (Ibn 'Abbās) narrated a tradition saying: A man passed by the Apostle of Allah (may peace be upon him) in a street, while he re turned from the toilet or just urinated. He (the man) saluted him, but the Prophet did not return the salutation. When the man was about to disappear (from sight) in the street he struck a wall with both of his hands and wiped his face with them. He then struck another stroke and wiped his arms. He then returned the man's salutation. Then he said: I did not return the salutation to you because I was not purified.

Abū Dāwūd said: I heard Aḥmad b. Ḥanbal say: Muhammad b. Thābit reported a rejected tradition.

148. There are traditions which indicate the wiping of the hands up to the shoulders; some fix the limit up to the wrist and others up to the elbows. A few mention the limit up to half the forearms. Hence the limit of wiping the hands is disputed. The following are a few opinions:

(1) The hands should be wiped up to the wrists. This is held by al-Awzā'ī, Aḥmad, Ishāq, the Ẓāhirīs (literalists) and the traditionists.

(2) The hands should be wiped up to the elbows (including them). This is the view of Abū Hanīfah, al-Thawrī, al-Laith, al-Shāfi'ī and Mālik.

(3) Wiping the hands up to the wrists is obligatory and up to the elbows is recommendatory (*sunnah*). This is held by Mālik.

(4) The hands should be wiped up to the shoulders and armpits. This is maintained by al-Zuhrī and Muhammad b. Salamah (*Ma'ārif al-Sunan*, I, 478-79).

149. This tradition shows that it is permissible to perform *tayammum* while one is staying at home and does not find water. Moreover, the Prophet (may peace be upon him) performed *tayammum* to return the salutation because he could not get water to perform ablution immediately. Although it is not necessary to perform ablution or *tayammum* for returning the salutation, the Prophet (may peace be upon him) did so as a remembrance of Allah because *Salām* is one of His names (*'Awn al-Ma'būd*, I. 129)

Ibn Dāsah said: Abū Dāwūd said: No one supported Muḥammad b. Thābit in respect of narrating this tradition as to striking the wall twice (for wiping) from the Prophet (may peace be upon him), but reported it as an action of Ibn 'Umar.

(331) Ibn 'Umar said: The Apostle of Allah (may peace be upon him) came from the privy. A man met him near Bīr Jamal and saluted him. The Apostle of Allah (may peace be upon him) did not return the salutation until he came to a wall and placed his hands on the wall and wiped his face and hands; he then returned the man's salutation.

Chapter 127

A PERSON WHO IS SEXUALLY DEFILED MAY PERFORM *TAYAMMUM*

(332) Abū Dharr said: A few goats got collected with the Apostle of Allah (may peace be upon him). He said: Abū Dharr, drive them to the wood. I drove them to Rabadhah (a place near Medina). I would have sexual defilement (during my stay there) and I would remain (in this condition) for five or six days. Then I came to the Apostle of Allah (may peace be upon him). He said: O Abū Dharr I kept silence. He then said: May your mother bereave you, Abu Dharr; woe be to your mother.[150] He then called a black slave-girl for me. She brought a vessel which contained water. She then concealed me by drawing a curtain and I concealed myself behind a she-camel, and took a bath. I felt as if I had thrown away a mountain from me. He said: Clean earth is a means of ablution for a Muslim, even for ten years (he does not find water); but when you find water, you should make it touch your skin, for that is better.[151]

The version of Musaddad has: "the goats (were collected) from the alms," and the tradition reported by 'Amr is complete.

(333) A man from Banū 'Āmir said: I embraced Islam and my (ignorance of the) religion made me anxious (to learn the essentials). I came to Abū Dharr. Abū Dharr said: The climate of Medina did not suit me. The Apostle of Allah (may peace be upon him) ordered me to have a few camels and goats. He said to me: Drink their milk. (The narrator Ḥammād said): I doubt whether he (the Prophet) said: "their urine." Abū Dharr said: I was away from the watering place and I had my family

150. This is an Arabic idiom used on the occasion of anger or sorrow. This is not a curse. The Prophet (may peace be upon him) in fact, expressed his sorrow for saying his prayer without purification (i.e. performing *tayammum*).

151. It is agreed upon by the jurists that *tayammum* is a substitute for bath as it is for ablution. There is no limit for the period. One may perform *tayammum* in the case of sexual defilement and say prayer for any length of time until one finds water.

with me. I would have sexual defilement and pray without purification. I came to the Apostle of Allah (may peace be upon him) at noon. He was resting in the shade of the mosque along with a group of his Companions. He (the Prophet) said: Abū Dharr. I said: Yes, I am ruined, Apostle of Allah. He said: What ruined you? I said: I was away from the watering place and I had my family with me. I used to be sexually defiled and pray without purification. He commanded (to bring) water for me. Then a black slave-girl brought a vessel of water that was shaking as the vessel was not full. I concealed myself behind a camel and took a bath and then came (to the Prophet). The Apostle of Allah (may peace be upon him) said: Abū Dharr, clean earth is a means of ablution, even if you do not find water for ten years. When you find water, you should make it touch your skin.

Abū Dāwūd said: This is transmitted by Ḥammād b. Zaid from Ayyūb. This version does not mention the words "their urine." This is not correct. The words "their urine" occur only in the version reported by Anas and transmitted only by the people of Baṣrah.

Chapter 128

IF A PERSON WHO IS SEXUALLY DEFILED FEARS COLD, SHOULD HE PERFORM *TAYAMMUM*?

(334) 'Amr b. al-'Āṣ said: I had a sexual dream on a cold night in the battle of Dhāt al-Salāsil. I was afraid, if I washed I would die. I, therefore, performed *tayammum* and led my companions in the dawn prayer. They mentioned that to the Apostle of Allah (may peace be upon him). He said: 'Amr, you led your companions is prayer while you were sexually defiled? I informed him of the cause which impeded me from washing. And I said: I heard Allah say: "Do not kill yourself, verily Allah is merciful to you." The Apostle of Allah (may peace be upon him) laughed and did not say anything.[152]

Abū Dāwūd said: 'Abd al-Raḥmān b. Jubair is an Egyptian and a freed slave of Khārijah b. Ḥudhāfah. He is not Jubair b. Nufair.

(335) Abū Qais, the freed slave of 'Amr b. al-'Āṣ, said 'Amr b. al-'Āṣ was in a battle. He then narrated the rest of the tradition. He then said: He washed his armpits and other joints where dirt was found, and he performed ablution like that for prayer. Then he led them in prayer. He then narrated the tradition in a similar way but did not make a mention of *tayammum*.

Abū Dāwūd said: This incident has also been narrated by al-Awzā'ī on the

152. This tradition shows that one should perform *tayammum* and say prayer if the night is severely cold and one cannot wash oneself in the case of seminal ejection.

authority of Hassān b. 'Aṭīyyah. This version has the words: Then he performed *tayammum*.

Chapter 129

A PERSON SUFFERING FROM SMALLPOX MAY PERFORM *TAYAMMUM*

(336) Jābir said: We set out on a journey. One of our people was hurt by a stone, that injured his head. He then had a sexual dream. He asked his fellow travellers: Do you find concession for me to perform *tayammum*? They said: We do not find any concession for you while you can use water. He took a bath and died. When we came to the Prophet (may peace be upon him), the incident was reported to him. He said: They killed him, may Allah kill them! Could they not ask when they did not know? The cure of ignorance is inquiry. It was enough for him to perform *tayammum* and to pour some drops of water or to bind a bandage over the wound (the narrator Mūsā was doubtful); then he should have wiped over it and washed the rest of his body.[153]

(337) 'Abd Allah b. 'Abbās said: A man was injured during the lifetime of the Apostle of Allah (may peace be upon him); he then had a sexual dream, and he was advised to wash and he washed himself. Consequently he died. When this was reported to the Apostle of Allah (may peace be upon him), he said: They killed him; may Allah kill them! Is not inquiry the cure of ignorance?

Chapter 130

IF A PERSON PRAYS ON ITS RIGHT TIME AFTER PERFORMING *TAYAMMUM*, AND HE FINDS WATER WHILE THE TIME OF PRAYER REMAINS (WHAT SHOULD HE DO?)

(338) Abū Sa'īd al-Khudrī said: Two persons set out on a journey. Meanwhile the time of prayer came and they had no water. They performed *tayammum* with clean

153. The topic of this chapter does not agree with the tradition. Some copies of Abū Dāwūd mention the topic "wounded" (*majrūḥ*) and others "disabled person" (*ma'dhūr*). These headings agree with the tradition.

This tradition indicates that a person who is injured may perform *tayammum* and wipe over the bandage. But this tradition indicates the combination of *tayammum* and washing. The author of *'Awn al-Ma'būd* observes that this is a weak tradition and it contradicts all other versions narrated by 'Aṭā' b. Abī Rabāḥ. This is transmitted by the narrator al-Zubair b. Khuraiq who is not very reliable.

This tradition also provides sanction for wiping over the bandage in the case of injury (*'Awn al-Ma'būd*, I, 132-33)

earth and prayed. Later on they found water within the time of the prayer. One of them repeated the prayer and ablution but the other did not repeat. Then they came to the Apostle of Allah (may peace be upon him) and related the matter to him. Addressing himself to the one who did not repeat, he said: You followed the ***sunnah*** (model behaviour of the Prophet) and your (first) prayer was enough for you. He said to the one who performed ablution and repeated: For you there is the double reward.[154]

Abū Dāwūd said: Besides Ibn Nāfi' this is transmitted by al-Laith from' Umairah b. Abī Nājīyyah from Bakr b. Sawādah on the authority of 'Aṭā' b. Yasār from the Prophet (may peace be upon him).

Abū Dāwūd said: The mention of (the name of the Companion) Abū Sa'īd in this tradition is not guarded. This is a *mursal* tradition (i.e. the Successor 'Aṭā' b. Yasār direcetly narrates it from the Prophet, leaving the name of the Companion in the chain).

(339) 'Aṭā' b. Yasār said: Two persons from the Companions of the Apostle of Allah (may peace be upon him); he then narrated the rest of the tradition to the same effect.

Chapter 131

ON TAKING A BATH ON FRIDAY

(340) Abū Hurairah said: While 'Umar b. al-Khaṭṭāb was making a speech on Friday (in the mosque), a man came in. 'Umar said: Are you detained from prayer? The man said: As soon as I heard the call for prayer, I performed ablution. Then 'Umar said: Only ablution? Did you not hear the Apostle of Allah (may peace be upon him) say: When any one of you comes for Friday (prayer) he should take a bath.[155]

(341) Abū Sa'īd al-Khudrī reported the Apostle of Allah (may peace be upon him) as saying: Taking a bath on Friday is necessary for every adult.

(342) Ḥafṣah reported: The Prophet (may peace be upon him) said: It is necessary for every adult (person) to go for (saying) Friday (prayer), and for everyone who

154. This tradition indicates that if one prays after performing *tayammum* and then finds water he need not perform ablution and repeat the prayer. It is not necessary; but if one does so, he will get a double reward.

155. Some other versions of this tradition indicate that the person who attended the mosque late for Friday prayer was 'Uthmān b. 'Affān.

Al-Khaṭṭābī observes that taking a bath on Friday for prayer is not obligatory. It is only recommended to take a bath for Friday prayer. Had it been obligatory 'Umar must have asked 'Uthmān to return and pray after taking a bath. Moreover, this happened in the presence of a large number of the Companions, who did not raise any objection to the performing of ablution only by 'Uthmān. Here the imperative indicates only emphasis and importance and not the obligatory nature of the duty (*'Awn al-Ma'būd*, I, 134).

goes for Friday (prayer) washing is necessary.

Abū Dāwūd said: If one takes a bath after sunrise, even though he washes because of seminal emission, that will be enough for him for his washing on Friday.

(343) Abū Sa'Id al-Khudrī and Abu Hurairah reported the Apostle of Allah (may peace be upon him) as saying: If anyone takes a bath on a Friday, puts on his best clothes, applies a touch of perfume if he has any, then goes to the congregational prayer (in the mosque), and takes care not to step over people, then prays what Allah has prescribed for him, then keeps silent from the time his *Imām* comes out until he finishes his prayer, it will atone for his sins during the previous week.

Abū Hurairah said: (It will atone for his sins) for three days more. He further said: One is rewarded ten times for doing a good work.

Abū Dāwūd said: The version narrated by Muḥammad b. Salamah is perfect, and Ḥammād did not make a mention of the statement of Abū Hurairah.

(344) 'Abd al-Raḥmān b. Abī Sa'Id al-Khudrī quotes his father as saying: The Prophet (may peace be upon him) said: Washing and the use of tooth-stick are necessary for every adult (person) on Friday; and everyone should apply perfume whatever one has. The narrator Bukair did not make a mention of 'Abd al-Raḥmān; and about perfume he said that even it might be of the kind used by women.

(345) Aws b. Aws al-Thaqafī reported: I heard the Apostle of Allah (may peace be upon him) say: If anyone makes (his wife) wash and he washes himself on Friday, goes out early (for Friday prayer), attends the sermon from the beginning, walking, not riding, takes his seat near the *Imām*, listens attentively, and does not indulge in idle talk, he will get the reward of a year's fasting and praying at night for every step he takes.

(346) Aws al-Thaqafī reported the Apostle of Allah (may peace be upon him) as saying: If anyone washes his head on a Friday and washes himself; and he narrated the rest of the tradition as above.

(347) 'Abd Allah b. 'Amr b. al-'Āṣ reported the Prophet (may peace be upon him) as saying: Whoever washes himself on Friday and applies the perfume of his wife if she has one, and wears good clothes and does not step over the necks of the people (in the mosque to sit in the front row) and does not indulge in idle talk during the sermon, that will atone (for his sins) between the two Fridays. But he who indulges in idle talk and steps over the necks of people (in the mosque), that (Friday) will be for him like the noon prayer.[156]

156. This tradition indicates that one should keep silent while the *Imām* is giving the Friday sermon on pulpit before prayer and should listen to the sermon attentively.

Furthermore, it is also necessary that one should take one's seat in the back rows where one finds a vacancy easily in case one is late in attending the mosque for Friday prayer. One should not try to go forward by stepping over the heads of the people.

(348) 'Ā ishah said: The Prophet (may peace be upon him) would take a bath because of sexual defilement on Friday, after opening a vein and after washing a dead body.[157]

(349) Makḥūl was asked about the meaning of words *ghassala* and *ightasala* (that occur in tradition 345) and he said : one should wash one's head and body well (and not that one should make one's wife wash).

(350) Explaining the meaning of the words *ghassala* and *ightasala* (that occur in tradition 345) Sa'īd (b. 'Abd al-'Azīz) said : One should wash one's head and body well (and not that one should make one's wife wash).

(351) Abū Hurairah reported the Apostle of Allah (may peace be upon him) as saying: Whoever takes a bath due to sexual defilement on Friday and goes out (for Friday prayer), is treated like one who offers a camel as sacrifice ; he who goes out in the second instance as one who offers a cow ; he who goes out in the third instance is treated as one who offers horned cow ; he who goes out in the fourth instance is treated as one who offers hen ; he who goes out in the fifth instance is treated as one who offers an egg. When the *Imām* comes out (for sermon), the angels too attend to listen to the sermon.

Chapter 132

CONCESSION FOR ABANDOING BATH ON FRIDAY

(352) 'Ā'ishah said : The people (mostly) were workers and they would come for Friday prayer in the same condition, so it was said to them : Would to God that you wash yourselves.[158]

(353) 'Amr b. Abī 'Amr and 'Ikrimah reported: Some people of Iraq came and said: Ibn 'Abbās, do you regard taking a bath on Friday as obligatory? He said: No, it is only a means of cleanliness, and is better for one who washes oneself. Anyone who

157. It should be noted that washing because of sexual defilement is necessary. But washing on Friday, after opening a vein and after washing a dead body is only recommended for the purpose of cleanliness ; it is not necessary.

158. Taking a bath on Friday for saying prayer in congregation is not obligatory to the extent that the prayer without it be not valid. It is not obligatory in the technical sense, yet its importance has been stressed.

In the earlier days of Islam people had no servants and they worked themselves. They wore woollen clothes, as the following tradition shows, which emitted a foul smell. When they got together in a mosque, the atmosphere would become stingy. Hence the Prophet (may peace be upon him) asked them to come to the mosque on Friday after taking a bath. It was in these circumstances that washing on Friday was stressed by him in so many traditions.

does not take a bath, it is not essential for him. I inform you how the bath (on Friday) commenced. The people were poor and used to wear woollen clothes, and would carry loads on their backs. Their mosque was small and its roof was lowered down. It was a sort of trellis of vine. The Apostle of Allah (may peace be upon him) once came out on a hot day and the people perspired profusely in the woollen clothes so much so that foul smell emitted from them and it caused trouble to each other. When the Apostle of Allah (may peace be upon him) found that foul smell, he said: O people, when this day (Friday) comes, you should take a bath and every one of you should anoint the best oil and perfume one has. Ibn 'Abbās then said: Then Allah, the Exalted, provided wealth (to the people) and they wore clothes other than the woollen, and were spared from work, and their mosque became vast. The foul smell that caused trouble to them became non-existent.

(354) Samurah reported the Apostle of Allah (may peace be upon him) as saying: If any one of you performs ablution (on Friday) that is all right; and if any of you takes a bath, that is better.

Chapter 133

THE INFIDEL WHO EMBRACES ISLAM SHOULD TAKE A BATH

(355) Qais b. 'Āṣim reported: I came to the Prophet (may peace be upon him) with the intention of embracing Islam. He commanded me to take a bath with water (boiled with) the leaves of the lote-tree.[159]

(356) 'Uthaim b. Kulaib reported from his father (Kuthair) on the authority of his grandfather (Kulaib) that he came to the Prophet (may peace be upon him): I have embraced Islam. The Prophet (may peace be upon him) said to him: Remove from yourself the hair that grew during the period of unbelief, saying "shave them."[160]

159. This tradition clearly indicates that washing after embracing Islam is necessary. But most of the scholars hold that it is desirable and not necessary to take a bath after entering the fold of Islam. Imām al-Shāfi'ī maintains that it is better for an unbeliever to take a bath after embracing Islam. If he does not do so, in case he is not sexually defiled, it is enough for him to perform ablution and he can pray. Aḥmad b. Ḥanbal, Mālik and Abū Thawr hold that washing is obligatory. The reason is, they argue, that an unbeliever might become sexually defiled in his state of disbelief, and his washing in this state was not valid. Hence it is necessary to take a bath when he embraces Islam in order to offer prayer. His prayer before washing will not be valid (*'Awn al-Ma'būd*, I. 139).

160. The Prophet (may peace be upon him) might have commanded to shave the hair for the purpose of cleanliness. Besides, sometimes the unbelievers have a particular type of hair-cut as a symbol of their religion. The Prophet (may peace be upon him) might have ordered him to shave the hair in order to eliminate the symbol of unbelief. It should be noted that normally it is not necessary for every unbeliever to have his hair shaved at the time of embracing Islam.

He further says that another person (other than the grandfather of 'Uthaim) reported to him that the Prophet (may peace be upon him) said to another person who accompanied him: Remove from yourself the hair that grew during the period of unbelief and get yourself circumcised.[161]

Chapter 134

SHOULD A MENSTRUATING WOMAN WASH HER CLOTHES THAT SHE WAS WEARING DURING HER MENSTRUAL PERIOD?

(357) Mu'ādhah said that 'Ā'ishah was asked about (washing) the clothes of a menstruating woman smeared with blood. She said: She should wash it; in case the mark is not removed she should change it by applying some yellow colour. I had three menstruations together while I lived with the Apostle of Allah (may peace be upon him), but I did not wash my clothes.

(358) 'Ā'ishah said: Each of us (wives of the Prophet) had only one clothe in which she would menstruate. Whenever it was smeared with blood, she would moisten it with her saliva and scratch it with the saliva.[162]

(359) Bakkār b. Yaḥyā said that his grandmother narrated to him: I entered upon Umm Salamah. A woman from the Quraish asked her about praying with the clothes which a woman wore while she menstruated. Umm Salamah said: We would menstruate in the lifetime of the Apostle of Allah (may peace be upon him). Then each one of us refrained (from prayer) during menstrual period. When she was purified, she would look at the clothe in which she menstruated. If it were smeared with blood, we would wash it and pray with it; if there were nothing in it, we would leave it and that would not prevent us from praying with it (the same clothe). As regards the woman who had plaited hair—sometimes each of us had plaited hair—when she washed, she would not undo the hair. She would instead pour three handfuls of water upon her head. When she felt moisture in the roots of her hair, she would rub them. Then she would pour water upon her whole body.

161. Circumcision is a symbol of being a Muslim. Its observance has been stressed from the hygienic viewpoint. Modern medical science has also accepted its usefulness.

According to al-Shāfi'ī and a number of scholars, circumcision is obligatory for both men and women. But in the opinion of Mālik, Abū Ḥanīfah and the majority of scholars it is only recommended (*sunnah*) and not obligatory. Al-Nāṣir and Imām Yaḥyā maintain that it is necessary for men and not for women. Moreover, al-Shāfi'ī thinks its observance necessary during minority. But the majority of scholars hold that no time limit is defined for circumcision. Its observance is not obligatory during the age of minority (***Nail al-Awṭār***, I. 109).

162. They scratched the blood in case its size was small. If the mark of the blood were large, they would wash it, as many other traditions indicate (***'Awn al-Ma'būd***, I. 140).

(360) Asmā' daughter of Abū Bakr said: I heard a woman asking the Apostle of Allah (may peace be upon him): What should any of us do with her clothe (in which she menstruated) when she becomes purified? Can she pray in that (clothe)? He said: She should see; if she finds blood in it, she should scratch it with some water and (in case of doubt) sprinkle upon it (some water) and pray so long as she does not find (any blood).

(361) Asmā' daughter of Abū Bakr said: A woman asked the Apostle of Allah (may peace be upon him): Apostle of Allah, what do you think if the clothe of any of us is smeared with the blood of menstruation; what should she do? He said: If (the clothe of) any of you is smeared with the blood of menstruation, she should scratch it; then she should sprinkle water upon it and then she may pray.

(362) This tradition has been transmitted by Hishām through a different chain of narrators to the same effect: Rub it off (with a stone), then scratch it (with finger) by pouring water, then sprinkle water upon it.

(363) Umm Qais daughter of Miḥṣan said: I asked the Prophet (may peace be upon him) about the blood of menstruation on the clothe. He said: Erase it off with a piece of wood and then wash it away with water and the leaves of the lote-tree.

(364) 'Ā'ishah said: One of us would have a shirt in which she would menstruate and in it she became sexually defiled. Then if she ever saw any drop of blood in it, she would rub it off by applying her saliva.

(365) Abū Hurairah reported that Khawlah daughter of Yasār came to the Prophet (may peace be upon him) and said: Apostle of Allah, I have only one clothe and I mentruate in it, how should I do? He said: When you are purified, wash it and pray in it. She asked: If the blood is not removed, (then what)? He said: It is enough for you to wash the blood, its mark will not do any harm to you.

Chapter 135

OFFERING PRAYER IN THE CLOTHE IN WHICH ONE HAS SEXUAL INTERCOURSE WITH ONE'S WIFE

(366) Mu'āwiyah b. Abī Sufyān asked his sister Umm Ḥabībah, the wife of the Prophet (may peace be upon him): Would the Apostle of Allah (may peace be upon him) pray in the clothe[163] in which he had an intercourse? She said: Yes, when he would not see any impurity in it.

163. The Arabic words in the *ḥadith* are *Shu'ur* and *luḥuf* meaning, respectively, a piece of cloth worn by a woman, and a quilt. *Shi'ār*—lying or sleeping together under one garment.

Chapter 136

OFFERING PRAYER IN THE WAIST-WRAPPERS OF WOMEN

(367) 'Ā'ishah said: The Apostle of Allah (may peace be upon him) would not pray in our wrappers or in our quilts.

'Ubaid Allah said: My father (Mu'ādh) doubted this.

(368) 'Ā'ishah said: The Prophet (may peace be upon him) would not pray in our quilts. Ḥammād said: I heard Sa'īd b. Abī Ṣadaqah say: I asked Muḥammad (b. Sīrīn) about it. He did not narrate it to me, but said: I heard it a long time ago and I do not know from whom I heard it. I do not know whether I heard it from a trustworthy person or not. Make an inquiry about it.[164]

Chapter 137

CONCESSION OF PRAYING IN THE CLOTHES OF WOMEN

(369) Maimūnah reported: The Prophet (may peace be upon him) prayed on a sheet of cloth partly put on by one of his wives who was menstruating. He was praying while (a part of) it was upon him.

(370) 'Ā'ishah said: The Apostle of Allah (may peace be upon him) would pray at night while I lay by his side during my menstrual period. A sheet of cloth would be partly on me and partly on him.

Chapter 138

THE LAW OF *SHARĪ'AH* ABOUT THE CLOTHE IF IT IS SMEARED WITH SEMEN

(371) Hammām b. al-Ḥārith reported, he had a sexual dream when he was staying with 'Ā'ishah. The slave-girl of 'Ā'ishah saw him while he was washing the mark of defilement, or he was washing his clothe. She informed 'Ā'ishah who said. He witnessed me rubbing off the semen from the clothe of the Apostle of Allah (may peace be upon him).[165]

164. This is a weak tradition because Muḥammad b. Sīrīn did not hear it from 'Ā'ishah directly. The person from whom he heard it is unknown.

165. There is a difference of opinion amongst scholars on the purity of semen. Al-Shāfi'ī and Aḥmad b. Ḥanbal take it as pure. According to Mālik and Abū Ḥanīfah, semen is impure. It is also disputed how it should be removed. According to Mālik, it should be washed in any case whether it is moist or dry. Abū Ḥanīfah maintains that it should be washed if it is moist, and be rubbed off if it is dry (*'Awn al-Ma'būd*, I, 143).

Abū Dāwūd said: Al-A'mash narrated it as narrated by al-Ḥakam.

(372) 'Ā'ishah reported: I used to rub off the semen from the clothe of the Apostle of Allah (may peace be upon him). He then would pray in it.

Abū Dāwūd said: Mughīrah, Abū Ma'shar and Wāṣil also narrated it to the same effect.

(373) Sulaimān b. Yasār reported: I heard 'Ā'ishah say that she would wash semen from the clothe of the Apostle of Allah (may peace be upon him). She added: Then I would see a mark or marks (after washing)

Chapter 139

HOW TO CLEAN THE CLOTHE SMEARED WITH THE URINE OF A CHILD

(374) Umm Qais daughter of Miḥṣan reported that she came to the Apostle of Allah (may peace be upon him) with her little son who had not attained the age of eating food. The Apostle of Allah (may peace be upon him) seated him in his lap, and he urinated on his clothe. He sent for water and sprayed it (over his clothe) and did not wash it.[166]

(375) Lubābah daughter of al-Ḥārith said: Al-Ḥusain b. 'Alī was (sitting) in the lap of the Apostle of Allah (may peace be upon him). He passed water on him. I said: Put on (another) clothe, and give me your wrapper to wash. He said: The urine of a female child should be washed (thoroughly) and the urine of a male child should be sprinkled over.

(376) Abū al-Samḥ said: I used to serve the Prophet (may peace be upon him). Whenever he intended to wash himself, he would say: Turn your back towards me, So I would turn my back and hide him. (Once) Ḥasan or Husain (may Allah be pleased with them) was brought to him and he passed water on his chest. I came to wash it. He said: It is only the urine of a female which should be washed; the urine of a male should be sprinkled over.

'Abbās (a narrator) said: Yaḥyā b. al-Walīd narrated the tradition to us. Abū Dāwūd said: He (Yaḥyā) is Abū al-Za'rā'. Ḥārūn b. Tamīm said on the authority of al-Ḥasan: All sorts of urine are equal.

166. There are different traditions which show that the urine of a female child should be cleaned by washing and that of a male child by sprinkling water. Hence scholars differed among themselves on this point. 'Aṭā' b. Abū Rabāḥ, al-Ḥasan al-Baṣrī, al-Shāfi'ī, Aḥmad b. Ḥanbal hold that the urine of a male child should be cleaned by sprinkling water until the age of eating, and the urine of a female child should be cleaned by washing. Al-Nakha'ī, Sufyān al-Thawrī and Abū Ḥanīfah maintain that the urine of both the male and female child should be cleaned by washing (*'Awn al-Ma'būd*, I, 145).

(377) 'Alī said: The urine of a female (child) should be washed and the urine of a male (child) should be sprinkled over until the age of eating.

(378) 'Alī b. Abī Ṭālib reported the Prophet (may peace be upon him) as saying: He narrated the tradition to the same effect, but he did not mention the words "until the age of eating." This version adds: Qatādah said: This is valid until the time they do not eat food; when they begin to eat, their urine should be washed.

(379) Al-Ḥasan reported on the authority of his mother that she saw Umm Salamah pouring water on the urine of the male child until the age when he did not eat food. When he began to eat food, she would wash (his urine). And she would wash the urine of the female child.

Chapter 140

THE EARTH SMEARED WITH URINE

(380) Abū Hurairah reported: A bedouin entered the mosque while the Apostle of Allah (may peace be upon him) was sitting. He offered two *rak'ahs* of prayer, according to the version of Ibn 'Abdah. He then said: O Allah, have mercy on me and on Muḥammad and do not have mercy on anyone along with us. The Prophet (may peace be upon him) said: You have narrowed down (a thing) that was broader. After a short while he passed water in a corner of the mosque. The people rushed towards him. The Prophet (may peace be upon him) prevented them and said: You have been sent to facilitate and not to create difficulties. Pour a bucket of water upon it.[167]

(381) 'Abd Allah b. Ma'qil b. Muqarrin reported: A bedouin prayed with the Prophet (may peace be upon him). He then narrated the rest of the tradition. This version adds: The Prophet (may peace be upon him) said: Remove the earth where he urinated and throw it away and pour water upon the place.

Abū Dāwūd said: This is a *mursal* tradition (i.e. the narrator quotes the Prophet directly, although he did not see him). Ibn Ma'qil did not see the Prophet (may peace be upon him).

Chapter 141

THE EARTH IS PURE WHEN IT BECOMES DRY

(382) Ibn 'Umar said: I used to sleep in the mosque in the lifetime of the

167. The version recorded in the *Ṣaḥiḥ* of al-Bukhārī and Muslim adds that the Prophet (may peace be upon him) called him and said: Mosques are not meant for urinating or easing oneself; they are meant for the remembrance of Allah and for reciting the Qur'ān.

Apostle of Allah (may peace be upon him) when I was young and bachelor. The dogs would urinate and frequently visit the mosque, and no one would sprinkle water over it.

Chapter 142

ON THE BORDER OF THE CLOTHE SMEARED WITH IMPURITY

(383) The slave-mother of Ibrāhīm b. 'Abd al-Raḥmān b. 'Awf asked Umm Salamah, the wife of the Prophet (may peace be upon him): I am a woman having a long border of clothe and I walk in filthy place; (then what should I do?). Umm Salamah replied: The Apostle of Allah (may peace be upon him) said: What comes after it cleanses it.[168]

(384) A woman of the Banu 'Abd al-Ashhal reported: I said Apostle of Allah, our road to the mosque has an unpleasant stench; what should we do when it is raining? He asked: Is there not a cleaner part after the filthy part of the road? She replied: Why not (there is one)! He said: It makes up for the other.

Chapter 143

ON THE SHOE BEING SMEARED WITH IMPURITY

(385) Abū Hurairah reported: The Apostle of Allah (may peace be upon him) said: When any of you treads with his sandal upon an unclean place, the earth will

168. The tradition clearly indicates that if a man walks in a filthy place and his clothe touches upon the filth, then he passes on the dry and clean land, the clothe will be purified by touching the dry earth. The point, however, is disputed in case the impurity is liquid. Al-Shāfi'ī holds that the clothe becomes purified only in case the impurity is dry. If the impurity is moistened, the clothe will be purified only by washing. Aḥmad b. Ḥanbal is of view that the tradition does not mean that if the clothe is smeared with urine, and it touches upon the dry earth, it will be purified. If only means that in case one passes by a filthy place and his clothe touches upon it and then he goes forward and the clothe touches upon the clean and dry land, then it will be purified. This will do for that. Mālik maintains that one part of earth purifies the other. If one treads upon a filthy place and then passes by a dry and clean place, then one part will purify the other. But in case the clothe is smeared with urine, or it drops on any part of the body, that will be purified only by washing. This is the view agreed upon by the community. Some scholars are of opinion that in all cases (whether the impurity is dry or liquid) the clothe will be purified by touching upon clean and dry earth (*'Awn al-Ma'būd*, I, 147).

render it purified.[169]

(386) Abū Hurairah reported a tradition to the same effect from the Prophet (may peace be upon him): When any of you treads with his shoes upon something unclean, they will be purified with the earth.

(387) 'Ā'ishah reported a similar tradition from the Apostle of Allah (may peace be upon him).

Chapter 144

ON REPEATING PRAYER OFFERED IN AN IMPURE GARMENT

(388) Umm Jaḥdar al-'Āmirīyyah said that she asked 'Ā'ishah about the blood of menses which drops on the clothe. She replied: I was (lying) with the Apostle of Allah (may peace be upon him) and we had our garment over us, and we had put a blanket over it. When the day broke, the Apostle of Allah (may peace be upon him) took the blanket, wore it and went out and offered the dawn prayer. He then sat (in the mosque among the people). A man said: Apostle of Allah, this is a spot of blood. The Apostle of Allah (may peace be upon him) caught hold of it from around and sent it to me folded in the hand of a slave and said: Wash it and dry it and then send it to me. I sent for my vessel and washed it; I then dried it and returned it to him. The Apostle of Allah (may peace be upon him) came at noon while he had the blanket over him.[170]

Chapter 145

DROPPING OF SALIVA ON THE CLOTHE

(389) Abū Naḍrah reported: The Apostle of Allah (may peace be upon him) spat

169. The majority of scholars have followed this tradition in its literal sense. If a shoe or a sandal is smeared with impurity and it is rubbed off with the earth and its major part is removed, then the shoe or the sandal is purified and prayer is valid in it. Al-Shāfi'ī earlier held this view but later changed it and maintained that washing is essential. Shāh Walī Allah is of opinion that a shoe or a sandal is purified by rubbing it with the soil. The reason is, he says that since their body is solid, the impurity does not penetrate into them. Obviously by impurity he means both kinds, dry and liquid (*'Awn al-Ma'būd*, I, 148).

170. It should be noted that there is no mention of repeating the prayer in the tradition. Therefore, Abū Dāwūd's argument for repeating the prayer, as the heading shows, is not obviously correct. It is, however, contended that the Prophet (may peace be upon him) might have repeated the prayer, but 'Ā'ishah could not know it. Or he might not have repeated the prayer as the mark of blood was very small. Had the mark of blood been large, the prayer would have been repeated (*'Awn al-Ma'būd*, I, 149).

on his clothe and scrubbed with a part of it.[171]

(390) A similar tradition has also been narrated by Anas from the Prophet (may peace be upon him) through a different chain of narrators.

171. Abū Naḍrah is a successor (*tābi'ī*). Hence this tradition is *mursal* (the link of the Companion between him and the Prophet is omitted). The Prophet (may peace be upon him) might have spat during prayer. It is evident from this tradition that if sometimes one is forced to eject saliva while praying, one can do so. It also shows that saliva is pure; likewise mucus is also pure (*'Awn al-Ma'būd*, I. 149).

II. KITĀB AL-ṢALĀT

[BOOK OF PRAYER]

Chapter 146

PRAYER IS OBLIGATORY ON MUSLIMS

(391) Ṭalḥah b. 'Ubaid Allah said: A man from among the people of Najd with dishevelled hair came to the Apostle of Allah (may peace be upon him). The humming sound of his voice could be heard but what he was saying could not be understood until he came near and it was then known that he was asking about Islam. The Apostle of Allah (may peace be upon him) said: Five times of prayer each day and night. He asked: Must I observe any more than them? He replied: No, unless you do it voluntarily. He (Ṭalḥah) said that the Apostle of Allah (may peace be upon him) mentioned fasting during the month of Ramaḍān. He asked: Must I observe anything else? He replied: No, unless you do it voluntarily. The Apostle of Allah (may peace be upon him) mentioned the *zakāt* to him. He asked: Must I pay anything else? He replied: No, unless you do it voluntarily. The man then turned away saying: I swear by Allah, I shall not add anything to this or fall short of it. The Apostle of Allah (may peace be upon him) said: The man will be successful if he speaks the truth.

(392) This tradition has also been reported by Abū Suhail Nāfi' b. Mālik b. Abī 'Āmir through a different chain of narrators. It adds: He will be successful, by his father, if he speaks the truth; he will enter Paradise, by his father, if he speaks the truth.

Chapter 147

THE TIMES OF PRAYER

(393) Ibn 'Abbās reported the Apostle of Allah (may peace be upon him) as saying: Gabriel (may peace be upon him) led me in prayer at the House (i.e. the Ka'bah). He prayed the noon prayer with me when the sun had passed the meridian to the extent of the thong of a sandal; he prayed the afternoon prayer with me when the shadow of everything was as long as itself; he prayed the sunset prayer with me when one who is fasting breaks fast; he prayed the night prayer with me when the

twilight had ended ; and he prayed the dawn prayer with me when food and drink become forbidden to one who is keeping fast. On the following day he prayed the noon prayer with me when his shadow was as long as himself ; he prayed the afternoon prayer with me when his shadow was twice as long as himself ; he prayed the sunset prayer at the time when one who is fasting breaks fast ; he prayed the night prayer with me when about the third of the night had passed ; and he prayed the dawn prayer with me when there was a fair amount of light. Then turning to me he said : Muḥammad, this is the time observed by the Prophets before you, and the time is anywhere between two times.[172]

(394) Ibn Shihāb said : 'Umar b. 'Abd al-'Azīz was sitting on the pulpit and he somewhat postponed the afternoon prayer. 'Urwah b. al-Zubair said to him : Gabriel informed Muḥammad (may peace be upon him) of the time of prayer. So 'Umar said to him : Be sure of what you are saying. 'Urwah then replied : I heard Bashīr b. Abū Mas'ūd say that he heard Abū Mas'ūd al-Anṣārī say that he heard the Apostle of Allah (may peace be upon him) say : Gabriel came down and informed me of the time of prayer, and I prayed along with him, then I prayed along with him, then I prayed

172. This tradition stands as a basis for the determination of the times of prayer. It describes the beginning and the end of the times. Scholars differ in some of the times ; some follow this tradition, others interpret it differently in the light of other traditions and the practice of his Companions. According to Ibn 'Abbās, Mālik, al-Thawrī, al-Shāfi'ī, Aḥmad b. Ḥanbal and Isḥāq, the time of the afternoon prayer begins when the shadow of everything becomes as long as itself. According to Abū Ḥanīfah, the time of the afternoon prayer begins when the shadow of everything becomes twice as long as itself But his disciples Abū Yūsuf and Muḥammad differ with him on this point ; they hold the same viewpoint as held by al-Shāfi'ī and others.

There is also a difference of opinion amongst scholars on the meaning of *shafaq* (twilight). In the opinion of Ibn 'Umar, Ibn 'Abbās, Makḥūl, Ṭāwūs, Mālik, al-Thawrī, Ibn Abī Laylā, Abū Yūsuf, Muḥammad, al Shāfi'ī, Aḥmad and Isḥāq, it stands for the redness of the horizon after sunset. The time of the sunset prayer ends when the redness of the horizon disappears. According to Abū Hurairah, 'Umar b. 'Abd al 'Azīz, Abū Ḥanīfah, and al-Awzā'ī, *shafaq* (twilight) whiteness of the horizon after sunset when the redness disappears. The time of the sunset prayer ends when this whiteness ends. The time of the sunset prayer according to this school, is longer than the one held by the former school. The whiteness lasts for about one and a quarter hour while the redness lasts for about half an hour.

The time of the night prayer ends when one-third of the night has passed. This is the view held by 'Umar, Abū Hurairah, 'Umar b. 'Abd al-'Azīz and al-Shāfi'ī. The other view is that it ends when half the night has passed. This is held by al-Thawrī, the Ḥanafī school, Ibn al-Mubārak and Isḥāq. Ibn 'Abbās maintains that it lasts all over the night and ends with the break of dawn.

The time of the dawn prayer ends with the sunrise. This is held by the Ḥanafī school. If a person offers the dawn prayer and the sun rises when he completes one *rak'ah* of the prayer, his prayer will be void according to the Ḥanafīs. But, according to al-Shāfi'ī, Mālik, Aḥmad, and Isḥāq, if the sun rises after the completion of one *rak'ah*, he may continue his prayer. His prayer will be valid even after the sunrise (*'Awn al-Ma'būd*, I, 151-52).

along with him, then I prayed along with him, then I prayed along with him, reckoning with his fingers five times of prayer. I saw the Apostle of Allah (may peace be upon him) offering the noon prayer when the sun had passed the meridian. Sometimes he would delay it when it was severe heat; and I witnessed that he prayed the afternoon prayer when the sun was high and bright before the yellowness had overcome it; then a man could go off after the prayer and reach Dhū'l-Ḥulaifah before the sunset, and he would pray the sunset prayer when the sun had set; and he would pray the night prayer when darkness prevailed over the horizon; sometimes he would delay it until the people assembled; and once he prayed the morning prayer in the darkness of dawn and at another time he prayed it when it became fairly light; but later on he continued to pray in the darkness of dawn until his death: he never prayed it again in the light of the dawn.

Abū Dāwūd said: This tradition has been transmitted from al-Zuhrī by Ma'mar, Mālik, Ibn 'Uyainah, Shu'aib b. Abī Ḥamzah, and al-Laith b. Sa'd and others; but they did not mention the time in which he (the Prophet) had prayed, nor did they explain it. And similarly it has been narrated by Hishām b. 'Urwah and Ḥabīb b. Abī Marzūq from 'Urwah like the report of Ma'mar and his companions. But Ḥabīb did not make a mention of Bashīr. And Wahb b. Kaisān reported on the authority of Jābir from the Prophet (may peace be upon him) the time of the sunset prayer. He said: Next day he (Gabriel) came to him at the time of the sunset prayer when the sun had already set. (He came both days) at the same time.

Abū Dāwūd said: Similarly, this tradition has been transmitted by Abū Hurairah from the Prophet (may peace be upon him). He said: Then he (Gabriel) led me in the sunset prayer next day at the same time.

Similarly, this tradition has been narrated through a different chain by 'Abd Allah b. 'Amr b al-'Āṣ, from Ḥassān b. 'Aṭīyyah, from 'Amr b. Shu'aib from his father, on the authority of his grandfather from the Prophet (may peace be upon him).

(395) Abū Mūsā reported: A man asked the Prophet (may peace be upon him) but he did not reply to him until he commanded Bilāl, who made the announcement for the beginning of the time of the dawn prayer when the dawn broke. He offered (the dawn prayer) when a man (due to darkness) could not recognise the face of his companion; or a man could not know the person who stood by his side. He then commanded Bilāl who made the announcement for the beginning of the time of the noon prayer when the sun had passed the meridian until someone said: Has the noon come? While he (the Prophet) knew (the time) well. He then commanded Bilāl who announced the beginning of the time of the afternoon prayer when the sun was white and high. When the sun set he commanded Bilāl who announced the beginning of the time of the sunset prayer. When the twilight disappeared he commanded Bilāl who

announced the beginning of the night prayer. Next day he offered the dawn prayer and returned until we said : Has the sun risen? He observed the noon prayer at the time he had previously observed the afternoon prayer. He offered the afternoon prayer at the time when the sun had become yellow or the evening had come. He offered the sunset prayer before the twilight had ended. He observed the night prayer when a third of the night had passed. He then asked: Where is the man who was asking me about the time of prayer. (Then replying to him he said): The time (of your prayer) lies within these two limits.

Abū Dāwūd said: Sulaimān b. Mūsā has narrated this tradition about the time of the sunset prayer from Mūsā from 'Aṭā' on the authority of Jābir from the Prophet (may peace be upon him). This version adds: He then offered the night prayer when a third of the night had passed, as narrated (he said the night prayer) when half the night had passed.

This tradition has been transmitted by Ibn Buraidah on the authority of his father from the Prophet (may peace be upon him) in a similar way.[173]

(396) 'Abd Allah b. 'Amr reported the Prophet (may peace be upon him) as saying: The time of the noon prayer is as long as the time of the afternoon prayer has not come; the time of the afternoon prayer is as long as the sun has not become yellow; the time of the sunset prayer is as long as the twilight has not ended; the time of the night prayer is up to midnight; and the time of the morning prayer is as long as the sun has not arisen.

Chapter 148

THE TIME OF THE PRAYER OF THE PROPHET (MAY PEACE BE UPON HIM) AND HOW HE USED TO OFFER THEM

(397) Muḥammad b. 'Amr b. al-Ḥasan reported: We asked Jābir about the time of the prayer of the Apostle of Allah (may peace be upon him). He said : He used to offer the noon prayer in the midday heat; the afternoon prayer when the sun was bright: the sunset prayer when the sun had completely set; the night prayer early when many people were present, but late if they were few; and the dawn prayer in the darkness (of the dawn).[174]

173. The Prophet (may peace be upon him) offered all prayers in the early hours and the next day in the late hour so that people might know the beginning and the end of the time of each prayer. A prayer is valid if it is offered within the limits explained in the tradition.

174. In the previous chapter the traditions dealt with the time of prayer in general. In this chapter the traditions point out the commendable times at which the Prophet (may peace be upon him) used to offer his prayers. Therefore, it is better to offer prayer at these times.

(398) Abū Barzah reported: The Apostle of Allah (may peace be upon him) would offer the noon prayer when the sun had passed the meridian; he would offer the afternoon prayer after which one of us would visit the skirts of Medina and return home while the sun was still bright; I forgot what he said about the sunset prayer; he did not fear postponing the night prayer until a third of night had passed, or he said: until the midnight had passed. He would dislike sleeping before it or talking after it: and he would offer the dawn prayer when a man could recognise his neighbour whom he recognised well; and he would recite from sixty to a hundred verses during it.

Chapter 149

THE TIME OF THE NOON PRAYER

(399) Jābir b. 'Abd Allah said: I would offer my noon prayer with the Apostle of Allah (may peace be upon him) and took a handful of gravels so that they might become cold in my hand and I placed them (before me) so that I may put my forehead on them at the time when I would prostrate. I did this due to the intensity of heat.[175]

(400) 'Abd Allah b. Mas'ūd said: The extent of the shadow when the Apostle of Allah prayed (the noon prayer) was three to five feet in summer and five to seven feet in winter.[176]

(401) Abū Dharr said: We were in the company of the Prophet (may peace be upon him). The *mu'adhdhin* (the person who calls for prayer) intended to call for the noon prayer. He said: Make it cooler. He then intended to call for prayer. He said twice or thrice: Make it cooler. We then witnessed the shadow of the mounds. He then said: The intensity of heat comes from the bubbling over of the Hell; so when the heat is violent, offer (the noon) prayer when it becomes cooler.[177]

(402) Abū Hurairah reported the Apostle of Allah (may peace be upon him) as saying: When the heat is violent, offer (the noon) prayer when it becomes fairly cool, for the violent heat comes from the bubbling over of the Hell.

(403) Jābir b. Samurah reported that Bilāl used to call for the noon prayer when

175. This tradition indicates that the Prophet (may peace be upon him) used to say his noon prayer in the early hours when the sun had passed the meridian.

176. Al-Khaṭṭābī said: The extent of shadow varies with the variance of cities and places. It is not equal in all places as indicated in this tradition. The variance in the extent of shadow depends on the rise and decline of the sun in different places according to their longitude and latitude (*'Awn al-Ma'būd*, I, 156).

177. There is no definite limit for the time when it becomes cooler. It depends on the situation (*'Awn al-Ma'būd*, I, 157).

the sun had declined.

Chapter 150

THE TIME OF THE AFTERNOON PRAYER

(404) Anas b. Mālik said that the Apostle of Allah (may peace be upon him) used to say the afternoon prayer when the sun was high and bright and living, then one would go off to al-'Awālī and get there while the sun was still high.[178]

(405) Al-Zuhrī said: Al-'Awālī is situated at a distance of two miles or three (from Medina). He (the narrator) said: I think he said: Or four miles.

(406) Khaythamah said: By the life of the sun is meant that you may find heat in it.

(407) 'Ā'ishah said: The Apostle of Allah (may peace be upon him) would offer the afternoon prayer while the sunlight was present in her apartment before it ascended (the walls).

(408) 'Alī b. Shaybān reported: We came upon the Apostle of Allah (may peace be upon him) in Medina. He would postpone the afternoon prayer as long as the sun remained white and clear.

Chapter 151

THE MIDDLE PRAYER

(409) 'Alī (may Allah be pleased with him) reported the Apostle of Allah (may peace be upon him) as saying on the day of the Battle of Khandaq (Trench):[179] They (the unbelievers) prevented us from offering the middle prayer,[180] i.e. afternoon prayer. May Allah fill their houses and their graves with Hell-fire.

(410) Abū Yūnus, the freed slave of 'Ā'ishah said: 'Ā'ishah commanded me to

178. Villages on heights outside Medina at a distance of about four miles.

179. On the occasion of the Battle of Khandaq (Trench) the Prophet (may peace be upon him) could not say the noon, afternoon, and sunset prayers due to heavy fighting all the day long. Hence he offered them all together along with the night prayer. As prayer is one of the important fundamentals of Islam, he could not tolerate its abandonment even in the battle. Hence, with all his mercifulness to mankind, he cursed the unbelievers who had kept him engaged in fighting.

180. The middle or the midmost prayer refers to the Qur'ānic expression *al-ṣalāt al-wusṭā* (ii. 238). The Qur'ān commands the Muslims to be careful particularly of this prayer. There is a difference of opinion amongst scholars on the meaning of the midmost prayer. The generally accepted view is that it means the afternoon prayer. This is the viewpoint held by a large number of the Companions, Successors, Abū Ḥanīfah, Aḥmad and Dāwūd. According to Mālik and al-Shāfi'ī, it stands for the dawn prayer. Some take it to mean the noon prayer, some sunset and some night prayer (*'Awn al-Ma'būd*, I, 158).

write for her some passage from the Qur'ān. She also added: When you reach the following verse, inform me: "Be guardians of your prayers and of the midmost prayer" (ii. 238). When I reached it, I informed her. She asked me to write: "Be guardians of your prayers, and of the midmost prayer, and of the afternoon prayer, and stand up with devotion of Allah" (ii. 238). 'A'ishah then said: I heard it from the Apostle of Allah (may peace be upon him).[181]

(411) Zaid b. Thābit said: The Apostle of Allah (may peace be upon him) used to offer the noon prayer in midday heat; and no prayer was harder on the Companions of the Apostle of Allah (may peace be upon him) than this one. Hence the revelation came down: "Be guardians of your prayers, and of the midmost prayer" (ii. 238). He (the narrator) said: There are two prayers before it and two prayers after it.

Chapter 152

HE WHO COMPLETES ONE *RAK'AH* OF PRAYER (BEFORE SUNRISE OR SUNSET) GETS THE WHOLE PRAYER

(412) Abū Hurairah reported the Apostle of Allah (may peace be upon him) as saying: If anyone says a *rak'ah* of the afternoon prayer before sunset, he has observed (the afternoon prayer): and if anyone performs a *rak'ah* of the dawn prayer, he has observed (the dawn prayer).[182]

181. This tradition indicates that *al-wusṭā* is not the afternoon prayer. It is some other because the conjunction "and" requires otherness. But to this objection various answers have been given. First, this is a rare (uncommon) reading of this Qur'ānic verse. The common reading agreed upon by the Muslims does not contain the phrase "and of the afternoon prayer." Hence it is no authority. Further, it is not a direct report from the Prophet (may peace be upon him) because the narrator does not clearly say that the phrase "and of the afternoon prayer" is a part of the Qur'ānic text. It should be noted that the text of the Qur'ān is established either by *tawātur* (continuous transmission from generation to generation) or by the consensus of the Muslims. The addition of this phrase is not supported by any of them. Secondly the conjunction "and" may be taken as an explanatory conjunction, explaining the word *al-wusṭā*. Thirdly, the conjunction "and" may be taken as redundant in this version of the tradition, since the version reported by Abū 'Ubaid contains no such conjunction. As such, the phrase "the afternoon prayer" would be an explanation of *'al-salāṭ al-wusṭā* (*'Awn al-Ma'būd*, I. 159).

182. It means that if a person begins his dawn prayer and completes one *rak'ah*, then the sun rises, he should complete the rest of the prayer. The prayer is valid. In case he does not complete one *rak'ah* and the sun rises before its completion, his prayer will not be valid. This is the viewpoint held by Mālik, al-Shāfi'ī, Aḥmad, and Isḥāq. But Abū Ḥanīfah holds that his prayer will be void if the sun rises even after the performance of one *rak'ah*. But Abū Ḥanīfah and all other jurists are agreed that in the case of the afternoon prayer it is valid if the sun sets after completion of one *rak'ah*. Abū Hanīfah distinguishes the dawn prayer from the afternoon prayer. The point of dis-

Chapter 153

THREAT ON DELAYING THE AFTERNOON PRAYER UNTIL THE SUN BECOMES YELLOW

(413) 'Alā b. 'Abd al-Raḥmān said: We came upon Anas b. Mālik after the noon prayer. He stood for saying the afternoon prayer. When he became free from praying, we mentioned to him about observing prayer in its early period, or he himself mentioned it. He said: I heard the Apostle of Allah (may peace be upon him) say: this is how the hypocrites pray; this is how the hypocrites pray; this is how the hypocrites pray: he sits (watching the sun), and when it becomes yellow and is between the horns of the devil,[183] or is on the horns of the devil, he rises and prays four *rak'ahs* quickly, remembering Allah only seldom during them.

Chapter 154

THREAT ON ABANDONING THE AFTERNOON PRAYER

(414) Ibn 'Umar reported the Apostle of Allah (may peace be upon him) as saying: Anyone who loses his afternoon prayer is like a person whose family has perished and whose property has been plundered.

Abū Dāwūd said: 'Abd Allah b. 'Umar narrated the word *utira* (instead of *wutira*, meaning perished). The dispute on this point goes back to Ayyūb. Al-Zuhrī reported from Sālim on the authority of his father from the Prophet (may peace be upon him) the word *'wutira'*.

(415) Al-Awzā'ī said: Delaying the afternoon prayer means that the sunshine becomes yellow on the earth.

tinction is that it is disapproved and undesirable (*makrūh*) to offer the afternoon prayer in the last moments when the sun becomes yellow. This shows that the whole time of the afternoon prayer is not perfectly valid for prayer due to the defect in the last moments. But this is not the case with the dawn prayer. Its whole time is perfectly valid for saying prayer. Hence one cannot be compared with the other (*Awn al-Ma'būd*. I, 152, 159).

183. Al-Khaṭṭābī said: This has been interpreted in manifold ways: (1) The devil comes near the sun when it begins to set. When it sets completely, he goes away. He does so at the time of sunrise and when the sun passes the meridian. Hence offering prayer is forbidden at these moments. (2) The horn of the devil means his power. At these three moments his power increases because the worshippers of the sun perform prostration in those moments. (3) The horns of the devil means his party and his companions who worship the sun. (4) This is a similitude. Anyone who delays the afternoon prayer until the sun becomes yellow does so with the inciting and exhorting of the devil. (5) The devil faces the sun at the time of its rise and takes it between both of his horns. As such, the sun rises between his horns. The worshippers who prostrate before the sun virtually prostrate before the devil and not the sun (*'Awn al-Ma'būd*, I, 160).

Chapter 155

THE TIME OF THE SUNSET PRAYER

(416) Anas b. Mālik said: We used to offer the sunset prayer with the Prophet (may peace be upon him) and then shoot arrows; one of us could see the place where the arrow would fall.

(417) Salamah b. al-Akwa' said: The Prophet (may peace be upon him) used to say the sunset prayer immediately after the sun had set when its upper side would disappear.

(418) Marthad b. 'Abd Allah said: When Abū Ayyūb came upon us to fight the infidels and in those days 'Uqbah b. 'Āmir was the Governor of Egypt, he ('Uqbah) delayed the sunset prayer. Hence Abū Ayyūb stood and said: What kind of prayer is this, 'Uqbah? He said: We were busy. He said: Did you not hear the Apostle of Allah (may peace be upon him) say: My community will remain well, or he said: will remain on its natural condition, so long as it would not delay the evening prayer until the stars shine brightly just like a network.

Chapter 156

THE TIME OF THE NIGHT PRAYER

(419) Nu'mān b. Bashīr said: I am the one who is best informed of the time of this prayer, i.e. the night prayer. The Apostle of Allah (may peace be upon him) used to offer it at the hour when the moon went down on its third night.

(420) 'Abd Allah b. 'Umar said: We remained one night waiting for the Apostle of Allah (may peace be upon him) to offer the night prayer. He came out to us when one-third of the night had passed or even after it. We did not know whether anything kept him occupied or there was some other matter. When he came out, he said: Are you waiting for this prayer? Were it not that it would impose a burden on my people, I would normally pray with them at this time. He then gave orders to the *mu'adhdhin* who declared that the time for prayer had come.

(421) Mu'ādh b. Jabal reported: We waited for the Prophet (may peace be upon him) to offer the night prayer. He delayed until people thought that he would not come out and some of us said that he had offered the prayer. At the moment when we were in this condition the Prophet (may peace be upon him) came out. People said to him as they were already saying. He said: Observe this prayer when it is dark, for by it you have been made superior to all the peoples, no people having observed it before you.

(422) Abū Sa'īd al-Khudrī said: We observed the prayer after nightfall with the

Apostle of Allah (may peace be upon him), and he did not come out till about half the night had passed. He then said: Take your places. We then took our places. Then he said: The people have prayed and gone to bed, but you are still engaged in prayer as long as you wait for the prayer. Were it not for the weakness of the weak and for the sickness of the sick, I would delay this prayer till half the night had gone.

Chapter 157

THE TIME OF THE DAWN PRAYER

(423) 'Ā'ishah reported: The Apostle of Allah (may peace be upon him) would say the dawn prayer after which the women would depart wrapped up in their woollen garments, being unrecognisable because of the darkness before dawn.

(424) Rāfi' b. Khadīj reported the Apostle of Allah (may peace be upon him) as saying: Offer morning prayer at dawn, for it is the most productive of rewards to you or most productive of reward.[184]

Chapter 158

REGULAR OFFERING OF PRAYERS

(425) 'Abd Allah b. Ṣunābihī reported: Abū Muḥammad fancies that *witr* prayer is essential. (Hearing this) 'Ubādah b. Ṣāmit said: Abū Muḥammad was wrong. I bear witness that I heard the Apostle of Allah (may peace be upon him) say: Allah, the Exalted, has made five prayers obligatory. If anyone performs ablution for them well, offers them at their (right) time, and observes perfectly their bowing and submissiveness in them, it is the guarantee of Allah that He will pardon him; if anyone does not do so, there is no guarantee for him on the part of Allah; He may pardon him if He wills, and punish him if He wills.

(426) Umm Farwah said: The Apostle of Allah (may peace be upon him) was asked: Which of the actions is best? He replied: Observing prayer early in its period.

Al-Khuzā'ī narrated in his version from his aunt named Umm Farwah who

184. This tradition shows that it is commendable to offer the morning prayer when the light is fair. This is the viewpoint of Abū Ḥanīfah who follows this tradition. The previous tradition indicates that the Prophet (may peace be upon him) used to offer the morning prayer in the darkness just after the break of the dawn. This tradition is followed by the traditionists and all other jurists. They also interpret the tradition which recommends saying the morning prayer in the light that it means the break of dawn and not the light of dawn. As such, both these traditions agree in meaning.

took the oath of allegiance to the Prophet (may peace be upon him): He was questioned.

(427) 'Umārah b. Ruwaibah said that a man from Baṣrah said: Tell me what you heard from the Apostle of Allah (may peace be upon him). He said: I heard the Apostle of Allah (may peace be upon him) say: No one will enter Hell who has prayed before the rising of the sun and before its setting (meaning the dawn and the afternoon prayers) He said three times: Have you heard it from him? He replied: Yes, each time saying: My ears heard it and my heart memorised it. The man then said: And I heard him (the Prophet) say that.

(428) 'Abd Allah b. Fuḍālah reported on the authority of his father: The Apostle of Allah (may peace be upon him) taught me and what he taught me is this: Observe the five prayers regularly. He said: I told (him): I have many works at these times; so give me a comprehensive advice which, if I follow, should be enough for me. He said: Observe the two afternoon prayers (*al-'aṣrain*). But the term *al-'aṣrain* (two afternoon prayers) was not used in our language. Hence I said: What is *al-'aṣrān*? He said: A prayer before the sunrise and a prayer before the sunset (i.e. the dawn and the afternoon prayers).

(429) Abū al-Darda' reported the Apostle of Allah (may peace be upon him) as saying: There are five things; if anyone observes them with faith, he will enter Paradise: He who prays the five times' prayer regularly, with the ablution for them, with their bowing, with their prostration, at their (right) times, keeps fast during Ramaḍān, performs *Ḥajj* (pilgrimage) to the House (*Ka'bah*), provided he has the ability for its passage, pays *zakāt* happily, and fulfils the trust (he will enter Paradise). People said: Abū al-Dardā', what is fulfilling the trust? He replied: Washing because of sexual defilement.

(430) Abū Qatādah b. Rab'ī reported the Apostle of Allah (may peace be upon him) as saying: Allah, the Exalted said: I made five times' prayers obligatory on your people, and I took a guarantee that if anyone observes them regularly at their times, I shall admit him to Paradise; if anyone does not offer them regularly, there is no such guarantee of Mine for him.

Chapter 159

IF THE IMĀM DELAYS THE PRAYER FROM ITS TIME

(431) Abū Dharr said: The Apostle of Allah (may peace be upon him) asked me: How will you act, Abū Dharr, when you are under rulers who kill prayer or delay it (beyond its proper time)? I said: Apostle of Allah, what do you command me? He replied: Offer the prayer at its proper time, and if you say it along with them, say it,

for it will be a supererogatory prayer for you.[185]

(432) 'Amr b. Maimūn al-Awdī said: Mu'ādh b. Jabal, the messenger of the Apostle of Allah (may peace be upon him) came to us in Yemen, I heard his *takbīr* (utterance of *Allah-u-akbar*) in the dawn prayer. He was a man with loud voice. I began to love him. I did not depart from him until I buried him dead in Syria (i.e. until his death). Then I searched for a person who had deep understanding in religion amongst the people after him. So I came to Ibn Mas'ūd and remained in his company until his death. He (Ibn Mas'ūd) said: The Apostle of Allah (may peace be uppon him) said to me: How will you act when you are ruled by rulers who say prayer beyond its proper time? I said: What do you command me, Apostle of Allah, if I witness such a time? He replied: Offer the prayer at its proper time and also say your prayer along with them as a supererogatory prayer.

(433) 'Ubādah b. al-Ṣāmit reported the Apostle of Allah (may peace be upon him) as saying: After me you will come under rulers who will be detained from saying prayer at its proper time by (their) works until its time has run out, so offer prayer at its proper time. A man asked him: Apostle of Allah, may I offer prayer with them? He replied: Yes, if you wish (to do so).

Sufyān (another narrator through a different chain) said: May I offer prayer with them if I get it with them? He said, Yes, if you wish to do so.

(434) Qabīṣah b. Waqqāṣ reported: The Apostle of Allah (may peace be upon him) said: After me you will be ruled by rulers who will delay the prayer and it will be to your credit but to their discredit. So pray with them so long as they pray facing the *qiblah*.

Chapter 160

ON A PERSON WHO OVERSLEEPS OR FORGETS PRAYER

(435) Abū Hurairah reported: When the Apostle of Allah (may peace be upon him) returned from the Battle of Khaibar, he travelled during the night. When we felt sleep, he halted for rest. Addressing Bilāl he said: Keep vigilance at night for us. But Bilāl who was leaning against the saddle of his mount was dominated by sleep. Neither the Prophet (may peace be upon him) nor Bilāl nor any of his Companions could get up till the sunshine struck them. The Apostle of Allah (may peace be upon

185. The Prophet (may peace be upon him) commanded to say all prayers in general twice if sometimes one has to do so. He did not distinguish one from another. But there are traditions which indicate the offering of the supererogatory prayer after the morning and afternoon prayers. In view of these traditions some scholars hold the opinion that only the noon, sunset and night prayers can be repeated and not all. But on the basis of this tradition another group of scholars argue that all prayers can be repeated (*'Awn al-Ma'būd*, I, 104).

him) got up first of all. The Apostle of Allah (may peace be upon him) was embarrassed and said: O Bilāl! He replied: He who detained your soul, detained my soul, Aposte of Allah, my parents be sacrificed for you. Then they drove their mounts to a little distance. The Prophet (may peace be upon him) performed ablution and commanded Bilāl who made announcement for the prayer. He (the Prophet) led them in the morning prayer. When he finished the prayer, he said: If anyone forgets saying prayer, he should observe it when he recalls it, for Allah has said (in the Qur'ān): "Establish prayer for my remembrance." Yūnus said: Ibn Shihāb used to recite this verse in a similar way (i.e. instead of reciting the word *li-dhikrī*—for the sake of My remembrance—he would recite *li-dhikrā*—when you remember). Aḥmad said: 'Anbasah (a reporter) reported on the authority of Yūnus the word *li-dhikrī* (for the sake of my remembrance). Ahmad said: The word *nu'ās* (occurring in this tradition) means "drowsiness."

(436) Abū Hurairah reported: Another version of the above tradition adds: The Apostle of Allah (may peace be upon him) said: Go away from this place of yours where inadvertence took hold of you. He then commanded Bilāl who called for prayer and announced that the prayer in congregation was ready (lit. he uttered the *iqāmah*), and he observed prayer.

Abū Dāwūd said: This tradition has been narrated by Mālik, Sufyān b. 'Uyainah, al-Awzā'ī and 'Abd al-Razzāq from Ma'mar and Ibn Isḥāq; none of them made a mention of the call for prayer (*adhān*) in this version of the tradition narrated by al-Zuhrī, and none of them attribute (this addition) to him except al-Awzā'ī and Abān al-'Aṭṭār on the authority of Ma'mar.

(437) Abū Qatādah reported: The Prophet (may peace be upon him) was on a journey. The Prophet (may peace be upon him) took a turn and I also took a turn with him He said: Look! I said: This is a rider; these are two riders; and these are three, until we became seven. He then said: Guard for us our prayer, i.e. the dawn prayer. But sleep dominated them and none could awaken them except the heat of the sun. They stood up and drove away a little. Then they got down (from their mounts) and performed ablution. Bilāl called for prayer and they offered two *rak'ahs* of the morning prayer (i.e. the *sunan* prayer) and then offered the morning prayer and mounted (their mounts). Some of them said to others: We showed negligence in prayer. The Prophet (may peace be upon him) said: There is no negligence in sleep. The negligence is in wakefulness. If any of you forgets saying prayer, he should offer it when he remembers it and next day (he should say it) at its proper time.

(438) Khālid b. Sumair said: 'Abd Allah b. Rabāh al-Anṣārī, whom the Ansār called *faqīh* (the jurist), came to us from Medina, and reported to us on the authority of Abū Qatādah al-Anṣārī, the horseman of the Apostle of Allah (may peace be upon him), saying: The Apostle of Allah (may peace be upon him) sent a military expedi-

tion consisting of the chief Companions. He then narrated the same story, saying Nothing awakened us except the rising sun. We stood up in bewilderment, for our prayer. The Prophet (may peace be upon him) said : Wait a little ; wait a little. When the sun rose high, the Apostle of Allah (may peace be upon him) said: Those who used to observe the two *rak'ahs* of morning prayer (i.e. *sunan* prayer before the obligatory prayer) should observe them. Then those who used to observe and those who would not observe stood up and said prayer. Then the Apostle of Allah (may peace be upon him) cammanded to call for prayer; the call for prayer was made accordingly. The Apostle of Allah (may peace be upon him) stood and led us in prayer. When he turned away (from the prayer) he said: We thank Allah for the fact that we were not engaged in any worldly affairs which detained us from our prayer; instead, our souls were in the hands of Allah ; He released them whenever He wished. If any one of you gets morning prayer tomorrow at its proper time, he should offer a similar prayer as an atonement.[186]

(439) This tradition has also been reported by Abū Qatādah through a different chain of narrators. He said: Allah detained your souls how He wished and returned when He wished. Stand up and call for prayer. They (the Companions) stood and performed ablution. When the sun rose high, the Prophet (may peace be upon him) stood and led the people in prayer.

(440) This tradition has been transmitted through a different chain by Abū Qatādah to the same effect. This version adds: "He performed ablution when the sun had arisen high and led them in prayer."

(441) Abū Qatādah reported the Apostle of Allah (may peace be upon him) as saying: There is no remissness in sleep, it is only when one is awake that there is remissness when you delay saying the prayer till the time for the next prayer comes.

(442) Anas b. Mālik reported the Prophet (may peace be upon him) as saying: If any one forgets a prayer or oversleeps, he should observe it when he remembers it; there is no expiation for it except that.

186. The narrator Khālid b. Sumair made a mistake in transmitting this tradition at three places. In the first place, he referred to the battle of Mūtah by saying that this was an expedition that consisted of the chief Companions. What is correct is that this incident happened on the way when they were returning from the Battle of Khaibar. Secondly, he reported that the Prophet (may peace be upon him) commanded only those persons who used to observe prayer to offer the *sunan* prayer. The other versions of this tradition indicate that he commanded them all Further, he might have given an option to say the *sunan* prayer due to journey. Hence he might have said that those who wished to offer them at that time should offer ; those who did not wish to offer due to the journey could avail of the concession. Thirdly, the other versions of this tradition state that he commanded to offer the morning prayer next day at its proper time and not to repeat a similar prayer along with it (*'Awn al-Ma'būd*. I, 168-69).

(443) 'Imrān b. Ḥuṣain said: The Apostle of Allah (may peace be upon him) was on his journey. They (the people) slept abandoning the morning prayer. They awoke by the heat of the sun Then they travelled a little until the sun rose high. He (the Prophet) commanded the *mu'adhdhin* (one who calls for prayer) to call for prayer. He then offered two *rak'ahs* of prayer (*sunan* prayer) before the (obligatory) morning prayer. Then he (the *mu'adhdhin*) announced for saying the prayer in conrgegation (lit. he uttered the *iqāmah*). Then he led them in the morning prayer.

(444) 'Amr b. Umayyah al-Ḍamrī said: We were in the company of the Apostle of Allah (may peace be upon him) during one of his journeys. He overslept abandoning the morning prayer until the sun had arisen. The Apostle of Allah (may peace be upon him) awoke and said: Go away from this place. He then commanded Bilāl (to call for prayer. He called for prayer. They (the people) performed ablution and offered two *rak'ahs* of the morning prayer (*sunan* prayer). He then commanded Bilāl (to utter the *iqāmah*, i.e. to summon the people to attend the prayer). He announced the prayer (i.e. uttered the *iqāmah*) and he led them in the morning prayer.

(445) Dhū Mikhbar al-Ḥabashī, who used to serve the Prophet (may peace be upon him), reported a version of the previous tradition. The Prophet (may peace be upon him) performed ablution in such a way that there was no mud on the earth. He then commanded Bilāl (to call for prayer). He called for prayer. The Prophet (may peace be upon him) stood and offered two *rak'ahs* of prayer unhurriedly.

This is narrated by Ḥajjāj on the authority of Yazīd b. Ṣulaiḥ from Dhū Mikhbar from a person of al-Ḥabashah (Ethiopia). 'Ubaid (a narrator) said: Yazīd b. Ṣāliḥ (instead of Yazīd b. Ṣulaiḥ).

(446) This tradition has also been transmitted through another chain of narrators by Dhū Mikhbar, the nephew of the Negus. This version adds: "He (Bilāl) called for prayer unhurriedly."

(447) 'Abd Allah b. Mas'ūd reported: We proceeded with the Apostle of Allah (may peace be upon him) on the occasion of al-Ḥudaibīyyah. The Apostle of Allah (may peace be upon him) said: Who will keep watch for us? Bilāl said: I (shall do). They overslept till the sun arose. The Prophet (may peace be upon him) awoke and said: Do as you used to do (i.e. offer prayer as usual). Then we did accordingly. He said: Anyone who oversleeps or forgets (prayer) should do similarly.

Chapter 161

ON BUILDING THE MOSQUES

(448) Ibn 'Abbās reported the Apostle of Allah (may peace be upon him) as saying: I was not commanded to build high mosques. Ibn 'Abbās said: You will

certainly adorn them as the Jews and Christians did.

(449) Anas reported the Prophet (may peace be upon him) as saying: The Last Hour will not come until people vie with one another about mosques.[187]

(450) 'Uthmān b. Abū al-'Āṣ reported: The Prophet (may peace be upon him) commanded him to build a mosque at Ṭā'if where the idols were placed.

(451) 'Abd Allah b. 'Umar reported: The mosque (of the Prophet) during his lifetime was built with bricks, its roof with branches of the palm-tree, and its pillars with palm-wood, as Mujāhid said; Abū Bakr did not add anything to it. But 'Umar added to it; he built it as it was built during the lifetime of the Apostle of Allah (may peace be upon him) with bricks and branches, and he changed its pillars. Mujāhid said: its pillars were made of wood. 'Uthmān changed it altogether with increasing addition. He built its walls with decorated stone and lime. And he built the pillars with decorated stone and its roof with teak. Mujāhid said: Its roof was made of teak.

Abū Dāwūd said: *Al-Qaṣṣah* means lime used as mortar.

(452) Ibn 'Umar reported: The pillars of the mosque of the Prophet (may peace be upon him) during the time of the Apostle of Allah (may peace be upon him) were made of the trunks of the palm-tree; they were covered from the above by twigs of the palm-tree; they decayed during the caliphate of Abū Bakr. He built it afresh with trunks and twigs of the palm-tree. But they again decayed during the caliphate of 'Uthmān. He, therefore, built it with bricks. That survives until today.

(453) Anas b. Mālik reported: The Apostle of Allah (may peace be upon him) came over to Medina and encamped at the upper side of Medina among the tribe known as Banū 'Amr b. 'Awf. He stayed among them for fourteen days. He then sent someone to call Banū al-Najjār. They came to him hanging their swords from the necks. Anas then said: As if I am looking at the Apostle of Allah (may peace be upon him) sitting on his mount and Abū Bakr seated behind him, and Banū al-Najjār standing around him He descended in the courtyard of Abū Ayyūb. The Apostle of Allah (may peace be upon him) would say his prayer wherever the time came and offer his prayer in the folds of the sheep and goats. He commanded us to build a mosque. He then sent for Banū al-Najjār and said to them: Banū al-Najjār, sell this land of yours to me for some price. They replied: By Allah, we do not want any price (from you) except from Allah. Anas said: I tell you what this land contained. It contained the graves of the disbelievers, dung-hills and some trees of date-palm. The Apostle of Allah (may peace be upon him) commanded and the graves of the

187. The Prophet (may peace be upon him) has predicted the approach of the Last Day at the time when people build high and magnificent mosques and vie with one another in respect of their grandeur and ornamentation. Excessive decoration of mosques is the sign of the Last Hour. Hence the Muslims are required not to decorate the mosques excessively (*'Awn al Ma'būd*, I, 171).

disbelievers were dug open, and the trees of date-palm were cut off. The wood of the date-palm were erected in front of the mosque; the door-steps were built of stone. They were reciting verses while carrying the stones. The Prophet (may peace be upon him) also joined them (in reciting verses) saying: O Allah, there is no good except the good of the Hereafter: do ye help the Helpers (*Anṣār*) and the Immigrants (*Muhājirah*)

(454) Anas b. Mālik said: The mosque (of the Prophet) was built in the land of Banū al-Najjār which contained crops, palm-trees and graves of the disbelievers. The Apostle of Allah (may peace be upon him) said: Sell it to me for some price. They (Banu al-Najjār) replied: We do not want (any price). The palm-trees were cut off, and the crops removed and the graves of the disbelievers dug opened. He then narrated the rest of the tradition. But this version has the word "forgive" in the verse, instead of the word "help." Mūsā said: 'Abd al-Wārith also narrated this tradition in a like manner. The version of 'Abd al-Wārith has the word "dung-hill" (instead of crop), and he asserted that he narrated this tradition to Ḥammād.

Chapter 162

BUILDING MOSQUES IN DIFFERENT LOCALITIES

(455) 'Ā'ishah said: The Apostle of Allah (may peace be upon him) commanded us to build mosques in different localities (i.e. in the locality of each tribe separately) and that they should be kept clean and be perfumed.

(456) Samurah reported that he wrote (a letter) to his sons: After (praising Allah and blessing the Prophet) that: The Apostle of Allah (may peace be upon him) used to command us to build mosques in our localities and to keep them well and clean.

Chapter 163

ON LIGHTING A LAMP IN THE MOSQUE

(457) Maimūnah, the freed slave-girl of the Prophet (may peace be upon him), reported that she said: Apostle of Allah, tell us the legal injunction about (visiting) Bait al-Muqaddas (the Dome of the Rock at Jerusalem). The Apostle of Allah (may peace be upon him) said: Go and pray there. All the cities at that time were effected by war. If you cannot visit it and pray there, then send some oil to be used in the lamps.

Chapter 164

ON SPREADING GRAVEL IN THE MOSQUE

(458) Abū al-Walīd said: I asked Ibn 'Umar about the gravel spread in the mosque. He replied: One night the rain fell and the earth was moistened. A man was bringing the gravel (broken stones) in his cloth and spreading it beneath him. When the Apostle of Allah (may peace be upon him) finished his prayer, he said: How fine it is!

(459) Abū Ṣāliḥ said: It was said that when a man removed gravels from the mosque, they adjured him.

(460) Abū Hurairah reported (Abū Bakr said that in his opinion he narrated this tradition from the Prophet): The gravels adjure the person who removes them from the mosque.

Chapter 165

ON SWEEPING THE MOSQUE

(461) Anas b. Mālik reported the Apostle of Allah (may peace be upon him) as saying: The rewards of my people were presented before me, so much so that even the reward for removing a mote by a person from the mosque was presented to me. The sins of my people were also presented before me. I did not find a sin greater than that of a person forgetting the Qur'ānic chapter or verse memorised by him.

Chapter 166

ON SEGREGATION OF WOMEN FROM MEN IN THE MOSQUES

(462) Ibn 'Umar reported the Apostle of Allah (may peace be upon him) as saying: If we left this door for women (it would have been better). Nāfi' said: Ibn 'Umar did not enter (the door) until his death. The others except 'Abd al-Wārith said: This was said by 'Umar (and not by Ibn 'Umar) and that is more correct.

(463) This tradition has been reported by 'Umar b. al-Khaṭṭāb through a different chain of narrators. He narrated it to the same effect and that is more correct.

(464) Nāfi' said: 'Umar b. al-Khaṭṭāb used to prohibit (men) to enter through the door reserved for women.

Chapter 167

WHAT SHOULD A MAN SAY WHEN HE ENTERS THE MOSQUE

(465) Abū Usaid al-Anṣārī reported the Apostle of Allah (may peace be upon him) as saying: When any of you enters the mosque he should invoke blessing on the Prophet (may peace be upon him) and then he should say: O Allah, open to me the gates of Thy mercy. And when he goes out, he should say: O Allah, I ask Thee out of Thine abundance.

(466) Haiwah b. Shuraiḥ reported: I met 'Uqbah b. Muslim and said to him: It has been reported to me that someone has narrated to you from the Prophet (may peace be upon him) that when he entered the mosque, he would say: I seek refuge in Allah, the Magnificent, and in His noble face, and in His eternal domain, from the accursed Devil. He asked: Is it so much only? I said: Yes. He said: When anyone says so, the devil says: He is protected from me all the day long.

Chapter 168

ON SAYING PRAYER IMMEDIATELY AFTER ENTERING THE MOSQUE

(467) Abū Qatādah reported the Apostle of Allah (may peace be upon him) as saying: When any one of you enters the mosque, he should pray two *rak'ahs* before sitting down.[188]

(468) This tradition has been narrated by Abū Qatādah through a different chain of transmitters to the same effect from the Prophet (may peace be upon him). This version adds: Then he may remain sitting (after praying two *rak'ahs*) or may go for his work

188. This prayer is known as *tahayyat al-masjid* (respect of mosque). This is commendable and not obligatory One can offer this prayer at any time after entering the mosque except in the three times when prayer is forbidden. It is also permissible to say this prayer when the *Imām* gives the sermon before the Friday prayer. This is the view held by al-Shāfi'ī, Ahmad b. Hanbal, Ishāq b. Rahwaih, al-Hasan al-Basrī and Makhūl. Another view goes that one should say this prayer on entering the mosque after the bręak of dawn and after the afternoon prayer. Moreover, when a person enters the mosque and the *Imām* is giving the sermon for the Friday prayer, he should sit down, and should not pray. This is the view held by Ibn Sīrīn, 'Aṭā' b. 'Alī Rabāḥ, al-Nakha'ī, Qatādah, the Hanafīs, Mālikīs and al-Thawrī (*'Awn al-Ma'būd* I, 176).

Chapter 169

THE EXCELLENCE OF SITTING IN THE MOSQUE

(469) Abū Hurairah reported the Apostle of Allah (may peace be upon him) as saying: The angels invoke blessings on any of you who remains sitting at the place where he says his prayer so long as he is defiled (needs ablution) or stands up, saying: O Allah, forgive him; O Allah, have mercy on him.

(470) Abū Hurairah reported the Apostle of Allah (may peace be upon him) as saying: One is considered to be at prayer so long as one is detained by prayer: nothing prevents one from going home to one's family except prayer.

(471) Abū Hurairah reported the Apostle of Allah (may peace be upon him) as saying: The servant (of Allah) is considered to be at prayer so long as he remains at the place of prayer waiting for prayer. The angels say: O Allah, forgive him? O Allah, take mercy on him, until he turns away, or he is defiled. He was asked: What is meant by defilement? He replied: He breaks wind gently or loudly.

(472) Abū Hurairah reported the Apostle of Allah (may peace be upon him) as saying: One shall have the thing for which one comes to the mosque.[189]

Chapter 170

ON DISAPPROVAL OF CRYING OUT IN THE MOSQUE ABOUT SOMETHING HE HAS LOST

(473) Abū Hurairah reported: I heard the Apostle of Allah (may peace be upon him) say: If anyone hears a man crying out in the mosque about something he has lost, he should say: May Allah not restore it to you, for the mosques were not built for this.[190]

Chapter 171

ON THE DISAPPROVAL OF SPITTING IN THE MOSQUE

(474) Anas b. Mālik reported the Prophet (may peace be upon him) as saying:

189. This refers to the correct intention while coming to the mosque. If one comes to the mosque with the intention of worship, one shall have the reward. If one comes with the intention of some other work, one will not get the reward (*'Awn al-Ma'būd*, I, 176).

190. This tradition clearly indicates that the mosques are not built for making a noise and speaking loudly. The atmosphere in the mosques should be calm and quiet so that people may concentrate on the remembrance of Allah. Another tradition states that the mosques are built for offering prayer and remembrance of Allah. Hence one should be careful in speaking loudly in the mosque.

Spitting in the mosque is a sin and it is expiated by burying the spittle.[191]

(475) Anas reported : The Apostle of Allah (may peace be upon him) said : Spitting in the mosque is a sin and it is expiated by burying the spittle.

(476) Anas b. Mālik reported : The Apostle of Allah (may peace be upon him) said : Spitting phlegm in the mosque. . . The narrator then transmitted the rest of the tradition to the same effect.

(477) Abū Hurairah reported : The Apostle of Allah (may peace be upon him) said : If anyone enters the mosque, and spits in it, or ejects phelgm, he should remove some earth and bury it there. It he does not do so, then he should spit in his clothe and not come out with it.

(478) 'Abd Allah al-Muḥāribī reported : The Apostle of Allah (may peace be upon him) said : When a man stands with the intention of saying prayer, or if any of you says prayer, he should not spit before him, nor at his right side ; but he should do so at his left side, if there is a place for it ; or he should spit under his left foot and then rub it off.

(479) Ibn 'Umar reported : One day while the Apostle of Allah (may peace be upon him) was giving sermon he suddenly saw phlegm on the wall towards the *qiblah* (the direction to which Muslims turn in prayer) of the mosque. So he became angry at people. He then scraped it and sent for saffron and staineo with it. He then said : When any of you prays, Allah, the Exalted, faces him ; he, therefore, should not spit before him.

(480) Abū Sa'īd al-Khudrī said : The Prophet (may peace be upon him) liked the twigs of date-plam, and he often had one of them in his hand. He entered the mosque and saw phlegm in the wall towards *qiblah* and he scraped it. He then turned towards people in anger and said : Is any one of you pleased to spit in his face? When any of you faces *qiblah*, he indeed faces his Lord, the Majestic and Glorious ; the angels are at his right side. Therefore, he should not spit on his right side nor before him towards *qiblah*. He should spit on his left side or beneath his foot. If he is in a hurry, he should do so-and-so. Describing it Ibn 'Ajlān said : He should spit in his cloth and fold a part of it over the other.

(481) 'Ubādah b. al-Sāmit said : We came to Jābir b. 'Abd Allah who was sitting in his mosque. He said : The Apostle of Allah (may peace be upon him) came to us in this mosque and he had a twig of date-palm of the kind of Ibn Ṭāb. He looked

191. Purity and cleanliness are the part of faith. The Prophet (may peace be upon him) has laid great emphasis on keeping the mosques neat and clean. Spitting anywhere is unhygienic. This should be avoided as far as possible, especially in the mosques. If someone is forced to spit while praying or does so by mistake he should bury it under the soil of the mosque. If there is no soil he should remove it and cleanse the place. If one spits during prayer one should do so beneath one's left foot and then rub it off (*'Awn al-Ma'būd*, I, 177).

and saw phlegm on the wall towards *qiblah.* He turned to it and scraped it with the twig. He then said: Who of you likes that Allah turns His face from him? He further said: When any of you stands for praying, Allah faces him. So he should not spit before him, nor on his right side. He should spit on his left side under his left foot. If he is in a hurry (i.e. forced to spit immediately), he should do with his cloth in this manner. He then placed the cloth on his mouth and rubbed it off. He then said: Bring perfume. A young man of the tribe stood and hurried to his house and returned with perfume in his palm. The Apostle of Allah (may peace be upon him) took it and put it at the end of the twig. He then stained the mark of phlegm with it. Jābir said: This is the reason you use perfume in your mosques.

(482) Abū Sahlat al-Sā'ib b. Khallād (Aḥmad said: He is one of the Companions) reported: A man led the people in prayer. He spat towards *qiblah* while the Apostle of Allah (may peace be upon him) was looking at him. The Apostle of Allah (may peace be upon him) said to him when he finished his prayer: He should not lead you in prayer (henceforth). Thenceforth he intended to lead them in prayer, but they forbade him and informed him of the prohibition of the Apostle of Allah (may peace be upon him). He mentioned it to the Apostle of Allah (may peace be upon him) who said to him: Yes. The narrator said: I think he (the Prophet) said: You did harm to Allah and His Apostle.

(483) Abū al-'Alā' reported on the authority of his father: I came to the Apostle of Allah (may peace be upon him) who was saying prayer. He spat beneath his left foot.[192]

(484) Abū al-'Alā' reported this tradition on the authority of his father to the same effect with a different chain of narrators. This version adds: "He then rubbed it with his shoe."

(485) Abū Sa'īd said: I saw Wāthilah b. al-Asqa' in the mosque of Damascus. He spat at the mat and then rubbed it with his foot. He was asked: Why did you do so? He said: Because I saw the Apostle of Allah (may peace be upon him) doing so.

Chapter 172

ON THE ENTERING OF A POLYTHEIST IN THE MOSQUE

(486) Anas b. Mālik reported: A man entered the mosque on camel and made it kneel down, and then tied his leg with rope. He then asked: Who among you is Muḥammad? The Apostle of Allah (may peace be upon him) was sitting leaning upon

192. Sometimes a man is forced to spit in avoidable circumstances. When a person is praying it does not look nice to spit; hence the Prophet (may peace be upon him) permitted it by his own action if at all it becomes necessary to do so.

something among them. We said to him: This white (man) who is leaning. The man said: O son of 'Abd al-Muṭṭalib. The Prophet (may peace be upon him) said: I already responded to you. The man (again) said: O Muḥammad, I am asking you. The narrator then narrated the rest of the tradition.[193]

(487) Ibn 'Abbās reported: Banū Sa'd b. Bakr sent Ḍamām b. Tha'labah to the Apostle of Allah (may peace be upon him). He came to him and made his camel kneel down near the gate of the mosque. He then tied its leg and entered the mosque. The narrator then reported in a similar way. He then said: Who among you is the son of 'Abd al-Muṭṭalib? The Apostle of Allah (may peace be upon him) replied: I am the son of Ibn 'Abd al-Muṭṭalib. He said: O son of 'Abd al-Muṭṭalib. The narrator then reported the rest of the tradition.

(488) Abū Hurairah said: The Jews came to the Prophet (may peace be upon him) and he was sitting in the mosque among his Companions. They said: O Abū al-Qāsim, a man and a woman have committed adultery.

Chapter 173

ON THE PLACES WHERE PRAYING IS UNLAWFUL

(489) Abū Dharr reported the Apostle of Allah (may peace be upon him) as saying: The earth has been made for me purifying and as a mosque (place for prayer).[194]

(490) Abū Ṣāliḥ al-Ghifārī reported: 'Alī (once) passed by Babylon during his travels. The *mu'adhdhin* (the person who calls for prayer) came to him to call for the afternoon prayer. When he passed by that place, he commanded to announce for the prayer. After finishing the prayer he said: My affectionate friend (i.e. the Prophet) prohibited me to say prayer in the graveyard. He also forbade me to offer prayer in Babylon because it is accursed.[195]

193. This tradition indicates that the unbelievers are allowed to enter the mosque. The Qur'ān tells us that the unbelievers are impure, and hence they are not allowed to enter the precincts of the Ka'bah (ix. 28). Here the impurity has been construed as the impurity of disbelief. Further the Qur'ān did not directly prevent them from entering the premises of the Ka'bah. That was only a prediction on the part of the Qur'ān that the dominance of the infidels will remain no longer.

194. It means that one can perform *tayammum* anywhere with pure earth. Likewise one can offer one's prayer at any place provided it is pure. The building of a mosque is not essential for the validity of pure.

195. According to al-Khaṭṭābī there may be something doubtful in the chain of this tradition. No scholar has ever prohibited from praying in Babylon. This tradition contradicts a more sound tradition which says that prayer is allowed on all the earth provided it is pure. Some scholars are of opinion that one is prohibited to pray there so that one might not stay there. The Prophet (may

(491) Abū Ṣāliḥ narrated this tradition with a different chain of transmitters to the same effect as reported by Sulaimān b. Dāwūd. But this version has the word *kharaja* (he went out) instead of *baraza* (proceeded).

(492) Sa'īd reported the Apostle of Allah (may peace be upon him) as saying and the narrator Mūsā said : As far as 'Amr thinks, the Prophet (may peace be upon him) said : The whole earth is a place of prayer except public baths and graveyards.

Chapter 174

PROHIBITION OF PRAYING AT PLACES WHERE THE CAMELS KNEEL DOWN

(493) Barā' b. 'Āzib reported : The Apostle of Allah (may peace be upon him) was asked about saying prayer at places where the camels kneel down. He replied: Do not say prayer at places where the camels kneel down because they are the places of devils. And he was asked about saying prayer in the fold of sheep. He replied : Pray there because they are the places of blessing.[196]

Chapter 175

IN WHAT AGE A BOY SHOULD BE COMMANDED TO PRAY

(494) 'Abd al-Malik b. al-Rabī' b. al-Saburah reported from his father on the authority of his grandfather : The Prophet (may peace be upon him) said: Command a boy to pray when he reaches the age of seven years. When he becomes ten years old, then beat him for prayer.

(495) 'Amr b. Shu'aib reported from his father on the authority of his grandfather : The Apostle of Allah (may peace be upon him) said : Command your children

peace be upon him) wanted that no Muslim should settle there. There is also the possibility that the prohibition is peculiar to 'Alī alone because the Prophet (may peace be upon him) was well aware that a great harm would be done to 'Alī at this place. Hence he prohibited him to pray (*'Awn al-Ma'būd*, I, 183).

196. A tradition recorded by Ibn Mājah says that camels have been created from devils. It should be noted that camels are naughty by nature. They become more dangerous when they flare up. They generally do not stay at their place, but run to and fro. Hence a man cannot pray with peace of mind and concentration. Above all, there is always a danger that some camel might injure the man at prayer. The sheep, on the contrary, are tame and generally remain at their places. They do not run to and fro like camels. Hence there is no danger to the man at prayer from them. Hence the Prophet (may peace be upon him) allowed to pray in their fold and prohibited to pray at the places of camels. Some commentators have expressed the view that the Prophet (may peace be upon him) might have prohibited to pray on the soft ground where the camels are kept and allowed to pray on the pebbly ground where the sheep are kept. The reason is that impurity might be mixed with the soil of the soft ground. But this is not the case with the pebbly ground. The impurity is manifest on its surface (*'Awn al-Ma'būd*, I, 184).

to pray when they become seven years old, and beat them for it (prayer) when they become ten years old; and arrange their beds (to sleep) separately.[197]

(496) This tradition has been narrated by Dāwūd b. Sawār al-Muzanī through a different chain of transmitters and to the same effect. This version adds: If any of you marries his slave-girl to his male-slave or his servant, he should not look at her private part below her navel and above her knees.[198]

Abū Dāwūd said: Wakī' misunderstood the name of Dāwūd b. Sawār. Abū Dāwūd al-Ṭayālisī has narrated this tradition from him. He said: Abū Ḥamzah Sawār al-Ṣairafī.

(497) Hishām b. Sa'd reported: We entered upon Mu'ādh b. 'Abd Allah b. Khubaib al-Juhanī. He said to his wife: When (at what age) should a boy pray? She replied: Some person of us reported: The Apostle of Allah (may peace be upon him) was asked about it; he said: When a boy distinguishes right hand from the left hand, then command him to pray.

Chapter 176

BEGINNING OF THE CALL TO PRAYER (*ADHĀN*)

(498) Abū 'Umair b. Anas reported on the authority of his uncle who was from the Anṣār (the helpers of the Prophet): The Prophet (may peace be upon him) was anxious as to how to gather the people for prayer. The people told him: Hoist a flag at the time of prayer; when they see it, they will inform one another. But he (the Prophet) did not like it. Then someone mentioned to him the horn. Ziyād said: A horn of the Jews. He (the Prophet) did not like it. He said: This is the matter of the Jews. Then they mentioned to him the bell of the Christians. He said: This is the matter of the Christians. 'Abd Allah b. Zaid returned anxiously from there because of the anxiety of the Apostle of Allah (may peace be upon him). He was then taught the call to prayer in his dream. Next day he came to the Apostle of Allah (may peace be upon him) and informed him about it. He said: Apostle of Allah, I was between sleep and wakefulness; all of a sudden a newcomer came (to me) and taught me the call to prayer. 'Umar b. al-Khaṭṭāb had also seen it in his dream before, but he kept

197. Although prayer is not obligatory on minors, the Prophet (may peace be upon him), in view of the significance of prayer, commanded to beat them if the children do not pray at the age of ten. If the children do not learn how to pray at the tender age, and if they are not accustomed of saying prayer before puberty, there is all likelihood that they may not pray even after adulthood. Commanding the children to pray at the age of seven and beating them at the age of ten is a sort of education and training. This applies equally both to male and female children.

198. The master is not allowed to have sexual intercourse with her slave-girl if she is married to some other person.

it hidden for twenty days. The Prophet (may peace be upon him) said to me ('Umar): What did prevent you from saying it to me? He said : 'Abd Allah b. Zaid had already told you about it before me : hence I was ashamed. Then the Apostle of Allah (may peace be upon him) said : Bilāl, stand up, and see what 'Abd Allah b. Zaid tells you (to do), then do it Bilāl then called to prayer.

Abū Bishr reported on the authority of Abū 'Umair : The Anṣār would think that if 'Abd Allah b. Zaid were not ill on that day, the Apostle of Allah (may peace be upon him) would have made him *mu'adhdhin*.

Chapter 177

HOW THE CALL TO PRAYER (*ADHĀN*) IS TO BE PRONOUNCED

(499) 'Abd Allah b. Zaid reported: When the Apostle of Allah (may peace be upon him) ordered a bell to be made so that it might be struck to gather the people for prayer, a man carrying a bell in his hand appeared to me while I was asleep, and I said: Servant of 'Abd Allah, will you sell the bell? He asked: What will you do with it? I replied : We shall use it to call the people to prayer. He said: Should I not suggest you something better than that. I replied : Certainly. Then he told me to say : Allah is most great, Allah is most great, Allah is most great, Allah is most great. I testify that there is no god but Allah, I testify that there is no god but Allah. I testify that Muḥammad is the Apostle of Allah. I testify that Muḥammad is the Apostle of Allah. Come to pray, Come to pray ; Come to salvation ; Come to salvation. Allah is most great, Allah is most great : There is no god but Allah. He then moved backward a few steps and said: When you utter the *iqāmah*, you should say: Allah is most great, Allah is most great. I testify that there is no god but Allah, I testify that Muhammad is the Apostle of Allah. Come to prayer, Come to salvation. The time for prayer has come, the time for prayer has come ; Allah is most great, Allah is most great There is no god but Allah. When the morning came, I came to the Apostle of Allah (may peace be upon him) and informed him of what I had seen in the dream. He said: It is a genuine vision, if Allah will; so get up along with Bilāl and teach him what you saw in the vision, and he then should use it to call people to prayer, for he has a louder voice than you have. So I got up along with Bilāl and began to teach it to him and he used it in making the call to prayer. 'Umar b. al-Khaṭṭāb (Allah be pleased with him) heard it while he was in his house and came out trailing his cloak and said : Apostle of Allah, by Him Who has sent you with the truth, I have also seen the kind of thing as has been shown to him. The Apostle of Allah (may peace be upon him) said: To Allah be the praise.

Abū Dāwūd said: Al-Zuhrī narrated this tradition in a similar way from Sa'īd b. al-Musayyib on the authority of 'Abd Allah b. Zaid. In this version Ibn Isḥāq narrated from al-Zuhrī: Allah is most great. Allah is most great. Allah is most great. Allah is most great. Ma'mar and Yūnus narrated from al-Zuhrī: Allah is most great, Allah is most great. They did not report it twice again.[199]

(500) Abū Maḥdhūrah reported: I said: Apostle of Allah, teach me the method of *adhān* (how to pronounce the call to prayer). He wiped my forehead (with his hand) and asked me to pronounce: Allah is most great, Allah is most great, Allah is most great, Allah is most great, raising your voice while pronouncing them (these words). Then you must say: I testify that there is no god but Allah; I testify that there is no god but Allah; I testify that Muḥammad is the Apostle of Allah, I testify that Muḥammad is the Apostle of Allah, lowering your voice while saying them (these words). Then you must raise your voice in making the testimony: I testify that there is no god but Allah, I testify that there is no god but Allah; I testify that Muḥammad is the Apostle of Allah, I testify that Muḥammad is the Apostle of Allah.[200] Come to prayer, come to prayer; come to salvation, come to salvation. If it is the morning prayer, you must pronounce: Prayer is better than sleep, prayer is better than sleep; Allah is most great, Allah is most great; there is no god but Allah.

199. There is a difference of opinion among the jurists about the number of phrases in *adhān* and *iqāmah* According to Sufyān al-Thawrī and Abū Ḥanīfah and other jurists of Kūfah, *adhān* contains fifteen phrases and *iqāmah* seventeen. The phrases of *adhān* ara as follows: In the beginning "Allah is most great" four times; "I testify that there is no god but Allah" twice; "I testify that Muḥammad is the Apostle of Allah" twice; "Come to prayer" twice; "Come to salvation" twice; "Allah is most great" twice; "there is no god but Allah" once in the last. The same phrases will be pronounced in *iqāmah* with the addition of the phrase "The time for prayer has come" twice after testification. This is also held by Aḥmad b. Ḥanbal. Mālik maintains that *adhān* contains seventeen phrases. "Allah is most great" twice in the beginning; repetition of testification (*tarji'*), i.e. four times once, and four times again; the rest is the same as narrated by 'Abd Allah b. Zaid.

According to al-Shāfi'ī, *adhān* contains nineteen phrases. It is same as held by Abū Ḥanīfah with the addition that the testification is repeated, i.e. in the beginning four times and again four times (*Ma'ārif al-Sunan*, II, 176).

200. This process of repeating the testification in a lower and then in a louder voice is called *tarji'* (repetition of testification). Al-Shāfi'ī, Mālik, Aḥmad b. Ḥanbal and most of the scholars hold that *tarji'* is necessary in *adhān*. They argue from the tradition reported by Abū Maḥdhūrah. Abū Ḥanīfah and his followers hold that '*tarji'* is not the essential part of *adhān*. It was taught to Abū Maḥdhūrah by the Prophet (may peace be upon him) for learning *adhān*. It is also contended that *tarji'* was taught to him to imprint the two important fundamentals of Islam. He continued it subsequently in his life ('*Awn al-Ma'būd*, I, 191).

According to another version, Aḥmad b. Ḥanbal does not hold *tarji'* in *adhān*. Sufyān al-Thawrī also does not follow repetition of testification. It is said that the difference of opinion on the question of *tarji'* doesm not ean lawfulness or unlawfulness. That is only a question of preference. There is no harm if one pronounces *tarji'* in *adhān* (*Ma'ārif al-Sunan*, II, 174).

(501) Abū Maḥdhūrah also narrated this tradition from the Prophet (may peace be upon him) to the same effect through a different chain of transmitters. This version has the additional wordings. The phrases "Prayer is better than sleep, prayer is better than sleep" are to be pronounced in the first *adhān* (i.e. not in *iqāmah*) of the morning prayer.

Abū Dāwūd said: The version narrated by Musaddad is more clear. It reads: He (the Prophet) taught me *iqāmah* (to pronounce each phrase) twice : Allah is most great, Allah is most great : I testify that there is no god but Allah, I testify that there is no god but Allah ; I testify that Muḥammad is the Apostle of Allah, I testify that Muḥammad is the Apostle of the Allah : come to prayer, come to prayer ; come to salvation, come to salvation ; Allah is most great, Allah is most great ; there is no god but Allah.

Abū Dāwūd said : The narrator 'Abd al-Razzāq said : You pronounce *iqāmah* for announcing the prayer ; you must say twice : The time for prayer has come, the time for prayer has come. (The Prophet said to Abū Maḥdhūrah) : Did you listen (to me) ? Abū Maḥdhūrah would not have the hair of his forehead cut, nor would he separate them (from him) because the Prophet (may peace be upon him) wiped over them.

(502) Abū Maḥdhūrah reported : The Apostle of Allah (may peace be upon him) taught him nineteen phrases in *adhān* and seventeen phrases in *iqāmah*. *Adhān* runs : Allah is most great, Allah is most great, Allah is most great, Allah is most great ; I testify that there is no god but Allah, I testify that there is no god but Allah ; I testify that Muḥammad is the Apostle of Allah, I testify that Muḥammad is the Apostle of Allah ; I testify that there is no god but Allah, I testify that there is no god but Allah ; I testify that Muḥammad is the Apostle of Allah, I testify that Muḥammad is the Apostle of Allah ; come to prayer, come to prayer ; come to salvation, come to salvation ; Allah is most great, Allah is most great ; there is no god but Allah. *Iqāmah* runs : Allah is most great, Allah is most great, Allah is most great, Allah is most great ; I testify that there is no god but Allah, I testify that there is no god but Allah ; I testify that Muḥammad is the Apostle of Allah, I testify that Muḥammad is the Apostle of Allah ; come to prayer ; come to prayer ; come to salvation, come to salvation ; the time for prayer has come, the time for prayer has come ; Allah is most great, Allah is most great ; there is no god but Allah. This is recorded in his collection (i.e. in the collection of the narrator Hammām b. Yaḥyā) according to the tradition reported by Abu Maḥdhūrah (i.e. *iqāmah* contains seventeen phrases.

(503) Abū Maḥdhūrah reported : The Apostle of Allah (may peace be upon him) himself taught me the call to prayer (*adhān*). He asked me to pronounce : Allah is most great. Allah is most great, Allah is most great, Allah is most great : I testify

that there is no god but Allah, I testify that there is no god but Allah ; I testify that Muḥammad is the Apostle of Allah, I testify that Muḥammad is the Apostle of Allah. Then repeat and raise your voice ; I testify that there is no god but Allah, I testify that there is no god but Allah ; I testify that Muhammad is the Apostle of Allah, I testity that Muhammad is the Apostle of Allah ; come to prayer, come to prayer ; come to salvation, come to salvation ; Allah is most great, Allah is most great ; there is no god but Allah.

(504) Abū Maḥdhūrah reported : The Apostle of Allah (may peace be upon him) taught me the call to prayer (*adhān*) verbatim : Allah is most great, Allah is most great, Allah is most great, Allah is most great ; I testify that there is no god but Allah, I testify that there is no god but Allah ; I testify that Muḥammad is the Apostle of Allah, I testify that Muḥammad is the Apostle of Allah : I testify that there is no god but Allah, I testify that there is no god but Allah ; I testify that Muhammad is the Apostle of Allah, I testify that Muḥammad is the Apostle of Allah ; come to prayer, come to prayer ; come to salvation, come to salvation. He used to pronounce "Prayer is better than sleep" in the dawn prayer.

(505) Abū Maḥdhūrah said that the Apostle of Allah (may peace be upon him) taught him the call to prayer (*adhān*), saying : Allah is most great, Allah is most great ; I testify that there is no god but Allah. He then narrated *adhān* like the one contained in the tradition transmitted by Ibn Juraij from 'Abd al-'Azīz b. 'Abd al-Mālik to the same effect. The version Mālik b. Dīnār has . I asked the son of Abū Mahdhūrah, saying : Narrate to me the *adhān* of your father narrated from the Apostle of Allah (may peace be upon him). He said : Allah is most great, Allah is most great, that is all. Similar is the version narrated by Ja'far b. Sulaimān from the son of Abū Maḥdhūrah from his uncle on the authority of his grandfather, excepting that he said : Then repeat and raise your voice, Allah is most great, Allah is most great.

(506) Ibn Abī Lailā said : Prayer passed through three stages.[201] And our people narrated to us that the Apostle of Allah (may peace be upon him) said : It is to my liking that the prayer of Muslims or believers should be united (i.e. in congregation), so much so that I intended to send people to the houses to announce the time of prayer ; and I also resolved that I should order people to stand at (the tops of) the forts and announce the time of the prayer for Muslims ; and they struck the bell or were about to strike the bell (to announce the time for prayer). Then came

201. When the Prophet (may peace be upon him) was in Mecca, he used to say prayer facing the Ka'bah. When he migrated to Medina, he began to pray facing Jerusalem towards which the Jews used to turn their faces in prayer. But the Prophet (may peace be upon him) had a yearning desire to face the Ka'bah in prayer. He prayed for sixteen months facing Jerusalem when the Qur'ānic verses were revealed to face the Ka'bah in prayer (*'Awn al Ma'būd* I, 197)

a person from among the Anṣār who said: Apostle of Allah, when I returned from you, as I saw your anxiety, I saw (in sleep) a person with two green clothes on him; he stood on the mosque and called (people) to prayer. He then sat down for a short while and stood up and pronounced in a like manner, except that he added: "The time for prayer has come." If the people did not call me (a liar), and according to the version of Ibn al-Muthannā, if you did not call me (a liar), I would say that I was awake; I was not asleep. The Apostle of Allah (may peace be upon him) said: According to the version of Ibn al-Muthannā, Allah has shown you a good (dream). But the version of 'Amr does not have the words: Allah has shown you a good (dream). Then ask Bilāl to pronounce the *adhān* (to call to prayer). 'Umar (in the meantime) said: I also had a dream like the one he had. But as he informed earlier, I was ashamed (to inform). Our people have narrated to us: When a person came (to the mosque during the prayer in congregation), he would ask (about the *rak'ahs* of prayer), and he would be informed about the number of *rak'ahs* already performed. They would stand (in prayer) along with the Apostle of Allah (may peace be upon him): Some in standing position; others bowing; some sitting and some praying along with the Apostle of Allah (may peace be upon him).[202]

Ibn al-Muthannā reported from 'Amr from Ḥuṣain b. Abī Lailā, saying: Until Mu'ādh came. Shu'bah said: I heard it from Ḥuṣain who said: I shall follow the position (in the prayer in which I find him [the Prophet]) . . . you should do in a similar way.

Abū Dāwūd said: I then turned to the tradition reported by 'Amr b. Marzūq. He said: Then Ma'ādh came and they (the people) hinted at him. Shu'bah said: I heard it from Ḥuṣain who said: Mu'ādh then said: I shall follow the position (in the prayer when I join it) in which I find him (the Prophet). He then said: Mu'ādh has introduced for you a *sunnah* (a model behaviour), so you should do in a like manner.[203]

202. In the early days of Islam when prayer was newly introduced, the people who came late to join the prayer in congregation used to ask the persons who attended the prayer from the beginning about the number of *rak'ahs* already completed. They first offered those *rak'ahs* of prayer, and then joined the congregation. Hence the people who came late could not follow the Prophet (may peace be upon him) in the prayer in the same position in which they would find him. But this was changed later on.

203. Mu'ādh b. Jabal did not follow the practice of completing the *rak'ahs* of prayer abandoned by him and then join the congregation. Instead, he preferred to join the congregation in the position he found the Prophet (may peace be upon him). He completed the *rak'ahs* left by him after the prayer was over, i.e. when the Prophet (may peace be upon him) pronounced *salām* (salutation). This action of Mu'ādh was approved by the Prophet (may peace be upon him) and made it a *sunnah* (a valid and recognised method) for the future generations. This is the established mode of completing the *rak'ahs* of prayer left by a person attending the congregation late (*'Awn al-Ma'būd*, I, 195).

He said: Our people have narrated to us: When the Apostle of Allah (may peace be upon him) came to Medina, he commanded them (the people) to keep fast for three days. Thereafter the Qur'ānic verses with regard to the fasts during Ramaḍān were revealed. But they were people who were not accustomed to keep fasts; hence the keeping of the fasts was hard for them; so those who could not keep fast would feed an indigent; then the following verse was revealed: "And whosoever of you is present, let him fast the month" (ii. 185). The concession was granted to the patient and the traveller; all were commanded to keep fast.

He said: Our people narrated to us: If a man broke fast and slept before eating anything, he would not eat until the morning. 'Umar b. al-Khaṭṭāb came and intended to cohabit with his wife, but she said: I have already slept. He thought that she was making an excuse; hence he had intercourse with her. A man from the Anṣār came and intended to take meals. They (the people) said: (Wait) till we make it warm: in the meantime he slept. Next day the following verse was revealed: "It is made lawful for you to go unto your wives on the night of the fast" (ii. 187).

(507) Mu'ādh b. Jabal said: Prayer passed through three stages[204] and fast also passed through three stages.[205] The narrator Naṣr reported the rest of the tradition

204. In the early period of Islam the Muslims used to pray individually. There was no congregation of prayer. The Prophet (may peace be upon him) was anxious about it. At last the call to prayer (*adhān*) was introduced and the Muslims began to gather in the mosque and to pray in congregation five times a day in Medina. This was the first stage. In the formative period of prayer, the people were allowed to talk during prayer. Further, when they joined the prayer in congregation, they would first complete the *rak'ahs* of prayer and then attended the congregation. There was no uniformity in positions in prayer. Some would stand, some bow and prostrate in the congregational prayer behind the Prophet (may peace be upon him). But later on the permission of talking during prayer was withdrawn and the people were ordered to keep silence in prayer. Further, as learnt from the tradition reported by Mu'ādh, the *rak'ahs* left by the late comers were to be completed after finishing the prayer by the *imām* and not in the beginning as practised earlier. This was the second stage. The third stage was the turning of the *qiblah*. The Prophet (may peace be upon him) prayed for about sixteen months facing Jerusalem in Medina. Thereafter he was commanded to face the Ka'bah.

There was also gradual change in the number and *rak'ahs* of prayer. The Muslims used to offer prayer three times at Mecca. But at Medina they would pray five times. Moreover, they would offer two *rak'ahs* in all prayers at Mecca. But at Medina the number of *rak'ahs* was precisely fixed for different prayers (*'Awn al-Ma'būd*, I, 194-97).

205. The fast also underwent a gradual change in three stages. When the Prophet (may peace be upon him) came to Medina, he would keep these fasts each month and the fast of the 10th of Muḥarram. This was the first stage. The fast during Ramaḍān was prescribed in the year 2 H. by revelation of the Qur'ānic verses. But in the beginning it was a little harder. People were not allowed to eat or drink after sleeping. The fast would begin after sleep. Further, there was option in keeping fast. One could feed an indigent if one could not fast. This was the second stage. At the third stage fast was made easy and the verses were revealed to begin the fast from the break of dawn and end it with sunset (*'Awn al-Ma'būd*, I, 196).

completely. The narrator Ibn al-Muthannā narrated the story of saying prayer facing towards the direction of Jerusalem. He said: The third stage is that the Apostle of Allah (may peace be upon him) came to Medina and prayed, i.e. facing Jerusalem for thirteen months.[206] Then Allah, the Exalted, revealed the verse: "We have seen thee turning of thy face to heaven (for guidance, O Muḥammad). And now verily We shall make thee turn (in prayer) toward a *qiblah* which is dear to thee. So turn thy face toward the Inviolable Place of Worship, and ye (O Muslims), wherever ye may be, turn your faces (when ye pray) toward it" (ii. 144). And Allah, the Reverend and the Majestic turned (them) towards the Ka'bah He (the narrator) completed his tradition. The narrator Naṣr mentioned the name of the person who had the dream, saying: And 'Abd Allah b. Zaid, a man from the Anṣār, came. The same version has: And he turned his face towards the *qiblah* and said: Allah is most great, Allah is most great; I testify that there is no god but Allah, I testify that there is no god but Allah; I testify that Muḥammad is the Apostle of Allah, I testify that Muḥammad is the Apostle of Allah; come to prayer (he pronounced) twice, come to salvation (he pronounced) twice; Allah is most great, Allah is most great. He then paused for a while, and then got up and pronounced in a like manner, except that after the phrase "Come to salvation" he added. "The time for prayer has come, the time for prayer has come." The Apostle of Allah (may peace be upon him) said: Teach it to Bilāl. Bilāl then pronounced *adhān* (call to prayer) with the same words.

As regards fast, he said: The Apostle of Allah (may peace be upon him) used to keep fast for three days every month, and would fast on the tenth of Muḥarram. Then Allah, the Exalted, revealed the verse: ". . . Fasting was prescribed for those before you, that ye may ward off (evil) . . . and for those who can afford it there is a ransom: the feeding of a man in need" (ii. 183-84). If someone wished to keep fast, he would keep fast; if someone wished to abandon the fast, he would feed an indigent every day: it would do for him. But this was changed. Allah the Exalted, revealed: "The month of Ramaḍān in which was revealed the Qur'an . . . (let him fast the same) number of other days" (ii. 185). Hence the fasts were prescribed for one who was present in the month (of Ramaḍān) and the traveller was required to atone (for them): and feeding (the indigent) was prescribed for the old man and woman who were unable to keep fast.

(The narrator Naṣr further reported): The Companion Sirmah came after finishing his day's work.[207] . . . and he narrated the rest of the tradition.

206. What is correct is that the Prophet (may peace be upon him) prayed for sixteen or seventeen months facing Jerusalem at Medina, as recorded in the collections of al-Bukhārī, Muslim and al-Nasā'ī. The tradition recorded by Abū Dāwūd is said to be weak (*'Awn al-Ma'būd*, I, 197).

207. The full text of this tradition goes: "A Companion, named Sirmah, who belonged to the Anṣār, kept on working all the day long while he was fasting. In the evening he returned home and

Chapter 178

ON THE PRONOUNCEMENT OF *IQĀMAH*

(508) Anas reported: Bilāl was commanded to pronounce ***adhān*** in double pairs and ***iqāmah*** in single pairs.

Hammām added in his version: "except ***iqāmah***."[208]

(509) Anas reported the tradition like that of Wuhaib. Ismā'īl said: I narrated this tradition to Ayyūb who said: "Except ***iqāmah***."[209]

(510) Ibn 'Umar said: The words of ***adhān*** were pronounced from the time of the Apostle of Allah (may peace be upon him) twice in pairs (i.e. four times) each, and the words of ***iqomah*** were pronounced once in pairs (twice each), except that the phrase "The time for prayer has come" would be pronounced twice. When we heard ***iqāmah***, we would perform ablution, and go out for prayer.

Shu'bah said: I did not hear Abū Ja'far narrating any other tradition except this one.

(511) This tradition has been narrated by Abū Ja'far, the ***mu'adhdhin*** of 'Uryān mosque (at Kūfah), from Abū al-Muthannā, the ***mu'adhdhin*** of Masjid al-Akbar (at Kūfah) on the authority of Ibn 'Umar. The rest of the tradition was transmitted in a like manner.

Chapter 179

ON THE PRONOUNCEMENT OF *ADHĀN* BY ONE PERSON AND *IQĀMAH* BY ANOTHER

(512) 'Abd Allah b. Zaid said: The Prophet (may peace be upon him) intended

offered night prayer and slept. He neither ate nor drank anything. The next morning he again kept fast. The Prophet (may peace be upon him) saw him feeling great hardship He said to him: Why do I see you in this hardship? He replied: Apostle of Allah, yesterday I worked (the whole day) and I returned home at the appointed time. Then I went to bed and slept. The next day I again kept fast. This tradition has been recorded by Aḥmad b. Ḥanbal in his *Musnad*.

When such incidents were reported to the Prophet (may peace be upon him) revelation as to the relaxation in fast came down (*'Awn al-Ma'būd*, I, 198 .

208. There is a difference of opinion among the jurists about the number of phrases of *iqāmah*. According to Abū Ḥanīfah, it contains phrases like those of ***adhān*** with an addition of the phrase "The time for prayer has come" twice. According to Mālik, it consists of ten phrases, pronouncing "Allah is most great" twice, and the rest of the phrases only once. The words "The time for prayer has come" will also be pronounced once. Aḥmad and al-Shāfi'ī hold that ***iqāmah*** contains eleven phrases. The phrase "Allah is most great" will be pronounced twice, and the rest of the phrases only once. The phrase "The time for prayer has come" will be uttered twice. All these jurists adduce traditions in support of their viewpoint, (***Ma'ārif al-Sunan***, II, 176).

209. This means that the words "The time for prayer has come" will be pronounced twice.

to do many things for calling (the people) to prayer, but he did not do any of them. Then 'Abd Allah b. Zaid was taught in a dream how to pronounce the call to prayer. He came to the Prophet (may peace be upon him) and informed him. He said: Teach it to Bilāl. He then taught him, and Bilāl made a call to prayer. 'Abd Allah said: I saw it in a dream and I wished to pronounce it, but he (the Prophet) said: You should pronounce *iqāmah*.

(513) This tradition has also been transmitted through a different chain of narrators by 'Abd Allah b. Zaid. He said: My grandfather pronounced the *iqāmah*.

Chapter 180

ONE WHO PRONOUNCES THE *ADHĀN* SHOULD PRONOUNCE THE *IQĀMAH*

(514) Ziyād b. al-Ḥārith al-Ṣudā'i said: When the *adhān* for the dawn prayer was initially introduced, the Prophet (may peace be upon him) commanded me to call the *adhān* and I did so. Then I began to ask: Should I utter *iqāmah*, Apostle of Allah? But he began to look at the direction of the east, (waiting) for the break of dawn, and said: No. When the dawn broke, he came down and performed ablution and he then turned to me; in the meantime his Companions joined him. Then Bilāl wanted to utter the *iqāmah*, but the Prophet (may peace be upon him) said to him: The man of Sudā' has called the *adhān*, and he who calls the *adhān* utters the *iqāmah*.[210]

Chapter 181

ON RAISING THE VOICE WHILE CALLING TO PRAYER

(515) Abū Hurairah reported the Prophet (may peace be upon him) as saying: The *mu'adhdhin* will receive forgiveness to the extent to which his voice reaches,[211] and every moist and dry place will testify on his behalf:[212] and he who attends (the con-

210. The previous tradition indicates that it is permissible to call the *adhān* by one person and to utter the *iqāmah* by another person. But this tradition tells that both the *adhān* and the *iqāmah* should be uttered by the same person. It should be noted that this is the question of preference and not of legitimacy. The previous tradition, it is said, is weak, and this tradition is sound and generally followed (*'Awn al-Ma'būd*, I, 200-201).

211. This statement has been interpreted in various ways. This means that the farther the voice of the *mu'adhdhin* reaches, the more forgiveness is granted to him; or this means that the sins of the *mu'adhdhin* are forgiven even if they are as many as fill up the distance his voice reaches (*'Awn al-Ma'būd*, I, 201-202).

212. All the objects of the universe, and all men and the jinn will bear witness to hearing the voice of the *mu'adhdhin* calling to prayer on the Day of Judgment (*'Awn al-Ma'būd*, I, 202).

gregation of) prayer will have twenty-five prayers recorded for him and will have expiation for sins committed between every two times of prayer.

(516) Abū Hurairah reported the Apostle of Allah (may peace be upon him) as saying: When the call to prayer is made, the devil turns his back and breaks wind so as not to hear the call being made; but when the call is finished, he turns round. When the second call to prayer (*iqāmah*) is made, he turns his back, and when the second call is finished, he turns round and suggests notions in the mind of the man (at prayer) to distract his attention, saying: Remember such and such, referring to something the man did not have in mind, with the result that he does not know how much he has prayed.[213]

Chapter 182

ON OBSERVING PUNCTUALITY IN TIME BY THE *MU'ADHDHIN* IN THE CALL TO PRAYER

(517) Abū Hurairah reported the Apostle of Allah (may peace be upon him) as saying: The *imām* is responsible[214] and the *mu'adhdhin* is trusted.[215] O Allah, guide the ***imāms*** and forgive the ***mu'adhdhins***.

(518) This tradition has also been transmitted through a different chain of narrators by Abū Hurairah who reported it in a similar manner from the Apostle of Allah (may peace be upon him).

Chapter 183

ON PRONOUNCING *ADHĀN* FROM THE MINARET

(519) 'Urwah b. al-Zubair reported on the authority of a woman from Banū al-

213. The devil who is the fatal enemy of man, particularly of a Muslim, is afraid of the call to prayer. Since man achieves much by offering prayer, he is never happy with his call to it. In this tradition, this simile indicates the severity of hatred of the devil for the summons to prayer. Further, it also shows that the devil makes his utmost endeavour to distract the attention of the man at prayer and thus vitiate his worship This tradition emphasises that one should concentrate on his prayer, and should not care for the notions one has during the prayer.

214. The validity of the prayer of the people who follow the *imām* depends on the validity of his prayer. He is in fact the representative of the people in prayer. Hence the *imām* should be immensely careful in purification and fulfil all the conditions of prayer perfectly (*'Awn al-Ma'būd*, I, 203-204).

215. The people rely on the *mu'adhdhin* in respect of the time for prayer, and for breaking the fast. Therefore the *mu'adhdhin* will be held responsible if he calls to prayer irregularly. He should check carefully before pronouncing *adhān* that he is doing so at the correct time (*'Awn al-Ma'būd*, I, 204).

Najjār. She said: My house was the loftiest of all the houses around the mosque (of the Prophet at Medina). Bilāl used to make a call to the morning prayer from it. He would come there before the break of dawn and wait for it. When he saw it, he would yawn and say: O Allah, I praise you and seek Your assistance for the Quraish so that they might establish Thine religion. He then would make the call to prayer. She (the narrator) said: By Allah, I do not know whether he ever left saying these words on any night.

Chapter 184

SHOULD THE *MU'ADHDHIN* TURN RIGHT AND LEFT DURING *ADHĀN*?

(520) Abū Juḥaifah reported: I came to the Prophet (may peace be upon him) at Mecca; he was sitting in a tent made of leather. Then Bilāl came out and called to prayer. I looked at his mouth following him this side and that side (i.e. right and left). Later on the Apostle of Allah (may peace be upon him) came out clad in a red suit, i.e. wearing the sheets of the Yemen, of the Qaṭrī design.[216] The version narrated by Mūsā has the words: "I saw Bilāl going towards al-Abṭaḥ."

He then made a call to prayer. When he reached the words "Come to prayer, come to salvation," he turned his neck right and left, respectively; he did not turn himself (with his whole body)[217] He then entered (his house) and came out with a lancet. The narrator then reported the rest of the tradition.

Chapter 185

ON SUPPLICATION BETWEEN THE *ADHĀN* AND THE *IQĀMAH*

(521) Anas b. Mālik reported the Apostle of Allah (may peace be upon him)

216. Ibn Qayyim is of opinion that the suit worn by the Prophet (may peace be upon him) was not purely red. It had red lines along with black colour. But others have refuted him saying that the Companion who reported this tradition clearly used the word "red," and being an Arab he must have been well aware of the meaning of the "red". Hence there seems no reason to interpret this tradition in a different way. On the basis of this tradition some scholars have allowed to wear red clothes. The matter, however, is disputed amongst scholars. There are seven viewpoints of scholars on the question of wearing red clothes (*'Awn al-Ma'būd*, I, 205).

217. It is agreed upon by scholars that a *mu'adhdhin* should turn his neck right and left while uttering the words "Come to prayer" and "Come to salvation". What is disputed is whether he should turn his body right and left. Some traditions indicate that Bilāl used to turn his whole body right and left; others show that he would not do it (*'Awn al-Ma'būd*, I 205).

as saying: The supplication made between the *adhān* and the *iqāmah* is not rejected.[218]

Chapter 186

WHAT SHOULD A PERSON SAY WHEN HE HEARS THE *ADHĀN*?

(522) Abū Sa'īd al-Khudrī reported the Apostle of Allah (may peace be upon him) as saying: When you hear the *adhān*, you should repeat[219] the same words as the *mu'adhdhin* pronounces.[220]

(523) 'Abd Allah b. 'Amr b. al-'Āṣ reported the Apostle of Allah (may peace be upon him) as saying: When you hear the *mu'adhdhin* repeat what he says, invoke a blessing on me, for everyone who invokes one blessing on me will receive ten blessings from Allah. Then ask Allah to give me the *wasīlah*, which is a rank in Paradise fitting for only one of Allah's servants, and I hope that I may be the one. If anyone asks Allah that I be given the *wasīlah*, he will be assured of my intercession.

(524) 'Abd Allah b. 'Amr reported : A man said : Apostle of Allah, the *mu'adhdhins* excel us.[221] The Apostle of Allah (may peace be upon him) said : Say (the same words) as they say, and when you come to the end, make a petition and that will be granted to you.

(525) Sa'd b. Abī Waqqāṣ reported the Apostle of Allah (may peace be upon him) as saying : If anyone says when he hears the *mu'adhdhin* : "And I testify that there is no god but Allah alone Who has no partner and that Muḥammad is His servant and apostle ; I am satisfied with Allah as Lord, with Muḥammad as apostle, and with Islam as religion," he will be forgiven.

(526) 'Ā'ishah said that when the Apostle of Allah (may peace be upon him) heard the *mu'adhdhin* uttering the testimony, he would say: "And I too, and I too."

(527) 'Umar b. al-Khaṭṭāb reported the Apostle of Allah (may peace be upon

218. There are some special timings and moments when one's supplication is certainly granted by Allah. One of these timings is a pause between the *adhān* and the *iqāmah*.

219. Response to the *adhān* is necessary according to the Ḥanafīs, Ahl al-Ẓāhir and Ibn Wahb. Others hold that it is desirable and not necessary to respond to the *adhān* (*'Awn al-Ma'būd*, I, 206).

220. If one hears the *adhān*, one should repeat all the phrases pronounced by the *mu'adhdhin*, except the words "Come to prayer" and "Come to salvation." When one hears these words, one should say: "There is no might and no power except in Allah, the High, the Mighty." And in the *adhān* for the morning prayer, when the *mu'adhdhin* says: "Prayer is better than sleep," one should make a response : "You spoke the truth, and you did a good work, and you pronounced what is right" (*'Awn al-Ma'būd*, I, 206).

221. This means that they get a great reward by making the call to prayer.

him) as saying: When the *mu'adhdhin* says: "Allah is most great, Allah is most great," and one of you says in response: Allah is most great, "Allah is most great."; then says: "I testify that there is no god but Allah," and he says in response: "I testify that there is no god but Allah"; then says: "I testify that Muḥammad is the Apostle of Allah," and he makes the response: "I testify that Muḥammad is the Apostle of Allah": then says: "Come to prayer," and he makes the response: "There is no might and no power except in Allah"; then says: "Come to salvation," and he makes the response: "There is no might and no power except in Allah"; then says: "Allah is most great, Allah is most great," and he makes the response: "Allah is most great", then says: "There is no god but Allah"; if he says this from his heart, he will enter Paradise.

Chapter 187

WHAT SHOULD A MAN SAY WHEN HE HEARS THE *IQĀMAH*

(528) Abū Umāmah, or one of the Companions of the Prophet (may peace be upon him), said that Bilāl began the *iqāmah*, and when he said: "The time for prayer has come," the Prophet (may peace be upon him) said: "May Allah establish it and cause it to continue." During the whole of the *iqāmah* he made such responses as are found in 'Umar's tradition about the *adhān*.

Chapter 188

SUPPLICATION AFTER *ADHĀN*

(529) Jābir b. 'Abd Allah reported the Apostle of Allah (may peace be upon him) as saying: If anyone says when he hears the call to prayer: "O Allah, Lord of this perfect call and of the prayer which is established for all time, grant Muḥammad the *wasīlah*[222] and excellency, and raise him up in a praiseworthy position which Thou hast promised,"[223] he will be assured of my intercession.

Chapter 189

WHAT SHOULD A MAN SAY WHEN HE HEARS THE *ADHĀN* FOR SUNSET PRAYER

(530) Umm Salamah said: The Apostle of Allah (may peace be upon him)

222. *Wasilah* is a rank in Paradise as explained in a previous tradition (No. 523).
223. Cf. Qur'ān, xvii. 79.

taught me to say when the *adhān* for the sunset prayer was called ; "O Allah, this is the time when Thy night comes on, Thy day retires, and the voices of Thy summoners are heard, so forgive me."

Chapter 190

ON TAKING CHARGES FOR CALLING *ADHĀN*

(531) 'Uthman b. Abū al-'Āṣ said : Apostle of Allah, appoint me the leader of the tribe in prayer. He said : You are their leader, but you should follow on who is the weakest of them :[224] and appoint a *mu'adhdhin* who does not charge for the calling of *adhān*.[225]

Chapter 191

ON CALLING THE *ADHĀN* BEFORE ITS PRESCRIBED TIME

(532) Ibn 'Umar reported : Bilāl made a call to prayer before the break of dawn ; the Prophet (may peace be upon him), therefore, commanded him to return and make a call : Lo ! the servant of Allah (i.e. I) had slept (hence this mistake). The version of Mūsā has the addition : He returned and made a call : Lo ! the servant of Allah had slept.

Abū Dāwūd said : None except Ḥammād b. Salamah has narrated this tradition from Ayyūb.

(533) Nāfi' reported : A *mu'adhdhin* of 'Umar, named Masrūḥ, called the *adhān* for the morning prayer before the break of dawn ; 'Umar commanded him (to repeat). The narrator reported the tradition in a similar way.

Abū Dāwūd said : This tradition has been narrated by al-Darāwardī from 'Ubaid Allah on the authority of Ibn 'Umar, saying : There was a *mu'adhdhin* of 'Umar, named Mas'ūd. He then narrated the rest of the tradition. This version is more correct than that one.

224 The leader in prayer does not follow anyone ; in fact, others follow him. This means that the *imām* should have consideration for a weak person in the congregation. He should recite small sūrahs and should not lengthen bowing and prostration. This is necessary for the *imām* because there are different sorts of people in the congregation.

225. According to the majority of scholars, the charges for calling *adhān* is disapproved. Only Mālik allows the taking of compensation for the pronouncement of *adhān* (*'Awn al-Ma'būd*, I, 209). In modern time some scholars have provided relaxation in taking charges for calling the *adhān*. According to them, it is permissible because sometimes a *mu'adhdhin* has to devote his whole time to the mosque.

(534) Bilāl reported that the Apostle of Allah (may peace be upon him) said to him: Do not call *adhān* until the dawn appears clearly to you in this way, stretching his hand in latitude.[226]

Abū Dāwūd said: Shaddād did not see Bilāl.

Chapter 192

ON CALLING THE *ADHĀN* BY A BLIND MAN

(535) 'Ā'ishah reported: Ibn Umm Maktūm was the *mu'adhdhin* of the Apostle of Allah (may peace be upon him) and he was blind.[227]

Chapter 193

ON GOING OUT FROM THE MOSQUE AFTER THE *ADHĀN* HAS BEEN PRONOUNCED

(536) Abū al-Sha'thā' said: We were sitting with Abū Hurairah in the mosque. A man went out of the mosque after the *adhān* for the afternoon prayer had been called. Abū Hurairah said: As regards this (man), he disobeyed Abū al-Qāsim,[228] i.e. the Prophet (may peace be upon him).

Chapter 194

ON THE WAITING OF *MU'ADHDHIN* FOR THE ARRIVAL OF THE *IMĀM*

(537) Jābir b. Samurah said: Bilāl would call the *adhān*, then he used to wait. When he would see that the Prophet (may peace be upon him) had come out (of his

226. It is disputed amongst the scholars whether the *adhān* for the morning prayer is valid before the break of dawn. Mālik, Ibn al-Mubārak, al-Shāfi'i, Aḥmad and Isḥāq are of opinion that it is valid and need not be repeated after the break of dawn. Sufyān al-Thawrī and Abū Ḥanīfah maintain that the *adhān* before the break of dawn is not valid; it should be repeated after the break of dawn (*'Awn al-Ma'būd*, I, 210-11).

227. This indicates that the *adhān* of a blind man is valid. In fact, Ibn Umm Maktūm was informed by the people about the break of dawn, saying: "The morning has come, the morning has come" (*'Awn al-Ma'būd*, I, 211).

228. In another tradition the Prophet (may peace be upon him) has expressly forbidden to go out of the mosque after the *adhān* has been called. But this prohibition applies to a man who goes out without any necessity. In case a person goes out of the mosque for a certain necessity, say, for taking a bath or for urination, etc., he is allowed to go out. There is no prohibition in the case of need (*'Awn al-Ma'būd* I, 211).

house), he would pronounce the *iqāma*.[229]

Chapter 195

ON CALLING THE PEOPLE TO PRAYER EVEN AFTER THE *ADHĀN* HAS BEEN PRONOUNCED (*TATHWĪB*)

(538) Mujāhid reported: I was in the company of Ibn 'Umar. A person invited the people for the noon or afternoon prayer (after the *adhān* had been called). He said: Go out with us (from this mosque) because this is an innovation (in religion).[230]

Chapter 196

IF THE *IQĀMAH* IS PRONOUNCED, AND THE *IMĀM* DOES NOT COME, THE PEOPLE SHOULD WAIT FOR HIM SITTING (AND NOT STANDING)

(539) Abū Qatādah reported on the authority of his father: The Prophet (may peace be upon him) said: When the *iqāmah* for prayer is pronounced, do not stand until you see me.[231]

Abū Dāwūd said: This has been narrated by Ayyūb and Ḥajjāj al-Ṣawwāf from Yaḥyā and Hishām al-Dustawā'ī in a similar way, saying: Yaḥya wrote to me (in this way). And this has been narrated by Mu'āwiyah b. Sallām and 'Alī b. al-Mubārak

229. Some other traditions show that the Prophet (may peace be upon him) remained in his house. When he heard the *iqāmah*, he would come out to lead in prayer.

230. The pronouncement of the words in addition to the words prescribed for the *adhān* is called *tathwib*. The *iqāmah* is also sometimes called *tathwib*. Similarly, the words "Prayer is better than sleep" are also known as *tathwib*. These words are recommended to be pronounced in the *adhān* for the morning prayer. If they are pronounced in the *adhān* for other prayers, this practice will be disapproved. Likewise, the practice prevalent in modern times to invite people for prayer after the *adhān* has been pronounced is disapproved ('*Awn al-Ma'būd*, I, 211).

231. It is permissible to pronounce the *iqāmah* in the absence of the *imām*. This tradition indicates that the people should remain sitting if the *imām* is not present in the mosque. They should stand in rows when the *imām* comes. If the *imām* is present in the mosque or in the congregation, the people are allowed to stand in rows from the beginning when the *iqāmah* is pronounced. According to Abū Ḥanīfah, it is commendable to stand in rows when the words 'Come to salvation" are pronounced, and when the words "The time for prayer has come", are uttered, the *imām* should pronounce the first *takbir* to begin the prayer. And according to Sa'īd b. al-Musayyib it is desirable to stand in rows when the *mu'adhdhin* utters "Allah is most great." When he utters "Come to prayer," the rows should be straightened and be ready for prayer. And when he pronounces "There is no god but Allah" the *imām* should pronounce takbīr to start the prayer ('*Awn al-Ma'būd*, I, 213).

from Yaḥyā: "Until you see me and show tranquillity."

(540) This tradition has also been reported through a different chain of narrators in a similar way. This ve sion says: "Until you see me that I have come out."

Abū Dāwūd said: No one except Ma'mar has narrated the words "that I have come out." And the version transmitted by Ibn 'Uyainah from Ma'mar does not mention the words "that I have come out."

(541) Abū Hurairah reported: When the *iqāmah* was pronounced for prayer during the time of the Apostle of Allah (may peace be upon him), the people would take their seats before the Prophet (may peace be upon him) came to his seat.[232]

(542) Ḥumaid reported: I asked Thābit al-Bunānī whether it was permissible for a man to talk after the *qāmah* had been pronounced He narrated a tradition on the authority of Anas: (Once) the *iqāmah* was pronounced, and a person came to the Apostle of Allah (may peace be upon him) and detained him after the *iqāmah* had been pronounced.

(543) 'Awn b. Kahmas reported on the authority of his father Kahmas: We stood for praying at Minā when the *imām* had not come out. Some of us sat down (and I too). An old man from Kūfah said to me: Why did you sit down? I said: Ibn Buraïdah, this is *sumud*[233] (i.e. waiting for the *imām* in the standing condition). The old man then narrated a tradition from 'Abd al-Raḥmān b. 'Awsajah on the authority of al-Barā' b. 'Āzib: We would stand in rows during the time of the Apostle of Allah (may peace be upon him) for a long time before he pronounced *takbīr*. He further said: Allah, the Exalted and Mighty, sends blessings and the angels invoke blessings for those who are nearer to the front rows. No step is more liking to Allah than a step which one takes to join the row (of the prayer).[234]

(544) Anas reported: The *iqāmah* was pronounced (for the night prayer) and the Apostle of Allah (may peace be upon him) remained engaged in talking (to a person) in the corner of the mosque. He did not begin prayer until the people slept.

(545) Abū al-Naḍr said: When the *iqāmah* was pronounced and the Apostle of Allah (may peace be upon him) saw that they (the people) were small in number, he

232. This means that the people would remain sitting at their seats until the Prophet (may peace be upon him) reached his seat.

233. *Sumūd* literally means "to stand raising one's head and projecting one's chest showing one's pride and conceit." It is reported about 'Alī that once he came out while the people were waiting for him standing in the rows for prayer. He disliked this practice, and said: How is it that I see you standing in a proud and conceited manner? Ibrāhīm al-Nakha'ī is reported to have said that it was disapproved to wait for the *imām* standing in the rows of prayer. This practice was called *sumūd* (*'Awn al-Ma'būd*, I, 213).

234. Many other traditions indicate that standing in the front rows of the prayer carries more reward than standing in the rear. Further, a number of traditions emphasise the straightening of the rows and standing tightly in the rows so that no room is left between two persons.

would sit down, and would not pray; but when he saw them (the people) large in number, he would pray.

(546) This tradition has been transmitted through a different chain of narrators in a similar way by 'Alī b. Abī Ṭālib.

Chapter 197

STRICT ORDERS THAT THE PRAYER IN CONGREGATION SHOULD NOT BE ABANDONED

(547) Abū al-Dardā' reported: I heard the Apostle of Allah (may peace be upon him) say: If there are three men in a village or in the desert among whom prayer is not offered (in congregation), the devil has got the mastery over them. So observe (prayer) in congregation, for the wolf eats only the straggling animal.

Sā'ib said: By the word *jamā'ah* he meant saying prayer in company or in congregation.

(548) Abū Hurairah reported the Apostle of Allah (may peace be upon him) as saying: I thought to give orders for arranging prayer in congregation, and then to have the *iqāmah* called for it, then to order a man to lead the people in prayer, then to go off in company of the people who have bundles of firewood to those people who are not present at the prayer and then to burn down their houses with fire.[235]

(549) Abū Hurairah reported the Apostle of Allah (may peace be upon him) as saying: I thought about giving orders to some youths for gathering a bundle of firewood, then going off to some people who offer their prayers in their homes without any excuse, and burning down their houses over them.

I (Yazīd b. Yazīd) said: I asked Yazīd b. al-Aṣamm: Abū 'Awf did he mean Friday (prayer) or any other? He replied: May my ears become deaf if I have not heard Abū Hurairah narrating it from the Apostle of Allah (may peace be upon him): He did not mention Friday (prayer) or any other.

(550) 'Abd Allah b. Mas'ūd said: Persevere in observing these five times of prayer where the announcement for them is made, because they are from the paths of right guidance. And Allah, the Mighty, the Majestic, has laid down for His Prophet (may peace be upon him) the paths of right guidance. I have seen the time when no one stayed away from prayer except a hypocrite whose hypocrisy was well

235. This and other traditions indicate the significance of offering prayer in congregation. The congregation is not obligatory. But it has been recommended most emphatically in the traditions of the Prophet (may peace be upon him). One can imagine the importance of congregation from this tradition. It is, however, permissible to abandon the congregation on account of some valid reason, say, illness, heavy rain, severe cold and similar other excuses The prayer is valid if one offers it at home without any excuse. But one will not get the reward for attending congregation.

known. I witnessed the time when a man would be brought swaying between two men till he was set up in the row (of the prayer). Every one of us has a mosque of his in his house. If you were to pray in your houses and stay away from your mosques, you would abandon the *sunnah* (practice) of your Prophet, and if you were to abandon the *sunnah* (practice) of your Prophet, you would become an unbeliever.[237]

(551) Ibn 'Abbās reported the Apostle of Allah (may peace be upon him) as saying: If anyone hears him who makes the call to prayer and is not prevented from joining the congregation by any excuse—he was asked what an excuse consisted of and replied that it was fear or illness—the prayer he offers will not be accepted from him.[238] Abū Dāwūd said: Abū Isḥāq has narrated from Maghrā'.

(552) Ibn Umm Maktūm asked the Prophet (may peace be upon him) saying: Apostle of Allah, I am a blind man, my house is far away (from the mosque), and I have a guide who does not follow me. Is it possible that permission be granted to me for saying prayer in my house? He asked: Do you hear summons (*adhān*)? He said: Yes. He said: I do not find any permission for you.[239]

(553) Ibn Umm Maktūm said: Apostle of Allah, there are many venomous creatures and wild beasts in Medina (so allow me to pray in my house because I am blind). The Prophet (may peace be upon him) said: Do you hear the call, "Come to prayer," "Come to salvation"? (He said: Yes.) Then you must come.

Abū Dāwūd said: Al-Qāsim al-Jarmī has narrated this tradition from Sufyān in a similar manner. But his version does not contain the words "Then you must come."

Chapter 198

EXCELLENCE OF PRAYING IN CONGREGATION

(554) Ubayy b. Ka'b said: The Apostle of Allah (may peace be upon him) led us

237. In this tradition great emphasis is laid on the adherence to the model behaviour and practice of the Prophet (may peace be upon him). A man does not become an unbeliever by abandoning a *sunnah* (practice) of the Prophet (may peace be upon him). This also shows the excellence and importance of praying in congregation.

238. This means that the prayer will not be accepted as fully as the prayer in congregation. This does not mean that the prayer will not be accepted at all.

It is worthy of note that the chain of this tradition is not sound. A narrator named Abū Janab is weak (*'Awn al-Ma'būd*, I, 216).

239. In the early days of Islam prayer in congregation was an important factor to integrate the Muslim community. Further, the Muslims used to learn about Islam from the Prophet (may peace be upon him) after the prayer. Had they absented themselves from the congregation, they would not have benefited from him. Hence the Prophet (may peace be upon him) did not allow Ibn Umm Maktūm to stay away from the congregation.

in the dawn prayer one day. And he said: Is so and so present? They said: No. He (again) asked: Is so and so present? They replied: No. He then said: These two prayers are the ones which are most burdensome to hypocrites. If you knew what they contain (i.e. blessings), you would come to them, even though you had to crawl on your knees. The first row is like that of the angels, and if you knew the nature of its excellence, you would race to join it. A man's prayer said along with another is purer than his prayer said alone, and his prayer with two men is purer than his prayer with one, but if there are more it is more pleasing to Allah, the Almighty, the Majestic.

(555) 'Uthmān b. 'Affān reported the Apostle of Allah (may peace be upon him) as saying: If anyone says the night prayer in congregation, he is like one who keeps vigil (in prayer) till midnight; and he who says both the night and dawn prayers in congregation is like one who keeps vigil (in prayer) the whole night.

Chapter 199

ON THE EXCELLENCE OF WALKING FOR PRAYER IN CONGREGATION

(556) Abū Hurairah reported the Prophet (may peace be upon him) as saying: The further one is from the mosque, the greater will be one's reward.[240]

(557) Ubayy b. Ka'b said: There was a certain person, out of all the people of Medina, who used to pray in the mosque. I do not know that any one of them lived at a farther distance than that man. Still he never missed the prayer in congregation in the mosque. I said: It would be better if you buy a donkey and ride it in heat and darkness. He said: I do not like that my house be by the side of the mosque. The discourse reached the Apostle of Allah (may peace be upon him). He asked him about it. He said: I did it so that my walking to the mosque and my return to my home when I return be recorded. He said: Allah has granted all this to you; Allah has granted all that you reckoned.

(558) Abū Umāmah reported the Apostle of Allah (may peace be upon him) said: If anyone goes out from his house after performing ablution for saying the prescribed prayer in congregation (in the mosque), his reward will be like that of one who goes for *Ḥajj* pilgrimage after wearing *iḥrām* (robe worn by the *Ḥajj* pilgrims). And he

240. Many other traditions indicate that one who walks to the mosque to pray in congregation, gets a blessing at every step. Therefore, the more distance one covers, the more blessings one gets.

who goes out to say the mid-morning (*ḍuḥā*) prayer,[241] and takes the trouble for this purpose, will take the reward like that of a person who performs *'Umrah.*[242] And a prayer followed by a prayer with no worldly talk during the gap between them will be recorded in *'illīyyīn.*[243]

(559) Abū Hurairah reported the Apostle of Allah (may peace be upon him) as saying: Prayer said by a man in congregation is twenty-five degrees more excellent than prayer said by him alone in his house or in the market. This is because when any of you performs ablution and does it perfectly, and goes out to the mosque having no intention except praying, and nothing moves him except prayer, then at every step which he takes his rank is elevated by one degree on account of this (walking), and one sin is remitted from him for this (walking), till he enters the mosque. When he enters the mosque, he will be reckoned as praying so long as he will be detained by the prayer. The angels keep on invoking blessings on any of you so long as he remains seated in the place he prayed, saying: O Allah, forgive him; O Allah, have mercy on him; O Allah, accept his repentance so long as he does not harm anyone, or breaks his ablution.

(560) Abū Sa'īd al-Khudrī reported the Apostle of Allah (may peace be upon him) as saying: Prayer in congregation is equivalent to twenty-five prayers (offered alone). If he prays in a jungle, and performs its bowing and prostrations perfectly, it becomes equivalent to fifty prayers (in respect of reward).[244]

Abū Dāwūd said: 'Abd al-Wāḥid b. Ziyād narrated in his version of this tradition: "Prayer said by a single person in a jungle is more excellent by multiplied degrees than prayer said in congregation."[245]

241. This is a supererogatory prayer offered after the sunrise or in mid-morning when the sun becomes hot and bright. The prayer said after the rise of the sun contains two or four *rak'ahs* and the prayer said in mid-morning consists of eight *rak'ahs*. Some traditions of the Prophet (may peace be upon him) indicate the excellence of this prayer and abundant reward for it.

242. *'Umrah* is performed after wearing *iḥrām* by circumambulating the Ka'bah and by running between the hills of Ṣafā' and Marwah at Mecca. There is no time specified for *'Umrah*. One can perform it at any time during the year.

243. *Illiyyin* literally means high places. This word occurs in the Qur'anic verses lxxxiii, 18-19. It has been interpreted as the place where the Register of the Righteous is kept. It contains every detail of the righteous. But this is all to be understood in a metaphorical sense. (See Eng. tr. of the Qur'ān by 'Abdullah Yūsuf 'Alī, footnote 6019.)

244. Some traditions recorded by Bukhārī and Muslim indicate that prayer said in congregation is twenty-seven degrees more excellent than prayer offered alone.

245. The reason is that one offers prayer in a jungle where no one sees him except Allah. Moreover, when he prays, the angels pray along with him. But it is necessary that such a person should pronounce the *adhān* and the *iqāmah*.

Chapter 200

ON THE EXCELLENCE OF WALKING FOR PRAYER IN DARKNESS

(561) Buraidah reported the Prophet (may peace be upon him) as saying : Give good tidings to those who walk to the mosques in darkness for having a perfect light on the Day of Judgment.

Chapter 201

IN WHAT MANNER SHOULD A MAN WALK TO THE MOSQUE FOR PRAYING ?

(562) Abū Thumamah al-Ḥannāṭ said that Ka'b b. 'Ujrah met him while he was going to the mosque ; one of the two (companions) met his companion (on his way to the mosque). And he met me crossing the fingers of my both hands. He prohibited me to do so, and said : The Apostle of Allah (may peace be upon him) has said : If any of you performs ablution, and performs his ablution perfectly, and then goes out intending for the mosque, he should not cross the fingers of his hands because he is already in prayer.[246]

(563) Sa'id b. al-Musayyib said : A person from the Anṣār (Helpers of the Prophet) was breathing his last. He said : I narrate to you a tradition, and I narrate it with the intention of getting a reward from Allah. I heard the Apostle of Allah (may peace be upon him) say : If any one of you performs ablution and performs it very well, and goes out for prayer, he does not take his right step but Allah records a good work (or blessing) for him, and he does not take his left step but Allah remits one sin from him. Any one of you may reside near the mosque or far from it ; if he comes to the mosque and prays in congregation, he will be forgiven (by Allah). If he comes to the mosque while the people had prayed in part, and the prayer remained in part, and he prays in congregation the part he joined, and completed the part he had missed, he will enjoy similarly (i.e. he will be forgiven). If he comes to the mosque when the people had finished prayer, he will enjoy the same.

246. In a number of traditions the act of crossing or snapping the fingers has been prohibited during prayer. This is the sign of laziness. One gets the reward of prayer when one goes out intending for the mosque. Hence the prohibition to cross the fingers after performing ablution.

Chapter 202

ON A PERSON WHO CAME OUT FROM HIS HOUSE INTENDING TO PRAY IN THE MOSQUE, BUT THE PRAYER IN CONGREGATION HAD BEEN FINISHED

(564) Abū Hurairah reported the Prophet (may peace be upon him) as saying: Whoever performs ablution, and performs his ablution perfectly, and then goes to the mosque and finds that the people had finished the prayer (in congregation), Allah will give him a reward like one who prayed in congregation and attended it; the reward of those who prayed in congregation will not be curtailed.

Chapter 203

ON WOMEN VISITING THE MOSQUE FOR PRAYER

(565) Abū Hurairah reported the Apostle of Allah (may peace be upon him) as saying: Do not prevent the female servants of Allah from visiting the mosques of Allah, but they may go out (to the mosque) having not perfumed themselves.[247]

(566) Ibn 'Umar reported the Apostle of Allah (may peace be upon him) as saying: Do not prevent the female servants of Allah from visiting the mosques of Allah.

(567) Ibn 'Umar reported the Apostle of Allah (may peace be upon him) as saying: Do not prevent your women from visiting the mosques; but their houses are better for them (for praying).[248]

(568) 'Abd Allah b. 'Umar reported the Prophet (may peace be upon him) as saying: Allow women to visit the mosques at night. A son of his (Bilāl) said: I swear by Allah, we shall certainly not allow them because they will defraud. I swear by Allah, we shall not allow them. He (Ibn 'Umar) abused him and became angry at him and said: I tell you that the Apostle of Allah (may peace be upon him) said: Allow them; yet you say: We shall not allow them.[249]

247. The attendance of women at the congregational prayer in the mosque after using scents is forbidden. Their attendance at the mosques without using perfume is disputed among the scholars. On the basis of this and similar other traditions a group of scholars allow them unconditionally to attend the mosques. Another group prohibits those who are too young and allow only those women who are old. A third group allow them to attend only the morning and night prayers and not all prayers. A fourth group do not allow them to attend the congregational prayer at all. All these views are supported by the traditions of the Prophet (may peace be upon him).

248. This shows that the Prophet (may peace be upon him) of course allowed women to attend the congregational prayer, but he never exhorted them to do so. Instead, he taught that it was better for women to pray in their houses.

249. Ibn 'Umar became angry because his son behaved imprudently with the tradition of the Prophet (may peace be upon him). His interpretation might be correct, but his tone and response were audacious.

Chapter 204

ON STRICT PREVENTION OF WOMEN FROM ATTENDING PRAYER IN THE MOSQUE

(569) 'Ā'ishah (Allah be pleased with her), the wife of the Prophet (may peace be upon him), said : If the Apostle of Allah (may peace be upon him) had seen what the women have invented, he would have prevented them from visiting the mosque (for praying), as the women of the children of Israel were prevented. Yaḥyā (the narrator) said : I asked 'Umrah : Were the women of Israel prevented ? She said : Yes.

(570) 'Abd Allah (b. Mas'ūd) reported the Prophet (may peace be upon him) as saying : It is more excellent for a woman to pray in her house than in her courtyard, and more excellent for her to pray in her private chamber than in her house.

(571) Ibn 'Umar reported the Apostle of Allah (may peace be upon him) as saying : If we reserve this door for women (it would be better). Nāfi' said : Ibn 'Umar did not enter through it (the door) till he died.

Abū Dāwūd said : This tradition has been narrated through a different chain of transmitters by 'Umar. And this is more correct.

Chapter 205

ON RUNNING FOR PRAYER

(572) Abū Hurairah said : I heard the Apostle of Allah (may peace be upon him) say : When the *iqāmah* is pronounced for prayer, do not come to it running, but come walking (slowly). You should observe tranquillity. The part of the prayer you get (along with the *imām*) offer it ; and the part you miss complete it (afterwards).

Abū Dāwūd said : The version narrated by al-Zubaidī, Ibn Abī Dhi'b, Ibrāhīm b. Sa'd, Ma'mar, Shu'aib b. Abī Ḥamzah on the authority of al-Zuhrī has the words : "the part you miss then complete it". Ibn 'Uyainah alone narrated from al-Zuhrī the words "then offer it afterwards". And Muḥammad b. 'Amr narrated from Abū Salamah on the authority of Abū Hurairah, and Ja'far b. Rabī'ah narrated from al-A'raj on the authority of Abū Hurairah the words "then complete it". And Ibn Mas'ūd narrated from the Prophet (may peace be upon him) and Abū Qatādah and Anas reported from the Prophet (may peace be upon him) the words "then complete it".

(573) Abū Hurairah reported the Prophet (may peace be upon him) as saying : Come to prayer with calmness and tranquillity. Then pray the part you get (along with the *imām*) and complete afterwards the part you miss.

Abū Dāwūd said : Ibn Sīrīn narrated from Abū Hurairah the words : "he should complete it afterwards". Similarly, Abū Rāfi' narrated from Abū Hurairah and Abū Dharr narrated from him the words "then complete it, and complete it afterwards." There is a variation of words in the narration from him.

Chapter 206

ON HOLDING THE CONGREGATIONAL PRAYER IN THE MOSQUE TWICE

(574) Abū Sa'īd al-Khudrī said: The Apostle of Allah (may peace be upon him) saw a person praying alone. He said: Is there any man who may do good with this (man) and pray along with him.[250]

Chapter 207

IF A MAN PRAYS IN HIS HOUSE, AND GETS CONGREGATIONAL PRAYER IN THE MOSQUE, HE SHOULD PRAY IN CONGREGATION

(575) Yazīd b. al-Aswad reported that he prayed along with the Apostle of Allah (may peace be upon him) when he was a young boy. When he (the Prophet) had prayed there were two persons (sitting) in the corner of the mosque; they did not pray (along with the Prophet). He called for them. They were brought trembling (before him). He asked: What prevented you from praying along with us? They replied: We have already prayed in our houses. He said: Do not do so. If any of you prays in his house and finds that the *imām* has not prayed, he should pray along wiih him; and that will be a supererogatory prayer for him.[251]

(576) Jābir b. Yazīd reported on the authority of his father: I said the morning

250. The question of establising the congregational prayer twice in the mosque is disputed among the scholars. This tradition indicates that it is permissible to pray in congregation twice in the mosque. This is held by Aḥmad b. Ḥanbal, Isḥāq and others. Some scholars maintain that it is not permissible to establish the congregational prayer again if it has been once held. Those who come late and miss the first congregation should say their prayer alone and not in congregation. This is maintained by Sufyān, Ibn al-Mubārak, Mālik and al-Shāfi'ī (*'Awn al-Ma'būd*, I, 225).

251. This shows that a person can repeat his prayer along with the *imām* if he has prayed alone in his house. There is no exception in favour of any prayer according to this tradition. This is held by Aḥmad b. Ḥanbal, Isḥāq, al-Shāfi'ī, al-Ḥasan and al-Zuhrī. Mālik and Sufyān al-Thawrī maintained that one should not repeat the sunset prayer in congregation if one has said it alone. Abū Ḥanīfah is of opinion that one should not repeat the morning, afternoon and sunset prayers if one has said them alone. According to him, the supererogatory prayer is not allowed after the morning and afternoon prayers. As regards the sunset prayer, it is not to be repeated because supererogatory prayer does not contain three *rak'ahs*. It contains only two or four *rak'ahs* (*'Awn al-Ma'būd*, I, 225).

prayer along with the Prophet (may peace be upon him) at Minā. He narrated the rest of the tradition to the same effect.

(577) Yazīd b. 'Āmir reported: I came while the Prophet (may peace be upon him) was saying the prayer. I sat down and did not pray along with them. The Apostle of Allah (may peace be upon him) turned towards us and saw that Yazīd was sitting there. He said: Did you not embrace Islam, Yazīd? He replied: Why not, Apostle of Allah; I have embraced Islam. He said: What prevented you from saying prayer along with the people? He replied: I have already prayed in my house, and I thought that you had prayed (in congregation). He said: When you come to pray (in the mosque) and find the people praying, then you should pray along with them, though you have already prayed. This will be a supererogatory prayer for you and that will be counted as obligatory.

(578) A man from Banū Asad b. Khuzaimah asked Abū Ayyūb al-Anṣārī: If one of us prays in his house, then comes to the mosque and finds that the *iqāmah* is being called, and if I pray along with them (in congregation), I feel something inside about it. Abū Ayyūb replied: We asked the Prophet (may peace be upon him) about it. He said: That is a share from the spoils received by the warriors (i.e. he will receive double the reward of the prayer).

Chapter 208

IF A MAN PRAYS IN CONGREGATION, THEN FINDS ANOTHER PRAYER IN CONGREGATION (IN ANOTHER MOSQUE), SHOULD HE REPEAT IT?

(579) Sulaimān, the freed slave of Maimūnah, said: I came to Ibn 'Umar at Bilāṭ (a place in Medina) while the people were praying. I said: Do you not pray along with them? He said: I heard the Apostle of Allah (may peace be upon him) say: Do not say a prayer twice in a day.[252]

Chapter 209

ON LEADING IN PRAYER AND ITS EXCELLENCE

(580) 'Uqbah b. 'Āmir said: I heard the Apostle of Allah (may peace be upon him) say: He who leads the people in prayer, and he does so at the right time, will receive, as well as those who are led (in prayer) will get (the reward). He who delays

252. This means that one should not pray twice an obligatory prayer. But one may say prayer twice in such a way that once he should say obligatory prayer and repeat it as supererogatory prayer and not obligatory. If a man has said prayer in congregation, he can repeat it in congregation as a supererogatory prayer (*'Awn al-Ma'būd*, I, 226).

(prayer) from the appointed time will be responsible (for this delay) and not those who are led in prayer.[253]

Chapter 210

ON DISAPPROVAL OF QUARRELLING ABOUT THE *IMĀMATE*

(581) Sulāmah daughter of al-Ḥurr and sister of Kharshah b. al-Ḥurr al-Fazārī said: I heard the Apostle of Allah (may peace be upon him) say: One of the signs of the Last Hour will be that people in a mosque will refuse to act as *imām* and will not find an *imām* to lead them in prayer.

Chapter 211

WHO IS MOST DESERVING FOR THE *IMĀMATE*

(582) Abū Mas'ūd al-Badrī reported the Apostle of Allah (may peace be upon him) as saying: The one of you who is most versed in the Book of Allah should act as *imām* for the people; and the one who is the earliest of them in reciting (the Qur'ān);[254] if they are equally versed in reciting it, then the earliest of them to emigrate (to Medina); if they emigrated at the same time, then the oldest of them. No man must lead another in prayer in his house[255] (i.e. in the house of the latter) or where the latter has authority,[256] or sit in his place of honour without his permission.[257] Shu'bah said: I asked Ismā'īl: What is the meaning of his place of honour? He replied: His throne.

253. If the *imām* leads the people in time, both the *imām* and the people who are led will get the reward. In the case of delay on the part of *imām* he will be sinful and not the people.

254. The other versions of this tradition, as expressed by Abū Dāwūd himself in the following traditions, have the words "the earliest of them to emigrate (to Medina)". According to the tradition recorded by Muslim, the order is as follows: One who is well versed in reciting the Qur'ān, then the one who has most knowledge of the *Sunnah*, then the one who is the earliest to emigrate, then the one who is the oldest of them (*'Awn al-Ma'būd*, I, 227).

255. This means that the owner of the house is more entitled for acting as *imām* than an outsider provided the owner is competent (*'Awn al-Ma'būd*, I, 227).

256. This applies to the Friday and festival prayers because the ruler or the governor leads the people in these prayers. They are the authorities who will act as *imām* on such occasions. As regards the obligatory prayers, one who is competent should lead the people in prayer. In case a ruler is a learned man, he may act as *imām* in obligatory prayers (*'Awn al-Ma'būd*, I, 227).

257. In a meeting or a gathering if there is an eminent person, who has a special place where he is generally seated and feels honour for this seat, others are not allowed to sit in his place without his permission. These are the ethics of a gathering taught by the Prophet (may peace be upon him).

(583) The version of this tradition narrated through a different chain by Shu'bah has the words: "A man should not lead another man in prayer."

Abū Dāwūd said: Yaḥyā al-Qaṭṭān narrated from Shu'bah in a similar way, i.e. the earliest of them in recitation.

(584) This tradition has been transmitted through a different chain by Abū Mas'ūd. This version has the words: "If they are equally versed in recitation, then the one who has most knowledge of the *Sunnah*; if they are equal with regard to (the knowledge of) the *Sunnah*, then the earliest of them to emigrate (to Medina)."[258] He did not narrate the words: "The earliest of them in recitation."

Abū Dāwūd said: Ḥajjāj b. Arṭāta reported from Ismā'īl: Do not sit in the place of honour of anyone except with his permission.

(585) 'Amr b. Salamah said: We lived at a place where the people would pass by us when they came to the Prophet (may peace be upon him). When they returned, they would again pass by us. And they used to inform us that the Apostle of Allah (may peace be upon him) said so-and-so. I was a boy with a good memory. From this (process) I memorised a large portion of the Qur'ān. Then my father went to the Apostle of Allah (may peace be upon him) along with a group of his clan. He (the Prophet) taught them prayer. And he said: The one of you who knows most of the Qur'ān should act as your *imām*. I knew the Qur'ān better than most of them because I had memorised it. They, therefore, put me in front of them, and I would lead them in prayer. I wore a small yellow mantle which, when I prostrated myself, went up on me, and a woman of the clan said: Cover the backside of your leader from us. So they bought an 'Ammānī shirt for me, and I have never been so pleased about anything after embracing Islam as I was about that (shirt). I used to lead them in prayer and I was only seven or eight years old.[259]

(586) This tradition has also been transmitted through a different chain by 'Amr b. Salamah. This version says: "I used to lead them in prayer with a sheet of cloth on me that was patched and torn. When I prostrated myself, my buttocks were disclosed."

258. During the lifetime of the Prophet (may peace be upon him) the Companions emigrated to Medina, some along with the Prophet (may peace be upon him) and others after him. The earlier one emigrated, the more honour, merit and excellence he deserved. But in modern times the merit due to emigration has ceased to exist. As such, a person whose ancestors embraced Islam earlier will deserve this merit (*'Awn al-Ma'būd*, I, 228).

259. It is disputed among the scholars whether a minor can lead the people in prayer. Al-Ḥasan al-Baṣrī and Isḥāq b. Rahwaih allow it. Al-Shāfi'ī maintains that a minor can lead the people in prayer provided he understands well how to say the prayer. But he does not allow a minor to act as *imām* in the Friday prayer. Those who do not allow are 'Aṭā', al-Sha'bī, Mālik, al-Thawrī, al-Awzā'ī and Abū Ḥanīfah. Two statements have been attributed to Aḥmad. They interpret this tradition by saying that 'Amr b. Salamah acted as *imām* without the knowledge and order of the Prophet (may peace be upon him) (*'Awn al-Ma'būd*, I, 228-29).

(587) 'Amr b. Salamah reported on the authority of his father (Salamah) that they visited the Prophet (may peace be upon him). When they intended to return, they said: Apostle of Allah, who will lead us in prayer? He said: The one of you who knows most of the Qur'an, or memorises most of the Qur'ān, (should act as your *imām*). There was none in the clan who knew more of the Qur'ān than I did. They, therefore, put me in front of them and I was only a boy. And I wore a mantle. Whenever I was present in the gathering of Jarm (name of his clan), I would act as their *imām*, and I lead them in their funeral prayers until today.

Abū Dāwūd said: This tradition has been narrated by 'Amr b. Salamah through a different chain of transmitters. This version has: "When my clan visited the Prophet (may peace be upon him). . . ." He did not report it on the authority of his father.

(588) Ibn 'Umar said: When the first emigrants came (to Medina), they stayed at al-'Aṣbah (a place near Medina) before the advent of the Apostle of Allah (may peace be upon him). Sālim, the client of Abū Ḥudhaifah, acted as their *imām*, as he knew the Qur'ān better than all of them, al-Haitham (the narrator) added: And 'Umar b. al-Khaṭṭāb and Abū Salamah b. 'Abd al-Asad were among them.

(589) Malik b. al-Ḥuwairith said that the Prophet (may peace be upon him) told him or some of his companions: When the time of prayer comes, call the *adhān*, then call the *iqāmah*, then the one who is oldest of you should act as your *imām*.

The version narrated by Maslamah goes: He said: On that day we were almost equal in knowledge.

The version narrated by Ismā'īl says: Khālid said: I said to Abū Qilābah: Where is the Qur'ān (i.e. why did the Prophet (may peace be upon him) not say: The one who knows the Qur'ān most should act as *imām*)? He replied: Both of them were equal in the knowledge of the Qur'ān.

(590) Ibn 'Abbās reported the Apostle of Allah (may peace be upon him) as saying: Let the best among you call the *adhān* for you, and the Qur'ān-readers act as your *imāms*.

Chapter 212

THE IMĀMATE OF WOMEN

(591) Umm Waraqah daughter of Nawfal reported: When the Prophet (may peace be upon him) proceeded for the Battle of Badr, I said to him: Apostle of Allah allow me to accompany you in the battle. I shall act as a nurse for your patients. It is possible that Allah might bestow martyrdom upon me. He said: Stay at your home. Allah, the Almighty, will bestow martyrdom upon you. The narrator said: Hence she was called martyr. She read the Qur'ān. She sought permission from the Prophet (may peace be upon him) to have a *mu'adhdhin* in her house. He, therefore,

permitted her (to do so).[260] She announced that her slave and slave-girl would be free after her death. One night they went to her and strangled her with a sheet of cloth until she died, and they ran away. Next day 'Umar announced among the people: Anyone who has knowledge about them, or has seen them, should bring them (to him). 'Umar (after their arrest) ordered (to crucify them) and they were crucified. This was the first crucifixtion at Medina.

(592) This tradition has also been narrated through a different chain of transmitters by Umm Waraqah daughter of 'Abd Allah b. al-Hārith. The first version is complete. This version goes: The Apostle of Allah (may peace be upon him) used to visit her at her house. He appointed a *mu'adhdhin* to call *adhān* for her; and he commanded her to lead the inmates of her house in prayer. 'Abd al-Rahmān said: I saw her *mu'adhdhin* who was an old man.

Chapter 213

ON THE PERSON WHO ACTS AS *IMĀM* FOR THE PEOPLE WHO DISLIKE HIM

(593) Ibn 'Umar reported the Apostle of Allah (may peace be upon him) as saying: There are three types of people whose prayer is not accepted by Allah: One who goes in front of people when they do not like him; a man who comes *dıbāran*, which means that he comes to it too late; and a man who takes into slavery an emancipated male or female slave.

Chapter 214

THE IMĀMATE OF THE PIOUS AND IMPIOUS

(594) Abū Hurairah reported the Apostle of Allah (may peace be upon him) as saying: The obligatory prayer is essential behind every Muslim, pious or impious.

260. In this tradition there is no indication that Umm Waraqah acted as *imām*. But the other version of this tradition which follows (No. 592) indicates that the Prophet (may peace be upon him) commanded her to lead the inmates of her house in prayer. On the basis of this tradition a group of scholars maintain that a woman can act as *imām* for the people who reside with her in her house, although they include males. The majority of scholars hold that a woman can lead the women alone in prayer and not men. They argue from a number of traditions which indicate that 'Ā'ishah and Umm Salamah led women in prayer, and they stood in the middle of the row, and not in front of them They led both obligatory and supererogatory prayers. The case of Umm Waraqah was of a special type which cannot be generalised (*Awn al-Ma'būd*, I. 230-31).

even if he has committed grave sins.[261]

Chapter 215

THE IMĀMATE OF A BLIND MAN

(595) Anas said that the Prophet (may peace be upon him) appointed Ibn Umm Maktūm as substitute to lead the people in prayer, and he was blind.[262]

Chapter 216

THE IMĀMATE OF A PERSON WHO COMES TO VISIT ANOTHER PERSON

(596) Abū 'Aṭīyyah, a freed slave of us, said: Mālik b. al-Ḥuwairith came to this place of prayer of ours, and the *iqāmah* for prayer was called. We said to him: Come forward and lead the prayer. He said to us: Put one of your own men forward to lead you in prayer. I heard the Apostle of Allah (may peace be upon him) say: If anyone visits people, he should not lead them in prayer, but some person of them should lead the prayer.[263]

Chapter 217

ON THE *IMĀM* STANDING IN A PLACE HIGHER THAN THAT OF THE PEOPLE

(597) Hammām said: Ḥudhaifah led the people in prayer in al-Madā'in standing on a shop (or a bench). Abū Mas'ūd took him by his shirt, and brought him down. When he (Abū Mas'ūd) finished his prayer, he said: Do you not know that they

261. This tradition has been narrated through a number of chains that are all weak No chain with this version is sound. The theme of this tradition is, however, corroborated by the traditions recorded by Bukhārī and Muslim. Bukhārī recorded a tradition narrated by 'Abd al-Karīm in his *Ta'rikh* which says: I found ten Companions of Muḥammad (may peace be upon him) who used to pray behind tyrannical rulers. The tradition recorded by Muslim says that if anyone says his prayer in its appointed time and he has to offer it again along with the rulers who delay it from its right time, he should say it once again along with them. This prayer will count as a supererogatory prayer. These traditions show that saying prayer behind any Muslim, pious or impious, is permissible (*Awn al-Ma'būd*, I, 31-32)

262. This tradition shows that a blind man can act as *imām*. There is no harm in it.

263. Most of the scholars are of opinion that a stranger and a visitor can lead the people in prayer if they permit him and are pleased with him. The other traditions of the Prophet (may peace be upon him) indicate that a person should lead the prayer with the consent of the people (*'Awn al-Ma'būd*, I, 232).

(the people) were prohibited to do so. He said : Yes, I remembered when you pulled me down.[264]

(598) 'Adī b. Thābit al-Anṣārī said : A man related to me that (once) he was in the company of 'Ammār b. Yāsir in al-Madā'in (a city near Kūfah). The *iqāmah* was called for prayer ; 'Ammār came forward and stood on a shop (or a bench) and prayed while the people stood on a lower place than he. Ḥudhaifah came forward and took him by the hands and 'Ammār followed him till Ḥudhaifah brought him down. When 'Ammār finished his prayer, Ḥudhaifah said to him : Did you not hear the Apostle of Allah (may peace be upon him) say : When a man leads the people in prayer, he must not stand in a position higher than theirs, or words to that effect ? 'Ammār replied : That is why I followed you when you took me by the hand.

Chapter 218

ON THE *IMĀM* WHO LEADS THE PEOPLE IN PRAYER WHILE HE HAD ALREADY SAID HIS PRAYER

(599) Jābir b. 'Abd Allah said : Mu'ādh b. Jabal would pray along with the Apostle of Allah (may peace be upon him) the night prayer, then go to his people and lead them in the same prayer.[265]

(600) Jābir b. 'Abd Allah said : Mu'ādh b. Jabal would pray along with the Prophet (may peace be upon him), then go and lead his people in prayer.

Chapter 219

ON THE *IMĀM* WHO LEADS PRAYER IN THE SITTING CONDITION

(601) Anas b. Mālik said : The Apostle of Allah (may peace be upon him) rode a

264. It is disapproved that the *imām* should stand on a higher place and the people who follow him stand on a lower place ; nor should the *imām* stand on a lower place and the people on a higher place. But it is permissible that the *imām* may stand on a higher place if some people pray along with him on the same place (*'Awn al-Ma'būd*, I, 232).

265. Mu'ādh might obviously have said his obligatory prayer along with the Prophet (may peace be upon him) and his supererogatory prayer with his people. Therefore, it has been inferred from this tradition that it is permissible to say the obligatory prayer behind a man who is saying the supererogatory prayer. But this is disputed among the jurists. According to al-Shāfi'ī, al-Awzā'ī and Aḥmad, it is permissible to say obligatory prayer behind an *imām* who is saying supererogatory prayer. This is also held by 'Aṭā' and Ṭāwūs. According to Abū Ḥanīfah, this is not permissible. He allows it in case the *imām* is saying obligatory prayer and the people supererogatory or obligatory prayer. Mālik maintains that if the intention of the *imām* and that of his followers differ, the prayer of the followers is not valid. They should repeat it. This is also held by al-Zuhrī and al-Rābi'ah (*'Awn al-Ma'būd*, I, 233).

horse and was thrown off it and his right side was grazed. He then prayed one of the prayers sitting and we prayed behind him sitting, and when he finished he said: The *imām* is appointed only to be followed ; so when he prays standing, pray standing, and when he bows, bow ; when he raises himself, raise yourselves ; when he says "Allah listens to him who praises Him," say "Our Lord ! to Thee be the praise" ; and when he prays sitting all of you pray sitting.[266]

(602) Jābir said : The Apostle of Allah (may peace be upon him) rode a horse in Medina. It threw him off at the root of a date-palm. His foot was injured. We visited him to inquire about his illness. We found him praying sitting in the apartment of 'Ā'ishah. We, therefore, stood (praying) behind him. He kept silent. We again visited him to inquire about his illness. He offered the obligatory prayer sitting. We, therefore, stood (praying) behind him ; he made a sign to us and we sat down. When he finished the prayer, he said : When the *imām* prays sitting, pray sitting ; and when the *imām* prays standing, pray standing, and do not act as the people of Persia used to act with their chiefs (i.e. the people stood and they were sitting).

(603) Abū Hurairah reported the Apostle of Allah (may peace be upon him) as saying: The *imām* is appointed only to be followed ; when he says "Allah is most great," say "Allah is most great" and do not say "Allah is most great" until he says "Allah is most great." When he bows, bow ; and do not bow until he bows. And when he says "Allah listens to him who praises Him," say "O Allah, our Lord, to Thee be the praise." The version recorded by Muslim goes : "And to Thee be the praise". And when he prostrates, prostrate ; and do not prostrate until he prostrates. When he prays standing, pray standing, and when he prays sitting, all of you pray sitting.

Ābū Dāwūd said : The words "O Allah, our Lord, to Thee be the praise" reported by Sulaimān were explained to me by some of our companions.

(604) Abū Hurairah reported the Prophet (may peace be upon him) as saying: The *imām* is appointed only to be followed. This version adds: "When he recites (the Qur'ān), keep silent".

Abū Dāwūd said : The addition of the words "When he recites, keep silent," in this version are not guarded. The misunderstanding, according to us, is on the part of Abū Khālid (a narrator).

266. Al-Khaṭṭābī says that Abū Dāwūd transmitted this tradition on the authority of Anas, Jābir and 'Ā'ishah, but he omitted the well-known event of the last prayer of the Prophet (may peace be upon him) during his illness when he led the prayer sitting while the people were standing behind him. In view of this last action of the Prophet (may peace be upon him), the earlier traditions reported by Anas and Jābir are considered to be abrogated. This is, however, disputed amongst the jurists. Abū Ḥanīfah, al-Shāfi'ī, Sufyān al-Thawrī and Abū Thawr hold that even if the *imām* if praying sitting, the people behined him should pray standing. Mālik does not allow anyone to lead the prayer sitting. Aḥmad b. Ḥanbal, Isḥāq b. Rahwaih and a group of the traditionists hold that if the *imām* prays sitting, the people behind him should also pray sitting as indicated by this tradition narrated by Anas (*'Awn al-Ma'būd*, I, 233-34).

(605) 'Ā'ishah said: The Apostle of Allah (may peace be upon him) prayed in his house sitting and the people prayed behind him standing. He made a sign to them (asking them) to sit down. When he finished the prayer, he said: The *imām* is appointed only to be followed; so when he prays standing, pray standing; and when he raises himself, raise yourselves; and when he prays sitting, pray sitting.

(606) Jābir said: When the Prophet (may peace be upon him) became seriously ill, we prayed behind him while he was sitting, and Abū Bakr was calling "Allah is most great" to cause the people to hear the *takbīr*. Then he (the narrator) narrated the rest of the tradition.

(607) Ḥuṣain reported on the authority of the children of Sa'd b. Mu'ādh that Usaid b. Ḥudair used to act as their *imām*. (When he fell ill) the Apostle of Allah (may peace be upon him) came to him inquiring about his illness. They said: Apostle of Allah, our *imām* is ill. He said: When he prays sitting, pray sitting.

Abū Dāwūd said: The chain of this tradition is not continuous (*muttaṣil*).

Chapter 220

IF ONE OF THE TWO PERSONS ACTS AS *IMĀM* FOR THE OTHER, WHERE SHOULD BOTH STAND?

(608) Anas said: The Apostle of Allah (may peace be upon him) entered upon Umm Ḥarām.[267] The people (in her house) brought some cooking oil and dates to him. He said: Put it (dates) back in its container and return it (cooking oil) to its bag, because I am keeping fast. He then stood and led us in prayer two *rak'ahs* of supererogatory prayer. Then Umm Sulaim[268] and Umm Ḥarām stood behind us (i.e. the men). Thābit (the narrator) said: I understand that Anas said: He (the Prophet) made me stand on his right side.[269]

(609) Anas said: The Apostle of Allah (may peace be upon him) led him and one of their women in prayer. He (the Prophet) put him on his right side and the woman behind him (Anas).

(610) 'Abd Allah b. 'Abbās said: When I was spending a night in the house of my maternal aunt Maimūnah, the Apostle of Allah (may peace be upon him) got up at night, opened the mouth of the water skin and performed ablution. He then closed the mouth of the water-skin and stood for prayer. Then I got up and performed ablution as he did; then I came and stood on his left side. He took my hand, turned

267. The maternal aunt of Anas.

268. The mother of Anas.

269. This tradition indicates that when two persons pray in congregation the *imām* should stand at the left side of the other person. The person who follows him should stand on the right side of the *imām*. Moreover, it is permissible to offer supererogatory prayer in congregation. Further, women should stand behind the row of men.

me round from behind his back and set me on his right side; and I prayed along with him.

(611) Another version of this tradition transmitted through a different chain of narrators by Ibn 'Abbās says: "He took my head or the hair of my head and made me stand on his right side."

Chapter 221

IF THERE ARE THREE PERSONS (IN CONGREGATIONAL PRAYER), HOW SHOULD THEY STAND?

(612) Anas b. Mālik said that his grandmother Mulaikah invited the Apostle of Allah (may peace be upon him) to take meals which she prepared for him. He took some of it and prayed. He said: Get up, I shall lead you in prayer. Anas said: I got up and took a mat which had become black on account of long use. I then washed it with water. The Apostle of Allah (may peace be upon him) stood upon it. I and the orphan (Ibn Abī Dumairah, the freed slave of the Prophet) stood in a row behind him. The old woman stood behind us. He then led us two *rak'ahs* in prayer and went away.[270]

(613) 'Abd al-Raḥmān b. al-Aswad reported on the authority of his father (al-Aswad): 'Alqamah and al-Aswad sought permission from 'Abd Allah (b. Mas'ūd) for admission, and we remained sitting at his door for a long time. A slave-girl came out and gave them permission (to enter). He (Ibn Mas'ūd) then got up and prayed (standing) between me (al-Aswad) and him (Alqamah). He then said: I witnessed the Apostle of Allah (may peace upon him) doing similarly.[271]

Chapter 222

THE *IMĀM* SHOULD TURN FROM THE DIRECTION OF THE KA'BAH AFTER UTTERING THE SALUTATION

(614) Jābir b. Yazīd b. al-Aswad reported on the authority of his father: I prayed behind the Apostle of Allah (may peace be upon him). When he finished the prayer,

270. This tradition indicates that women in congregational prayer should stand behind children. The order of the people in congregational prayer will be as follows: (1) men, (2) children, (3) women. Women will stand behind all the participants. If there is one man and one child, then the child will stand on the right side of the man.

271. If there are three persons in a congregational prayer, the *imām* may either go forward and set the two persons behind him or stand between them in the same row. If there are more than two persons in addition to the *imām*, it is essential to stand in front of them

he would turn (his face from the direction of the Ka'bah).[272]

(615) Al-Barā' b. 'Āzib said: When we would pray behind the Apostle of Allah (may peace be upon him), we liked to be on his right side. He (the Prophet) would sit turning his face towards us (and back towards the Ka'bah):[273] (may peace be upon him).

Chapter 223

THE *IMĀM* SHOULD NOT SAY THE SUPEREROGATORY PRAYER AT THE PLACE WHERE HE SAID THE OBLIGATORY PRAYER

(616) Mughīrah b. Shu'bah reported the Apostle of Allah (may peace be upon him) as saying: The *imām* should not pray at the place where he led the prayer until he moves (from there).[274]

Abū Dāwūd said: 'Aṭā' al-Khurāsānī did not see Mughīrah b. Shu'bah. (This tradition i , therefore, *munqaṭi'*, i.e. a link is missing in the chain).

Chapter 224

IF THE *IMĀM* BECOMES DEFILED AFTER RAISING HIS HEAD FROM THE PROSTRATION OF THE LAST *RAK'AH* OF THE PRAYER, IS HIS PRAYER COMPLETE (BEFORE UTTERING SALUTATION) OR NOT?

(617) 'Abd Allah b. 'Amr reported the Apostle of Allah (may peace be upon him) as saying: When the *imām* completes the prayer and sits (for reciting *tashahhud*), and then becomes defiled (i.e. his ablution becomes void) before he speaks (to someone), his prayer becomes complete. And those who prayed behind him also complete

272. This tradition shows that when the *imām* utters the salutation, he should turn his face from the direction of the Ka'bah.

273. This tradition indicates that the *imām* shou.d turn his face from the Ka bah after uttering the salutation He should sit with his face towards the people for supplication.

274. Another tradition reported by Abū Hurairah says that one should move forward or backward or on the right or left side of the *imām* when one finishes the obligatory prayer in congregation. The reason is, as some commentators observe, that in this way one should pray in different places and thus increase the number of the places of prostration. The places where one prostrates will bear witness on the Day of Judgment (*'Awn al-Ma'būd*, I, 238).

the prayer.[275]

Chapter 225

ON THE BEGINNING AND END OF THE PRAYER

(618) 'Alī reported the Apostle of Allah (may peace be upon him) as saying: The key of prayer is purification; *takbīr* (saying "Allah is most great") makes (all acts which break prayer) unlawful and *taslīm* (uttering the salutation) makes (all such acts) lawful [276]

Chapter 226

A MAN WHO IS LED IN PRAYER SHOULD FOLLOW THE *IMĀM* STRICTLY

(619) Mu'āwiyah b. Abū Sufyān reported the Apostle of Allah (may peace be upon him) as saying: Do not try to outstrip me in bowing and prostrating because however earlier I bow you will join me when I raise (my head from bowing); I have become bulky.

(620) Al-Barā' who is not a liar said: When they (the Companions) raised their heads from bowing along with the Apostle of Allah (may peace be upon him), they would stand up, and when they saw him that he went down in prostration, they would prostrate (following the Prophet).

(621) Al-Barā' b. 'Āzib said: We used to pray along with the Prophet (may peace be upon him); none of us bowed his back until he saw that the Prophet (may peace be upon him) bowed (his back).

(622) Al-Barā' (b. 'Āzib) said: They (the Companions) used to pray along with

275. Al-Khaṭṭābī said: This is a weak tradition. The experts of *Ḥadīth* have criticised some of its narrators. This also contradicts all those sound traditions which indicate that recitation of *tashahhud* and the utterance of salutation are necessary for the validity of prayer. None of the jurists has followed this tradition in its literal sense. Even the Ḥanafīs hold that it is necessary to sit after the last prostration as long as one recites *tashahhud*. No one holds that the prayer is complete immediately after the completion of the last prostration. Al-Tirmidhī also criticised the chain of this tradition (*'Awn al-Ma'būd*, I. 238).

276. *Takbir* i.e. saying *Allah-o-Akbar*, "Allah is most great," marks the beginning of prayer and *taslim* (uttering the salutation) marks the end of it. Al-Khaṭṭābi said: This tradition indicates that *taslim* is an essential part of prayer like *takbir*. The prayer is finished by the utterance of the salutation and not by defilement before it. Further, prayer begins by the pronouncement of *takbir* and not by uttering any other words. This is held by the majority of scholars. Abū Ḥanīfah maintains that prayer begins by uttering any words of exaltation. But this tradition refutes him, because it shows that it is essential to pronounce *takbir* (*'Awn al-Ma'būd*, I. 238)

the Apostle of Allah (may peace be upon him). When he bowed, they bowed; and when he said, "Allah listens to him who praises him," they remained standing until they saw that he placed his forehead on the ground: then they would follow him (may peace be upon him).[277]

Chapter 227

THREAT FOR A PERSON WHO RAISES HIMSELF BEFORE THE *IMĀM* OR PLACES HIS HEAD BEFORE HIM

(623) Abū Hurairah reported the Apostle of Allah (may peace be upon him) as saying: Does he who raises his head while the *imām* is prostrating not fear that Allah may change his head into a donkey's or his face into a donkey's face.[278]

Chapter 228

ON LEAVING THE MOSQUE BEFORE THE *IMĀM* WHEN THE PRAYER IS OVER

(624) Anas said: The Prophet (may peace be upon him) persuaded them to say prayer in congregation and prohibited them to leave before he goes away from the prayer.[279]

Chapter 229

ADEQUACY OF CLOTHES FOR THE VALIDITY OF PRAYER

(625) Abū Hurairah said: The Apostle of Allah (may peace be upon him) was

277. This shows that the people behind the *imām* should follow him in every action after he has started praying. It is disputed amongst the jurists whether the people who are led in prayer should start the different actions simultaneously with the *imām* or after a short while. According to Aḥmad and al-Shāfi'ī the people behind the *imām* should begin their actions after the *imām* has begun. According to Mālik and Abū Ḥanīfah, they should start simultaneously (*'Awn al Ma'būd*, III, 58-60).

278. This tradition gives a warning to a person who goes ahead of the *imām*; one should start his action either along with the *imām* simultaneously or after he has started the action. One becomes sinful if one goes before the *imām* The changing of the head into a donkey's is a threat for doing such an action.

If someone outstrips the *imām*, his prayer is valid according to all the jurists, though he commits a grave sin. He should, however, come back and follow the *imām*. If one outstrips by mistake or inadvertently, he will not be sinful (*Ma'ārif al Sunan*, III, 55).

279 The reason for prohibiting the Companions before him was that the women would first leave the mosque. When they all left, the Prophet (may peace be upon him) would stand and go out and the Companions also followed him (*'Awn al-Ma'būd*, I, 240).

asked about the validity of prayer in a single garment. The Prophet (may peace be upon him) said: Does every one of you has two garments?[280]

(626) Abū Hurairah reported the Apostle of Allah (may peace be upon him) as saying: None of you should pray in a single garment of which no part comes over the shoulders.[281]

(627) Abū Hurairah reported the Apostle of Allah (may peace be upon him) as saying: If anyone prays in a single (piece of) cloth, he should cross the two ends.

(628) 'Umar b. Abū Salamah said: I saw the Apostle of Allah (may peace be upon him) praying girded with a single (piece of) cloth, place its two ends over his shoulders.[282]

(629) Qais b. Ṭalq reported on the authority of his father: We came to the Prophet (may peace be upon him), and a man came and said: Prophet of Allah, what do you say if one prays in a single garment? The Apostle of Allah (may peace be upon hin) then took off his wrapper and combined it with his sheet, and put it on them. He got up and the Prophet of Allah (may peace be upon him) led us in prayer. When he finished the prayer, he said: Does every one of you have two garments?

Chapter 230

ON A MAN WHO TIES THE CLOTH OVER HIS NAPE AND THEN PRAYS

(630) Sahl b. Sa'd said: I saw the people tying their wrappers over their necks like children due to the narrowness of the wrappers behind the Apostle of Allah (may peace be upon him) during prayer.[283] Someone said: Body of women, do not

280. This tradition shows that prayer is valid in a single garment if it covers the private parts. But it is better to wear a suitable dress for prayer.

281. This does not mean that if one does not cover one's shoulders, the prayer will not be valid. Mālik, Abū Ḥanīfah and al-Shāfi'ī hold that the prayer will be valid with abomination if one does not cover the shoulders. They argue from the tradition reported by Jābir. It says that one should cover one's shoulders if one's cloth is large; in case it is small, one should cover the private parts. Aḥmad b. Ḥanbal, according to one version, holds that the prayer is not valid if one does not cover the shoulder; according to another version it is valid in his opinion (*'Awn al-Ma'būd*, I, 241).

282. The ends were each over a shoulder and under the other armpit tied over the chest.

283. In the early decade of Islam poverty prevailed among the Muslims. There were very few people who had two garments to wear. Further, even one piece of cloth sometimes was so narrow that they could not tie them over their chest, but tied over their napes. Hence the Prophet (may peace be upon him) permitted the Muslims to pray in a single piece of cloth.

raise your heads until the men raise (their heads).[284]

Chapter 231

ON A MAN WHO PRAYS IN A SINGLE PIECE OF CLOTH WHOSE ONE PART LIES OVER THE OTHER PERSON

(631) 'Ā'ishah said: The Prophet (may peace be upon him) prayed in a single (piece of) cloth whose one part was upon me.

Chapter 232

ON A MAN WHO PRAYS IN A SINGLE SHIRT

(632) Salamah b. al-Akwa' said: I said: Apostle of Allah, I am a man who goes out hunting; may I pray in a single shirt? He replied: Yes, but fasten it even if it should be with a thorn.

(633) 'Abd al-Raḥmān b. Abū Bakr reported on the authority of his father: Jābir b. 'Abd Allah led us in prayer in a single shirt, having no sheet upon him. When he finished the prayer he said: I witnessed the Apostle of Allah (may peace be upon him) praying in a shirt.[285]

Chapter 233

IF THE CLOTH IS TIGHT, IT SHOULD BE USED AS A WRAPPER

(634) 'Ubādah b. al-Ṣāmit said: We came to Jābir b. 'Abd Allah. He said: I (Jābir) accompanied the Apostle of Allah (may peace be upon him) in a battle. He got up to pray. I had a sheet of cloth upon me, and I began to cross both the ends, but they did not reach (my shoulders). It had fringes which I turned over and crossed the two ends, and bowed down retaining it with my neck lest it should fall down. Then I came and stood on the left side of the Apostle of Allah (may peace be upon him). He then took my hand and brought me around him and set me on his right side. Then Ibn Ṣakhr came and stood on his left side. He then took us with his both hands and made us stand behind him. The Apostle of Allah (may peace be upon him) began to look at me with furtive glances, but I could not understand.

284. He prevented them to do so lest the women should see the private parts as the man prayed in a single garment wearing no wrapper.

285. Prayer in a single shirt is permissible provided the private parts are not disclosed.

When I understood, he hinted at me to tie the wrapper. When the Apostle of Allah (may peace be upon him) finished the prayer, he said (to me): O Jābir. I said: Yes, Apostle of Allah. He said: If it (the sheet) is wide, cross both its ends (over the shoulders); if it is tight, tie it over your loins.

(635) Ibn 'Umar reported the Apostle of Allah (may peace be upon him) as saying, or reported 'Umar as saying (the narrator is doubtful): If one of you has two (pieces of) cloth, he should pray in them; if he has a single (piece of) cloth, he should use it as a wrapper, and should not hang it upon the shoulder like the Jews.[286]

(636) 'Abd Allah b. Buraidah reported on the authority of his father: The Apostle of Allah (may peace be upon him) prohibited us to pray in a sheet of cloth without crossing both its ends, and he also prohibited us to pray in a wrapper without putting on a sheet.[287]

Chapter 234

ON TRAILING GARMENT DURING PRAYER

(637) Ibn Mas'ud said: I heard the Apostle of Allah (may peace be upon him) say: He who lets his garment trail during prayer out of pride, Allah, the Almighty, has nothing to do with pardoning him and protecting him from Hell.[288]

(638) Abū Hurairah said: While a man was praying letting his lower garment trail, the Apostle of Allah (may peace be upon him) said to him: Go and perform ablution. He, therefore, went and performed ablution and then returned. He (the Prophet) again said: Go and perform ablution. He again went, performed ablution and returned. A man said to him (the Prophet): Apostle of Allah, why did you order him to perform ablution? He said: He was praying with lower garment trailing,

286. The Jews used to hang a piece of cloth upon the shoulders without tying its ends upon the breast. They let loose both the ends of the cloth. Such a practice was prohibited by the Prophet (may peace be upon him).

287. In a number of traditions the Prophet (may peace be upon him) has permitted the Muslims to pray in a single garment. They can use it as a wrapper if it is tight. But in case one has two (pieces of) cloth, one should use both of them, and should not pray in a single garment.

288. The trailing of a lower garment beyond the ankles displays pride and self-conceit. Hence the Prophet (may peace be upon him) forbade this practice. Prayer is, however, valid if one prays trailing one's lower garment. But he will commit a sin. The trailing of the lower garment during prayer is disapproved according to Abū Ḥanīfah and al-Shāfi'ī. Mālik holds that it is permissible during prayer but not permissible during walking as it exhibits one's pride which is condemned by Allah (*'Awn al-Ma'būd*, I, 243).

and Allah does not accept the prayer of a man who lets his lower garment trail.[289]

Chapter 235

IN HOW MANY CLOTHES A WOMAN WOULD PRAY?

(639) Zaid b. Qunfudh said that his mother asked Umm Salamah: In how many clothes should a woman pray? She replied: She would pray wearing a veil and a long shirt which covers the surface of her feet.[290]

(640) Umm Salamah said that she asked the Prophet (may peace be upon him): Can a woman pray in a shirt and veil without wearing a lower garment? He replied: If the shirt is ample and covers the surface of her feet.

Abū Dāwūd said: This tradition has been transmitted by Mālik b. Anas, Bakr b. Muḍar, Ḥafṣ b. Ghiyāth, Ismā'īl b. Ja'far, Ibn Abī Dhi'b, and Ibn Isḥāq from Muḥammad b. Zaid on the authority of his mother who narrated from Umm Salamah. None of these narrators mention the name of the Prophet (may peace be upon him). They reported it directly from Umm Salamah.

Chapter 236

ON A WOMAN WHO PRAYS WITHOUT WEARING A VEIL

(641) 'Ā'ishah reported the Prophet (may peace be upon him) as saying: Allah does not accept the prayer of a woman who has reached puberty unless she wears a veil.[291]

Abū Dāwūd said: This tradition has been narrated by Sa'īd b. Abū 'Arūbah from Qatādah on the authority of al-Hasan from the Prophet (may peace be upon him).

289. This means that his prayer is not as perfect as required by Allah. It would be perfect if he prayed it while wearing his lower garment above his ankles. One should not let one's lower garment trail beyond the ankles during prayer. If one does so the prayer is valid, and the man will be sinful. The other versions of this tradition indicate the threat of the punishment of Hell-fire for such an action.

290. There is a difference of opinion amongst the jurists about the parts of body of a free woman to be covered during prayer. Al-Shāfi'ī and al-Awzā'ī maintain that a woman should cover all her body except her face and hands (up to the wrist). Abū Bakr b. 'Abd al Raḥmān holds that a woman should cover all her body, even her nails. This is the view of Aḥmad b. Ḥanbal. According to Abū Ḥanīfah, she should cover her whole body except her face, hands and feet. Mālik is of opinion that a woman should repeat her prayer within the time if she discloses her hair or the surface of her feet. A slave girl can disclose her hair (*'Awn al-Ma'būd*, I, 244)

291. A woman uses a veil (*khimār*) to cover her head and breasts. Since it is necessary to cover the head by a woman during prayer, she should wear a veil when she prays.

(642) Muḥammad said: 'Ā'ishah came to Safīyyah Umm Ṭalḥat al-Ṭalḥāt and seeing her daughters she said: The Apostle of Allah (may peace be upon him) entered (into the house) and there was a girl in my apartment. He gave his lower garment (wrapper) to me and said: Tear it into two pieces and give one-half to this (girl) and the other half to the girl with Umm Salamah. I think she has reached puberty, or (he said) I think they have reached puberty.

Abū Dāwūd said: Hishām has narrated it similarly from Muḥammad b. Sīrīn.

Chapter 237

ON TRAILING THE GARMENT DURING PRAYER

(643) Abū Hurairah said: The Apostle of Allah (may peace be upon him) forbade trailing garments during prayer[292] and that a man should cover his mouth.[293]

Abū Dāwūd said: This tradition has also been narrated by 'Isl on the authority of 'Aṭā' from Abū Hurairah: The Prophet (may peace be upon him) forbade trailing garments during prayer.

(644) Ibn Juraij said: I often saw 'Aṭā' praying while letting his garment trail.

Abū Dāwūd said: This (practice of 'Aṭā') weakens the tradition (narrated by Abū Hurairah).

Chapter 238

ON SAYING PRAYER UPON THE SHEETS OF CLOTH OF WOMEN

(645) 'Ā'ishah said: The Apostle of Allah (may peace be upon him) would not

292. The Arabic word *sadl* (trailing) has been interpreted variantly: (1) to hang a cloth on the body and let it loose to touch the ground; (2) to let the garment trail without tying both of its ends over the chest; (3) to wrap a cloth upon the body and to enter the hands inside it leaving the sleeves hanging and with such a cloth one bows and prostrates; (4) to place the cloth upon the head from the middle and let its both ends loose on the left and right sides without covering the shoulders with them; (5) literally, it means to let a cloth trail loosely.

The tradition covers all these meanings of *sadl* prohibited by the Prophet (may peace be upon him). This was forbidden by him because this practice was prevalent among the Jews. Some scholars like 'Aṭā', Makḥūl, al-Zuhrī, al-Hasan, Ibn Sīrīn and Mālik allow trailing garments during prayer. But Sufyān and al-Shāfi'ī disapprove of it (*'Awn al-Ma'būd*, I, 245).

293. The Arabs used to cover their mouths with their turbans. Hence the Prophet (may peace be upon him) prohibited it, especially during prayer (*'Awn al-Ma'būd*, I, 245).

pray on our sheets of cloth or on our quilts.[294] 'Ubaid Allah said: My father doubted.[295]

Chapter 239

ON A MAN WHO PRAYS TYING THE BACK KNOT OF HIS HAIR

(646) Sa'id b. Abū Sa'īd al-Maqburī reported on the authority of his father that he saw Abū Rāfi', the freed slave of the Prophet (may peace be upon him), passing by Ḥasan b. 'Alī (Allah be pleased with them) when he was standing offering his prayer. He had tied the back knot of his hair. Abū Rāfi' untied it. Ḥasan turned to him with anger. Abū Rāfi' said to him: Concentrate on your prayer and do not be angry; I heard the Apostle of Allah (may peace be upon him) say: This is the seat of the devil, referring to the back knot of the hair.[296]

(647) Kuraib, the freed slave of Ibn 'Abbās, reported: 'Abd Allah b. 'Abbās saw 'Abd Allah b. al-Ḥārith praying having the back knot of the hair. He stood behind him and began to untie it. He remained standing unmoved (stationary). When he finished his prayer he came to Ibn 'Abbās and said to him: What were you doing with my head? He said: I heard the Apostle of Allah (may peace be upon him) say: A man who prays with the black knot of hair tied is the one praying pinioned.

Chapter 240

ON PRAYING IN SANDALS

(648) 'Abd Allah b. al-Sā'ib said: I saw the Prophet (may peace be upon him) praying on the day of the conquest of Mecca and he had placed his shoes at his left side.

(649) 'Abd Allah b. al-Sā'ib said: The Apostle of Allah (may peace be upon him) led us in the morning prayer at Mecca. He began to recite Sūrah al-Mu'minīn and while he came to description of Moses and Aaron or the description of Moses and Jesus—the narrator Ibn 'Abbād doubts or other narrators differed amongst themselves on this word—the Prophet (may peace be upon him) coughed and gave up (recitation) and then bowed. 'Abd Allah b. al-Sā'ib was present seeing all this

294. The Prophet (may peace be upon him) would not pray upon the clothes of women worn by them or used by them at the time of sleep. The reason is that the clothes used by women might be smeared with impurity.

295. He doubted whether 'Ā'ishah said sheets or quilts.

296. The scholars are agreed upon the disapproval of prayer if one offers having the back-knot of the hair. But the prayer is valid; the man will be sinful (*'Awn al-Ma'būd*, I, 247).

(incident).[297]

(650) Abū Sa'īd al-Khudrī said : While the Apostle of Allah (may peace be upon him) was leading his Companions in prayer, he took off his sandals and laid them on his left side ; so when the people saw this, they removed their sandals. When the Apostle of Allah (may peace be upon him) finished his prayer, he asked : What made you remove your sandals? They replied : We saw you remove your sandals, so we removed our sandals. The Apostle of Allah (may peace be upon him) then said : Gabriel came to me and informed me that there was filth in them. When any of you comes to the mosque, he should see ; if he finds filth on his sandals, he should wipe it off and pray in them.[298]

(651) This tradition has also been transmitted through a chain by Bakr b. 'Abd Allah. This version has the word *khubuth* (filth) and in two places the word *khubuthan* (filth).

(652) Shaddād b. Aws reported on the authority of his father : The Apostle of Allah (may peace be upon him) said : Act differently from the Jews, for they do not pray in their sandals or their shoes.

(653) 'Amr b. Shu'aib, on his father's authority, said that his grandfather reported : I saw the Apostle of Allah (may peace be upon him) praying both barefooted and wearing sandals.

Chapter 241

WHEN A PERSON WHO IS GOING TO PRAY TAKES OFF HIS SANDALS, WHERE SHOULD HE PLACE THEM?

(654) Abū Hurairah reported the Apostle of Allah (may peace be upon him) as saying : When any of you prays, he should not place his sandals on his right side or on his left so as to be on the right side of someone else, unless no one is at his left, but should place them between his feet.[299]

(655) Abū Hurairah reported the Apostle of Allah (may peace be upon him) as saying : When any of you prays and takes off his sandals, he should not harm anyone by them. He should place them between his feet or pray with them on.

297. It should be noted that this tradition and the previous one contain the same theme ; the former is abridged and the latter is detailed. Although this tradition has no mention of the shoes, it should be taken as the same as the previous one (*'Awn al-Ma'būd*, I, 246-47).

298. This tradition indicates that it is permissible to pray in sandals if they are free from impurity or filth. If not, one should wipe it off, or wash it if necessary and then pray (*'Awn al-Ma'būd*, I, 247).

299. When there is no one on the left side, one should place one's sandals on the left. But if there are persons on one's both sides, then one should place them between one's feet.

Chapter 242

ON PRAYING ON A SMALL MAT

(656) Maimūnah bint al-Ḥārith reported : The Apostle of Allah (may peace be upon him) used to pray while I was by his side in the state of menstruation. Sometimes his cloth would touch me when he prostrated. He would pray on a small mat.

Chapter 243

ON PRAYING ON A MAT

(657) Anas b. Mālik reported : A man from the Anṣār said : I am a corpulent man—and he was (actually) a fat man ; I cannot pray along with you. He prepared food for him and invited him to his house. (He said :) (Please) pray (here) so that I may see how you pray, and then I would follow you. They (the people) washed one side of their mat. He (the Prophet) then got up and prayed two *rak'ahs*. Ibn al-Jārūd asked Anas b. Mālik : Would he (the Prophet) say the forenoon prayer ? He replied : I did not see him offering this prayer except that day.

(658) Anas b. Mālik said : The Prophet (may peace be upon him) used to visit Umm Sulaim. Sometimes the time for prayer would come and he would pray on our carpet that was really a mat. She (Umm Sulaim) used to wash it with water.

(659) Al-Mughīrah b. Shu'bah said : The Apostle of Allah (may peace be upon him) used to pray on a mat[300] and on a tanned skin.[301]

Chapter 244

ON A PERSON WHO PROSTRATES ON HIS CLOTH

(660) Anas b. Mālik said : We used to pray along with the Apostle of Allah (may peace be upon him) in intense heat. When any of us could not rest his face on bare ground (while prostrating due to intense heat) he spread his cloth and would prostrate on it.

300. All these traditions indicate that it is not necessary to pray on bare ground. One can say prayer on a carpet, mat or a tanned skin.

301. A number of traditions show that one should not use a skin before it is tanned . It becomes pure when it is tanned.

Chapter 245

STRAIGHTENING THE ROWS

(661) Jābir b. Samurah reported the Apostle of Allah (may peace be upon him) as saying: Why do you not stand in rows as the angels do in the presence of their Lord? We asked: How do the angels stand in rows in the presence of their Lord? He replied: They make the first row complete and keep close together in the row.

(662) Al-Nu'mān b. Bashīr said: The Apostle of Allah (may peace be upon him) paid attention to the people and said three times: Straighten your rows (in prayer); by Allah, you must straighten your rows, or Allah will certainly put your faces in contrary directions. I then saw that every person stood (in prayer) keeping his shoulder close to that of the other, and his knee close to that of the other, and his ankle close to that of the other.

(663) Al-Nu'mān b. Bashir said: The Prophet (may peace be upon him) used to straighten us in the rows (of prayer) as the arrow is straightened, until he thought that we had learned it from him and understood it. One day he turned towards us, and when he saw a man whose chest projected from the row, he said: You must straighten your rows, or Allah will certainly put your faces in contrary directions.

(664) Al-Barā' b. 'Āzib said: The Apostle of Allah (may peace be upon him) used to pass through the row from one side to the other; he used to set our chests and shoulders in order, and say: Do not be irregular. And he would say: Allah and His angels bless those who are near the first rows.

(665) Al-Nu'mān b. Bashīr said: The Apostle of Allah (may peace be upon him) used to straighten our rows when we stood up to pray, and when we were straight, he said: Allah is most great.

(666) 'Abd Allah b. 'Umar reported the Apostle of Allah (may peace be upon him) as saying: Set the rows in order, stand shoulder to shoulder, close the gaps, be pliant in the hands of your brethren, and do not leave openings for the devil. If anyone joins up a row, Allah will join him up, but if anyone breaks a row, Allah will cut him off.[302]

Abū Dāwūd said: The name of Abū Shajrah is Kathīr b. Murrah.

(667) Anas b. Mālik reported the Apostle of Allah (may peace be upon him) as saying: Stand close together in your rows, bring them near one another, and stand neck to neck, for by Him in Whose hand my soul is, I see the devil coming in through openings in the row just like a small black sheep.

302. This means that people in the rows of prayer should be pliant to move backward or forward if anyone moves them to set the row in order. This may also mean that the people in the rows should provide space leniently to a person who joins it or should take a person out of the row and stand with him.

(668) Anas reported the Apostle of Allah (may peace be upon him) as saying: Straighten your rows, for the straightening of the rows is part of perfecting the prayer.[303]

(669) Muḥammad b. Muslim b. al-Sā'ib said: One day I prayed by the side of Anas b. Mālik. He said: Do you know why this stick is placed here? I said: No, by Allah. He said: The Apostle of Allah (may peace be upon him) used to put his hand upon it and say: Keep straight and straighten your rows.

(670) This tradition has also been narrated by Anas through a different chain of transmitters. This version goes: When the Apostle of Allah (may peace be upon him) stood for prayer, he took it (the stick) in his right hand and turning (to the right side) said: Keep straight and straighten your rows. He then took it in his left hand and said: Keep straight and straighten your rows.

(671) Anas reported the Apostle of Allah (may peace be upon him) as saying: Complete the front row, then the one that comes next, and if there is any incompleteness, let it be in the last row.

(672) Ibn 'Abbās reported the Apostle of Allah (may peace be upon him) as saying: The best of you are those whose shoulders are soft in prayer.[304]

Chapter 246

THE SETTING OF THE ROWS OF PRAYER BETWEEN THE PILLARS

(673) 'Abd al-Ḥamīd b. Maḥmūd said: I offered the Friday prayer along with Anas b. Mālik. We were pushed to the pillars (due to the crowd of people). We, therefore, stopped forward and backward. Anas then said: We used to avoid it (setting a row between the pillars) during the time of the Apostle of Allah (may peace be upon him.[305]

303. This means that straightening the rows does not fall outside the prayer. It is in fact a part of perfect prayer. The prayer will not be considered to be perfect if the rows are not in order. Hence the significance of straightening the rows in prayer.

304. This means that they do not annoy others in prayer. Some commentators have taken it to mean that they easily move if they are moved by someone in prayer.

305. This tradition shows that praying between the pillars is disapproved. Explaining the reason Abū Bakr b. al-'Arabī says that this was due either to the break of the row or that it is the place where sandals are generally placed. Aḥmad and Isḥāq hold that it is disapproved to set a row of prayer between the pillars. But Abū Ḥanīfah and al-Shāfi'ī allow it arguing from the fact that the Prophet (may peace be upou him) prayed between the two pillars within the Ka'bah Some scholars are of opinion that it is prohibited to offer congregational prayer between the pillars but not the prayer which is offered individually. One is allowed to say prayer alone between the pillars (*'Awn al-Ma'būd*, I, 252).

Chapter 247

ON A MAN WHO LIKES TO STAND IN THE ROW OF PRAYER NEAR THE *IMĀM* AND THE DISAPPROVAL OF STANDING FAR AWAY (FROM HIM)

(674) Abū Mas'ūd reported the Apostle of Allah (may peace be upon him) as saying: Let those of you who are sedate and prudent be near me, then those who are next to them, then those who are next to them.

(675) This tradition has also been transmitted by 'Abd Allah (b. Mas'ūd) through a different chain of narrators. This version adds: "Do not be irregular, so have your hearts irregular, and beware of tumult such as found in markets."

(676) 'Ā'ishah reported the Apostle of Allah (may peace be upon him) as saying: Allah and His angels bless those who are on the right flanks of the rows.[306]

Chapter 248

THE POSITION OF CHILDREN IN THE ROWS

(677) Abū Mālik al-Ash'arī said: Should I not tell you how the Apostle of Allah (may peace be upon him) led the prayer? He said: He had the *iqāmah* announced, drew the men up in line and drew up the youths behind them, then led them in prayer. He then mentioned how he conducted it, and said: Thus is the prayer of. . . .[307] 'Abd al-A'lā said: I think he must have said: My people.

Chapter 249

THE WOMEN'S ROW AND THEIR POSITION IN THE BACK AWAY FROM THE FIRST ROW

(678) Abū Hurairah reported the Apostle of Allah (may peace be upon him) as saying: The best of the men's row is the first and the worst of them is the last, but the best of the women's rows is the last and the worst of them is the first.[308]

(679) 'Ā'ishah reported the Apostle of Allah (may peace be upon him) as saying:

306 One should stand in the front row of prayer as far as possible, and, if possible, on the right side of the *imām* If it is not possible, then one should try to stand in the row nearer to the *imām*. Moreover, those who have a good knowledge of religion should stand close to the *imam* so that they may correct him if he commits any mistake.

307. The wording of the tradition is incomplete, 'Abd al A'lā who is a later narrator in the chain supplies the missing words.

308. The last row of men is the worst because it is close to the row of women. The first row of women is the worst because it is close to the row of men.

The people will continue to keep themselves away from the front row until Allah will keep them away (from the front) in the Hell-fire.[309]

(680) Abū Sa'īd al-Khudrī said : The Apostle of Allah (may peace be upon him) saw a tendency among his Companions to go to the back. He said to them : Come forward and follow my lead, and let those who come after you follow your lead. People will continue to keep to the back till Allah would put them at the back.[310]

Chapter 250

THE POSITION OF THE *IMĀM* IN THE ROW

(681) Abū Hurairah reported the Apostle of Allah (may peace be upon him) as saying : Have the *imām* in the centre and close up the gaps.

Chapter 251

ON A MAN WHO PRAYS ALONE BEHIND THE ROW

(682) Wābiṣah said : The Apostle of Allah (may peace be upon him) saw a man praying alone behind the row. He ordered him to repeat. Sulaimān b. Harb said : The prayer.[311]

(683) Abū Bakrah said that he came to the mosque when the Prophet (may peace be upon him) was bowing. So I bowed outside the row (before joining it). The Prophet (may peace be upon him) said : May Allah increase your eagerness ! But do not do it again.[312]

(684) Al-Ḥasan reported : Abū Bakrah came when the Apostle of Allah (may peace be upon him) was bowing. So he bowed without the row (before joining it). He then went to the row. When the Prophet (may peace be upon him) finished his prayer, he said : Which of you bowed without the row, and then went to the row ? Abū Bakrah said : It was I. The Prophet (may peace be upon him) said : May Allah increase your eagerness ! But do not do it again.

309 This tradition points to the significance of standing in the front row of the prayer.

310. This means that they will be deprived of the reward, mercy and blessings endowed upon those who stand in the front row.

311. Scholars hold divergent opinions about the validity of the prayer offered alone behind the row. According to al-Nakha'ī, al-Ḥasan b. Ṣāliḥ, Aḥmad, Isḥāq, Ḥammād, Ibn Abī Lailā and Wakī', if one says prayer alone behind the row, it is not valid. But al-Ḥasan al-Baṣrī, Al-Awzā'ī, Mālik, al-Shāfi'ī and Abū Ḥanīfah maintain that it is valid. Both the views have been supported by traditions (*'Awn al-Ma'būd*, I, 254).

312. Al-Khaṭṭābī observes that this tradition indicates that offering the prayer alone outside the row is valid and permissible. The advice of the Prophet (may peace be upon him) not to repeat it in future was a direction for a better action. It the prayer were not valid, he would order him to repeat it (*'Awn al-Ma'būd*, I, 254).

Chapter 253

ON THE SCREEN (*SUTRAH*)[313] WHICH A MAN AT PRAYER SETS BEFORE HIM

(685) Ṭalḥah b. 'Ubaid Allah reported the Apostle of Allah (may peace be upon him) as saying: When you place in front of you something such as the back of a saddle, then there is no harm to you if someone passes in front of you (i.e. on the other side of it).[314]

(686) 'Aṭā' said : The back of the saddle is (about) one cubit (in height) or more than that.[315]

(687) Ibn 'Umar said : When the Apostle of Allah (may peace be upon him) would go out (for prayer) on the day of 'Īd, he ordered to bring a lance, it was then set up in front of him and he would pray in its direction,[316] and the people (stood) behind him. He used to do so during journey ; hence the rulers would take it (lance) (with them).[317]

(688) Abū Juḥaifah said : The Prophet (may peace be upon him) led them in prayer at al-Baṭḥā', with a staff set up in front of him. (He prayed) two *rak'ahs* of the noon prayer and two *rak'ahs* of the afternoon prayer. The women and the donkeys would pass in front of the staff.

Chapter 254

THE WORSHIPPER SHOULD DRAW A LINE WHEN HE DOES NOT FIND A STAFF

(689) Abū Hurairah reported the Apostle of Allah (may peace be upon him) as saying : When one of you prays, he should put something in front of his face, and if he can find nothing, he should set up his staff ; but if he has no staff, he should

313. *Sutrah* is a screen or a covering which a man at prayer places in front of him in the direction of the Ka bah so that a man may pass in front of him

314. It is forbidden to pass in front of a man who is praying. If someone passes he will be sinful. But if the man who is praying places a *sutrah* (i.e. screen, staff or any object which serves as covering), then there is no harm if one passes on the other side of this covering. In all cases the prayer will be valid.

315. From this tradition it is inferred that the minimum height of the *sutrah* is one cubit.

316. This shows that the *sutrah* set up in front of the *imām* is sufficient. It is not necessary to hoist the *sutrah* in front of all the people of the congregation.

317. The caliphs in the later days of Islam made it a fashion to have a lance when they went out for the 'Īd prayer.

draw a line ; then what passes in front of him will not harm him.[318]

(690) This tradition has also been reported by Abū Hurairah through a different chain of narrators.

Abū Hurairah reported : The Prophet (may peace be upon him) said : . . . . He then narrated the tradition about drawing the line.

Sufyān said : We did not find anything by which we could reinforce this tradition, and this has been narrated only through this chain.

He ('Alī b. al-Madīnī, a narrator) said : I said to Sufyān : There is a difference of opinion on the name (Abū Muḥammad b. 'Amr). He pondered for a moment and then said : I do not remember except Abū Muḥammad b. 'Amr. Sufyān said : A man had come to Kūfah after the death of Ismā'īl b. Umayyah ; he was seeking Abū Muḥammad until he found him. He asked him (about this tradition) but he became confused. Abū Dāwūd said : I heard Aḥmad b. Ḥanbal who was questioned many times how the line should be drawn. He replied : In this way, horizontally like crescent.

Abū Dāwūd said : I heard Musaddad say : Ibn Dāwūd said : The line should be drawn perpendicularly.

Abū Dāwūd said : I heard Aḥmad b. Hanbal describing many times how the line should be drawn. He said: In this way horizontally in a round semi-circular form like the crescent, that is (the line should be) a curve.[319]

(691) Sufyān b. 'Uyainah said : I saw Sharīk who led us in the afternoon prayer during a funeral ceremony. He placed his cap in front of him, that is, for saying the obligatory prayer the time of which had come.

Chapter 255

THE OFFERING OF PRAYER FACING THE RIDING BEAST

(692) Ibn 'Umar said: The Prophet (may peace be upon him) used to pray facing his camel.[320]

318. This tradition has been followed by Aḥmad b. Ḥanbal and some other scholars. According to them, it is permissible to draw a line on the ground in front of the man at prayer perpendicularly if one does not find anything to set up. But the rest of the jurists, Abū Ḥanīfah, Mālik and al-Shāfi'ī do not follow it, arguing that there is overt confusion in the chain of this tradition. Hence the tradition is not sound (*'Awn al-Ma'būd*, I, 256).

319. It is disputed amongst scholars how the line should be drawn According to Ibn Ḥanbal it should be in the form of a semi-circle. According to others, it should be drawn perpendicularly.

320. The Prophet (may peace be upon him) did so during a journey. He used the sitting camel as a *sutrah* for prayer. The version of al-Bukhārī adds that he used to take the saddle, put it straight, and pray facing the back of it. This he did so that the camel might not move away.

Chapter 256

IF ONE PRAYS FACING A PILLAR OR SOMETHING LIKE IT, HOW SHOULD ONE FACE IT?

(693) Al-Miqdād b. al-Aswad said: I never saw the Apostle of Allah (may peace be upon him) praying in front of a stick, a pillar, or a tree, without having it opposite his right or left eyebrow, and not facing it directly.[321]

Chapter 257

ON SAYING PRAYER FACING THE PERSONS WHO ARE TALKING OR SLEEPING

(694) 'Abd Allah b. 'Abbās reported the Prophet (may peace be upon him) as saying: Do not pray behind a sleeping or a talking person.[322]

Chapter 258

ON KEEPING CLOSE TO THE *SUTRAH*

(695) Sahl b. Abī Ḥathmah reported the Prophet (may peace be upon him) as saying: When one of you prays facing a *sutrah* he should keep close to it, and not let the devil interrupt his prayer.

Abū Dāwūd said: This tradition has also been narrated by Wāqid b. Muḥammad from Ṣafwān from Muḥammad b. Sahl on the authority of his father, or on the authority of Muḥammad b. Sahl from the Prophet (may peace be upon him). Some have narrated it from Nāfi' b. Jubair on the authority of Sahl b. Sa'd. There is a variation in the chain of its narrators.

(696) Sahl said: The distance between the place where the Prophet (may peace be upon him) stood and the *qiblah* (i.e. the *sutrah* or the wall of the mosque) was as much

321. This tradition indicates that it is commendable to face the *sutrah* at the side of one's left or right eyebrow and one should not face it directly so that it might be likened to the worshipping of the idols. But it should be noted that the chain of this tradition is weak as a narrator named Abū 'Ubaid al-Walīd is not reliable (*'Awn al-Ma'būd*, I, 257).

322. The chain of this tradition is weak. Further it contradicts the tradition which says that the Prophet (may peace be upon him) used to pray facing 'Ā'ishah who was sleeping in front of him. Al-Shāfi'ī and Aḥmad b. Ḥanbal, however, think that praying in front of a talking person is disapproved because his attention is distracted by talking (*'Awn al-Ma'būd*, I, 257).

as to allow a goat to pass.[323]

Chapter 259

IF SOMEONE PASSES IN FRONT OF THE MAN WHO PRAYS, HE SHOULD STOP HIM

(697) Abū Sa'īd al-Khudrī reported the Apostle of Allah (may peace be upon him) as saying: When one of you prays, he should not let anyone pass in front of him; he should turn him away as far as possible; but if he refuses (to go), he should fight him, for he is only a devil.[324]

(698) Abū Sa'īd al-Khudrī reported the Apostle of Allah (may peace be upon him) as saying: When one of you prays, he should pray facing the *sutrah* (screen or covering) and he should keep himself close to it. He then narrated the tradition to the same effect.

(699) Abū 'Ubaid said: I saw 'Aṭā' b. Yazīd al-Laithī praying in a standing posture. So I went to him passing in front of him; he, therefore, turned me away. He then said to me: Abū Sa'īd al-Khudrī reported the Apostle of Allah (may peace be upon him) as saying: If any one of you can do that he should not let anyone pass between him and the *qiblah*, he should do it.

(700) Abū Ṣāliḥ said: I narrate what I witnessed from Abū Sa'īd and heard from him. Abū Sa'īd entered upon Marwān and said: I heard the Apostle of Allah (may peace be upon him) say: When one of you prays facing any object which conceals him from people, and someone wishes to pass in front of him, he should strike him at his chest; if he refuses (to go), he should fight him; he is only a devil.[325]

Chapter 260

PROHIBITION FROM PASSING IN FRONT OF A MAN WHO IS PRAYING

(701) Abū Juhaim reported the Apostle of Allah (may peace be upon him) as

323. This distance has been reckoned as three cubits. It is, therefore, commendable to leave the distance of three cubits between the man who prays and the *sutrah* or the wall at the most. It is reported that when the Prophet (may peace be upon him) prayed in the Ka'bah, he left the distance of three cubits between him and the wall. Some have interpreted it by saying that the minimum distance is the passing of a goat to a maximum of three cubits (*'Awn al-Ma'būd*, I, 257).

324. This means that the devil instigates him to pass in front him. One should not fight physically because this would make the prayer null and void. This is an emphasis to indicate that the man should be turned away forcibly (*'Awn al-Ma'būd*, I, 258).

325. While praying one should not try to turn him away by force, but one should signal him to go away. After finishing the prayer one can give him warning or tell him harshly.

saying: If one who passes in front of a man who is praying knew the responsibility he incurs, he would prefer to stand still for forty . . . rather than pass in front of him. Abū al-Naḍr said: I do not know whether he said forty days, or months, or years.[326]

Abū Dāwūd: Sufyān al-Thawrī said: If a man passes proudly in front of me while I am praying, I shall stop him, and if a weak man passes, I shall not stop him.

Chapter 261

ON THE THINGS IF THEY PASS IN FRONT OF A MAN WHO IS PRAYING THAT CUT OFF THE PRAYER

(702) Ḥafṣ reported the Apostle of Allah (may peace be upon him) as saying, and the other version of this tradition transmitted through a different chain has: Abū Dharr said (and not the Prophet): If there is not anything like the back of a saddle in front of a man who is praying, then a donkey, a black dog, and a woman cut off his prayer.[327] I asked him: Why has the black dog been specified, distinguishing it from a red, a yellow and a white dog? He replied: My nephew, I also asked the Apostle of Allah (may peace be upon him) the same question as you asked me. He said: The black dog is a devil.[328]

(703) Qatādah said: I heard Jābir b. Zaid who reported on the authority of Ibn 'Abbās; and Shu'bah reported the Prophet (may peace be upon him) as saying: A menstruating woman and a dog cut off the prayer.

326. In the *Ṣaḥiḥ* of Ibn Ḥibbān another version of this tradition mentions one hundred years. This shows that forty or hundred years, or any length of time have been mentioned only for emphasis. Any definite length of time in itself does not count.

This tradition indicates that passing in front of a man who is praying is a grave sin. This applies equally to the obligatory and supererogatory prayers. But it is permissible to pass in front of him at a distance covered by three rows or more. If a man passes in front of him at a distance which is less than the distance covered by three rows he will be sinful.

327. There is a difference of opinion amongst scholars on the fact that prayer becomes void by the passing of a woman, an ass and a black dog in front of a man who is praying. Some scholars take this tradition literally and hold that the prayer becomes void. Aḥmad b. Ḥanbal is of opinion that a black dog cuts off the prayer if it passes, but he is doubtful about an ass and a woman. Mālik, Abū Ḥanīfah and al-Shāfi'ī and the majority of scholars maintain that none of these things or anything else cuts off the prayer if it passes in front of the man at prayer. According to them, by cutting off the prayer in this tradition is meant the distraction of mind by the passing of these things. Therefore, the prayer becomes defective and not void (*'Awn al-Ma'būd*, I, 259).

328. Some scholars have interpreted it literally by saying that the devil sometimes appears in the shape of a black dog. Others are of opinion that black dog is more dangerous than ordinary dogs. Hence it has been described as devil (*'Awn al-Ma'būd*, I, 259).

Abū Dāwūd said : Sa'īd, Hishām, and Hammām narrated this tradition from Qatādah on the authority of Jābir b. Zaid as a statement of Ibn 'Abbās.

(704) 'Ikrimah reported on the authority of Ibn 'Abbās, saying : I think the Apostle of Allah (may peace be upon him) said : When one of you prays without a *sutrah*, a dog, an ass, a pig, a Jew, a Magian, and a woman cut off his prayer, but it will suffice if they pass in front of him at a distance of over a stone's throw. [329]

Abū Dāwūd said : There is something about this tradition in my heart. I used to discuss it with Ibrāhīm and others. I did not find anyone who narrated it from Hishām and knew it. I did not know anyone who reported it from Hishām and knew it. I did not know anyone who related it from Hishām. I think the confusion is on the part of Ibn Abī Samīnah that is, Muḥammad b. Ismā'īl al-Baṣrī, the freed slave of Banū Hāshim. In this tradition the mention of the words "a Magian" is rejected ; the mention of the words "at a stone's throw" and "a pig" are rejected.

Abū Dāwūd said : I did not hear this tradition except from Muḥammad b. Ismā'īl b. Samurrah and I think he was mistaken because he used to narrate to us from his memory.

(705) Yazīd b. Namrān said : I saw a crippled man at Tabūk. He (the man) said : I passed riding a donkey in front of the Prophet (may peace be upon him) who was praying. He said (cursing him) : O Allah, cut off his walking. Thenceforth I could not walk.

(706) This tradition has also been reported by Sa'īd through the same chain of narrators and to the same effect. He added : He cut off our prayer, may Allah cut off his walking.

Abū Dāwūd said : The version narrated by Mushir on the authority of Sa'īd has : He cut off our prayer.

(707) Sa'īd b. Ghazwān reported on the authority of his father that he made his stay at Tabūk (during his journey) for performing *Ḥajj*. All of a sudden he saw a crippled man and asked him about his condition. He said : I relate to you a tradition, but do not narrate it to anyone so long as I am alive : The Apostle of Allah (may peace be upon him) encamped at Tabūk near a date-palm and he said : This is our *qiblah* (direction for praying). He then offered prayer facing it. I came running, when I was a boy, until I passed the place between him and the tree. He said (cursing): He cut off our prayer, may Allah out off his walking. I could not, therefore, stand upon them (feet) until today.

329. The distance beyond a stone's throw has been measured as three cubits. If these things pass in front of the man at prayer at a distance of three cubits or more, there is no need of erecting a *sutrah*, nor will they cut off the prayer (*'Awn al-Ma'būd*, I, 259).

Chapter 262

THE *SUTRAH* (CURTAIN) PLACED BEFORE THE *IMĀM* IS SUFFICIENT FOR THOSE WHO PRAY BEHIND HIM

(708) 'Amr b. Shu'aib reported from his father on the authority of his grandfather : We came down from the mountain pass of Adhākhir in the company of the Apostle of Allah (may peace be upon him). The time of prayer came and he prayed facing a direction for prayer, and we were (standing) behind him. Then a kid came and passed in front of him. He kept on stopping it until he brought his stomach near the wall (to detain it), and at last it passed behind him, or as Musaddad said.

(709) Ibn 'Abbās said : The Prophet (may peace be upon him) was (once) praying. A kid went passing in front of him and he kept on stopping it.

Chapter 263

A VIEW THAT IF A WOMAN PASSES IN FRONT OF A WORSHIPPER, SHE DOES NOT CUT OFF THE PRAYER

(710) 'Ā'ishah said : I was sleeping in front of the Prophet (may peace be upon him) with my legs between him and the *qiblah*. Shu'bah said : I think she said : I was menstruating.[330]

Abū Dāwūd said : This tradition has been narrated by al-Zuhrī, 'Aṭā', Abū Bakr b. Ḥafṣ, Hishām b. 'Urwah, 'Irāk b. Mālik, Abū al-Aswad and Tamīm b. Salamah ; all transmitted from 'Urwah on the authority of 'Ā'ishah ; Ibrāhīm narrated from al-Aswad on the authority of 'Ā'ishah ; Abū al-Ḍuḥā narrated from Masrūq on the authority of 'Ā'ishah ; al-Qāsim b. Muḥammad and Abū Salamah narrated from 'Ā'ishah. All these narrators did not mention the words : "And I was menstruating."

(711) 'Urwah reported on the authority of 'Ā'ishah : The Apostle of Allah (may peace be upon him) used to pray at night and she ('Ā'ishah) would lie between him and the *qiblah*, sleeping on the bed on which he would sleep. When he wanted to offer the *witr*[331] prayer, he awakened her and she offered the *witr* prayer.

(712) 'Ā'ishah said : I used to sleep with my legs in front of the Apostle of Allah (may peace be upon him) when he would offer his prayer at night (i.e. *tahajjud* prayer

330. This tradition indicates that if a woman passes in front of a woman, this will do no harm to the prayer.

331. *Witr* is an additional prayer offered after the night prayer. The number of *rak'ahs* it contains is disputed amongst the jurists.

offered towards the end of night). When he prostrated himself he struck my legs, and I drew them up and he then prostrated.

(713) 'Ā'ishah said: I used to sleep lying between the Apostle of Allah (may peace be upon him) and the *qiblah*. The Apostle of Allah (may peace be upon him) used to pray when I (was lying) in front of him. When he wanted to offer the *witr* prayer—added by the narrator 'Uthmān—he pinched me—then the narrators are agreed—and said : Set aside.

Chapter 264

A VIEW THAT IF A DONKEY PASSES IN FRONT OF THE WORSHIPPER, IT DOES NOT CUT OFF THE PRAYER

(714) Ibn 'Abbās said : I came riding a donkey. Another version has : Ibn 'Abbās said : When I was near the age of the puberty I came riding a she-ass and found the Apostle of Allah (may peace be upon him) leading the people in prayer at Minā. I passed in front of a part of the row (of worshippers), and dismounting left my she-ass for grazing in the pasture, and I joined the row, and no one objected to that.

Abū Dāwūd said : These are the words of al-Qa'nabī, and are complete. Mālik said : I take it as permissible at the time when the *iqāmah* for prayer is pronounced.

(715) Abū al-Ṣahbā' said : We discussed the things that cut off the prayer according to Ibn 'Abbās. He said : I and a boy from Banū 'Abd al-Muṭṭalib came riding a donkey, and the Apostle of Allah (may peace be upon him) was leading the people in prayer. He dismounted and I also dismounted. I left the donkey in front of the row (of the worshippers). He (the Prophet) did not pay attention to that. Then two girls from Banū 'Abd al-Muṭṭalib came and joined the row in the middle, but he paid no attention to that.

(716) The above-mentioned tradition has also been narrated by Manṣūr through a different chain of narrators. This version has : Then two girls from Banu 'Abd al-Muṭṭalib came fighting together. He caught them. 'Uthmān (a narrator) said : He separated them. And Dāwūd (another narrator) said : He pulled away one from the other, but he paid no attention to that.

Chapter 265

A VIEW THAT THE PASSING OF A DOG IN FRONT OF A WORSHIPPER DOES NOT CUT OFF THE PRAYER

(717) Al-Faḍl b. 'Abbās said : The Apostle of Allah (may peace be upon him)

came to us accompanied by 'Abbās when we were in open country belonging to us. He prayed in a desert with no *sutrah* in front of him, and a she-ass and a bitch of ours were playing in front of him, but he paid no attention to that.

Chapter 266

A VIEW THAT THE PASSING OF ANYTHING IN FRONT OF THE WORSHIPPER DOES NOT CUT OFF THE PRAYER

(718) Abū Sa'īd reported the Apostle of Allah (may peace be upon him) as saying: Nothing interrupts prayer, but repulse as much as you can anyone who passes in front of you, for he is just a devil.

(719) Abū al-Waddāk said: A youth from the Quraish passed in front of Abū Sa'īd al-Khudrī who was praying. He repulsed him. He returned again. He then repulsed him for the third time. When he finished his prayer, he said: Nothing cuts off prayer; but the Apostle of Allah (may peace be upon him) said: Repulse as much as you can, for he is just a devil.

Abū Dāwūd said: If the two traditions of the Prophet (may peace be upon him) conflict, the practice of his Companions after him should be taken into consideration.[332]

CHAPTERS ON THE DETAILS OF COMMENCING PRAYER

Chapter 267

RAISING THE HANDS

(720) Sālim reported on the authority of his father (Ibn 'Umar): I saw the

332. The majority of the Companions maintain that the passing of anything does not cut off prayer. A number of traditions indicate that the passing of a dog, an ass, a woman, or any other animal does not interrupt prayer. Al-Tirmidhī said: Most of the Companions and their Successors hold that nothing interrupts prayer. Sufyān and al-Shāfi'ī also hold the same view. But a group of scholars hold that prayer is interrupted if a black dog, or a woman, or an ass passes in front of the worshipper. It seems that Abū Dāwūd himself prefers the view that prayer is not interrupted by the passing of anything. Al-Ṭaḥāwī and others appear to have inclined towards the view that the tradition narrated by Abū Dharr has been abrogated by the tradition narrated by 'Ā'ishah. Al-Shāfi'ī and some other scholars have interpreted the tradition reported by Abū Dharr by saying that by cutting off is meant the distraction of attention and not the cutting off the prayer itself. Some scholars hold that the tradition narrated by Abū Dharr is earlier to the tradition reported by 'Ā'ishah. Both can be reconciled (*'Awn al-Ma'būd*, I. 262).

Apostle of Allah (may peace be upon him) that when he began prayer, he used to raise his hands opposite his shoulders,[333] and he did[334] so when he bowed, and raised his head after bowing. Sufyān (a narrator) once said: "When he raised his head"; and after he used to say: "When he raised his head after bowing. He would not raise (his hands) between the two prostrations."

(721) 'Abd Allah b. 'Umar said: The Apostle of Allah (may peace be upon him) used to raise his hands opposite his shoulders when he began prayer, then he uttered *takbīr* (Allah is most great) in the same condition, and then he bowed. And when he raised his back (head) after bowing he raised them opposite his shoulders, and said: "Allah listens to him who praises Him." But he did not raise his hand when he prostrated himself; he rather raised them when he uttered the *takbīr* (Allah is most great) before bowing until his prayer is finished.

(722) 'Abd al-Jabbār b. Wā'il (b. Ḥujr) said: I was a small boy and I did not understand the prayer of my father. So Wā'il b. 'Alqamah reported Wā'il b. Ḥujr as saying: I offered prayer along with the Apostle of Allah (may peace be upon him). He used to raise his hands when he pronounced the *takbīr* (Allah is most great), then pulled his garment round him, then placed his right hand on his left, and entered his hands in his garment. When he was about to bow he took his hands out of his garment, and then raised them. And when he raised his head after bowing, he raised his hands. He then prostrated himself and placed his face (forehead on the ground) between his hands. And when he raised his head after prostration,[335] he also raised

333. There is a difference of opinion amongst the jurists on the point whether the utterance of *takbir* and raising the hands should be done simultaneously or the hands should be raised before pronouncing the *takbir*. According to the traditionists and most of the scholars, it is preferable to raise the hands and utter the *takbir* simultaneously. One should not be done after the other. Al-Shāfi'ī and Mālik also hold the same view. According to Abū Hanīfah the hands should be raised first, then the *takbir* should be uttered.

The point of raising the hands opposite the shoulders is also disputed among the scholars. According to al-Shāfi'ī and the majority of scholars, the hands should be raised opposite the shoulders. This equally applies to man and woman. According to Abū Ḥanīfah, men should raise the hands opposite the ears, and women opposite the shoulders.

334. The raising of hands just before and after bowing is commendable according to al-Shāfi'ī, Aḥmad and Mālik. Abū Ḥanīfah does not validate it except at the beginning of prayer. He follows the tradition reported by Ibn Mas'ūd, which says that he saw the Prophet (may peace be upon him) raising his hands at the beginning of prayer, but he did not repeat it. There are many arguments adduced in support of both views (*'Awn al Ma'būd*, I, 262).

335. The tradition reported by Ibn 'Umar clearly indicates that the Prophet (may peace be upon him) did not raise his hands between the two prostrations. Some scholars have harmonised these two traditions by saying that the Prophet (may peace be upon him) used to raise his hands between the prostrations. But later on he gave up this practice. Hence it is now considered to be abrogated.

his hands until he finished his prayer. Muhammad (a narrator) said: I mentioned it to al-Ḥasan b. Abū al-Ḥasan who said: This is how the Apostle of Allah (may peace be upon him) offered prayer; some did it and others abandoned it.

Abū Dāwūd said: This tradition has been narrated by Hammām from Ibn Juḥādah, but he did not mention the raising of hands after he raised his head at the end of prostration.

(723) Wā'il b. Ḥujr said that he saw the Apostle of Allah (may peace be upon him) raise his hands when he uttered the *takbīr* (Allah is most great).

(724) Wā'il b. Ḥujr said: He saw that when the Prophet (may peace be upon him) stood up to pray he raised his hands till they were in front of his shoulders and placed his thumbs opposite his ears; then he uttered the *takbīr* (Allah is most great).

(725) Wā'il b. Ḥujr said: I purposely looked at the prayer of the Apostle of Allah (may peace be upon him), how he offered it. The Apostle of Allah (may peace be upon him) stood up, faced the direction of the *qiblah* and uttered the *takbīr* (Allah is most great) and then raised his hands in front of his ears, then placed his right hand on his left (catching each other). When he was about to bow, he raised them in the same manner. He then placed his hands on his knees. When he raised his head after bowing, he raised them in the like manner. When he prostrated himself he placed his forehead between his hands. He then sat down and spread his left foot and placed his left hand on his left thigh, and kept his right elbow aloof from his right thigh. He closed his two fingers and made a circle (with the fingers). I ('Āṣim b. Kulaib) saw him (Bishr b. al-Mufaḍḍal) say in this manner. Bishr made the circle with the thumb and the middle finger and pointed with the forefinger.

(726) The above tradition has been transmitted by 'Āṣim b. Kulaib through a different chain of narrators and to the same effect. This version has: "He then placed his right hand on the back of his left palm and his wrist and forearm." This also adds: "I then came back afterwards in a season when it was severe cold. I saw the people putting on heavy clothes moving their hands under the clothes (i.e. raised their hands before and after bowing)."

(727) Wā'il b. Ḥujr said: I witnessed the Prophet (may peace be upon him) raise his hands in front of his ears when he began to pray. I then came back and saw them (the people) raising their hands up to their chests when they began to pray. They wore long caps and blankets..

Chapter 268

THE BEGINNING OF PRAYER

(728) Wā'il b. Ḥujr said: I came to the Prophet (may peace be upon him) during

winter; I saw his Companions raise their hands in their clothes in prayer.[336]

(729) Abū Ḥumaid al-Sā'idī once told a company of ten of the Companions of the Apostle of Allah (may peace be upon him); Abū Qatādah was one of them: I am one among you who is more informed of the way the Apostle of Allah (may peace be upon him) prayed. They said: Why, by Allah, you did not follow him more than us, nor did you remain in his company longer than us? He said: Yes. They said: Then describe (how the Prophet prayed). He said: When the Apostle of Allah (may peace be upon him) stood up to pray, he raised his hands so as to bring them opposite his shoulders, and uttered the *takbir* (Allah is most great), until every bone rested in its place properly; then he recited (some verses from the Qur'ān); then he uttered the *takbīr* (Allah is most great), raising his hands so as to bring them opposite to his shoulders; then he bowed; placing the palms of his hands on his knees and keeping himself straight, neither raising nor lowering his head; then raised his head saying: "Allah listens to him who praises Him"; then raised his hands so as to bring them exactly opposite to his shoulders; then uttered: "Allah is most great"; then lowered himself to the ground (in prostration), keeping his arms away from his sides; then raised his head, bent his left foot and sat on it, and opened the toes when he prostrated; then he uttered: "Allah is most great"; then raised his head, bent his left foot and sat on it so that every bone returned to its place properly; then he did the same in the second (*rak'ah*). At the end of the two *rak'ahs* he stood up and uttered the *takbīr* (Allah is most great), raising his hand so as to bring them opposite to his shoulders; then he bowed, placing the palms of his hands on his knees and keeping himself straight, neither raising nor lowering his head: then raised his head saying: "Allah listens to him who praises Him"; then raised his hands so as to bring them exactly opposite to his shoulders; then uttered: "Allah is most great"; then lowered himself to the ground (in prostration), keeping his arms away from his sides; then raised his head, bent his left foot and sat on it, and opened the toes when he prostrated himself; then he prostrated; then uttered "Allah is most great"; then raised his head, bent his left foot and sat on it so that every bone returned to its place properly; then he did the same in the second (*rak'ah*). At the end of the two *rak'ahs* he stood up and uttered the *takbir* (Allah is most great), raising his hand so as to bring them opposite to his shoulders in the way he had uttered the *takbir* (Allah is most great) at the beginning of the prayer; then he did that in the remainder of his prayer; and after the prostration which is followed by the *taslīm* (salutation) he put out his left foot and sat on his left hip.[337] They said: You have spoken the truth. This is

336. They did not take out their hands due to severe cold.

337. Al-Khaṭṭābī said: It is a *sunnah* (recommended) that the man who prays four *rak'ahs* should sit on his left foot after two *rak'ahs* in the middle and should sit on his left hip putting out his left foot at the end of the four *rak'ahs* in the last sitting, and should not sit on the sole of his

how he (may peace be upon him) used to pray.

(730) 'Amr al-'Āmirī said: I (once) attended the meeting of the Companions of the Apostle of Allah (may peace be upon him). They began to discuss his prayer. Abū Humaid then narrated a part of the same tradition and said: When he bowed he clutched his knees with his palms, and he opened his fingers; then he bent his back without raising him upwards, and did not turn his face (on any side). When he sat at the end of two *rak'ahs* he sat on the sole of his left foot and raised the right, and after the fourth he placed his left hip on the ground and spread out both his feet on one side.

(731) The above-mentioned tradition has also been reported by Muḥammad b. 'Amr b. 'Aṭā' through a different chain of narrators. This version adds: "When he prostrated himself he neither placed his arms on the ground nor closed them; putting forward his fingers towards the *qiblah*."

(732) Abbās or 'Ayyāsh b. Sahl al-Sā'idī said that he was present in a meeting which was attended by his father who was one of the Companions of the Prophet (may peace be upon him), Abū Hurairah, Abū Ḥumaid al-Sā'idi and Abū Usaid. He then narrated the same tradition with a slight addition or deletion. He said: He then raised his head after bowing and uttered: "Allah listens to him who praises Him, to Thee, our Lord, be the praise," and raised his hands. He then uttered: "Allah is most great"; then he prostrated himself and rested on his palms, knees, and the end of his toes while prostrating: then he uttered the *takbīr* (Allah is most great , and sat down on his hips and raised his other foot; then he uttered the *takbīr* and prostrated himself; then he uttered the *takbir* and stood up, but did not sit on his hips. He (the narrator) then narrated the rest of the tradition. He further said: Then he sat down at the end of two *rak'ahs*; when he was about to stand after two *rak'ahs*, he uttered the *takbir*; then he offered the last two *rak'ahs* of the prayer. The narrator did not mention about his sitting on the hips spreading out his feet.

(733) 'Abbās b. Sahl said: Abū Ḥumaid, Abū Usaid, Sahl b. Sa'd and Muḥammad b. Maslamah (once) got together and discussed how the Apostle of Allah (may peace be upon him) used to offer his prayer. Abū Ḥumaid said: I am more informed than any of you regarding the prayer offered by the Apostle of Allah (may peace be upon him). Then he mentioned a part of it, and said: He then bowed and placed his hands upon his knees as if he caught hold of them; and bent them, keeping (his arms) away from his sides. He then prostrated himself and placed his nose and forehead (on the ground); and kept his arms away from his sides, and placed

left foot as he did after two *rak'ahs*. This is held by al-Shāfi'ī, Aḥmad b. Ḥanbal and Isḥāq. Mālik maintains that he should sit on his hips in both sittings, and not on his foot. Abū Ḥanīfah and Sufyān al-Thawrī are of the view that he should sit on his left foot in both the sittings and not on his hip (*'Awn al-Ma'būd*, I, 266)

his palms (on the ground) opposite his shoulders; he then raised his head that every bone returned to its proper place; (he then prostrated twice) until he finished (his prostrations). Then he sat down and spread out his left foot, putting forward the front of his right foot towards the *qiblah* placing the palm of his right hand on his right knee, and the palm of his left hand on his left knee, and he pointed with his finger.[338]

Abū Dāwūd said: This tradition has been narrated by Ibn al-Mubārak from Fulaiḥ who heard 'Abbās b. Sahl narrating it; but I do not remember it. I think he made the mention of 'Īsā b. 'Abd Allah who heard 'Abbās b. Sahl saying: I accompanied Abū Ḥumaid al-Sā'idī.

(734) Abī Ḥumaid reported to the same effect. He said: When he (the Prophet) prostrated he kept his thighs wide and did not let his belly touch the thighs.

Abū Dāwūd says that Ibn Mubārak narrated this *hadīth* from 'Abbās b. Sahl, which he did not remember well. It is thought that he has mentioned 'Īsā b. 'Abd Allah, 'Abbās b. Sahl and Abū Ḥumaid al-Sā'idī.

(735) Wā'il b. Ḥujr reported in this tradition from the Prophet (may peace be upon him): When he prostrated, his knees touched the ground before his palms touched it; when he prostrated himself, he placed his forehead on the ground) between his palms, and kept his armpits away from his sides.

Ḥajjāj reported from Hammām and Shaqīq narrated a similar tradition to us from 'Āṣim b. Kulaib on the authority of his father from the Prophet (may peace be upon him).

And the version narrated by one of them has—and I think in all probability that this version has been narrated by Muḥammad b. Juhādah—when he got up (after prostration), he got up with his knees and gave his weight on his thighs.

(736) Wā'il b. Ḥujr said: I saw the Apostle of Allah (may peace be upon him) raising his thumbs in prayer up to the lobes of his ears.

(737) Abū Hurairah said: When the Apostle of Allah (may peace be upon him) uttered the *takbīr* (Allah is most great) for prayer (in the beginning), he raised his hands opposite to his shoulders; and when he bowed, he did like that; and when he raised his head to prostrate, he did like that; and when he got up at the end of two *rak'ahs*, he did like that.

(738) Maimūn al-Makkī said: that he saw 'Abd Allah b. al-Zubair leading in prayer. He pointed with his hands (i.e. raised his hands opposite to the shoulders) when he stood up, and when he bowed and when he prostrated, and when he got up

338 The pointing with the finger signifies the Unity of Allah and sincerity of the worshipper. Hence the Prophet (may peace be upon him) prohibited to point with two fingers.

The other versions of this tradition clearly state that he pointed with his forefinger and he raised it reciting the words "There is no god but Allah." Some traditions indicate that the Prophet (may peace be upon him) used to move his fingers and others show that he did not do so (*'Awn al-Ma'būd*, I. 267)

after prostration, he pointed with his hands (i.e. raised his hands). Then I went to Ibn 'Abbās and said (to him): I saw Ibn al-Zubair praying that I never saw anyone praying. I then told him about the pointing with his hands (raising his hands). He said: If you like to see the prayer of the Apostle of Allah (may peace be upon him) follow the prayer as offered by 'Abd Allah b. al-Zubair.

(739) Naḍr b. Kathīr al-Sa'dī said: 'Abd Allah b. Ṭāwūs prayed at my side in the mosque of al-Khaif. When he made the first prostration, he raised his head after it and raised his hands opposite to his face. This came as something strange for me. I, therefore, said it to Wuhaib b. Khālid. Then Wuhaib b. Khālid said to him: You are doing a thing that I did not see anyone do. Ibn Ṭāwūs then replied: I saw my father doing it, and my father said: I saw Ibn 'Abbās doing it. I do not know but he said: The Prophet (may peace be upon him) used to do it.[339]

(740) Nāfi' said on the authority of Ibn 'Umar that when he began prayer, he uttered the *takbir* (Allah is most great) and raised his hands; and when he bowed (he raised his hands); and when he said: "Allah listens to him who praises Him," (he raised his hands); and when he stood up at the end of two *rak'has*, he raised his hands. He (Ibn 'Umar) traced that back to the Apostle of Allah (may peace be upon him)

Abū Dāwūd said: What is correct is that the tradition reported by Ibn 'Umar does not go back to the Prophet (may peace be upon him).

Abū Dāwūd said: The narrator Baqīyyah reported the first part of this tradition from 'Ubaid Allah and traced it back to the Prophet (may peace be upon him); and the narrator al-Thaqafī reported it from 'Ubaid Allah as a statement of Ibn 'Umar himself (not from the Prophet). In this version he said: When he stood at the end of two *rak'has* he raised them up to his breasts. And this is the correct version.

Abū Dāwūd said: This tradition has been transmitted as a statement of Ibn 'Umar (and not of the Prophet) by al-Laith b. Sa'd, Mālik, Ayyūb, and Ibn Juraij; and this has been narrated as a statement of the Prophet (may peace be upon him) by Ḥammād b. Salamah alone on the authority of Ayyūb. Ayyūb and Mālik did not mention his raising of hands when he stood after two prostrations, but al-Laith mentioned it in his version. Ibn Juraij said in this version: I asked Nāfi': Din Ibn 'Umar raise (his hands) higher for the first time? He said: No. I said: Point out to me. He then pointed to the breasts or lower than that.

(741) Nāfi' said: When 'Abd Allah b. 'Umar began his prayer, he raised his hands opposite to his shoulders; and when he raised his head after bowing, he raised them

339. This tradition shows that raising the hands between the two prostrations is commendable. This is maintained by Abū Bakr b. al-Mundhir, Abū 'Alī al-Ṭabarī, one of the followers of al-Shāfi'ī, and a group of traditionists. But what is correct is that this tradition is weak because the narrator al-Naḍr b. Kathīr al-Sa'dī is objectionable in narrating the traditions. Moreover, a number of sound traditions indicate clearly that the Prophet (may peace be upon him) did not raise hands between the two prostrations (*'Awn al-Ma'būd*, I, 269-70)

lower than that.

Abū Dāwūd said: So far as I know, no one narrated the words "he raised them lower than that" except Mālik.

Chapter 269

THE VIEW THAT HE (THE PROPHET) RAISED HIS HANDS WHEN HE STOOD AT THE END OF TWO *RAK'AHS*

(742) Ibn 'Umar said: When the Apostle of Allah (may peace be upon him) stood at the end of two *rak'ahs*, he uttered the *takbīr* (Allah is most great) and raised his hands.

(743) 'Alī b. Abī Ṭālib said: When the Apostle of Allah (may peace be upon him) stood for offering the obligatory prayer, he uttered the *takbīr* (Allah is most great) and raised his hands opposite to his shoulders; and he did like that when he finished recitation (of the Qur'ān) and was about to bow; and he did like that when he rose after bowing; and he did not raise his hands in his prayer while he was in his sitting position; and when he stood up from his prostrations (at the end of two *rak'ahs*), he raised his hands likewise and uttered the *takbir* (Allah is most great) and raised his hands so as to bring them up to his shoulders, as he uttered the *takbir* in the beginning of the prayer.

(744) Mālik b. al-Ḥuwairith said: I saw the Prophet (may peace be upon him) raise his hands when he uttered the *takbīr* (Allah is most great), when he bowed and when he raised his head after bowing until he brought them to the lobes of his ears.

(745) Abū Hurairah said: If I were in front of the Prophet (may peace be upon him), I would see his armpits.[340]

Ibn Mu'ādh added that Lāḥiq said: Do you not see, Abū Hurairah could not stand in front of the Prophet (may peace be upon him) while he was praying?[341] Mūsā added: When he uttered the *takbīr*, he raised his hands.

(746) 'Abd Allah b. Mas'ūd said: The Apostle of Allah (may peace be upon him) taught us how to pray. He then uttered the *takbir* (Allah is most great) and raised his hands; when he bowed, he joined his hands and placed them between his knees. When this (report) reached Sa'd, he said: My brother said truly. We used to do this; then we were later on commanded to do this, that is, to place the hands on the knees.

340. One can see the armpits if the man raises his hands. Abū Hurairah meant that he saw the Prophet (may peace be upon him) raise the hands.

341. This is the expression of doubt about the statement of Abū Hurairah from the narrator Lāḥiq. Abū Hurairah prayed behind the Prophet (may peace be upon him) who led the people in prayer. Hence how could he stand in front of him and see him raise the hands?

Chapter 270

THE VIEW THAT DOES NOT SUPPORT THE RAISING OF HANDS JUST BEFORE BOWING

(747) 'Alqamah said: 'Abd Allah b. Mas'ūd said: Should I pray in the way the Apostle of Allah (may peace be upon him) had performed it? He said: He prayed, raising his hands only once.[342]

(748) This tradition has also been transmitted by Sufyān through a different chain of narrators. This version has: He then raised his hands once in the beginning. Some narrated: (raised his hands) once only.

(749) Al-Barā' said: When the Apostle of Allah (may peace be upon him) began prayer, he raised his hands up to his ears, then he did not repeat.[343]

(750) This tradition has been narrated by Sufyān through a different chain of transmitters. This version does not have the words "then he did not repeat". Sufyān said: The words "then he did not repeat" were narrated to us later on at Kūfah by him (Yazīd).

Abū Dāwūd said: This tradition has also been transmitted by Hushaim, Khālid, and Ibn Idrīs from Yazīd. They did not mention the words "then he did not repeat".

(751) Al-Barā' b. 'Āzib said: I saw that the Apostle of Allah (may peace be upon him) raised his hands when he began prayer, but he did not raise them until he finished (prayer).

Abū Dāwūd said: This tradition is not sound.

(752) Abū Hurairah said: When the Apostle of Allah (may peace be upon him) began his prayer, he raised his hands extensively.

342. The Ḥanafīs argue with this tradition in support of their view not to raise hands before bowing. But their argument is not correct as this tradition is weak according to Ibn Ḥajar, Ibn al-Mubārak, Ibn Abī Ḥātim, Ibn Ḥanbal, al-Bukhārī, Abū Dāwūd, al-Dāraquṭnī, Ibn Ḥibbān. The narrators 'Āṣim b. Kulaib is not trustworthy. Ibn Ma'īn and al-Tirmidhī regard this tradition as good (*ḥasan*). But this tradition contradicts a large number of traditions, established as sound, which clearly indicate that the Prophet (may peace be upon him) used to raise his hands before bowing and after it. According to al-Khaṭṭābī these traditions are more sound than the one reported by Ibn Mas'ūd. Moreover, raising hands before and after bowing is commendable and not obligatory. It is possible that the Prophet (may peace be upon him) might have left this on some occasions, and Ibn Mas'ūd could remember this practice only. He also forgot the practice of placing hands on the knees while bowing and he continued to place them between the knees, though this practice was abrogated later on (*'Awn al-Ma'būd*, I, 272-73).

343. This tradition is weak according to al-Madīnī, Ibn Ḥanbal, and al-Dāraquṭnī. The narrator Yazīd b. Ziyād is not trustworthy (*'Awn al-Ma'būd*, I, 273).

Chapter 271

PLACING THE RIGHT HAND ON THE LEFT HAND IN PRAYER

(753) Zur'ah b. 'Abd al-Raḥmān said: I heard Ibn al-Zubair say: Setting the feet right and placing one hand on the other is a *sunnah*.

(754) Abū 'Uthmān al-Nahdī said: When Ibn Mas'ūd prayed he placed his left hand on the right. The Prophet (may peace be upon him) saw him and placed his right hand on his left one.[344]

(755) Abū Juḥaifah said: 'Alī said that it is a *sunnah* to place one hand on the other in prayer below the navel.[345]

(756) Ibn Jarīr al-Ḍabbī reported on the authority of his father: I saw 'Alī (Allah be pleased with him) catching hold of his left hand by his right hand on the wrist above the navel.

Abū Dāwūd said: Sa'īd b. Jubair narrated the words: "above the navel". Abū Mijlaz reported the words: "below the navel". This has also been narrated by Abū Hurairah. But that is not strong.

(757) Abū Hurairah said: (The established way of folding hands is) to hold the hands by the hands in prayer below the navel.

Abū Dāwūd said: I heard Aḥmad b. Ḥanbal say: The narrator 'Abd al-Raḥmān b. Isḥāq al-Kūfī is weak (i.e. not reliable).

(758) Ṭāwūs said: The Apostle of Allah (may peace be upon him) used to place his right hand on his left hand, then he folded them strictly on his chest in prayer.[346]

344. There is no difference of opinion amongst the jurists that it is the *sunnah* of the Prophet (may peace be upon him) to place the right hand on the left hand. No tradition which contradicts it has been reported from the Prophet (may peace be upon him).

345. The question of folding hands in prayer below the navel is disputed amongst the jurists. According to Abū Ḥanīfah, Sufyān al-Thawrī, Isḥāq b. Rahwaih, Abū Isḥāq al-Marwazī, the hands should be folded below the navel. This tradition is followed by them According to al-Shāfi'ī, the hands should be placed below the chest. Al-Nawawī says that this is the view of the majority of the jurists. Two statements have been attributed to Aḥmad b. Ḥanbal. According to the third view ascribed to him he does not give any preference to any of these two views. One has the choice of placing the hands. Mālik is also reported to have held two different views. According to one version, the hands should be placed below the chest. According to the second, he held that one should leave the hands in their natural position without folding them. One should not fold them placing one on the other (*'Awn al-Ma'būd*, I, 275).

346. This is a *mursal* tradition, as Ṭāwūs is a successor and the name of the Companion has been omitted. According to the traditionists, the tradition is sound. Hence folding hands on the chest in prayer, in their opinion, is the established *sunnah* of the Prophet (may peace be upon him). The traditions regarding the folding of hands below or above the navel are not established as coming from the Prophet (may peace be upon him) (*'Awn al-Ma'būd*, I, 275-77).

Chapter 272

WHAT SUPPLICATIONS SHOULD BE RECITED AFTER THE BEGINNING OF PRAYER

(759) 'Alī b. Abī Ṭālib said: When the Apostle of Allah (may peace be upon him stood up for prayer,[347] he uttered the *takbir* (Allah is most great), then said: I have turned my face, breaking with all others, towards Him Who created the heavens and the earth, and I am not a polytheist. My prayer and my devotion, my life and my death belong to Allah, the Lord of the Universe, Who has no partner. That is what I have been commanded, and I am first of Muslims (those who surrender themselves). O Allah, Thou art the King. There is no god but Thee. Thou art my Lord and I am Thy servant. I have wronged myself, but I acknowledge my sin, so forgive me all my sins; Thou Who alone canst forgive sins; and guide me to the best qualities, Thou Who alone canst guide to the best of them; and turn me from evil ones. Thou Who alone canst turn from evil qualities. I come to serve and please Thee. All good is in Thy hands, and evil does not pertain to Thee. I seek refuge in Thee and turn to Thee, Who art blessed and exalted. I ask Thy forgiveness and turn to Thee in repentance. When he bowed, he said: O Allah, to Thee I bow, in Thee I trust, and to Thee I submit myself. My hearing, my sight, my brain, my bone, and my sinews humble themselves before Thee. When he raised his head, he said: Allah listens to him who praises Him. O our Lord, and all praise be to Thee in the whole of the heavens and the earth, and what is between them, and in whatever Thou createst afterwards. When he prostrated himself, he said: O Allah, to Thee I prostrate myself, to Thee I trust, and to Thee I submit myself. My face prostrated itself before Him Who created it, fashioned it, and fashioned it in the best shape, and brought forth its hearing and seeing. Blessed is Allah, the best of the creators. When he saluted at the end of the prayer, he said: O Allah, forgive me my former and my latter sins, my open and my secret sins, my sins in exceeding the limits, and what Thou knowest better than I. Thou art He Who puts forward and puts back. There is no deity but Thee.

347. In their versions of this tradition Ibn Ḥibbān, al-Shāfi'ī and some other scholars of tradition have clearly mentioned the word (obligatory prayer). This shows that the Prophet (may peace be upon him) recited all these supplications in the obligatory prayer. But Muslim in his *Ṣaḥiḥ* indicated the words "ṣalāt al-laif" (prayer at night in small hours) and added the words "min jawf al-lail" (at midnight or dead of night). This shows that he used to recite all these supplications in the supererogatory prayer of *tahajjud* in the middle or towards the end of night. This is held by the Ḥanafī school. It is, however, possible that the Prophet (may peace be upon him) might have recited these supplications sometimes in obligatory prayer and at times in supererogatory prayer (*'Awn al-Ma būd*, I, 277).

(760) 'Alī b. Abī Ṭālib said: When the Apostle of Allah (may peace be upon him) stood up for (offering) obligatory prayer,[348] he uttered the *takbir* (Allah is most great) and raised his hands opposite to his shoulders, and he did so when he finished the recitation (of the Qur'ān) and when he was about to bow; and he did like that when he raised (his head) after bowing He did not raise his hands in prayer when he was sitting. When he stood at the end of two *rak'ahs*, he raised his hands in a similar way and uttered the *takbīr* and supplicated in a more or less the same manner as narrated by 'Abd al-'Azīz in his version. This version does not mention the words "All good is in Thy hands and evil does not pertain to thee." And this adds: He said when he finished the prayer: "O Allah, foregive me my former and latter sins, my open and secret sins; Thou art my deity; there is no god but Thee.

(761) Shu'aib b. Abī Ḥamzah said: Ibn al-Munkadir, Ibn Abī Farwah and a number of the jurists of Medina said to me: When you recite the supplication "I am first of the Muslims," say instead; "I am one of the Muslims.[349]

(762) Anas b. Mālik said: A man came panting to join the row of worshippers, and said: Allah is most great; praise be to Allah, much praise, good and blessed. When the Apostle of Allah (may peace be upon him) finished his prayer, he asked: Which of you is the one who spoke the words? He said nothing wrong. Then the man said: I (said), Apostle of Allah (may peace be upon him); I came and had difficulty in breathing, so I said them. He said: I saw twelve angels racing against one another to be the one to take them up to Allah.

The narrator Ḥumaid added: When any of you comes for praying, he should walk as usual (i.e. he should not hasten and run quickly); then he should pray as much as he finds it (along with the *imām*), and should offer the part of the prayer himself (when the prayer is finished) which the *imām* had offered before him.

(763) Jubair b. Muṭ'im said that he saw the Apostle of Allah (may peace be upon him) observing prayer. The narrator 'Amr said: I do not know which prayer he was offering. He (the Prophet) said: Allah is altogether great; Allah is altogether great; Allah is altogether great; and praise be to Allah in abundance; and praise be to Allah in abundance; and praise be to Allah in abundance. Glory be to Allah in the morning and afternoon (saying it three times). I seek refuge in Allah from the accursed devil, from his puffing up (*nafkh*), his spitting (*nafth*) and his evil suggestion (*hamz*).

He ('Amr) said: His *nafth* it poetry, his *nafkh* is pride, and his *hamz* is madness.

348. This version of the tradition clearly indicates that the Prophet (may peace be upon him) used to recite all these supplications in obligatory prayers

349. The reason is that it was the Prophet (may peace be upon him) who was the first Muslim.

(764) The above-mentioned tradition has also been reported by Jubair b. Muṭ'im through a different chain of narrators. This version adds: I heard the Prophet (may peace be upon him) uttering (all these supplications) in a supererogatory prayer; he narrated the tradition in a similar manner.

(765) 'Āṣim b. Ḥumaid said: I asked 'Ā'ishah: By what words the Apostle of Allah (may peace be upon him) would begin his supererogatory prayer at night? She replied: You ask me about a thing of which no one asked me before you. When he stood up, he uttered the *takbīr* (Allah is most great) ten times, and uttered "Praise be to Allah" ten times, and uttered "Glory be to Allah" ten times, and uttered "There is no god but Allah" ten times, and sought forgiveness ten times, and said: O Allah, forgive me, and guide me, and give me sustenance, and keep me well, and he sought refuge in Allah from the hardship of standing before Allah on the Day of Judgment.

Abū Dāwūd said: This tradition has also been narrated by Khālid b. Ma'dān from Rabī'ah al-Jarashī on the authority of 'Ā'ishah.

(766) Abū Salamah b. 'Abd al-Raḥmān b. 'Awf said: I asked 'Ā'ishah: By what words the Prophet (may peace be upon him) used to begin his prayer when he stood up at night (to offer *tahajjud* prayer). She said: When he stood up at night, he began his prayer by saying: O Allah, Lord of Jibrā'īl, Lord of Mikā'īl, Lord of Isrāfīl, Creator of the heavens and the earth, the Knower of what is seen and of what is unseen; Thou decidest between Thy servants in which they used to differ. Guide me to the Truth where there is a difference of opinion by Thy permission. Thou guidest anyone Thou wishest to the right path.

(767) The above-mentioned tradition has been reported by 'Ikrimah with a different chain of narrators. This version adds: When he stood up, he said the *takbīr* (Allah is most great) and said. . . .

(768) Mālik said: There is no harm in uttering supplication in prayer, in its beginning, in its middle, and in the end, in obligatory prayer or other.

(769) Rifā'ah b. Rāfi' said: One day we were praying behind the Apostle of Allah (may peace be upon him). When the Apostle of Allah (may peace be upon him) raised his head after bowing, he said: Allah listened to him who praised Him. A man behind the Apostle of Allah (may peace be upon him) said: O Allah, Our Lord, and to Thee be praise, much p aise, good and blessed. When the Apostle of Allah (may peace be upon him) finished his prayer, he asked: Which of you is the one who spoke (the words) just now. The man said: I (uttered) these words, Prophet of Allah. The Apostle of Allah (may peace be upon him) said: I saw more than thirty angels racing against one another to be the one to write them first.

(770) Ibn 'Abbās said: When the Apostle of Allah (may peace be upon him) stood up for praying at midnight, he said: O Allah, be praise to Thee; Thou art the

light of the heavens and the earth ; and to Thee be praise ; Thou are the maintainer of the heavens and the earth ; and to Thee be praise, Thou art the heavens and the earth and what is between them ; Thou art the truth, and Thy statement is truth ; and Thy promise is the truth ; and the visitation with Thee is true ; and the Paradise is true and the Hell-fire is true and the Hour is true ; O Allah, to Thee I submitted, and in Thee I believed, and in Thee I trusted, and to Thee I turned my attention, and by Thee I disputed, and to Thee I brought forth my case, so forgive me my former and my latter sins, and my secret and open sins, Thou art my deity, there is no deity but Thou.

(771) Ibn 'Abbās said : The Apostle of Allah (may beace be upon him) used to say in his *tahajjud* prayer (i.e. supererogatory prayer offered in or after the midnight) after he said the *takbīr* ; he then narrated the tradition to the same effect.

(772) Rifā'ah b. Rāfi' said : I offered prayer behind the Apostle of Allah (may peace be upon him). Rifā'ah sneezed. The narrator Qutaibah did not mention the name Rifā'ah (but he said : I sneezed). So I said : Praise be to Allah, praise much, good and blessed therein, blessed thereupon, as our Lord likes and is pleased. When the Apostle of Allah (may peace be upon him) finished his prayer, he turned and said : Who was the speaker in prayer? He then narrated the rest of the tradition like that of Mālik and completed it.

(773) Rabī'ah said : A young man from the Anṣār sneezed behind the Apostle of Allah (may peace be upon him) while he was praying. He then said : Praise be to Allah, much, good, blessed, till our Lord is pleased (with us) in the affairs relating to this world and to the other world. When the Apostle of Allah (may peace be upon him) finished his prayer, he said : Who was the speaker of these words (in prayer)? The young man kept silence. He again asked : Who was the speaker of these words? He did not say wrong. He said : Apostle of Allah, I said these (words). I did not intend by them but good. He said : These words did not stay below the Throne of the Compassionate (Allah).

Chapter 273

THE VIEW THAT THE SUPPLICATION "GLORY BE TO THEE, O ALLAH," AND "PRAISE BE TO THEE . . ." SHOULD BE RECITED AFTER UTTERING THE FIRST *TAKBĪR*

(774) Abū Sa'īd al-Khudrī said : When the Apostle of Allah (may peace be upon him) got up to pray at night (for *tahajjud* prayer) he uttered the *takbīr* and then said : "Glory be to Thee, O Allah," and "Praise be to Thee," and "Blessed is Thy name," and Exalted is Thy greatness." and "There is no god but Thee." He then said :

"There is no god but Allah" three times; he then said: "Allah is altogether great" three times: "I seek refuge in Allah, All-Hearing and All-Knowing from the accursed devil, from his evil suggestion *(hamz)*, from his puffing up *(nafkh)*, and from his spitting *(nafth)* " He then recited (the Qur'ān).

Abū Dāwūd said: It is said that this tradition has been narrated by 'Alī b. 'Alī from al-Ḥasan omitting the name of the Companion of the Prophet (may peace be upon him) The misunderstanding occurred on the part of Ja'far.[350]

(775) 'Ā'ishah said: When the Apostle of Allah (may peace be upon him) began his prayer, he said: "Glory be to Thee, O Allah," and ' Praise be to Thee," and "Blessed is Thy name, and Exalted is Thy greatness, and there is no god but Thee."[351]

Abū Dāwūd said: This tradition is not well known from 'Abd al-Salām b. Ḥarb. No one narrated this except Ṭalq b. Ghannām. A group of narrators reported the description of prayer from (the narrator) Budail; they did not mention therein this supplication.

Chapter 274

ON PERIOD OF SILENCE IN THE BEGINNING OF PRAYER

(776) Samurah (b. Jundub) said: I remember two periods of silence in prayer, one when the *imām* said the *takbīr*; and one when he finished reciting the *Fātiḥah* and the *surah* when he was about to bow. But 'Imrān b. Ḥuṣain took it as some thing strange. So they wrote about it to Ubayy (b. Ka'b) in Medina. He verified the statement of Samurh.

Abū Dāwūd said: Ḥumaid also narrated in this tradition the words "and one period of silence when he finished the recitation (of the Qur'ān)"

(777) Samurah b. Jundub said: The Prophet (may peace be upon him) had two periods of silence; when he began his prayer and when he finished the recitation (of

350. Al-Tirmidhī said that critical remarks have been made about this tradition. The expert of tradition Yaḥyā b. Sa'īd criticised the narrator 'Alī b. 'Alī. Aḥmad b. Ḥanbal is of opinion that this tradition is not sound (*'Awn al-Ma'būd*, I, 282).

351 A number of traditionists state that 'Umar used to recite this supplication in the beginning of prayer loudly so that people might learn it. Abū Bakr also used to recite it in prayer. 'Uthmān and Ibn Mas'ūd also recited it. This practice of the Companions shows that it is better to recite this supplication in the beginning of prayer, and this also shows that the Prophet (may peace be upon him) might have recited it in prayer. It is, however, worthy of remark that the traditions coming direct from the Prophet (may peace be upon him) about the supplication to be recited in the beginning of prayer are those reported by Abū Hurairah and 'Alī. The tradition reported by Ā'ishah has been criticised (*'Awn al-Ma'būd*, I, 282).

the Qur'ān). He then narrated the tradition like the version of Yūnus.

(778) Samurah b. Jundub and 'Imrān b. Ḥuṣain had a discussion (about the periods of silence in prayer). Samurah then said that he remembered two periods of silence from the Apostle of Allah (may peace be upon him): one when he uttered the *takbīr* and the other when he finished reciting: "Not of those with whom Thou art angry, nor of those who go astray" (i. 7). Samurah remembered that, but 'Imrān b. Ḥuṣain rejected it. Then they wrote about it to Ubayy b. Ka'b. He wrote a letter to them and gave a reply to them that Samurah remembered correctly.

(779) Samurah (b. Jundub) said: I remember from the Apostle of Allah (may peace be upon him) two periods of silence. Sa'īd said: We asked Qatādah: What are those two periods of silence? He said: (One) when he began his prayer, and (one) when he finished the recitation. Then he added: When he finished reciting (the closing verse of the *Fātiḥah*): "Not of those with whom Thou art angry, nor of who go astray."

(780) Abū Hurairah said: The Apostle of Allah (may peace be upon him) kept silence[352] between the *takbīr* and the recitation of the Qur'ān. So I asked him, for whom I would give my father and mother as ransom: What do you say during your period of silence between the *takbīr* and the recitation? He replied (that he said): O Allah, remove my sins far from me as Thou hast removed the east far from the west. O Allah, purify me from sins as a white garment is purified from filth. O Allah, wash away my sins with snow, water and hail.

Chapter 275

THE VIEW THAT "IN THE NAME OF ALLAH, THE COMPASSIONATE, THE MERCIFUL" SHOULD NOT BE RECITED LOUDLY

(781) Anas said: The Prophet (may peace be upon him), Abū Bakr, 'Umar and 'Uthmān used to begin the recitation with "Praise be to Allah, the Lord of the Universe."[353]

(782) 'Ā'ishah said: The Apostle of Allah (may peace be upon him) began prayer

352. The different traditions in this chapter indicate that the Prophet (may peace be upon him) used to observe three periods of silence in prayer: One after uttering the *takbir*; the other after reciting the *Fātiḥah*; and the third after reciting the *sūrah*. Al-Awzā'ī al-Shāfi'ī, Aḥmad and Isḥāq maintain that it is commendable to observe three periods of silence in prayer. Mālik and Abū Ḥanīfah are of opinion that three periods of silence are disapproved. There is only one period of silence after the *takbir* (*'Awn al-Ma'būd*, I, 283).

353. This tradition shows that the Prophet (may peace be upon him) and the three Caliphs recited the *tasmiyah* (In the name of Allah . . .) quietly. They began recitation with the *Fātiḥāh* and not with *tasmiyah*.

with the *takbīr* (Allah is most great) and with reciting "Praise be to Allah, the Lord of the Universe." And when he bowed, he neither raised up nor lowered down his head, but kept it between the two (conditions). And when he raised his head after bowing, he did not prostrate himself until he stood up straight; and when he raised his head after prostration, he did not prostrate (the second time) until he sat down properly; and he recited *al-taḥīyyat* after every pair of *rak'ahs*; and when he sat, he spread out his left foot and raised his right. He forbade to sit like the sitting of the devil,[354] and to spread out the hands (on the ground in prostration) like animals [355] He used to finish prayer with uttering the salutation.

(783) Anas b. Mālik said: The Apostle of Allah (may peace be upon him) said: A *sūrah* has just been revealed to me. He then recited: "In the name of Allah, the Compassionate, the Merciful. Lo! We have given thee Abundance" (cviii. 1) until he finished it. Then he asked: Do you know what Abundance (*al-Kawthar*) is? They replied: Allah and His Apostle know it better. He said: It is a river of which my Lord, the Exalted, the Majestic, has promised me to give in Paradise.

(784) 'Urwah reported on the authority of 'Ā'ishah mentioning the incident of slander. She said: The Apostle of Allah (may peace be upon him) sat and unveiled his face and said: "I take refuge in Allah, All-Hearing, All-Knowing, from the accursed devil. Lo! they who spread the slander are a gang among you" (xxiv. 11).[356]

Abū Dāwūd said: This is a rejected (*munkar*) tradition. A group of narrators have reported this tradition from al-Zuhrī; but they did not mention this detail. I am afraid the phrase concerning "seeking refuge in Allah" is the statement of Ḥumaid.

Chapter 276

THE VIEW THAT *TASMIYAH* (IN THE NAME OF ALLAH) SHOULD BE RECITED LOUDLY IN PRAYER

(785) Yazīd al-Fārisī said: I heard Ibn 'Abbās say: I asked 'Uthmān b. 'Affān:

354. This means that one should not sit on hips and raise one's knees like a dog.

355. According to this tradition, it is prohibited to spread out hands on the ground like animals in prostration. One should place only palms on the ground and keep the hands aloof from the ground and from the sides.

356. There is a difference of opinion amongst scholars on the point that *tasmiyah* (In the name of Allah) should be recited loudly. According to Abū Ḥanīfah, Aḥmad and Isḥāq, it should be recited quietly. According to al-Shāfi'ī, it should be recited loudly. Those who maintain that *tasmiyah* (In the name of Allah) should be recited loudly take it as part of the *sūrah*, while, the opponent think that it is not a part of the *sūrah* but placed between the two *sūrahs*, in the Qur'ān to distinguish between them. What is correct is that the Prophet (may peace be upon him) recited it somethimes loudly and at times quietly (*'Awn al-Ma'būd*, I, 286-89).

What moved you to put the (Sūrah) al-Barā'ah which belongs to the ***mi'īn*** (*sūrahs*)[357] (containing one hundred verses) and the (Sūrah) al-Anfāl which belongs to the *mathānī* (*Sūrahs*)[358] in the category of *al-sab'u al-ṭiwal*[359] (the first long *sūrahs* or chapters of the Qur'ān), and you did not write "In the name of Allah, the Compassionate, the Merciful" between them? 'Uthmān replied: When the verses of the Qur'ān were revealed to the Prophet (may peace be upon him), he called someone to write them for him and said to him: Put this verse in the *sūrah* in which such-and-such has been mentioned; and when one or two verses were revealed, he used to say similarly. (Sūrah) al-Anfāl is the first *sūrah* that was revealed at Medina, and (*Sūrah*) al-Barā'ah was revealed last in the Qur'ān, and its contents were similar to those of al-Anfāl. I, therefore, thought that it is a part of al-Anfāl. Hence I put them in the category of *al-sab'u al-ṭiwal* (the seven lengthy *sūrahs*), and I did not write "In the name of Allah, the Compassionate, the Merciful" between them.

(786) The above-mentioned tradition has been reported by Ibn 'Abbās through a different chain of narrators to the same effect. This version adds: The Apostle of Allah (may peace be upon him) died, but he did not mention to us that Sūrah al-Barā'ah is a part of al-Anfāl.[360]

Abū Dāwūd said: Al-Sha'bī, Abū Mālik, Qatādah, and Thābit b. 'Umarah said: The Prophet (may peace be upon him) did not write "In the name of Allah, the Compassionate, the Merciful" until Sūrah al-Naml was revealed. This is the meaning of what they said. Further, this is a *mursal* tradition (omitting the name of the Companion).

(787) Ibn 'Abbās said: The Prophet (may peace be upon him) did not distinguish between the two *sūrahs* until the words "In the name of Allah, the Compassionate, the Merciful" was revealed to him. These are the words of Ibn al-Sarḥ.[361]

357. The *sūrahs* (chapters) of the Qur'ān have been divided into three categories, viz. *ṭiwal*, *mi'in* and *mathānī*. *Mi'in* are those chapters which contain one hundred verses. They are shorter than *ṭiwal* which are lengthy *sūrahs*. By this question it was meant that al Barā'ah was a shorter chapter; why did he include it in the lengthy *sūrahs* ?

358 *Mathānī* are those chapters of the Qur'ān which are shorter than *mi'in* and longer than *mufaṣṣal*.

359. This means the seven lengthy *sūrahs* in the beginning of the Qur'ān. The order of the chapters in respect of length are as follows: (1) *ṭiwal* (seven lengthy *sūrahs*); (2) *mi'in* (containing one hundred verses); (3) *mathānī* (shorter than *mi'in*); and (4) *mufaṣṣal* (the shortest chapters). (*'Awn al-Ma'būd*, I, 287).

360. The reason is that the words "In the name of Allah, the Compassionate, the Merciful" are the part of Sūrah al-Naml.

361. All these traditions indicate that the words "In the name of Allah, the Compassionate, the Merciful" were part of the *sūrahs*. Hence one should, according to one view, recite these words loudly, in prayer along with the *sūrahs*.

Chapter 277

HASTENING IN PRAYER IF AN INCIDENT OCCURS

(788) Abū Qatādah reported the Apostle of Allah (may peace be upon him) as saying: I stand up to pray and intend to prolong it; but when I hear the cry of a boy I shorten it for fear that his mother might be distressed.[362]

Chapter 278

LOSS IN PRAYER

(789) 'Ammār b. Yāsir said: I heard the Apostle of Allah (may peace be upon him) say: A man returns after saying his prayer while a tenth part of his prayer, or a ninth part, or an eighth part, or a seventh part, or a sixth part, or a fifth part, or a third part, or half of it, is recorded for him.[363]

Chapter 279

OFFERING PRAYER LIGHTLY

(790) Jābir said: Mu'ādh b. Jabal used to pray along with the Prophet (may peace be upon him); then he returned and led us in prayer. Sometimes he (the narrator) said: then he returned and led his people in prayer. One night the Prophet (may peace be upon him) delayed the prayer. Sometimes he (the narrator) mentioned the word "the night prayer". Then Mu'ādh prayed along with the Prophet (may peace be upon him), then returned to his people and led them in prayer, and recited Sūrah al-Baqarah. A man turned aside and prayed alone. The people said to him: Have you become a hypocrite, so and so? He replied: I did not become a hypocrite. He then came to the Prophet (may peace be upon him) and said (to him): Apostle of Allah, Mu'ādh prays along with you and then returns and leads us in prayer. We look after camels used for watering and work by day. He came to us leading us in prayer, and he recited Sūrah al-Baqarah (in prayer). He (the Prophet) said: Mu'adh, are you a

362. This tradition indicates that the *imām* should be lenient towards those who follow him in prayer. He should not prolong the prayer so much so that prayer becomes a burden on them He should lead in a way that none of the participants should feel tired or become bored. He should shorten it and make it lighter if there occurs any incident during prayer (*'Awn al-Ma'būd*, I, 290).

363. This tradition indicates that one receives his reward according to the perfection of the prayer. The more perfectly one offers the prayer, the more reward one gets. If one prays carelessly, paying no attention to the performance of all its actions and details, one will get less reward as mentioned in this tradition (*'Awn al-Ma'būd*, I, 290).

trouble-maker? Recite such and such; recite such and such (*surahs*).[364] The narrator Abū al-Zubair said: (Recite) "Glorify the name of the most high Lord", (Sūrah lxxxvii.) and "By the night when it covers over" (Sūrah xcii.). We mentioned this to 'Amr. He said: I think he mentioned it (the names of some *surahs*).

(791) Ḥazm b. Ubayy b. Ka'b said that he came to Mu'ādh b. Jabal who was leading the people in the sunset prayer. According to this version, the Apostle of Allah (may peace be upon him) said: O Mu'ādh, do not become a trouble, because the aged, the weak, the needy and the traveller pray behind you.

(792) Abū Ṣāliḥ reported, on the authority of some Companions of the Prophet (may peace be upon him): The Prophet (may peace be upon him) said to a person: What do you say in prayer? He replied: I first recite *tashahhud* (supplication recited in sitting position), and then I say: O Allah, I ask Thee for Paradise, and I seek refuge in Thee from Hell-fire, but I do not understand your sound and the sound of Mu'ādh (what you say or he says in prayer). The Prophet (may peace be upon him) said: We too go around it (Paradise and Hell-fire).

(793) Jābir narrated the story of Mu'ādh and said: The Prophet (may peace be upon him) said to a youth: My nephew, what do you do in prayer? He replied: I recite *Fātiḥat al-Kitāb* and I ask Allah for Paradise and seek in Him refuge from Hell-fire I do not understand well your sound and the sound of Mu'ādh. The Prophet (may peace be upon him) said: I and Mu'ādh go around both (Paradise and Hell-fire), or he said something similar.

(794) Abū Hurairah reported the Prophet (may peace be upon him) as saying: When one of you leads the people in prayer, he should be brief, for among them are the weak, the sick, and the aged. But when one of you prays by himself, he may pray as long as he likes.

(795) Abū Hurairah reported the Prophet (may peace be upon him) as saying: When one of you leads the people in prayer, he should be brief, for among them are the sick, the aged and the needy.

Chapter 280

RECITATION DURING THE NOON PRAYER

(796) Abū Hurairah said: In every prayer there is a recitation. We make you listen what the Apostle of Allah (may peace be upon him) made us listen, and we

364. This tradition shows that the *imām* should lead the people in prayer lightly. He should not recite such lengthy *sūrahs* of the Qur'ān that the people behind become tired and then detest prayer. A number of traditions indicate that the *imām* should take into consideration all sorts of people participating in the congregation, such as the sick, the weak, children, women and persons having work to attend at home

keep hidden from you what he kept hidden from us.[365]

(797) Abū Qatādah said: The Apostle of Allah (may peace be upon him) used to lead us in prayer and recite in the first two *rak'ahs* of the noon prayer *Fātiḥat al-Kitāb* and two *surahs*, and he would sometimes recite loud enough for us to hear the verse. He would prolong tne first *rak'ah* of the noon prayer and shorten the second; and he did so in the morning prayer.

Abū Dāwūd said: Musaddad did not mention the words *Fatiḥat al-Kitāb* and *surah*.

(798) The above-mentioned tradition has been reported by Abū Qatādah through a different chain of narrators. This version adds: He would recite *Fātiḥat al-Kitāb* in the last two *sūrahs*. Hammām added: He would prolong the first *rak'ah* but would not prolong the second so much; and he did so similarly in the afternoon prayer, and so in the morning prayer.

(799) Abū Qatādah said: We thought that by this (prolonging the first *rak'ah*), he (the Prophet) meant that the people might join the first *rak'ah*.

(800) Abū Ma'mar said: We asked Khabbāb: Did the Apostle of Allah (may peace be upon him) recite (the Qur'ān) in the noon and afternoon prayers? He replied: Yes. We then asked: How did you know this? He said: By the shaking of his beard, may peace be upon him.

(801) 'Abd Allah b. Abī Awfā said: The Prophet (may peace be upon him) used to stand in the *rak'ah* of prayer so much so that no sound of steps was heard.[366]

Chapter 281

BRIEF RECITATION IN THE LAST TWO *RAK'AHS* OF PRAYER

(802) Jābir b. Samurah reported: 'Umar said to Sa'd: People complain against you for everything, even for prayer. He replied: I prolong the first two *rak'ahs* of prayer and make the last two *rak'ahs* brief; I do not fall short of following the prayer offered by the Apostle of Allah (may peace be upon him). He said: I think so about you.

(803) Abū Sa'īd al-Khudrī said: We used to estimate how long the Apostle of Allah (may peace be upon him) stood in the noon and the afternoon prayer, and we

365. During the noon and afternoon prayers the Prophet (may peace be upon him) used to recite the Qur'ān quietly, and during the morning, sunset and night prayers he would recite loudly. By this statement Abū Hurairah meant that one should recite the Qur'ān in all prayers; in some prayers loudly, and in others quietly.

366. This means that all the people joined the prayer in the first *rak'ah* and no one remained. From this it is obvious that he prolonged the first *rak'ah*.

estimated that he stood in the first two *rak'ahs* of the noon prayer as long as it takes to recite thirty verses (of the Qur'ān), such as A.-L.-M. Tanzīl al-Sajdah. And we estimated that he stood in the last two *rak'ahs* half the time he stood in the first two *rak'ahs*. We estimated that he stood in the first two *rak'ahs* of the afternoon prayer as long as he did in the last two at noon; and we estimated that he stood in the last two *rak'ahs* of the afternoon prayer half the time he did in first two.

Chapter 282

HOW MUCH ONE SHOULD RECITE IN THE NOON AND AFTERNOON PRAYERS

(804) Jābir b. Samurah said: The Apostle of Allah (may peace be upon him) used to recite in the noon and afternoon prayers: "By the Heaven and the Morning Star" (Sūrah lxxxvi.) and "By the Heaven, holding mansion of the stars" (Sūrah lxxxv.) and similar *sūrah* of equal length.

(805) Jābir b. Samurah said: When the sun declined, the Apostle of Allah (may peace be upon him) offered the noon prayer and recited *sūrahs* like "By the night when it covers over" (Sūrah xcii.) and (recited similar *sūrahs*) in the afternoon prayer, and in other prayers except the dawn prayer which he used to prolong.

(806) Ibn 'Umar said: The Prophet (may peace be upon him) prostrated himself in the noon prayer; then he stood up and bowed, and we knew that he recited Ṭanzīl al-Sajdah (Sūrah xxxii).

Ibn 'Īsā said: No one narrated this tradition to Umayyah except Mu'tamir.

(807) 'Abd Allah b. 'Ubaid Allah said: I went to Ibn 'Abbās accompanying some youths of Banū Hāshim. We said to one of them: Ask Ibn 'Abbās: Did the Apostle of Allah (may peace be upon him) recite (the Qur'ān) in the noon and afternoon prayers? He replied: No.[367] People said to him: Perhaps he might recite the Qur'ān quietly. He said: May your face be scratched (a kind of curse)! This (statement) is worse than the former. He was only a servant (of Allah) receiving Commands from Him. He preached (the divine) message which he brought with him. He did not command anything to us (Banū Hāshim) specially excluding other people except three points: he commanded us to perform ablution perfectly, and not to

367. Since Ibn 'Abbās was a child during the lifetime of the Prophet (may peace be upon him), he used to stand in the last row of worshippers. Hence he could not know whether the Prophet (may peace be upon him) recited the Qur'ān in the noon and afternoon prayers. Three statements about this point have been attributed to him. In one, he negates the recitation absolutely; in the second, he is doubtful; and in the third, he accepts. The tradition in which he accepts the recitation of the Qur'ān in these prayers by the Prophet (may peace be upon him) has been narrated by Ibn al-Mundhir and al-Ṭaḥāwī. This tradition is preferable to others in which he denies (*'Awn al-Ma'būd* I, 297).

accept charity and not to make pairing of donkey with horse.

(808) Ibn 'Abbās said: I do not know whether the Apostle of Allah (may peace be upon him) would recite the Qur'ān at the noon and afternoon prayer or not.

Chapter 283

AMOUNT OF THE RECITATION OF THE QUR'AN IN THE EVENING PRAYER

(809) Umm al-Faḍl daughter of al-Ḥārith said: I heard Ibn 'Abbās reciting *wa'l-Mursalāt 'Urfan* (Sūrah lxxvii.). She said; Sonny you have reminded me of this *sūrah* by your recitation. Thie is the last *sūrah* which I heard the Apostle of Allah (may peace be upon him) reciting in the sunset prayer.

(810) Jubair b. Muṭ'im said: I heard the Apostle of Allah (may peace be upon him) reciting al-Ṭūr (Sūrah lii) in the sunset prayer.

(811) Marwān b. al-Ḥakam said: Zaid b. Thābit asked me: Why do you recite short *sūrahs* in the sunset prayer? I saw the Apostle of Allah cmay peace be upon him) reciting two long *sūrahs* at the sunset prayer. I asked him: Which are those two long *sūrahs*? He replied: Al-A'rāf (Sūrah vii) and al-An'ām (Sūrah vi.). I (the narrator Ibn Juraij) asked Ibn Abī Mulaikah (about these *sūrahs*): He said on his own accord: Al-Mā'idah (Sūrah v.) and al-A'rāf (Sūrah vii.).[368]

Chapter 284

THE VIEW THAT ONE CAN RECITE SHORT *SŪRAHS* DURING THE SUNSET PRAYER

(812) Hishām b. 'Urwah said that his father ('Urwah) used to recite the *sūrahs* as you recite like Wa'l-'Ādiyāt (Sūrah c).

Abū Dāwūd said: This indicates that those (traditions indicating long *sūrahs*) are abrogated, and this is a more sound tradition.

(813) 'Amr b. Shu'aib, on his father's authority, quoted his grandfather as saying: There is no short or long *sūrah* in *al-Mufaṣṣal* which I have not heard the Apostle of Allah (may peace be upon him) reciting when he led the people in the prescribed prayer.

368. This and similar other traditions indicate that the Prophet (may peace be upon him) used to recite long *sūrahs* in the sunset prayer. But a number of traditions also indicate that he would recite short *sūrahs* in the evening prayer. These sets of traditions can be reconciled by saying that he recited different *sūrahs* in different situations. Sometimes he recited long *sūrahs* and at other times he recited short *sūrahs*. Hence one should not stick to the practice of reciting short *sūrahs* alone (*'Awn al-Ma'būd*, I, 298).

(814) Abū 'Uthmān al-Nahdī said that he offered the sunset prayer behind Ibn Mas'ūd, when he recited "Say: He is Allah, the One" (Sūrah cxii.).

Chapter 285

ON REPEATING THE SAME *SŪRAH* BY A MAN IN THE FIRST TWO *RAK'AHS* OF PRAYER

(815) Mu'ādh b. 'Abd Allah al-Juham said that a man of Juhainah told him that he had heard the Prophet (may peace be upon him) reciting "When the earth is shaken" (Sūrah xcix.) in both *rak'ahs* of the morning prayer. But I do not know whether he had forgotten, or whether he recited it on purpose.[369]

Chapter 286

THE RECITATION OF THE QUR'ĀN IN THE MORNING PRAYER

(816) 'Amr b. Ḥuraith said: As if I am hearing the voice of the Prophet (may peace be upon him) who would recite at the morning prayer "Oh, but I call to witness the planets, the stars which rise and set" (Sūrah lxxxi. 15-16).[370]

Chapter 287

ON A PERSON WHO DOES NOT RECITE AL-FĀTIḤAH DURING THE PRAYER

(817) Abū Sa'īd said: We were commanded to recite *Fātiḥat al-Kitāb*[371] and whatever was convenient (from the Qur'ān during the prayer).

(818) Abū Hurairah reported the Apostle of Allah (may peace be upon him) as saying: Go out and announce in Medina that prayer is not valid but by the recitation

369. It is worthy of note that the Prophet (may peace be upon him) never did anything out of forgetfulness in religious matters. If he did so sometimes, he corrected it. Therefore, his action will be taken to mean that he did so purposely to teach the people (*'Awn al-Ma'būd*, I, 299).

370. This means that he used to recite the *sūrah* in which this verse occurs.

371. This and similar other traditions indicate that the recitation of Sūrah al-Fātiḥah in every *rak'ah* of prayer is neccessary. The recitation of this *sūrah* in the prayer has been specified and no other *sūrah* can be substituted. If anyone gives up its recitation in the prayer, his prayer will not be valid. This is held by Mālik, al-Shāfi'ī, and Aḥmad, and majority of the scholars. Abū Ḥanīfah holds that what is necessary is the recitation of a verse from the Qur'ān and not specifically Sūrah al-Fātiḥah. He takes these traditions to mean that it is necessary for the *imām* and not for the followers (*'Awn al-Ma'būd*, I, 300).

of the Qur'ān even though it might be *Fātiḥat al-Kitāb* and something more.[371]

(819) Abū Hurairah said: The Apostle of Allah (may peace be upon him) commanded me to announce that prayer is not valid but with the recitation of *Fātiḥat al-Kitāb* and something more.

(820) Abū Hurairah reported the Apostle of Allah (may peace be upon him) as saying: If anyone observes a prayer in which he does not recite *Umm al-Qur'ān*, it is incomplete, it is incomplete, it is incomplete, and deficient. (The narrator said) I said: Abū Hurairah, sometime I pray behind the *imām* (then what should I do)? Pressing my hand he replied: O Persian, recite it inwardly, for I heard the Apostle of Allah (may peace be upon him) as saying that Allah, Most High, has said: I have divided the prayer into two halves between Me and My servant, and the half is for Me and the half for My servant and My servant will receive what he asks. The Apostle of Allah (may peace be upon him) said: Recite. When the servant says: "Praise be to Allah, the Lord of the Universe," Allah, Most High says: "My servant has praised Me." When the servant says: "The Compassionate, the Merciful," Allah Most High says : "My servant has lauded me." When the servant says: "Owner of the Day of Judgment," Allah, Most High, says: "My servant has glorified Me." When the servant says: "Thee do we worship and of Thee we ask help," (Allah says :) "This is between Me and My servant, and My servant will receive what he asks." When the servant says: "Guide us to the Straight Path, the path of those whom Thou hast favoured, not (the path) of those who earn Thine anger nor of those who go astray," (Allah says:) "This is for My servant, and My servant will receive what he asks."[372]

(821) 'Ubādah b. al-Ṣāmit reported the Apostle of Allah (may peace be upon him) as saying: The prayer is not valid if one does not recite *Fātiḥat al-Kitāb* and something more, Sufyān (the narrator) said: This applies to a man who prays alone.[373]

371 The recitation of a *sūrah* or some verses from the Qur'ān in addition to Sūrat al-Fātiḥah is commendable according to the majority of scholars But Abū Ḥanīfah maintains that it is necessary to recite both al-Fātiḥah and some other *sūrah* or verses from the Qur'ān. Prayer is not valid if one gives up either of them. But it should be noted that the Fātiḥah and the *sūrah* should be recited in the first two *rak'ahs* of prayer. In the last one or two *rak'ahs* of the prescribed or obligatory prayer, one may recite the Fātiḥah but not the *sūrah* (*'Awn al-Ma'būd*, I, 300-01).

372. Opinion is divided whether the expression "In the name of Allah. . ." is a part of al-Fātiḥah or not. The traditionists and majority of the scholars maintain that this is a part of al-Fātiḥah and this is also a verse like other verses. Mālik and a group of scholars hold that this is an independent verse and not a part of al-Fātiḥah (*'Awn al-Ma'būd*, I, 302).

373. The recitation of Sūrat al-Fātiḥah during the prayer when offered alone is necessary according to all the jurists. Even according to the Ḥanafīs the recitation of al-Fātiḥah and some verses from the Qur'ān in the prayer is also necessary (*wājib*), though not obligatory (*farḍ*).

The question of its recitation during the congregational prayer behind the *imām* by the worshippers is disputed. According to Abū Ḥanīfah, Aḥmad, Mālik, al-Zuhrī, Sufyān al-Thawrī, Ibn

(822) 'Ubādah b. al-Ṣāmit said: We were behind the Apostle of Allah (may peace be upon him) at the dawn prayer, and he recited (the passage), but the recitation became difficult for him. Then when he finished, he said: Perhaps you recite behind your *imām*? We replied: Yes, it is so, Apostle of Allah. He said: Do not do so except when it is *Fātiḥat al-Kitāb*, for he who does not recite it is not credited with having prayed.[374]

(823) Nāfi' b. Maḥmūd b. al-Rabī' al-Anṣārī said: 'Ubādah b. al-Ṣāmit came late to lead the morning prayer. Abū Nu'aim, the *mu'adhdhin*, pronounced the *takbīr* and he led the people in prayer. Then 'Ubādah came and I was with him. We joined the row behind Abū Nu'aim, while Abū Nu'aim was reciting the Qur'ān loudly. Then 'Ubādah began to recite the *Umm al-Qur'ān* (i.e. Sūrah al-Fātiḥah). When he finished, I said to 'Ubādah: I heard you reciting the *Umm al-Qur'ān* while Abū Nu'aim was reciting the Qur'ān loudly. He replied: Yes. The Apostle of Allah (may peace be upon him) led us in a certain prayer in which the Qur'ān is recited loudly, but he became confused in the recitation. When he finished he turned his face to us and said: Do you recite when I recite the Qur'ān loudly? Some of us said: We do so; this is why I said to myself: What is that which confused me (in the recitation of) the Qur'ān. Do not recite anything from the Qur'ān when I recite it loudly except the *Umm al-Qur'ān*.[375]

(824) The above-mentioned tradition has been transmitted through a different chain of narrators by 'Ubādah b. al-Ṣāmit like the version of al-Rabī' b. Sulaimān. This version adds: Makḥūl used to recite Sūrah al-Fātiḥah at the sunset, night and morning prayers quietly in every *rak'ah*. Makḥūl said: Recite *Fātiḥat al-Kitāb* quietly in the prayers in which the *imām* recites the Qur'ān loudly when he observes the period of silence. If he does not observe the period of silence, recite it before him (i.e. before his recitation), or along with him or after him; do not give it up in any case.

'Uyainah and Isḥāq b. Rahwaih, it is not necessary to recite Sūrah al-Fātiḥah behind the *imām* by the persons led by him in the congregational prayer. According to al-Shāfi'ī and the traditionists, it is necessary to recite the Fātiḥah behind the *imām*. There is again a difference of opinion on its recitation during the prayers in which the *imām* recites the Qur'ān loudly, i.e. the morning, sunset and night prayers, and at the prayers in which the Qur'ān is recited quietly, i.e. the noon and afternoon prayers. Abū Ḥanīfah, Mālik, Aḥmad, al-Awzā'ī, Laith b. Sa'd, Ibn al-Mubarak, Isḥāq b. Rahwaih and al-Shāfi'ī, according to his former view which he revised later on, maintain that it is not necessary to recite the Fātiḥah behind the *imām* in the prayers in which the Qur'ān is recited loudly. But during the prayers in which the Qur'ān is recited quietly the worshippers should recite the Fātiḥah behind the *imām* according to al-Shāfi'ī, the traditionists and the early Ḥanafī jurists. The later Ḥanafī jurists regard its recitation as disapproved (*Ma'ārif al-Sunan*, III, 184-90).

374. This tradition shows that it is necessary to recite the Fātiḥah behind the *imām*.

375. This tradition also clearly indicates that it is necessary to recite the Fātiḥah behind the *imām*.

Chapter 288

THE VIEW THAT THE WORSHIPPERS SHOULD NOT RECITE THE FĀTIḤAH BEHIND THE *IMĀM* WHEN HE RECITES THE QUR'ĀN LOUDLY

(825) Abū Hurairah said: When the Apostle of Allah (may peace be upon him) finished a prayer in which he had recited (the Qur'ān) loudly, he asked: Did any of you recite along with me just now? A man replied: Yes, Apostle of Allah. He said: I am wondering what is the matter with me that I have been contended with reciting the Qur'ān. He said: When the people heard that from the Apostle of Allah (may peace be upon him) they ceased reciting[376] (the Qur'ān) along with him at the prayers in which he recited aloud.

Abū Dāwūd said: This tradition reported by Ibn Ukaimah has also been narrated by Ma'mar, Yūnus, and Usāmah b. Zaid on the authority of al-Zuhrī similar to the tradition of Mālik.

(826) Abū Hurairah said: The Apostle of Allah (may peace be upon him) led us in prayer, that was, we think, the dawn prayer. He further narrated this tradition up to the words "what is the matter with me that I have been contended with in (the recitation of) the Qur'ān."

Abū Dāwūd said: Musaddad in his tradition said that Ma'mar said: The people ceased to recite (the Qur'ān) at the prayers in which the Apostle of Allah (may peace be upon him) recited aloud. Ibn al-Sarḥ said in his version that Ma'mar reported from al-Zuhrī on the authority of Abū Hurairah. Then the people ceased (to recite behind the *imām*). Another version says: Sufyān said: Al-Zuhrī spoke a word that I could not hear. Then Ma'mar said: He said: Then people ceased (to recite the Qur'ān).

Abū Dāwūd said: This tradition has been narrated by 'Abd al-Raḥmān b. Isḥāq on the authority of al-Zuhrī. This version ends at the words: "What is the matter with me that I am contended with in (the recitation of) the Qur'ān. Al-Awzā'ī also narrated it on the authority of al-Zuhrī. This version has: Al-Zuhrī said: The Muslims took lesson from that and thenceforth they did not recite (the Qur'ān) at the prayers in which he (the Prophet) recited aloud.

376. The phrase "when the people heard. . . they ceased reciting" is not part of the tradition. This is the statement of al-Zuhrī. Imām al-Bukhārī added to this tradition the words "and they recited inwardly during the prayers in which the *imām* recites quietly". On the basis of this tradition a group of scholars argue that one should not recite the Qur'ān behind the *imām* during the prayers in which he recites loudly. But it should be noted that this tradition is not sound, and this has been criticised by most of the traditionists. The narrator Ukaimah is said to be unknown, and hence weak. Further, Abū Hurairah himself narrates the tradition to the effect that the prayer of one who prays and does not recite al-Fātiḥah is incomplete. Further, he said that one should recite inwardly if one is behind the *imām* (*'Awn al-Ma'būd*, I. 305-06).

Abū Dāwūd said : I heard Muḥammad b. Yaḥyā b. Fāris say : The words "the people ceased to recite (the Qur'ān)" is a statement of al-Zuhrī.

Chapter 289

THE VIEW THAT ONE SHOULD RECITE (AL-FĀTIḤAH) BEHIND THE *IMĀM* DURING THE PRAYERS IN WHICH THE QUR'ĀN IS NOT RECITED LOUDLY

(827) 'Imrān b. Ḥuṣain said : The Prophet (may peace be upon him) led (us) in the noon prayer, and a man came and recited behind him "Glorify the name of thy Lord, the Most High" (Sūrah lxxxvii.) When he finished (the prayer), he said : Which of you recited ? They (the people) said : A man (recited). He said : I knew that some one of you confused me in it (in the recitation of the Qur'ān).

Abū Dāwūd said: Abū al-Walīd said in his version : Shu'bah said : I asked Qatādah ; Did Sa'īd not say : Listen attentively to the Qur'ān? He replied : (Yes), but that applies to the prayers in which it (the Qur'ān) is recited aloud. Ibn Kathīr said in his version : I said to Qatādah : Perhaps he (the Prophet) disliked it (recitation). He said : If he had disliked it, he would have prohibited it.

(828) 'Imrān b. Ḥuṣain reported that the Prophet of Allah (may peace be upon him) led them in the noon prayer. When he finished it, he said : Which of you did recite the Sūrah "Glorify the name of thy Lord, the Most High" (Sūrah lxxxvii.). A man said : I. He said : I knew that some one of you confused me in it (i.e. in the recitation of the Qur'ān) [377]

Chapter 290

ON THE AMOUNT OF RECITATION OF THE QUR'ĀN WHICH IS SUFFICIENT FOR AN UNLETTERED AND A NON-ARAB DURING PRAYER

(829) Jābir b. 'Abd Allah said : The Apostle of Allah (may peace be upon him) came out to us while we were reciting the Qur'ān, and there were among us bedouins and the non-Arabs. He said : Recite, all is well. In the near future there will appear

377. This shows that one should not recite the *sūrah* in the prayers in which the *imām* recites the Qur'ān loudly. But this does not indicate that one should not recite even al-Fātiḥah. Some scholars, however, argue on the basis of this tradition that one should not recite the Qur'ān behind the *imām*.

people who will straighten it (the Qur'ān) as an arrow is straightened.[378] They will recite it quickly and not slowly (or it means that they will get the reward in this world and not in the Hereafter).[379]

(830) Sahl b. Sa'd al-Sā'idī said: The Apostle of Allah (may peace be upon him) one day came out to us while we were reciting the Qur'ān. He said: Praise be to Allah. The Book of Allah is one, and among you are the red, and among you are the white, and among you are the black. Recite it before there appear people who will recite it and straighten it as an arrow is straightened. They will get their reward for it in this world and will not get it in the Hereafter.

(831) 'Abd Allah b. Abī Awfā said: A man came to the Prophet (may peace be upon him) and said: I cannot memorise anything from the Qur'ān; so teach me something which is sufficient for me. He said: Say: Glory be to Allah, and praise be to Allah, and there is no god but Allah, and Allah is most great, and there is no might and no strength but in Allah.[380] He said: Apostle of Allah, this is for Allah, but what is for me? He said: Say: O Allah have mercy on me, and sustain me, and keep me well, and guide me. When he stood up, he made a sign with his hand (indicating that he had earned a lot). The Apostle of Allah (may peace be upon him) said: He filled up his hand with virtues.

(832) Jābir b. 'Abd Allah said: We used to offer supererogatory prayers and recite supplications while we were standing, and would glorify Allah while bowing and prostrating.[381]

(833) The above-mentioned tradition has also been tramsmitted through a different chain of narrators by Ḥumaid, but he did not mention the word "supererogatory prayer" This version has: Al-Ḥasan (al-Baṣrī) would recite *Fātiḥat al-Kitāb* in the noon and afternoon prayers while he led in prayer or he was behind the *imām*, and

378. This means that they will lay much emphasis on pronouncing the words of the Qur'ān correctly.

379. They will lose their reward in the Hereafter because, by pronouncing the words of the Qur'ān correctly, they would aim at earning their name and fame and not pleasure of Allah. If one does not do an act sincerely to seek the pleasure of Allah, one will not get its reward in the Hereafter.

380. This means that the man had to offer his prayer immediately at that moment, but he did not learn any part or passage of the Qur'ān. Hence the Prophet (may peace be upon him) allowed him to recite these words for the time being until he memorised the verses of the Qur'ān. One should try to learn the Qur'ān by heart as much as possible, and until he learns he may recite these words in prayer (*'Awn al-Ma'būd*, I. 308-09).

381. This tradition indicates that the recitation of the Qur'ān is not necessary in the supererogatory prayers. But it should be noted that the chain of this tradition is broken. Al-Ḥasan al-Baṣrī did not hear traditions from Jābir. Hence a link between Ḥasan and Jābir is missing. Further, this tradition contradicts more sound and established traditions narrated by al-Bukhārī and Muslim which indicate that prayer is not valid without reciting al-Fātiḥah (*'Awn al-Ma'būd*, I. 309).

would glorify Allah, and would repeatedly say : "Allah is most great" and "There is no god but Allah" (i.e. *takbīr* and *tahlīl*) equal to the amount one recites al-Qāf (Sūrah l.) and al-Dhāriyāt (Sūrah li.).

Chapter 291

ON UTTERING THE *TAKBĪR* DURING PRAYER

(834) Muṭarrif said : I and 'Imrān b. Ḥuṣain offered prayer behind 'Alī b. Abī Ṭālib (may Allah be pleased with him). When he prostrated, he uttered the *takbīr* (Allah is most great) and when he bowed, he uttered the *takbīr* and when he stood up at the end of two *rak'ahs*, he uttered the *takbīr*. When we finished our prayer, 'Imrān caught hold of my hand, and said : He has led us in prayer just now like the prayer offered by Muḥammad (may peace be upon him).

(835) Abū Bakr b. 'Abd al-Raḥmān and Abū Salamah said : Abū Hurairah would utter the *takbīr* in every prayer, whether obligatory or non-obligatory. He would utter the *takbīr* when he stood, and he would utter the *takbīr* when he bowed, then he would say : "Allah listens to him who praises Him"; he then would say before prostrating himself; "Our Lord, to Thee be praise"; then he would say while falling in prostration : "Allah is most great"; he then would utter the *takbīr* when he raised his head after prostration, and then utter the *takbīr* when he prostrated, and then utter the *takbīr* when he stood up at the end of two *rak'ahs* after sitting down. He used to do so in every *rak'ah* until he finished his prayer. Then he would say at the end of the prayer : By Him in Whose hands lies my life, I am closer to the Apostle of Allah (may peace be upon him) in respect of his prayer. Such was the prayer he used to offer until he departed from the world.

Abū Dāwūd said : Mālik, al-Zubaidī and others have narrated so that they form the last words from al-Zuhrī on the authority of 'Alī b. Ḥusain. And this is supported by the version reported by 'Abd al-A'lā from Ma'mar and Shu'aib b. Abī Ḥamzah on the authority of al-Zuhrī.

(836) 'Abd al-Raḥmān b. Abzā said that he offered prayer along with the Apostle of Allah (may peace be upon him) but he did not complete the *takbīr*.[382]

Abū Dāwūd said : This means that when he raised his head after bowing and when he was about to prostrate, he did not utter the *takbir*, and when he stood up after prostration, he did not utter the *takbīr*.

382. This tradition contradicts all other sound traditions which indicate that the Prophet (may peace be upon him) used to utter the *takbir* at the time of all movements except raising the head after bowing. Hence this tradition is not followed.

Chapter 292

HOW SHOULD A WORSHIPPER PLACE HIS KNEES (ON THE GROUND) BEFORE PLACING HIS HANDS

(837) Wā'il b. Ḥujr said : I saw that the Prophet (may peace be upon him) placed his knees (on the ground) before placing his hands when he prostrated himself. And when he stood up, he raised his hands before his knees.

(838) The above-mentioned tradition has also been transmitted by Wā'il b. Ḥujr through a different chain of narrators. This version has : When he prostrated himself, his knees fell on the ground before his hands had fallen. Hammām said : This tradition has also been transmitted by 'Āṣim b. Kulaib through a different chain of narrators to the same effect. And one of these two versions, and probably the version narrated by Muḥammad b. Juḥādah, has the words : When he stood up (after prostration), he stood up on his knees taking the support of his thighs.

(839) Abū Hurairah reported the Apostle of Allah (may peace be upon him) as saying : When one of you prostrates himself he must not kneel in the manner of a camel, but should put down his hands before his knees.[383]

(840) Abū Hurairah reported the Apostle of Allah (may peace be upon him) as saying: (Does) one of you kneel down in his prayer as a camel kneels down (i.e. put his knees before his hands). ?[384]

Chapter 293

ON STANDING UP AFTER THE FIRST AND THE THIRD *RAK'AH* OF THE PRAYER

(841) Abū Qilābah said: Abū Sulaimān Mālik b. al-Ḥuwairith came to our

383. This tradition indicates that one should put his hands on the ground before his knees when one goes to prostrate oneself. This is held by al-Awzā'ī, Mālik, Ibn Ḥazm and Aḥmad according to a version. Al-Ḥazimī said : I found people placing their hands on the ground before placing their knees. This is also held by the traditionists. Ibn Sayyid al-Nās thinks that the traditions which indicate the placing of hands before knees are more established and preferable. But al-Khaṭṭābi is of opinion that the tradition reported by Wā'il b. Ḥujr is better established because it is supported by several other sound traditions. Ibn Khuzaimah observes that the tradition of Abū Hurairah has been abrogated. He reports a tradition on the authority of Sa'd b. Abī Waqqāṣ : We used to place our hands (on the ground) before our knees, but later on we were commanded to place our knees before our hands (*'Awn al-Ma'būd*, I, 311-12).

384. There is a difference of opinion amongst the jurists on this point. Abū Ḥanīfah, al-Shāfi'ī and Aḥmad maintain that one should place knees before hands. And this seems to be more convenient. Mālik, al-Awzā'ī and Ibn Ḥazm hold that one should place hands before knees (*'Awn al-Ma'būd*, I, 312).

mosque and said : By Allah, I shall offer prayer ; and I do not intend to pray, but I intend to show you how I saw the Apostle of Allah (may peace be upon him) offering prayer. He (the narrator Ayyūb) said : I asked Abū Qilābah : How did he pray ? He replied : Like the prayer of this master of ours, namely, 'Amr b. Salamah, their *imām*. He then said : When he raised his head after the last prostration in the first *rak'ah*, he used to sit, and then stand up.[385]

(842) Abū Qilābah said: Abū Sulaimān Mālik b. al-Ḥuwairith came to our mosque, and said : By Allah, I shall offer prayer, though I do not intend to pray ; I only intend to show you how I saw the Apostle of Allah (may peace be upon him) praying. The narrator said : (He then prayed and) he sat at the end of the first *rak'ah* when he raised his head after the last prostration.

(843) Abū Qilābah said : Mālik b. al-Ḥuwairith saw that the Prophet (may peace be upon him) would not stand at the end of the first or the third *rak'ah* until he sat down straight.

Chapter 294

SITTING ON HEELS BETWEEN THE TWO PROSTRATIONS

(844) Ṭāwūs said : We asked Ibn 'Abbās about sitting on heels between the two prostrations. He said : It is the *sunnah*. We said : We look upon it as a pressure on the foot. He said : This is the *sunnah* of your Prophet (may peace be upon him).[386]

Chapter 295

WHAT SHOULD BE SAID WHEN ONE RAISES ONE'S HEAD AFTER BOWING

(845) 'Abd Allah b. Abī Awfā said : When the Apostle of Allah (may peace be upon him) raised his head after bowing, he said : Allah listens to him who praises

385. It is disputed amongst the jurists whether one should sit and then stand after the first and the third *rak'ah* of the prayer. Al-Shāfi'ī and the traditionists hold that one should sit and then stand after the first and the third *rak'ah*. But Abū Ḥanīfah, Mālik and Aḥmad maintain that one should not sit after the first and the third *rak'ah* (*'Awn al-Ma'būd*, I, 313).

386. The original Arabic word *iq'ā'* means to sit on one's hips by raising the knees and spreading forearms on the ground like a dog. Sitting in such a position has been disapproved by the Prophet (may peace be upon him). The other meaning of *iq'ā'* is to sit on one's heels. This was practised by the Prophet (may peace be upon him) and his Companions. Al-Shāfi'ī regards it as commendable. The Prophet (may peace be upon him) might have done so in his old age due to infirmity. The tradition which prohibits *iq'ā'* goes : I like for you, 'Alī, what I like for myself, and I dislike for you what I dislike for myself ; do not sit on your heels between the two prostrations. This refers to the original meaning of *iq'ā'* (*'Awn al-Ma'būd*, I, 314).

Him. O Allah, our Lord, to Thee be the praise in the heavens and in all the earth, and all that it pleases Thee to create afterwards.

Abū Dāwūd said: Sufyān al-Thawrī and Shu'bah b. al-Ḥajjāj reported on the authority of 'Ubaid b. al-Ḥasan: There is no mention of the words "after bowing" in this tradition. Sufyān said: We met al- Shaikh 'Ubaid b. al-Ḥasan; he did not say the words "after bowing" in it.

Abū Dāwūd said: Shu'bah narrated this from Abī 'Iṣmah, from al-A'mash, on the authority of 'Ubaid, saying: "after bowing".

(846) Abū Sa'īd al-Khudrī said: When the Apostle of Allah (may peace be upon him) said;"Allah listens to him who praises Him," he also said: O Allah, our Lord, to Thee be the praise in all heavens. Mu'ammil said (in his version): "In all the heavens, and in all the earth, and in all that it pleases Thee to create aftewards. O Thou Who art worthy of praise and glory, most worthy of what a servant says, and we are all Thy servants, no one can withhold what Thou givest or give what Thou withholdest." The narrators then were agreed on the words: "And riches cannot avail a wealthy person with Thee."[387]

(847) Abū Hurairah reported the Apostle of Allah (may peace be upon him) as saying: When the *imām* says: "Allah listens to him who praises Him," say: "O Allah, our Lord, to Thee be the praise," for if what anyone says synchronises with what the angels say, he will be forgiven his past sins.

(848 'Āmir said: The people behind the *imām* should not say: "Allah listens to him who praises Him," but they should say: "Our Lord, to Thee be the praise."

Chapter 296

SUPPLICATION BETWEEN TWO PROSTRATIONS

(849) Ibn 'Abbās reported that the Prophet (may peace be upon him) used to say between the two prostrations: "O Allah, forgive me, show mercy to me, guide me, heal me, and provide for me."

Chapter 297

WHEN SHOULD THE WOMEN PRAYING ALONG WITH THE *IMĀM* RAISE THEIR HEADS AFTER PROSTRATION?

(850) Asmā' daughter of Abū Bakr said: I heard the Apostle of Allah (may peace be upon him) say: One of you who believes in Allah and in the Last Day should not

387. This means that only obedience to Allah will avail him or protect him from Allah's punishment.

raise her head until the men raise their heads (after prostration) lest they should see the private parts of men.[388]

Chapter 298

HOW LONG SHOULD ONE STAND AFTER BOWING AND SIT BETWEEN THE TWO PROSTRATIONS

(851) Al-Barā' said: The prostration observed by the Apostle of Allah (may peace be upon him), his bowing, and his sitting between the two prostrations were nearly equal.

(852) Anas b. Mālik said: I did not offer prayer behind anyone more brief than the one offered by the Apostle of Allah (may peace be upon him) and that was perfect. When the Apostle of Allah (may peace be upon him) said: "Allah listens to him who praises Him," he stood so long that we thought that he had omitted something; then he would say *takbīr* (Allah is most great) and prostrate, and would sit between the two prostrations so long that we thought that he had omitted something.[389]

(853) Al-Barā' b. 'Āzib said: I witnessed Muḥammad (may peace be upon him) —Abū Kāmil's version has the wording: The Apostle of Allah (may peace be upon him)—during his prayer. I found his standing like his bowing and prostration and his moderation in bowing was like that of his prostration, and his sitting between the two prostrations and his prostration (and his sitting[390] between the salutation) and going away (after finishing the prayer) were nearly equal to one another.[391]

Abū Dāwūd said: Musaddad said: His bowing and his moderation in bowing and prostration, and his prostration and his sitting between the two prostrations, and his

388. During the time of the Prophet (may peace be upon him) the people would tie wrappers instead of wearing trousers While prostrating the private parts were likely to be disclosed and seen by the women who stood in the row behind the children. Hence the Prophet (may peace be upon him) commanded women to raise their heads after the men had raised.

389. This tradition shows that the Prophet (may peace be upon him) would observe bowing, prostration, standing after bowing and sitting between the prostrations for a long duration, But his prayer would be brief and perfect for he recited short *sūrahs* in the prayer and did not make haste in the observance of bowing and prostration.

390. This shows that the Prophet (may peace be upon him) used to sit for a short while after finishing the prayer.

391 The observance of moderation in different positions in prayer is obligatory according to al-Shāfi'ī and Aḥmad b. Ḥanbal. If one observes bowing and prostration hurriedly, one's prayer will not be valid. This tradition clearly shows that the Prophet (may peace be upon him) used to perform all the acts during the prayer moderately and gave long duration after bowing and between the two prostrations. The Prophet (may peace be upon him) sometimes recited long *sūrahs* and at times short *sūrahs* during the prayer, but performed bowing and prostrations moderately and unhurriedly.

prostration and sitting between the salutation and going away (after finishing the prayer) were nearly equal.

Chapter 299

ON THE PRAYER OF ONE WHO DOES NOT KEEP ONE'S BACK STEADY DURING BOWING AND PROSTRATION

(854) Abū Mas'ūd al-Badrī reported the Apostle of Allah (may peace be upon him) as saying: A man's prayer does not avail him unless he keeps his back steady when bowing and prostrating.

(855) Abū Hurairah said: When the Apostle of Allah (may peace be upon him) entered the mosque, a man also entered it and prayed. He then came and saluted the Apostle of Allah (may peace be upon him). The Apostle of Allah (may peace be upon him) returned the salutation and said to him: Go back and pray, for you have not prayed. The man returned and prayed as he prayed before. He then came to the Prophet (may peace be upon him) and saluted him. The Apostle of Allah (may peace be upon him) said to him: "And upon you be peace." Go back and pray, for you have not prayed. He did so three times. Then the man said: By Him Who has sent you (as a Prophet) with truth; I cannot do better than this; so teach me. He said: When you get up to pray, utter the *takbīr* (Allah is most great); then recite a convenient portion of the Qur'ān; then bow and remain quietly in that position; then raise yourself and stand erect: then prostrate yourself and remain quietly in that position; then sit and remain quietly in that position; then do that throughout all your prayer.

Abū Dāwūd said: Al-Qa'nabī reported this tradition from Sa'īd b. Abī Sa'īd on the authority of Abū Hurairah. This version has the wording in the last: When you do this, then your prayer is completed. If you omit anything from this, you will omit that much from your prayer. This version also has the wording: When you get up for praying, perform the ablution perfectly.[392]

(856) 'Alī b. Yaḥyā b. Khallād reported on the authority of his uncle: A man entered the mosque. He then narrated the tradition like the one narrated above. This version goes: The Prophet (may peace be upon him) said: The prayer of anyone is not perfect unless he performs ablution perfectly; he then should utter the *takbīr*, and praise Allah, the Exalted, and admire Him; he then should recite the Qur'ān as much as he desires. He then should say: "Allah is Most Great". He then

392. This tradition shows the obligation of the observance of moderation in all the acts of prayer. One should not offer prayer hurriedly. All the major acts of prayer such as standing, bowing, standing after bowing, prostration and sitting between the prostrations should be performed moderately.

should bow so that all his joints return to their proper places. Then he should say: "Allah listens to him who praises Him", and stand erect. He then should say: "Allah is most great," and should prostrate himself so that all his joints are at rest properly. Then he should say: "Allah is most great"; he should raise his head (at the end of prostration) till he sits erect. Then he should say: "Allah is most great"; then he should prostrate himself till all his joints return to their proper places. Then he should raise his head and say the *takbīr*. When he does so, then his prayer is completed.

(857) Rifā'ah b. Rāfi' reported the above-mentioned tradition through a different chain of narrators to the same effect. This version goes: The Apostle of Allah (may peace be upon him) said: The prayer of any of you is not complete until he performs ablution perfectly, as Allah, the Exalted, has ordered you. He should wash his face and hands up to the elbows, and wipe his head and (wash) his feet up to the ankles. Then he should exalt Allah and praise Him. Then he should recite the Qur'ān as much as it is convenient for him. He then narrated the tradition like Ḥammād. He said: He then should utter the *takbīr* and prostrate himself so that his face is at rest. Hammām said: Sometimes he reported: so that his forehead is at rest on the ground, and his joints return to their places and are loosened. Then he should say the *takbīr* and then sit right on his hips and erect his back. He described the nature of prayer in this way by offering four *rak'ahs* until he finished it. The prayer of any of you is not complete unless he does so.

(858) This tradition has also been transmitted through a different chain of narrators by Rifā'ah b. Rāfi'. This version goes: When you get up and face the *qiblah*, say the *takbīr* (Allah is most great). Then recite the *Umm al-Qur'ān* (Sūrah i.) and what Allah wishes you to recite. And when you bow, put your palms on your knees and stretch out your back. When you prostrate yourself, do it completely (so that you are at rest). When you raise yourself then sit on your left thigh.

(859) This tradition has also been transmitted by Rifā'ah b. Rāfi' through a different chain of narrators. This version has: When you get up to pray, say the *takbīr*, exalting Allah; then recite the Qur'ān as much as it is convenient for you. The version adds: When you sit in the middle of the prayer, do it completely (so that you are at rest) and spread your left thigh; then recite the *tashahhud*.[393] Then if you get up (again), do in a similar way until you finish your prayer.

(860) Rifā'ah b. Rāfi' has also narrated this tradition through a different chain from the Apostle of Allah (may peace be upon him). This version goes: Then perform ablution in a way Allah, the Exalted, has commanded you, then say the *shahādah*[394]

393. This means the supplication *taḥiyyah*, i.e. *al-taḥiyyāt-u-lillāhi*. . . . The details will follow in due course.

394. A testimony that there is no deity but Allah, and that Muḥammad (may peace be upon him) is His prophet.

and get up and say the *takbīr*. Then if you know any of the Qur'ān, recite it; otherwise say: "Praise be to Allah"; "Allah is most great"; "There is no god but Allah". He (the narrator) also said in this version: If some defect remains in this, that defect will remain in your prayer.

(861) 'Abd al-Raḥmān b. Shibl said: The Apostle of Allah (may peace be upon him) prohibited to peck[395] like a crow, and to spread (the forearms) like a wild beast,[396] and to fix a place in the mosque like a camel which fixes its place. These are the wordings of Qutaibah.

(862) Sālim al-Barrād said: We came to Abū Mas'ūd 'Uqbah b. 'Amr al-Anṣārī and said to him: Tell us about the prayer of the Apostle of Allah (may peace be upon him). He stood up before us in the mosque and said the *takbīr*. When he bowed, he placed his hands upon his knees and put his fingers below, and kept his elbows (arms) away from his sides, so everything returned properly to its place. Then he said: "Allah listens to him who praises Him"; then he stood up so that everything returned properly to its place; then he said the *takbīr* and prostrated and put the palms of his hands on the ground; he kept his elbows (arms) away from his sides, so that everything returned to its proper place. Then he raised his head and sat so that everything returned to its proper place; he then repeated it in a similar way. Then he offered four *rak'ahs* of prayer like this *rak'ah* and completed his prayer. Then he said: Thus we witnessed the Apostle of Allah (may peace be upon him) offering his prayer.

Chapter 300

THE SAYING OF THE PROPHET (MAY PEACE BE UPON HIM): "IF A MAN CANNOT OFFER HIS (OBLIGATORY) PRAYER PERFECTLY, THE DEFECT WILL BE COMPENSATED BY THE SUPEREROGATORY PRAYER"

(863) Anas b. Ḥakīm al-Ḍabbī said that he feared Ziyād or Ibn Ziyād; so he came to Medina and met Abū Hurairah. He attributed his lineage to me and I became a member of his lineage. Abū Hurairah said (to me): O youth, should I not narrate a tradition to you? I said: Why not, may Allah have mercy on you? Yūnus (a narrator) said: I think he narrated it (the tradition) from the Prophet (may peace be upon him):

395. This means to offer prayer hurriedly so that one may not perform bowing, prostration and standing in prayer quietly with pause and moderation. He bows and prostrates hastily like the pecking of a crow. This shows that observance of moderation and tranquillity is necessary in prayer.

396. While prostrating men should not place their forearms on the ground. This is permissible for women.

The first thing about which the people will be called to account out of their actions on the Day of Judgment is prayer. Our Lord, the Exalted, will say to the angels—though He knows better: Look into the prayer of My servant and see whether he has offered it perfectly or imperfectly. If it is perfect, that will be recorded perfect. If it is defective, He will say: See there are some optional prayers offered by My servant. If there are optional prayers to his credit, He will say: Compensate the obligatory prayer by the optional prayer for My servant. Then all the actions will be considered similarly.[397]

(864) The above-mentioned tradition has also been transmitted by Abū Hurairah through a different chain of narrators to the same effect.

(865) Tamīm al-Dārī reported this tradition from the Prophet (may peace be upon him) to the same effect. This version adds: Then *zakāt* will be considered in a similar way. Then all the actions will be considered accordingly.

Chapter 301

CHAPTERS ON THE SUB-RULES OF BOWING AND PROSTRATION AND ON PUTTING THE HANDS ON THE KNEES (IN BOWING POSITION)

(866) Mus'ab b. Sa'd said: I prayed by the side of my father. I put both of my hands between my knees (in bowing condition). He prohibited me from it. I then repeated; so he said: Do not do so, because we used to do so, but we were prohibited to do that, and commanded to put our hands on the knees.

(867) 'Abd Allah (b. Mas'ūd) said: When any of you bows, he should spread his arms on his thighs and clap both his palms (placing them between the knees), as if I am seeing the variation of the fingers of the Apostle of Allah (may peace be upon him).[398]

Chapter 302

WHAT A MAN SHOULD RECITE IN HIS BOWING AND PROSTRATION

(868) 'Uqbah b. 'Āmir said: When "Glorify the name of your mighty

397. This shows that one should not neglect offering optional or supererogatory prayers and similar other actions in addition to the obligatory duties. All other obligatory duties such as *zakāt* and fasting will be compensated by the voluntary actions.

398. This action of placing the hands between the knees while bowing is called *taṭbiq* which was allowed in the early days of Islam. But later on *taṭbiq* was annulled and people were commanded to put their hands on their knees. But 'Abd Allah b. Mas'ūd remembered the previous injunction and he followed this practice persistently throughout his life.

Lord''[399] was revealed, the Apostle of Allah (may peace be upon him) said: Use it when bowing, and when "Glorify the name of your most high Lord"[400] was revealed, he said: Use it when prostrating yourself.

(869) The above-mentioned tradition has also been reported through a different chain of narrators by 'Uqbah b. 'Āmir to the same effect. This version adds: When the Apostle of Allah (may peace be upon him) bowed, he said: "Glory and praise be to my mighty Lord" three times, and when he prostrated himself, he said: "Glory and praise be to my most high Lord" three times.

Abū Dāwūd said: We are afraid the addition of the word "praise" is not guarded.

(870) Ḥudhaifah said that he prayed along with the Prophet (may peace be upon him), and that he said when bowing, "Glory be to my mighty Lord," and when prostrated himself, "Glory be to my most high Lord"; when he came to a verse which spoke of mercy, he stopped and made supplication, and when he came to a verse which spoke of punishment, he stopped and sought refuge in Allah.

(871) 'Ā'ishah said that the Prophet (may peace be upon him) used to say when bowing and prostrating, "All-Glorious, All-Holy, Lord of the angels and spirit."[401]

(872) 'Awf b. Mālik al-Ashja'ī said: I stood up to pray along with the Apostle of Allah (may peace be upon him); he got up and recited Sūrah al-Baqarah (Sūrah ii.); when he came to a verse which spoke of mercy, he stopped and made supplication, and when he came to a verse which spoke of punishment, he stopped and sought refuge in Allah; then he bowed and paused as long as he stood (reciting Sūrah al-Baqarah), and said while bowing, "Glory be to the Possessor of greatness, the Kingdom, grandeur and majesty."[402] Then he prostrated himelf and paused as long as he stood up and repeated while prostrating the same supplication. Then he stood up and recited Sūrah Āl-i-'Imrān (Sūrah iii.) and then recited many *sūrahs* one after another.

(873) Ḥudhaifah said that he saw the Apostle of Allah (may peace be upon him) praying at night. He said: "Allah is most great" three times, "Possessor of kingdom, grandeur, greatness and majesty." He then began (his prayer) and recited Sūrah al Baqarah; then he bowed and he paused in bowing as long as he stood up; he said while bowing, "Glory be to my mighty Lord," "Glory be to my mighty Lord";

399. Qur'ān, lvi. 74, 96.

400. Qur'ān, lxxxvii. 1.

401. The Prophet (may peace be upon him) might have recited this supplication while bowing and prostrating before the revelation of the *sūrhas* mentioned in tradition 868 narrated by 'Uqbah b. 'Āmir. After the revelation of these *sūrhas* this supplicatoin was replaced by the supplications "Glory be to my mighty Lord," and by "Glory be to my most high Lord."

402. The Prophet (may peace be upon him) used to recite different supplications while bowing and prostrating until the *sūrahs* mentioned by 'Uqbah b. 'Āmir in his tradition were revealed.

then he raised his head, after bowing; then he stood up and he paused as long as he paused in bowing and said, "Praise be to my Lord"; then he prostrated and paused in prostration as long as he paused in the standing position; he said while prostrating: "Glory be to my most high Lord"; then he raised his head after prostration, and sat as long as he prostrated, and said while sitting: "O my Lord forgive me." He offered four *rak'ahs* of prayer and recited in them Sūrah al-Baqarah, Āl-i-'Imrān, al-Nisā', al-Mā'idah, or al-An'ām.[403] The narrator Shu'bah doubted.

Chapter 303

MAKING SUPPLICATION WHILE BOWING AND PROSTRATING

(874) Abū Hurairah reported the Apostle of Allah (may peace be upon him) as saying: The nearest a servant comes to his Lord is when he is prostrating himself, so make supplication often.[404]

(875) Ibn 'Abbās said: The Prophet (may peace be upon him) lifted the curtain (and saw that) the people were standing in rows (of prayer) behind Abū Bakr.[405] He said: O people, there remained nothing that gives good tidings from prophethood except a true dream which a Muslim has himself or which another Muslim has for him.[406] I have been prohibited to recite the Qur'ān while bowing or prostrating. As regards bowing, exalt the Lord in it, and as to prostration, make supplication with exertion in it, that is worthy of being accepted.

(876) 'Ā'ishah said: The Apostle of Allah (may peace be upon him) often said while bowing and prostrating himself; "Glory be to Thee, O Allah, our Lord," and "Praise be to Thee, O Allah, forgive me," thus interpreting the (command in the Qur'ān).[407]

(877) Abū Hurairah said: The Prophet (may peace be upon him) used to say when prostrating himself: "O Allah, forgive me all my sins, small and great, first and last." The narrator Ibn al-Sarḥ added: "Open and secret."

403. This was the *tahajjud* prayer which the Prophet (may peace be upon him) used to offer at the dead of night or towards the end. Hence he prolonged it extraordinarily.

404. Prostration is the highest form of worship It displays the utmost submission and humbleness of a servant, Hence this position is liked most by Allah, and hence He strictly prohibited to prostrate before anyone other than Him. The supplication is generally accepted by Allah when one is prostrating.

405. This refers to the death sickness of the Prophet (may peace be upon him) when Abū Bakr led the people in prayer in his absence.

406. This means that there will be no prophet after him. A Muslim may have a true dream only.

407. This refers to Sūrah al-Naṣr (cx. 3).

(878) 'Ā'ishah said: One night I missed the Apostle of Allah (may peace be upon him) and when I sought him on the spot of prayer I found him in prostration with his feet raised, and he was saying: "(O Allah), I seek refuge in Thy good pleasure from Thy anger, and in Thy forgiveness from Thy punishment, and I seek refuge from Thee in Thee;[408] I cannot reckon Thy praise; Thou art as Thou hast lauded Thyself."

Chapter 304

MAKING SUPPLICATION DURING PRAYER

(879) 'Ā'ishah said: The Apostle of Allah (may peace be upon him) used to make supplication during the prayer saying: "O Allah, I seek refuge in Thee from the punishment of the grave; I seek refuge in Thee from the trial of the Antichrist; I seek refuge in Thee from the trial of life and the trial of death; O Allah, I seek refuge in Thee from sin and debt." Someone said to him: How often you seek refuge from debt! He replied: When a man is in debt, he talks and tells lies, makes promises and breaks them.[409]

(880) Ibn Abī Lailā said: I prayed by the side of the Apostle of Allah (may peace be upon him) in the supererogatory prayer and I heard him say: "I seek refuge in Allah from the Hell-fire; woe to the inmates of the Hell-fire!"

(881) Abū Hurairah said: The Apostle of Allah (may peace be upon him) got up for prayer and we also stood up along with him. A bedouin said during prayer: O Allah, show mercy to me and to Muḥammad and do not show mercy to anyone along with us. When the Apostle of Allah (may peace be upon him) uttered the salutation, he said to the bedouin: You narrowed down a vast (thing). By this he meant the mercy of Allah.

(882) Ibn 'Abbās reported: When the Prophet (may peace be upon him) recited: "Glorify the name of thy Lord, the Most High," he would say: "Glory be to Allah, the Most High."

Abū Dāwūd said: In this tradition the other narrators have differed from the narrator Wakī'. This has been narrated by Wakī', and Shu'bah from Abū Isḥāq, from Sa'īd b. Jubair, from Ibn 'Abbās as his own statement (and not from the Prophet).

(883) 'Ā'ishah said: A man used to pray on the roof of his house. When h recited the verse "Is not He (Who doth so) able to bring the dead to life?" (lxxv. 40) he would say: "Glory be to Thee, then, why not?" The people asked him about it.

408. This means that only Allah can give refuge from His anger.

409. The Prophet (may peace be upon him) used to make these supplications in the sitting position after reciting *tashahhud* and invoking blessing.

He replied: I heard it from the Apostle of Allah (may peace be upon him).

Abū Dāwūd said: Aḥmad (b. Ḥanbal) said: It is pleasing to me that one should recite in the obligatory prayer those supplications which have occurred in the Qur'ān.

Chapter 305

DURATION OF THE BOWING AND PROSTRATION

(884) Sa'dī reported that he heard his father or his uncle say: I witnessed the Prophet (may peace be upon him) while offering prayer. He used to stay in his bowing and his prostration as long as one utters the words "Glory be to Allah and praise be to Him" three times.

(885) 'Abd Allah b. Mas'ūd reported the Apostle of Allah (may peace be upon him) as saying: When one of you bows, he should say three times: "Glory be to my mighty Lord," and when he prostrates, he should say: "Glory be to my most high Lord" three times. This is the minimum number.

Abū Dāwūd said: The chain of this tradition is broken. The narrator 'Awn did not see 'Abd Allah (b. Mas'ūd).

(886) Abū Hurairah reported the Apostle of Allah (may peace be upon him) as saying: When one of you recites "By the fig and the olive" (Sūrah xcv.) and comes to its end "Is not Allah the best of judges?" (verse 8) he should say: "Certainly, and I am one of those who testify to that." When one recites "I swear by the day of resurrection" (Sūrah lxxv.), and comes to "Is not that one able to raise the dead to life" (verse 40), he should say: "Certainly." And when one recites "By those that are sent" (Sūrah lxxvii.), and comes to "Then in what message after that will they believe?" (verse 50), he should say: "We believe in Allah."[410]

The narrator Ismā'īl (b. Umayyah) said: I began to repeat (this tradition) before the bedouin (who reported this tradition) so that I might see whether he (was mistaken). He said: My nephew, do you think that I did not remember it? I performed sixty *Ḥajj* (pilgrimages); there is no *Ḥajj* but I recognise the camel on which I performed it.

(887) Mālik b. Anas said: I did not offer behind anyone after the Apostle of Allah (may peace be upon him) a prayer like the prayer offered by the Apostle of Allah (may peace be upon him) than this youth, i.e. 'Umar b. 'Abd al-'Azīz. We

410. It is commendable to recite the supplications after the verses mentioned in this tradition during the prayer as well as when one is not praying. But this tradition is weak because the name of the bedouin who narrated this tradition is not known (*'Awn al-Ma'būd*, I, 331).

estimated reciting glorification ten times in his bowing, and in his prostration ten times.[411]

Abū Dāwūd said: Aḥmad b. Ṣāliḥ said: I asked him ('Abd Allah) whether the name Mānūs is correct or Mābūs. He replied: 'Abd al-Razzāq used to say Mābūs, but I remember Mānūs (i.e. the narrator Wahb b. Mānūs). These are the words of Ibn Rāfi'. It has also been narrated by Aḥmad from Sa'īd b. Jubair on the authority of Anas b. Mālik.

Chapter 306

THE LIMBS WHICH TOUCH THE GROUND WHILE PROSTRATING

(888) Ibn 'Abbās reported the Prophet (may peace be upon him) as saying: I have been commanded. According to the version of Ḥammād: Your Prophet (may peace be upon him) was commanded to prostrate on seven (bones),[412] and not to fold back the hair or the clothing.[413]

(889) Ibn 'Abbās reported the Prophet (may peace be upon him) as saying: I have been commanded, and sometimes the narrator said: Your Prophet (may peace be upon him) was commanded to prostrate on seven limbs.

(890) 'Abbās b. 'Abd al-Muṭṭalib said that he heard the Apostle of Allah (may peace be upon him) as saying: When a servant (of Allah) prostrates himself, the seven limbs, i.e. his face,[414] his palms, his knees and his feet prostrate along with him.

(891) Ibn 'Umar reported the Prophet (may peace be upon him) as saying: Both hands prostrate as the face prostrates. When one of you puts his face (on the ground) he should put his hands too (on the ground). And when he raises it, he should raise them too.

411. This shows that the *imām* can recite the glorification in bowing and prostration even up to ten times. But this is permissible in case the people behind the *imām* are not tired. If so, he should recite only three times. A person praying alone can recite glorification as many times as he can (*'Awn al-Ma'būd*, I, 331).

412. I.e. the forehead, the hands, the knees and the toes of the feet.

413. It is disapproved to fold back or roll up the clothing or to have back knot or hair during prayer (*'Awn al-Ma'būd*. I. 337).

414. The face includes both forehead and nose. If one puts only his forehead on the ground and not his nose, the prostration will be valid. In case he puts only his nose on the ground, it is disputed whether his prostration will be valid. According to Abū Ḥanīfah, his prostration will be valid if he puts only his nose on the ground. According to others, that will not be valid.

Chapter 307

WHAT SHOULD A MAN DO WHEN HE FINDS THE *IMĀM* PROSTRATING

(892) Abū Hurairah reported the Apostle of Allah (may peace be upon him) as saying: When you come to pray while we are prostrating ourselves, you must prostrate yourselves, and do not reckon it anything (i.e. as a full *rak'ah*) or a part of the prayer; and if anyone is present while bowing (*rak'ah*) he has been present at the prayer.[415]

Chapter 308

PUTTING THE NOSE AND THE FOREHEAD ON THE GROUND WHILE PROSTRATING

(893) Abū Sa'Id al-Khudrī said : The mark of earth was seen on the forehead and nose of the Apostle of Allah (may peace be upon him) due to the prayer in which he led the people.[416]

(894) The above-mentioned tradition has also been transmitted by Ma'mar through a different chain of narrators to the same effect.

Chapter 309

HOW TO PROSTRATE ONESELF

(895) Al-Barā' b. 'Āzib described to us (the nature of prostration). He placed his

415. This means that if anyone comes late and joins the congregation while the *imām* is bowing, he will be considered to have been present at the full *rak'ah*, and he is not required to offer this *rak'ah*. This is the view of the majority of the scholars. The traditionists hold that one should recite the *Fātiḥah* in every *rak'ah*, and no prayer is valid without reciting the *Fātiḥah*. Hence one must recite the *Fātiḥah*.

If one joins the congregation while the *imām* is prostrating one will not be considered to have been present at the full *rak'ah*. One will have to offer this *rak ah* after the salutation of the *imām* (*'Awn al-Ma'būd*, I, 332-36).

416. There is a difference of opinion on prostrating on the nose and the forehead. According to Aḥmad b. Ḥanbal, al-Awzā'ī Isḥāq and al-Shāfi'ī, it is necessary to place both the nose and the forehead on the ground during prostration. The majority of the scholars are of opinion that what is necessary during prostration is to put one's forehead and not the nose. Abū Ḥanīfah maintains that it is sufficient for prostration to place the nose on the ground. But Ibn al-Mundhir has reported the consensus of the Companions of the Prophet (may peace be upon him) on the fact that the prostration will not be valid if one puts one's nose alone on the ground and not the forehead (*'Awn al-Ma'būd*, I, 338).

hands (palms), reclined on his knees, and raised his hips ; he said : This is how the Apostle of Allah (may peace be upon him) used to prostrate himself.

(896) Anas reported the Apostle of Allah (may peace be upon him) as saying : Adopt a moderate position when prostrating yourselves, and see that none of you stretches out his forearms (on the ground) like a dog.[417]

(897) Maimūnah said : When the Prophet (may peace be upon him) prostrated himself, he kept his arms so far away from his sides that if a lamb had wanted to pass under his arms, it could have done so.

(898) Ibn 'Abbās said : I came to the Prophet (may peace be upon him) from behind. I saw the whiteness of his armpits and he kept his arms away from his sides and raised his stomach (from the ground).

(899) Aḥmar b. Jaz' said : When the Apostle of Allah (may peace be upon him) prostrated himself, he kept his arms far away from his sides so much so that we took pity on him.

(900) Abū Hurairah reported the Prophet (may peace be upon him) as saying : When one of you prostrates himself, he should not stretch out his forearms (on the ground) like a dog and he should join both of his thighs.[418]

Chapter 310

PERMISSION TO PLACE THE FOREARMS ON THE GROUND WHILE PROSTRATING

(901) Abū Hurairah said : The Companions of the Prophet (may peace be upon him) complained to the Prophet (may peace be upon him) about the hardship when they kept their forearms far away from their sides while prostrating. He said : Take help with the elbows (by spreading them on the ground and sticking them to the sides).[419]

417. The moderate position of prostration is that one should place his palms, knees, nose and forehead on the ground, and should raise the forearms from the ground, keeping them away from the sides and keep the thighs separate from the stomach (*'Awn al-Ma'būd, I,* 339).

418. This might apply to woman. The other traditions indicate that the Prophet (may peace be upon him) used to keep his thighs separate from each other, and also kept them away from his stomach.

419. This shows that in congregational prayer if there is congestion among the rows and people feel hardship in keeping their forearms away from their sides, they are allowed to spread them on the ground and stick them to the sides.

Chapter 311

PUTTING THE HANDS ON THE WAIST AND TO SIT RAISING THE FEET AND SPREADING THE HANDS ON THE GROUND DURING PRAYER

(902) Sa'īd b. Ziyād b. Ṣubaiḥ al-Ḥanafī said : I prayed by the side of Ibn 'Umar and I put my hands on my waist. When he finished his prayer, he said : This is a cross in prayer ; the Apostle of Allah (may peace be upon him) used to forbid it.[420]

Chapter 312

WEEPING DURING PRAYER

(903) Muṭarrif reported on the authority of his father (Abd Allah b. al-Shikhkhīr); I saw the Apostle of Allah (may peace be upon him) praying and a sound came from his breast like the rumbling of a mill owing to weeping.[421]

Chapter 313

DISAPPROVAL OF THE EVIL SUGGESTIONS AND TALKING TO ONESELF QUIETLY DURING PRAYER

(904) Zaid b. Khālid al-Juhanī reported the Prophet (may peace be upon him) as saying : Anyone who performs ablution and performs his ablution well, and then he offers two *rak'ahs* of prayer in a way that he does not forget (anything in it), will be forgiven all his past sins.

(905) 'Uqbah b. 'Āmir al-Juhanī reported the Apostle of Allah (may peace be upon him) as saying: Any one performs ablution and performs the ablution perfectly and then offers two *rak'ahs* of prayer concentrating on them with his heart and face but Paradise will necessarily fall to his lot.

420. To put the hands on the waist during prayer is disapproved according to the majority of the scholars. The literalist (*ahl al-ẓāhir*) take it as forbidden. There may be several reasons for the prohibition of this act during prayer (*'Awn al-Ma'būd*, I, 340) :

(1) resemblance to satan ;

(2) resemblance to the Jews ;

(3) comfort of those who go to Hell (as another tradition shows) ;

(4) an action of proud and self-conceited people ;

(5) resembles the people who are suffering from miseries.

421. Aḥmad narrates that when the Holy Prophet (may peace be upon him) offered prayer a sound like that of a boiling cauldron came from within him because of his weeping. This means that the prayer is not affected by weeping.

Chapter 314

CORRECTING THE *IMĀM* DURING PRAYER (IF HE MAKES A MISTAKE)

(906) Al-Miswar b. Yazīd al-Mālikī said : The Apostle of Allah (may peace be upon him). The narrator Yaḥyā said : Sometimes he (al-Miswar) said : I prayed along with the Apostle of Allah (may peace be upon him) and witnessed that he recited the Qur'ān during the prayer and omitted something (i.e. some verses inadvertently) which he did not recite. A man said to him : Apostle of Allah, you omitted such-and-such verse. The Apostle of Allah (may peace be upon him) said : Why did you not remind me of it ? The narrator Sulaimān said in his version : He (the man) said : I thought that it (the verse) was repealed. Sulaimān said : Yaḥyā b. Kathīr narrated it to us.

(907) Ibn 'Umar said : The Prophet (may peace be upon him) prayed and recited the Qur'ān in it. He was then confused in it (in his recitation). When he finished (his prayer), he said to Ubayy (b. Ka'b) : Did you pray along with us ? He said : Yes. He said : What prevented you (from correcting me) ?[422]

Chapter 315

PROHIBITION OF INSTRUCTING THE *IMĀM*

(908) 'Alī (Allah be pleased with him) reported the Apostle of Allah (may peace be upon him) as saying : 'Alī, do not instruct the *imām* during the prayer.

Abū Dāwūd said : The narrator Abū Isḥāq heard only four traditions from al-Ḥārith ; this tradition is not one of them.[423]

422. If the *imām* forgets some verses while reciting the Qur'ān in the prayer, the person who remembers them behind him should recite to him loudly to correct him. The permission in these two traditions is unconditional. One can correct the *imām* during the prayer whether he recites aloud or quietly. Further, if he makes a mistake in any other action of prayer, he should be corrected by clapping by women, and by glorifying Allah if men correct him (*'Awn al-Ma'būd*. I, 342).

423. This tradition is weak because a link is missing from its chain. The scholars, however, differ on this point. 'Uthmān and Ibn 'Umar hold that it is permissible to instruct the *imām* during the prayer. This is also the opinion of 'Aṭā', al-Ḥasan, Ibn Sīrīn, Mālik, al-Shāfi'ī, Aḥmad and Isḥāq b. Rāhwaih. Ibn Mas'ūd is reported to have disapproved of instructing the *imām* during the prayer. This is also the view of al-Sha'bī and Sufyān al-Thawrī. Abū Ḥanīfah maintains that if the *imām* requires instruction, he should be given ; otherwise not. In his opinion giving instruction to the *imām* during prayer is like speaking which breaks the prayer (*'Awn al-Ma'būd*, I. 342).

Chapter 316

LOOKING BY TURNING THE NECK DURING PRAYER

(909) Abū Dharr reported the Apostle of Allah (may peace be upon him) as saying: Allah, the Most High, continues to turn favourably towards a servant while he is engaged in prayer as long as he does not look to the side (by turning the neck), but if he does so, He turns away from him.[424]

(910) 'Ā'ishah said: I asked the Apostle of Allah (may peace be upon him) about looking to the sides during prayer. He said: It is something which the devil snatches from a servant's prayer

Chapter 317

PROSTRATING ON THE NOSE

(911) Abū Sa'īd al-Khudrī said: The mark of earth was seen on the forehead and nose of the Apostle of Allah (may peace be upon him) who had led the people in prayer.

Abū 'Alī[425] said: Abū Dāwūd did not recite this tradition when he recited his collection (of the *Sunan*) for the fourth time.

Chapter 318

LOOKING TO ANY DIRECTION DURING PRAYER

(912) Jābir b. Samurah said (this is the version of the narrator 'Uthmān): The Apostle of Allah (may peace be upon him) entered the mosque and saw there some people praying raising their hands towards the heaven. (This is the common version:) He said: People must stop raising their eyes to the heaven. The narrator Musaddad said: During prayer, otherwise their sight will be taken away.[426]

(913) Anas b. Mālik reported the Apostle of Allah (may peace be upon him) as

424. This tradition indicates that one should not look to the sides by turning the neck about during prayer. This action is looked upon as disapproved by the jurists. In case one turns one's chest from the direction of the *qiblah*, the prayer would become void. Looking to the sides distracts the attention of the worshipper and disturbs his concentration during prayer (*'Awn al-Ma'būd*, I, 342).

425. His name is Muḥammad b. Aḥmad b. 'Amr al-Lu'lu' al-Baṣrī. He has narrated the *Sunan* of Abū Dāwūd from the author himself. He means that Abū Dāwūd finally deleted this tradition from his collection, as he has already mentioned it.

426. This tradition shows that one should not raise one's eyes to the heaven in prayer. All the scholars are agreed that looking to the heaven in prayer is abominable.

saying: What is the matter that people raise their eyes (upwards) in prayer. He then said sternly: They should stop doing that, otherwise their sight will be snatched away.[427]

(914) 'Ā'ishah said: The Apostle of Allah (may peace be upon him) once prayed with a sheet of cloth upon him. It had prints and paintings. He said: The prints of this (sheet) distracted my attention; take it to Abū Jahm and bring a blanket to me.[428]

(915) The above-mentioned tradition has also been narrated by 'Ā'ishah through a different chain of transmitters. This version adds: He (the Prophet) took a kind of sheet of cloth known as *kurdī* which belonged to Abū Jahm. The people told him: Apostle of Allah, the (former) sheet of cloth was better than this kind of *kurdī* sheet.

Chapter 319

PERMISSION FOR LOOKING TO THE SIDES DURING PRAYER

(916) Sahl b. al-Ḥanẓalīyyah said: The *iqāmah* for the morning prayer was pronounced and the Apostle of Allah (may peace be upon him) began to offer prayer while he was looking at the mountain-pass.

Abū Dāwūd said: He sent a horseman to the mountain-pass at night in order to keep watch.[429]

Chapter 320

WHAT MAY OR MAY NOT BE DONE DURING PRAYER

(917) Abū Qatādah said: The Apostle of Allah (may peace be upon him) was

427. This is a threat against raising one's eyes to the heaven in prayer. The reason for this prohibition is that by raising eyes to the heaven, a worshipper keeps himself away from the direction of the *qiblah* and remains no longer in the proper condition of prayer According to some scholars, it is forbidden to raise eyes to the heaven. Al-Shāfi'ī is of opinion that it is disapproved (*'Awn al-Ma'būd*, I. 343).

428. He is a well-known Companion of the Prophet (may peace be upon him). He presented the sheet to him. Hence he asked to return it to him.

This tradition shows that one should not wear such clothes as disturb one's concentration in prayer.

429 This tradition indicates that there is no harm if one looks to the sides without turning neck in prayer. This is the opinion of 'Aṭā', Mālik, Abū Ḥanīfah, and al-Awzā'ī. It is also said that looking to the sides was earlier permissible. But when the opening verses of Sūrah al-Mū'minun were revealed, the permission was withdrawn. The people were commanded to look to the spot of prostration while standing (*'Awn al-Ma'būd*, I, 344).

leading the people in prayer with Umāmah daughter of Zainab daughter of the Apostle of Allah (may peace be upon him) (in his lap). When he prostrated, he put her down, and when he got up (after prostration) he lifted her up.[430]

(918) Abū Qatādah said: We were sitting in the mosque when the Apostle of Allah (may peace be upon him) came upon us carrying Umāmah daughter of Abū al-'Āṣ b. al-Rabī'. Her mother was Zainab daughter of the Apostle of Allah (may peace be upon him). She (Umāmah) was a child and he (the Prophet) was carrying her on his shoulder. The Apostle of Allah (may peace be upon him) led (the people) in prayer while she was on his shoulder. When he bowed he put her down and took her up when he got up. He kept on doing so until he finished his prayer.

(919) Abū Qatādah al-Anṣārī said: I saw the Apostle of Allah (may peace be upon him) leading the people in prayer with Umāmah daughter of Abū al-'Āṣ on his neck (shoulder). When he prostrated, he put her down.

Abū Dāwūd said: The narrator Makhramah did not hear from his father except one tradition.[431]

(920) Abū Qatādah, a Companion of the Apostle of Allah (may peace be upon him), said: While we were waiting for the Apostle of Allah (may peace be upon him) for the noon or afternoon prayer, and Bilāl had already called him for prayer, he came upon us with Umāmah daughter of Abū al-'Āṣ and daughter of his daughter on his neck. The Apostle of Allah (may peace be upon him) stood at the place of prayer and we stood behind him and she (Umāmah) (all this time) was in her place. He uttered the *takbīr* and we also uttered. When the Apostle of Allah (may peace be upon him) intended to bow, he took her and put her down, and then he bowed and prostrated till he finished his prostration. He then got up and took her and returned her to her place. The Apostle of Allah (may peace be upon him) kept on doing that in every *rak'ah* until he finised his prayer. May peace be upon him.

(921) Abū Hurairah reported the Apostle of Allah (may peace be upon him) as saying: Kill the two black things during prayer, the snake and scorpion.[432]

(922) 'Ā'ishah said: The Apostle of Allah (may peace be upon him) was praying with his door bolted. I came and asked to have the door opened. He walked and opened the door for me. He then returned to his place for prayer. He (the narrator

430. This shows that this much action or doing something similar in prayer is negligible. This applies equally to obligatory, supererogatory and optional prayers and to the prayer offered in congregation or alone (*'Awn al Ma'būd*, I, 345).

431. He heard the only tradition about *witr* from his father. The chain of this tradition is, therefore, broken (*mursal* tradition).

432. The black snake and the black scorpion are generally venomous and dangerous. Hence the Prophet (may peace be upon him) specially permitted to kill them during prayer. The action of killing does not break the prayer. Analogy with these two venomous insects can be extended to similar other insects killing which does not require much struggle and exertion.

'Urwah) mentioned that the door faced the *qiblah*.[433]

Chapter 321

THE RETURNING OF SALUTATION DURING PRAYER

(923) 'Abd Allah (b. Mas'ūd) said: We used to salute the Apostle of Allah (may peace be upon him) while he was engaged in prayer and he would respond to our salutation, but when we returned from the Negus,[434] we saluted him and he did not respond to us. He said: Prayer demands one's whole attention.[435]

(924) 'Abd Allah (b. Mas'ūd) said: We used to salute during prayer and talk about our needs. I came to the Apostle of Allah (may peace be upon him) and found him praying. I saluted him, but he did not respond to me. I recalled what happened to me in the past and in the present. When the Apostle of Allah (may peace be upon him) finished his prayer, he said to me: Allah, the Almighty, creates new command as He wishes, and Allah, the Exalted, has sent a fresh command that you must not talk during prayer. He then returned my salutation.

(925) Ibn 'Umar reported on the authority of Ṣuhaib: I passed by the Apostle of Allah (may peace be upon him) who was praying. I saluted him and he returned it by making a sign. The narrator said: I do not know but that he said: He made a sign with his finger.[436] This is the version reported by Qutaibah.

(926) Jābir said: The Prophet of Allah (may peace be upon him) sent me to Banū al-Muṣṭaliq. When I returned to him, he was praying on his camel. I talked to him; he made a sign to me with his hand like this. I again talked to him; he made a

433. This shows that it is permissible to walk a few steps during supererogatory prayer for some necessity. Moreover, all the traditions of this chapter indicate that there is no harm if one walks a few steps, or opens the door, or kills a snake or a scorpion with a stick, or puts a child on the shoulder during prayer (*'Awn al-Ma'būd* I, 346-47).

434. This refers to the return of the Muslims who migrated from Mecca to Abyssinia when Muslims were being persecuted. 'Abd Allah b Mas'ūd was one of them who emigrated.

435. Prayer underwent certain changes by degrees at different stages. In the beginning the return of salutation during prayer was permitted, but later on the practice was forbidden. There is, however, a difference of opinion on this question amongst the jurists. A group of scholars, like Sa'īd b. al-Musayyib, al-Ḥasan al-Baṣrī, Qatādah, and Abū Hurairah hold the opinion that one can respond to the salutation during prayer. But the majority of scholars do not allow it. Ibn 'Umar is reported to have returned the salutation by making a sign. 'Aṭā', al-Sha'bī, al-Nakha'ī, Sufyān al-Thawrī maintain that one should return the salutation after the prayer. Abū Ḥanīfah holds that one should not respond to the salutation during prayer either by expression or by making a sign (*'Awn al-Ma'būd*, I, 347).

436. This tradition shows the approval of returning the salutation by making a sign during prayer. This is held by al-Shāfi'ī and most of the scholars.

sign to me with his hand like this. I was hearing him reciting the Qur'ān, and he was making a sign with his head. When he finished his prayer, he said: What did you do about the mission for which I had sent to you; nothing prevented me from talking to you except that I was praying.[437]

(927) 'Abd Allah b. 'Umar said: The Apostle of Allah (may peace be upon him) went to Qubā' to offer prayer. Then the Anṣār (the Helpers) came to him and gave him a salutation while he was engaged in prayer. I asked Bilāl: How did you find the Apostle of Allah (may peace be upon him) responding to them when they saluted him while he was engaged in prayer. He replied: In this way, and Ja'far b. 'Awn demonstrated by spreading his palm, and keeping its inner side below and its back side above.

(928) Abū Hurairah reported the Prophet (may peace be upon him) as saying: There is no loss in prayer nor in salutation. Aḥmad (b. Ḥanbal) said: This means, I think, that you do not salute nor you are saluted by others. The loss of a man in his prayer is that a man remains doubtful about it when he finishes it.[438]

(929) Abū Hurairah reported the Prophet (may peace be upon him) as saying: There is no loss in salutation and in prayer.

Abū Dāwūd said: According to the version of Ibn Mahdī, this tradition has been narrated by Ibn Fuḍail as a statement of Abū Hurairah and not as a saying of the Prophet (may peace be upon him).

Chapter 322

RESPONSE TO SNEEZING DURING PRAYER

(930) Mu'āwiyah b. al-Ḥakam al-Sulamī said: I was praying with the Apostle of Allah (may peace be upon him). A man in the company sneezed, and I said: May Allah have mercy on you! The people gave me disapproving looks, so I said: Woe is to me! What do you mean by looking at me? They began to strike their hands on their thighs; then I realised that they were urging me to be silent. When the Apostle of Allah (may peace be upon him) finished his prayer—for whom I would give my father and mother as ransom—he did not beat, scold, or revile me, but said: No talk to

437. This tradition indicates that it is permissible to make a sign or to make a minor movement to return the salutation or for any other purpose during prayer.

438. Loss in prayer and loss in salutation have been interpreted by scholars differently. Loss in prayer might mean that one does not perform all the actions of prayer properly. It may also mean that, as interpreted by Aḥmad, that one doubts the number of *rak'ahs* one offered in prayer. Loss in salutation might mean that one does not return the salutation perfectly as one who saluted him. The other meaning is that one salutes another person, but he does not return it.

people is lawful in this prayer,[439] for it consists only in glorifying Allah, declaring His greatness, and reciting the Qur'ān[440] or words to that effect said by the Apostle of Allah (may peace be upon him). I said: Apostle of Allah, we were only recently pagans, but Allah has brought Islam to us, and among us there are men who have recourse to soothsayers (*kāhins*). He replied: Do not have recourse to them. I said: Among us there are men who take omens. He replied: That is something which they find, but let it not turn them away (from what they intended to do). I said: Among us there are men who draw lines. He replied: There was a prophet who drew lines; so if the line of anyone tallies with his line, that might come true. I said: A slave-girl of mine used to tend goats before (the mountain) Uḥud and al-Jawānīyyah. Once when I reached her (suddenly) I found that a wolf had taken away a goat of them. I am a human being; I feel grieved as others do. But I gave her a good knocking. This was unbearable for the Apostle of Allah (may peace be upon him). I asked: Should I set her free? He replied: Bring her to me. So I brought her to him. He asked (her): Where is Allah? She said: In the heaven. He said: Who am I? She replied: You are the Apostle of Allah. He said: Set her free, for she is believer.

(931) Mu'āwiyah b. al-Ḥakam al-Sulamī said: When I came to the Apostle of Allah (may peace be upon him) I learnt many things about Islam. One of the things that I was taught was that it was pointed out to me: When you sneeze, praise Allah (i.e. say "Praise be to Allah"); and when someone sneezes and praises Allah, say "May Allah have mercy on you." Meanwhile I was standing along with the Apostle of Allah (may peace be upon him) during prayer, all of a sudden a man sneezed, and he praised Allah. So I said, "May Allah have mercy on you," in a loud voice. The people gave me disapproving looks so much so that I took ill of it. So I said: What do you mean by looking at me with furtive glances. Then they glorified Allah. When the Prophet (may peace be upon him) finished his prayer, he asked: Who was the

439. This tradition indicates that talking during prayer is forbidden. If the *imām* commits a mistake, the people behind should not speak; if the person who instructs him is a man, he should glorify Allah. In case a woman instructs him, she should clap hands. This is the view held by the majority of scholars. Al-Awzā'ī holds that talking during prayer is permissible if it is done in the context or interest of prayer. If a man talks or speaks during prayer inadvertently, his prayer will not break according to the majority of scholars. Abū Ḥanīfah maintains that if one talks during prayer, whether intentionally or inadvertently, his prayer will become void (*'Awn al-Ma'būd*, I, 349).

440. This shows the prohibition of response to the one who sneezes during prayer and says "Praise be to Allah." The response is "May Allah have mercy on you." Praising Allah after sneezing and its response by another person are commendable when one is not praying. The response by another person to the sneezing during prayer is considered equivalent to talking which breaks prayer. According to al-Shāfi'ī, if one sneezes during prayer, one should praise Allah quietly. But Ibn 'Umar, al-Nakha'ī, Aḥmad and Mālik hold that one should praise Allah loudly. The former view is more correct because all the supplications in prayer are made quietly (*'Awn al-Ma'būd*, I, 349).

speaker? The people told him: This bedouin. The Apostle of Allah (may peace be upon him) called me and said to me: Prayer is meant for the recitation of the Qur'ān, and making mention of Allah. When you are in it (prayer), this should be your work therein. I never saw an instructor more lenient than the Apostle of Allah (may peace be upon him).

Chapter 323

SAYING *ĀMĪN* BEHIND THE *IMĀM*

(932) Wā'il b. Ḥujr said: When the Apostle of Allah (may peace be upon him) recited the verse "Nor of those who go astray" (Sūrah al-Fāṭiḥah, verse 7), he would say *Āmīn*, and raised his voice (while uttering this word).[441]

(933) Wā'il b. Ḥujr said that he prayed behind the Apostle of Allah (may peace be upon him), and he said *Āmīn* loudly and saluted at his right and left sides until I saw the whiteness of his cheek.

(934) Abū Hurairah said: When the Apostle of Allah (may peace be upon him) recited the verse "Not of those with whom Thou art angry, nor of those who go astray," he would say *Āmīn* so loudly that those near him in the first row would hear it.

(935) Abū Hurairah reported the Prophet (may peace be upon him) as saying: When the *imām* recites "Not of those with whom Thou art angry, nor of those who go astray" (Sūrah al-Fātiḥah, verse 7), say *Āmīn*, for if one's words (utterance of *Āmīn*) synchronise with those of the angels, he will be forgiven his past sins.[442]

(936) Abū Hurairah reported the Apostle of Allah (may peace be upon him) as saying: When the *imām* says *Āmīn*, say *Āmīn*, for if anyone's utterance of *Āmīn* synchronises with that of the angels, he will be forgiven his past sins.

Ibn Shihāb (al- Zuhrī) said: The Apostle of Allah (may peace be upon him) used to say *Āmīn* (at the end of the Fātiḥah)

(937) Bilāl reported that he said: Apostle of Allah, do not say *Āmīn* before me.[443]

441. This tradition show that saying *Āmīn* at the end of Sūrah al-Fātiḥah by the *imām* and the people behind him is recommended (*sunnah*). This is held by most of the Companions, their successors, and by al-Shāfi'ī, Aḥmad and Isḥāq. Mālik, according to one version, and Abū Ḥanīfah maintain that *Āmīn* should be said quietly (*'Awn al-Ma'būd*, I, 351-52).

442. Some other traditions of the Prophet (may peace be upon him) indicate that the angels also utter *Āmīn* when the *imām* utters it.

443. Bilāl by this request meant that his utterance of *Āmīn* should synchronise with that of the Prophet (may peace be upon him). It is reported about Abū Hurairah that when he entered the mosque while the *imām* was leading the prayer, he would say loudly: Do not say *Āmīn* before me. He wanted to recite al-Fātiḥah (*'Awn al-Ma'būd*, I, 353).

(938) Abū Miṣbaḥ al-Muqra'ī said: We used to sit in the company of Abū Zuhair al-Numairī. He was a Companion of the Prophet (may peace be upon him), and he used to narrate good traditions. Once a man from among us made a supplication. He said: End it with the utterance of *Āmīn*, for *Āmīn* is like a seal on the book. Abū Zuhair said: I tell you about that. We went out with the Apostle of Allah (may peace be upon him) one night and came upon a man who made supplication with persistence. The Prophet (may peace be upon him) waited to hear him. The Prophet (may peace be upon him) said: He will have done something which guarantees (Paradise for him) if he puts a seal to it. One of the people asked: What should he use for a seal? He replied: *Āmīn*, for if he ends it with *Āmīn*, he will do something which guarantees (Paradise for him). Then the man who questioned the Prophet (may peace be upon him) came to the man who was supplicating, and said to him: So-and-so, end it with *Āmīn* and have the good news. These are the words of Maḥmūd.

Abū Dāwūd said: Al-Muqra'ī is a clan of Ḥimyar.

Chapter 324

CLAPPING DURING PRAYER

(939) Abū Hurairah reported the Apostle of Allah (may peace be upon him) as saying: Glorifying Allah applies to men and clapping applies only to women.[444]

(940) Sahl b. Sa'd said: The Apostle of Allah (may peace be upon him) went to Banū 'Amr b. 'Awf[445] to effect reconciliation between them. In the meantime the time of prayer came and the *mu'adhdhin* came to Abū Bakr and asked: Will you lead the people in prayer? I pronounce the *iqamah*. He said: Yes. So Abū Bakr led the prayer, and the Apostle of Allah (may peace be upon him) came back while the people were praying. He penetrated through the rows and stood in the first row. The people clapped but Abū Bakr did not pay any attention to it during prayer. When the people clapped increasingly, he paid attention. He saw the Apostle of Allah (may peace be upon him). The Apostle of Allah (may peace be upon him) made a sign to him (saying): Stay at your place. Abū Bakr raised his hands and praised Allah for the commandment the Apostle of Allah (may peace be upon him) had given him (to lead the people in prayer). Abū Bakr then stepped back and stood in the row. The Apostle of Allah (may peace be upon him) stepped forward and led the prayer. When

444. If anything happens during prayer, say, a man calls one who is praying, or the person praying behind the *imām* wants to inform him about something, or desires to correct him, in all such cases men should say "Glory be to Allah," and women should clap hands by striking the outer part of the left hand with the inner part of the right hand They should not utter any word like men. But it should be noted that women should no clap hands in ordinary sense as one does in applause. If they do so, the prayer will become void (*'Awn al-Ma'būd*, I, 354).

445. A clan of the tribe Aws.

he finished the prayer, he said: Abū Bakr, what prevented you from staying (at your place) when I already commanded you to do so? Abū Bakr said: It was not befitting for the son of Abū Quḥāfah (Abū Bakr) to lead the prayer in the presence of the Apostle of Allah (may peace be upon him). The Apostle of Allah (may peace be upon him) said: What is the matter that I saw you clapping frequently during prayer? If anything happens to someone during prayer, he should say "Glory be to Allah," for when he glorifies Allah, He pays attention to him. Clapping applies only to women.[446]

Abū Dāwūd said: This is operative in the obligatory prayer.

(941) Sahl b. Sa'd said: Fighting took place amongst the tribe of Banū 'Amr b. 'Awf. This (the news) reached the Prophet (may peace be upon him). He came to them for their reconciliation after the noon prayer. He said to Bilāl: If the time of the afternoon prayer comes, and I do not return to you, then ask Abū Bakr to lead the people in prayer. When the time of the afternoon prayer came, Bilāl called the *adhān* and pronounced the *iqāmah* and then asked Abū Bakr (to lead the prayer). He stepped forward. The narrator reported this tradition to the same effect. In the end he (the Prophet) said: If anything happens to you during prayer, the men should say "Glory be to Allah," and the women should clap.

(942) 'Īsā b. Ayyūb said: Clapping by women means that one should strike her left hand with the two fingers of her right hand.

Chapter 325

TO MAKE A SIGN DURING PRAYER

(943) Anas b. Mālik said: The Prophet (may peace be upon him) used to make a sign during prayer.[447]

(944) Abū Hurairah reported the Apostle of Allah (may peace be upon him) as

446. Al-Khaṭṭābī said that this tradition indicates a number of rules of law: (1) prayer should be offered early in its period because this tradition shows that the people did not wait for the return of the Prophet (may peace be upon him); (2) prayer does not break by looking at the side until one turns to the right or left side; (3) the Prophet (may peace be upon him) did not ask men who clapped during prayer to repeat their prayer; (4) clapping applies to women; (5) stepping backward or forward for some necessity does not harm prayer; (6) permission for raising the hands during prayer and praising Allah for His favour; (7) permissibility for leading the prayer by two *imāms* one after the other; (8) permissibility for joining the congregation by one who did not join in the beginning; (9) it is a *sunnah* for men to glorify Allah if something happens during prayer; (10) to utter glorification by men to inform the *imām* does not break prayer (*'Awn al-Ma'būd* I, 355).

447. This tradition shows that one can make a sign during prayer in the case of some necessity.

saying: Saying "Glory be to Allah" applies to men during prayer and clapping applies to women. Anyone who makes a sign during his prayer, a sign which is intelligible by implication, should repeat it (i.e. his prayer).

Abū Dāwūd said: This tradition is a misunderstanding.[448]

Chapter 326

REMOVING PEBBLES DURING PRAYER

(945) Abū Dharr reported the Prophet (may peace be upon him) as saying: When one of you gets up to pray, he must not remove pebbles, for mercy is facing him.[449]

(946) Mu'aiqib reported the Prophet (may peace be upon him) as saying: Do not remove pebbles while you are praying: If you do it out of sheer necessity, do it only once to smooth the pebbles.[450]

Chapter 327

PUTTING HANDS ON THE WAIST DURING PRAYER

(947) Abū Hurairah said that the Apostle of Allah (may peace be upon him) forbade putting hands on the waist during prayer.[451]

Abū Dāwūd said: The word *ikhtisar* means to put one's hands on one's waist.

Chapter 328

RESTING ON A STAFF DURING PRAYER

(948) Hilāl b. Yasāf said: I came to al-Raqqah (a place in Syria). One of my

448. This is a weak tradition. It contradicts a number of the traditions which indicates that the Prophet (may peace be upon him) made a sign which was intelligible. For example, he returned the salutation by making a sign. Supposing the tradition is sound, then it means that making an intelligible sign during prayer is allowed for returning the salutation or some necessity and not for ordinary things (*'Awn al-Ma'būd*, I, 356).

449. Most of the scholars consider it disapproved to remove pebbles during prayer for it distracts the attention of the worshipper. Mālik does not see any harm in removing pebbles and smoothing the ground during prayer (*'Awn al-Ma'būd*, I, 356).

450. This tradition shows that it is permissible to remove pebbles to smooth the ground only once during prayer.

451. The commentators have mentioned many reasons for the prohibition of putting hands on the waist during prayer. This resembles the practice of the Jews; this is an act of satan; it is said that the Devil fell down from Paradise in this condition; this is a sign of self-conceit and pride (*'Awn al-Ma'būd*, I, 357).

companions said to me: Do you want to see any of the Companions of the Prophet (may peace be upon him)? I said: A good opportunity. So we went to Wābiṣah. I said to my friend: Let us first see his mode of living He had a cap with two ears stuck (to his head), and wearing a brown silken robe. He was resting on a staff during prayer. We asked him (about resting on the staff) after salutation; He said: Umm Qais daughter of Miḥṣan said to me that when the Apostle of Allah (may peace be upon him) became aged and the flesh grew increasingly on him, he took a prop at his place of prayer and rested on it.[452]

Chapter 329

PROHIBITION OF SPEECH DURING PRAYER

(949) Zaid b Arqam said: One of us used to speak to the man standing by his side during prayer. Then the Qur'ānic verse "And stand up with devotion to Allah" (ii. 238) was revealed. So we were commanded to keep silence (during prayer) and prohibited from speaking.[453]

Chapter 330

ON OFFERING PRAYER IN SITTING CONDITION

(950) 'Abd Allah b. 'Amr said: It has been narrated to me that the Apostle of Allah (may peace be upon him) said: The prayer of a man in sitting condition is half the prayer (wins him half the reward of prayer). I came to him and found him praying in sitting condition. I placed my hand on my head (in surprise). He said: What is the matter, 'Abd Allah b. 'Amr? I said: Apostle of Allah, you have been reported to me as saying: The prayer of a man in sitting condition is half the prayer, but you are praying in sitting condition. He said: Yes, but I am not like one of you.[454]

452. This shows the permissibility of resting on a staff or leaning against a wall and having some prop during prayer for some valid reason (*'Awn al-Ma'būd*. I, 357).

453. There is a difference of opinion amongst scholars on the question of prohibition of speech whether it took place in Mecca or Medina. The tradition of Ibn Mas'ūd clearly indicates that it took place in Medina when he returned from Abyssinia and the Prophet (may peace be upon him) was making preparations for the Battle of Badr (*'Awn al-Ma'būd*, I, 358).

454. It is permissible to offer supererogatory prayer in sitting condition without any excuse or valid reason. But one gets half the reward. In case one prays obligatory prayer in sitting condition without any excuse or valid reason, his prayer will not be valid. He should offer his prayer in standing condition. But if one offers obligatory prayer in sitting condition for some reason or excuse, one will get the full reward. A sick man, for instance, is allowed to offer obligatory prayer in sitting condition if he is unable to do so standing (*'Awn al-Ma'būd*, I, 359).

(951) 'Abd Allah b. Buraidah said: 'Imrān b. Ḥuṣain asked the Prophet (may peace be upon him) about the prayer a man offers in sitting condition. He replied: His prayer in standing condition is better than his prayer in sitting condition, and his prayer in sitting condition is half the prayer he offers in standing condition, and his prayer in lying condition[455] is half the prayer he offers in sitting condition.

(952) 'Imrān b. Ḥuṣain said: I had a fistula; so I asked the Prophet (may peace be upon him). He said: Offer prayer in standing condition; if you are unable to do so, then in sitting condition; if you are unable, then at your side (i.e. in lying condition).

(953) 'Ā'ishah said: I never saw the Apostle of Allah (may peace be upon him) reciting the Qur'ān in his prayer at night in sitting condition until he became old. Then he used to sit in it (the prayer) and recite the Qur'ān until forty or thirty verses ramained, then he stood and recited them and prostrated himself.

(954) 'Ā'ishah, wife of the Prophet (may peace be upon him), said: When the Prophet (may peace be upon him) prayed sitting, he recited the Qur'ān in sitting condition. When the amount of his recitation remained about thirty or forty verses he stood up and recited them standing. He then bowed and prostrated and then did so in the second *rak'ah* of the prayer.[456]

Abū Dāwūd said: 'Alqamah b. Waqqaṣ narrated this tradition on the authority of 'Ā'ishah from the Prophet (may peace be upon him) to the same effect.

(955) 'Ā'ishah said: The Apostle of Allah (may peace be upon him) used to pray standing at night for a long time, and used to pray sitting at night for a long time. When he prayed standing, he bowed standing, and when he prayed sitting, he bowed sitting.

(956) 'Abd Allah b. Shaqīq said: I asked 'Ā'ishah whether the Apostle of Allah (may peace be upon him) recited a whole *surah* (of the Qur'ān) in one *rak'ah* of the prayer. She replied: (He recited from among) the *mufaṣṣal*[457] *surahs*. I asked: Did he pray (at night) sitting? She replied: (He prayed sitting) when the people made him old.

455. Al-Khaṭṭābī said that he did not remember any one of the scholars who hold that it is permissible to offer supererogatory prayer in lying condition in the case when one has the ability to offer it in sitting or standing condition. The point, however, is disputed amongst the scholars. Some allowed it on the basis of this tradition and others prohibited it (*'Awn al-Ma'būd*, I, 359).

456. This tradition shows that it is permissible for a man who is offering supererogatory prayer to commence it sitting and then he can stand before bowing.

457. *Mufaṣṣal sūrahs* are the short *sūrahs* of the Qur'ān beginning from Sūrah al-Qāf up to the end.

Chapter 331

HOW SHOULD ONE SIT WHEN ONE RECITES *TASHAHHUD*

(957) Wā'il b. Ḥujr said: I said that I should look at the prayer of the Apostle of Allah (may peace be upon him) how he prays. The Apostle of Allah (may peace be upon him) stood up and faced the *qiblah* (i.e. the direction of Ka'bah) and uttered the *takbir* (Allah is most great); then he raised his hands till he brought them in front of his ears; then he caught hold of his left hand with his right hand (i.e. folded his hands). When he was about to bow, he raised them (his hands) in a like manner. Then he sat, stretched out his left foot (to sit on it), placed his left hand on his left thigh, and kept away the tip of his right elbow from his right thigh, joined two fingers,[458] formed a ring,[459] to do so.[460] And the narrator Bishr made a ring with the thumb and the middle finger.

Chapter 332

SITTING ON HIPS IN THE FOURTH *RAK'AH* OF PRAYER

(958) Abū Ḥumaid al-Sā'idī said (in the presence of ten Companions of the Prophet): I am more informed than any of you regarding the manner in which the Apostle of Allah (may peace be upon him) offered his prayer. They said: Present it. The narrator then reported the tradition, saying: He bent the toes of his feet turning them towards the *qiblah* when he prostrated, then he uttered "Allah is most great," and raised (his head), and bent his left foot and sat on it, and he did the same in the second *rak'ah*. The narrator then transmitted the tradition, and added: In the prostration (i.e. the *rak'ah*) which ended at the salutation, he sat on the hips at the left side. Aḥmad (b. Ḥanbal) added: They said: You are right. This is how he used to

458. I.e. the little finger and the ring finger.

459. I.e. with the thumb and the middle finger.

460. There are different traditions of the Prophet (may peace be upon him) which indicate various positions of placing the right hand on the right thigh while reciting *tashahhud* in sitting condition: (1) to form a ring with the thumb and the middle finger as this tradition indicates; (2) a tradition narrated by Muslim says that the Prophet (may peace be upon him) placed his right hand on his right knee and put the thumb below the forefinger; (3) a tradition reported also by Muslim says that he folded all his fingers and pointed with his forefinger; (4) another tradition indicates that he pointed with his forefinger by placing his thumb on his middle finger and caught hold of his left knee with his left hand; (5) a tradition says that he placed his right hand on his right thigh and pointed with his forefinger without making a ring or folding the fingers (*'Awn al-Ma'būd*, I, 361).

pray.[461] They (Aḥmad and Musaddad) did not mention in their versions how he sat after offering two *rak'ahs* of prayer.

(959) Muḥammad b. 'Amr b. 'Aṭā' was sitting in the company of a few Companions of the Apostle of Allah (may peace be upon him). He then narrated this tradition, but he did not mention the name of Abū Qatādah. He said: When he (the Prophet) sat up after the two *rak'ahs* he sat on his left foot; and when he sat up after the last *rak'ah* he put out his left foot and sat on his hip.

(960) Muḥammad b. 'Amr al-'Āmirī said: I was sitting in the company (of the Companions). He then narrated this tradition saying: When he (the Prophet) sat up after two *rak'ahs*, he sat on the sole of his left foot and raised his right foot. When he sat up after four *rak'ahs*, he placed his left hip on the ground and put out his both feet on one side.

(961) 'Abbās or 'Ayyāsh b. Sahl al-Sā'idī said that he attended a company in which his father was also present. He then narrated this tradition saying: He (the Prophet) prostrated himself, he depended on his palms, knees and the toes of his feet. When he sat up, he sat on his hips, and raised his other foot. He then uttered the *takbīr* (Allah is most great) and prostrated himself. He uttered the *takbīr* and stood up and did not sit on his hips. Then he repeated (the same) and offered the second *rak'ah*; he uttered the *takbīr* in the same manner, and sat up after two *rak'ahs*. When he was about to stand up, he stood up after saying the *takbīr*. Then he offered the last two *rak'ahs*. When he saluted, he saluted on his right and left sides.

Abū Dāwūd said: In this tradition there is no mention of sitting on hips and raising hands when he stood after two *rak'ahs* as narrated by 'Abd al- Ḥamid.

(962) 'Abbās b. Sahl said: Abū Ḥumaid, Abū Usaid, Sahl b. Sa'd and Muḥammad b. Maslamah got together. Then he narrated this tradition. He did not mention the raising of hands when he stood after two *rak'ahs*, nor did he mention sitting. He said: When he finished (his prostration), he spread his foot (on the ground) and turned the toes of his right feet towards the *qiblah* (and then he sat on his left foot).[462]

461. The tradition narrated by Abū Ḥumaid clearly indicates that it is commendable (*sunnah*) to sit on the feet in the first sitting and to sit on the hips in the second or last sitting during prayer for reciting *tashahhud*. This is the opinion of al-Shāfi'ī. The scholars differ on the point whether sitting on the hips is better or sitting on the feet. According to Mālik and a group of scholars, sitting on hips is better in both the sittings. Abū Ḥanīfah maintains that sitting on the feet is better in both sittings. According to al-Shāfi'ī and a group of scholars, one should sit on one's feet in the first sitting and on one's hips in the last sitting (*'Awn al-Ma'būd*, 1, 363).

462. This tradition is followed by Abū Ḥanifah. To sit on the left foot in both the sittings is commendable during prayer in his opinion.

Chapter 333

AL-TASHAHHUD[463]

(963) 'Abd Allah b. Mas'ūd said: When we (prayed and) sat up during prayer along with the Apostle of Allah (may peace be upon him), we said: "Peace be to Allah before (it is supplicated for) His servants; peace be to so and so." The Apostle of Allah (may peace be upon him) said: Do not say "Peace be to Allah," for Allah Himself is peace. When one of you sits (during the prayer), he should say: The adorations of the tongue[464] are due to Allah, and acts of worship and all good things. Peace be upon you, O Prophet, and Allah's mercy and His blessings. Peace be upon us and upon Allah's upright servants. When you say that, it reaches every upright servant in heaven and earth or between heaven and earth. I testify that there is no god but Allah, and I testify that Muḥammad is His servant and apostle. Then he may choose any supplication which pleases him and offer it.

(964) 'Abd Allah (b. Mas'ūd) said: We did not know what we should say when we sat during prayer. The Apostle of Allah (may peace be upon him) was taught (from Allah). He then narrated the tradition to the same effect.

Sharīk reported from Jāmi', from Abū Wā'il on the authority of 'Abd Allah (b. Mas'ūd) something similar. He said: He used to teach us also some other words, but he did not teach them as he taught us the *tashahhud*: O Allah, join our hearts, and mend our social relationship, and guide us to the path of peace, and bring us from darkness to light, and save us from obscenities, outward or inward, and bless our ears, our eyes, our hearts, our wives, our children, and relent toward us, Thou art the Relenting, the Merciful. And make us grateful for Thy blessing and make us praiser of it while accepting it and give us full of it.

(965) 'Alqamah said that 'Abd Allah b. Mas'ūd caught hold of his hand saying that the Apostle of Allah (may peace be upon him) caught hold of his (Ibn Mas'ūd's) hand and taught him the *tashahhud* during prayer. He then narrated the tradition like that reported by al-A'mash. This version adds: When you say this or finish this, then you have completed your prayer.[465] If you want to stand up, then stand, and if

463. *Tashahhud* means to recite supplication beginning with the words *al-Taḥiyyāt lillāhi* at the end of two or four *rak'ahs* in the sitting position during prayer.

464. The Arabic word *taḥiyyāt* is the plural of *taḥiyyah* meaning originally "long living" and it is taken in its usual meaning of salutation. This phrase in the context of prayer has been variously explained. Figuratively it is taken to mean "endless existence," or "dominion," or "kingship," or "freedom from all evils," or "freedom from all causes of cessation of existence" belong to Allah.

465. Al-Khaṭṭābī said: It is disputed whether these are the words of the Prophet (may peace be upon him) or of Ibn Mas'ūd. If these are the words of the Prophet (may peace be upon him), then the prayer is finished after the recitation of the *tashahhud* and the recitation of the blessing on

you want to remain sitting, then remain sitting.[466]

(966) Ibn 'Umar reported the Apostle of Allah (may peace be upon him) as saying: The adorations of the tongue are due to Allah, and acts of worship, all good things. Peace be upon you, O Prophet, and Allah's mercy and His blessings. Ibn 'Umar said: I added:[467] "And Allah's blessings, peace be upon us, and upon Allah's upright servants. I testify that there is no god but Allah." Ibn 'Umar said: I added to it: He is alone, no one is His associate, and I testify that Muḥammad is His servant and His Apostle.

(967) Ḥiṭṭān b. 'Abd Allah al-Ruqāshī said: Abū Mūsā al-Ash'arī led us in prayer. When he sat at the end of his prayer, one of the people said: Prayer has been established by virtue and purity. When Abū Mūsā returned (from his prayer or finished his prayer), he paid his attention to the people, and said: Which of you is the speaker of such and such words? The people kept silence. Which of you is the speaker of such and such words? The people kept silence. He said: You might have said them, Ḥiṭṭān. He replied: I did not say them. I was afraid you might punish me. One of the people said: I said them and I did not intend by them (anything) except good. Abū Mūsā said: Do you not know how you utter (them) in your prayer? The Apostle of Allah (may peace be upon him) addressed us and taught us and explained to us our way of doing and taught us our prayer. He said: When you pray (congregational prayer), straighten your rows, then one of you should lead you in prayer. When he says the *takbīr* (Allah is most great), say the *takbīr*. and when he recites verses "Not of those upon whom is Thy anger, nor of those who err" (i.e. the end of Sūrah i.), say *Āmīn*; Allah will favour you. When he says "Allah is most great," and bows, say "Allah is most great" and bow, for the *imām* will bow before you, and will raise (his head) before you The Apostle of Allah (may peace be upon him) said: This is for that.[468] When he says "Allah listens to him who praises Him," say: "O Allah,

the Prophet (may peace be upon him) is not necessary. Abū Bakr al-Khaṭṭābī said: These are the words of Ibn Mas'ūd and not of the Prophet (may peace be upon him). These words are not the part of the tradition, but included later on (*'Awn al-Ma'būd*, I, 367).

466. Standing up or going away here means to finish the prayer by uttering the salutation. The salutation is necessary. One may remain sitting or go away after salutation, one's prayer is complete after uttering the *tashahhud* after salutation, provided these are the words of the Prophet (may peace be upon him) (*'Awn al-Ma'būd*, I, 367).

467. The additions made by Ibn 'Umar in this tradition are the words of the Prophet (may peace be upon him) according to the other versions of this tradition recorded by Muslim in his *Ṣaḥīḥ*. These additions may not be taken as the words of Ibn 'Umar but of the Prophet (may peace be upon him) (*'Awn al-Ma'būd*, I, 367).

468. This phrase has been interpreted variantly by the commentators. According to some, this means that "say your *takbir* for bowing and your bowing should take place after the *takbir* and bowing of the *imām*". Likewise, you should raise your heads after the *imām* has raised his head after

our Lord, to Thee be the praise," Allah will listen to you, for Allah, the Exalted, said by the tongue of His Prophet (may peace be upon him): "Allah listens to him who praises Him." When he says "Allah is most great" and prostrates, say: "Allah is most great" and prostrate, for the *imām* prostrates before you and raises his head before you. The Apostle of Allah (may peace be upon him) said: This is for that. When he sits, each one of you should say "The adorations of the tongue, all good things, acts of worship are due to Allah, peace be upon you, O Prophet, and Allah's mercy and His blessings. Peace be upon us and upon Allah's upright servants. I testify that there is no god but Allah, and I testify that Muḥammad is His servant and apostle."

The version of Aḥmad does not mention the words "and His blessings" nor the phrase "and I testify"; instead, it has the words "that Muḥammad."

(968) This tradition has also been transmitted by Ḥiṭṭān b. 'Abd Allah al-Ruqāshī through a different chain of narrators. This version adds: When he (the *imām*) recites the Qur'ān, keep silence (and listen attentively). And in the *tashahhud* this version adds after the words "I testify that there is no god but Allah" the words "He is alone, and there is no associate of Him."

Abū Dāwūd said: His word "And keep silence" is not guarded; it has been narrated by Sulaimān al-Taimī alone in his version.

(969) Ibn 'Abbās said: The Apostle of Allah (may peace be upon him) used to teach us the *tashahhud* as he would teach us the Qur'ān, and would say: The blessed adorations of the tongue, acts of worship (and) all good things are due to Allah. Peace be upon you, O Prophet, and Allah's mercy and His blessings. Peace be upon us and upon Allah's upright servants. I testify that there is no god but Allah, and I testify that Muḥammad is Allah's apostle (peace be upon him).

(970) Samurah b. Jundub said: The Apostle of Allah (may peace be upon him) commanded us (to recite) when we sit in the middle of the prayer or at its end before the salutation: The adorations of the tongue, all good things, acts of worship, and the Kingdom are due to Allah.[469] Then give salutation to the right side; then salute your reciter (i.e. the *imām*) and yourselves.

Abū Dāwūd said: Sulaimān b. Mūsā hails from Kūfah and he lived in

bowing. Al-Khaṭṭābī says that this means that your prayer depends on the prayer of your *imām*. Therefore, follow him literally and do not differ from him (*'Awn al-Ma'būd*, I, 368).

469. The *tashahhud* has been narrated from the Prophet (may peace be upon him) by Ibn Mas'ūd, Ibn 'Abbās and 'Umar in different versions. Among these versions the one narrated by Ibn Mas'ūd has been considered to be more sound and authentic. This is followed by the majority of scholars and Companions, and by Abū Ḥanīfah and Aḥmad b. Ḥanbal. Al-Shāfi'ī follows the version of Ibn 'Abbās and Mālik the version of 'Umar. But it should be noted that one can recite any version of the *tashahhud*; the difference being of excellence and not of validity (*'Awn al-Ma'būd*, I, 366)

Damascus.

Abū Dāwūd said: This collection of traditions indicates that al-Ḥasan (al-Baṣrī) heard traditions from Samurah (b. Jundub).[470]

Chapter 334

BLESSING ON THE PROPHET (MAY PEACE BE UPON HIM)

(971) Ka'b b. 'Ujrah said: We said or the people said: Apostle of Allah, you have commanded us to invoke blessing on you and to salute you. As regards salutation we have already learnt it. How should we invoke blessing on you? He said: Say: "O Allah, bless Muhammad and Muḥammad's family as Thou didst bless Abraham and Abraham's family. O Allah, grant favours to Muḥammad and Muḥammad's family as Thou didst grant favours to Abraham; Thou art indeed praiseworthy and glorious."[471]

(972) This tradition has also been reported by Shu'bah through a different chain of narrators. This version adds: Bless Muḥammad and Muḥammad's family as Thou didst bless Abraham.

(973) This has been transmitted by al-Ḥakam through a different chain of narrators. This version has: O Allah, bless Muḥammad and Muḥammad's family as Thou didst bless Abraham. Thou art indeed praiseworthy and glorious. O Allah grant favours to Muḥammad and Muḥammad's family as Thou didst grant favour to Abraham's family. Thou art indeed praiseworthy and glorious.

Abū Dāwūd said: This tradition has been narrated by al-Zubair b. 'Adī as narrated by Mis'ar, except that his version goes: As Thou didst bless Abraham's family. Thou art indeed praiseworthy and glorious. And grant favours to Muhammad. He then narrated the tradition in full.

(974) Abū Ḥumaid al-Sā'idī said: Some people asked: Apostle of Allah, how should we invoke blessings on you? He said: Say, "O Allah, bless Muḥammad, his

470. Samurah b. Jundub, a well-known Companion of the Prophet (may peace be upon him), wrote letters to his children and narrated to them the traditions through these letters. These letters were collected and developed in the form of a collection of tradition narrated by Samurah. By this expression Abū Dāwūd means to say that his son Sulaimān b. Samurah heard traditions from his father, likewise al-Ḥasan al-Baṣrī heard traditions from him through this collection (*'Awn al-Ma'būd*, I, 369).

471. To invoke blessing on the Prophet (may peace be upon him) and on his family after the *tashahhud* during prayer is obligatory in the opinion of 'Umar, Ibn 'Umar, Ibn Mas'ūd, Jābir b. Zaid, al-Sha'bī, Muḥammad b. Ka'b al-Quraẓī, Abū Ja'far al-Bāqir, al-Shāfi'ī, Aḥmad b. Ḥanbal, Isḥāq b. Rahwaih and al-Qāḍī Abū Bakr b. al-'Arabī. Most of the scholars, however, maintain that it is not obligatory, but commendable or recommended (*sunnah*). This view is held by Abū Ḥanīfah, Mālik, al-Thawrī, al-Awzā'ī and others (*'Awn al-Ma'būd*, I, 370).

wives and his offspring, as Thou didst bless Abraham's family, and grant favours to Muḥammad's family, his wives and offspring, as Thou didst grant favours to Abraham's family. Thou art indeed praiseworthy and glorious.

(975) Abū Mas'ūd al-Anṣārī said: The Apostle of Allah (may peace be upon him) came to us in a meeting of Sa'd b 'Ubādah. Bashīr b. Sa'd said to him: Allah has commanded us to invoke blessing on you, Apostle of Allah. How should we invoke blessing on you? The Apostle of Allah (may peace be upon him) kept silence so much so that we wished he would not ask him. Then the Apostle of Allah (may peace be upon him) said: Say. He then narrated the tradition like that of Ka'b b. 'Ujrah. This version adds in the end: In the universe, Thou art praiseworthy and glorious.

(976) This tradition has also been reported by 'Uqbah b. 'Amr through a different chain of narrators. This version adds: Say, O Allah, bless Muḥammad, the Prophet, the unlettered, and Muḥammad's family.

(977) Abū Hurairah reported the Prophet (may peace be upon him) as saying: If anyone would like to have the fullest measure granted to him when he invokes blessings on us, the members of the Prophet's family, he should say: O Allah, bless Muḥammad, the unlettered Prophet, his wives who are the mothers of the faithful, his offspring, and the people of his house as Thou didst bless the family of Abraham. Thou art indeed praiseworthy and glorious.

Chapter 335

WHAT ONE SHOULD RECITE AFTER THE *TASHAHHUD*

(978) Abū Hurairah reported the Apostle of Allah (may peace be upon him) as saying: When one of you finishes the last *tashahhud*, he should seek refuge in Allah from four things: the punishment in Hell, the punishment in the grave, the trial of life and death, and the evil of Antichrist.[472]

(979) Ibn 'Abbās said: The Prophet (may peace be upon him) used to say after the *tashahhud*: "O Allah, I seek refuge in Thee from the punishment in Hell, and I seek refuge in Thee from the punishment in the grave, and I seek refuge in Thee from the trial of Antichrist, and I seek refuge in Thee from the trial of life and

472. Ibn Ḥazm and the Ẓāhirī school maintain that reciting supplication about taking refuge in Allah after the *tashahhud* and the blessing on the Prophet (may peace be upon him) is obligatory. They interpret such traditions literally. But the majority of the scholars hold the view that reciting supplication about taking refuge in Allāh after *tashahhud* is commendable and not obligatory (*'Awn al-Ma'būd*, I, 373).

death.[473]

(980) Miḥjan b. al-Adra' said: The Apostle of Allah (may peace be upon him) entered the mosque and saw a man who had finished his prayer, and was reciting the *tashahhud* saying: O Allah, I ask you, O Allah, the One, the eternally besought of all, He begetteth not, nor was He begotten, and there is none comparable unto Him, that you may forgive me my sins, you are Most Forgiving, Merciful. He said: He was forgiven (repeating three times).

Chapter 336

RECITATION OF THE *TASHAHHUD* QUIETLY

(981) 'Abd Allah (b. Mas'ūd) said: It pertains to the *sunnah*[474] to utter the *tashahhud* quietly.

Chapter 337

POINTING WITH THE FINGER DURING THE *TASHAHHUD*

(982) 'Abd al-Raḥmān al-Mu'āwī said: 'Abd Allah b. 'Umar saw me playing with pebbles during prayer. When he finished his prayer, he forbade me (to do so) and said: Do as the Apostle (may peace be upon him) used to do. I asked him: How would the Apostle of Allah (may peace be upon him) do? He said: When he sat during the prayer (for reciting the *tashahhud*), he placed his right hand on his right thigh,

473. The Prophet (may peace be upon him) has taught Muslims a large number of supplications to be made within and without the prayer. The punishment in Hell and the punishment in the grave are most horrible so much so that one cannot even listen to it. Hence the Prophet (may peace be upon him) is reported to seek refuge in Allah from the punishment in Hell and in the grave frequently.

The appearance of the Antichrist will also be a great trial for the Muslims. He will call people to disbelief and he will possess all sorts of comforts of life at a time when the people will have none. The Prophet (may peace be upon him), in a number of traditions, has reportedly predicted the appearance of the Antichrist and warned against his illusionment. Seeking refuge in Allah from his trial during prayer indicates the gravity of the test which the Muslims have to undergo after his appearance.

The trial of life and death is also immensely serious, for a Muslim has to face it every moment in his life. He has to prove himself during his practical life that he is a true Muslim. Likewise, he will be put to death at the time of his death and he will be questioned about faith in the grave.

474. When a Companion says: "It pertains to the *sunnah*," this is tantamount to his saying: "The Apostle of Allah (may peace be upon him) said." By such a phrase he means to narrate a tradition from the Prophet (may peace be upon him). This is the view about the phrase *sunnah* of the majority of the traditionists and the jurists. Some of the scholars take it as a statement of the Companion himself and not of the Prophet (may peace be upon him) (*'Awn al-Ma'būd*, I, 374).

and clenched all his fingers, and pointed with the finger which is adjacent to the thumb, and he placed his left hand on his left thigh.

(983) 'Abd Allah b. al-Zubair said: When the Apostle of Allah (may peace be upon him) sat during the prayer (at the *tashahhud*), he placed his left foot under his right thigh and shin and spread his right foot and placed his left hand on his left knee and placed his right hand on his right thigh, and he pointed with his finger. The narrator 'Abd al-Wāḥid demonstrated it to us and pointed with his forefinger [475]

(984) 'Abd Allah b. al-Zubair said: The Prophet (may peace be upon him) used to point with his finger (at the end of the *tashahhud*) and he would not move it.[476]

(985) 'Abd Allah b. al-Zubair narrated the above-mentioned tradition on the authority of his father saying: He kept his look fixed[477] on the finger he was pointing.

(986) Mālik b. Numair al-Khuza'ī reported on the authority of his father: I saw the Prophet (may peace be upon him) placing his right hand on his right thigh and raising his forefinger curving it a little.

475. Different positions of the Prophet (may peace be upon him), while sitting at the *tashahhud*, have been described in different traditions: (1) He would place the end of his right elbow on his right thigh, and clench his two fingers and make a circle. He would then raise his forefinger and move it towards the end of the *tashahhud*. (2) He would place his right hand on his right knee, count fifty-three on his knuckles, and point with his forefinger. (3) He clenched all his fingers and pointed with his forefinger. (4) He placed his right hand on the right thigh and his left hand on the left thigh and pointed with his forefinger, and placed his thumb on his middle finger and clutched his knee with his left hand. (5) He placed his right hand on his right thigh without clenching the fingers and pointed with his forefinger.

It should be noted that the Prophet (may peace be upon him) sometimes adopted one position and sometimes another. The position of placing hands and pointing with the finger changed in different situation. There are three positions of pointing with the finger: (1) He clenched his small finger, ring finger, and middle finger and left the forefinger free. He then joined the thumb with the root of the forefinger. This is the method of counting fifty-three on fingers. (2) He attached the thumb to the clenched middle finger, counting twenty-three on fingers. (3) He clenched his small and ring finger and left the forefinger out and made a circle with his thumb and the middle finger.

Al-Shāfi'ī is of opinion that one should point with the forefinger when one recites the words "I testify that there is no god but Allah," especially at the moment of uttering the words "but Allah". The pointing with the finger refers to the unity of Allah (*'Awn al-Ma'būd*, I, 375).

476. This shows that the Prophet (may peace be upon him) would not move his finger while pointing with it. This is followed by Abū Ḥanīfah. But some other traditions indicate that he would move it. This is the view of Mālik and of the majority of the scholars (*'Awn al-Ma'būd*, I, 375).

477. This means that one should look at the finger at the moment of pointing and should not look at the heaven as some people do.

Chapter 338

ABOMINATION OF LEANING ON HAND DURING PRAYER

(987) Ibn 'Umar said: The Apostle of Allah (may peace be upon him) prohibited, according to the version of Aḥmad b. Ḥanbal, that a person should sit during prayer while he is leaning on his hand. (According to the version of Ibn Shibwaih), he prohibited that a man should lean on his hand during prayer. (According to the version of Ibn Rāfi') he prohibited that a man should pray while he is leaning on his hand, and he mentioned this tradition in the chapter on "Raising the head after prostration." According to the version of Ibn 'Abd al-Malik, he prohibited that a man should lean on his hand when he stands up after prostration.[478]

(988) Ismā'īl b. Umayyah said: I asked about a man who intertwines his fingers while he is engaged in prayer. He said that Ibn 'Umar had said: This is the prayer of those who earn the anger of Allah.[479]

(989) Nāfi' said: Ibn 'Umar saw a man resting on his left hand while he was sitting during prayer. The version of Hārūn b. Zaid goes: He was lying on his left side. The agreed version goes: He said to him: Do not sit like this, because those who are punished sit like this.

Chapter 339

SHORT DURATION OF THE FIRST SITTING IN PRAYER

(990) Abū 'Ubaidah reported on the authority of his father (Ibn Mas'ūd): The Prophet (may peace be upon him) was in the first two ***rak'ahs*** as though he were on heated stones.[480] He (the narrator Shu'bah) said: We said: Till he (the Prophet)

478. The version of Aḥmad b. Ḥanbal shows that one should not sit after prostration while leaning on one's hand. The versions of Ibn Shibwaih and Ibn Rāfi' are unconditional and should be interpreted in the light of Ibn 'Abd al-Malik which says that one should not stand up after prostration while leaning on one's hand. According to Abū Ḥanīfah and Mālik, one should not lean on one's hand while standing after prostration. Al-Shāfi'ī and the traditionists maintain, arguing from the tradition reported by Mālik b. al-Ḥuwairith, that one should lean no one's hands while standing after prostration (*'Awn al-Ma'būd*. I, 376-77).

479. To intertwine fingers during prayer is abominable. This is the statement of Ibn 'Umar, but it is supported by a tradition of the Prophet (may peace be upon him) : Ka'b b. 'Ujrah reported the Apostle of Allah (may peace be upon him) as saying : When one of you performs ablution and does it well, then goes out making for the mosque, he must not intertwine his fingers for he is engaged in prayer (***Musnad Aḥmad***, al-Tirmidhī).

480. This is a figurative phrase to indicate the shortening of the sitting after the first two *rak'ahs* during the ***tashahhud.***

got up. He (the narrator Sa'd b. Ibrāhīm) said : We said : Till he got up.[481]

Chapter 340

ON SALUTATION AT THE END OF PRAYER

(991) 'Abd Allah (b. Mas'ūd) said : The Prophet (may peace be upon him) used to give the salutation to his left and right sides until the whiteness of his cheek was seen, (saying) : "Peace be upon you and mercy of Allah" twice.[482]

Abū Dāwūd said : This is a version of the tradition reported by Abū Sufyān. The version of Isrā'īl did not explain it.

Abū Dāwūd said : This tradition has been narrated by Zubair from Abū Isḥāq and Yaḥyā b. Ādam from Isrā'īl from Abū Isḥāq from 'Abd al-Raḥmān b. al-Aswad from his father from 'Alqamah on the authority of 'Abd Allah (b. Mas'ūd).

Abū Dāwūd said : Shu'bah used to reject this tradition, the tradition narrated by Abū Isḥāq as coming from the Prophet (may peace be upon him).

(992) 'Alqamah b. Wā'il said on the authority of his father : I offered prayer along with the Prophet (may peace be upon him). He would give the salutation to his right side (saying) : Peace be upon you and mercy of Allah ; and to his left side (saying) : Peace be upon you and mercy of Allah.

(993) Jābir b. Samurah said : When we prayed behind the Apostle of Allah (may peace be upon him), one of us gave the salutation and pointed with his hand to the man to his right side and left side. When he finished his prayer, he said : What is the matter that one of you points with his hand (during prayer) just like the tails of restive horses. It is sufficient for one of you, or is it not sufficient for one of you to say in this manner? And he pointed with his finger ; one sould salute his brother at his

481. This indicates that one should recite only the *tashahhud* after the first two *rak'ahs*. When the prayer consists of three or four *rak'ahs*, one should not recite anything else except the *tashahhud* during the first sitting. In case one recites anything else along with the *tashahhud* in the first sitting, one should prostrate on account of forgetfulness (*'Awn al-Ma'būd*, I, 377).

482. This shows that giving the salutation at the end of the prayer is necessary. There is a difference of opinion amongst the scholars on the point whether salutation at the end of the prayer is necessary (*wājib*) or recommended (*sunnah*). According to al-Shafi'ī, salutation is necessary (*wājib*) and in the opinion of Abū Ḥanīfah and others it is recommended (*sunnah*). Mālik holds that only one salutation is recommended (*sunnah*) at the end of the prayer and not two. He argues from the practice of the people of Medina. Al-Shāfi'ī takes one salutation as necessary and the other as recommended. Abū Ḥanīfah considers both salutations as recommended. The way of giving the one salutation is that one should utter the words of salutation with one's face towards the *qiblah* and then turn one's head a little to the right side (*'Awn al-Ma'būd*, I, 381). Salutation at the end of prayer is *wājib* according to Abū Hanīfah, as *sunnah* includes *wājib* too (*al-Hidāyah*, I, 96).

right and left side.[483]

(994) The aforesaid tradition has also been narrated by Mis'ar through a different chain of transmitters to the same effect. This version adds: Is it not sufficient for one of you or for one of them that he puts his hand on his thigh, and then gives the salutation to his brother to his right and left sides.

(995) Jābir b. Samurah said: The Apostle of Allah (may peace be upon him) entered upon us while the people were raising their hands. The narrator Zubair said: I think (they were raising the hand) during prayer. He (the Prophets) said: What is the matter, I see you raising your hands as if they are the tails of restive horses! Maintain tranquillity during prayer.[484]

Chapter 341

RESPONDING TO THE SALUTATION OF THE *IMĀM*

(996) Samurah reported: The Prophet (may peace be upon him) commanded us to respond to the salutation of the *imām*, and to love each other, and to salute each other.[485]

Chapter 342

TO PRONOUNCE THE *TAKBĪR* ALOUD AFTER PRAYER

(997) Ibn 'Abbās said: The end of the prayer of the Apostle of Allah (may peace be upon him) was known by the *takbīr* (pronounced aloud).[486]

(998) Ibn 'Abbās said: To raise the voice for making the mention of Allah after

483. This means that one should utter the words of salutation on both sides and should not point with his hand only. By pointing with the finger the Prophet (may peace be upon him) meant that one should place one's hands on one's thighs and point with the finger while reciting the *tashahhud*. It does not mean that he allowed to point with the finger while giving the salutation (*'Awn al-Ma'būd*, I, 381-82).

484. This means that the Prophet (may peace be upon him) prohibited them from raising hands at the time of salutation towards the end of the prayer. This does not mean that he prohibited from raising hands before and after bowing.

485. According to Abū Ḥanīfah, the people on both the right and left sides of the *imām* should have the intention of responding to the salutation of the *imām*. In the opinion of Mālik one should repeat the same words of salutation uttered by the *imām*. As such, the follower behind the *imām* should give three salutations, namely, one salutation facing the *qiblah* by which he ends his prayer; the second for the *imām* and the third for the Muslims on his left side (*'Awn al-Ma'būd*, I, 382)

486. This does not mean that only the *takbīr* was pronounced after finishing the prayer. A tradition indicates that the Companions used to make mention of Allah for a short period after the prayer was over.

the people had finished their obligatory prayer was in vogue during the time of the Apostle of Allah (may peace be upon him).[487]

Ibn 'Abbās said: I used to know by it when they finished the prayer and would listen to it (making the mention of Allah).[488]

Chapter 343

THE SHORTENING OF SALUTATION[489]

(999) Abū Hurairah reported the Apostle of Allah (may peace be upon him) as saying: Shortening the salutation is *sunnah* (commendable).

The narrator 'Īsā said: Ibn al-Mubārak prohibited me from reporting this tradition as a statement of the Prophet (may peace be upon him).

Abū Dāwūd said: I heard Abū 'Umar 'Īsā b. Yūnus al-Fakhurī al-Ramlī saying: When al-Firyābī returned from Mecca, he gave up narrating this tradition as a statement of the Prophet (may peace be upon him). He said: Aḥmad b. Ḥanbal forbade to report this tradition directly from the Prophet (may peace be upon him).

Chapter 344

A MAN BREAKING WIND DURING PRAYER SHOULD REPEAT IT

(1000) 'Alī b. Ṭalq reported the Apostle of Allah (may peace be upon him) as saying: When any of you breaks wind during prayer, he must withdraw, perform ablution, and repeat the prayer.[490]

487. Al-Shāfi'ī observes that the Companions made the mention of Allah aloud after prayer for a short period. This was done only for teaching. Afterwards they made the mention of Allah quietly. This is the recognised practice (*'Awn al-Ma'būd*, I, 383).

488. Ibn 'Abbās was a child, he did not sometimes attend the congregational prayer. And when he attended, he stood in the last row of prayer. Hence he would not know the end of the prayer by salutation, but would hear the *takbir* which the people pronounced loudly at the end of the prayer.

489. This means that one should not prolong one's breath while giving the salutation. Instead, one should pronounce it quicky in a short breath. Prolongation of pronouncing the salutation is abominable (*'Awn al-Ma'būd*, I, 383-84)

490. If one breaks wind during congregational prayer one should hold one's nose and withdraw as another tradition indicates. If one is doubtful about breaking wind, one's doubt will not be taken into consideration. One must hear the sound, or feel the smell.

Chapter 345

ON A MAN WHO OFFERS SUPEREROGATORY PRAYER ON THE SPOT WHERE HE OFFERED OBLIGATORY PRAYER

(1001) Abū Hurairah reported the Apostle of Allah (may peace be upon him) as saying : Cannot any one of you (according to the version of the narrator 'Abd al-Wārith) step forward or backward or at his right or left. The version of Ḥammād added : during prayer ; that is, in supererogatory prayer.[491]

(1002) Al-Azraq b. Qais said: An *imām* of ours whose *kunyah* (surname) was Abū Rimthah led us in prayer and said : I prayed this prayer, or one like it, along with the Prophet (may peace be upon him). Abū Bakr and 'Umar were standing in the front row on his right and there was a man who had been present at the first *takbīr* in the prayer. The Prophet of Allah (may peace be upon him) offered the prayer, then gave the salutation to his right and his left so that we saw the whiteness of his cheeks, then turned away as Abū Rimthah (meaning himself) has done. The man who had been present with him at the first *takbīr* in the prayer then got up to pray another prayer, whereupon 'Umar leaped up and, seizing him by the shoulders, shook him and said : Sit down, for the People of the Book perished for no other reason than that there was no interval between their prayers. The Prophet (may peace be upon him) raised his eyes and said : Allah has made you say what is right, son of al-Khaṭṭāb.[492]

Abū Dāwūd said : Sometimes the name Abū Umayyah is narrated instead of Abū Rimthah.

Chapter 346

PROSTRATIONS DUE TO FORGETFULNESS DURING PRAYER

(1003) Abū Hurairah said : The Apostle of Allah (may peace be upon him) led us

491. This tradition indicates that after offering obligatory prayer one should move backward or forward or to the left or right for offering supererogatory prayer. The Prophet (may peace be upon him) commanded to change the place so that different places may testify to his prayer.

492. It is commendable to give a short interval between the obligatory and supererogatory prayers. The Prophet (may peace be upon him) used to make mention of Allah after the obligatory prayer and thus would give an interval between two prayers. Abū Ḥanīfah maintains that the *sunan* prayers are part of obligatory prayers, offered for their consummation ; hence one should offer them immediately after the obligatory prayers. He considers making mention of Allah desirable after those obligatory prayers which are not followed by *sunan* prayers like morning and afternoon prayers.

in one of the two evening (*'ashīy*) prayers, noon or afternoon. He led us in two *rak'ahs* and gave the salutation. He then got up going towards a piece of wood which was placed in the front part of the mosque. He placed his hands upon it, one on the other, looking from his face as if he were angry. The people came out hastily saying : The prayer has been shortened ; the prayer has been shortened. Abū Bakr and 'Umar were among the people, but they were too afraid to speak to him. A man whom the Apostle of Allah (may peace be upon him) would call "the possessor of arms" (Dhū al-Yadain) stood up (asking him) : Have you forgotten, Apostle of Allah, or has the prayer been shortened ? He said : I have neither forgotten nor has it been shortened. He said : Apostle of Allah, you have forgotten. The Apostle of Allah (may peace be upon him) turned towards the people and asked : Did the possessor of arms speak the truth ? They made a sign, that is, yes. The Apostle of Allah (may peace be upon him) returned to his place and prayed the remaining two *rak'ahs*, then gave the salutation ; he then uttered the *takbīr* and prostrated himself as usual or prolonged. He then raised his head and uttered the *takbīr* ; then he uttered the *takbīr* and made prostration as usual or made longer (prostration). Then he raised his head and uttered the *takbīr* (Allah is most great). The narrator Muḥammad was asked : Did he give the salutation (while prostrating) due to forgetfulness ?[493] He said : I do not remember it from Abū Hurairah. But we are sure that 'Imrān b. Ḥuṣain (in his version) said : He then gave the salutation.

(1004) This tradition has been narrated through a different chain of transmitters ; but the version of Ḥammād is more perfect. This version goes : Then the Apostle of Allah (may peace be upon him) prayed ; it does not have the words, "led us (in prayer)," nor the words "they made a sign". Thereupon the people said : Yes. He then raised his head. The version does not mention the words "he uttered the *takbīr*. He then uttered the *takbīr* and made the prostration as usual or prolonged it. He then raised his head." The narrator then finished the tradition and did not mention the words that follow it. He did not mention the words "they made a sign," but Ḥammād b. Zaid mentioned them in his version.

Abū Dāwūd said : Anyone who narrated this tradition did not mention the words "then he uttered the *takbīr*," nor the words "he returned"

493. There is a difference of opinion amongst the jurists on the question whether one should prostrate due to forgetfulness before salutation or after it. According to Abu Ḥanīfah prostrations due to forgetfulness should be made after salutation, and according to al-Shāfi'ī before salutation. Mālik holds that in the case of excess of an act in prayer by forgetfulness one should prostrate after salutation, and in the case of omission of something in prayer one should prostrate before salutation. According to the traditionists, one should follow the traditions of the Prophet (may peace be upon him) about forgetfulness strictly. In cases where the Prophet (may peace be upon him) prostrated before salutation one should prostrate before it, and where he (the Prophet) prostrated after salutation, one should follow him in the same manner (*'Awn al-Ma'būd*, I, 390).

(1005) Abū Hurairah said : The Apostle of Allah (may peace be upon him) led us in prayer. He then narrated the same version reported by Ḥammād up to the words "we are sure that 'Imrān b. Ḥuṣain said : Then he gave the salutation." The narrator said : I asked : What about the *tashahhud*? He replied : I did not hear anything about the *tashahhud*, but it is more liking to me that one should recite the *tashahhud*. This version has not the words "whom he called the possessor of arms (*Dhu al-Yadain*)," nor the words "they made a sign," nor the word "anger." The tradition narrated by Ḥammād from Ayyūb is more perfect.

(1006) The above-mentioned tradition has also been narrated by Abū Hurairah through a different chain of transmitters. This version goes : The Prophet (may peace be upon him) uttered the *takbīr* and prostrated himself (in a tradition relating to the incidence of the possessor of arms [*Dhu al-Yadain*]). The narrator Hishām, i.e. Ibn Ḥassān said : He uttered the *takbīr* ; then he uttered the *takbīr* and prostrated himself.

Abū Dāwūd said : This tradition has also been narrated by Ḥabīb b. al-Shahīd, Ḥumaid, Yūnus, and 'Āṣim b. al-Aḥwal, from Muḥammad on the authority of Abū Hurairah. None of them mentioned what Ḥammād b. Zaid mentioned from Hishām that he uttered the *takbīr* ; then uttered the *takbīr* and prostrated himself. Ḥammād b. Salamah and Abū Bakr b. 'Ayyāsh also narrated this tradition from Hishām, but they did not narrate from him what Ḥammād b. Zaid narrated that he uttered the *takbīr* and again uttered the *takbīr*.

(1007) This tradition has also been transmitted by Abū Hurairah through a different chain of narrators. This version goes : He did not make two prostrations (at the end of prayer) due to forgetfulness until Allah gave him satisfaction about it.

(1008) Ibn Shihāb (al-Zuhrī) reported on the authority of Abū Bakr b. Sulaimān b. Abī Hathmah that the Apostle of Allah (may peace be upon him) did not make two prostrations which are made when one is doubtful until the people met him.

Ibn Shihāb said : Sa'īd b. al-Musayyib narrated this tradition to me on the authority of Abū Hurairah. He said : This tradition has been narrated to me by Abū Salamah b. 'Abd al-Raḥmān, Abū Bakr b. al-Ḥārith b. Hishām and 'Ubaid Allah b. 'Abd Allah.

Abū Dāwūd said: This tradition has also been narrated by Yaḥyā b. Kathīr and 'Imrān b. Abī Anas from Abū Salamah b. 'Abd al-Rahmān and by al-'Aṭā' b. 'Abd al-Raḥmān from his father on the authourity of Abū Hurairah. They did not mention that he made two prostrations.

Abū Dāwūd said: This tradition has also been narrated by al-Zāhidī from al-Zuhrī from Abū Bakr b. Sulaimān b. Abī Ḥathmah from the Prophet (may peace be upon him). This version goes: He did not make two prostrations on account of forgetfulness.

(1009) Abū Hurairah reported: The Prophet (may peace be upon him) offered the noon prayer and he gave the salutation at the end of two *rak'ahs*. He was asked : Has the prayer been shortened? Then he offered two *rak'ahs* of prayer and made two prostrations (at the end of it).

(1010) Abū Hurairah said: When the Prophet (may peace be upon him) finished two *rak'ahs* of an obligatory prayer, a man asked him: Apostle of Allah, has the prayer been shortened, or have you forgotten? He replied: I did not do all that. The people said: Apostle of Allah, you did that. Therefore, he offered another two *rak'ahs* of prayer and did not make two prostrations due to forgetfulness.

Abū Dāwūd said: This tradition has also been narrated by Dāwūd b. al-Ḥusain from Abū Sufyān, freed slave of Ibn Abī Aḥmad on the authority of Abū Hurairah from the Prophet (may peace be upon him). This version goes: He then made two prostrations while he was sitting after the salutation.

(1011) Abū Hurairah reported: He then made two prostrations on account of forgetfulness after he had given the salutation.

(1012) Ibn 'Umar said: The Apostle of Allah (may peace be upon him) led us in prayer and gave the salutation after two *rak'ahs* of prayer. He narrated this tradition like that of Ibn Sīrīn from Abū Hurairah. This version adds: He gave the salutation and prostrated two prostrations due to forgetfulness.

(1013) 'Imrān b. Ḥuṣain said: The Apostle of Allah (may peace be upon him) gave the salutation at the end of three *rak'ahs* in the afternoon prayer, then went into the apartment (according to the version of Maslamah). A man called al-Khirbāq who had long arms got up and said: Has the prayer been shortened, Apostle of Allah? He came out angrily trailing his cloak and said: Is he telling the truth? They said: Yes. He then prayed that *rak'ah*, then gave the salutation, then made two prostrations, then gave the salutation.

Chapter 347

ON OFFERING FIVE INSTEAD OF FOUR *RAK'AHS* DURING PRAYER

(1014) 'Abd Allah (b. Mas'ūd) said: The Apostle of Allah (may peace be upon him) prayed five *rak'ahs* in the noon prayer. He was asked whether the prayer had been extended. He asked what they meant by that. The people said: You prayed five *rak'ahs*. Then he made two prostrations after having given the salutation.[494]

(1015) 'Abd Allah (b. Mas'ūd) said: The Apostle of Allah (may peace be upon

494. Abū Ḥanīfah argues from this tradition that prostration should be made after salutation. It should be noted that the Prophet (may peace be upon him) sometimes prostrated before salutation and sometimes after salutation. This is all established by a number of traditions. Hence this tradition cannot be generalised.

him) offered prayer. The version of the narrator Ibrāhīm goes: I do not know whether he increased or decreased (the *rak'ahs* of prayer). When he gave the salutation, he was asked: Has something new happened in the prayer, Apostle of Allah? He said: What is that? They said: You prayed so many and so many (*rak'ahs*). He then relented his foot and faced the *qiblah* and made two prostrations. He then gave the salutation. When he turned away (finished the prayer), he turned his face to us and said: Had anything new happened in prayer, I would have informed you. I am only a human being and I forget just as you do; so when I forget, remind me, and when any of you is in doubt about his prayer he should aim at what is correct, and complete his prayer in that respect, then give the salutation and afterwards make two prostrations.

(1016) This tradition has also been transmitted by 'Abd Allah (b. Mas'ūd) through a different chain of narrators. This version goes: When one of you forgets (in his prayer), he should perform two prostrations. Then he turned away, and performed two prostrations (due to forgetfulness).

Abū Dāwūd said: The narrator Ḥuṣain also reported it like al-A'mash.

(1017) 'Abd Allah (b. Mas'ūd) said: The Apostle of Allah (may peace be upon him) led us in five *rak'ahs* of prayer. When he turned away (i.e. finished his prayer), the people whispered among themselves. He asked: What is the matter with you? They said: Apostle of Allah, has (the number of the *rak'ahs* of) the prayer been increased? He said: No. They said: You have offered five *rak'ahs* of prayer. He then turned away and performed two prostrations, and afterwards gave the salutation. He then said: I am only a human being, I forget, as you forget.

(1018) Mu'āwiyah b. Khudaij said: One day the Apostle of Allah (may peace be upon him) prayed and gave the salutation while a *rak'ah* of the prayer remained to be offered. A man went to him and said: You forgot to offer one *rak'ah* of prayer. Then he returned and entered the mosque and ordered Bilāl (to utter the *Iqāmah*). He uttered the *iqamah* for prayer. He then led the people in one *rak'ah* of prayer. I stated it to the people. They asked me: Do you know who he was? I said: No, but I can recognise him if I see him. Then the man passed by me, I said: It is he. The people said: This is Talḥah b. 'Ubaid Allah.[495]

495. The various traditions about the prostration of forgetfulness indicate that the people at the end of the prayer talked to the Prophet (may peace be upon him) and to each other. The Prophet (may peace be upon him) himself talked to the people. He then completed the one *rak'ah* of the prayer which he had omitted. All this shows that finishing the prayer incompletely by forgetfulness does not invalidate it. One can complete it by saying the omitted *rak'ahs*. Similarly, talking by forgetfulness or talking by a man who thinks by mistake that he has completed the prayer also does not harm the prayer. This is the view held by the majority of the scholars, classical and modern. This is the opinion held by Ibn 'Abbās, Ibn al-Zubair, 'Uwrah, and 'Aṭā' al-Ḥasan al-Baṣrī. This is maintained by al-Shāfi'ī and Aḥmad and by all the traditionists. According to the Ḥanafī school,

Chapter 348

IF A PERSON IS DOUBTFUL WHETHER HE HAS PRAYED TWO *RAK'AHS* OR THREE, A VIEW GOES THAT HE SHOULD THROW AWAY THE DOUBT

(1019) 'Aṭā' b. Yasār said that Abū Sa'īd al-Khudrī reported the Apostle of Allah (may peace be upon him) as saying: When one of you is in doubt about his prayer (i.e. how much he has prayed), he should throw away his doubt and base his prayer on what he is sure of. When he is sure about the completion of his prayer, he should make two prostrations (at the end of the prayer). If the prayer is complete, the additional *rak'ah* and the two prostrations will be supererogatory prayer. If the prayer is incomplete, the additional *rak'ahs* will compensate it,[496] and the two prostrations will be a disgrace for the devil.[497]

(1020) Ibn 'Abbās said: The Prophet (may peace be upon him) named the two prostrations of forgetfulness disgraceful for the devil.

(1021) 'Aṭā' b. Yasār reported the Apostle of Allah (may peace be upon him) as saying: When one of you is in doubt about his prayer, and does not know how much he has prayed, three or four *rak'ahs*, he should pray one (additional) *rak'ah* and make two prostrations while sitting before giving the salutation. If the (additional) *rak'ah* which he prayed is the fifth one, he will make it an even number by these two prostrations. If it is the fourth one, the two prostrations will be a disgrace for the devil.

(1022) Zaid b. Aslam reported on the authority of the chain of Mālik: The Prophet (may peace be upon him) said: If one of you is in doubt about his prayer, and if he is sure that he has prayed three *rak'ahs*, he should stand and complete one *rak'ah*

talking during prayer whether deliberately or inadvertently, makes it void. They argue on the basis of the traditions reported by Ibn Mas'ūd and Zaid b. Arqam about the prohibition of talking during prayer. In their opinion the traditions about the permission of talking during prayer have been abrogated by those traditions. But it should be noted that the tradition of Ibn Mas'ūd about prohibition of speech is prior to the traditions of forgetfulness which allow speech during prayer by forgetfulness or to correct the prayer. Hence the tradition of Ibn Mas'ūd is not abrogated (*'Awn al-Ma'būd*, I, 386).

496. There are three views about the doubt in the *rak'ahs* of prayer: (1) One should make two prostrations at the end of the prayer; (2) one should throw away the doubt and base his prayer on the least—for instance, one should base one's prayer on one *rak'ah* if the doubt is about one or two *rak'ahs*, and on two *rak'ahs* if the doubt is about two or three *rak'ahs*, and on three *rak'ahs* if one is doubtful about three or four *rak'ahs*. (3) One should follow what is highly probable in one's opinion. In case there is no such probability, one should follow what is the least.

497. This is because there is no harm from the evil suggestions of the devil. The worshipper gets the reward of the complete prayer and additional reward for additional *rak'ahs* and prostrations.

along with its prostrations. Then he should sit and recite the *tashahhud*. When he finishes the prayer, and there remains nothing except salutation, he should make two prostrations while he is sitting and afterwards should give the salutation. The narrator then narrated the tradition similar to that of Mālik.

Abū Dāwūd said: Similarly, this tradition has been narrated by Ibn Wahb from Mālik, Ḥafṣ b. Maisarah, Dāwūd b. Qais and Hishām b. Sa'd. But Hishām projected it to Abū Sa'īd al-Khudrī.

Chapter 349

IN THE CASE OF DOUBT ABOUT THE NUMBER OF *RAK'AHS*, A VIEW GOES THAT ONE SHOULD FOLLOW WHAT IS HIGHLY PROBABLE IN ONE'S OPINION

(1023) Abū 'Ubaidah reported, on the authority of his father 'Abd Allah (b. Mas'ūd), the Apostle of Allah (may peace be upon him) as saying: When you offer the prayer, and you are in doubt about the number of *rak'ahs* whether offered three or four, and you have prayed four *rak'ahs* in all probability in your opinion, you should recite *tashahhud* and make two prostrations while you are sitting before giving the salutation. Afterwards you should recite the *tashahhud* and give the salutation again.[498]

Abū Dāwūd said: This tradition has been narrated by 'Abd al-Wāḥid from Khuṣaif, but he did not report it as a statement of the Prophet (may peace be upon him). The version of 'Abd al-Wāḥid has been corroborated by Sufyān, Sharīk, and Isrā'īl. They differed amongst themselves about the text of the tradition and they did not narrate it with the continuous chain up to the Prophet (may peace be upon him).[499]

(1024) Abū Sa'īd al-Khudrī reported the Apostle of Allah (may peace be upon him) as saying: When one of you prays, and he does not know whether he prayed more or less *rak'ahs* (than those prescribed by the *Sharī'ah*), he should perform two prostrations while he is sitting. If the devil comes to him, and tells him (suggests him): "You have been defiled," he should say: "You have told a lie," except that he

498. According to the Ḥanafīs, one should follow what is highly probable. In case one is sure, one should base one's prayer on surety Al-Shāfi'ī is of opinion that a man should base his prayer on what he is sure of in all conditions. Again, Mālik and Abū Ḥanīfah hold the view that one who has the doubt frequently should follow what is highly probable in one's opinion. But if doubt does not happen to someone frequently, he should follow what is sure in his opinion. This is the view of al-Shāfi'ī and the majority of scholars (*'Awn al-Ma'būd*, I, 394).

499. 'Ubaid Allah did not hear any tradition from his father Ibn Mas'ūd. Hence this tradition has the broken chain (*'Awn al-Ma'būd*, I, 395).

feels smell with his nose, or sound with his ears (then his ablution will break). These are the wordings of the tradition reported by Abān.

Abū Dāwūd said: Ma'mar and 'Abī b. al-Mubārak mentioned the name "Iyāḍ b. Hilāl and al-Awzā'ī mentioned the name 'Iyāḍ b. Abī Zuhair

(1025) Abū Hurairah reported the Apostle of Allah (may peace be upon him) as saying: When one of you stands up to pray, the devil comes to him and confuses him so that he does not know how much he has prayed. If any of you has such an experience, he should perform two prostrations while he is sitting.

Abū Dāwūd said: This tradition has been narrated in a similar manner by Ibn 'Uyainah, Ma'mar and al-Laith.

(1026) This tradition has also been transmitted by Muḥammad b. Muslim through a different chain of narrators. This version adds: "While he is sitting before he gives the salutation."

(1027) This traditions has also been narrated by Muḥammad b. Muslim al-Zuhrī through a different chain of transmitters and to the same effect. This version adds: He should perform two prostrations before giving the salutation.

Chapter 350

THE VIEW THAT ONE SHOULD PERFORM PROSTRATION OF FORGETFULNESS AFTER GIVING THE SALUTATION

(1028) 'Abd Allah b. Ja'far reported the Apostle of Allah (may peace be upon him) as saying: Anyone who is in doubt in his prayer should make two prostrations after giving the salutation.[500]

500. There are four points of views about the making of prostration of forgetfulness: (1) One should make the prostration after giving the salutation. This view is supported by the tradition reported by Dhū al-Yadain. This is held by 'Alī, Sa'd, Ibn al-Zubair, al-Ḥasan, al-Nakha'ī, Ibn Abī Lailā, al-Thawrī, al-Ḥasan b. Ṣāliḥ and Abū Ḥanīfah. (2) The prostration due to forgetfulness should be performed before giving the salutation. This is corroborated by the traditions narrated by Ibn Buḥainah, Abū Sa'īd al-Khudrī and Mu'āwiyah. This is maintained by al-Shāfi'ī. (3) If prostration of forgetfulness is made due to excess in prayer, one should perform it after the salutation, as indicated by the tradition reported by Dhū al-Yadain. In case the prostration is made due to deficiency in prayer, one should perform it before the salutation as indicated by the tradition of Abū Sa'īd al-Khudrī. This is held by Mālik b. Anas. (4) If one forgets sitting at the end of two *rak'ahs* and stands up for praying the third *rak'ah*, one should perform the prostration before giving the salutation. The same thing should be done in case one remains doubtful in prayer in the beginning but becomes sure later on. If one gives the salutation by forgetfulness at the end of two *rak'ahs*, one should make the prostration after giving the salutation. One should also do so in case one remains doubtful. This is the opinion of Aḥmad b. Ḥanbal. Al-Nawawī observes that the most sound

Chapter 351

ON STANDING UP AT THE END OF *RAK'AHS* BY FORGETFULNESS WITHOUT SITTING AND RECITING THE *TASHAHHUD* DURING PRAYER

(1029) 'Abd Allah b. Buḥainah[501] said: The Apostle of Allah (may peace be upon him) led us in prayer praying two *rak'ahs*. When he stood up and did not sit (at the end of two *rak'ahs*) the people stood up along with him. When he finished the prayer and we expected him to give the salutation, he said: "Allah is most great." While sitting and made two prostrations before giving the salutation. Then he gave it.[502]

(1030) This tradition (mentioned above) has also been transmitted by al-Zuhrī through a different chain of narrators to the same effect. This version adds: Some of us recited the *tashahhud* while they were standing.

Abū Dāwūd said: Ibn al-Zubair made two prostrations before giving the salutation in a similar way when he stood up at the end of two *rak'ahs*. This is the opinion of al-Zuhrī.

Chapter 352

ON A PERSON WHO FORGETS TO RECITE THE *TASHAHHUD* AND SITTING AT THE END OF TWO *RAK'AHS*

(1031) Al-Mughīrah b. Shu'bah reported the Apostle of Allah (may peace be

view is the one held by Mālik, then the one held by al-Shāfi'ī. Al-Qāḍī 'Iyāḍ opines that the difference of opinion on this question is of preference and not of validity. If one makes prostration, before or after the salutation, the prayer will be valid (*'Awn al-Ma'būd*, I, 397).

501. 'Abd Allah b. Buḥainah was a Companion of the Prophet (may peace be upon him). Buḥainah was the name of his mother. The name of his father was Mālik who was also a Companion (*'Awn al-Ma'būd*, I, 397).

502. Al-Nawawī observes that this tradition contains a number of the rules of law: (1) The prostration of forgetfulness should be made before giving the salutation either generally in all cases or in the case of deficiency in prayer. (2) The sitting and the recitation of the *tashahhud* at the end of two *rak'ahs* are not necessary parts of prayer (*rukn*). Had they been the necessary parts of prayer, they would not have been compensated by making the two prostrations. This is the view held by Mālik, Abū Ḥanīfah and al-Shāfi'ī. (3) One must say "Allah is most great" before making the prostration of forgetfulness. (4) In case one makes the prostration after giving the salutation, according to al-Shāfi'ī, one should give the salutation and should not recite the *tashahhud*. (5) Muḥammad b. Ismā'īl says: This tradition shows that if one omits the sitting and the *tashahhud* at the end of two *rak'ahs*, they can be compensated by the prostration of forgetfulness (*'Awn al-Ma'būd*, I, 398).

upon him) as saying: When an *imām* stands up at the end of two *rak'ahs*, if he remembers before standing straight up, he should sit down, but if he stands straight up, he must not sit down, but perform the two prostrations of forgetfulness.[503]

(1032) Ziyād b. 'Ilāqah said: Al-Mughīrah b. Shu'bah led us in prayer and he stood up at the end of two *rak'ahs*. We said: Glory be to Allah; he also said: Glory be to Allah, and he proceeded. When he finished the prayer and gave the salutation, he made two prostrations of forgetfulness. When he turned (to us) he said: I saw the Apostle of Allah (may peace be upon him) doing so as I did.

Abū Dāwūd said: Ibn Abī Lailā narrated this tradition in a similar manner from al-Sha'bī from al-Mughīrah b. Shu'bah. Abū 'Umais narrated it from Thābit b. 'Ubaid saying: "Al-Mughīrah b. Shu'bah led us in prayer, like the tradition reported by Ziyād b. 'Ilāqah.

Abū Dāwūd said: Abū 'Umais is the brother of al-Mas'ūdī. And Sa'd b. Abī Waqqāṣ did the same as done by al-Mughīrah, 'Imrān b. Ḥuṣain, Ḍaḥḥāk b. Qais and Mu'āwiyah b. Abī Sufyān. Ibn 'Abbās and 'Umar b. 'Abd al-'Azīz issued legal verdict to the same effect.

Abū Dāwūd said: This applies to a person who stands up at the end of two *rak'ahs* and makes prostration after giving the salutation.

(1033) Thawbān reported the Prophet (may peace be upon him) as saying: For each forgetfulness there are two prostrations after giving the salutation.[504] No one except 'Amr (b. 'Uthmān) mentioned the words "from his father" (in the chain 'Abd al-Raḥmān b. Jubair b. Nufair from Thawbān).

Chapter 353

ON RECITING THE *TASHAHHUD* AND GIVING THE SALUTATION AFTER MAKING THE PROSTRATIONS OF FORGETFULNESS

(1034) 'Imrān b. Ḥuṣain said that the Prophet (may peace be upon him) led them in prayer and forgot something, so he made two prostrations and uttered the

503. This means that if he stands up by forgetfulness, he should make two prostrations. If he is near the sitting, he should sit down, and the prostration should not be made (*'Awn al-Ma'būd*, I, 399).

504. The experts of traditions have criticised this tradition and declared it as weak. It is agreed upon amongst the jurists that if a person makes several mistakes during the prayer, the two prostrations of forgetfulness are sufficient for compensation. There is no need of making prostrations severally for each mistake (*'Awn al-Ma'būd*, I, 401).

tashahhud, then gave the salutation.[505]

Chapter 354

ON THE RETURNING OF WOMEN FROM CONGREGATIONAL PRAYER BEFORE THE RETURNING OF MEN

(1035) Umm Salamah said: When the Apostle of Allah (may peace be upon him) gave the salutation, he stayed for a while. By this people thought that women should return earlier than men.[506]

Chapter 355

TO WHICH SIDE ONE SHOULD TURN AFTER FINISHING THE PRAYER?

(1036) Qabīṣah b. Halb reported on the authority of his father that he prayed along with the Prophet (may peace be upon him). He used to turn to both his sides (sometimes to the left and sometimes to the right).[507]

(1037) 'Abd Allah (b. Mas'ūd) said: One of you should not give a share from his prayer to the devil, that he does not turn away except to his right side. I saw the Apostle of Allah (may peace be upon him) often turning away to his left side. The narrator 'Umārah said: I came to Medina afterwards and saw that the houses of the

505. The question of uttering the *tashahhud* after making the prostrations of forgetfulness has been discussed earlier. Opinion is divided on this point. Some hold the view that one should recite the *tashahhud* and give the salutation. Another group opines that there is no recitation of the *tashahhud* and the salutation. If one makes prostration before giving the salutation, one should not recite the *tashahhud*. This is the opinion of Aḥmad and Isḥāq (*'Awa al-Ma'būd*, I, 402).

506. This shows that men and women should not have mixed gathering. During the time of the Prophet (may peace be upon him) women used to leave the mosque at the end of the prayer before men so that men might not see them. The modernists in our day misinterpret the text of the Qur'ān and the *sunnah* to project their view that veil is not necessary for women. But this and many other traditions show that the Prophet (may peace be upon him) always emphasised seclusion of women from men in Muslim society.

507. This shows that no particular direction is fixed for turning away after finishing the prayer. One can go by his right or left side. The Prophet (may peace be upon him) would turn away sometimes to his left and sometimes to his right as he felt the need. This tradition also indicates that one should not fix any direction for leaving the mosque after finishing the prayer (*Awn al-Ma'būd*, I, 402).

Prophet (may peace be upon him) were (built) on the left.[508]

Chapter 356

OFFERING THE SUPEREROGATORY PRAYER BY A PERSON IN HIS HOUSE

(1038) Ibn 'Umar reported the Apostle of Allah (may peace be upon him) as saying: Offer some of your prayers[509] in your houses, and do not make them graves.[510]

(1039) Zaid b. Thābit reported the Prophet (may peace be upon him) as saying: The prayer a man offers in his house is more excellent than his prayer in this mosque of mine except obligatory prayer.[511]

Chapter 357

ON A PERSON WHO OFFERS HIS PRAYER IN A DIRECTION OTHER THAN THE *QIBLAH*, AND AFTERWARDS KNOWS THE RIGHT DIRECTION

(1040) Anas said: The Prophet (may peace be upon him) and his Companions used to pray in the direction of Jerusalem. When the following verse was revealed: "So turn thy face towards the inviolable mosque" ; and Ye (O Muslims), wheresoever ye may be, turn your faces towards it" (ii. 144), a man passed by the people of Banū Salamah. He called them while they were bowing in the morning prayer facing Jerusalem: Lo, the *qiblah* (direction of prayer) has been changed towards the Ka'bah. He called them twice. So they turned their faces towards the Ka'bah while they were bowing.[512]

508. This shows that it is abominable to consider the turning away to the right or to the left necessary. One has the choice of direction which has not been fixed by the Prophet (may peace be upon him).

509. This refers to the supererogatory prayer, for it is better to offer obligatory prayer in the mosque in congregation. A tradition of the Prophet (may peace be upon him) goes: Pray, O people, in your houses, for the best prayer is the one which a man offers in his house except the obligatory prayer.

510. This means that one should not make one's house like the graveyard where praying is forbidden. One should, instead, offer optional and supererogatory prayer at home. During the time of the Prophet (may peace be upon him) people used to offer *sunan* prayers at their homes.

511. This tradition indicates that one should offer obligatory prayer in the mosque. The optional and additional prayers are to be offered at home.

512. This shows that the prayer which they offered in the direction of Jerusalem by their ignorance was valid. From this it can be inferred that if one prays in some other direction due to ignorance, his prayer will be valid, and it is not necessary to repeat it.

Chapter 358

INJUNCTIONS ABOUT THE PRAYER ON FRIDAY

(1041) Abū Hurairah reported the Apostle of Allah (may peace be upon him) as saying: The best day on which the sun has risen is Friday; on it Adam was created, on it he was expelled (from Paradise), on it his contrition was accepted, on it he died, and on it the Last Hour will take place. On Friday every beast is on the outlook from dawn to sunrise from fear of the Last Hour, but not jinn and men, and it contains a time at which no Muslim prays and asks anything from Allah but He will give it to him. Ka'b said: That is one day every year. So I said: It is on every Friday. Ka'b read the Torah and said: The Apostle of Allah (may peace be upon him) has spoken the truth. Abū Hurairah said: I met 'Abd Allah b. Salām and told him of my meeting with Ka'b. 'Abd Allah b. Salām said: I know what time it is. Abū Hurairah said: I asked him: Tell me about it. 'Abd Allah b. Salām said: It is at the very end of Friday. I asked: How can it be when the Apostle of Allah (may peace be upon him) had said: "No Muslim finds it while he is praying. . ." and this is the moment when no prayer is offered. 'Abd Allah b. Salām said: Has the Apostle of Allah (may peace be upon him) not said: "If anyone is seated waiting for the prayer, he is engaged in the prayer until he observes it." I said: Yes, it is so.[513]

(1042) Aus b. Aus reported the Apostle of Allah (may peace be upon him) as saying: Among the most excellent of your days is Friday; on it Adam was created, on it he died, on it the last trumpet will be blown, and on it the shout will be made, so invoke more blessings on me that day, for your blessings will be submitted to me. The people asked: Apostle of Allah, how can it be that our blessings will be submitted to you while your body is decayed? He replied: Allah, the Exalted, has prohibited the earth from consuming the bodies of Prophets.[514]

513. This does not mean that he is actually praying. But this means that he is sitting prior to prayer.

There is much difference of opinion about the exact moment on Friday when one's supplication is accepted by Allah. Some scholars take the statement of 'Abd Allah b. Salām as right. Others are of opinion that this hour starts when the *imām* is seated for preaching and lasts till the end of the prayer. This view is supported by the traditions of the Prophet (may peace be upon him). The author of *Fatḥ al-Bārī* has quoted forty-two opinions about this hour. The purpose of hiding this moment on Friday is that people should remain engaged in supplication and prayer all the day long. Had it been unfolded, people would not have made efforts in seeking it.

514. This means that they are alive in their graves. They hear the speech and the salutation made to them. The actions of their community and their blessings are presented to them and by their blessings they are pleased and pray for them.

Chapter 359

WHICH IS THE HOUR ON FRIDAY WHEN THE PRAYER IS ACCEPTED BY ALLAH ?

(1043) Jābir b. 'Abd Allah reported the Apostle of Allah (may peace be upon him) as saying : Friday is divided into twelve hours. Amongst them there is an hour in which a Muslim does not ask Allah for anything but He gives it to him. So seek it in the last hour after the afternoon prayer.

(1044) Abū Burdah b. Abī Mūsā al-Asha'rī said : 'Abd Allah b. 'Umar said to me : Did you hear your father narrating a tradition from the Apostle of Allah (may peace be upon him) about an hour on Friday (when supplication is accepted by Allah)? I said : Yes, I heard it. I heard the Apostle of Allah (may peace be upon him) say : This hour is found during the period when the *imām* is seated (for giving Friday sermon) until the prayer is finished.

Abū Dāwūd said : By sitting is meant sitting on the pulpit.

Chapter 360

THE EXCELLENCE OF FRIDAY

(1045) If anyone performs ablution, doing it well, then comes to the Friday prayer, listens and keeps silence, his sins between that time and the next Friday will be forgiven, with three days extra ;[515] but he who touches pebbles has caused an interruption.[516]

(1046) 'Alī said on the pulpit in the mosque of Kūfah : When Friday comes, the devils go to the markets with their flags, and involve people in their needs and prevent them from the Friday prayer. The angels come early in the morning, sit at the door of the mosque, and record that so-and-so came at the first hour, and so-and-so came at the second hour until the *imām* comes out (for preaching). When a man sits in a

515. A Muslim is most fortunate in getting the reward for his virtues. If he does one good act, he gets its reward ten times more according to the Qur'ān This refers to the same theory that one gets reward ten times for one's good action. A week contains seven days. Hence three days more were added to them to make the reward ten times. Thus by offering the Friday prayer Allah forgives the sins of a Muslim for ten days (*'Awn al-Ma'būd*, I, 406).

516. This refers to removing or playing with the pebbles while the *imām* is delivering the sermon. It is necessary to keep silence when the sermon is delivered. If one removes the pebbles or plays with them or does a similar action, one violates the rules of sermon as if one speaks during sermon. The basic meanings of *lagha* are "he has spoken" or "deviated from what is right". The idea seems to be that one who makes a sound by removing pebbles during the sermon has hindered others from hearing it (*'Awn al-Ma'būd*, I, 406).

place where he can listen (the sermon) and look (at the *imām*), keeps silence and does not interrupt, he will get a double reward. If he keeps himself away, and sits in a place where he cannot listen (to the sermon), and keeps silence, and does not interrupt, he will get the reward only once. If he sits in a place where he can listen (to the sermon) and look (at the *imām*), and he did not keep silence, he will have the burden of it. If anyone says to his companion sitting beside him to be silent (while the *imām* is preaching), he is guilty of idle talk. Anyone who interrupts (during the sermon), will get nothing (no reward) on that Friday. Then he (the narrator) says in the end of this tradition: I heard the Apostle of Allah (may peace be upon him) say so.

Abū Dāwūd said: This tradition has been narrated by al-Walīd b Muslim from Ibn Jābir. This version adds: *bi'l-rabā'ith* (instead of *al-rabā'ith*, needs preventing the people from prayer). Further, this adds: Freed slave of his wife Umm 'Uthmān b. 'Aṭā'.

Chapter 361

THREAT FOR LEAVING THE FRIDAY PRAYER

(1047) Al-Ja'd al-Ḍamrī who was a Companion reported the Apostle of Allah (may peace be upon him) as saying: He who leaves the Friday prayer (continuously) for three Fridays on account of slackness, Allah will print a stamp on his heart.[517]

Chapter 362

EXPIATION FOR LEAVING THE FRIDAY PRAYER

(1048) Samurah b. Jundub reported the Prophet (may peace be upon him) as saying: If anyone omits the Friday prayer without excuse, he must give a dīnār in alms, or if he does not have as much, then half a dīnār.

Abū Dāwūd said: Khālid b. Qais reported this tradition in this manner, but he disagreed in respect of chain (of transmitters) and agreed in respect of the text.

(1049) Qudāmah b. Wābirah reported the Apostle of Allah (may peace be upon him) as saying: If anyone omits the Friday prayer without excuse, he must give one

517. This means that sometimes a man commits a sin and he is deprived of many virtues because of that sin. The giving up of the Friday prayer is a great sin. If a person leaves it for three weeks or more, he becomes hard-hearted and does not feel the graveness of the sin.

dirham or half a dirham, or one ṣā‘ or half a ṣā‘ of wheat, in alms.[518]

Abū Dāwūd said: Sa‘īd b. Bashīr reported this tradition in a like manner, except that he narrated "one mudd or half a mudd" (instead of ṣā‘). He narrated it from Samurah.

Chapter 363

THE PERSONS ON WHOM THE FRIDAY PRAYER IS OBLIGATORY

(1050) ‘Ā'ishah, the wife of the Prophet (may peace be upon him), said: The people used to attend the Friday prayer from their houses and from the suburbs of Medina.[519]

(1051) ‘Abd Allah b. ‘Amr reported the Prophet (may peace be upon him) as saying: The Friday prayer is obligatory on him who hears the call.[520]

Abū Dāwūd said: This tradition has been transmitted by a group of narrators from Sufyān. They did not narrate it as a statement of the Prophet (may peace be upon him); only Qabīṣah has transmitted it as a saying of the Prophet (may peace be upon him).

518. This shows that nothing has been prescribed for atonement for the omission of the Friday prayer. One can give one dīnār or half a dīnār, one dirham or half a dirham, one ṣā' or half a ṣā' and one mudd or half a mudd of wheat. But this expiation will only alleviate the acrimony of the sin. It will not totally remove it. Therefore, one must repent for one's sin along with the expiation. Further, the expiation, giving something in alms, is not necessary. It is only commendable (*‘Awn al-Ma‘būd*, I, 407).

519. The original Arabic word is *‘awālī* which means the highlands at a distance of three or four miles form Medina towards the east. The area extended to eight miles. The people residing in this locality used to attend the Friday prayer in Medina.

This tradition shows that people residing at a distance of three or four miles should attend the mosque to offer Friday prayer in the city. Those who live at a long distance may offer Friday prayer in their own locality. The people of Qubā' in the suburb of Medina held their Friday congregation in their own locality during the time of the Prophet (may peace be upon him). Against this tradition the Ḥanafīs hold that it is not permissible to offer the Friday prayer in a small village. The congregation of the Friday prayer can be held, in their opinion, in big cities.

Further, this tradition also indicates that all the Muslims of a city should offer the Friday prayer in one mosque. This is the view of Abū Ḥanīfah. Mālik and al-Shāfi‘ī'. Aḥmad b. Ḥanbal allows to offer it in separate mosques if the city is densely populated (*‘Awn al-Ma‘būd*. I, 408-09).

520. This does not mean that one who does not hear the call is not required to offer the Friday prayer. This means that one must leave one's work after the call and proceed for prayer as required by the Qur'ān. The Friday prayer is obligatory on all those who live in the city, whether they hear the call or not. This tradition is weak and has been criticised by the experts of traditions (*‘Awn al-Ma‘būd*, I, 409).

Chapter 364

FRIDAY PRAYER ON A RAINY DAY

(1052) Abū al-Malīḥ reported on the authority of his father ('Āmir b. Usāmah):[521] The rain was falling on the day when the Battle of Ḥunain took place. The Prophet (may peace be upon him), therefore, commanded that the people should offer their prayer in their camps.[522]

(1053) Abū al-Malīḥ said: That took place on a Friday.[523]

(1054) Abū al-Malīḥ reported on the authority of his father that he attended the Prophet (may peace be upon him) on the occasion of the treaty of al-Ḥudaibīyah on Friday. The rain fell as little as the soles of the shoes of the people were not wet. He (the Prophet) commanded them to offer Friday prayer in their dwellings.

Chapter 365

PERMISSION TO KEEP AWAY FROM ATTENDING THE CONGREGATIONAL PRAYER ON A COLD NIGHT

(1055) Nāfi' said: Ibn 'Umar stayed at Ḍajnān (a place between Mecca and Medina) on a cold night. He commanded an announcer (to announce). He announced that the people should offer prayer in their dwellings. Ayyūb said: Nafi' narrated on the authority of Ibn 'Umar that whenever there was a cold or rainy night, the Apostle of Allah (may peace be upon him) commanded the announcer (to announce). He announced to offer prayer in the dwellings.[524]

(1056) Nāfi' reported: Ibn 'Umar made the call to prayer at Ḍajnān (a place between Mecca and Medina). Then he announced: "Offer prayer in your dwellings." He then narrated a tradition from the Apostle of Allah (may peace be upon him). He used to command an announcer who made the call to prayer. He then announced: "Pray in your dwellings" on a cold or rainy night during journey.

Abū Dāwūd said: This tradition has been narrated by Ḥammād b. Salamah from Ayyūb and 'Ubaid Allah. In his version he added: During journey on a cold

521. Opinion is divided about the name of his father: 'Āmir b. Usāmah, Zaid b. Usāmah, Usāmah b. 'Āmir, 'Umair b. Usāmah. He came from the tribe of Huzail and lived in Basrah (*'Awn al-Ma būd*, I, 410).

522. Another tradition indicates that this incident happened on a Friday. This refers to the Friday prayer. The Prophet (may peace be upon him) provided convenience to the people by granting them concession to offer prayer at home on a rainy day.

523. Since there was no mention of Friday in the tradition, the narrator explained it.

524. This indicates that the Prophet (may peace be upon him) did not want to put the people to hardship. He granted concession to the people due to rain or cold to offer prayer at home.

or a rainy night.

(1057) Nāfi' said: Ibn 'Umar made the call to prayer at Ḍajnān (a place between Mecca and Medina), on a cold and windy night. He added the words at the end of the call: "Lo! pray in your dwellings. Lo! pray in the dwellings." He then said: The Apostle of Allah (may peace be upon him) used to command the *mu'adhdhin* to announce, "Lo! pray in your dwellings," on a cold or rainy night during journey.

(1058) Nāfi' said: Ibn 'Umar made the call to prayer on a cold and windy night. He then said: "Lo! pray in the dwellings." Afterwards he said: Whenever there was a cold or rainy night, the Apostle of Allah (may peace be upon him) used to command the *mu'adhdhin* to announce: "Lo! pray in the dwellings."

(1059) Ibn 'Umar said: The announcer of the Apostle of Allah (may peace be upon him) announced for that (to pray at homes) at Medina on a rainy night or a cold morning.

Abū Dāwūd said: This tradition has also been narrated by Yaḥyā b. Sa'īd al-Anṣārī from al-Qāsim from Ibn 'Umar from the Prophet (may peace be upon him). This version adds the words "During the journey."

(1060) Jābir said: We were in the company of the Apostle of Allah (may peace be upon him) during a journey. The rain fell upon us. The Apostle of Allah (may peace be upon him) said: Anyone who wants to pray in his dwelling may pray.

(1061) Ibn Sīrīn said: Ibn 'Abbās said to his *mu'adhdhin* on a rainy day: "When you utter the words 'I testify that Muḥammad is the Apostle of Allah," do not say, "Come to prayer" but say "Pray at your homes." By this (announcement) the people were surprised. He said: One who was better than me has done it. The Friday prayer is an obligatory duty. But I disliked to put you to hardship so that you might walk in mud and rain.

Chapter 366

THE RULE OF LAW ABOUT OFFERING THE FRIDAY PRAYER BY A SLAVE AND A WOMAN

(1062) Ṭāriq b. Shihāb reported the Prophet (may peace be upon him) as saying: The Friday prayer in congregation is a necessary duty for every Muslim,[525] with four

525. The Friday prayer is valid only in congregation. If one misses the congregation one should offer the noon prayer alone and not the Friday prayer. The number of persons required for the validity of the congregation of the Friday prayer is disputed. According to Abū Ḥanīfah, the minimum number is three excluding the *imām*. According to others, it is necessary that forty persons should be present in the congregation of the Friday prayer. The traditionists hold that the congregation of the Friday prayer is valid by the attendance of the persons less than forty (*'Awn al-Ma'būd*, I, 412, 415).

exceptions; a slave, a woman, a boy, and a sick person.[526]

Abū Dāwūd said: Ṭāriq b. Shihāb had seen the Prophet (may peace be upon him) but not heard anything from him.

Chapter 367

ON OFFERING THE FRIDAY PRAYER IN A VILLAGE

(1063) Ibn 'Abbās said: The Friday prayer first offered in Islam after the Friday prayer offered in the mosque of the Apostle of Allah (may peace be upon him) is the Friday prayer offered at Juwāthā, a village from the villages of al-Baḥrain. The narrator 'Uthmān said: It is a village from the villages of the tribe of 'Abd al-Qais.[527]

(1064) 'Abd al-Raḥmān b. Ka'b b. Mālik said: When Ka'b b. Mālik heard the call to prayer on Friday, he prayed for As'ad b. Zurārah. I asked him: What is the matter that when you hear the call to prayer, you pray for As'ad b. Zurārah? He replied: This is because he held the Friday prayer for the first time for us at Hazm al-Nabīt of Ḥarrah belonging to Banū Bayāḍah in Naqī', called Naqī' al-Khadumāt.[528]

526. Friday prayer is not obligatory on a traveller. But in case he hears the call to the Friday prayer, he should attend it (*'Awn al-Ma'būd*, I, 413).

527. This indicates that offering the Friday prayer in a village is permissible. But this depends on the fact that Juwāthā was a village. It is disputed whether Juwāthā was a village or a city. According to al-Jawharī and al-Zamakhsharī, Juwāthā was a fort in al-Baḥrain, Abū al-Ḥasan al-Lakhmī holds the view that it was a city. It is possible that Juwāthā might be a small village in the beginning; later on it might have been developed into a city. It should be noted that the word *qaryah* applies to both the city and the village. Hence it cannot be argued from this tradition that the Friday prayer is permissible in a small village.

There is a difference of opinion amongst the jurists on the validity of the Friday prayer in a village. According to Abū Ḥanīfah, the Friday prayer is not permissible in a village. It is valid only in a city or a big town. The other jurists hold that it is also valid in a village. Both groups adduce arguments in support of their view (*'Awn al-Ma'būd*, I 413).

528. Name of a place in Medina where water collected in large quantity.

It should be noted that this place was a part of Medina and not a separate locality. Hence this cannot be adduced in support of the validity of holding the Friday prayer in a village. The best way of proving the validity of the Friday prayer in a village is that one should say that the Friday prayer is obligatory on the authority of the Qur'ān and the *Sunnah*. The injunction of the Qur'ān is absolute and unconditioned. There is no mention of the word "the city" in the Qur'ānic verse The Ḥanafīs argue from the tradition reported by 'Alī: No *tashriq* (uttering a supplication on the occasion of 'Īd al-Aḍḥā) and Friday prayer are valid except in a city. But this tradition is not a statement of the Prophet (may peace be upon him). On the contrary, 'Umar wrote to the people of al-Baḥrain: Offer Friday prayer wherever you might be. Moreover, al-Baihaqī reported a tradition of the Prophet (may peace be upon him): The Friday prayer is obligatory on the people of every village although there live four persons. Further, it is already established that the Companions

I asked him: How many were you at that time? He said: Forty.[529]

Chapter 368

SYNCHRONISATION OF THE FRIDAY PRAYER AND THE 'ĪD PRAYER

(1065) Iyās b. Abī Ramlah al-Shāmī said: I witnessed Mu'āwiyah b. Abī Sufyān asking Zaid b. Arqam: Did you offer along with the Apostle of Allah (may peace be upon him) the Friday and 'Īd prayers synchronised on the same day? He said: Yes. He asked: How did he do? He replied: He offered the 'Īd prayer, then granted concession to offer the Friday prayer, and said: If anyone wants to offer it, he may offer.[530]

(1066) 'Aṭā' b. Abī Rabāḥ said: Ibn al-Zubair led us in the 'Īd prayer on Friday early in the morning. When we went to offer the Friday prayer, he did not come out to us. So we prayed ourselves alone. At that time Ibn 'Abbās was present in al-Ṭā'if. When he came to us, we mentioned this (incident) to him. He said: He followed the *sunnah*.[531]

(1067) 'Aṭā' said: The Friday and the 'Īd prayers synchronised during the time of Ibn al-Zubair. He said: Two festivals ('Īd and Friday) synchronised on the same day. He combined them and offered two *rak'ahs* in the morning and did not add anything to them until he offered the afternoon prayer.

(1068) Abū Hurairah reported the Apostle of Allah (may peace be upon him) as saying: Two festivals ('Īd and Friday) have synchronised on this day. If anyone

offered the Friday prayer both in a jungle and a city. This is the view held by traditionists, al-Shāfi'ī, Aḥmad, and Isḥāq.

529. This shows that forty persons are required for the validity of the Friday prayer. But other traditions indicate that only four persons are sufficient.

530. This shows that it is not necessary to offer the Friday prayer for those who offer the 'Īd prayer. But they are not exempted from offering the noon (*ẓuhr*) prayer. This is held by a group of scholars. Al-Shāfi'ī, and some other scholars maintain that it is necessary to offer both the Friday and the 'Īd prayers. This tradition in their opinion, is weak (*'Awn al-Ma'būd*, I, 416).

531. Al-Shawkānī observes: What is more correct in the opinion of al-Shāfi'ī is that it is necessary for the people of a city to offer both the 'Īd and the Friday prayers. But it is not necessary for the people who come from the villages and from the outskirts of the city to offer the Friday prayer They may offer it if they like. According to Abū Ḥanīfah, it is necessary for the people of a city to offer both the 'Īd and the Friday prayers. According to Aḥmad b. Ḥanbal, to offer the Friday prayer is necessary neither for the people of a city nor for the people of the villages in case they offer the 'Īd prayer. The Friday prayer is exonerated from them by offering the 'Īd prayer. But they should offer the noon prayer. 'Aṭā' is of opinion that it is not necessary to offer both the Friday and the noon prayer if the people had offered the 'Īd prayer. They should offer the afternoon prayer (*'Awn al-Ma'būd*, I, 417).

does not want to offer the Friday prayer, the 'Id prayer is sufficient for him. But we shall offer the Friday prayer.

This tradition has been narrated by 'Umar from Shu'bah.[532]

Chapter 369

WHAT IS RECITED IN THE MORNING PRAYER ON FRIDAY

(1069) Ibn 'Abbās said: The Apostle of Allah (may peace be upon him) used to recite in the morning prayer on Friday Sūrah Tanzīl al-Sajdah (xxxii.) and Sūrah al-Dahr (lxxvi.).[533]

(1070) This tradition has also been transmitted through a different chain of narrators. This version adds: In the Friday prayer he would recite Sūrah al-Jumu'ah (lxii.) and Sūrah al-Munāfiqūn (lxiii.).[534]

Chapter 370

WEARING CLEAN DRESS FOR OFFERING THE FRIDAY PRAYER

(1071) 'Abd Allah b. 'Umar said: 'Umar b. al-Khaṭṭāb saw a silken suit sold at the gate of the mosque. He said: Apostle of Allah, would that you purchase this suit and wear it on Friday and on the occasion when a delegation (from the outside) comes to you. The Apostle of Allah (may peace be upon him) said: One who has no share in the afterlife will put on this (suit). Afterwards suits of similar nature were brought to the Apostle of Allah (may peace be upon him). He gave 'Umar b. al-Khaṭṭāb one of these suits. 'Umar said: Apostle of Allah, you are giving it to me for use while you had told me such-and-such about the suit of 'Uṭārid (i.e. sold by 'Uṭārid). The Apostle of Allah (may peace be upon him) said: I did not give it to you that you should wear it. Hence 'Umar gave it to his brother who was a disbeliever at Mecca for wearing.[535]

532. This shows that it is better to offer the Friday prayer. There is no harm if one does not offer. But it is necessary to offer the noon prayer.

533. It is to be noted that the recitation of these *sūrahs* in the morning prayer is only commendable and not necessary. There is no harm if one recites other *sūrahs*.

534. To recite these *sūrahs* in the Friday prayer is also commendable. One may recite other *sūrahs* too.

535. It is not lawful for men to wear silken clothes. Hence the Prophet (may peace be upon him) forbade 'Umar to wear it. But other traditions of the Prophet (may peace be upon him) indicate that it is permissible for women to wear silken clothes.

(1072) 'Abd Allah b. 'Umar said: 'Umar b. al-Khaṭṭāb saw a suit of silken cloth being sold in the market. He took it and brought it to the Apostle of Allah (may peace be upon him), and said: Purchase it and decorate with it on 'Īd and on the occasion of the arrival of some delegations. The narrator then narrated the tradition. The former version is complete.

(1073) Muḥammad b. Yaḥyā b. Ḥabbān reported the Apostle of Allah (may peace be upon him) as saying: What is the harm if any of you has two garments, if he can provide, for Friday (prayer) in addition to the two garments for his daily work?[536]

'Amr reported from Ibn Ḥabīb from Mūsā b. Sa'd from Ibn Ḥabbān from Ibn Salām who heard this (tradition) from the Apostle of Allah (may peace be upon him) on the pulpit.

Abū Dāwūd said: This tradition has been reported by Yūsuf b. 'Abd Allah b. Salām from the Prophet (may peace be upon him) through a different chain of narrators.

Chapter 371

ON MAKING A CIRCLE (IN THE MOSQUE) ON FRIDAY BEFORE OFFERING THE PRAYER

(1074) 'Amr b. Shu'aib reported from his father on the authority of his grandfather: The Apostle of Allah (may peace be upon him) prohibited buying and selling in the mosque, announcing aloud about a lost thing, the recitation of a poem in it, and prohibited sitting in a circle (in the mosque) on Friday before the prayer.[537]

Chapter 372

ON THE CONSTRUCTION OF A PULPIT

(1075) Abū Ḥāzim b. Dīnār said: People came to Sahl b. Sa'd al-Sā'idī, when they were doubtful about the kind of wood of the pulpit (in the mosque of the

536. This shows that it is commendable to change the clothes for offering the Friday prayer. The Prophet (may peace be upon him) advised to have a separate suit of clothes for Friday prayer because the clothes used every day become dirty by daily work. This tradition indicates that one should wear a clean dress on Friday for offering prayer.

537. There were no separate buildings for education during the time of the Prophet (may peace be upon him). The people used to sit in circles in the mosques and received religious knowledge. As the Prophet (may peace be upon him) exhorted the people to come early in the mosque for the Friday prayer, he prohibited them from sitting in circles for the acquisition of knowledge for it might interrupt the people in prayer (*'Awn al-Ma'būd*, I, 419).

Prophet). They asked him about it. He said: By Allah, I know (the wood) of which it was made; I saw it the first day when it was placed there, and the first day when the Apostle of Allah (may peace be upon him) sat on it. The Apostle of Allah (may peace be upon him) sent for a woman whom Sahl named and asked her: Order your boy,[538] the carpenter, to construct for me a wooden pulpit so that I sit on it when I deliver a speech to the people. So she ordered him and he made a pulpit of a wood called ṭarfā taken from al-Ghābah (a place at a distance of nine miles from Medina). He brought it to her. She sent it to the Apostle of Allah (may peace be upon him). He ordered and that was placed here. I saw the Apostle of Allah (may peace be upon him) praying on it: he said: "Allah is most great"; he then bowed while he was on it; then he returned and prostrated in the root of the pulpit; he then returned (to the pulpit). When he finished (the prayer), he addressed himself to the people and said: O people, I did this so that you may follow me and know my prayer.[539]

(1076) Ibn 'Umar said: When the Prophet (may peace be upon him) became fat, Tamīm al-Dārī said to him: Should I make for you a pulpit, Apostle of Allah, that will bear the burden of your body? He said: Yes. So he made a pulpit consisting of two steps.[540]

Chapter 373

THE PLACE OF THE PULPIT

(1077) Salamah b. al-Akwa' said: The space between the pulpit of the Apostle of Allah (may peace be upon him) and the wall (of the mosque) was such that a goat could pass.[541]

Chapter 374

THE OFFERING OF PRAYER ON FRIDAY BEFORE MERIDIAN

(1078) Abū Qatādah said: The Prophet (may peace be upon him) disapproved of

538. The name of this boy who was a carpenter was Maimun.

539. This tradition shows that the *imām* should recite the sermon or deliver a lecture on the pulpit in the mosque. Further, the Prophet (may peace be upon him) offered prayer on the pulpit to display the actions of the prayer to the people on a higher place.

540. It should be noted that Tamīm al-Dārī himself did not make the pulpit. He got it constructed by some carpenter and he was Maimūn.

The other point is that many other traditions show that the pulpit of the Prophet (may peace be upon him) consisted of three steps while this tradition indicates only two. The commentators have reconciled these traditions by saying that the narrator did not count the step on which the Prophet used to sit (*'Awn al-Ma'būd*, I, 421).

541. This means that the pulpit was not stuck to the wall. It was placed at a distance from it.

the offering of prayer at the meridian except on Friday. The Hell-fire is kindled except on Friday.[542]

Abū Dāwūd said : This is a *mursal* tradition (i.e. the successor is narrating it directly from the Prophet). Mujāhid is older than Abū al-Khalīl, and Abū al-Khalīl did not hear (any tradition from) Abū Qatādah.

Chapter 375

THE TIME OF FRIDAY PRAYER

(1079) Anas b. Mālik said : The Apostle of Allah (may peace be upon him) used to offer the Friday prayer when the sun declined.[543]

(1080) Salamah b. al-Akwa' reported on the authority of his father : We used to offer the Friday prayer along with the Apostle of Allah (may peace be upon him) and return (to our homes) while no shade of the walls was seen (at that time).[544]

(1081) Sahl b. Sa'd said : We had a siesta or lunch after the Friday prayer.[545]

Chapter 376

THE CALL TO PRAYER ON FRIDAY

(1082) Al-Sā'ib b. Yazīd said: During the time of the Prophet (may peace be upon him) and Abū Bakr and 'Umar the call to the Friday prayer was first made at the time when the *imām* was seated on the pulpit (for giving the sermon). When the time of 'Uthmān came, and the people became abundant, 'Uthmān ordered to make a third[546] call to the Friday prayer. It was made on al-Zaurā' (a house in Medina). The rule of action continued to the same effect.

(1083) Sā'ib b. Yazīd said : The call to the (Friday) prayer was made at the gate of the mosque in front of the Apostle of Allah (may peace be upon him) when he sat on the pulpit, and of Abū Bakr and 'Umar. The narrator then repeated the same tradition as reported by Yūnus.

542. It is disapproved to offer supererogatory prayer at meridian except on Friday.

543. According to Abū Ḥanīfah, Mālik and al-Shāfi'ī, the time of the Friday prayer is after the sun passes the meridian. It is not lawful before it. But, according to Aḥmad b. Ḥanbal, the Friday prayer is lawful even before the meridian (*'Awn al-Ma'būd*, I, 422).

544. This tradition apparently corroborates the viewpoint of Aḥmad b. Ḥanbal that the Friday prayer is permissible before the meridian.

545. This also shows that the Prophet (may peace be upon him) used to offer the Friday prayer in the early hours either just after the sun had passed the meridian or before it.

546. The third call refers to the *adhān* which is pronounced in the beginning on Friday. The second call is uttered when the *imām* gives the sermon. The third call is the *iqāmah* made just before the prayer.

(1084) Sā'ib said: There was no other *mu'adhdhin* (pronouncer) of the Apostle of Allah (may peace be upon him) except Bilāl.

The narrator then reported the tradition to the same effect.

(1085) Sā'ib b. Yazīd said: There was only one *mu'adhdhin* of the Apostle of Allah (may peace be upon him). He then narrated the tradition which is incomplete.[547]

Chapter 377

IT IS PERMISSIBLE FOR THE *IMAM* TO SPEAK TO A CERTAIN PERSON DURING THE DELIVERY OF THE SERMON FOR THE FRIDAY PRAYER

(1086) Jābir said: When the Apostle of Allah (may peace be upon him) seated himself on the pulpit on a Friday he said, Sit down. Ibn Mas'ūd heard that and sat down at the door of the mosque, and when the Apostle of Allah (may peace be upon him) saw him, he said: Come here, 'Abd Allah b. Mas'ūd.

Abū Dāwūd said: This tradition is known as *mursal* (the successor reports directly from the Prophet, omitting the name of the Companion). The people narrated it from the Prophet (may peace be upon him) on the authority of 'Aṭā'. Makhlad is his teacher.[548]

Chapter 378

THE *IMĀM* SHOULD FIRST SEAT HIMSELF ON THE PULPIT WHEN HE ASCENDS IT

(1087) Ibn 'Umar said: The Prophet (may peace be upon him) used to deliver two sermons. He would sit down when he ascended the pulpit till he (I think he meant the *mu'adhdhin*) finished. He would then stand up and preach, then sit down

547. This means that only one *mu'adhdhin*, i.e. Bilāl, used to pronounce the *adhān* on Friday in Medina. Ibn Umm Maktūm was also a *mu'adhdhin*, but he did not make a call to the Friday prayer. The Prophet (may peace be upon him) appointed Abū Muḥdhūrah a *mu'adhdhin* at Mecca and Sa'd at Mecca.

It should be noted that the additional call to the Friday prayer initiated by 'Uthmān during his caliphate is also a part of the *sunnah*. Those who pronounce one call to the Friday prayer in fact follow the *sunnah* of the Prophet (may peace be upon him) Abū Bakr and 'Umar. Those who pronounce two calls follow the *sunnah* of the Caliph 'Uthmān, who was a rightly-guided Caliph.

548. This shows that the *imām* is allowed to speak to the people while giving the sermon on Friday if he feels the necessity to do so.

and say nothing, then stand up and preach.[549]

Chapter 379

ON GIVING FRIDAY SERMON STANDING

(1088) Jābir b. Samurah said: The Apostle of Allah (may peace be upon him) used to deliver the sermon standing, then he would sit down, then stand and preach standing. If anyone tells you he preached sitting, he is lying. I swear by Allah that I offered along with him more than two thousand prayers.[550]

(1089) Jābir b. Samurah said: The Apostle of Allah (may peace be upon him) gave two sermons between which he sat,[551] recited the Qur'ān and gave the people an exhortation.[552]

(1090) Jābir b. Samurah said: I saw that the Prophet (may peace be upon him) would deliver the sermon standing, then sit down without saying anything. The narrator then reported the tradition in full.

549. It is commendable to sit down on the pulpit when the *mu'adhdhin* makes a call to the prayer. The *imām* should wait till he finishes the call. When the call is over he should stand and deliver the sermon. After delivering the first sermon he should sit for a short while and then stand and deliver a second sermon. It is *sunnah* (recommended) to deliver the sermon standing.

550. This includes the Friday prayers too. This does not refer to the Friday prayers in totality. Further, it should be noted that giving the sermon standing on Friday is necessary according to the majority of scholars but recommended in the opinion of Abū Ḥanīfah. Abu Bakr and 'Umar would not preach sitting. It is Mu'āwiyah who first preached sitting on the pulpit (*'Awn al-Ma'būd*, I, 427).

551. The Friday prayer is valid by giving two sermons and sitting between them. Two sermons are necessary for the Friday prayer according to the majority opinion (*'Awn al-Ma'būd*, I, 427).

552. According to al Shāfi'ī, the Friday sermon should contain the praise of Allah, blessing on the Prophet (may peace be upon him) and preaching and exhortation to the people. These three things are necessary for the validity of the Friday sermon.

According to a group of scholars, recitation of a Qur'ānic verse in the first sermon and prayer for the believers in the second are necessary. Mālik and Abū Ḥanīfah maintain that a speech or preaching to which these terms apply in their true sense is sufficient. There is no condition prescribed for preaching.

It is worthy of remark that this tradition clearly indicates that the Friday sermon was designed to teach the people the fundamentals of Islam, the laws of the *Sharī ah*, the prescriptions, and prohibitions and to explain to them the Islamic way of life. The Prophet (may peace be upon him) would preach in Arabic because his audience were Arabs. But in the non-Arab countries the *imām* should preach in the language which the people understand. In such countries a part of the sermon should consist of the Qur'ānic verses, blessing on the Prophet (may peace be upon him) and traditions and prayer for the community at large. The major part should be in the local language so that the people may understand the preaching. This is the view of the traditionists (*'Awn al-Ma'būd*, I. 428)

Chapter 380

DELIVERING SERMON ON FRIDAY LEANING ON A BOW

(1091) Shu'aib b. Zuraiq al-Ṭā'ifī said: I sat with a man who had been in the company of the Apostle of Allah (may peace be upon him). He was called al-Ḥakam b. Ḥazn al-Kulafī. He began to narrate a tradition to us saying: I came to the Apostle of Allah (may peace be upon him) in a delegation consisting of seven or nine persons. We entered upon him and said: Apostle of Allah, we have visited you, so pray Allah what is good for us. He ordered to give us some dates. The Muslims in those days were weak. We stayed there for several days and offered the Friday prayer along with the Apostle of Allah (may peace be upon him). He stood leaning on a staff or a bow.[553] He praised Allah and exalted Him in light, pure, and blessful words. Then he said: O people, you have no power to obey or you cannot obey what you are ordered. But be straight and give good tidings.

Abū 'Alī said: Did you hear Abū Dāwūd? He said: Some of my companions reminded me of some words that were omitted from writing on the paper.

(1092) Ibn Mas'ūd said: When the Apostle of Allah (may peace be upon him) addressed, he would say: Praise be to Allah, from Whom we seek help and pardon, and we seek refuge in Allah from the evils of our souls. He whom Allah guide has no one who can lead him astray, and he whom He leads astray has no one to guide him. And I bear witness that there is no god but Allah, and I bear witness that Muḥammad is His servant and apostle. He sent him before the coming of the last hour with truth giving good tidings and warning. He who obeys Allah and His Apostle follows the right path; and he who disobeys them shall harm none except himself, and he will not harm Allah in the least.[554]

(1093) Yūnus asked Ibn Shihāb about the address of the Apostle of Allah (may peace be upon him) on Friday. He mentioned it in like manner. He added: Anyone who disobeys them (Allah and His Apostle) goes astray. We beseech Allah, our Lord, to make us from those who obey Him and obey His Apostle, and follow what He likes, and abstain from His anger; we are due to Him and we belong to Him.

(1094) 'Adī b. Ḥātim said: A speaker delivered a speech in the presence of the Prophet (may peace be upon him). He said: Anyone who obeys Allah and His Apostle, and one who disobeys them. He said: Go away, you are a bad

553. This tradition shows that it is commendable to lean on a sword, a staff, or a bow while giving the Friday sermon.

554. The Prophet (may peace be upon him) used to deliver this speech on Friday, on the occasion of marriage and on some other significant occasions and in case of some need.

speaker.[555]

(1095) Bint al-Ḥārith b. al-Nu'mān said: I memorised Sūrah al-Qāf (l) from the mouth of the Apostle of Allah (may peace be upon him); he would recite it in his speech on every Friday. Our oven and his oven were the same.

Abū Dāwūd said: Rawḥ b. 'Ubādah reported on the authority of Shu'bah the name Bint Ḥārithah b. al-Nu'mān; and Ibn Isḥāq reported the name Umm Hishām bint Ḥārithah b. al-Nu'mān.

(1096) Jābir b. Samurah said: The prayer offered by the Apostle of Allah (may peace be upon him) was moderate, and the sermon given by him was (also) moderate. He would recite a few verses from the Qur'ān and exhort the people.[556]

(1097) 'Umrah reported on the authority of her sister: I memorised Sūrah al-Qāf (b) from the mouth of the Apostle of Allah (may peace be upon him); he used to recite it on every Friday.

Abū Dāwūd said: This tradition has been narrated in a similar way by Yaḥyā b. Ayyūb, Ibn Abū al-Rijāl, from Yaḥyā b. Sa'īd, from 'Umrah from Umm Hishām bint Ḥārithah b. al-Nu'mān.

(1098) This tradition has also been transmitted to the same effect through a different chain of narrators by 'Umrah from her sister 'Umrah daughter of 'Abd al-Rahmān who was older than her.

Chapter 381

RAISING HANDS ON THE PULPIT

(1099) 'Umārah b. Ruwaibah said that he saw Bishr b. Marwān (on the pulpit) praying on Friday (by raising his hands). 'Umārah said: May Allah reject these hands! I have seen the Apostle of Allah (may peace be upon him) on the pulpit gesturing no more than this pointing with his forefinger.[557]

(1100) Sahl b. Sa'd said: I never saw the Apostle of Allah (may peace be upon him) raising his hands and praying on the pulpit or otherwise. But I saw him saying (doing) this way, and he would point with his forefinger making a circle by joining the

555. The reason is that he combined the words Allah and His Apostle in a single word (i.e. them) The speech requires elucidation and elaboration of the teaching, and not hints, allusions and brevity.

556. The jurists are agreed upon the fact that the Friday sermon should be short so that the people may not be bored. The length of the preaching is of course disputed.

557. This tradition indicates that, while delivering a speech, one should not point with both of one's hands. A speaker should point with his forefinger of his right hand as the Prophet (may peace be upon him) would do.

middle finger with his thumb.[558]

Chapter 382

SHORTENING THE SERMON

(1101) 'Ammār b. Yāsir said: The Apostle of Allah (may peace be upon him) commanded us to shorten the speeches.[559]

(1102) Jābir b. Samurah al-Suwā'i said: The Apostle of Allah (may peace be upon him) would not lengthen the sermon on Friday. He would say a few words.

Chapter 383

THE SITTING OF AUDIENCE NEAR THE *IMĀM* AT THE TIME OF SERMON

(1103) Samurah b. Jundub reported the Apostle of Allah (may peace be upon him) as saying: Attend the sermon (on Friday) and sit near the *imām*, for a man keeps himself away until he will be left behind at the time of entering Paradise though he enters it.[560]

Chapter 384

THE *IMĀM* MAY SUSPEND THE SERMON IF ANYTHING HAPPENS

(1104) 'Abd Allah b. Buraidah reported on the authority of his father: The Apostle of Allah (may peace be upon him) delivered a speech to us; meanwhile al-Ḥasan and al-Ḥusain came upon there stumbling, wearing red shirts. He came down from the pulpit, took them and ascended it with them. He then said: Allah truly said: "Your property and your children are only trial" (lxiv. 15). I saw both of them,

558. The Prophet (may peace be upon him) would not raise his hands for prayer while delivering the Friday sermon. But it should be noted that there are certain traditions which indicate that the Prophet (may peace be upon him) used to raise his hands for prayer to Allah when he prayed for rain (*'Awn al-Ma'būd*, I, 431).

559. Muslim reported a tradition on the authority of 'Ammār : The length of a man's prayer and the shortness of his sermon are a sign of his understanding ; so make the prayer long and the sermon short, for there is magic in eloquence. These traditions indicate that the Friday sermon should be shorter than the prayer. One should not lengthen the sermon.

560. This means that one should sit in the first row near the *imām* so that he may hear the preaching easily and attentively. One may be deprived of higher degrees in Paradise though he enters it by sitting behind.

and I could not wait. Afterwards he resumed the speech.[561]

Chapter 385

SITTING ON HIPS BY ERECTING FEET, STICKING THEM TO THE STOMACH AND HOLDING THEM WITH HANDS OR TYING THEM WITH A CLOTH WHILE THE *IMĀM* IS DELIVERING THE SERMON

(1105) Anas said: The Apostle of Allah (may peace be upon him) prohibited to sit on hips by erecting feet, sticking them to the stomach and holding them with hands on Friday while the *imām* is delivering the sermon.[562]

(1106) Ya'la b. Shaddād b. Aws said: I came to Mu'āwiyah in Jerusalem. He led us in the Friday prayer. I saw that most of the people in the mosque were the Companions of the Prophet (may peace be upon him). I saw them sitting in *iḥtibā'* condition, i e. sitting on hips erecting the feet and sticking them to the stomach and holding them with hands or tying them with the cloth to the back, while the *imām* was giving sermon.

Abū Dāwūd said: Ibn 'Umar used to sit in *iḥtibā'* position while the *imām* gave the Friday sermon. Anas b. Mālik, Shuraiḥ, Ṣa'ṣa'ah b. Ṣawḥān, Sa'īd b. al-Musayyib, Ibrāhīm al-Nakha'ī, Makḥūl, Ismā'īl b. Muḥammad b. Sa'd, and Nu'aim b. Sulāmah said: There is no harm in sitting in *iḥtibā'* position.

Abū Dāwūd said: I do not know whether anyone considered it disapproved except 'Ubādah b. Nasayy.[563]

Chapter 386

SPEAKING WHILE THE *IMĀM* GIVES THE FRIDAY SERMON

(1107) Abū Hurairah reported the Apostle of Allah (may peace be upon him) as

561. It is permissible to break the Friday sermon if something serious happens during it. The *imām* may give instructions to someone during the sermon if he thinks it necessary to do so.

562. The original Arabic word is *ḥabwah* or *iḥtibā'*. This refers to the position of sitting like a dog, i.e. to sit on hips by erecting feet and sticking them to the stomach, and holding them with hands or tying them with a cloth. The Arabs used to sit in this position when they had to sit for a long time. The Prophet (may peace be upon him) prohibited to sit in this manner because a man feels sleep in this position and his ablution breaks.

563. According to the majority of scholars, sitting in *iḥtibā'* position while the *imām* is giving the sermon is permissible. In the opinion of a group of scholars including 'Ubādah b. Nusayy, it is disapproved (*'Awn al-Ma'būd*, I, 432).

saying: When you tell (your brother on Friday) to be silent while the *imām* is giving the sermon you are guilty of idle talk.[564]

(1108) 'Abd Allah b. 'Amr reported the Prophet (may peace be upon him) as saying: Three types of people attend Friday prayer: one is present in a frivolous way and that is all he gets from it; another comes with a supplication, Allah may grant or refuse his request as He wishes; another is present silently and quietly without stepping over a Muslim or annoying anyone, and that is an atonement for his sins till the next Friday and three days more, the reason being that Allah, the Exalted, says: "He who does a good deed will have ten times as much" (vi. 160).

Chapter 387

SEEKING PERMISSION FROM THE *IMĀM* BY A MAN WHOSE ABLUTION BREAKS

(1109) 'Ā'ishah reported the Prophet (may peace be upon him) as saying: When one of you becomes defiled during prayer, he should hold his nose and then turn away.[565]

Abū Dāwūd said: This tradition has been narrated by Ḥammād b. Salamah and Abū Usāmah from Hishām on the authority of his father from the Prophet (may peace be upon him). They did not mention the name of 'Ā'ishah.

Chapter 388

WHAT SHOULD A MAN DO WHEN HE ENTERS THE MOSQUE WHILE THE *IMĀM* IS GIVING THE FRIDAY SERMON

(1110) Jābir said: I came (to the mosque) while the Prophet (may peace be upon him) was giving the (Friday) sermon. He asked: Did you pray, so-and-so? He replied: No. He said: Stand and pray.

(1111) Jābir and Abū Ṣāliḥ reported on the authority of Abū Hurairah: Sulaik al-Ghaṭafānī came (to the mosque) while the Apostle (may peace be upon him) was giving the (Friday) sermon. He asked him: Did you pray something? He said: No.

564. This tradition indicates that all the people in the mosque should keep silence when the *imām* gives the Friday sermon. It is not permissible to recite anything, or to talk to one's companion or to give any instruction to him.

565. This is a manner by which the *imām* will understand that the man has become defiled. The other people will understand that the man has the bleeding of his nose. If anyone breaks his ablution by any way, he should hold his nose and turn away from the rows of the prayer to perform ablution afresh.

He said : Offer two *rak'ahs* of prayer and make them short.

(1112) This tradition has also been transmitted through a different chain of narrators by Jābir b. 'Abd Allah. This version adds : He (the Prophet) turned to the people and said : When one of you comes (on Friday) while the *imām* is preaching, he should pray two *rak'ahs* and make them short.[566]

Chapter 389

STEPPING OVER THE PEOPLE IN THE MOSQUE ON FRIDAY

(1113) Abū al-Zāhirīyyah said : We were in the company of 'Abd Allah b. Busr, the Companion of the Prophet (may peace be upon him), on a Friday. A man came and stepped over the people. 'Abd Allah b. Busr said : A man came and stepped over the people while the Prophet (may peace be upon him) was giving the sermon on Friday. The Prophet (may peace be upon him) said : Sit down, you have annoyed (the people).[567]

Chapter 390

WHAT SHOULD A MAN DO IF HE DOZED WHILE THE *IMĀM* IS GIVING THE SERMON ON FRIDAY?

(1114) Ibn 'Umar reported the Apostle of Allah (may peace be upon him) as saying : When any of you dozes in the mosque (on Friday), he should change his place.[568]

566. Al-Nawawī said : All such traditions strongly corroborate the view held by al-Shāfi'ī, Aḥmad, Isḥāq and the traditionists. When a man enters the mosque while the *imām* is giving the sermon he should offer two *rak'ahs* of prayer. It is disapproved to sit before praying. But one should make the prayer short to listen to the sermon (*'Awn al-Ma'būd*, I, 435).

567. It is disapproved to step over the people in the congregation of the Friday prayer in order to sit in the front rows. If one wants to sit in the front row, one should come earlier. Some scholars have allowed to step over the people to fill in the gaps in the front row or for some other necessity. Normally, one should avoid to do so (*'Awn al-Ma'būd*, I, 435).

568. If one feels sleepy in the mosque while one is waiting for the prayer, one should change one's place. This will remove the sleep and make the man alert. Sleep is sometimes attributed to devil. Once during a journey the whole caravan remained sleeping. The Prophet (may peace be upon him) ordered them to move from that place. This shows that the change of place removes laziness and averts the influence of the devil.

Chapter 391

THE *IMAM* MAY SPEAK AFTER HE DESCENDS FROM THE PULPIT

(1115) Anas said: I saw the Apostle (may peace be upon him) would descend from the pulpit and a man stop him for his need. He would remain standing with him until his need was fulfilled. Then he would stand and pray.

Abū Dawud said: This tradition is not well known from the narrator Thābit. Jarīr b. Ḥazim is the only narrator of this tradition.[569]

Chapter 392

ON A PERSON WHO OBTAINS ONE *RAK'AH* OF THE FRIDAY PRAYER

(1116) Abū Hurairah reported the Apostle of Allah (may peace be upon him) as saying: If anyone obtains a *rak'ah* in the prayer (along with the *imām*), he has obtained the whole prayer.[570]

Chapter 393

WHAT IS RECITED FROM THE QUR'ĀN IN THE FRIDAY PRAYER

(1117) Al-Nu'mān b. Bashīr said: The Apostle of Allah (may peace be upon him) used to recite at the two 'Ids (festivals) and on Friday, "Glorify the name of your most high Lord" (Surah lxxxvii.) and "Has the story of the overwhelming event reached you?" (Sūrah lxxxviii.) He said: When a festival ('Īd) and a Friday coincided,

569. It is permissible to the *imām* to talk to the people and fulfil their need when the sermon is over on Friday. The *imām* may stay for a short while to talk to the people or for some other necessity at the end of the sermon before the prayer (*'Awn al-Ma'būd*, I, 436).

570. This tradition shows that if a person obtains one *rak'ah* of the Friday prayer or of any prayer in general, he should offer the remaining *rak'ah* of the Friday prayer or the omitted *rak'ahs* of other prayers after salutation. In case he does not obtain any *rak'ah* along with the *imām* but joins the congregation in the last sitting position during the *tashahhud*, he should offer all the *rak'ahs* after salutation. According to Mālik, al-Shāfi'ī, and Aḥmad if a person obtains no *rak'ah* of the Friday prayer, but joins the prostration or the *tashahhud*, he should complete four *rak'ahs* of the noon prayer instead of the two *rak'ahs* of the Friday prayer. Abū Ḥanīfah maintains that he should offer only two *rak'ahs* of prayer after the salutation of the *imām* even if he joins the prostration or the *tashahhud* of the Friday prayer.

he recited them both (at the two prayers).[571]

(1118) Al-Ḍaḥḥāk b. Qais asked al-Nu'mān b. Bashīr: What did the Apostle of Allah (may peace be upon him) recited on Friday after reciting the Sūrah al-Jumu'ah (lxii.)? He replied: He used to recite, "Has the story of the overwhelming event reached you?" (Sūrah lxxxviii.).

(1119) Ibn Abī Rāfi' said: Abū Hurairah led us in the Friday prayer and recited Sūrah al-Jumu'ah and "When the Hypocrites come to you" (lxiii.) in the last *rak'ah*. He said: I met Abū Hurairah when he finished the prayer and said to him: You recited the two *surahs* that 'Alī used to recite at Kūfah. Abū Hurairah said: I heard the Apostle of Allah (may peace be upon him) reciting them on Friday.

(1120) Samurah b. Jundub said: The Apostle of Allah (may peace be upon him) used to recite in the Friday prayer: "Glorify the name of your most high Lord" (lxxxvii.) and "Has the story of the overwhelming event reached you?" (Sūrah lxxxviii.).

Chapter 394

ON A PERSON WHO FOLLOWS THE *IMĀM* IN A PLACE WHERE A WALL STANDS BETWEEN THEM

(1121) 'Ā'ishah said: The Apostle of Allah (may peace be upon him) offered the prayer in his apartment and the people were following him behind the apartment.[572]

Chapter 395

THE *SUNAN* PRAYER AFTER THE FRIDAY PRAYER

(1122) Nāfi' said: Ibn 'Umar saw a man praying two *rak'ahs* after the Friday prayer on the same place (where he offered the Friday prayer). He pushed him and said: Do you offer four *rak'ahs* of the Friday prayer? 'Abd Allah (b. 'Umar) used to

571. Besides these *sūrahs* the Prophet (may peace be upon him) is reported to have recited other *sūrahs* too on Friday and on the two festivals ('Īds). Hence one may recite any *sūrah* during these prayers. It is, however, recommended (*sunnah*) to recite the *sūrahs* recited by the Prophet (may peace be upon him) during the Friday and 'Īd prayers.

572. This tradition indicates that if the *imām* is outside the mosque and there is some screen or a wall between him and the people, they can follow him in the prayer. This is the view held by Mālik. The other scholars argue that the apartment mentioned in this tradition does not refer to the apartment of 'Ā'ishah or the apartments of the wives of the Prophet (may peace be upon him). This refers to a small cell that he built within the mosque. Hence, in their opinion it is necessary that the *imām* should be present in the mosque. In such a case if a wall stands between him and the people, they can follow him and their prayer will be valid. In case he stands outside the mosque and a wall stands between them, the people cannot follow him (*'Awn al-Ma'būd*, I, 437).

pray two *rak'ahs* in his house after the Friday prayer, and he used to say: This is how the Apostle of Allah (may peace be upon him) did.[573]

(1123) Nāfi' said: Ibn 'Umar used to lengthen his prayer before the Friday prayer[574] and would offer two *rak'ahs* after it in his house. He used to say that the Apostle of Allah (may peace be upon him) would do that.

(1124) 'Umar b. 'Aṭā' b. Abū al-Khuwār said that Nāfi' b. Jubair sent him to al-Sā'ib b. Yazīd b. Ukht Namir to ask him about something Mu'āwiyah had seen him do in prayer. He said: I offered the Friday prayer along with him in the enclosure.[575] When I uttered the salutation I stood up in my place and prayed. When he went in, he sent me a message saying: Never again do what you have done. When you pray the Friday prayer, you must not join another prayer to it till you have engaged in conversation or gone out,[576] for the Prophet of Allah (may peace be upon him) gave the precise command not to join on a prayer till you had engaged in conversation or gone out.

(1125) 'Aṭā' said: When Ibn 'Umar offered the Friday prayer in Mecca he would go forward and pray two *rak'ahs*, he would then go forward and pray four *rak'ahs*;

573. There are other traditions which indicate that the Prophet (may peace be upon him) used to offer four *rak'ahs* of prayer in the mosque after the Friday prayer. The scholars are of opinion that it is better to offer four *rak'ahs* instead of two *rak'ahs* of *sunan* prayer after the Friday prayer. Ibn Taimīyyah has harmonised these traditions by saying that one should say two *rak'ahs* after the Friday prayer if one says in one's house. If one offers the *sunan* prayer in the mosque after the Friday prayer one should offer four *rak'ahs* (*'Awn al-Ma'būd*, I, 439-40).

574. It should be noted that to offer *sunan* prayer before the Friday prayer is not established on the basis of sound traditions. The traditions which indicate that the Prophet (may peace be upon him) would offer four *rak'ahs* before the Friday prayer are weak. Ibn Mas'ūd is reported to have offered four *rak'ahs*, Ibn 'Umar twelve *rak'ahs* and Ibn 'Abbās eight *rak'ahs* before the Friday prayer. In fact, the people during the lifetime of the Prophet (may peace be upon him) used to attend the mosque in the early hours and would offer supererogatory prayers until the Friday prayer was offered. Hence there is no *sunan* prayer before the Friday prayer as a part of it. But one may offer two or four *rak'ahs* before it. This is not disapproved (*'Awn al-Ma'būd*, I, 438-39).

575. The enclosure (*maqṣūrah*) was a private part in the mosque. It was designed to protect the life of the caliph. Hence it was reserved for him. Mu'āwiyah is reported to have innovated it. Scholars differ on the validity of its construction in the mosque. Al-Ḥasan, al-Qāsim b. Muḥammad and Sālim and others allow its construction in the mosque, while Ibn 'Umar, al-Sha'bī, Aḥmad and Isḥāq disapprove of its construction. Another view goes that if this enclosure is allowed to be used by all, the Friday prayer is valid in it. In case it is reserved for some people, the Friday prayer is not valid (*'Awn al-Ma'būd*, I, 439).

576. This shows that there should be a break between the obligatory and *sunan* prayers. This is done in many ways. The best way is that one should offer *sunan* prayer at home. In case one offers *sunan* prayer in the mosque, one should change the place. If one offers this prayer at the same place, one should engage in conversation or do an action which separates the obligatory prayer from the *sunan* prayer. It is, however, to be emphasised that obligatory and voluntary prayers should not be joined together (*'Awn Ma'būd*, I, 439).

but when he was in Medina, he offered the Friday prayer, then returned to his house and prayed two *rak'ahs*, not praying them in the mosque. Someone mentioned this to him and he replied that the Apostle of Allah (may peace be upon him) used to do it.[577]

(1126) Abū Hurairah reported the Apostle of Allah (may peace be upon him) as saying (this is the version of the narrator Ibn al-Ṣabbāḥ): If any of you prays after the Friday prayer, he should say four *rak'ahs*. According to the version of the narrator Ibn Yūnus, the tradition goes: When you have offered the Friday prayer, pray after it four *rak'ahs*. He said: My father said to me: My son, if you have said two *rak'ahs* in the mosque, then you come to your house, pray two *rak'ahs* more.[578]

(1127) Ibn 'Umar said: The Apostle of Allah (may peace be upon him) used to pray two *rak'ahs* in his house after the Friday prayer.

Abū Dāwūd said: This tradition has been transmitted in a similar way by 'Abd Allah b. Dīnār from Ibn 'Umar.

(1128) Ibn Juraij said: 'Aṭā' told me that he saw Ibn 'Umar pray after the Friday prayer. He moved a little from the place where he offered the Friday prayer. Then he would pray two *rak'ahs*. He then walked far away from that place and would offer four *rak'ahs*. I asked 'Aṭā': How many times did you see Ibn 'Umar do that? He replied: Many times. Abū Dāwūd said: This has been narrated by 'Abd al-Malik b. Abī Sulaimān, but did not narrate it completely.[579]

Chapter 396

TO SIT BETWEEN THE TWO SERMONS

(1129) Ibn 'Umar said: The Prophet (may peace be upon him) used to give two sermons. He would sit down when he ascended the pulpit till he (I think he meant the *mu'adhdhin*) had finished. He would then stand up and preach, then sit down and say nothing, then stand up and preach.

577. It should be noted that the Prophet (may peace be upon him) is not reported to have offered the Friday prayer at Mecca. By the attribution to him Ibn 'Umar might have meant his action at Medina. It should be noted that the traditions indicate that the Prophet (may peace be upon him) had offered both two and four *rak'ahs* of prayer after the Friday prayer (*'Awn al-Ma būd*, I, 439-40).

578. This shows that it is recommended to pray two *rak'ahs* in the house as the Prophet (may peace be upon him) used to do.

579. One may say either two or four *rak'ahs* of *sunan* prayer after the Friday prayer. But it is better to say four *rak'ahs*. One may also combine both. One should, however, pray two *rak'ahs* in the house and four in the mosque.

Chapter 397

THE PRAYER AT THE TWO 'ĪDS (FESTIVALS)

(1130) Anas said: When the Apostle of Allah (may peace be upon him) came to Medina, the people had two days on which they engaged in games. He asked: What are these two days (what is the significance)? They said: We used to engage ourselves on them in the pre-Islamic period. The Apostle of Allah (may peace be upon him) said: Allah has substituted for them something better than them, the day of sacrifice and the day of the breaking of the fast.

Chapter 398

THE TIME OF PROCEEDING FOR OFFERING 'ĪD PRAYER

(1131) Yazīd b. Khumair al-Raḥbī said: 'Abd Allah b. Busr, the Companion of the Apostle of Allah (may peace be upon him) came out along with the people on the day of the breaking of the fast or on the day of sacrifice (to offer the prayer). He disliked the delay of the *imām*, and said: We would finish (our 'Īd prayer) at this moment, that is, at the time of forenoon.[580]

Chapter 399

THE COMING OUT OF THE WOMEN FOR OFFERING THE 'ĪD PRAYER

(1132) Umm 'Aṭīyyah said: The Apostle of Allah (may peace be upon him) commanded us to bring out the secluded women on the day of 'Īd (festival). He was asked: What about the menstruous women? He said: They should be present at the place of virtue and the supplication of the Muslims. A woman said: Apostle of Allah, what should we do if one of us does not possess an outer garment? He replied: Let

580. This tradition indicates that it is better to offer the 'Id prayer in the forenoon in the early hours after the sunrise. The other traditions of the Prophet (may peace be upon him) show that it is commendable to offer the prayer on the day of the breaking of the fast. The reason is that the people have to slaughter the sacrificial animals on the day of sacrifice. Hence the prayer on this occasion should be offered earlier than the prayer offered on the day of breaking the fast (*'Awn al-Ma'būd*, I, 441-42).

her friend lend a part of her garment.[581]

(1133) This tradition has also been narrated by Umm 'Aṭīyyah in a similar manner through a different chain. She added: The menstruating women should keep themselves away from the place of prayer of the Muslims. She did not mention the garment. She narrated this tradition from Ḥafṣah mentioning a woman who asked about another woman saying: O Apostle of Allah. . . . She then reported the tradition like that narrated by Mūsā mentioning the garment.

(1134) This tradition has also been narrated by Umm 'Aṭīyyah through a different chain of transmitters. She said: We were commanded to go out (for offering the 'Īd prayer). She further said: The menstruating women stood behind the people and they uttered the *takbīr* (Allah is most great) along with the people.[582]

(1135) Umm 'Aṭīyyah said: When the Apostle of Allah (may peace be upon him) came to Medina, he gathered the women of Anṣār in a house, and sent to us (to them) 'Umar b. al-Khaṭṭāb. He stood at the door and gave the salutation to us and we returned it (the salutation) to him. Thereupon, he said: I am the messenger of the Apostle of Allah (may peace be upon him) to you. He commanded us to bring out the menstruating women and the virgins for both the 'Īd prayers, and that the Friday prayer is not obligatory on us. He prohibited us to accompany the funeral procession.[583]

Chapter 400

DELIVERING THE SERMON ON 'ĪD

(1136) Abū Sa'īd al-Khudrī said: Marwān[584] brought out the pulpit on the 'Īd.

581. It is disputed whether or not the women should attend the congregational prayer of 'Īd. Abū Bakr, 'Alī and Ibn 'Umar consider it necessary for the women to attend the 'Īd prayer in the congregation 'Urwah al-Qāsim, Yaḥyā al-Anṣārī, Mālik and Abū Yūsuf maintain that the women should not attend the congregational prayer of 'Īd. The tradition, however, indicates that women should attend the congregational prayer of 'Īd. (*'Awn al-Ma'būd*, I, 442).

582 It is permissible for menstruating women to utter the *takbīr*, but they should not offer prayer.

The *takbīr* is pronounced on the day of 'Īd at four occasions, viz. (1) on the way while going towards the place of prayer ; (2) during the prayer ; (3) during the sermon ; (4) after the prayer. The majority of the jurists consider it commendable to utter the *takbīr* on the way to the place of 'Īd prayer. As regards the *takbīr* pronounced by the people along with the *imām* during the sermon, it is held only by Mālik, and rejected by others (*'Awn al-Ma'būd*, I, 443).

583. The reason of prohibition is obvious. Women are generally weak-hearted and cannot bear the calamity, and thus they might weep and cry and disturb others.

584. Marwān b. al-Ḥakam was the Umayyad Caliph, 64-65 H.

He began preaching before the prayer.[585] A man stood and said: You opposed the *sunnah*, O Marwān. You brought out the pulpit on the 'Īd; it was not brought out before; and you began preaching before the prayer. Abū Sa'īd al-Khudrī said: Who is this (man)? They (the people) said: So-and-so son of so-and-so. He has performed his duty. I heard the Apostle of Allah (may peace be upon him) say: He who observes an evil deed should change it with his hand if he can do so; if he cannot do, (he should change it) then with his tongue; if he cannot do, then (he should change it) with his heart, and that is the weakest degree of the faith.

(1137) Jābir b. 'Abd Allah said: The Prophet (may peace be upon him) stood on the day of the breaking of the fast ('Īd) and offered prayer. He began the prayer before the sermon. He then addressed the people. When the Prophet (may peace be upon him) finished the sermon, he descended (from the pulpit) and went to women. He gave them an exhortation while he was leaning on the hand of Bilāl. Bilāl was spreading his garment in which women were putting alms; some women put their rings and others other things.

(1138) Ibn 'Abbās said: The Apostle of Allah (may peace be upon him) came out on 'Īd (the festival day). He first offered the prayer and then delivered the sermon. He then went to women, taking Bilāl with him. The narrator Ibn Kathīr said: The probable opinion of Shu'bah is that he commanded them to give alms. So they began to put (their jewellery).

(1139) The above-mentioned tradition has also been narrated by Ibn 'Abbās to the same effect through a different chain of transmitters. This version adds: He (the Prophet) thought that women could not hear (his sermon). So he went to them and Bilāl was in his company. He gave them an exhortation and commanded them to give alms. Some women put their ear-rings and others their rings in the garment af Bilāl.

(1140) The above-mentioned tradition has also been transmitted by Ibn 'Abbās through a different chain of narrators. This version adds: The women began to give their ear-rings and rings in alms. Bilāl began to collect them in his garment. He (the Prophet) then distributed them among the poor Muslims.[586]

585. The sermon on the occasion of the 'Īd should be delivered after the prayer as the Prophet (may peace be upon him) used to do himself. Marwān changed this practice for certain reasons. Al-Bukhārī has recorded his reply to Abū Sa'īd al-Khudrī. He said: The people did not stay to hear the sermon after the prayer. Hence the practice was changed. It is said that during the caliphate of Marwān the people did not hear the sermon of the 'Īd prayer deliberately because it contained the condemnation of some people and exaggerated praise of others. The people contempted this practice and left the congregation after the prayer was over (*'Awn al-Ma'būd*, I, 443).

586. This tradition with its versions contains many rules of action First, the sermon on the 'Īd festival should be given after the prayer. Second, women should participate in the congregational prayer of 'Īd. Thirdly, women should observe seclusion from men. Fourthly, the *imām* should give them an exhortation and an admonition separately if they are unable to hear the

Chapter 401

DELIVERING SERMON WHILE LEANING ON A BOW

(1141) Al-Barā' said : Someone presented a bow to the Prophet (may peace be upon him) on the 'Īd (festival). So he preached leaning upon it.

Chapter 402

ABANDONING THE *ADHĀN* FOR THE 'ĪD PRAYER

(1142) 'Abd al-Raḥmān b. 'Ābis said : A man asked Ibn 'Abbās : Have you been present at the 'Īd prayer along with the Apostle of Allah (may peace be upon him)? He replied : Yes. Had there been no dignity for me in his eyes, I would not have been present with him due to my minority. Then the Apostle of Allah (may peace be upon him) came to the point that was near the house of Kathīr b. al-Ṣalt. He prayed and afterwards preached. He (Ibn 'Abbās) did not mention the *adhān* (call to prayer) and the *iqāmah*. He then commanded to give alms. The women began to point to their ears and throats (to give their jewellery in alms).[587]

(1143) Ibn 'Abbās said : The Apostle of Allah (may peace be upon him) offered the 'Īd prayer without the *adhān* and the *iqāmah*. Abū Bakr and 'Umar or 'Uthmān also did so. The narrator Yaḥyā is doubtful about 'Uthmān.

(1144) Jābir b. Samurah said : I prayed the 'Īd prayer with the Prophet (may peace be upon him) not once or twice (but many times) without the *adhān* and the *iqāmah*.

Chapter 403

ON THE NUMBER OF *TAKBĪRS* DURING THE 'ĪD PRAYER

(1145) 'Ā'ishah said : The Apostle of Allah (may peace be upon him) would say the *takbīr* (Allah is most great) seven times in the first *rak'ah* and five times in the second *rak'ah* on the day of the breaking of the fast and on the day of sacrifice (on

sermon along with men. Fifthly, women may give alms voluntarily without the permission of their husbands. Sixthly, the *imām* may demand contribution for the poor and the needy (*'Awn al-Ma'būd*, I, 144).

587. This tradition indicates that no *adhān* (call to prayer) and *iqāmah* are to be pronounced for the 'Īd prayers.

the occasion of both the 'Īd prayers, the two festivals).[588]

(1146) The above-mentioned tradition has also been narrated by Ibn Shihāb through a different chain of transmitters to the same effect. This version adds: "Except the two *takbīrs* pronounced at the time of bowing".

(1147) 'Abd b. 'Amr b. al-'Āṣ said : The Prophet of Allah (may peace be upon him) said : There are seven *takbīrs* in the first *rak'ah* and five in the second *rak'ah* of the prayer offered on the day of the breaking of the fast.

(1148) 'Amr b. Shu'aib reported from his father on the authority of his grandfather : The Prophet (may peace be upon him) used to say on the day of the breaking of the fast seven *takbirs* in the first *rak'ah* and then recite the Qur'ān, and utter the *takbīr* (Allah is most great). Then he would stand, and utter the *takbīr* four times. Thereafter he would recite the Qur'ān and bow.

Abū Dāwūd said : This has been narrated by Wakī' and Ibn al-Mubārak. Their version goes : "Seven (in the first *rak'ah*) and five (in the second)."

(1149) Abū 'Ā'ishah said : Sa'īd b. al-'Āṣ asked Abū Mūsā al-Asha'rī and Ḥudhaifah b. al-Yamān : How would the Apostle of Allah (may peace be upon him) utter the *takbīr* (Allah is most great) in the prayer on the day of sacrifice and of the breaking of the fast. Abū Mūsā said : He uttered the *takbīr* four[589] times as he did at funerals. Ḥudhaifah said : He is correct. Then Abū Mūsā said : I used to utter the *takbīr* in a similar way when I was the governor of Baṣrah. Abū 'Ā'ishah said : I was present there when Sa'īd b. al-'Āṣ asked.

588. There are different views about the number of *takbirs* during the 'Īd prayer. First, there are seven *takbirs* before the recitation of the Qur'ān in the first *rak'ah*, and five *takbirs* before the recitation of the Qur'ān in the second *rak'ah*. This is held by most of the Companions of the Prophet (may peace be upon him) and by the seven jurists of Medina, 'Umar b. 'Abd al-'Azīz, al-Zuhrī and Makḥūl. This is also the view of Mālik, al-Auzā'ī, al-Shāfi'ī, Aḥmad and Isḥāq. It is, however, to be noted that al-Shāfi'ī, al-Auzā'ī, and Isḥāq exclude the *takbir* for the beginning of the prayer in the first *rak'ah* (*takbirat al-taḥrim*). Second, the seven *takbirs* in the first *rak'ah* include the *takbīr* for the beginning of the prayer. This is held by Mālik, Aḥmad, and al-Muzanī. Third, there are seven *takbirs* in the first *rak'ah* and seven in the second. This is reported to have been held by Anas b. Mālik, al-Mughīrah b. Shu'bah, Ibn 'Abbās, Sa'īd b. al-Musayyib and al-Nakha'ī. Fourth, there are three *takbirs* in the first *rak'ah* before the recitation of the Qur'ān after the *takbirat al-taḥrim*, and three *takbirs* in the second *rak'ah* after the recitation of the Qur'ān. This is held by Ibn Mas'ūd and Abū Mūsā and Abū Mas'ūd al-Anṣārī, al-Thawrī and Abū Ḥanīfah. Fifth, there are six *takbirs* in the first *rak'ah* before the recitation of the Qur'ān after the *takbirat al-taḥrim* and five *takbirs* in the second *rak'ah* after the recitation of the Qur'ān. This is one of the opinions ascribed to Aḥmad b. Ḥanbal. One should raise one's hands at the time of pronouncing the *takbir*. But this is not established on the basis of traditions directly reported from the Prophet (may peace be upon him). This is based on the statements and practice of his Companions (*'Awn al-Ma'būd*, I, 448).

589. This refers to one *takbir* of *taḥrim* and three of the 'Īd prayer. Abū Ḥanīfah argues from this tradition. But this is a weak tradition. The narrator 'Abd al-Raḥmān b. Thawbān is weak and Abū 'Ā'ishah is unknown (*'Awn al-Ma'būd*, I, 447).

Chapter 404

WHAT IS RECITED DURING THE PRAYER ON THE DAY OF SACRIFICE AND ON THE DAY OF THE BREAKING OF THE FAST

(1150) 'Ubaid Allah b. 'Abd Allah b. 'Utbah b. Mas'ūd said : 'Umar b. al-Khaṭṭāb asked Abū Wāqid al-Laithī : What did the Apostle of Allah (may peace be upon him) recite during the prayer on the day of sacrifice and on the breaking of the fast ? He replied : He recited at both of them Surāh al-Qāf, "By the Glorious Qur'ān" (l.) and the Sūrah "The Hour[590] is nigh" (liv.).

Chapter 405

TO SIT FOR LISTENING TO THE SERMON AT THE 'ĪD PRAYER

(1151) 'Abd Allah b. al-Sā'ib said : I attended the 'Īd prayer along with the Apostle of Allah (may peace be upon him). When he finished the prayer, he said : We shall deliver the sermon ; he who likes to sit for listening to it may sit and he who likes to go away may go away.[591]

Abū Dāwūd said : This is a *mursal* tradition (i.e. the successor 'Aṭā' directly reporting from the Prophet and omitting the link of the Companions).

Chapter 406

ON GOING FOR THE 'ĪD PRAYER BY ONE ROAD AND RETURNING BY ANOTHER

(1152) Ibn 'Umar said : The Apostle of Allah (may peace be upon him) went out by one road on the day of the 'Īd (festival) and returned by another.[592]

590. It is commendable to recite these *sūrahs* during the 'Īd prayer, but not necessary.

591. This tradition shows that delivering sermon at 'Īd prayer is not necessary. That is only recommended (*sunnah*), while the sermon on Friday is necessary.

592. It is commendable to go for offering the 'Īd prayer by one road and to return by another. There may be various reasons for the change of roads, one of them being that both the roads will bear witness on the Day of Judgment.

Chapter 407

IF THE *IMĀM* DOES NOT GO OUT TO OFFER THE 'ĪD PRAYER ON ONE DAY, HE SHOULD GO OUT TO OFFER IT THE NEXT DAY

(1153) Abū 'Umair b. Anas said on the authority of some of his paternal uncles who were Companions of the Prophet (may peace be upon him): Some men came riding to the Prophet (may peace be upon him) and testified that they had sighted the new moon the previous day. He, (the Holy Prophet), therefore, commanded the people to break the fast and to go out to their place of prayer in the morning.[593]

(1154) Bakr b. Mubashshir al-Anṣārī said: I used to go to the place of prayer on the day of the breaking of the fast, and on the day of sacrifice along with the Companions of the Apostle of Allah (may peace be upon him). We would walk through a valley known as Baṭn Baṭḥān till we came to the place of prayer. Then we would pray along with the Apostle of Allah (may peace be upon him) and return through Baṭn Baṭḥān to our house.[594]

Chapter 408

TO OFFER PRAYER AFTER THE 'ĪD PRAYER

(1155) Ibn 'Abbās said: The Apostle of Allah (may peace be upon him) came out on the day of the breaking of the fast and prayed two *rak'ahs*, before and after which he did not pray.[595] He then went to women, taking Bilāl with him, and commanded

593. The moon could not be sighted in Medina on the 29th of Ramaḍān. Some people came to the Prophet (may peace be upon him) the next day and informed him that they had sighted the moon. It appears that they might have come in the afternoon. Hence the Prophet (may peace be upon him) postponed the 'Īd prayer till the next day. If the people are informed about the moon after the passing of the time of the 'Īd prayer, it can be postponed for the next day. This is held by al-Awzā'ī, al-Thawrī, Aḥmad, Isḥāq, Abū Ḥanīfah, and al-Shāfi'ī (*'Awn al-Ma'būd*, I, 450).

594. This shows that there is no harm if one goes to the place of the 'Īd prayer by one road and return by the same. The change of roads in going and returning is only commendable and not necessary.

595. The majority of scholars are of opinion that it is disapproved to offer any prayer on the place of the 'Īd prayer before and after it. There are many other views about this question. One goes that it is permissible to pray after the 'Īd prayer and not before it. This is held by al-Awzā'ī, al Thawrī, and Abū Ḥanīfah. This has been the practice of the people of Kūfah. Another view goes that it is permissible to pray before the 'Īd prayer and not after it. This has been the practice of the people of Baṣrah and held by al-Ḥasan al-Baṣrī and a group of scholars. A third view says that it is not permissible to pray before and after the 'Īd prayer. This is maintained by al-Zuhrī, Ibn Juraij, Aḥmad and Mālik and practised by the people of Medina. Mālik has prohibited to pray at

them to give alms. So one began to put her ear-ring and another her necklace (in the garment of Bilāl).

Chapter 409

ON OFFERING THE 'ĪD PRAYER IN THE MOSQUE IF THE RAIN IS FALLING

(1156) Abū Hurairah said: The rain fell on the day of 'Īd (festival), so the Prophet (may peace be upon him) led them (the people) in the 'Īd prayer in the mosque.[596]

Chapter 410

PRAYER FOR RAIN AND DETAILED INJUNCTIONS ABOUT IT

(1157) 'Abbād b. Tamīm (al-Mūzinī) reported on the authority of his uncle: The Apostle of Allah (may peace be upon him) took the people out (to the place of prayer) and prayed for rain. He led them in two *rak'ahs* of prayer[597] in the course of which he recited from the Qur'ān in a loud voice. He turned round his cloak[598] and

the place of the 'Īd prayer. but permitted to do so in the mosque according to a version attributed to him (*'Awn al-Ma'būd*, I, 451).

596. The Prophet (may peace be upon him) used to offer the 'Īd prayer usually in a vast ground outside the city. Whenever there was rain, he would say it in the mosque of Medina. But at Mecca the 'Īd prayer is usually offered in the mosque around the Ka'bah. In case the mosque of the city is immensely vast, then it is disputed whether the 'Īd prayer should be offered in the mosque or in the ground outside the city Al-Shāfi'ī holds that it is better to pray in the mosque and, according to Mālik, it is better to pray in the ground (*'Awn al-Ma'būd*, I, 451-52).

597. The majority of scholars hold that it is recommended (*sunnah*) to offer two *rak'ahs* of prayer for rain in congregation when it is dry. Abū Ḥanīfah maintains that the prayer is not commendable for rain. The people should get together and make supplication to Allah for rain. He argues from those traditions which mention only supplication and not prayer. But what is correct is to offer prayer for rain. The supplication for rain can be made in three ways: (1) to make supplication by the people together for rain without offering prayer; (2) to make supplication to Allah for rain during the sermon of the Friday prayer or after the obligatory prayers; this is better than the former; (3) to offer two *rak'ahs* of prayer collectively in a vast ground outside the city and to deliver two sermons. This prayer should be preceded by giving alms, keeping fast, repentance, doing good works and avoiding bad ones. This is the perfect way of supplication for rain (*'Awn al-Ma'būd*, I, 452).

598. By turning round the cloa kmeant to put its right side on the left shoulder and its left side on the right shoulder. Further it is turned over by making the inner side out and the outer side in. The Prophet (may peace be upon him) did so to show the change in the prevailing condition.

raised his hands, prayed for rain and faced the *qiblah*.

(1158) 'Abbād b. Tamīm al-Māzinī said on the authority of his uncle ('Abd Allah b. Zaid b 'Āṣim) who was a Companion of the Apostle of Allah (may peace be upon him): One day the Apostle of Allah (may peace be upon him) went out to make supplication for rain. He turned his back towards the people praying to Allah, the Exalted. The narrator Sulaimān b. Dāwūd said: He faced the *qiblah* and turned round his cloak and then offered two *rak'ahs* of prayer. The narrator Ibn Abī Dhi'b said: He recited from the Qur'ān in both of them. The version of Ibn al-Sarḥ adds: By it he means in a loud voice.

(1159) The above-mentioned tradition has also been transmitted by Muḥammad b. Muslim through a different chain of narrators. But there is no mention of prayer in this version. The version adds: "He turned round his cloak, putting its right side on his left shoulder and its left side on his right shoulder. Thereafter he made supplication to Allah."

(1160) 'Abd Allah b. Zaid said: The Apostle of Allah (may peace be upon him) prayed for rain wearing a black robe with ornamented border. The Apostle of Allah (may peace be upon him) wanted to reverse it from bottom to top by holding the bottom. But when it was too heavy he turned it round on his shoulders.

(1161) 'Abd Allah b. Zaid said: The Apostle of Allah (may peace be upon him) went out to the place of prayer to pray for rain. When he wanted to make supplication, he faced the *qiblah* and turned round his cloak.

(1162) 'Abd Allah b. Zaid al-Māzinī said: The Apostle of Allah (may peace be upon him) went out to the place of prayer and made supplication for rain, and turned round his cloak when he faced the *qiblah*.

(1163) Hishām b. Isḥāq b. 'Abd Allah b. Kinānah reported on the authority of his father: Al-Walīd b. 'Utbah or (according to the version of 'Uthmān) al-Wālīd b. 'Uqbah, the then governor of Medina, sent me to Ibn 'Abbās to ask him about the prayer for rain offered by the Apostle of Allah (may peace be upon him). He said: The Apostle of Allah (may peace be upon him) went out wearing old clothes in a humble and lowly manner until he reached the place of prayer. He then ascended the pulpit, but he did not deliver the sermon as you deliver (usually).[599] He remained engaged in making supplication, showing humbleness (to Allah) and uttering the *takbīr* (Allah is most great). He then offered two *rak'ahs* of prayer as done on the 'Īd (festival).

Abū Dāwūd said: This is the version of al-Nufailī. What is correct is Ibn

599. This does not mean that he did not deliver the sermon. This means that he did not deliver two sermons like that of the Friday prayer. He preached only once. Hence Abū Yūsuf holds that only one sermon is commendable at the prayer for rain. Muḥammad al-Shaibānī differs with him (*'Awn al-Ma'būd*, I, 453).

Utbah's.

Chapter 411

ON RAISING THE HANDS WHILE MAKING SUPPLICATION FOR RAIN

(1164) 'Umair, the client of Abū al-Laḥm, said that he saw the Prophet (may peace be upon him) praying for rain at Aḥjār al-Zait[600] near al-Zaurā',[601] standing, making supplication, praying for rain and raising his hands in front of his face, but not lifting them above his head.[602]

(1165) Jābir b. 'Abd Allah said: The people came to the Prophet (may peace be upon him) weeping (due to drought). He said (making supplication): O Allah! give us rain which will replenish us, abundant, fertilising and profitable, not injurious, granting it now without delay. He (the narrator) said: Thereupon the sky became overcast.

(1166) Anas said: The Prophet (may peace be upon him) was not accustomed to raise his hands in any supplication he made except when praying for rain. He would then raise them high enough so much so that the whiteness of his armpits was visible.[603]

(1167) Anas reported: The Prophet (may peace be upon him) used to make supplication for rain in this manner. He spread his hands keeping the inner side (of hands) towards the earth, so I witnessed the whiteness of his armpits.

(1168) Muḥammad b. Ibrāhīm said: A man who witnessed the Prophet (may peace be upon him) reported to me that he saw the Prophet (may peace be upon him) praying at Aḥjār al-Zait spreading his hands.

(1169) 'Ā'ishah said: The people complained to the Apostle of Allah (may peace be upon him) of the lack of rain, so he gave orders for a pulpit: It was then set up for him in the place of prayer. He fixed a day for the people on which they should come out. 'Ā'ishah said: The Apostle of Allah (may peace be upon him), when the rim of the sun appeared, sat down on the pulpit, and having pronounced the greatness of Allah and expressed His praise, he said: You have complained of drought in your abodes, and of delay in receiving rain at the beginning of its season. Allah has ordered you to supplicate Him and promised that He would answer your prayer. Then he

600. This is the name of a part of Medina It got this name because of the black stones there which seemed as if they had been smeared with oil.

601. A village near Medina.

602. This shows that one should not lift one's hands above the head while supplicating to Allah.

603 The Prophet (may peace be upon him) used to raise his hands while praying for rain a little higher than usual. It is commendable to raise hands higher while making prayer for rain.

said: Praise be to Allah, the Lord of the Universe, the Compassionate, the Merciful, the Master of the Day of Judgment. There is no god but Allah Who does what He wishes. O Allah, Thou art Allah, there is no deity but Thou, the Rich, while we are the poor. Send down the rain upon us and make what Thou sendest down a strength and satisfaction for a time. He then raised his hands, and kept raising them till the whiteness under his armpits was visible. He then turned his back to the people and inverted or turned round his cloak while keeping his hands aloft. He then faced the people, descended and prayed two *rak'ahs*. Allah then produced a cloud, and the storm of thunder and lightning came on. Then the rain fell by Allah's permission, and before he reached his mosque streams were flowing. When he saw the speed with which the people were seeking shelter, he (may peace be upon him) laughed till his back teeth were visible. Then he said: I testify that Allah is Omnipotent and that I am Allah's servant and apostle.

Abū Dāwūd said: This is a *gharīb* (rare) tradition, but its chain is sound. The people of Medina recite "*maliki*' (instead of *māliki*) *yawm al-dīn*" (the master of the Day of Judgment). But this tradition (in which the word *mālik* occurs) is an evidence for them.

(1170) Anas said: The people of Medina had drought during the time of the Prophet (may peace be upon him). While he was preaching on a Friday, a man stood and said: Apostle of Allah, the horses perished, the goats perished, pray Allah to give us water: He spread his hands and prayed. Anas said: The sky was like mirror (there was no cloud). Then the wind blasted; a cloud appeared (in the sky) and it spread over; the sky poured down the water. We came out (from the mosque after the prayer) passing through the water till we reached our homes. The rain continued till the next Friday. The same or some other person stood up and said: Apostle of Allah, the houses have been demolished, pray Allah to stop it. The Apostle of Allah (may peace be upon him) smiled and said: (O Allah), the rain may fall around us and not upon us. Then I looked at the cloud which dispersed around Medina just like a crown.

(1171) The above-mentioned tradition has been narrated by Anas through a different chain of transmitters. This version goes like the tradition reported by 'Abd al-'Azīz. It goes: The Apostle of Allah (may peace be upon him) raised his hands in front of his face and said: O Allah! give us water. The narrator then reported the tradition like the former.

(1172) 'Amr b. Shu'aib, on his father's authority, quoted his grandfather as saying: When the Apostle of Allah (may peace be upon him) prayed for rain, he said: O Allah! provide water for Thy servants and Thy cattle, display Thy mercy and give life to Thy dead land.

Chapter 412

PRAYER AT AN ECLIPSE

(1173) 'Ā'ishah said : There was an eclipse of the sun in the time of the Prophet (may peace be upon him). The Prophet (may peace be upon him) stood for a long time, accompanied by the people. He then bowed, then raised his head, then he bowed and then he raised his head, and again he bowed and prayed two *rak'ahs* of prayer. In each *rak'ah* he bowed three times. After bowing for the third time he prostrated himself.[604] He stood for such a long time that some people became unconscious on that occasion and buckets of water had to be poured on them. When he bowed, he said, Allah is most great ; and when he raised his head, he said, Allah listens to him who praises Him, till the sun became bright. Then he said : The sun and the moon are not eclipsed on account of anyone's death or on account of anyone's birth, but they are two of Allah's signs ; He produces dread in His servants by means of them. When they are eclipsed, hasten to prayer.

Chapter 413

THE VIEW THAT ONE SHOULD BOW FOUR TIMES (IN TWO *RAK'AHS* IN THE PRAYER AT AN ECLIPSE).[605]

(1174) Jābir b. 'Abd Allah said : There was an eclipse of the sun in the time of the Apostle of Allah (may peace be upon him). This was the day when Ibrāhīm, the son of the Apostle of Allah (may peace be upon him), had died. The people began to say that there was an eclipse on account of the death of Ibrāhīm. The Prophet (may peace be upon him) stood up and led the people in prayer performing six bowings and four prostrations. He said : Allah is most great, and then recited from the

604. This tradition shows that it is recommended (*sunnah*) to offer two *rak'ahs* of prayer in congregation in the event of eclipse and bow three times in every *rak'ah*. Sufyān al-Thawrī and the Ḥanafīs maintain that one should bow only once in each *rak'ah* as usual. The traditions are variant on this subject. A tradition goes that the Prophet (may peace be upon him) prayed two *rak'ahs* and bowed four times and prostrated four times (two bowings and two prostrations in each *rak'ah*). This is the view held by Mālik, al-Shāfi'ī, and Aḥmad b. Ḥanbal. The other traditions indicate that he bowed twice and prostrated four times in two *rak'ahs* ; that he bowed six times and prostrated four times in two *rak'ahs* ; and that he bowed ten times and prostrated four times in two *rak'ahs*. It appears from these various traditions that the Prophet (may peace be upon him) prolonged the prayer and bowed many times as the eclipse was prolonged ; and he shortened the prayer and bowed in a less number of times in case the eclipse became clear shortly. From this it can be inferred that the prayer at an eclipse can be long or short according to the situation (*'Awn al-Ma'būd*, I, 457-58).

605. This is the view of Mālik, al-Shāfi'ī, and Aḥmad and other scholars of Ḥijāz.

Qur'ān and prolonged the recitation. He then bowed nearly as long as he stood. He then raised his head and recited from the Qur'ān, but it was less than the first (recitation). He then bowed nearly as long as he stood. He then raised his head and then recited from the Qur'ān for the third time, but it was less than the second recitation. He then bowed nearly as long as he stood. Then he raised his head and went down for prostration. He made two prostrations. He then stood and made three bowings before prostrating himself, the preceding bowing being more lengthy than the following, but he bowed nearly as long as he stood. He then stepped back during the prayer and the rows (of the people) too stepped back along with him, Then he stepped forward and stood in his place, and the rows too stepped forward.[606] He then finished the prayer and the sun had become bright. He said : O people, the sun and the moon are two of Allah's signs ; they are not eclipsed on account of a man's death. So when you see anything of that nature, offer prayer until the sun becomes bright. The narrator then narrated the rest of the tradition.

(1175) Jābir said : There was an eclipse of the sun in the time of the Apostle of Allah (may peace be upon him) on a hot day. The Apostle of Allah (may peace be upon him) led his Companions in prayer and prolonged the standing until the people began to fall down. He then bowed and prolonged it ; then he raised his head and prolonged (the stay) ; then he bowed and prolonged it ; then he raised his head and prolonged (the stay) ; then he made two prostrations and then stood up ; then he did in the same manner. He thus performed four bowings and four prostrations.[607] Then the narrator narrated the rest of the tradition.

(1176) 'Ā'ishah, wife of the Prophet (may peace be upon him), said: There was an eclipse of the sun during the lifetime of the Apostle of Allah (may peace be upon him) came to the mosque; he stood up and uttered the *takbīr* (Allah is most great); the people stood in rows behind him; the Apostle of Allah (may peace be upon him) recited from the Qur'ān for a long time; then he uttered the *takbir* (Allah is most great) and performed bowing for a long time; then he raised his head and said: Allah listens to him who praises Him; our Lord, and to Thee be praise; then he stood up and recited from the Qur'ān for a long time, but it was less than the first (recitation); he then bowed for a long time, but it was less than the first bowing; he then said, Allah listens to him who praises Him; our Lord, and to Thee be praise. He then did so in the second *rak'ah*. He thus completed four bowings and four prostrations. The sun had become bright before he departed.

606 Some commentators have interpreted this by saying that he stepped backward when Hell was shown to him, and stepped forward when Paradise was presented to him.

607. These different traditions indicate that the Prophet (may peace be upon him) offered prayer at eclipse on various occasions in different ways. The number of bowings varied from time to time. Hence the difference of opinion amongst the jurists on the number of bowings.

(1177) 'Abd Allah b. 'Abbās said: The Apostle of Allah (may peace be upon him) prayed at the solar eclipse as reported in the tradition narrated by 'Urwah from 'Ā'ishah from the Apostle of Allah (may peace be upon him) that he offered two *rak'ahs* of prayer bowing twice in each *rak'ah*.

(1178) Ubayy b. Ka'b said: An eclipse of the sun took place in the time of the Apostle of Allah (may peace be upon him). The Prophet (may peace be upon him) led them (the people) in prayer. He recited one of the long *surahs*, bowing five times and prostrating himself twice. He then stood up for the second *rak'ah*, recited one of the long *surahs*, bowed five times, prostrated himself twice, then sat where he was facing the *qiblah* and made the supplication till the eclipse was over.

(1179) Ibn 'Abbās said: The Prophet (may peace be upon him) prayed at solar eclipse; he recited from the Qur'ān and then bowed; then he recited from the Qur'ān and then bowed; he then recited from the Qur'ān and bowed; he then recited from the Qur'ān and bowed. Then he prostrated himself and performed the second *rak'ah* similar to the first.

(1180) Samurah b. Jundub said: When I and a boy from the Anṣār were shooting (arrows) towards two of our marks, the sun was sighted by the people at two or three lances height the horizon. It became black like the black herb called *tannumah*. One of us said to his companion: Let us go to the mosque; by Allah, this incident of the sun will surely bring something new in the community of the Apostle of Allah (may peace be upon him). As we reached there, we suddenly saw he (the Prophet) had already come out (of his house). He stepped forward for a long time as much as he could do so in the prayer. But we did not hear his voice. He then performed a bowing and prolonged it as much as he could do in the prayer. But we did not hear his voice. He then prostrated himself with us and prolonged it which he never did in the prayer before. But we did not hear his voice.[608] He then did similarly in the second *rak'ah*. The sun became bright when he sat after the second *rak'ah*. Then he uttered the salutation. He then stood up, praised Allah, and extolled Him, and testified that there is no god but Allah and testified that he is His servant and apostle. Aḥmad b. Yūnus then narrated the address of the Prophet (may peace be upon him).

(1181) Qabīṣah al-Hilālī said: There was an eclipse of the sun in the time of the Apostle of Allah (may peace be upon him). He came out bewildered pulling his garment, and I was in his company at Medina. He prayed two *rak'ahs* and stood for a

608. This tradition indicates that the Prophet (may peace be upon him) recited the Qur'ān quietly in the prayer at the eclipse. This is the view of Abū Ḥanīfah and al-Shāfi'ī. But there is another tradition narrated by 'Ā'ishah which shows that he recited the Qur'ān loudly. This tradition has been transmitted by al-Bukhārī. The view that the Qur'ān should be recited loudly is held by Aḥmad, Isḥāq, Ibn Khuzaimah and Ibn al-Mundhir. Al-Nawawī has stated that al-Shāfi'ī, Mālik, Abū Ḥanīfah, al-Laith b. Sa'd and the majority of the jurists hold that one should recite the Qur'ān quietly at the solar eclipse and loudly at the lunar eclipse (*'Awn al-Ma'būd*, I, 460).

long time in them. He then departed and the sun became bright. He then said: There are the signs by means of which Allah, the Exalted, produces dread (in His servants). When you see anything of this nature, then pray as you are praying a fresh obligatory prayer.

(1182) Qabīṣah al-Hilālī said: The solar eclipse took place. . . . The narrator then narrated the tradition like that of Mūsā. The narrator again said: Until the stars appear (in the heaven).

Chapter 414

THE RECITATION OF THE QUR'ĀN IN THE PRAYER AT AN ECLIPSE

(1183) 'Ā'ishah said: There was an eclipse of the sun in the time of the Apostle of Allah (may peace be upon him). The Apostle of Allah (may peace be upon him) came out and led the people in prayer. He stood up and I guessed that he recited Sūrah al-Baqarah. The narrator then further transmitted the tradition. He (the Prophet) then prostrated himself twice, and then stood up and prolonged the recitation. Then I guessed his recitation and knew that he recited Sūrah Āl-i-'Imrān.[609]

(1184) 'A'ishah said: The Apostle of Allah (may peace be upon him) recited from the Qur'ān in a loud voice in the prayer at an eclipse.[610]

(1185) Ibn 'Abbās said: An eclipse of the sun took place. The Apostle of Allah (may peace be upon him) prayed along with the people. He stood up for a long time nearly equal to the recitation of Sūrah al-Baqarah. He then bowed. The narrator then transmitted the rest of the tradition.

Chapter 415

TO CALL THE PEOPLE FOR PRAYER AT AN ECLIPSE

(1186) 'Ā'ishah said: There was an eclipse of the sun. The Apostle of Allah (may peace be upon him) commanded a man who summoned: "The prayer will be held in congregation."[611]

609. On the basis of this and similar other traditions, Mālik, al-Shāfi'ī and Abū Ḥanīfah hold the view that one should recite the Qur'ān quietly in prayer at an eclipse.

610 This is the most sound tradition and it is followed by the majority of the traditionists. Aḥmad b. Ḥanbal, Isḥāq b. Rahwaih and a large number of scholars from among the traditionists hold the view that one should recite the Qur'ān in the prayer at an eclipse in a loud voice.

611. This tradition indicates that there is no *adhān* and *iqāmah* to be pronounced for the prayer at an eclipse. Someone may summon the people informally.

Chapter 416

TO GIVE ALMS AT AN ECLIPSE

(1187) 'Ā'ishah said: The sun and the moon are not eclipsed on account of anyone's death or on account of anyone's birth. So when you see that, supplicate Allah, declare His greatness, and give alms.[612]

Chapter 417

THE MANUMISSION OF SLAVES AT AN ECLIPSE

(1188) Asmā' said: The Prophet (may peace be upon him) used to command us to free slaves on the occasion of an eclipse.

Chapter 418

TO PERFORM BOWING TWICE IN EACH *RAK'AH* IN THE PRAYER AT AN ECLIPSE

(1189) Al-Nu'mān b. Bashīr said: There was an eclipse of the sun in the time of the Prophet (may peace be upon him). He began to pray a series of pairs of *rak'ahs* enquiring about the sun (at the end of them) till it became clear.[613]

(1190) 'Abd Allah b. 'Amr said: There was an eclipse of the sun in the time of the Apostle of Allah (may peace be upon him). The Apostle of Allah (may peace be upon him) stood up and he was not going to perform bowing till he bowed; and he was not going to raise his head till he raised (after bowing); and he was not going to prostrate himself till he prostrated himself; and he was not going to raise his head till he raised (at the end of prostration); he did similarly in the second *rak'ah*; he then puffed in the last prostration saying: Fie, Fie! He then said: My Lord, didst Thou not promise me that Thou wouldst not punish them so long as I will remain among them? Didst Thou not promise me that Thou will not punish them so long as they continue to beg pardon of Thee. The Apostle of Allah (may peace be upon him) finished the prayer, and the sun was clear. The narrator then narrated the tradition (in full).

(1191) 'Abd al-Raḥmān b. Samurah said: During the lifetime of the Apostle of

612. It is commendable to remain devoted in the prayer, supplication, remembrance of Allah and for the rich to give alms on the occasion of eclipse.

613. The word *rak'ah* might also mean bowing as this word has been used in some tradition in the same meaning. If we construe this word as bowing, then it means that the Prophet (may peace be upon him) performed bowing twice in each *rak'ah*.

Allah (may peace be upon him) I was shooting some arrows when an eclipse of the sun took place. I, therefore, threw them (the arrows) away and said: I must see how the Apostle of Allah (may peace be upon him) acts in a solar eclipse today. So I came to him; he was standing (in prayer) raising his hands, glorifying Allah, praising Him, acknowledging that He is the only Deity, and making supplication till the sun was clear. He then recited two *sūrahs* and prayed two *rak'ahs*.[614]

Chapter 419

TO OFFER PRAYER WHEN OVERWHELMING DARKNESS PREVAILS OR SOME OTHER SIMILAR CALAMITY COMES ABOUT

(1192) 'Ubaid Allah b. al-Naḍr reported on the authority of his father: Darkness prevailed in the time of Anas b. Mālik. I came to Anas and said (to him): Abū Ḥamzah, did anything like this happen to you in the time of the Apostle of Allah (may peace be upon him)? He replied: Take refuge in Allah. If the wind blew violently, we would run quickly towards the mosque for fear of the coming of the Day of Judgment.[615]

614. This does not mean that the Prophet (may peace be upon him) recited two *sūrahs* and prayed two *rak'ahs* after the eclipse came to an end. In fact, 'Abd al-Raḥmān b. Samurah found him praying and he related the story of his praying, i.e. reciting the Qur'ān, making mention of Allah and praising Him The later narrators reported the story in such a way as if he had prayed after the sun was clear. He started his prayer when the sun was eclipsed and completed one *rak'ah*; the eclipse was over when he was praying the second *rak'ah* (*'Awn al-Ma'būd*, I, 463).

615. The mosque is a central place in Muslim society. It is an important symbol of Islam. The practice of the Prophet (may peace be upon him) and his Companions shows that in the event of any calamity, such as tempest, earthquake, rainfall, flood, cyclone and eclipse, the Muslims, besides taking preventive measures, used to rush towards the mosque. This indicates that a Muslim should combine both practical means and supplication to Allah in the case of a calamity and in doing all his works.

It is reported that once in the time of the Prophet (may peace be upon him) the wind blasted. A man began to abuse it. The Prophet (may peace be upon him) said: Do not abuse it. It has been commanded by Allah. But say: I ask Thee for the good of it, and what is good in it and the good of what Thou commanded; and I take refuge in Thee from its evil, and what is evil in it, and the evil of what Thou commanded. In the case of the calamity the Muslims in the early decades of Islam remained engaged in prayer, making mention of Allah begging pardon of Him. Sometimes they used to pronounce the *takbir* (Allah is most great) in a loud voice, especially in the case of fire (*'Awn al-Ma'būd*, I, 463-64).

Chapter 420

TO PERFORM PROSTRATION IN THE EVENT OF AN ACCIDENT

(1193) 'Ikrimah said: Ibn 'Abbās was informed that so-and-so, a certain wife of the Prophet (may peace be upon him), had died. He fell down prostrating himself. He was questioned: Why do you prostrate yourself this moment? He said: The Apostle of Allah (may peace be upon him) said: When you see a portent[616] (an accident), prostrate[617] yourselves. And which portent (accident) can be greater than the death of a wife of the Prophet (may peace be upon him)?

DETAILED RULES OF LAW ABOUT THE PRAYER DURING JOURNEY

Chapter 421

THE PRAYER OF A TRAVELLER

(1194) 'Ā'ishah said: The prayer was prescribed as consisting of two *rak'ahs* both when one was resident and when travelling. The prayer while travelling was left according to the original prescription and the prayer of one who was resident was enhanced.[618]

616 The original Arabic word is *āyah* which here means a sign or indication which produces dread in the hearts of the people or predicts about the coming of a calamity.

617. This may mean both prostration and prayer. In the case of an eclipse this means prayer and in the case of other accidents this may refer to the prostration alone (*'Awn al-Ma'būd*. I, 463-64).

618. There is a difference of opinion amongst the jurists about the shortening of prayer while travelling. Al-Shāfi'ī, Mālik and majority of the scholars hold the view that both the shortening and offering the complete prayer are permissible during journey, though shortening is better. Abū Ḥanīfah maintains that the shortening of prayer is necessary during journey and to offer complete prayer is not permissible. He argues that the Prophet (may peace be upon him) mostly shortened his prayer while travelling. Al-Shāfi'ī and others contend that the Companions used to travel in the company of the Prophet (may peace be upon him) and some of them shortened their prayer and some offered them completely. Further, some of them kept fasts and others did not; but they did not criticise each other. Moreover, 'Uthmān and 'Ā'ishah did not shorten their prayers while travelling (*'Awn al-Ma'būd*, I, 464).

As regards the prescription of two *rak'ahs* of prayer, it should be noted that prayer was originally prescribed in Mecca—night prayer (*tahajjud*), then prayer for two times and then three times. These three times were morning, evening and night prayers. Five times prayer was prescribed at

(1195) Ya'lā b. Umayyah said : I remarked to 'Umar b. al-Khaṭṭāb: Have you seen the shortening of the prayer by the people today while Allah has said ; "If you fear that those who are infidels may afflict you" (iv. 101), whereas those days are gone now? He replied: I have wondered about the same matter for which you wondered. So I mentioned this to the Apostle of Allah (may peace be upon him). He said: It is an act of charity which Allah has done to you, so accept his charity.[619]

(1196) The above-mentioned tradition has also been narrated through a different chain of transmitters by 'Abd Allah b. Abī 'Ammār who narrated it in like manner.

Abū Dāwūd said: This has been transmitted by Abū 'Āṣim and Ḥammād b. Mas'adah as transmitted by Ibn Bakr.

Chapter 422

WHEN SHOULD A TRAVELLER SHORTEN HIS PRAYER?

(1197) Yaḥyā b. Yazīd al-Hannānī said: I asked Anas b. Mālik about the shortening of the prayer (while travelling). He said: When the Apostle of Allah (may peace be upon him) went out on a journey of three miles or three farsakh[620] (the narrator Shu'bah doubted), he used to pray two *rak'ahs*.[621]

the time of *Mi'raj* (Ascension) at Mecca in the ninth year before migration to Medina. At Mecca only two *rak'ahs* were prescribed, but at Medina the number of *rak'ahs* was increased to four in the noon, afternoon and night prayers (*Sirat al-Nabi*, II, 109-11).

619. Ya'lā b. Umayyah expressed his doubt that the shortening of prayer during journey was confined to the time of danger as the Qur'ānic verse indicates. The Prophet (may peace be upon him) explained it to 'Umar who had the same doubt by saying that it was a reward and blessing from Allah for the Muslims. They may shorten the prayer while travelling in normal conditions too.

According to Abū Ḥanīfah, the shortening of prayer during journey is obligatory. This is the view held by 'Alī, 'Umar, Ibn 'Umar, Ibn 'Abbās, 'Umar b. 'Abd al-'Azīz, Qatādah, al-Ḥasan. If one offers the complete prayer during journey, that should be repeated. Al-Shāfi'ī, Aḥmad and Mālik hold that one may offer complete prayer during journey, but it is better to shorten it. This view is held by 'Ā'ishah, 'Uthmān and Ibn 'Abbās. Further, it is agreed upon that the morning and evening prayers should not be shortened. Only the noon, afternoon and night prayers will be shortened and only two *rak'ahs* of the obligatory prayer will be offered (*'Awn al-Ma'būd*, I, 465).

620. There is a difference of opinion about the length of a mile. The well-known opinion is that it contains 5250 yards. A farsakh is equivalent to three miles.

621. Opinion is divided about the distance at which the prayer should be shortened during the journey. Al-Shāfi'ī, Mālik, al-Laith, al-Awzā'ī and the traditionists maintain that the prayer during the journey should be shortened in a journey covering the distance of two postal-stages (*marḥalah*) which are equivalent to forty-eight miles. According the Abū Ḥanīfah, one should shorten the prayer on a journey covering three postal-stages (*marāḥil*). In terms of days, al-Awzā'ī holds that it should be one full day's journey. According to Mālik, Isḥāq, al-Shāfi'ī, al-Ḥasan and al-Zuhrī, it should be two days' journey. In the opinion of Sufyān al-Thawrī and the Ḥanafīs that should be three days' journey (*'Awn al-Ma'būd*, I, 466).

(1198) Anas b. Mālik said: I prayed along with the Apostle of Allah (may peace be upon him) four *rak'ahs* at the noon prayer at Medina and two *rak'ahs* at the afternoon prayer in Dhū al-Ḥulaifah.[622]

Chapter 423

TO PRONOUNCE THE *ADHĀN* WHILE TRAVELLING

(1199) 'Uqbah b. 'Āmir said: I heard the Apostle of Allah (may peace be upon him) say: Allah is pleased with a shepherd of goats who calls to prayer at the peak of a mountain, and offers prayer. Allah, the Exalted, says: Look at this servant of Mine: he calls to prayer and offers it and he fears Me. So I forgive him and admit him to paradise.[623]

Chapter 424

ON OFFERING PRAYER BY A TRAVELLER DURING JOURNEY WHILE HE HAS DOUBTS ABOUT ITS CORRECT TIMING

(1200) Mishāj b. Mūsā said: I asked Anas b. Mālik: Narrate to us what you heard the Apostle of Allah (may peace be upon him) say. He said: When we travelled along with the Apostle of Allah (may peace be upon him), we would say: Did the sun pass the meridian or not? But he (the Prophet) would offer the noon prayer and then proceed.[624]

(1201) Anas b. Mālik said: When the Apostle of Allah (may peace be upon him) halted at a certain place (while on a journey), he would not leave that place till he offered the noon prayer. A man said to him: Even if in the middle of the day? He

622. Dhū al-Ḥulaifah lies at a distance of six miles from Medina. Some scholars have argued from this tradition that it is permissible to shorten prayer in a journey covering only six miles. But this is not correct. The Prophet (may peace be upon him) was indeed going to Mecca and he stopped at Dhū al-Ḥulaifah for prayer. The shortening of prayer should be started when one leaves the boundary and the last dwelling of the city (*'Awn al-Ma'būd*, I, 466).

623. It is not necessary but commendable to pronounce the *adhān* and the *iqāmah* if a person prays alone. In case many people offer prayer while travelling, they should call the *adhān* and the *iqāmah*.

624. This means that the Companions who accompanied the Prophet (may peace be upon him) during the journey were doubtful about the time of the noon prayer. But the Prophet (may peace be upon him) was well-acquainted with the definite timings of the prayer ; hence he knew the time and prayed. This does not mean that the Prophet (may peace be upon him) prayed the noon prayer before the sun had passed the meridian. From this it can be inferred that if the *imām* is familiar with the time of the prayer, the doubt of other persons will be neglected (*'Awn al-Ma'būd*, I. 467).

replied: Even if in the middle of the day.[625]

Chapter 425

ON COMBINATION OF TWO PRAYERS AT A TIME

(1202) Mu'ādh b. Jabal said: They (the Companions) proceeded on the expedition of Tabūk along with the Apostle of Allah (may peace be upon him). He combined the noon and afternoon prayers and the sunset and night prayers. One day he delayed the prayer and came out (of his dwelling) and combined the noon and the afternoon prayers. He then went in and then came out and combined the sunset and night prayers.[626]

(1203) Ibn 'Umar said that he was informed about the death of Ṣafīyyah (the wife of the Prophet) when he was at Mecca. He proceeded till the sun set and the stars shined. He said: When the Prophet (may peace be upon him) was in a hurry about something while on a journey, he would combine both these prayers. He pro-

625. This does not mean that he (the Prophet) prayed the noon prayer before the sun had passed the meridian. This only implies that the Prophet (may peace be upon him) would offer the noon prayer in the early hours just after the sun had passed the meridian. To say the noon prayer early during the journey is therefore, commendable.

626. It should be noted that all the scholars are agreed upon the fact that during the days of Ḥajj the noon and the afternoon prayers should be combined on 'Arafah and the evening and night prayers at Muzdalifah.

But there is a difference of opinion amongst the jurists about the combination of the noon and afternoon prayers, and of the sunset and night prayers while travelling and resident. There are three forms of combination, namely: (1) Apparent combination and not real (*jam' sūri*). This means that the noon or the sunset prayer should be delayed till the last hour. It should be offered in the last moment of its time and the next prayer, i.e. afternoon or the night prayer should be offered in the early moments of its time. In this way both should be offered at their right times. This is held by Abū Ḥanīfah. Sa'd b. Abī Waqqāṣ is also reported to have combined the two prayers in this way. (2) Another form of combination is to offer the afternoon prayer at the time of noon prayer and to offer the night prayer at the time of the evening prayer, thus combining both at one time. This is known as the combination of prayers at the time of preceding prayer (*jam 'taqdim*). (3) The third form is that the noon prayer should be delayed and offered at the time of the afternoon prayer and combined with it. Similarly, the evening prayer should be delayed and offered along with the night prayer at night. This is known as combination of two prayers by delaying the preceding one (*jam' ta'khir*). Both these forms are not allowed by Abū Ḥanīfah. The majority of scholars allow such a combination. The noon and afternoon prayers can be combined at noon or afternoon Likewise, the evening and the night prayers, can be combined at sunset or night. This is held by Ibn 'Abbās, 'Aṭā' b. Abī Rabāḥ, Sālim b. 'Abd Allah, Ṭāwūs, Mujāhid, al-Shāfi'ī. Isḥāq b. Rahwaih and Aḥmad b. Ḥanbal. According to the four orthodox legal scholars, these prayers can be combined while on a journey and not while resident in normal conditions. Mālik allows this in the case of heavy rain or danger. According to the traditionists, one can combine these prayers while resident due to one's heavy engagement in one's work (*'Awn al-Ma'būd*, I, 467-68).

ceeded till twilight had disappeared. He then combined both of them (the prayers).

(1204) Mu'ādh b. Jabal said: On the expedition to Tabūk if the sun had passed the meridian before the Apostle of Allah (may peace be upon him) moved off, he combined the noon and the afternoon prayers; but if he moved off before the sun had passed the meridian, he delayed the noon prayer till he halted for the afternoon prayer. He acted similarly for the sunset prayer; if the sun set before he moved off, he combined the sunset and the night prayers, but if he moved off before sunset, he delayed the sunset prayer till he halted for the night prayer and then combined them.

Abū Dāwūd said: Hishām b. 'Urwah narrated this tradition from Ḥusain b. 'Abd Allah, from Kuraib on the authority of Ibn 'Abbās from the Prophet (may peace be upon him) like the tradition narrated by Mufaḍḍal and al-Laith.

(1205) Ibn 'Umar said: The Apostle of Allah (may peace be upon him) never combined the sunset and night prayers while on a journey except once.

Abū Dāwūd said: This has been narrated by Ayyūb from Nāfi' from Ibn 'Umar as a statement of Ibn 'Umar. Ibn 'Umar was never seen combining these two prayers except on the night he was informed about the death of Ṣafīyyah. The tradition narrated by Makḥūl from Nāfi' indicates that he (Nāfi') saw Ibn 'Umar doing so once or twice.

(1206) 'Abd Allah b. 'Abbās said: The Apostle of Allah (may peace be upon him) combined the noon and afternoon prayers, and combined the sunset and night prayers without any danger or journey. Mālik said: I think it so happened during rain.[627]

Abū Dāwūd said: Ḥammād b. Salamah narrated in like manner from Abū al-Zubair; it has also been narrated by Qurrah b. Khālid from Abū al-Zubair. He said: It so happened in a journey that we made to Tabūk.

(1207) Ibn 'Abbās said: The Apostle of Allah (may peace be upon him) combined the noon and afternoon prayers, and the sunset and night prayers at Medina without any danger and rain: He was asked: What did he intend by it? He replied: He intended that his community might not fall into hardship.[628]

627. This tradition indicates clearly that it is permissible to combine two prayers when resident without any, excuse, i.e. danger or rain. Opinion is divided on the combination of two prayers while it is raining heavily. Combination of two prayers is permissible during rain according to Ibn 'Umar, 'Urwah, Ibn al-Musayyib, 'Umar b. 'Abd al-'Azīz, Abū Bakr b. 'Abd al-Rahmān and the jurists of Medina in general. This is held by Mālik, al-Shāfi'ī and Aḥmad (*'Awn al-Ma'būd*, I, 469).

628. This shows that the combination of two prayers at a time has been allowed by the Prophet (may peace be upon him) unconditionally. Sometimes a person is engaged in his work immensely, and he finds no time to offer the prayers severally; he is permitted to combine the noon and afternoon prayers, and the evening and night prayers. But it is not appreciable to do so in normal circumstances or to accustom oneself of it. This is a sort of privilege for busy people.

(1208) 'Abd Allah b. Wāqid said: The *mu'adhdhin* of Ibn 'Umar said: Prayer (i.e. the time of prayer has come). He said: Go ahead. He then alighted before the disappearance of twilight and offered the sunset prayer. He then waited till the twilight disappeared. He then offered the night prayer. He then said: When the Apostle of Allah (may peace be upon him) was in a hurry about something, he would do as I did. Then he travelled and covered a distance of three days' journey on that day.

Abū Dāwūd said: A similar tradition has been transmitted by Ibn Jābir from Nāfi' with the same chain.

(1209) This tradition has also been transmitted by Ibrāhīm b. Mūsā al-Rāzī, from 'Īsā, on the authority of Ibn Jābir to the same effect.

Abū Dāwūd said: 'Abd Allah b. al-'Alā' narrated on the authority of Nāfi', saying: When the twilight was about to disappear, he alighted and combined both (the prayers).

(1210) Ibn 'Abbās said: The Apostle of Allah (may peace be upon him) led us in prayer at Medina eight and seven *rak'ahs*, in the noon and afternoon prayers, and the sunset and night prayers. The narrators Sulaimān and Musaddad did not say the words "led us".

Abū Dāwūd said: The aforesaid tradition has also been narrated by Ṣāliḥ, the client of Tū'mah on the authority of Ibn 'Abbās, saying: "Not during rain."

(1211) Jābir said: When the sun set at Mecca, the Apostle of Allah (may peace be upon him) combined the two prayers at Sarif.[629]

(1212) Hishām b. Sa'd said: There was a distance of ten miles between them, that is, between Mecca and Sarif.

(1213) 'Abd Allah b. Dīnār said: The sun set when I was with 'Abd Allah b. 'Umar. We proceeded, and when we saw that the evening came, we said prayer. He went on travelling until the twilight disappeared and the stars became thick. He then alighted and combined the two prayers. Then he said: I saw the Apostle of Allah (may peace be upon him); when he hastened his travelling, he would pray like this prayer of mine. He said: He would combine the two prayers after the passing of a part of night. Abū Dāwūd said: This has been transmitted by 'Āṣim b. Muḥammad from his brother on the authority of Sālim and this has also been narrated by Ibn Abī Najīḥ from Ismā'īl b. 'Abd al-Raḥman b. Dhuwaib saying that Ibn 'Umar would combine the two prayers after the disappearance of twilight.

(1214) Anas b. Mālik said: When the Apostle of Allah (may peace be upon him) proceeded before the sun had declined, he delayed the noon prayer till the time of the afternoon prayer; he would then alight and combine the two prayers. If the sun declined before he moved off, he would offer the noon prayer and rode (the beast)—may peace be upon him.

629. A place near Mecca.

Abū Dāwūd said: The narrator Mufaḍḍal was the judge of Egypt. His supplication was accepted by Allah; he was the son of Fuḍālah.

(1215) The above-mentioned tradition has also been reported by 'Uqail through a different chain of narrators. He said: He would delay the evening prayer till he combined the evening and the night prayers when the twilight disappeared.

(1216) Mu'ādh b. Jabal said: The Prophet (may peace be upon him) was engaged in the Battle of Tabūk. If he moved off before the sun had declined, he would delay the noon prayer till he would combine it with the afternoon prayer and would offer them together. If he moved off after the sun had declined, he would combine the noon and afternoon prayers, and then he proceeded; if he moved off before the evening prayer, he would delay the evening prayer; he would offer it along with the night prayer. If he moved off after the evening prayer, he would offer the night prayer earlier and offer it along with the evening prayer.

Abū Dāwūd said: This tradition has not been narrated by anyone except by Qutaibah

Chapter 426

ON SHORTENING THE RECITATION OF THE QUR'ĀN DURING PRAYER WHILE TRAVELLING

(1217) Al-Barā' said: We went out on a journey along with the Apostle of Allah (may peace be upon him). He led us in the night prayer and he rcited in one of the *rak'ahs*: "By the fig and the olive" (Sūrah xcv.).

Chapter 427

TO OFFER SUPEREROGATORY PRAYER WHILE TRAVELLING

(1218) Al-Barā' said: I accompanied the Apostle of Allah (may peace be upon him) on eighteen journeys and I never saw him fail to pray two *rak'ahs* when the sun had passed the meridian before offering the noon prayer.[630]

(1219) Ḥafṣ b. 'Āṣim said: I accompanied Ibn 'Umar on the way (on a journey). He led us in two *rak'ahs* of (the noon) prayer. Then he proceeded and saw some people standing. He asked: What are they doing? I replied: They are glorifying Allah (i.e. offering supererogatory prayer). He said: If I had offered the supererogatory prayer (while travelling), I would have completed prayer, my cousin. I accompanied

630. The Prophet (may peace be upon him) might have offered these two *rak'ahs* of prayer out of gratitude or he might have prayed the *sunan* prayer before the noon prayer.

the Apostle of Allah (may peace be upon him) during the journey, he did not pray more than two *rak'ahs* until his death. I also accompanied Abū Bakr, and he prayed two *rak'ahs* and nothing more until he died. I also accompanied 'Umar, and he prayed two *rak'ahs* and nothing more until he died. I also accompanied 'Uthmān and prayed two *rak'ahs* and nothing more until he died. Allah, the Exalted, said: "Certainly you have in the Messenger of Allah an excellent exemplar" (xxxiii.).[631]

Chapter 428

TO OFFER THE SUPEREROGATORY PRAYER AND *WITR* PRAYER ON A RIDING-BEAST

(1220) Ibn 'Umar said: While travelling the Apostle of Allah (may peace be upon him) would pray voluntary prayer on his riding-beast in whatever direction it turned; and he would observe a *witr* prayer, but he did not offer the obligatory prayers upon it.[632]

(1221) Anas b. Mālik said: When the Apostle of Allah (may peace be upon him) was on a journey and wished to say voluntary prayer, he made his she-camel face the *qiblah* and uttered the *takbīr* (Allah is most great), then prayed in whatever direction his mount made him face.

(1222) 'Abd Allah b. 'Umar said: I saw the Apostle of Allah (may peace be upon him) praying on a donkey while he was facing Khaibar.[633]

(1223) Jābir said: The Apostle of Allah (may peace be upon him) sent me on some business, and when I came to him he was praying on (the back of) his riding beast (moving) towards the east and making the prostration lower than the bowing.[634]

631. It is not necessary to offer *sunan* prayer while travelling. But one is allowed to offer supererogatory prayer if one likes. In the opinion of al-Shāfi'ī and some other scholars, it is commendable to offer the *sunan* prayers while travelling. According to others, it is not even commendable to offer the *sunan* prayers during journey (*'Awn al-Ma'būd*, I, 473).

632. This shows that it is permissible to offer supererogatory prayer on a riding-beast. It is not necessary that the mount should face the *qiblah*. But it is not permissible to offer the obligatory prayers on a mount. This tradition also shows that the *witr* prayer is supererogatory; otherwise the Prophet (may peace be upon him) would not have prayed it on a mount (*'Awn al-Ma'būd*, I, 473).

633. Khaibar is not in the direction of Ka'bah from Medina.

634. This shows that he was performing prostration and bowing by making a sign. But he bowed in prostration lower than he did in bowing.

Chapter 429

TO OFFER THE OBLIGATORY PRAYER ON A RIDING-BEAST ON ACCOUNT OF SOME EXCUSE?

(1224) 'Āṭā' b. Abī Rabāḥ asked 'Ā'ishah: Can women offer prayer on a riding-beast? She replied: They were not permitted to do so in hardship or comfort. Muḥammad b. Shu'aib said: This (prohibition) applies to the obligatory prayers.

Chapter 430

WHEN SHOULD A TRAVELLER OBSERVE COMPLETE PRAYER?

(1225) 'Imrān b. Ḥuṣain said: I went on an expedition with the Apostle of Allah (may peace be upon him), and I was present with him at the conquest. He stayed eighteen days in Mecca and prayed only two *rak'ahs* (at each time of prayer). And he said: You who live in the town must pray four; we are travellers.[635]

(1226) Ibn 'Abbās said: The Apostle of Allah (may peace be upon him) had a stop of seventeen days in Mecca and he shortened the prayer (i.e. prayed two *rak'ahs* at each time of prayer). Ibn 'Abbās said: He who stays seventeen days should shorten the prayer; and he who stays more than that should offer complete prayer.[636]

Abū Dāwūd said: The other version transmitted by Ibn 'Abbās through a different

635. There is a difference of opinion amongst the jurists on the number of days in which a traveller stays at a place and observes complete prayer. Sufyān al-Thawrī and Abū Ḥanīfah maintain that if a traveller stays at a place fifteen days or more, he should observe complete prayer (i.e. four *rak'ahs*). Al-Awzā'ī holds that he should pray completely if he stays twelve days. According to Mālik, al-Shāfi'ī and Aḥmad if he stays four days, he should observe complete prayer. The number of days of stay, in the opinion of Isḥāq, is nineteen. All this depends on the intention of staying at a place. In case one does not intend to stay at a place, one should shorten the prayer though many years elapse. The difference of opinion in the number of days of stay is due to various traditions which indicate different number of days the Prophet (may peace be upon him) stayed at Mecca at the time of its fall (*'Awn al-Ma būd*, I, 475).

636. There are four versions about the period of the staying of the Prophet (may peace be upon him) in Mecca, namely, seventeen, eighteen, nineteen and fifteen days. To reconcile these varying versions it has been said that those who take nineteen days as correct add two days of coming and going to seventeen days. But those who consider seventeen days to be correct omit these two days. The advocates of eighteen days add only one day to seventeen days. Al-Nawawī regards the tradition indicating fifteen days as weak. In case it is taken as sound, it can be said that it is possible that the narrator might have considered seventeen days as correct, and omitted two days of coming and going from it. The tradition preferable out of these versions is the one which indicates nineteen days. The reason is that the majority of the sound traditions on this subject indicate the same number. Hence it was adopted by Isḥāq b. Rahwaih (*'Awn al-Ma'būd*, I, 475).

chain adds: He (the Prophet) had a stop of nineteen days (in Mecca).

(1227) Ibn 'Abbās said: The Apostle of Allah (may peace be upon him) stayed fifteen days in Mecca in the year of the Conquest, shortening the prayer.

Abū Dāwūd said: This tradition has also been transmitted by 'Abdah b. Sulaimān, Aḥmad b. Khālid al-Wahbī, and Salamah b. al-Faḍl on the authority of Ibn Isḥāq; but they did not mention the name of Ibn 'Abbās.

(1228) Ibn 'Abbās said: The Apostle of Allah (may peace be upon him) stayed in Mecca seventeen days and prayed two *rak'ahs* (at each time of prayer).

(1229) Anas b. Mālik said: We went out from Medina to Mecca with the Apostle of Allah (may peace be upon him) and he prayed two *rak'ahs* (at each time of prayer) till we returned to Medina. We (the people) said: Did you stay there for some time? He replied: We stayed there ten days.[637]

(1230) Muḥammad reported from his father 'Umar on the authority of his grandfather 'Alī b. Abī Ṭālib: When 'Alī travelled, he kept on travelling till it became nearly dark. He then alighted and offered the sunset prayer. Then he would call for his dinner and take it. Then he prayed the night prayer and then moved off. He would say: This is how the Apostle of Allah (may peace be upon him) used to do.

The narrator 'Uthmān transmitted on the authority of 'Abd Allah b. Muḥammad b. 'Umar b. 'Alī: I heard Abū Dāwūd say: Usāmah b. Zaid reported from Ḥafṣ b. 'Ubaid Allah, the son of Anas b. Mālik: Anas would combine them (the evening and night prayer) when the twilight disappeared. He said: The Prophet (may peace be upon him) used to do so. Al-Zuhrī also reported similarly on the authority of Anas from the Prophet (may peace be upon him).

Chapter 431

ON SHORTENING THE PRAYER WHEN ENCAMPED IN ENEMY TERRITORY

(1231) Jābir b. 'Abd Allah said: The Apostle of Allah (may peace be upon him) stayed at Tabūk twenty days; he shortened the prayer (during his stay).

Abū Dāwūd said: No one narrates this tradition with continuous chain except Ma'mar.[638]

637. This tradition does not contradict the tradition reported by Ibn 'Abbās because the former relates to the Farewell Pilgrimage, while the latter to the conquest of Mecca. The Prophet (may peace be upon him) on the occasion of Ḥajj stayed for ten days at Mecca (*'Awn al-Ma'būd*, I, 476).

638. If a traveller intends to stay at a certain place he should offer his prayer in full. But if he does not intend to stay, but vacillate to depart from that place, he should shorten the prayer, no matter how long he remains in this condition.

Chapter 432

PRAYER IN TIME OF DANGER

A view that the imām *should lead all the people in prayer and they should stand in two rows. He then should utter the* takbīr *(Allah is most great) along with them and bow together. Then the* imām *and the row near him should prostrate themselves, while the row behind them (i.e. the second row) should stand guard over them. Then the people in the front row should take the place of the second row, and the people in the second row should step forward in their place (in the front row). The* imām *then should bow and all of them (i.e. both the rows) should bow along with him. He then should prostrate and the row near him should also prostrate. The people in the second row should stand guard over them. When the* imām *and the row which is near him sit (for the* tashahhud*) the people in the second row should perform prostration. Then all of them should sit and the* imām *should utter the salutation along with them.*

Abū Dāwūd said : This is the opinion of Sufyān.

(1232) Abu 'Ayyāsh al-Zuraqī said : We accompanied the Apostle of Allah (may peace be upon him) at 'Usfān,[639] and Kālid b. al-Walid was the chief of unbelievers. We offered the noon prayer. Thereupon, the unbelievers said : We suffered from negligence ; we became careless. We should have attacked them while they were praying. Thereupon the verse relating to the shortening of the prayer (in time of danger) was revealed between the noon and afternoon (prayers). When the time of the afternoon prayer came, the Apostle of Allah (may peace be upon him) stood facing *qiblah*, and the unbelievers were standing in front of him. The people stood in a row behind the Apostle of Allah (may peace be upon him) and there was another row behind this row. The Apostle of Allah (may peace be upon him) bowed and all of them bowed. He then prostrated and also the row near him prostrated. The other people in the second row remained standing and stood guard over them. When they performed two prostrations and stood up, those who were behind them prostrated. The people in the front row near him then stepped backward taking the place of the people in the second row and the second row took the place of the first row. The Apostle of Allah (may peace be upon him) then bowed and all of them bowed together. Then he and the row near him prostrated themselves. The other people in the second row remained standing and stood guard over them. When the Apostle of Allah (may peace be upon him) and the row near him (i.e. the front row) were seated, the people in the second row behind them prostrated themselves. Then all of them were seated. He (the Prophet) then uttered the salutation upon all of them. He prayed in this manner at 'Usfān as well as at the territory of Banū Sulaim.

639. A place between Mecca and Medina.

Abū Dāwūd said : This tradition has been narrated by Ayyūb and Hishām from Abū al-Zubair on the authority of Jābir to the same effect from the Prophet (may peace be upon him). Similarly, this has been transmitted by Dāwūd b. Ḥuṣain from 'Ikrimah, on the authority of Ibn 'Abbās. This has also been reported by 'Abd al-Malik, from 'Aṭā' from Jābir in like manner. This has also been narrated by Qatādah from al-Ḥasan from Ḥiṭṭān on the authority of Abū Mūsā in a similar way. Similarly, this has been reported by 'Ikrimah b. Khālid from Mujāhid from the Prophet (may peace be upon him). This has also been reported by Hishām b. 'Urwah from his father from the Prophet (may peace be upon him). This is the opinion of al-Thawrī.[640]

Chapter 433

A SECOND VIEW GOES THAT THE PEOPLE SHOULD FORM A ROW ALONG WITH THE *IMĀM* AND FORM THE OTHER ROW FACING THE ENEMY. THE *IMĀM* SHOULD LEAD THE PEOPLE WHO ARE WITH HIM IN ONE *RAK'AH* AND THEN SHOULD REMAIN STANDING SO THAT THOSE WHO ARE WITH HIM MIGHT COMPLETE THE OTHER *RAK'AH*. THESE PEOPLE SHOULD THEN TURN AWAY AND FORM A ROW FACING THE ENEMY. THE OTHER SECTION SHOULD THEN COME AND THE *IMĀM* SHOULD LEAD THEM IN ONE *RAK'AH* AND HE SHOULD REMAIN SEATED IN HIS PLACE UNTIL THEY COMPLETE THE OTHER *RAK'AH* BY THEMSELVES. THE *IMĀM* SHOULD THEN UTTER THE SALUTATION ALONG WITH ALL OF THEM

(1233) Sahl b. Abī Ḥathmah said: The Prophet (may peace be upon him) prayed in time of danger and divided them (the people) behind him in two rows. He then led those who were near him in one *rak'ah*. Then he stood and remained standing till those who were in the second row offered one *rak'ah*. Thereafter they came forward and those who were in front of them (in the first row) stepped backward. The Prophet (may peace be upon him) led them in one *rak'ah* of prayer. He sat down till those

640. Al-Khaṭṭābī said : The Prophet (may peace be upon him) offered the prayer in time of danger on different occasions in different ways. In all these prayers he aimed at preserving the form of prayer as much as possible and to offer it in a way that guarded them by all means. The form of prayer mentioned in this tradition is generally adopted when the enemy is between them and the *qiblah* (*'Awn al-Ma'būd*, I. 478) :

who were in the second row completed one *rak'ah*. He then uttered the salutation.

Chapter 434

A THIRD VIEW GOES THAT WHEN THE *IMĀM* COMPLETES ONE *RAK'AH* ALONG WITH ONE SECTION, HE SHOULD REMAIN STANDING, AND THE PEOPLE BEHIND HIM SHOULD COMPLETE THE SECOND *RAK'AH* BY THEMSELVES AND UTTER THE SALUTATION. THEN THEY SHOULD TURN AWAY AND TAKE THEIR POSITION FACING THE ENEMY. OPINION IS DIVIDED ABOUT THE UTTERANCE OF THE SALUTATION

(1234) Ṣāliḥ b. Khawwāt reported on the authority of a person who offered the prayer in time of danger along with the Apostle of Allah (may peace be upon him) at the Battle of Dhat al-Riqā'.[641] One section of people stood in the row of prayer along with the Apostle of Allah (may peace be upon him) and the other section remained standing in front of the enemy. He led those who were with him in one *rak'ah* and remained standing (in his place) and they completed (the second *rak'ah*) by themselves. Then they turned away and arrayed before the enemy. Thereafter the other section came and he led them in the *rak'ah* which remained from his prayer. He then remained sitting (in his place) and they completed their one *rak'ah* by themselves. He then uttered the salutation along with them.

Mālik said: I like the tradition reported by Yazīd b. Rūmān (i.e. the present tradition) more than (other versions) I heard.[642]

(1235) Sahl b. Ḥathmah al-Anṣārī said: The prayer in time of danger should be offered in the following way: The *imām* should stand (for prayer) and a section of the people should stand along with him. The other section should stand facing the enemy. The *imām* should perform bowing and prostrate himself along with those who are with him. He then should stand (after prostration) and, when he stands straight, he should remain standing. They (the people) should (in the meantime) complete their remaining *rak'ah* (i.e. the second one). Then they should utter the salutation, and turn away while the *imām* should remain standing. They should go before the enemy. Thereafter those who did not pray should come forward and utter the *takbīr* (Allah is most great) behind the *imām*. He should bow and prostrate along with them and utter the salutation. Then they should stand and complete their remaining *rak'ah*, and utter the salutation.

641. This battle took place in 5 H.

642. This tradition is followed by Mālik and al-Shāfi'ī in the case when the enemy is behind the Muslim army. But Abū Ḥanīfah follows the tradition transmitted by Ibn 'Umar (*'Awn al-Ma'būd*, I, 479).

Abū Dāwūd said: The tradition reported by Yaḥyā b. Sa'īd from al-Qāsim is similar to the one transmitted by Yazīd b. Rūmān except that he differed with him in salutation. The tradition reported by 'Ubaid Allah is like the one reported by Yaḥyā b. Sa'īd, saying: He (the Prophet) remained standing.

Chapter 435

A FOURTH VIEW GOES THAT ALL THE PEOPLE SHOULD UTTER THE FIRST *TAKBĪR* TOGETHER, THOUGH THEIR BACK IS TOWARDS THE *QIBLAH*. THEN A SECTION OF THEM SHOULD OFFER ONE *RAK'AH* ALONG WITH THE *IMĀM*, AND GO TO THE PLACE OF THEIR COMPANIONS (FACING THE ENEMY) AND THE OTHER SECTION SHOULD COME AND OFFER ONE *RAK'AH* BY THEMSELVES. THE *IMĀM* THEN SHOULD LEAD THEM IN ONE *RAK'AH*. THEREAFTER THE SECTION WHICH STANDS BEFORE THE ENEMY SHOULD COME FORWARD AND OFFER ONE *RAK'AH* BY THEMSELVES, WHILE THE *IMĀM* SHOULD REMAIN SEATED. (WHEN THEY COMPLETE ONE *RAK'AH*) HE SHOULD UTTER THE SALUTATION ALONG WITH ALL OF THEM

(1236) 'Urwah b. al-Zubair reported that Marwān b. al-Hakam asked Abū Hurairah: Did you pray in time of danger along with the Apostle of Allah (may peace be upon him)? Abū Hurairah replied: Yes. Marwān then asked: When? Abū Hurairah said: On the occasion of the Battle of Najd.[643] The Apostle of Allah (may peace be upon him) stood up to offer the afternoon prayer. One section stood along with him (to pray) and the other was standing before the enemy, and their backs were towards the *qiblah*. The Apostle of Allah (may peace be upon him) uttered the *takbīr* and all of them too uttered the *takbīr*, i.e. those who were with him and those who were facing the enemy. Then the Apostle of Allah (may peace be upon him) offered one *rak'ah* and the section that was with him also prayed one *rak'ah*. He then prostrated himself and those who were with him also prostrated, while the other section was standing before the enemy. The Apostle of Allah (may peace be upon him) then stood up and the section with him also stood up. They went and faced

643. This is another name of the battle of Dhat al-Riqā' which took place twice. Abū Hurairah participated in the second battle.

the enemy and the section that was previously facing the enemy stepped forward. They bowed and prostrated while the Apostle of Allah (may peace be upon him) was standing in the same position. Then they stood up and the Apostle of Allah (may peace be upon him) prayed another *rak'ah* and all of them bowed and prostrated along with him. Thereafter the section that was standing before the enemy came forward and they bowed and prostrated, while the Apostle of Allah (may peace be upon him) remained seated and also those who were with him. The salutation then followed. The Apostle of Allah (may peace be upon him) uttered the salutation and all of them uttered it together. The Apostle of Allah (may peace be upon him) prayed two *rak'ahs* and each of the two sections prayed one *rak'ah* with him (and the other by themselves).

(1237) Abū Hurairah said: We went out with the Apostle of Allah (may peace be upon him) to Najd. When we reached Dhāt al-Riqā'[644] at Nakhl[645] (or in a valley with palm trees) he met a group of the tribe of Ghaṭafān. The narrator then reported the tradition to the same effect, but his version is other than that of Ḥaiwah. He added to the words "when he bowed along with those who were with him and prostrated" the words "when they stood up, they retraced their footsteps to the rows of their companions". He did not mention the words "their back was towards the *qiblah*".

Abū Dāwūd said: This tradition has been transmitted by 'Ā'ishah through a different chain of narrators. She said: The Apostle of Allah (may peace be upon him) uttered the *takbīr* and the section that were in the same row with him also uttered the *takbīr*. He then bowed and they also bowed, and he prostrated and they also prostrated. Then he raised his head and they also raised (their heads). The Apostle of Allah (may peace be upon him) then remained seated. They prostrated alone and stood up and retraced their footsteps and stood behind them. Thereafter the other section came; they stood up and uttered the *takbīr* and bowed by themselves. The Apostle of Allah (may peace be upon him) prostrated himself and they also prostrated along with him. Then the Apostle of Allah (may peace be upon him) stood up and they performed the second prostration by themselves. Then both the sections stood up and prayed with the Apostle of Allah (may peace be upon him). He bowed and they also bowed, and then he prostrated himself and they also prostrated themselves. Then he returned and performed the second prostration and they also prostrated along with him as quickly as possible, showing no slackness in quick prostration.

644. Many interpretations have been given about the name of Dhāt al-Riqā'. It is said that it is the name of a tree at that place; or it is the name of a mountain. What is correct is that it is the name of a place. Al-Nawawī says that this battle was fought in 5 H. on the land of Ghaṭafān in Najd. This battle is called Dhāt al-Riqā' because the Muslims had blisters on their feet due to walking over a long distance. They had to tie them with pieces of cloth. It is also said that they tied pieces of cloth in their flags (*'Awn al-Ma'būd*, I, 481).

645. This is the name of a place at a distance of two days' journey from Medina.

The Apostle of Allah (may peace be upon him) then uttered the salutation. Thereafter the Apostle of Allah (may peace be upon him) stood up. Thus all the people participated in the entire prayer.

Chapter 436

A FIFTH VIEW GOES THAT THE *IMĀM* SHOULD LEAD EACH OF THE SECTIONS IN ONE *RAK'AH*; THEN HE SHOULD UTTER THE SALUTATION. EACH SECTION THEN SHOULD STAND AND COMPLETE ONE *RAK'AH* BY THEMSELVES

(1238) Ibn 'Umar said: The Apostle of Allah (may peace be upon him) led one section in one *rak'ah* of prayer and the other section was facing the enemy. Then they turned away and took the position of the other section. They (the other section) came and he (the Prophet) led them in the second *rak'ah*. He then uttered the salutation. Thereafter they stood up and completed the remaining *rak'ah*; they went away and the other section completed their remaining *rak'ah*.[646]

Abū Dāwūd said: This tradition has been narrated by Nāfi' and Khālid b. Ma'dān from Ibn 'Umar in like manner from the Prophet (may peace be upon him). This has also been transmitted similarly by Masrūq and Yūsuf b. Mihrān on the authority of Ibn 'Abbās. This has been narrated by Yūnus from al-Hasan from Abū Mūsā something similarly, saying that Abū Mūsā had done so.

Chapter 437

A SIXTH VIEW GOES THAT THE *IMĀM* SHOULD LEAD EACH SECTION IN ONE *RAK'AH* AND THEN UTTER THE SALUTATION. THEREAFTER THOSE BEHIND HIM SHOULD COMPLETE THEIR SECOND *RAK'AH* BY THEMSELVES. THE OTHER SECTION THEN SHOULD TAKE THEIR PLACE AND OFFER ONE *RAK'AH*[647]

(1239) 'Abd Allah b. Mas'ūd said: The Apostle of Allah (may peace be upon him) led us in prayer in the time of danger. They (the people) stood in two rows. One row was behind the Apostle of Allah (may peace be upon him) and the other faced the enemy. The Apostle of Allah (may peace be upon him) led them in one *rak'ah*,

646. Abū Ḥanīfah follows this tradition.

647. The difference between the previous tradition reported by Ibn 'Umar and this tradition reported by Ibn Mas'ūd is that in the former case both the sections completed their prayer by themselves in the same condition and the *imām* was like a guard for them. But in the latter case they completed their prayer severally ramaining in the state of prayer (*'Awn al-Ma'būd*, I, 482).

and then the other section came and took their place; they went and faced the enemy. The Prophet (may peace be upon him) led them in one *rak'ah* and uttered the salutation. They stood up and prayed the second *rak'ah* by themselves and uttered the salutation and went away; they took the place of the other section facing the enemy. They came back and took their place. They prayed one *rak'ah* by themselves and then uttered the salutation.

(1240) This tradition has been transmitted by Khuṣaif with a different chain of narrators and to the same effect. This version adds: The Prophet of Allah (may peace be upon him) uttered the *takbīr* and both the rows uttered the *takbīr* together.

Abū Dāwūd said: This tradition has been narrated by al-Thawrī to the same effect on the authority of Khuṣaif. 'Abd al-Raḥmān b. Samurah also prayed in like manner. But the section which he (the Prophet) led in one *rak'ah* and then uttered the salutation and went and took the place of their companions. They came and prayed one *rak'ah* by themselves. Then they returned to their place and they prayed (one *rak'ah*) by themselves.

Abū Dāwūd said: Muslim b. Ibrāhīm reported from 'Abd al-Ṣamad b. Ḥabīb on the authority of his father that they had fought a battle at Kābul along with 'Abd al-Raḥmān b. Samurah. He led us in prayer in time of danger.

Chapter 438

A SEVENTH VIEW THAT THE *IMĀM* SHOULD LEAD EACH SECTION IN ONE *RAK'AH* SEVERALLY AND THEY SHOULD NOT PRAY THE SECOND *RAK'AH* BY THEMSELVES

(1241) Tha'labah b. Zahdam said: We accompanied Sa'īd b. al-'Āṣ at Ṭabaristān. He stood and said: Which of you prayed along with the Apostle of Allah (may peace be upon him) in time of danger? Ḥudhaifah said: I. Then he led one section in one *rak'ah* and the other section in one *rak'ah*. They did not pray the second *rak'ah* by themselves.

Abū Dāwūd said: This tradition has been transmitted by 'Ubaid Allah b. 'Abd Allah and Mujāhid on the authority of Ibn 'Abbās from the Prophet (may peace be upon him) in like manner. This has also been narrated by 'Abd Allah b. Shaqīq from Abū Hurairah from the Prophet (may peace be upon him). Yazīd al-Faqīr and Abū Mūsā also narrated this tradition from Jābir from the Prophet (may peace be upon him). Some of the narrators said in the version narrated by Yazīd al-Faqīr that they completed their second *rak'ah*. This has also been narrated by Simāk al-Ḥanafī on the authority of Ibn 'Umar from the Prophet (may peace be upon him) something similar. Zaid b. Thābit also narrated from the Prophet (may peace be upon him) in like manner. This version adds: The people prayed one *rak'ah* and the Prophet (may peace be upon him) prayed two *rak'ahs*.[648]

(1242) Ibn 'Abbās said: Allah, the Exalted, prescribed prayer for you, through the tongue of your Prophet (may peace be upon him), four *rak'ahs* while resident, two *rak'ahs* while travelling and one *rak'ah* in time of danger.[649]

Chapter 439

AN EIGHTH VIEW GOES THAT THE *IMĀM* SHOULD LEAD EACH SECTION IN TWO *RAK'AHS*

(1243) Abū Bakrah said: The Prophet (may peace be upon him) offered the noon prayer in time of danger. Some of the people formed a row behind him and others arrayed themselves against the enemy. He led them in two *rak'ahs* and then he uttered the salutation. Then those who were with him went away and took the position of their companions before the enemy. Then they came and prayed behind him. He led them in two *rak'ahs* and uttered the salutation. Thus the Apostle of Allah (may peace be upon him) offered four *rak'ahs* and his companions offered two *rak'ahs*. Al-Ḥasan used to give legal verdict on the authority of this tradition.

Abū Dāwūd said: This will be so in the sunset prayer. The *imām* will offer six *rak'ahs* and the people three *rak'ahs*.

Abū Dāwūd said: Yaḥyā b. Abī Kathīr narrated from Abū Salamah from Jābir from the Prophet (may peace be upon him) something similar. Sulaimān al-Yashkurī reported it from Jābir from the Prophet (may peace be upon him) in like manner.[650]

648. This shows that it is permissible to pray one *rak'ah* along with the *imām* in time of danger. This is held by al-Thawrī, Isḥāq, Abū Hurairah and Abū Mūsā al-Ash'arī. Some scholars allow one *rak'ah* in acute danger. The majority of scholars do not allow to offer one *rak'ah*. They interpret this tradition by saying that they prayed one *rak'ah* along with the Prophet (may peace be upon him) and one *rak'ah* by themselves. The text of this iradition contradicts their viewpoint (*Awn al Ma'būd*, I. 483).

649. Al-Nawawī said: Scholars like al-Ḥasan al-Baṣrī al-Daḥḥāk and Isḥāq b. Rahwaih followed this tradition literally, Mālik, al-Shāfi'ī and the majority of scholars are of opinion that the prayer in time of danger is like the one offered in time of peace in respect of the number of *rak'ahs*. If it is prayed while resident. four *rak'ahs* are necessary. In case it is offered while travelling, only two *rak'ahs* should be prayed. But in no circumstances one should offer one single *rak'ah* (*'Awn al-Ma'būd*, I, 484).

650. This shows that in time of danger the *imām* should lead each section separately in two *rak'ahs*. His first two *rak'ahs* will be obligatory and the next two supererogatory. This is also held by al Shāfi'ī, and a similar view is attributed to al-Ḥasan. Al-Taḥāwī said that this tradition has been abrogated. But there is no evidence for its abrogation (*'Awn al-Ma'būd*, I, 484).

Chapter 440

PRAYER OF A PURSUER

(1244) 'Abd Allah b. Unais said : The Apostle of Allah (may peace be upon him) sent me to Khālid b. Sufyān al-Hudhalī. This was towards 'Uranah and 'Arafāt.[651] He (the Prophet) said : Go and kill him. I saw him when the time of the afternoon prayer had come. I said : I am afraid if a fight takes place between me and him (Khālid b. Sufyān), that might delay the prayer. I proceeded walking towards him while I was praying by making a sign.[652] When I reached near him, he said to me : Who are you ? I replied : A man from the Arabs ; it came to me that you were gathering (any army) for this man (i.e. the Prophet). Hence I came to you in connection with this matter. He said : I am (engaged) in this (work). I then walked along with him for a while ; when it became convenient for me, I dominated him with my sword until he became cold (dead).

Chapter 441

THE DETAILED INJUNCTIONS ABOUT THE SUPEREROGATORY PRAYER AND THE *RAK'AHS* OF THE *SUNAN* PRAYERS

(1245) Umm Ḥabībah reported the Prophet (may peace be upon him) as saying : If anyone prays in a day and a night twelve *rak'ahs* voluntarily (supererogatory prayer), a house will be built for him in Paradise on account of these (*rak'ahs*).[653]

651. Name of a valley opposite to 'Arafāt.

652. If a man goes out in pursuit of an enemy or he is pursued by him, and there is a danger that he will be killed in case he stays a moment anywhere to pray, he is allowed to pray walking or running facing any direction. While he is walking he should make a sign of bowing and prostration. According to Abū Ḥanīfah, if a man is pursued by an enemy, there is no harm in praying while walking. But if he himself pursues it is not permissible to pray while walking. Mālik maintains that a man can offer prayer on his mount while walking. It matters little whether he pursues or is pursued by an enemy. Al-Shāfi'ī and al-Awzā'ī hold the same view as that of Abū Ḥanīfah. This is also held by 'Aṭā', al-Ḥasan, al-Thawrī, Aḥmad and Abū Thawr. Al-Shāfi'ī thinks that if a pursuer fears that he will miss the enemy, he can pray while walking. If this is not the case, he should pray in the usual manner (*'Awn al-Ma'būd*, I. 485).

653. The other traditions indicate the details of these twelve *rak'ahs*. They are : four before and two after the noon prayer, two after the sunset prayer, two after the night prayer, and two before the dawn prayer. These *sunan* prayers are called *rawātib* (prayers regularly offered by the Prophet along with the obligatory prayers and abandoned due to some valid reason or while travelling). Great emphasis has been placed on offering these *sunan* prayers in the Prophetic traditions. Hence one should not abandon them except in the case of excuse.

(1246) Abd Allah b. Shaqīq said : I asked 'Ā'ishah about the voluntary prayers offered by the Apostle of Allah (may peace be upon him). She replied : Before the noon prayer he would pray four *rak'ahs* in my house,[654] then go out and lead the people in prayer, then return to my house and pray two *rak'ahs*. He would lead the people in the sunset prayer, then return to my house and pray two *rak'ahs*. Then he would lead the people in the night prayer, and enter my house and pray two *rak'ahs*. He would pray nine *rak'ahs* during the night, including *witr* (prayer).[655] At night he would pray for a long time standing and for a long time sitting. When he recited the Qur'ān while standing, he would bow and prostrate himself from the standing position ; and when he recited while sitting, he would bow and prostrate himself from the sitting position ; and when dawn came he prayed two *rak'ahs*, then he would come out and lead the people in the dawn prayer.

(1247) 'Abd Allah b. 'Umar said : The Apostle of Allạh (may peace be upon him) would pray two[656] *rak'ahs* before and two after the noon prayer, two after the sunset prayer in his house, and two after the night prayer. He would not pray after the Friday prayer till he departed. He would then pray two *rak'ahs*.

(1248) 'Ā'ishah said : The Prophet (may peace be upon him) never omitted four *rak'ahs* before the noon prayer, and two *rak'ahs* before the dawn prayer.

Chapter 442

ON OBSERVING THE TWO *RAK'AHS* BEFORE THE DAWN PRAYER

(1249) 'Ā'ishah said : The Apostle of Allah (may peace be upon him) was more particular about observing the supererogatory *rak'ahs* before the dawn prayer than about observing any of the other supererogatory prayers.[657]

654. It is commendable to offer the *sunan* prayer in the house.

655. Literally, single or odd This is an additional prayer offered after the night prayer. This is necessary (*wājib*) according to Abū Ḥanīfah, but recommended emphatically according to others. Opinion is divided about the number of its odd *rak'ahs*.

656. The Prophet (may peace be upon him) would pray sometimes two *rak'ahs* and sometimes four *rak'ahs sunan* prayer before the noon prayer. The more preferable version is that he often used to pray four *rak ahs* before the noon prayer (*'Awn al-Ma'būd*, I, 486).

657. This tradition shows the significance of observing the *sunan* prayer before the dawn prayer. Hence some scholars, like al-Ḥasan al-Baṣrī, consider these two *rak'ahs* to be necessary (*'Awn al-Ma'būd*, I, 486).

Chapter 443

ON OBSERVING THE *SUNAN* PRAYER AT DAWN LIGHTLY

(1250) 'Ā'ishah said : The Prophet (may peace be upon him) would pray two *rak'ahs* before the dawn prayer lightly so much so that I would say : Did he recite Sūrah al-Fātiḥah in them.[658]

(1251) Abū Hurairah said : The Prophet (may peace be upon him) would recite in both *rak'ahs* of the dawn prayer : "Say, O unbelievers" (Sūrah cix.) and "Say : He is Allah, the One" (Sūrah cxii.).[659]

(1252) Ziyādat al-Kindī reported on the authority of Bilāl that he (Bilāl) came to the Apostle of Allah (may peace be upon him) to inform him about the dawn prayer. 'Ā'ishah kept Bilāl engaged in a matter which she asked him till the day was bright and it became fairly light. Bilāl then stood up and called him to prayer and called him repeatedly. The Apostle of Allah (may peace be upon him) did not yet come out. When he came out, he led the people in prayer and he (Bilāl) informed him that 'Ā'ishah had kept him engaged in a matter which she asked him till it became fairly light ; hence he became late in reaching him (in time). He (Bilāl) said : Apostle of Allah, the dawn became fairly bright. He said : If the dawn became brighter than it is now, I would pray them (the two *rak'ahs* of the *sunan* prayer), offer them well and in a more beautiful manner.

(1253) Abū Hurairah reported the Apostle of Allah (may peace be upon him) as saying : Do not omit them (the two *rak'ahs* before the dawn prayer) even if you are driven away by the horses.[660]

(1254) 'Abd Allah b. 'Abbās said : The Apostle of Allah (may peace be upon

658. As the Prophet (may peace be upon him) used to prolong the supererogatory prayers, the shortening of these two *rak'ahs* surprised her. This does not mean that he would not recite Sūrah al-Fātiḥah. This is a way of expressing the light observance.

659. It is commendable to recite these two *sūrahs* in the two *rak'ahs* before the prayer. One, however, is allowed to recfte any *sūrah* one wishes.

660. This tradition has been interpreted variantly. First, one should not omit these two *rak'ahs* even if the caravan leaves one behind. A man should pray these two *rak'ahs* even if the caravan departs and he remains behind. As such he will fall into hardship and danger. This shows the importance of these two *rak'ahs* ; one should pray them at the cost of one's life and property. Second, if a man is seeking shelter from an enemy and the enemy is running after him, even in such a situation he must not omit these *rak'ahs*. The expression is only a way of underlining the regularity in offering these *rak'ahs*. Third, if a man is riding his beast, and he is pursued by his enemy, he should pray these *rak'ahs* on the mount, in any direction he might be facing.

This tradition puts a great emphasis on saying the *sunan* prayer before the dawn prayer while travelling or resident, and in peace and danger (*'Awn al-Ma'būd*, I, 487).

him) used to recite in both *rak'ahs* of the dawn prayer: "Say: We believe in Allah and in the revelation given to us" (ii. 136). This is in the first *rak'ah*; and in the second *rak'ah* (he recited): "We believe in Allah and bear thou witness that we are submitting ones" (iii. 51).

(1255) Abū Hurairah said that he heard the Prophet (may peace be upon him) recite in both *rak'ahs* of the dawn: "Say: We believe in Allah, and in the revelation given to us" (ii. 136). This is in the first *rak'ah*. In the second *rak'ah* (he recited) this verse: "Our Lord, we believe in that which Thou hast revealed and we follow the messenger, so write us down with those who bear witness" (iii. 53); or he recited: "Surely, We have sent thee with the truth as a bearer of good news and as a warner, and thou wilt not be called upon to answer for the companions of the flaming fire" (ii. 119). Al-Darāwardī doubted (which of the verses he recited).

Chapter 444

ON LYING AFTER PRAYING THE TWO *RAK'AHS* BEFORE THE DAWN PRAYER

(1256) Abū Hurairah reported the Apostle of Allah (may peace be upon him) as saying: If any of you prays two *rak'ahs* before the dawn prayer, he should lie at his right side.[661] Marwān b. al-Ḥakam said to him: Is it not enough that one of us walks to the mosque until he lies at his right side? According to the version of 'Ubaid Allah, he (Abū Hurairah) replied: No. This statement (of Abū Hurairah) reached Ibn 'Umar. He said: Abū Hurairah exceeded limits on himself. He was asked: Do you look askance at what he says? He replied: No, but he dared and we showed cowardice. This (criticism of Ibn 'Umar) reached Abū Hurairah. He said: What is my sin if I remembered and they forgot?

(1257) 'Ā'ishah said: When the Apostle of Allah (may peace be upon him) finished his prayer late in the night, he would see. If I was awake, he would talk to

661. This tradition shows that lying on the right side is recommended (*sunnah*) after offering the *sunan* prayer before the dawn prayer. This has been narrated by 'Ā'ishah, Abū Hurairah, 'Abd Allah b. 'Abbās and 'Abd Allah b. 'Amr. This is, however, a disputed issue. Those who issued a verdict in favour of its legitimacy were Abū Mūsā al-Ash'arī, Rāfi' b. Khadīj, Anas b. Mālik and Abū Hurairah. A number of scholars from the Successors are said to have held this view. They were Ibn Sīrīn, Sa'īd b. al-Musayyib, al-Qāsim b. Muḥammad, 'Urwah b. al-Zubair Abū Bakr b. 'Abd al-Raḥmān, Khārijah b. Zaid, 'Ubaid Allah b 'Abd Allah and Sulaimān b. Yasār. Al-Shāfi'ī also held this viewpoint (*'Awn al-Ma'būd*, I. 488).

According to al-Shāfi'ī, this is recommended (*sunnah*); Mālik holds that it is innovation (*bid'āh*); Aḥmad takes it to be approved (*mustaḥabb*); it is permissible in the opinion of Abū Ḥanīfah for a man who is tired of his *tahajjud* prayer. But, according to Ibn Ḥazm, lying is necessary condition for the validity of the dawn prayer.

me. If I was sleeping, he would awaken me, and pray two *rak'ahs*, then he would lie down as long as the *mu'adhdhin* came to him and call him for the dawn prayer. Then he would pray two *rak'ahs* lightly and come out for prayer.

(1258) 'Ā'ishah said : When the Prophet (may peace be upon him) prayed the two *rak'ahs* of the dawn prayer, he would lie down if I was asleep ; in case I was awake, he would talk to me.[662]

(1259) Abū Bakrah said : I came out with the Prophet (may peace be upon him) to offer the dawn prayer. When he passed by a sleeping man he called him for prayer or moved him with his foot. The narrator Ziyād said : This tradition has been reported to us by Abū al-Faḍl.

Chapter 445

ON PRAYING THE TWO *RAK'AHS* OF THE *SUNAN* PRAYER AT THE TIME WHEN THE *IMĀM* IS LEADING THE PEOPLE IN THE OBLIGATORY PRAYER OF THE DAWN

(1260) 'Abd Allah b. Sarjas said : A man came while the Prophet (may peace be upon him) was leading the people in the dawn prayer. He prayed the two *rak'ahs* and then joined the congregational prayer led by the Prophet (may peace be upon him). When he finished the prayer, the Prophet (may peace be upon him) said : So-and-so, which was your real prayer, the one you prayed alone or the one offered with us ?[663]

(1261) Abū Hurairah reported the Apostle of Allah (may peace be upon him) as saying : When the *iqāmah* is pronounced for prayer, no prayer is valid except the obligatory prayer.[664]

662. This tradition shows that it is permissible to give a pause between the supererogatory prayer and the obligatory prayer at dawn. It is also permissible to have a talk with some person.

663. This tradition indicates that one should not offer the *sunan* prayer in the mosque when the *imām* is leading the obligatory prayer of any time. This covers all the *sunan* prayers. In the case of the dawn prayer, if a man enters the mosque and the *imām* is leading the prayer, he should join the congregation and postpone the *sunan* prayer. He may offer the *sunan* prayer after the congregational prayer is over, or after sunrise. This is the view held by al-Shāfi'I and the traditionists. But Abū Ḥanīfah maintains that in the case of the dawn prayer, one can offer the *sunan* prayer in the mosque at some distance from the congregational prayer if he expects to get at least one *rak'ah* along with the *imām*. But if he fears that he will miss both *rak'ahs* along with the *imām* if he is engaged in the *sunan* prayer, he should postpone the *sunan* prayer and join the congregation. He should not offer the *sunan* prayer at the end of the congregational prayer, as al-Shāfi'I holds. Instead, he should pray them after sunrise.

664. This applies to all the *sunan* prayers including the dawn prayer.

Chapter 446

WHEN SHOULD A PERSON OFFER THE TWO *RAK'AHS* OF THE DAWN PRAYER (*SUNAN* PRAYER) IF HE MISSES THEM?

(1262) Qais b. 'Amr said: The Apostle of Allah (may peace be upon him) saw a person praying after the congregational prayer at dawn was over. The Apostle of Allah (may peace be upon him) said: There are two *rak'ahs* of the dawn prayer (i.e. the prescribed *rak'ahs*). The man replied: I did not pray the two *rak'ahs* before the dawn prayer . Hence I offered them now. The Apostle of Allah (may peace be upon him) kept silent.[665]

(1263) This tradition has also been transmitted by 'Aṭā' b. Abī Rabāḥ on the authority of Sa'd b. Sa'īd through a different chain of narrators.

Abū Dāwūd said: 'Abd Rabbihī and Yaḥyā b. Sa'īd also narrated this tradition from the Prophet (may peace be upon him) omitting the name of the Companion (*mursal*). Their grandfather Zaid prayed along with the Prophet (may peace be upon him).

Chapter 447

THE FOUR *RAK'AHS* BEFORE AND FOUR AFTER THE NOON PRAYER

(1264) Umm Ḥabībah reported the Apostle of Allah (may peace be upon him) as saying: If anyone keeps on praying regularly four *rak'ahs* before and four after the noon prayer, he will not enter the Hell-fire.[666]

(1265) Abū Ayyūb reported the Prophet (may peace be upon him) as saying: The

665. If a person misses the two *rak'ahs* of the *sunan* prayer before the dawn prayer, it is disputed when he should offer them. Ibn 'Umar used to offer them after the congregational prayer of dawn. This view is also held by 'Aṭā', Ṭāwūs and Ibn Juraij and al-Shāfi'ī according to his earlier statement. Another view goes that these two *rak'ahs* should be offered after sunrise. This is maintained by al Qāsim b. Muḥammad, al-Awzā'ī, al-Shāfi'ī, Aḥmad, and Isḥāq. According to the Ḥanafis, one should pray them after the sun rises higher in the sky. If one does not offer them, there is no harm because it is supererogatory prayer. Mālik maintains that one should offer them in the forenoon before the sun passes the meridian But one should not offer them after it passes the meridian (*'Awn al-Ma'būd*, I. 498).

666. Some traditions indicate that the Prophet (may peace be upon him) prayed two *rak'ahs* before the noon prayer, and others indicate that he offered four. Similar is the case with the *rak'ahs* of the *sunan* prayer after the noon prayer. What is generally preferred is that there are four *rak'ahs* before and two after the noon prayer. The two additional *rak'ahs* after the noon prayer are not emphasised.

gates of heaven are opened for four *rak'ahs* containing no *taslīm* (salutation) before the noon prayer.

Abū Dāwūd said: Yaḥyā b. Sa'īd al-Qaṭṭān said: If I were to narrate any tradition from 'Ubaidah, I would narrate this tradition.

Abū Dāwūd said: 'Ubaidah is weak.

Abū Dāwūd said: The name of the narrator Ibn Minjāb is Sahm.

Chapter 448

THE *SUNAN* PRAYER BEFORE THE AFTERNOON PRAYER

(1266) Ibn 'Umar reported the Apostle of Allah (may peace be upon him) as saying: May Allah show mercy to a man who prays four *rak'ahs* before the afternoon prayer.[667]

(1267) 'Alī said that the Prophet (may peace be upon him) used to pray two *rak'ahs* before the afternoon prayer.[668]

Chapter 449

TO OFFER THE SUPEREROGATORY PRAYER AFTER THE AFTERNOON PRAYER

(1268) Kuraib, the client of Ibn 'Abbās, said that 'Abd Allah b. 'Abbās, 'Abd al-Raḥmān b. Azhar and al-Miswar b. Makhramah sent him to 'Ā'ishah, wife of the Prophet (may peace be upon him). They said: Convey our regards to her from all of us and ask her about the two *rak'ahs* after the afternoon prayer; and tell her that we have been informed that she prays them; and we are told that the Apostle of Allah (may peace be upon him) prohibited them. I entered upon her and told her that for which they had sent me to her. She said: Ask Umm Salamah. I returned to them (Ibn 'Abbās and others) and informed them about her opinion. They sent me back to Umm Salamah with the same mission for which they had sent me to 'Ā'ishah. Umm Salamah said: I heard the Apostle of Allah (may peace be upon him) prohibiting them, but later on I saw him praying them. When he prayed them, he had offered the afternoon prayer. He then came to me while a number of women from Banū Ḥarām from the Anṣār were sitting with me. He prayed these two *rak'ahs*. I sent a slave-girl

667. To pray four *rak'ahs* or two *rak'ahs* before the afternoon prayer carries much reward as this tradition shows. But this is a voluntary prayer, not much emphasised. Hence it depends on one's choice to pray or leave it.

668. The version recorded by al-Tirmidhī indicates that he would pray four *rak'ahs* separating them with a salutation.

to him and I told her: Stand beside him and tell him that Umm Salamah has asked: Apostle of Allah, I heard you prohibiting these two *rak'ahs* (after the afternoon prayer) but I see you praying them yourself. If he makes a sign with his hand, step backward from him. The slave-girl did so. He (the Prophet) made a sign with his hand; she turned away from him. When he finished his prayer, he said: O daughter of Abū Umayyah,[669] you asked about the praying of two *rak'ahs* after the afternoon prayer; in fact, some people of 'Abd al-Qais had come to me with the news that their people had embraced Islam. They hindered me from praying the two *rak'ahs* after the noon prayer. It is those two *rak'ahs* (which I offered after the afternoon prayer).[670]

Chapter 450

THE VIEW THAT THE PRAYING OF THE TWO *RAK'AHS* AFTER THE AFTERNOON PRAYER IS PERMISSIBLE WHEN THE SUN IS AT ITS HEIGHT

(1269) 'Alī said: The Prophet (may peace be upon him) prohibited to offer prayer after the afternoon prayer except at the time when the sun is high up in the sky.[671]

(1270) 'Alī said: The Apostle of Allah (may peace be upon him) would offer two *rak'ahs* after every obligatory prayer except the dawn and the afternoon prayer.[672]

(1271) Ibn 'Abbās said: Some reliable people testified before me, and among them was 'Umar b. al-Khaṭṭāb, and most reliable in my eyes was 'Umar: The Prophet of Allah (may peace be upon him) said: There is no prayer after the dawn

669. The name of Umm Salamah's father.

670. This tradition shows that it is only recommended to atone for the *sunan* prayers, i.e. to offer them after the passing of the time. The version of al-Ṭaḥāwī adds: I asked: Apostle of Allah, should we pray these *sunan* prayers after the passing of the time if we miss them? He said: No. This indicates that this was peculiar with the Prophet (may peace be upon him). One is not allowed to offer *sunan* or supererogatory prayer after the afternoon prayer until the sun sets. This is the view held by Abū Ḥanīfah. Dāwūd al-Ẓāhirī maintains that it is permissible to offer supererogatory prayer after the dawn, afternoon prayer, and when the sun is at its height at midday. Al-Shāfi'ī also does not allow to pray supererogatory prayer in these timings without any reason. If one is to fulfil one's vow or to atone for a prayer one can do so. It is also permissible to offer funeral prayer after the dawn and afternoon prayer (*'Awn al-Ma'būd*, I, 492).

671. This applies equally to all prayers—missing obligatory prayer, *sunan*, supererogatory or funeral prayer (*'Awn al Ma'būd*, I, 492).

672. The Prophet (may peace be upon him) did not offer these two *rak'ahs* after the afternoon prayer in the mosque. He is, however, reported to have prayed them in the house of 'Ā'ishah. 'Alī might not have known it (*'Awn al-Ma'būd*, I, 492).

prayer until the sun rises; and there is no prayer after the afternoon prayer until the sun sets.[673]

(1272) 'Amr b. 'Anbasat al-Sulamī said: I asked: Apostle of Allah, in which part of night the supplication is more likely to be accepted? He replied: In the last part: pray as much as you like, for the prayer is attended by the angels and it is recorded[674] till you offer the dawn prayer; then stop praying when the sun is rising till it is high up about the length of one lance or two lances, for it rises between the two horns of the devil,[675] and the infidels offer prayer for it (at that time). Then pray as much as you like, because the prayer is witnessed and recorded till the shadow of a lance becomes equal to it;[676] then cease prayer, for at that time the Hell-fire is heated up and doors of the Hell are opened. When the sun declines, pray as much as you like, for the prayer is witnessed till you pray the afernoon prayer; then cease prayer till the sun sets, for it sets between the horns of the devil, and (at that time) the infidels offer prayer for it. He narrated a lengthy tradition. 'Abbās said: Abū Salām narrated this tradition in like manner from Abū Umāmah. If I committed a mistake unintentionally, I beg pardon of Allah and repent to Him.

(1273) Yasār, the client of Ibn 'Umar, said: Ibn 'Umar saw me praying after the break of dawn. He said: O Yasār, the Apostle of Allah (may peace be upon him) came to us while we were offering this prayer. He (the Prophet) said: Those who are present should inform those who are absent: Do not offer any prayer after (the break of) dawn except two *rak'ahs*.

(1274) Al-Aswad and Masrūq said: We bear witness that 'Ā'ishah said: Not a day passed but the Prophet (may peace be upon him) prayed two *rak'ahs* after the afternoon prayer.[677]

673. It is disapproved to offer prayer at the time of sunrise, sunset and at the midday. One should not say supererogatory prayer after the dawn and afternoon prayer. But one may offer the abandoned prayers after the dawn and the afternoon prayer. If one begins the dawn or afternoon prayer and the sun rises or sets during the offering, the prayer is valid according to al-Shāfi'ī and the traditionists; Abū Ḥanīfah allows only the afternoon prayer and not the dawn prayer in such a case.

674. This means that the angels attend the prayer and record the reward of the worshippers.

675. The horns of the devil have been interpreted variantly. This means the party and the followers of the devil; or this refers to the domination and spread of corruption by the followers of the devil; the more probable interpretation is that the devil brings his head near the sun at these times so that those who worship the sun look as if they were prostrating before him.

676. This means that the shadow stands opposite to the lance in the north, moving neither towards east or west. This is the situation at midday.

677. It is not generally permissible to offer supererogatory prayer after the afternoon prayer. This might be the peculiarity of the Prophet (may peace be upon him). Some interpret it by saying that the Prophet (may peace be upon him) could not say the *sunan* prayer after the noon prayer; he offered this prayer at this time, as the tradition reported by Umm Salamah indicates. According to

(1275) Dhakwān, the client of 'Ā'ishah, reported on the authority of 'Ā'ishah: The Apostle of Allah (may peace be upon him) used to pray after the afternoon prayer but prohibited others from it; and he would fast continuously but forbid others to do so.[678]

Chapter 451

PRAYER BEFORE THE SUNSET PRAYER

(1276) 'Abd Allah al-Muzanī reported: The Apostle of Allah (may peace be upon him) said: Pray two *rak'ahs* before the sunset prayer. He then said (again): Pray two *rak'ahs* before the sunset prayer; it applies to those who wish to do so. That was because he feared that the people might treat it as a *sunnah*.[679]

(1277) Anas b. Mālik said: I offered two *rak'ahs* of prayer before the sunset prayer (i.e. obligatory) during the time of the Apostle of Allah (may peace be upon him). I (the narrator al-Mukhtār b. Fulful) asked Anas: Did the Apostle of Allah (may peace be upon him) see you? He replied: Yes, but he neither commanded us nor forbade us (to do so).[680]

(1278) 'Abd Allah b. Mughaffal reported the Apostle of Allah (may peace be upon him) as saying: Between the two *adhāns* there is a prayer; between the two *adhāns* there is a prayer for one who desires (to offer).[681]

(1279) Ṭāwūs said: Ibn 'Umar was asked about praying two *rak'ahs* before the sunset prayer. He replied: I did not see anyone praying them during the time of the Apostle of Allah (may peace be upon him). He permitted to pray two *rak'ahs* after the afternoon prayer.[682]

a group of scholars, it is permissible to offer supererogatory prayer after the dawn and afternoon prayers.

678 Both these things were peculiar to the Prophet (may peace be upon him). The people in general were not allowed to do so.

679. It is disputed whether it is commendable to offer two *rak'ahs* after sunset before the sunset prayer. A group of the Companions and the Successors hold that it is commendable to offer two *rak'ahs* before the sunset prayer. This is held by Aḥmad and Isḥāq. Others maintain that it is not commendable to do so, for it causes delay in offering the sunset prayer. This is held by most of the scholars and jurists (*'Awn al-Ma'būd*, I, 495).

680. This shows the permissibility of praying two *rak'ahs* before the sunset prayer.

681. This tradition indicates the desirability of offering two *rak'ahs* of prayer in general irrespective of any time between the *adhān* and the *iqāmah*. Here the two *adhāns* mean the *adhān* and the *iqāmah*.

682. According to Ibn Ḥazm, the chain of this tradition is not sound. How can the tradition be sound when a number of the Companions like Anas, 'Abd Allah b. Mughaffal and 'Uqbah b. 'Āmir narrated the permission of the Prophet (may peace be upon him) for praying these two *rak'ahs*? Moreover, Anas, 'Abd al-Raḥmān b. 'Awf, Ubayy b. Ka'b, Abū Ayyūb al-Anṣārī, Abū al-Dardā', and Jābir b. 'Abd Allah used to pray these *rak'ahs* (*'Awn al-Ma'būd*, I, 495).

Abū Dāwūd said: I heard Yaḥyā b. Ma'īn say: The correct name of the narrator Abū Shu'aib is Shu'aib. Shu'bah made a mistake in narrating his name.

Chapter 452

PRAYER IN THE FORENOON[683]

(1280) Abū Dharr reported the Prophet (may peace be upon him) as saying: In the morning alms are due from every bone in man's body. His salutation to everyone he meets is alms; his enjoining good is alms; his forbidding what is evil is alms; the removal of a harmful thing from the way is alms; to have sexual intercourse with one's wife is alms; and two *rak'ahs* which one prays in the forenoon serve instead of that.

Abū Dāwūd said: The tradition narrated by 'Abbād is more perfect (than the version narrated by Musaddad). Musaddad did not mention in his version "the command (of good) and the prohibition (of evil)". Instead, he added in his version saying: "Such and such." Ibn Ma'nā added in his version: "They (the people) said: Apostle of Allah, how is it that one of us fulfils his desire and still there are alms for him (i.e. is rewarded)? He replied: What do you think if he had had unlawful sexual intercourse; would he not have been a sinner?

(1281) Abū al-Aswad al-Dailanī said: While we were present with Abū Dharr, he said: in the morning alms are due from every bone in a man's fingers and toes. Every prayer is alms for him; every fast is alms; every pilgrimage is alms; every utterance of "Glory be to Allah" is alms; every utterance of "Allah is most great" is alms; every utterance of "Praise be to Allah" is alms. The Apostle of Allah (may peace be upon him) recounted all such good works. He then said: Two *rak'ahs* which one prays in the forenoon serve instead of that.

(1282) Mu'ādh b. Anas al-Juhanī reported the Apostle of Allah (may peace be upon him) as saying: If anyone sits in his place of prayer when he finishes the dawn prayer till he prays the two *rak'ahs* of the forenoon, saying nothing but what is good, his sins will be forgiven even if they are more than the foam of the sea.

(1283) Abū Umāmah reported the Apostle of Allah (may peace be upon him) as saying: Prayer followed by a prayer with no idle talk between the two is recorded in

683. The original Arabic word is *ḍuḥā* which means the beginning of day when the sun is high up in the sky and becomes fairly bright spreading its rays on earth. The time of prayer in the forenoon (*ḍuḥā*) lasts till midday before the sun passes the meridian. The early part of this time is called *ishrāq* and the later part is known as *ḍuḥā*. Al-Nawawī observes: The minimum *rak'ahs* of this prayer are two, the maximum are eight, and the medium are four or six (*'Awn al-Ma'būd*, I, 495-96).

'illiyyin.[684]

(1284) Nu'aim b. Hammār said: I heard the Apostle of Allah (may peace be upon him) say: Allah, the Exalted, says: Son of Adam, do not be helpless in performing four *rak'ahs* for Me at the beginning of the day; I will supply what you need till the end of it.

(1285) Umm Hānī b. Abū Ṭālib said: The Apostle of Allah (may peace be upon him) prayed on the day of the Conquest (of Mecca) eight *rak'ahs* saluting after every two *rak'ahs*.

Abū Dāwūd said: Aḥmad b. Ṣāliḥ said that the Apostle of Allah offered the prayer in the forenoon on the day of the Conquest of Mecca, and he narrated something similar. Ibn al-Sarḥ reported that Umm Hānī said: The Apostle of Allah (may peace be upon him) entered upon me. This version does not mention the prayer in the forenoon.

(1286) Ibn Abī Lailā said: No one told us that the Prophet (may peace be upon him) had offered the prayer in the forenoon except Umm Hānī. She said that the Prophet (may peace be upon him) had taken a bath in her house on the day of the Conquest of Mecca and prayed eight *rak'ahs*. But no one saw him afterwards praying these *rak'ahs*.

(1287) 'Abd Allah b. Shaqīq said: I asked 'Ā'ishah: Did the Apostle of Allah (may peace be upon him) pray in the forenoon? She replied: No, except when he returned from his journey. I then asked: Did the Apostle of Allah (may peace be upon him) recite the *surahs* combining each other? She said: He would do so in the *mufaṣṣal surahs*.[685]

(1288) 'Ā'ishah, the wife of the Prophet (may peace be upon him), said: The Apostle of Allah (may peace be upon him) never offered prayer in the forenoon, but I offer it. The Apostle of Allah (may peace be upon him) would give up an action, though he liked it to do, lest the people should continue it and it is prescribed for them.[686]

(1289) Simāk said: I asked Jābir b. Samurah: Did you sit in the company of the

684. " *'Illiyin* : the oblique form of the nominative *'illiyūn* in the next verse [lxxxiii. 19]. It is in contrast to the *sijjin* which occurs in verse 7 above. . . . Literally, it means the 'High Places', but probably not the same as the 'Heights' (*A'rāf*) mentioned in vii. 46. . . . We may interpret it as the Place where is kept the Register of the Righteous. (A. Yusūf 'Ali, *English Translation of the Holy Qur-ān*, footnote 6019 to lxxxiii. 18).—"Of course, we must not understand a material Register. . . . The whole description is figurative of the inescapable record which sin creates." (ibid,, footnote 6014 to lxxxiii. 9).

685. The small *sūrahs* beginning from Sūrah al-Ḥujurāt to the end of the Qur'ān.

686. This means that he would not pray it regularly. There are many statements of 'Ā'ishah concerning the prayer in the forenoon. Muslim in his collection recorded from 'Ā'ishah that the Prophet (may peace be upon him) prayed four *rak'ahs* in the forenoon.

Apostle of Allah (may peace be upon him)? He replied; Yes, very often. He would not stand from the place he prayed the dawn prayer till the sunrise. When the sun rose, he would stand (to pray in the forenoon).

Chapter 453

PRAYER BY DAY

(1290) ... 'Umar reported the Prophet (may peace be upon him) as saying: Prayer by night and day should consist of pairs of *rak'ahs*.[687]

(1291) Muṭṭalib reported the Prophet (may peace be upon him) as saying: Prayer is to be offered in two *rak'ahs*; and you should recite the *tashahhud* at the end of two *rak'ahs*,[688] and express your distress and humility and raise your hands and say praying: O Allah, O Allah.[689] He who does not do so does not offer a perfect prayer.

Abū Dāwūd was asked about offering prayer at night in two *rak'ahs*. He said: They may be two if you like and four if you like.

Chapter 454

PRAYER GLORIFYING ALLAH

(1292) Ibn 'Abbās reported that the Apostle of Allah (may peace be upon him) said to al-'Abbās b. 'Abd al-Muṭṭalib: 'Abbās, my uncle, shall I not give you, shall I not present you, shall I not donate you, shall I not produce in you ten things? If you act upon them, Allah will forgive you your sins, first and last, old and new, involuntary and voluntary, small and great, secret and open. These are the ten things:

687. Ibn 'Umar, Nāfi', Ṭāwūs and 'Abd Allah b. Dīnār also narrated this tradition, but they did not mention the word "by day". The Prophet (may peace be upon him) said this about the supererogatory prayers offered at night or in the day. Mālik, al-Shafi'ī and Aḥmad b. Ḥanbal are of opinion that the supererogatory prayers should be offered in two *rak'ahs*. It is desirable to offer the supererogatory prayer whether in the day or night in two *rak'ahs* ending each pair in salutation. A tradition narrated by 'Ā'ishah indicates that sometimes the Prophet (may peace be upon him) offered supererogatory prayer in four *rak'ahs* at night. By this she meant that he recited the *tashahhud* at the end of two *rak'ahs*, and gave the salutation at the end of four *rak'ahs*. This tradition can also be interpreted as meaning the recitation of the *tashahhud* at the end of two *rak'ahs* or giving the salutation. Both mean two *rak'ahs* (*'Awn al-Ma'būd*, I, 498 99)

688. This shows that two *rak'ahs* mean to recite the *tashahhud* at the end of two *rak'ahs* and not necessarily the finishing of the prayer by giving the salutation. If a man offers four *rak'ahs* of supererogatory prayer by day or by night and he recites the *tashahhud* at the end of two *rak'ahs*, according to this tradition he prays in pairs of *rak'ahs*.

689 This means that he should do so while making supplication in prayer (*qunūt*), or after finishing the prayer.

you should pray four *rak'ahs* reciting in each one *Fātiḥat al-Kitāb* and a *surah*, and when you finish the recitation in the first *rak'ah* you should say fifteen times while standing, "Glory be to Allah"; "Praise be to Allah": "There is no god but Allah"; "Allah is most great". Then you should bow and say it ten times while bowing. Then you should raise your head after bowing and say it ten times. Then you should get down in prostration and say it ten times while prostrating yourself. Then you should raise your head after prostration and say it ten times. Then you should prostrate yourself and say it ten times. Then you should raise your head after prostrating and say it ten times in every *rak'ah*. You should do that in four *rak'ahs*. If you can observe it once daily, do so; if not, then once weekly; if not, then once a month; if not, then once a year; if not, then once in your lifetime.[690]

(1293) Abū al-Jauzā' said: A man who attended the company of the Prophet (may peace be upon him) narrated to me it is thought that he was 'Abd Allah b. 'Amr: The Prophet (may peace be upon him) said to me: Come to me tomorrow; I shall give you; I shall give you; I shall reward you; I shall donate you. I thought that he would give me some present. He said (to me when I came to him): When the day declines, stand up and pray four *rak'ahs*. He then narrated something similar. This version adds: Then you should raise your head after the second prostration and sit down upright. Do not stand until you glorify Allah ten times, and praise Him ten times, and exalt Him ten times, and say, "There is no god but Allah" ten times. Then you should do that in four *rak'ahs*. If you are the greatest sinner on earth, you will be forgiven (by Allah) on account of this (prayer). I asked: If I cannot pray this on this appointed hour, (what should I do)? He replied: Pray that by night or by day (at any time).

Abū Dāwūd said: Ḥabbān b. Hilāl is the maternal uncle of Hilāl al-Rā'ī.

Abū Dāwūd said: This tradition has been narrated by al-Mustamir b. al-Riyyān from Ibn al-Jawzā' from 'Abd Allah b. 'Amr without referring to the Prophet (may peace be upon him),—narrated as a statement of 'Abd Allah b. 'Amr himself (*mauqūf*). This has also been narrated by Rawḥ b. al-Musayyab, and Ja'far b. Sulaimān from 'Amr b. Mālik al-Nakrī from Abū al-Jauzā' from Ibn 'Abbās as his own statement (and not the statement of the Prophet). But the version of Rawḥ has the words: "The tradition of the Prophet (may peaçe be upon him)."

(1294) 'Urwah b. Ruwaim said that an al-Anṣārī[691] narrated to him: The Apostle

690 Ibn al-Jauzī calls this tradition spurious because the narrator Mūsā b. 'Abd al-'Azīz is obscure. But this is not correct. Ibn Ḥajar al-'Asqalānī observes that his reliability has been confirmed by Ibn Ma'īn and al-Nasā'ī and Ibn Ḥibbān. This has been called good (*ḥasan*) tradition by a number of the experts of traditions. Moreover, al-Bukhārī has recorded it in his treatise on "The Recitation of Sūrah al-Fātiḥah behind the *Imām*" (*'Awn al-Ma'būd*, I, 499-500).

691. This refers either to Jābir b. 'Abd Allah or Abū Kabshah (*'Awn al-Ma'būd*, I, 501).

of Allah (may peace be upon him) said to Ja'far. He then narrated the tradition in like manner. This version has the words: "In the second prostration of the first *rak'ah*," in addition to the words transmitted by Mahdī b. Maimūn (in the previous tradition).

Chapter 455

WHERE SHOULD THE TWO *RAK'AHS* OF THE *SUNAN* PRAYER OF THE SUNSET PRAYER BE OFFERED?

(1295) Ka'b b. 'Ujrah said: The Prophet (may peace be upon him) came to the mosque of Banū 'Abd al-Ashhal. He prayed the sunset prayer there. When they finished the prayer, he saw them praying the supererogatory prayer after it. He said: This is the prayer to be offered in the houses.[692]

(1296) Ibn 'Abbās said: The Apostle of Allah (may peace be upon him) used to prolong the recitation of the Qur'ān in the two *rak'ahs* after the sunset prayer until the people praying in the mosque dispersed.[693]

Abū Dāwūd said: This has been reported by Naṣr al-Mujaddir from Ya'qūb al-Qummī with the same chain of narrators.

Abū Dāwūd said: Muḥammad b. 'Isā b. al-Ṭabbā' transmitted from Nāṣr al-Mujaddir from Ya'qūb in like manner.

(1297) Sa'īd b. Jubair reported this tradition from the Prophet (may peace be upon him) without mentioning the name of the Companion in the chain (in the *mursal* form).

Abū Dāwūd said: I heard Muḥammad b. Ḥumaid say: I heard Ya'qūb say: Anything I narrated you from Ja'far on the authority of Sa'īd b. Jubair from the Prophet (may peace be upon him) is directly coming from Ibn Abbās from the Prophet (may peace be upon him).

Chapter 456

PRAYER AFTER THE NIGHT PRAYER

(1298) Shuraiḥ b. Hānī said: I asked 'Ā'ishah about the prayer of the Apostle of Allah (may peace be upon him). She said: The Apostle of Allah (may peace be upon him) never offered the night prayer and thereafter came to me but he offered four or

692. It is not binding to offer the *sunan* prayer of the sunset prayer at home. It is commendable to do so. The Prophet (may peace be upon him) recommended to offer the *sunan* prayer at home so that the houses too are blessed with prayer.

693. The Prophet (may peace be upon him) would sometimes offer the *sunan* prayer after the sunset prayer in the mosque and sometimes in the house.

six *rak'ahs* of prayer. One night the rain fell, so we spread a piece of leather (for his prayer), and now I see as if there is a hole in it from which the water is flowing. I never saw him protecting his clothes from the earth (as he did on that occasion).

CHAPTERS ON PRAYER AT NIGHT

Chapter 457

ABROGATION OF THE PRAYER AT NIGHT AND CONVENIENCE IN IT

(1299) Ibn 'Abbās said: In Sūrat al-Muzzammil (lxxiii.), the verse: "Keep vigil in the night but a little, a half thereof" (2-3) has been abrogated by the verse therein: "He knoweth that ye count it not, and turneth unto you in mercy. Recite then of the Qur'ān that which is easy for you" (v. 20). The phrase "the vigil of the night" (*nāshi'at al-lail*) means the early hours of night. They (the Companions) would pray (the *tahajjud* prayer) in the early hours of night. He (Ibn 'Abbās) says: It is advisable to offer the prayer at night (*tahajjud*), prescribed by Allah for you (in the early hours of the night). This is because when a person sleeps, he does not know when he will awake. The words "speech more certain (*aqwamu qīlan*) means that this time is more suitable for the understanding of the Qur'ān. He says: The verse: "Lo, thou hast by day a chain of business" (v. 7) means engagement fo long (in the day's works).[694]

(1300) Ibn 'Abbās said: When the opening verses of Sūrah al-Muzzammil (lxxiii.) were revealed, the Companions would pray as long as they would pray during Ramaḍān until its last verses were revealed. The period between the revelation of its opening and the last verses was one year.

Chapter 458

PRAYER AND VIGIL AT NIGHT

(1301) Abū Hurairah reported the Apostle of Allah (may peace be upon him)

694. In the early days of Islam when the Prophet (may peace be upon him) was at Mecca vigil and prayer at night were prescribed by Allah on him and on the Companions. They were required to pray at night (*tahajjud* prayer) for one-third or at the most two-third of night. Sometimes they could not exactly determine the parts of night prescribed for them for prayer, and they would remain engaged in prayer from evening till morning. The result was that their feet were inflamed. Hence the vigil at night and prayer for long hours were abrogated later on. One view goes that the prayer at night and its vigil were abrogated for the Prophet (may peace be upon him) as well as for the Companions. Another view says that it was abrogated for the Companions and not for the Prophet (may peace be upon him). Hence he regularly offered this prayer till his last days.

as saying: When one of you sleeps, the devil ties three knots at the back of his neck, sealing every knot with, "You have a long night, so sleep," So if one awakes and mentions Allah, a knot will be loosened; if he performs ablution, another knot will be loosened; and if he prays, the third knot will be loosened; and in the morning he will be active and in good spirits; otherwise he will be in bad spirits and sluggish.[695]

(1302) 'Ā'ishah said: Do not give up prayer at night, for the Apostle of Allah (may peace be upon him) would not leave it. Whenever he fell ill or lithargic, he would offer it sitting.[696]

(1303) Abū Hurairah reported the Apostle of Allah (may peace be upon him) as saying: May Allah have mercy on a man who gets up at night and prays, and awakens his wife; if she refuses, he should sprinkle water on her face. May Allah have mercy on a woman who gets up at night and prays, and awakens her husband; if he refuses, she should sprinkle water on his face.

(1304) Abū Sa'īd and Abū Hurairah reported the Apostle of Allah (may peace be upon him) as saying: If a man awakens his wife at night, and then both pray or both offer two *rak'ahs* together, the (name of the) man will be recorded among those who mention the name of Allah, and the (name of the) woman will be recorded among those who mention the name of Allah. Ibn Kathīr did not narrate this tradition as a statement of the Prophet (may peace be upon him), but he reported it as a statement of Abū Sa'īd.

Abū Dāwūd said: This tradition has been narrated by Ibn Mahdī from Sufyān. and I think he mentioned the name of Sufyān. He also said: The tradition transmitted by Sufyān is a statement of the Companion (and not that of the Prophet).

Chapter 459

DOZING DURING PRAYER

(1305) 'Ā'ishah, wife of the Prophet (may peace be upon him), reported him as saying: When one of you dozes in prayer he should sleep till his sleep is gone, for when one of you prays while he is dozing, perhaps he might curse himself if he begs

695. Tying the knots at the back of a sleeping person by the devil is a figurative expression to show one's slackness in the offering of the prayer at night. This sluggishness is removed by mentioning the name of Allah, performing ablution and offering prayer. This is a sort of exhortation to offer the prayer at night. If one remains sleeping, he in a sense is controlled by the devil.

Some scholars are of opinion that the devil actually ties the knot like a magician (*'Awn al-Mu'būd*, I, 504).

696. This shows that it is permissible to offer supererogatory prayer in sitting position. But one gets half reward if one prays sitting without any valid reason. The Prophet (may peace be upon him), on the contrary, got full reward even when he prayed in sitting position.

pardon of Allah.[697]

(1306) Abū Hurairah reported the Apostle of Allah (may peace be upon him) as saying: When one of you gets up by night (to pray), and falters in reciting the Qur'ān (due to sleep), and he does not understand what he utters, he should sleep.

(1307) Anas said: The Apostle of Allah (may peace be upon him) entered the mosque (and saw that) a rope was tied between two pillars. He asked: What is this rope (for)? The people told him: This is (for) Ḥamnah b. Jaḥsh who prays (here). When she is tired, she reclines on it. The Apostle of Allah (may peace be upon him) said: She should pray as much as she has strength. When she is tired, she should sit down.

The version of Ziyād has: He said: What is this? The people told him: This is for Zainab who prays. When she becomes lazy, or is tired, she holds it. He said: Undo it. One of you should pray in good spirits. When he is lazy or tired, he should sit down.

Chapter 460

ON A PERSON WHO MISSES HIS DAILY ROUND OF RECITAL

(1308) 'Umar b. al-Khaṭṭāb reported the Apostle of Allah (may peace be upon him) as saying: He who misses him daily round of recital or a part of it due to sleep and he recites it between the dawn and the noon prayers, will be reckoned as if he recited it at night.[698]

Chapter 461

ON A PERSON WHO MAKES THE INTENTION OF GETTING UP AND PRAYING AT NIGHT BUT REMAINS SLEEPING

(1309) 'Ā'ishah, wife of the Apostle of Allah (may peace be upon him), reported him as saying: Any person who offers prayer at night regularly but (on a

697. This applies to all kinds of prayer, obligatory, supererogatory, optional, whether offered by day or by night. But some scholars have stipulated that if one sleeps, the time of the obligatory prayer should not pass. Mālik says that this applies only to the supererogatory prayer at night and not to obligatory prayer. It should, however, be noted that the Prophet (may peace be upon him) has emphasised concentration in prayer (*'Awn al-Ma'būd*, I, 505).

698. The daily recital (*ḥizb*) refers either to the recitation of the Qur'ān or the prayer at night regularly.

certain night) he is dominated by sleep will be given the reward of praying. His sleep will be almsgiving.[699]

Chapter 462

WHICH PART OF NIGHT IS BETTER (FOR PRAYER)?

(1310) Abū Hurairah reported the Apostle of Allah (may peace be upon him) as saying: Our Lord who is blessed and exalted descends every night to the lowest heaven when the last one-third of the night remains, and says: Who supplicates Me so that I may answer him? Who asks of Me so that I may give to him? Who asks My forgiveness so that I may forgive him?[700]

Chapter 463

THE TIME WHEN THE PROPHET (MAY PEACE BE UPON HIM) USED TO GET UP AT NIGHT FOR PRAYER

(1311) 'Ā'ishah said: Allah, the Exalted, would awaken the Apostle of Allah (may peace be upon him) at night. When the dawn came, he would finish his daily round of recital.

(1312) Masrūq said: I asked 'Ā'ishah about the prayer of the Apostle of Allah (may peace be upon him), and I said to her: At what time he prayed at night? She said: When he heard the cock crow, he got up and prayed.[701]

(1313) 'Ā'ishah said: When he was with me he would sleep at dawn. By this she

699. This is the mercy of Allah that He does not deprive a man of the reward of prayer if he misses it due to some valid reason. In fact, Allah gives reward on a Muslim's intention though he may not act upon it due to some excuse.

700. It should be noted that the verses and the traditions which indicate the actions and qualities of Allah like those of men should be interpreted literally without knowing how (*bilā kaif*) they are. Abū Ḥanīfah was once asked about the descending of Allah to the lowest heaven. He replied: He descends but how He descends is not known to us. This is the view held by the majority of scholars and traditionists. Moreover, it is not advisable to interpret such traditions figuratively. As the essence of Allah is not similar to man, His actions and qualities too do not correspond to those of man. How Allah acts is beyond the understanding of man. Hence it is better to believe in the actions and attributes of Allah as they are mentioned in the texts (*'Awn al-Ma'būd*, I, 506-07)

701. This means either midnight or a little after midnight. Some scholars are of the view that this means the last part of the night when probably one-third of the night remains (*'Awn al-Ma'būd*, I, 507).

referred to the Prophet (may peace be upon him).[702]

(1314) Ḥudhaifah said: When anything distressed the Prophet (may peace be upon him), he prayed.[703]

(1315) Rabī'ah b. Ka'b al-Aslamī said: I used to live with the Apostle of Allah (may peace be upon him) at night; I would bring water for his ablution and his need. He said: Ask me. I said: Your company in Paradise. He said: Is there anything other than that? I said: It is only that. He said: Help me for yourself by making prostrations abundantly.[704]

(1316) Anas b. Mālik said (explaining the meaning) of the following Qur'ānic verse "Who forsake their beds to cry unto their Lord in fear and hope, and spend of what We have bestowed on them" (xxxii. 16): The people used to remain awake between the sunset and the night prayers and would pray. Al-Ḥasan used to say: (This verse means) the prayer and vigil at night.

(1317) Anas said (explaining the meaning) of the following Qur'ānic verse "They used to sleep but little of the night" (ii. 17): They (the people) used to pray between the sunset and night prayers. The version of Yaḥyā adds: The verse *tatajāfā junūbuhum* also means so.

Chapter 464

BEGINNING OF THE PRAYER AT NIGHT WITH TWO *RAK'AHS*

(1318) Abū Hurairah reported the Apostle of Allah (may peace be upon him) as saying: When one of you gets up at night, he should begin the prayer with two short *rak'ahs*.[705]

702. The Prophet (may peace be upon him) used to pray in the long hours of night. Hence he would sleep after his prayer and vigil at night (i.e. *tahajjud* prayer). When the dawn came he would get up and offer the dawn prayer.

703. This tradition is not relevant to this chapter. This might be interpreted that he would pray at night on such occasions. Moreover, it is important to note that one should pray when one is faced by distress and calamity. The Prophet (may peace be upon him) presented a model behaviour in every situation. In times of danger, distress and calamity a Muslim should pray to Allah to remove the calamity. This is in addition to making efforts and adopting means to eradicate the distress.

704. By this he meant that he should offer supererogatory prayer frequently. The Prophet (may peace be upon him) could intercede for him, but he required him to do good actions, particularly prayer in abundance. This shows that one should do good works himself and then should expect intercession of the Prophet (may peace be upon him).

705. The Prophet (may peace be upon him) would pray these two *rak'ahs* after performing the ablution. These two *rak'ahs* were of course part of the prayer at night. They were offered shortly so that one gets used to the prayer by degrees. Afterwards one is allowed to prolong as one can (*'Awn al-Ma'būd*, I, 508).

(1319) This tradition has also been transmitted by Abū Hurairah through a different chain of narrators to the same effect. This version adds: He should then prolong it afterwards as much as he likes.

Abū Dāwūd said: This tradition has been transmitted by Ḥammād b. Salamah, Zuhair b. Mu'āwiyah and a group of narrators from Hishām. They transmitted it as a statement of Abū Hurairah himself (*mauquf*).

This tradition has also been transmitted by Ibn 'Awn from Muḥammad (b. Sīrīn). This version has the wordings : These two *rak'ahs* were short.

(1320) 'Abd Allah b. Ḥabashī al-Khath'amī said: The Prophet (may peace be upon him) was asked: Which is the best action? He replied: To stand in prayer for a long time [706]

Chapter 465

THE PRAYER AT NIGHT IS TO BE OFFERED IN PAIRS OF *RAK'AHS* EACH TIME

(1321) 'Abd Allah b. 'Umar said: A man asked the Apostle of Allah (may peace be upon him) about the prayer at night. The Apostle of Allah (may peace be upon him) said: Prayer during the night should consist of pairs of *rak'ahs*, but if one of you fears the morning is near he should pray one *rak'ah* which will make his prayer an odd number for him.[707]

Chapter 466

RECITATION OF THE QUR'ĀN IN LOUD VOICE DURING THE PRAYER AT NIGHT

(1322) Ibn 'Abbās said: The Prophet's (may peace be upon him) recitation was loud enough for one who was in the inner chamber to hear it when he was in the

706. This tradition shows that to stand for a long time in prayer is better than to offer a large number of *rak'ahs* of the supererogatory prayers. It is better to say, for instance, two *rak'ahs* of prayer in which one should recite long *sūrahs* of the Qur'ān and thus stand for a long time in prayer. A group of scholars opine that to say supererogatory prayer abundantly is better than to prolong the *rak'ahs* of prayer.

707. There is no difference of opinion in the legitimacy of offering of two or four *rak'ahs* each time of supererogatory prayer by day or by night. The dispute is over the preference. According to al-Shāfi'ī, it is preferable to offer supererogatory prayer in pairs by day and by night. Abū Ḥanīfah holds that it is better to offer four *rak'ahs* each time by day and by night. Muḥammad b. al-Ḥasan and Abū Yūsuf hold that one should pray in pairs at night and four *rak'ahs* each time by day (*'Awn al-Ma'būd*, I, 409).

house.[708]

(1323) Abū Hurairah said : The Prophet's (may peace be upon him) recitation at night was partly in a loud voice and partly in a low voice.

Abū Dāwūd said : The name of Abū Khālid al-Wālibī is Hurmuz.

(1324) Abū Qatādah said : The Prophet (may peace be upon him) went out at night and found Abū Bakr praying in a low voice, and he passed 'Umar b. al-Khaṭṭāb who was raising his voice while praying. When they both met the Prophet (may peace be upon him) together, the Prophet (may peace be upon him) said : I passed by you, Abū Bakr, when you were praying in a low voice. He replied : I made Him hear with Whom I was holding intimate converse, Apostle of Allah. He (the Prophet) said to 'Umar : I passed by you when you were praying in a loud voice. He replied : Apostle of Allah, I was awakening the drowsy and driving away the devil. Al-Ḥasan added in his version : The Prophet (may peace be upon him) said : Raise your voice a little, Abū Bakr, and he said to 'Umar : Lower your voice a little.[709]

(1325) This tradition has also been transmitted by Abū Hurairah through a different chain of narrators. This version does not mention that the Prophet (may peace be upon him) said to Abū Bakr : Raise your voice a little ; or he said to 'Umar : Lower your voice a little. But this version adds : (The Prophet said :) I heard you, Bilāl, (reciting) ; you were reciting partly from this *sūrah* and partly from that *sūrah*. He said : This is all good speech ; Allah has combined one part with the other. The Prophet (may peace be upon him) said : All of you were correct.

(1326) 'Ā'ishah said : A man got up at night and recited the Qur'ān in a loud voice. When the dawn came, the Apostle of Allah (may peace be upon him) said : May Allah have mercy on so-and-so who reminded me many verses that I had nearly forgotten.[710]

Abū Dāwūd said : Hārūn al-Naḥwī transmitted from Ḥammad b. Salamah the Qur'ānic verse of Sūrah Āl'Imrān : "How many of the prophets fought (in Allah's way)" (iii. 146).

(1327) Abū Sa'īd said : The Apostle of Allah (may peace be upon him) retired to the mosque. He heard them (the people) reciting the Qur'ān in a loud voice. He removed the curtain and said : Lo ! every one of you is calling his Lord quietly. One

708. This means that his recitation was moderate, neither at the top of his voice nor quietly during his prayer at night.

709. The Prophet (may peace be upon him) taught that one should recite the Qur'ān in the prayer at night (*tahajjud*) in a moderate voice. We find the same instructions in the Qur'ān : "Neither speak thy prayer aloud nor speak it in a low tone, but seek a middle course between" (xvii. 110).

710. This probably means that the Prophet (may peace be upon him) forgot these verses while reciting the Qur'ān in prayer. One should not be surprised on the forgetfulness of the Prophet (may peace be upon him) as it was just possible for he was a human being.

should not trouble the other and one should not raise the voice in recitation or in prayer over the voice of the other.

(1328) 'Uqbah b. 'Āmir al-Juhanī reported the Apostle of Allah (may peace be upon him) as saying : One who recites the Qur'ān in a loud voice is like one who gives alms openly ; and one who recites the Qur'ān quietly is one who gives alms secretly.

Chapter 467

ON THE NUMBER OF *RAK'AHS* OF THE PRAYER AT NIGHT

(1329) 'Ā'ishah said : The Apostle of Allah (may peace be upon him) used to pray ten *rak'ahs* during the night, and would observe the *witr* with one *rak'ah* ; he then prayed two *rak'ahs* of the dawn prayer. Thus he prayed thirteen *rak'ahs* in all.[711]

(1330) 'Ā'ishah, wife of the Prophet (may peace be upon him), said : The Apostle of Allah (may peace be upon him) used to pray eleven *rak'ahs* (at night, observing the *witr* with one *rak'ah*. When he finished it (the prayer), he would lie down on his right side.

(1331) 'Ā'ishah said : Between the time when the Apostle of Allah (may peace be upon him) finished the night prayer till the dawn broke, he used to pray eleven *rak'ahs*, uttering the salutation at the end of every two and observing the *witr* with a single one, and during that he would make a prostration about as long as one of you would take to recite fifty verses before raising his head. When the *mu'adhdhin* finished making the call for the dawn prayer, he stood up and prayed two short *rak'ahs* ; then he lay down on his right side till the *mu'adhdhin* came to him.

(1332) This tradition has been transmitted by Ibn Shihāb through a different chain of narrators to the same effect. This version adds: He would observe *witr* with a single *rak'ah* and make a prostration about as long as one of you would take to recite fifty verses before raising his head. When the *mu'adhdhin* finished his call for the dawn prayer and the dawn became clear to him. . . . Then the narrator transmitted the rest of the tradition to the same effect.

Some narrators added something more in their version.

(1333) 'Ā'ishah said: The Apostle of Allah (may peace be upon him) used to pray thirteen *rak'ahs* during the night, observing a *witr* out of that with five ; he did

711. There are a number of traditions about the *rak'ahs* that the Prophet (may peace be upon him) used to pray at night (i.e. *tahajjud* prayer). He prayed sometimes fifteen, sometimes thirteen and sometimes eleven *rak'ahs*. In fact, there is no contradiction between them. This depended on his convenience and time. The number of *rak'ahs* varied according to his convenience and the time at his disposal.

not sit during the five except during the last and then gave the salutation.[712]

(1334) 'Ā'ishah said: The Apostle of Allah (may peace be upon him) used to pray thirteen *rak'ahs* during the night; he then offered two light *rak'ahs* of prayer when he heard the call to the dawn prayer.

(1335) 'Ā'ishah said: The Prophet of Allah (may peace be upon him) used to pray thirteen *rak'ahs* during the night. He would offer eight *rak'ahs* observing the *witr* with one *rak'ah*. Then he prayed (the narrator Muslim said) two *rak'ahs* after *witr* prayer in sitting position. When he wished to bow, he stood up and bowed. He used to pray two *rak'ahs* between the call to the dawn prayer and the *iqāmah*.

(1336) Abū Salamah b. 'Abd al-Raḥman asked 'Ā'ishah, wife of the Prophet (may peace be upon him): How did the Apostle of Allah (may peace be upon him) pray during Ramaḍān? She said: The Apostle of Allah (may peace be upon him) did not pray more than eleven *rak'ahs* during Ramaḍān and other than Ramaḍān.[713] He would pray four *rak'ahs*.[714] Do not ask about their elegance and length. He then would pray four *rak'ahs*. Do not ask about their elegance and length. Then he would pray three *rak'ahs*. 'A'ishah said: I asked: Apostle of Allah, do you sleep before observing *witr*? He replied: 'Ā'ishah, my eyes sleep, but my heart does not sleep.

(1337) Sa'd b. Hishām said: I divorced my wife. I then came to Medina to sell my land that was there so that I could buy arms and fight in battle. I met a group of the Companions of the Prophet (may peace be upon him). They said: Six persons of us intended to do so (i.e. to divorce their wives and purchase weapons), but the Prophet (may peace be upon him) prohibited them. He said: For you in the Apostle of Allah there is an excellent model. I then came to Ibn 'Abbās and asked him about the *witr* observed by the Prophet (may peace be upon him). He said: I point to you a person who is most familiar with the *witr* prayer observed by the Apostle of Allah (may peace be upon him). Go to 'Ā'ishah. While going to her I asked Ḥakīm b. Aflaḥ to accompany me. He refused, but I adjured him. He, therefore, went along with me. We sought permission to enter upon 'Ā'ishah. She said: Who is this? He said: Ḥakīm b. Aflaḥ. She asked: Who is with you? He replied: Sa'd b. Hishām. She said: Hishām son of 'Amir who was killed in the Battle of Uḥud. I said: Yes. She said: What a

712. This shows that the Prophet (may peace be upon him) sometimes offered five *rak'ahs* of *witr* prayer. The number of *rak'ahs* of *witr* prayer is disputed. According to Abū Ḥanīfah, it comprises only three *rak'ahs*. Al-Shāfi'ī and other jurists hold that it is permissible to offer one, three or five *rak'ahs* of *witr* prayer.

713. He would pray eight *rak'ahs* of *tahajjud* prayer or *tarāwiḥ* and three *rak'ahs* of *witr*. Some traditions indicate that he also prayed thirteen *rak'ahs*. In fact, these included two *rak'ahs* of the dawn prayer.

714. Another tradition indicates that the Prophet (may peace be upon him) prayed during the night in pairs of *rak'ahs*. Sometimes he prayed in two *rak'ahs* and sometimes in four *rak'ahs*. There is no contradiction between the two reports.

good man 'Āmir was! I said: Mother of the faithful, tell me about the character of the Apostle of Allah (may peace be upon him). She asked: Do you not recite the Qur'ān? The character of the Apostle of Allah (may peace be upon him) was the Qur'ān.[715] I asked: Tell me about his vigil and prayer at night. She replied: Do you not recite: "O thou folded in garments" (lxxiii. 1). I said: Why not?

When the opening verses of this *sūrah* were revealed, the Companions stood praying (most of the night) until their feet swelled; and the concluding verses were not revealed for twelve months from heaven. At last the concluding verses were revealed and so the prayer at night became voluntary after it was obligatory. I said: Tell me about the *wit* of the Prophet (may peace be upon him) She replied: He used to pray eight *rak'ahs*, sitting only during the eighth of them. Then he would stand up and pray another *rak'ah*. He would sit only after the eighth and the ninth *rak'ahs*. He would utter the salutation only after the ninth *rak'ah*. He would then pray two *rak'ahs* sitting,[716] and that made eleven *rak'ahs*, sonny. But when he grew old and became fleshy he observed a *witr* of seven, sitting only in sixth and seventh *rak'ahs*, and would utter the salutation only after the seventh *rak'ah*. He would then pray two *rak'ahs* sitting, and that made nine *rak'ahs*, sonny. The Apostle of Allah (may peace be upon him) would not pray through a whole night, or recite the whole Qur'ān in a night, or fast a complete month except in Ramaḍān. When he offered a prayer, he would do that regularly. When he was overtaken by sleep at night, he would pray twelve *rak'ahs*.

The narrator said: I came to Ibn 'Abbās and narrated all this to him. By Allah, this is really a tradition. Had I been on speaking terms with her, I would have come to her and heard it from her mouth. I said: If I knew that you were not on speaking terms with her, I would have never narrated it to you.[717]

(1338) The above-mentioned tradition has also been narrated by Qatādah through a different chain of narrators. This version adds: He (the Prophet) used to pray eight *rak'ahs* during which he did not sit except after the eighth *rak'ah*. He would sit, make

715. This means that the Prophet (may peace be upon him) translated the teachings of the Qur'ān into action in his own life His character was a mirror of the Qur'ān.

716. The Prophet (may peace be upon him) sometimes prayed two *rak'ahs* sitting after *witr* prayer. But he did not pray them regularly. It is said that he had done so to show their permissibility. Most of the traditions narrated by al-Bukhārī and Muslim indicate that the last prayer of the Prophet (may peace be upon him) during night was *witr*. Aḥmad and al-Awzā'ī permitted to pray two *rak'ahs* sitting after *witr*, but Mālik did not allow (*'Awn al-Ma'būd*, I, 513).

717. This shows that Ibn 'Abbās was not on speaking terms with 'Ā'ishah perhaps due to her quarrel with 'Alī. Ibn 'Abbās was siding 'Alī in the Battle of Jamal. There may be other reasons for this matter. But it should be noted that the action of Ibn Abbās is not a model for others for it contradicts a number of traditions of the Prophet (may peace be upon him). He prohibited to abandon speaking to a Muslim for more than three days (*'Awn al-Ma'būd*, I, 513).

mention of Allah, supplicate Him and then utter the salutation so loudly that we could hear it. He would then pray two *rak'ahs* sitting after he had uttered the salutation. Then he would pray one *rak'ah*, and that made eleven *rak'ahs*, sonny. When the Apostle of Allah (may peace be upon him) grew old and became fleshy, he offered seven *rak'ahs* of *witr*, and then he would pray two *rak'ahs* sitting after he had uttered the salutation. The narrator narrated the tradition to the same effect till the end.

(1339) The above tradition has also been transmitted by Yahyã b. Sa'îd to the same effect. The version adds the words: "He uttered the salutation so loudly that we could hear it."

(1340) This tradition has also been transmitted by Sa'îd through a different chain of narrators to the same effect. Ibn Bashshãr narrated the tradition like that of Yahyã b. Sa'îd. His version has: He uttered the salutation in a way that we could hear it.

(1341) Zurãrah b. Awfã said that 'Ã'ishah was asked about the prayer of the Apostle of Allah (may peace be upon him) in the midnight. She said: He used to offer his night prayer in congregation and then return to his family (in his house) and pray four *rak'ahs*. Then he would go to his bed and sleep, but the water for his ablution was placed covered near his head and his tooth-stick was also kept there until Allah awakened him at night. He then used to tooth-stick and performed ablution perfectly and came to the place of prayer and would pray eight *rak'ahs*, in which he would recite Sûrah al-Fãtihah, and a *sûrah* from the Qur'ãn as Allah willed. He would not sit during any of them but sit after the eighth *rak'ah*, and would not utter the salutation, but recite (the Qur'ãn) during the ninth *rak'ah* and then would sit and supplicate as long as Allah willed, and beg Him and devote his attention to Him; and he would utter the salutation once in a loud voice so much so that the inmates of the house were almost awakened by his loud salutation. He would then recite Sûrah al-Fãtihah while sitting and bow while sitting, and then recite the Qur'ãn during the second *rak'ah*, and would bow and prostrate while sitting, and supplicate Allah as long as He willed, and then utter the salutation and turn away. This much prayer of the Apostle of Allah (may peace be upon him) continued till he became fleshy. During that period he retrenched two *rak'ahs* from nine and began to pray six and seven *rak'ahs* standing and two *rak'ahs* sitting. This continued till he died.

(1342) The above-mention tradition has also been narrated by Banu al-Hakîm through a different chain of narrators. This version adds: He (the Prophet) would offer the night prayer and go to his bed. In this version there is no mention of praying four *rak'ahs*. The narrator then transmitted the rest of the tradition. This version further says: He would pray eight *rak'ahs* during which his recitation of the Qur'ãn, bowing and prostration were all equal. He would sit only after the eighth *rak'ah*, and then stand up without uttering the salutation, and pray one *rak'ah* observing *witr* prayer and then give the salutation raising his voice so much so that we were about to awake. The narrator then transmitted the tradition to the same effect.

(1343) Zurārah b. Awfā said that 'Ā'ishah was asked about the prayer of the Apostle of Allah (may peace be upon him). She said: He used to lead the people in the night prayer and return to his family and pray four *rak'ahs* and go to his bed. The narrator then transmitted the tradition in full. This version does not mention the words: "During them (the *rak'ahs*) he equated all the recitation of the Qur'ān, bowing and recitation." This also does not mention the words about the salutation: "Till he almost awakened us."[718]

(1344) This tradition has also been transmitted by 'Ā'ishah through a different chain of narrators. But the tradition narrated by Ḥammād b. Salamah is not equal to the tradition narrated by others.

(1345) 'Ā'ishah said: The Apostle of Allah (may peace be upon him) used to pray thirteen *rak'ahs* during the night, observing the *witr* prayer with nine (or as she said). He used to pray two *rak'ahs* while sitting and pray two *rak'ahs* of the dawn prayer between the *adhān* and the *iqāmah*.

(1346) 'Ā'ishah said: The Apostle of Allah (may peace be upon him) used to observe the *witr* prayer with nine *rak'ahs*. Then he used to pray seven *rak'ahs* (of *witr* prayer). He would pray two *rak'ahs* sitting after the *witr* in which he would recite the Qur'an (sitting). When he wished to bow, he stood up and bowed and prostrated.

Abū Dāwūd said: These two traditions have been transmitted by Khālid b. 'Abd Allah al-Wāsiṭī. In his version he said: 'Alqamah b. Waqqāṣ said: O mother, how did he pray the two *rak'ahs*? He narrated the rest of the tradition to the same effect.

(1347) Sa'd b. Hishām said: I came to Medina and entered upon 'Ā'ishah, and said to her: Tell me about the prayer of the Apostle of Allah (may peace be upon him). She said: The Apostle of Allah (may peace be upon him) used to lead the people in the night prayer, and then go to his bed and sleep. When the midnight came he got up and went to answer the call of nature and to the ablution water. He

718. The number of *rak'ahs* prayed by the Prophet (may peace be upon him) during the night vary as narrated by Ibn 'Abbās, 'Ā'ishah, Zaid and other Companions. The reason of variance is that each Companion narrated according to his observation. Even 'Ā'ishah narrated several traditions on this subject which indicate a different number of *rak'ahs* of *tahajjud* prayer. It is said that generally the Prophet (may peace be upon him) prayed eleven *rak'ahs* at night. Occasionally he changed this number. He prayed the maximum number of fifteen *rak'ahs* including two *rak'ahs* of the dawn prayer, and the minimum he prayed were seven *rak'ahs*. All this depended on his convenience and duration. But it should be noted that the number of *rak'ahs* of *tahajjud* prayer is not defined. One may pray more or less than the *rak'ahs* mentioned in the traditions. The more one prays, the more reward one will get. The difference is over the number of *rak'ahs* prayed by the Prophet (*'Awn al-Ma'būd*, I, 515).

then performed ablution and thereafter entered the mosque and prayed eight *rak'ahs*. To my mind he performed the recitation of the Qur'ān, bowing and prostrating equally. He then observed *witr* with one *rak'ah* and prayed two *rak'ahs* sitting. Then he lay down on the ground. Sometimes Bilāl came to him and called him for prayer. He then napped, and sometimes I doubted whether he napped or not, till he (Bilāl) called him for prayer. This is the prayer he offered till he grew old or became fleshy. She then mentioned how he became fleshy as Allah wished.

(1348) 'Abd Allah b. 'Abbās said that he slept with the Prophet (may peace be upon him). He saw that he (the Prophet) awoke, used tooth-stick, performed ablution, and recited: "In the creation of the heavens and the earth"[719] to the end of the *surah*. Then he stood up and prayed two *rak'ahs* in which he prolonged the standing, bowing, prostration; he then turned away and slept till he began to snore. This he did three times. This made six *rak'ahs* in all. He would use tooth-stick, then perform ablution, and recite those verses. He then observed the *witr* prayer. The version of 'Uthmān has: with three *rak'ahs*. The *mu'adhdhin* then came to him and he went out for prayer. The version of Ibn 'Īsā adds: He then observed *witr* prayer; then Bilāl came to him and called him for prayer when the dawn broke. He then prayed the two *rak'ahs* of the dawn prayer. He then went out for prayer. Then both the narrators were agreed: He began to supplicate saying: O Allah, place light in my heart, light in my tongue, light in my hearing, light in my eyesight, light on my right hand, light on my left hand, light in front of me, light behind me, light below me; O Allah, give me abundant light.

(1349) The above tradition has also been transmitted by Ḥuṣain through a different chain of narrators in like manner, This version has the words: "And give me abundant light."

Abū Dāwūd said: This tradition has been transmitted by Abū Khālid al-Dālānī from Ḥabīb and Salamah b. Kuhail from Abū Rishdīn from Ibn 'Abbās in a similar manner.

(1350) Faḍl b. 'Abbās said: I spent a night with the Prophet (may peace be upon him) to see how he prayed. He got up, performed ablution and prayed two *rak'ahs*. His standing was like his bowing (i.e. equal in duration), and his bowing was like his prostration (equal in length). Then he slept. Afterwards he awoke, performed ablution, and used tooth-stick. He then recited five verses from Sūrah Āl 'Imrān; In the creation of the heavens and the earth and the alternation of night and day. He went on doing so till he prayed ten *rak'ahs*. He then stood up and prayed one *rak'ah* observing *witr* with it. In the meantime the *mu'adhdhin* called to prayer. The Apostle of Allah (may peace be upon him) stood up after the *mu'adhdhin* had kept silent. He prayed two light *rak'ahs* and remained sitting till he offered the dawn prayer.

719. Qur'ān, iii. 190.

Abū Dāwūd said : A part of the tradition transmitted by Ibn Bashshār remained hidden from me.

(1351) Ibn 'Abbās said : I spent a night with my maternal aunt Maimūnah. The Apostle of Allah (may peace be upon him) came after the evening had come. He asked : Did the boy pray ? She said : Yes. Then he lay down till a part of night had passed as much as Allah willed ; he got up, performed ablution and prayed seven or five *rak'ahs*, observing *witr* with them. He uttered the salutation only in the last of them.

(1352) Ibn 'Abbās said : I spent a night in the house of my maternal aunt Maimūnah, daughter of al-Ḥārith. The Prophet (may peace be upon him) offered the night prayer. He then came and prayed four *rak'ahs* and slept. He then stood up and prayed. I stood at his left side. He made me go round and made me stand at his right side. He then prayed five *rak'ahs* and slept, and I heard his snoring. He then got up and prayed two *rak'ahs*. Afterwards he came out and offered the dawn prayer.

(1353) Sa'īd b. Jubair said that Ibn 'Abbās told him : He (the Prophet) got up and prayed eight *rak'ahs* in pairs, and then observed *witr* with five *rak'ahs* and he did not sit between them.

(1354) 'A'ishah said : The Apostle of Allah (may peace be upon him) used to pray thirteen *rak'ahs*, observing six *rak'ahs* in pairs including the two *rak'ahs* of the dawn prayer. He woud observe *witr* with five *rak'ahs*. He sat only in the last of them.

(1355) 'Ā'ishah said : The Prophet (may peace be upon him) used to pray thirteen *rak'ahs* during the night including the two *rak'ahs* of the dawn prayer.

(1356) 'Ā'ishah said : The Apostle of Allah (may peace be upon him) offered the night prayer and then prayed eight *rak'ahs* standing, and two *rak'ahs* between the two *adhans* (i.e. the *adhān* for the dawn prayer and the *iqāmah*). He never left them

Ja'far b. Musāfir said in his version : (He prayed) the two *rak'ahs* sitting between the two *adhāns*. He added the word "sitting".

(1357) 'Abd Allah b. Abī Qais said that he asked 'Ā'ishah : How many *rak'ahs* would the Apostle of Allah (may peace be upon him) pray observing the *witr* ? She said : He used to observe the *witr* with four and three, six and three, eight and three and ten and three *rak'ahs* never observing less than seven or more than thirteen.

The narrator Aḥmad added in his version : He would not observe the *witr* with two *rak'ahs* before the dawn. I asked : With what would he observe the *witr*? She said : He would never leave it. The version of Aḥmad does not mention the words "six and three (*rak'ahs*)".

(1358) Al-Aswad b. Yazīd said that he entered upon 'Ā'ishah and asked her about the prayer of the Apostle of Allah (may peace be upon him) during the night. She said : He used to pray thirteen *rak'ahs* during the night. Then he began to pray eleven *rak'ahs* and left two *rak'ahs*. When he died, he would pray nine *rak'ahs* during the night. His last prayer during the night was *witr.*

(1359) The client of Ibn 'Abbās said that he asked him: How would the Apostle of Allah (may peace be upon him) pray during the night? He replied: I spent a night with him when he was with Maimūnah. He slept and awoke when half the night or one-third of it had passed. He stood up and went to a leather-bag containing water. He performed ablution and I also performed ablution with him. He then stood up and I also stood at his left side. He made me stand at his right side. He then put his hand upon my head, as he was touching my ear and awakening me. He then prayed two light *rak'ahs* and recited Sūrah al-Fātiḥah in each of them, and uttered the salutation. He then prayed eleven *rak'ahs* observing the *witr* and slept. Then Bilāl came to him and said: Prayer, Apostle of Allah. He got up and prayed two *rak'ahs*, and then led the people in prayer.

(1360) Ibn 'Abbās said: I spent a night with my maternal aunt Maimūnah. The Prophet (may peace be upon him) got up to pray at night. He prayed thirteen *rak'ahs* including two *rak'ahs* of the dawn prayer. I guessed that he stood in every *rak'ah* as long as one could recite Sūrah al-Muzzammil.

The version of Nūḥ does not mention the two *rak'ahs* of the dawn prayer.

(1361) Khālid al-Juhanī said: I shall watch the prayer of the Apostle of Allah (may peace be upon him) at night. I slept at the threshold of his door or of his tent. The Apostle of Allah (may peace be upon him) prayed two light *rak'ahs*, and then he prayed two long, long, long *rak'ahs*. He then prayed two *rak'ahs* that were not so long as the two *rak'ahs* before them; he then prayed two *rak'ahs* that were less in duration, than the *rak'ahs* before them; again he prayed two *rak'ahs* that were less in length than the preceding *rak'ahs*; he again prayed two *rak'ahs* that were less in length than the previous *rak'ahs*. This made altogether thirteen *rak'ahs*.

(1362) 'Abd Allah b. 'Abbās said that he spent a night with Maimūnah, wife of the Prophet (may peace be upon him), who was also his (Ibn 'Abbās's) maternal aunt. I lay towards the width of the pillow and the Apostle of Allah (may peace be upon him) and his wife slept towards its length. The Apostle of Allah (may peace be upon him) slept. When half the night passed, or a little before it or a little after it, the Apostle of Allah (may peace be upon him) awoke and began to rub his face (eyes) to remove the sleep. He then recited ten verses from the last part of Sūrah 'Āl 'Imrān. He then came to a bag of water that was hanging. He performed ablution from it and performed his ablution well. He then stood up and prayed. I also got up and did as he did. I then went and stood at his side. The Apostle of Allah (may peace be upon him) placed his right hand upon my head and took me by my ear twisting it. He then prayed two *rak'ahs*, then two *rak'ahs*, then two *rak'ahs*, then two *rak'ahs*, then two *rak'ahs*, then two *rak'ahs*. The narrator al-Qa'nabī said: Six times. He observed the *witr* prayer, and then slept until the *mu'adhdhin* came. He got up and prayed two light *rak'ahs* ; and then he came out and offered the dawn prayer.

Chapter 468

THE COMMANDMENT OF OBSERVING MODERATION IN PRAYER

(1363) 'Ā'ishah reported the Apostle of Allah (may peace be upon him) as saying : Choose such actions as you are capable of performing, for Allah does not grow weary till you do. The acts most pleasing to Allah are those which are done most continuously, even if they amount to little. Whenever he began an action, he would do it continuously.[720]

(1364) 'Ā'ishah said : The Prophet (may peace be upon him) called 'Uthmān b. Maẓ'ūn. When he came to him, he said : 'Uthmān, did you dislike my practice ? He said : No, by Allah, but I seek your practice. He said : I sleep, I pray, I keep fast, I (sometimes) leave fast, and I marry women. Fear Allah, 'Uthmān, your wife has a right on you, your guest has a right on you, your self has a right on you ; you should keep fast and (sometimes) leave fast, and pray and sleep.[721]

(1365) 'Alqamah said : 'Ā'ishah was asked about the actions of the Apostle of Allah (may peace be upon him). Did he perform some actions exclusively on some particular days ? She said : No, he performed his actions regularly. Which of you has the strength as much as the Apostle of Allah (may peace be upon him) had ?

DETAILED INJUNCTIONS ABOUT RAMADĀN

Chapter 469

NIGHT PRAYERS DURING RAMAḌĀN

(1366) Abū Hurairah said : The Apostle of Allah (may peace be upon him) used to commend prayer at night during Ramaḍān, but did not command it as a duty. He would say : If anyone prays during the night in Ramaḍān because of faith and

720. This tradition indicates that Allah likes those actions that are performed regularly, in good spirit and with pleasure. One should not undertake an action that one cannot perform easily so that one is tired and grows weary, and then leaves that action. This applies equally to all good actions and includes worship.

721. The Prophet (may peace be upon him) taught moderation in observing prayer, keeping fasts and in similar other acts of piety. There is no monasticism in Islam. Islam does not allow to leave all the business of life and retire in a lonely place for worship. A Muslim should perform all the works of daily life in accordance with the injunctions of Islam ; they will earn reward for him like acts of worship.

seeking his reward from Allah, his previous sins will be forgiven to him. When the Apostle of Allah (may peace be upon him) died, this was the practice, and it continued thus during Abū Bakr's caliphate and early part of 'Umar's.[722]

Abū Dāwūd said: This tradition has been transmitted by 'Uqail, Yūnus and Abū Uwais in like manner. The version of 'Uqail goes: He who fasts during Ramaḍān and prays during the night.

(1367) Abū Hurairah reported the Prophet (may peace be upon him) as saying: If anyone fasts during Ramaḍān because of faith and in order to seek his reward from Allah, his previous sins will be forgiven to him. If any one prays in the night of power (*lailat al-qadr*)[723] because of faith and in order to seek his reward from Allah his previous sins will be forgiven to him.

Abū Dāwūd said: This tradition has been transmitted in a similar manner by Yaḥyā b. Abī Kathīr and Muḥammad b. 'Amr from Abū Salamah.

(1368) 'Ā'ishah, wife of the Prophet (may peace be upon him), offered (*tarāwīḥ*) prayer in the mosque and the people also prayed along with him. He then prayed on the following night, and the people gathered in large numbers. They gathered on the third night too, but the Apostle of Allah (may peace be upon him) did not come out to them. When the morning came, he said: I witnessed what you did, and nothing prevented me from coming out to you except that I feared that this (prayer) might be prescribed for you. That was in Ramaḍān.[724]

(1369) 'Ā'ishah said: The people used to pray (*tarawīḥ* prayer) in the mosque during Ramaḍān severally. The Apostle of Allah (may peace be upon him) commanded me (to spread a mat). I spread a mat for him and he prayed upon it. The narrator then transmitted the same story. The Prophet (may peace be upon him) said: O people, praise be to Allah, I did not pass my night carelessly, nor did your position

722. In the beginning the Prophet (may peace be upon him) prayed the *tarāwiḥ* prayer in Ramaḍān in congregation for two days. He did not come out from his house on the third day, and told them in the morning that he had not come out to lead them in this prayer for the fear that it might be prescribed by Allah upon them in Ramaḍān. Hence the people offered it in their houses during his lifetime, during Abū Bakr's caliphate and in the early part of 'Umar's. 'Umar then made the arrangement of offering *tarāwiḥ* prayer in congregation, calling it a good innovation (*bid'ah*.) Hence Abū Ḥanīfah, al-Shāfi'ī and Aḥmad and most of the scholars take it better to offer *tarāwiḥ* prayer in congregation. According to Abū Yūsuf and Mālik, it is better to offer this prayer alone in the house.

723. *L ilat al-Qadr* literally means Night of Power or Honour. This is a significant night which generally falls in the last ten days of Ramaḍān. Allah grants mercy, forgiveness and much reward to those who worship in this night.

724. The Prophet (may peace be upon him) abandoned the congregational prayer of *tarāwiḥ* for fear that it might be prescribed as a duty. This might put them into hardship. Now after the death of the Prophet (may peace be upon him) there is no fear of prescription. Hence there is no harm in offering the *tarāwiḥ* prayer in congregation.

remain hidden from me.

(1370) Abū Dharr said : We fasted along with the Apostle of Allah (may peace be upon him) during Ramaḍān, but he did not make us get up at night for prayer at any time during the month till seven nights remained ; then he made us get up for prayer till a third of the night had passed. When the sixth remaining nights came, he did not make us get up for prayer. When the fifth remaining night came, he made us get up for prayer till a half of the night had gone, so I said : Apostle of Allah, I wish you had led us in supererogatory prayers during the whole of this night. He said : When a man prays with an *imām* till he goes he is reckoned as having spent a whole night in prayer. On the fourth remaining night he did not make us get up. When the third remaining night came, he gathered his family, his wives, and the people and prayed with us till we were afraid we would miss the *falāḥ* (success). I said : What is *falaḥ* ? He said : Meal before daybreak. Then he did not make us get up for prayer during the remainder of the month.[725]

(1371) 'Ā'ishah said : When the last ten days of Ramaḍān came, the Prophet (may peace be upon him) kept vigil and prayed during the whole night, and tied the wrapper tightly, and awakened his family (to pray during the night).

Abū Dāwūd said : The name of Abū Ya'fūr is 'Abd al-Raḥmān b. 'Ubaid b. Nisṭās.

(1372) Abū Hurairah said : The Apostle of Allah (may peace be upon him) came out and saw that the people were praying during (the night of) Ramaḍān in the corner of the mosque. He asked : Who are these people ? It was said to him that those were people who had not learnt the Qur'ān. But Ubayy b. Ka'b is praying and they would pray behind him. The Prophet (may peace be upon Him) said : They did right and it is good what they did.

Abū Dāwūd said : This tradition is not strong ; the narrator Muslim b. Khālid is weak.

725. If the month of Ramaḍān is counted for thirty days, the remaining seven nights begin from the twenty-fourth of Ramaḍān. If it is taken for twenty-nine days, the remaining seven nights begin from the twenty-third of Ramaḍān. If is most probable that he prayed on twenty-third, twenty-fifth and twenty-seventh night of Ramaḍān because they are odd number. The night of power (*lailat al-qadr*) generally happens on odd nights in the last ten days of Ramaḍān.

As regards the number of *rak'ahs* of the *tarāwiḥ* prayer, it should be noted that the most authentic and sound traditions indicate that the Prophet (may peace be upon him) prayed eleven *rak'ahs*, i.e. eight *rak'ahs*, for *tarāwiḥ* and three for *witr* prayer. The traditions which indicate twenty *rak'ahs* are weak.

According to Abū Ḥanīfah, Mālik, al-Shāfi'ī and Aḥmad, there are twenty *rak'ahs* in the *tarāwiḥ* prayer. The traditionists maintain that there are only eight *rak'ahs* in the *tarāwiḥ* prayer. Both groups proffer evidence in support of their point of view (*'Awn al-Ma'būd*, I, 521-22).

Chapter 470

LAILAT AL-QADR

(1373) Zirr (b. Ḥubaish) said : I said to Ubayy b. Ka'b : Tell me about *lailat al-qadr*, O Abū al-Mundhir,[726] for our companion (Ibn Mas'ūd) was questioned about it, and he said : Anyone who gets up for prayer every night all the year round will hit upon it (i.e. *lailat al-qadr*). He replied : May Allah have mercy on Abū 'Abd al-Raḥmān.[727] By Allah, he knew that it was in Ramaḍān, (Musaddad's version goes) but he disliked that the people should content themselves (with that night alone) ; or he liked that the people should not content themselves (with that night alone). According to the agreed version : By Allah, it is the twenty-seventh night of Ramaḍān, without any reservation. I said : How did you know that, Abū al-Mundhir? He replied : By the indication (or sign) of which the Apostle of Allah (may peace be upon him) informed us. I asked Zirr : What is that sign ? He replied : The sun rises like a vessel of water in the morning following that night ; it has no ray until it rises high up.[728]

(1374) 'Abd Allah b. Unais said : I was present in the gathering of Banū Salamah, and I was the youngest of them. They (the people) said : Who will ask the Apostle of Allah (may peace be upon him) for us about *lailat al-qadr* ? That was the twenty-first of Ramaḍān. I went out and said the sunset prayer along with the Apostle of Allah (may peace be upon him). I then stood at the door of his house. He passed by me and said : Come in. I entered (the honse) and the dinner was brought for him. I was prevented from taking food as it was scanty. When he finished his dinner, he said to me : Give me my shoes. He then stood up and I also stood up with him. He said : Perhaps you have some business with me. I said : Yes. Some people of Banū Salamah have sent me to you asking you about *lailat al-qadr*. He asked : Which is the night today? I said : Twenty-second. He said : This is the very night. He then

726. This is the ***kunyah*** of Ubayy b. Ka'b.

727. ***Kunyah*** of Ibn Mas ūd

728. ***Lailat al-qadr*** is a significant night in the last ten days of Ramaḍān. Its merit and importance has been mentioned in the Qur'ān in Sūrah al-Qadr (xcvii.). Anyone who prays and worships in this night gets the reward of prayer and worship of one thousand months. The prayer and worship in this night are far better than worshipping for one thousand months. This is called ***lailat al-qadr*** (night of power, honour or destination) because decisions about peoples sustenance, birth, death and similar other matters take place during this night. Or it is called so due to its prominence and grandeur among all the nights.

There is a great difference of opinion amongst scholars as to when it comes. It is generally established that one can get it on the odd number of nights in the last ten days of Ramaḍān. It is also said that among these odd number of nights twenty-seventh night of Ramaḍān is certainly ***lailat al-qadr***. The Prophet (may peace be upon him) did not pinpoint it so that people should seek by observing prayer and worship on different nights (***'Awn al-Ma'būd***, I, 523).

withdrew and said : Or the following night referring to the twenty-third night.

(1375) 'Abd Allah b. Unais al-Juhanī said : Apostle of Allah, I have a place in the desert where I live and in which I pray, with the praise of Allah ; but give me command about a night when I come to this mosque. He replied : Come on the twenty-third night. I (Muhammad b. Ibrāhīm) said to his ('Abd Allah b. Unais's) son : How would your father act ? He replied : He used to enter the mosque when he had offered the afternoon prayer, and did not leave it for any purpose till he prayed the morning prayer. Then when he had prayed the morning prayer, he found his riding beast at the door of the mosque, mounted it and got back to his desert.

(1376) Ibn 'Abbās reported the Prophet (may peace be upon him) as saying: Seek *lailat al-qadr* in the last ten nights of Ramaḍān : when nine (nights) remain (i.e. on the twenty-first), when seven (nights) remain (i.e. on the twenty-third), and when five (nights) remain (i.e. on the twenty-fifth).

Chapter 471

THE VIEW THAT THE TWENTY-FIRST NIGHT OF RAMAḌĀN IS *LAILAT AL-QADR*

(1377) Abū Sa'īd al-Khudrī said : The Apostle of Allah (may peace be upon him) used to spend the middle ten days of Ramaḍān in retirement and devotion (*i'tikāf*) in the mosque. One year he had retirement and devotion in the mosque (as usual) ; when the twenty-first night came, and this is the night when he used to come out of his devotion in the mosque, he said : He who has engaged himself in devotion along with me should do so during the last ten days ; I saw that night, then was caused to forget it, but I have seen myself prostrating in water and mud on the morning following (that night), so seek it in the last ten days and seek it in every night with an odd number. Abū Sa'īd said : Rain fell that night, the mosque that was a thatched building dripped, and my eyes saw the Apostle of Allah (may peace be upon him) with traces of water and mud, on his forehead on the morning following the twenty-first night.

(1378) Abū Sa'īd al-Khudrī reported the Apostle of Allah (may peace be upon him) as saying : Seek it (*lailat al-qadr*) in the last ten days of Ramaḍān. Seek it on the ninth, seventh and fifth night. I (Abū Naḍrah) said : You know counting better than us, Abū Sa'īd. He said : Yes. I asked : What do you mean by the ninth, seventh and fifth night ? He said : When the twenty-first night passes, the night which follows it is the ninth ; when the twenty-third night passes, the night which follows it is the seventh ; when the twenty-fifth passes, the night which follows it is the fifth.[729]

Abū Dāwūd said : I do not know whether anything remained hidden from me or not.

Chapter 472

THE TRADITION THAT THE SEVENTEENTH NIGHT OF RAMAḌĀN IS *LAILAT AL-QADR*

(1379) Ibn Mas'ūd said : The Apostle of Allah (may peace be upon him) said to us : Seek it (*lailat al-qadr*) on the seventeenth night of Ramaḍān, and on the twenty-first night, and on the twenty-third night. He then kept silence.

Chapter 473

THE TRADITION THAT *LAILAT AL-QADR* FALLS DURING THE LAST SEVEN NIGHTS OF RAMAḌĀN

(1380) Ibn 'Umar reported the Apostle of Allah (may peace be upon him) as saying : Seek *lailat al-qadr* in the last seven nights.

Chapter 474

THE VIEW THAT THE TWENTY-SEVENTH NIGHT OF RAMAḌĀN IS *LAILAT AL-QADR*

(1381) Mu'āwiyah b. Abī Sufyān reported the Prophet (may peace be upon him) as saying : *Lailat al-qadr* is the twenty-seventh night (of Ramaḍān).

Chapter 475

THE VIEW THAT *LAILAT AL-QADR* IS IN THE WHOLE OF RAMAḌĀN

(1382) 'Abd Allah b. 'Umar said : The Apostle of Allah (may peace be upon him) was asked about *lailat al-qadr* and I was hearing. He said : It is during the whole of

729. These nights are not odd in number. Many traditions indicate that the people should seek *lailat al-qadr* in the nights odd in number during Ramaḍān. The Prophet (may peace be upon him) might have called them odd in consideration of the end of the month.

Ramaḍān.[730]

Abū Dāwūd said: Sufyān and Shu'bah narrated this tradition from Abū Isḥāq as a statement of Ibn 'Umar himself; they did not transmit it as a saying of the Prophet (may peace be upon him).

Chapter 476

IN HOW MANY DAYS SHOULD ONE COMPLETE THE RECITATION OF THE QUR'ĀN

(1383) 'Abd Allah b. 'Amr reported the Prophet (may peace be upon him) as saying to him: Complete the recitation of the Qur'ān in one month. He said: I have more strength. He (the Prophet) said: Complete the recitation in twenty days. He again said: I have more energy. He said: Recite in fifteen days. He again said: I have more energy. He said: Recite in ten days. He again said: I have more energy. He said: Recite in seven days; do not add to it.[731]

Abū Dāwūd said: The tradition narrated by Muslim is more perfect.

(1384) 'Abd Allah b. 'Amr said: The Apostle of Allah (may peace be upon him) said to me: Keep fast for three days every month, and finish the recitation of the Qur'ān in one month. I and he differed among ourselves on period of time.[732] He said: Fast one day and give it up the other day. The narrator 'Aṭā' said: The people differed from my father (in narrating the period of time). Some narrated seven days and others five.

(1385) Yazīd b. 'Abd Allah said that 'Abd Allah b. 'Amr said: In how many days should I finish the recitation of the Qur'ān, Apostle of Allah? He replied: In one month. He said: I am more energetic to complete it in a period less than this. He kept on repeating these words and lessening the period until he said: Complete its recitation in seven days. He again said: I am more energetic to complete it in a period less than this. He said: He who finishes the recitation of the Qur'ān in less than three

730. What is more correct is that *lailat al-qadr* falls on the twenty-seventh night of Ramaḍān. The correct date is, however, disputed.

731. It is commendable to finish the recitation of the whole of the Qur'ān in seven days. By this the Prophet (may peace be upon him) meant the observance of moderation in acts of worship. It is, however, not forbidden to finish the reading of the Qur'ān in less than seven days. Another tradition indicates that one can finish it in three days. In fact, mere recitation is not enough; one should understand it too. For this much time is required.

732 This means that 'Abd Allah b. 'Amr wanted to lessen the period of completing the recitation of the Qur'ān, but the Prophet (may peace be upon him) wished to increase it. He wished to keep more fasts, but the Prophet (may peace be upon him) wanted to lessen them. Another version has the word *nāqaḍani* instead of *nāqaṣani*. This means that he wanted "to change my action and I wanted to persist on it."

days does not understand it.[733]

(1386) Khaithamah reported that 'Abd Allah b. 'Amr said: The Apostle of Allah (may peace be upon him) said to me: Recite the Qur'ān in one month. I said: I have (more) energy. He said: Recite it in three days.

Abū 'Alī said: I heard Abū Dāwūd say: I heard Aḥmad b. Ḥanbal say: The narrator 'Īsā b. Shādhān is a sane person.

Chapter 477

ON FIXING A PART FROM THE QUR'ĀN FOR DAILY RECITATION

(1387) Ibn al-Hād said: Nāfi' b. Jubair asked me: In how many days do you recite the Qur'ān? I said: I have not fixed any part from it for daily round. Nāfi' said to me: Do not say: I do not fix any part of it for daily round, for the Apostle of Allah (may peace be upon him) said: I recited a part of the Qur'ān.[734]

The narrator Ibn al-Hād said: I think I have transmitted this tradition from al-Mughīrah b. Shu'bah.

(1388) Aws b. Ḥudhaifah said: We came upon the Apostle of Allah (may peace be upon him) in a deputation of Thaqīf. The signatories of the pact came to al-Mughīrah b. Shu'bah as his guest. The Apostle of Allah (may peace be upon him) made Banū Mālik stay in a tent of his. Musaddad's version says: He was in the deputation of Thaqīf which came to the Apostle of Allah (may peace be upon him). He used to visit and have a talk with us every day after the night prayer. The version of Abū Sa'īd goes: He remained standing for long (talking to us) so much so that he put his weight sometimes on one leg and sometimes on the other due to his long stay. He mostly used to state to us how his people, the Quraish, behaved with him. He would say: We were not equal; we were weak and degraded at Mecca (according to the Musaddad's version). When we came over to Medina the fight began between us; sometimes we suppressed them and at other times they suppressed us. One night he came late and did not come at the time he used to come. We asked him: You came late tonight? He said: I could not recite the fixed part of the Qur'ān that I used to recite everyday. I disliked to come till I completed it. Aws said: I asked the Com-

733. This shows that it is commendable to complete the recitation of the Qur'ān in seven days. One can complete in three days too if one is able to do so. It is worthy to note that the Prophet (may peace be upon him) stressed the understanding of the Qur'ān, and not the recitation alone. The more slowly a man reads the Qur'ān, the more he can understand it.

734. The Qur'ān was not divided into thirty parts in the lifetime of the Prophet (may peace be upon him). He might have fixed some portion of the Qur'ān for recitation. One is allowed to fix any number of verses or *sūrahs* he is easily able to recite every day.

panions of the Apostle of Allah (may peace be upon him): How do you divide the Qur'ān for daily recitation? They said: Three *surahs*; five *surahs*; eleven *surahs*; thirteen *surahs*: *mufaṣṣal surahs*.[735]

Abū Dāwūd said: The version of Abū Sa'īd is complete.

(1389) 'Abd Allah b. 'Amr reported the Apostle of Allah (may peace be upon him) as saying: He who recites the Qur'ān in a period less than three days does not understand it.[736]

(1390) Wahb b. Munabbih said: 'Abd Allah b. 'Amr asked the Prophet (may peace be upon him): In how many days should one complete the recitation of the Qur'ān? He said: In forty days. He then said: In one month. He again said: In twenty days. He then said: In fifteen days. He then said: In ten days. Finally he said: In seven days.

(1391) 'Alqamah and al-Aswad said: A man came to Ibn Mas'ūd. He said: I recite the *mufaṣṣal*[737] *surahs* in one *rak'ah*. You might recite it quickly as one recites the verse (poetry) quickly, and/or as the dried dates fall down (from the tree). But the Prophet (may peace be upon him) used to recite two equal *surahs* in one *rak'ah*; he would recite (for instance) Sūrahs al-Najm and al-Raḥmān in one *rak'ah*, Sūrahs Iqtarabat and al-Ḥāqqah in one *rak'ah*, Sūrahs al-Ṭūr and al-Dhāriyat in one *rak'ah*, Sūrahs Idhā Waqa'at and Nūn in one *rak'ah*, Sūrahs Sa'ala Sā'il and al-Nāzi'āt in one *rak'ah*, Sūrahs Wailun li'l-Muṭaffifīn and 'Abasa in one *rak'ah*, Sūrahs al-Muddaththir and al-Muzzammil in one *rak'ah*, Sūrahs Hal Atā and Lā Uqsimu bi Yawm al-Qiyāmah in one *rak'ah*, Sūrahs 'Amma Yatasā'alūn and wa al-Mursalāt in one *rak'ah*, Sūrahs al-Dukhān and Idhā al-Shamsu Kuwwirat in one *rak'ah*.

Abū Dāwūd said: This is the arrangement of Ibn Mas'ūd himself.[738]

(1392) 'Abd al-Raḥmān b. Yāzīd said: I asked Abū Mas'ūd while he was making circumambulation of the Ka'bah (about the recitation of some verses from the Qur'ān). He said: The Apostle of Allah (may peace be upon him) said: If anyone recites two verses from the last of Sūrah al-Baqarah at night, they will be sufficient for him.[739]

735. The Qur'ān has been divided into seven stages (*manāzil*). One has to recite one stage (*manzil*) daily and thus finish the Qur'ān in one week. This was generally the practice prevalent in the lifetime of the Prophet (may peace be upon him). The seven stages found in the Qur'ān are the same in which the Qur'ān was divided in the time of the Prophet (may peace be upon him).

736. This shows that it is advisable to recite the Qur'ān in three days. If one does so, one understands it. If a person finishes the Qur'ān in less than three days, he cannot understand it due to quick recitation.

737. The *sūrahs* from Qāf to the end of the Qur'ān.

738. Similar was the arrangement of the *sūrahs* in the codex of Ibn Mas'ūd.

739. This either means that the recitation of these verses is enough for him; he is not required to keep vigil and pray at night, or it means that they will be sufficient for him in distress and misery.

(1393) 'Abd Allah b. 'Amr b. al-'Āṣ reported the Apostle of Allah (may peace be upon him) as saying: If anyone prays at night reciting regularly ten verses, he will not be recorded among the negligent; if anyone prays at night and recites a hundred verses, he will be recorded among those who are obedient to Allah; and if anyone prays at night reciting one thousand verses, he will be recorded among those who receive huge rewards.[740]

Abū Dāwūd said: The name of Ibn Ḥujairah al-Aṣghar is 'Abd Allah b. 'Abd al-Raḥmān b. Ḥujairah.

(1394) 'Abd Allah b. 'Amr said: A man came to the Apostle of Allah (may peace be upon him) and said: Teach me to read the Our'ān, Apostle of Allah. He said: Read three *surahs* which begin with A.L.R. He said: My age is advanced, my mind has become dull (i.e. memory has grown weak), and my tongue has grown heavy). So he said: Then read three *surahs* which begin with Ḥ.M. He repeated the same words. So he said: Read three *surahs* which begin with the "Glorification of Allah". But he repeated the same excuse. The man then said: Teach me a comprehensive *surah*, Apostle of Allah. The Prophet (may peace be upon him) taught him Sūrah (xcix.). "When the earth is shaken with her earthquake". When he finished it, the man said: By Him Who sent you with truth, I shall never add anything to it. The man then went away. The Prophet (may peace be upon him) said twice: The man got salvation.

Chapter 478

ON THE NUMBER OF VERSES IN A *SŪRAH*

(1395) Abū Hurairah reported the Prophet (may peace be upon him) as saying: A *surah* of the Qur'ān containing thirty verses will intercede its reader till he will be forgiven. That is: "Blessed is He in Whose Hand is the sovereignty" (Sūrah lxvii.).

CHAPTERS ON PROSTRATION WHILE REСITING THE QUR'ĀN

Chapter 479

HOW MANY PLACES ARE THERE IN THE QUR'ĀN WHERE PROSTRATION IS REQUIRED

(1396) 'Amr b. al-'Āṣ said: The Prophet (may peace be upon him) taught me

740. This refers to the recitation of *sūrahs* in the prayer at night (*tahajjud*). Some *sūrahs* have their particular characteristics in accordance with their theme. Hence one gets particular reward from Allah on their recitation.

fifteen prostrations while reciting the Qur'ān, including three in al-Mufaṣṣal[741] and two in Sūrah al-Ḥajj.[742]

Abū Dāwūd said: Abū al-Dardā' has reported eleven prostrations from the Prophet (may peace be upon him), but the chain of this tradition is weak.

(1397) 'Uqbah b. 'Āmir reported: I said to the Apostle of Allah (may peace be upon him): Are there two prostrations in Sūrah al-Ḥajj? He replied: Yes; if anyone does not make two prostrations, he should not recite them.[743]

Chapter 480

A VIEW THAT THERE IS NO PROSTRATION IN *MUFAṢṢAL SŪRAHS*

(1398) Ibn 'Abbās said: The Apostle of Allah (may peace be upon him) did not make a prostration at any verse in *al-Mufaṣṣal* from the time he moved to Medina.[744]

(1399) Zaid b. Thābit said: I recited to the Apostle of Allah (may peace be upon him) Sūrah al-Najm, but he did not prostrate himself.[745]

(1400) This tradition has also been transmitted by Zaid b. Thābit through a different chain of narrators to the same effect.

741. A title given to the *sūrahs* from xlix. to the end. Here this refers to the Sūrahs al-Najm, Idha al-Samā' Unshaqqat and 'Alaq (Iqrā').

742. Surah xxii.

It should be noted that the number of the places in the Qur'ān where one should prostrate is disputed among the jurists According to Aḥmad and Ibn al-Mubārak, there are fifteen places where prostration is required, as shown by this tradition. Al-Shāfi'ī and Abū Ḥanīfah maintain fourteen. But al-Shāfi'ī excludes the prostration in Sūrah Ṣād and Abū Ḥanīfah excludes one prostration in Sūrah al-Ḥajj. Mālik excludes the prostration in the *mufaṣṣal sūrahs*. Thus he takes eleven prostrations into consideration excluding prostration in Ṣād.

To make prostration while reciting the Qur'ān one has to fulfil all the conditions required for prayer If one does not make prostration at the time of recitation of the Qur'ān, one should prostrate later on. This will remain due on him.

743. This tradition clearly shows that there are two prostrations in Sūrah al-Ḥajj. But Abū Ḥanīfah excludes one prostration from al-Ḥajj. His view goes against this tradition. Al-Tirmidhī has, however, said that the chain of this tradition is weak (*'Awn al-Ma'būd*, I, 530).

744. Mālik argues on the basis of this tradition. But this tradition is weak, for the narrators Abū Qudāmah and Maṭar al-Warrāq are not reliable.

745. The Mālikīs argue from this tradition. In reply to them, it is said that this tradition does not indicate that the Prophet (may peace be upon him) never prostrated when he recited this *sūrah*. At that moment he might have left prostration for some excuse. Al-Bukhārī narrated a tradition which shows that the Prophet (may peace be upon him) recited Sūrah al-Najm and prostrated and along with him prostrated the Muslims, unbelievers and the jinn (*'Awn al-Ma'būd*, I, 530).

Abū Dāwūd said: Zaid was *imām* (in a prayer) and he did not make prostration.[746]

Chapter 481

A VIEW THAT THERE IS PROSTRATION IN *MUFAṢṢAL SURAHS*

(1401) 'Abd Allah (b. Mas'ūd) said: The Apostle of Allah (may peace be upon him) recited Sūrah al-Najm and prostrated himself. No one remained there who did not prostrate (along with him). A man[747] from the people took a handful of pebbles or dust and raised it to his face saying: This is enough for me. 'Abd Allah (b. Mas'ūd) said: I later saw him killed as an infidel.

Chapter 482

PROSTRATION IN SŪRAHS INSHIQĀQ (LXXXIV.) AND IQRĀ' (XCVI.)

(1402) Abū Hurairah said: We prostrated ourselves along with the Apostle of Allah (may peace be upon him) on account of: "When the sky is rent asunder" (lxxxiv.) and "Recite in the name of your Lord Who created" (xcvi).[748]

(1403) Abū Rāfi' said: I offered the night prayer behind Abū Hurairah. He recited Sūrah Inshiqāq ("When the sky is rent asunder") and prostrated himself. I asked him: What is this prostration? He replied: I prostrated myself on account of this (*surah*) behind Abū al-Qāsim (i.e. the Prophet). I shall continue prostrating on account of this till I meet him.

Chapter 483

PROSTRATION IN SŪRAH ṢĀD

(1404) Ibn 'Abbās said: A prostration when reciting Ṣād is not one of those which are divinely commanded, but I have seen the Apostle of Allah (may peace be upon him) prostrate himself.[749]

(1405) Abū Sa'īd al-Khudrī said: The Apostle of Allah (may peace be upon him)

746. The Prophet (may peace be upon him) did not prostrate in Sūrah al-Najm for he was following Zaid in prayer.

747. He was Umayyah b. Khalaf.

748. This shows the legality of prostrating while reciting the Qur'ān. This prostration, in the opinion of Abū Ḥanīfah, is necessary (*wājib*), but all the other jurists maintain that it is recommended (*sunnah*). It is necessary for the reciter and the listener to prostrate.

749. According to Mālik and al-Shāfi'ī, there is no prostration in Sūrah Ṣād.

recited Sūrah Ṣād on the pulpit. When he reached the place of prostration (in the *surah*), he descended and prostrated himself and the people prostrated with him. When the next day came, he recited it. When he reached the place of prostration (in the *surah*), the people became ready for prostration. Thereupon the Apostle of Allah (may peace be upon him) said: This is the repentance of a Prophet; but I saw you being ready for prostration. So he descended and prostrated himself and the people prostrated along with him).

Chapter 484

IF A PERSON LISTENS TO A VERSE IN WHICH A PROSTRATION OCCURS, AND HE IS RIDING (THE BEAST), WHAT SHOULD HE DO?

(1406) Ibn 'Umar said: In the year of Conquest the Apostle of Allah (may peace be upon him) recited a verse at which a prostration should be made and all the people prostrated themselves. Some were mounted, and some were prostrating themselves on the ground, and those who were mounted prostrated themselves on their hands.

(1407) Ibn 'Umar said: The Apostle of Allah (may peace be upon him) would recite to us a *surah* (according to the version of Ibn Numair) outside the prayer (the agreed version goes), then he would prostrate along with him, and none of us could find a place for his forehead.[750]

(1408) Ibn 'Umar said: The Apostle of Allah (may peace be upon him) used to recite the Qur'ān to us. When he came upon the verse containing prostration, he would utter the *takbīr* (Allah is most great) and we would prostrate ourselves along with him.

The narrator 'Abd al-Razzāq said: Al-Thawrī liked this tradition very much.

Abū Dāwūd said: This was liked by him for this contains the uttering of *takbīr*.

Chapter 485

WHAT SHOULD ONE SAY WHEN ONE PROSTRATES?

(1409) 'Ā'ishah said: The Apostle of Allah (may peace be upon him) prostrated himself at night when reciting the Qur'ān. He said repeatedly: My face prostrates

750. The place was so crowded that they could not make room for prostration. Another tradition indicates that they prostrated on the backs of the people. This is the view of Aḥmad and Abū Ḥanīfah. One is allowed to prostrate on another man's back in such a situation. Mālik holds that the people should wait till the men before them raise their heads; they should then prostrate themselves (*'Awn al-Ma'būd*, I, 532).

itself to Him Who created it and brought forth its hearing and seeing by His might and power.[751]

Chapter 486

WHEN SHOULD A PERSON PROSTRATE IF HE RECITES A QUR'ĀNIC VERSE CONTAINING PROSTRATION?

(1410) Abū Tamīmah al-Hujaimī said: When we came to Medina accompanying the caravan, I used to preach after the dawn prayer, and prostrate on account of the recitation of the Qur'ān. Ibn 'Umar prohibited me three times, but I did not cease doing that. He then repeated (his prohibition) saying: I prayed behind the Apostle of Allah (may peace be upon him), Abū Bakr, 'Umar and 'Uthmān; they would not prostrate (on account of the recitation of the Qur'ān) till the sun had risen.[752]

DETAILED INJUNCTIONS ABOUT *WITR*[753]

Chapter 487

TO OBSERVE THE *WITR* IS COMMENDABLE

(1411) 'Alī reported the Apostle of Allah (may peace be upon him) as saying: Allah is single (*witr*) and loves what is single, so observe the *witr*, you who follow the Qur'ān.[754]

(1412) The above-mentioned tradition has also been narrated by 'Abd Allah (b.

751. This is the supplication and praise of Allah which the Prophet (may peace be upon him) used to make in his prostrations while praying at night. This supplication is not peculiar to the prostrations made on account of the recitation of the Qur'ān. One may recite the usual supplication made in the prostration while praying, namely, "Glory be to my Lord, the Most High."

752. The prostration on account of the recitation of the Qur'ān after the morning and the afternoon prayers is prohibited according to Mālik, al-Shāfi'ī and Aḥmad b. Ḥanbal. The Ḥanafīs allow to make prostration after the morning and afternoon prayers. This tradition, in their opinion, is weak.

753. Literally, single or odd. This is an additional prayer observed after the prayer at night. This is necessary (*wājib*) according to Abū Ḥanīfah but not obligatory (*farḍ*) like the five prayers. Mālik, al-Shāfi'ī and Aḥmad hold that it is recommended (*sunnah*).

754. This refers to the prayer at night (*tahajjud*) in which the Qur'ān is recited for long. He addressed those who were Qur'ān-readers or memorised the Qur'ān by heart. By observing the *witr* the Prophet (may peace be upon him) meant to offer the prayer at night (*tahajjud*) and to make the *rak'ahs* odd by praying one, three or five *rak'ahs* of the *witr* in the end. This would make nine, eleven or thirteen *rak'ahs* of the prayer at night.

Mas'ūd) through a different chain of narrators to the same effect. This version adds: A bedouin said: What are you saying? He replied: This is neither for you, nor for your companions.

(1413) Khārijah b. Ḥudhafah al-'Adawī said: The Apostle of Allah (may peace be upon him) came out to us and said: Allah the Exalted has given you an extra prayer which is better for you than the red camels (i.e. high breed camels). This is the *witr* which Allah has appointed for you between the night prayer and the daybreak.

Chapter 488

ON A PERSON WHO DOES NOT OBSERVE THE *WITR* PRAYER

(1414) Buraidah said: I heard the Apostle of Allah (may peace be upon him) say: The *witr* is a duty, so he who does not observe it does not belong to us; the *witr* is a duty, so he who does not observe it does not belong to us; the *witr* is a duty, so he who does not observe it does not belong to us.[755]

(1415) Ibn Muḥairīz said: A man from Banū Kinānah, named al-Makhdajī, heard a person called Abū Muḥammad in Syria, saying: The *witr* is a duty. Al-Makhdajī said: So I went to 'Ubādah b. al-Ṣāmit and informed him. 'Ubādah said: Abū Muḥammad told a lie. I heard the Apostle of Allah (may peace be upon him) say: There are five prayers[756] which Allah has prescribed on His servants. If anyone offers them, not losing any of them, and not treating them lightly, Allah guarantees that He will admit him to Paradise. If anyone does not offer them, Allah does not take any responsibility for such a person. He may either punish him or admit him to Paradise.

Chapter 489

HOW MANY *RAK'AHS* ARE THERE IN THE *WITR*?

(1416) Ibn 'Umar said: A man who lived in the desert asked the Apostle of Allah (may peace be upon him) about the prayer at night. He made a sign with his two

755. This does not mean that the *witr* is an obligatory duty. It is of course a duty immensely emphasised by the Prophet (may peace be upon him). This is recommended (*sunnah*) according to Mālik, al-Shāfi'ī and Aḥmad, but necessary in the opinion of Abū Ḥanīfah.

756. As the Prophet (may peace be upon him) did not mention the *witr* among these prayers, the *witr* cannot be taken as a binding duty like five prayers. Those who maintain that the *witr* is recommended argue from this tradition.

fingers—in this way in pairs. The *witr* consists of one *tak'ah* towards the end of night.[757]

(1417) Abū Ayyūb al-Anṣārī reported the Apostle of Allah (may peace be upon him) as saying: The *witr* is a duty for every Muslim so if anyone wishes to observe it with five *rak'ahs*, he may do so; if anyone wishes to observe it with three, he may do so, and if anyone wishes to observe it with one, he may do so.[758]

Chapter 490

WHAT IS RECITED IN THE *WITR*

(1418) Ubayy b. Ka'b said: The Apostle of Allah (may peace be upon him) used to observe *witr* with (reciting) "Glorify the name of thy Lord, the most High" (Sūrah lxxxvii.), "Say O disbelievers" (Sūrah cix.), and "Say, He is Allah, the One, Allah, the eternally besought of all" (cxii.).[759]

(1419) 'Abd al-'Azīz b. Juraij said: I asked 'Ā'ishah, mother of the believers: With which (*sūrah*) the Apostle of Allah (may peace be upon him) used to observe *witr*? The narrator then narrated the tradition to the same effect. This version adds: In the third *rak'ah* he would recite: "Say, He is Allah, the One" (Sūrah cxii.), and "Say, I seek refuge in the Lord of daybreak" (Sūrah cxiii.), and "Say, I seek refuge in the Lord of mankind" (Sūrah cxiv.).

Chapter 491

SUPPLICATION DURING THE *WITR*

(1420) Al-Ḥasan b. 'Alī said: The Apostle of Allah (may peace be upon him)

757. The number of *rak'ahs* of the *witr* prayer is disputed amongst scholars. According to some, it consists of only one *rak'ah*. This view is held by 'Uthmān, Sa'd b. Abī Waqqāṣ, Abū Mūsā al-Ash'arī, Ibn 'Abbās, 'Ā'ishah, Ibn al-Zubair, Ibn al-Musayyib, Aṭā', Mālik, al-Awzā'ī, al-Shāfi'ī, Aḥmad and Isḥāq. Mālik, al-Shāfi'ī, Aḥmad and Isḥāq maintain that one may offer two *rak'ahs* and observe the *witr* along with them with one *rak'ah*. If one offers only one *rak'ah* independently, that is permissible according to al-Shāfi'ī, Aḥmad and Isḥāq. But Mālik disapproves of it. Abū Ḥanīfah maintains that the *witr* contains three *rak'ahs* without severing by uttering the salutation. Sufyān al-Thawrī holds that the *witr* consists of three, five, seven, nine or eleven *rak'ah*. Al-Awzā'ī holds the view that if one separates the first two *rak'ahs* from the last one *rak'ahs*, it is all right; if not, that is well and good. According to Mālik, it is necessary to separate the two *rak'ah* from one *rak ah*. If one forgets to separate two *rak'ahs* from one *rak'ah*, one should make two prostrations at the end of the prayer on account of forgetfulness (*'Awn al-Ma'būd*, I, 534).

758. This tradition clearly shows that the *witr* does not consist of any fixed number of *rak'ahs*. One may offer one, three or five *rak'ahs*. One may pray these *rak'ahs* either separately or in combination with the prayer at night (*tahajjud*).

759. The Ḥanafīs argue from this tradition that the *witr* consists of three *rak'ahs*.

taught me some words that I say during the *witr*. The version of Ibn Jawwās has: I say them in the supplication of the *witr*. They were: "O Allah, guide me among those Thou hast guided, grant me security among those Thou hast granted security, take me into Thy charge among those Thou nast taken into Thy charge, bless me in what Thou hast given, guard me from the evil of what Thou hast decreed, for Thou dost decree, and nothing is decreed for Thee. He whom Thou befriendest is not humbled. Blessed and Exalted art Thou, our Lord." [760]

(1421) The aforesaid tradition has been transmitted by Abū Isḥāq with the same chain and to the same effect. In the last of this tradition he said: The version has the words: "He would recite in the supplication of the *witr*." He did not mention the words: "I say them in the *witr*."

Abū Dāwūd said: The name of Abū al-Hawrā' is Rabī'ah b. Shaibān.

(1422) 'Alī b. Abī Ṭālib said: The Apostle of Allah (may peace be upon him) used to say at the end of his *witr*: "O Allah, I seek refuge in Thy good pleasure from Thy anger, and in Thy forgiveness from Thy punishment, and I seek refuge in Thy mercy from Thy wrath.[761] I cannot reckon the praise due to Thee. Thou art as Thou hast praised Thyself."

Abū Dāwūd said: Hishām is the earliest teacher of Ḥammād. Yaḥyā b. Ma'īn said: No one is reported to have narrated traditions from him except Ḥammād b. Salamah.

Abū Dāwūd said: Ubayy b. Ka'b said: The Apostle of Allah (may peace be upon him) recited supplication in the *witr* before bowing.

760. According to Abū Ḥanīfah, supplication in the third *rak'ah* of the *witr* prayer is necessary before bowing after the recitation of the Qur'ān. The rest of the jurists take it to be recommended (*sunnah*) in the third *rak'ah* of the *witr* prayer after bowing. It is, however, disputed whether the supplication should be recited before bowing or after it. The traditions narrated by al-Baihaqī indicate that the Prophet (may peace be upon him) used to recite supplication in the *witr* after bowing. This is also corroborated by the practice of the first four Caliphs. The traditions recorded by al-Nasā'ī indicate that he would recite supplications before bowing. But these traditions are said to be weak.

The supplication is also disputed. The traditions indicate that the Prophet (may peace be upon him) used to recite different supplications in the *witr* prayer on different occasions. Hence all the supplications reported are recommended to be recited in the *witr*. However, the most authentic tradition on the subject is the one narrated by al-Ḥasan b. 'Alī. The supplication contained in this tradition is followed by other jurists. Abū Ḥanīfah follows a different supplication known as *khal'* and *ḥafd* beginning from : "O Allah, we seek help from You."

The recitation of the supplication in the morning prayer is disputed. According to Mālik, al-Shāfi'ī, Aḥmad and Isḥāq, the supplication should be recited in the morning prayer in the second *rak'ah* after bowing. Abū Ḥanīfah maintains that the supplication should not be recited in the morning prayer except in time of danger or on occasions when some calamity befalls Muslims (*'Awn al-Ma'būd*, I, 536).

761. Literally, "in Thee from Thee"

Abū Dāwūd said: This tradition has also been narrated by 'Īsā b. Yūnus through a different chain of narrators from Ubayy b. Ka'b He also narrated it through a different chain of narrators on the authority of Ubayy b. Ka'b that the Apostle of Allah (may peace be upon him) recited the supplication in the *witr* before bowing.

Abū Dāwūd said: The chain of narrators of the tradition of Sa'īd from Qatādah goes: Yazīd b. Zurai' narrated from Sa'īd, from Qatādah, from 'Azrah, from Sa'īd b. 'Abd al-Raḥmān b. Abzā, on the authority of his father, from the Prophet (may peace be upon him). This version does not mention the supplication and the name of Ubayy. This tradition has also been narrated by 'Abd al-A'lā and Muḥammad b. Bishr al-'Abdī. He heard traditions from 'Īsā b. Yūnus at Kūfah. They did not mention the supplication in their version.

This tradition has also been narrated by Hishām al-Dastuwā'ī and Shu'bah from Qatādah. They did not mention the supplication in their version. The tradition of Zubaid has been narrated by Sulaimān al-A'mash, Shu'bah, 'Abd al-Mālik b. Abī Sulaimān, and Jarīr b. Ḥāzim; all of them narrated on the authority of Zubaid. None of them mention the supplication in his version, except in the tradition transmitted by Hafṣ b. Ghiyāth from Mis'ar from Zubaid; he narrated in his version that he (the Prophet) recited supplication before bowing.

Abū Dāwūd said: This version of tradition is not well known. There is a doubt that Ḥafṣ might have narrated this tradition from some other narrator than Mis'ar.

Abū Dāwūd said: It is reported that Ubayy (b. Ka'b) used to recite the supplication (in the *witr*) in the second half of Ramaḍān.[762]

(1423) Muḥammad reported on the authority of some of his teachers that Ubayy b. Ka'b led them in prayer during Ramaḍān. He used to recite the supplication (in the *witr*) during the second half of Ramaḍān.

(1424) Al-Ḥasan reported: 'Umar b al-Khaṭṭāb (may Allah be pleased with him) gathered the people (in *tarāwīḥ* prayer) behind Ubayy b. Ka'b (who led them). He used to lead them for twenty days (during Ramaḍān, and would not recite the supplication except in the second half of it (i.e. Ramaḍān). When the last ten days remained, he kept away from them, and prayed in his house. They used to say: Ubayy ran away.[763]

Abū Dāwūd said: This tradition shows that whatever has been reported about

762. This is also the view of al-Shāfi'ī and Aḥmad. Supplication is to be made in the *witr*, according to them, in the second half of Ramaḍān. Abū Ḥanīfah holds that this should be recited throughout the year.

763. Al-Ḥasan al-Baṣrī was born in 21 A.H. and 'Umar died in 24 A.H. Al-Ḥasan did not see 'Umar. Hence this tradition has a missing link between al-Hasan and 'Umar. Al-Nawawī says that this tradition is weak (*'Awn al-Ma'būd*, I, 538).

the recitation of the supplication is not tenable. Moreover, these two traditions from Ubayy b. Ka'b indicate that another tradition wh ch tells that the Prophet (may peace be upon him) recited the supplication in the *witr* is weak.

Chapter 492

SUPPLICATION AFTER THE *WITR* PRAYER

(1425) Ubayy b. Ka'b said: When the Apostle of Allah (may peace be upon him) offered salutation in the *witr* prayer, he said: Glory be to the king most holy.[764]

(1426) Abū Sa'īd reported the Apostle of Allah (may peace be upon him) as saying: If anyone oversleeps and misses the *witr*, or forgets it, he should pray when he remembers.[765]

Chapter 493

ON OBSERVING THE *WITR* BEFORE SLEEPING

(1427) Abū Hurairah said: My friend (i.e. the Prophet) instructed me to observe three practices that I do not leave while travelling nor while resident; to pray two *rak'ahs* in the forenoon, to fast three days every month and not to sleep but after observing the *witr*.[766]

(1428) Abū al-Dardā' said: My friend (i.e. the Prophet) instructed me to observe three practices which I never leave: he instructed me to fast three days every month, and not to sleep but after observing the *witr*, and to observe the supererogatory prayer in the forenoon while travelling and while resident.

(1429) Abū Qatādah said: The Prophet (may peace be upon him) asked Abū Bakr: When do you observe the *witr*? He said: I observe the *witr* prayer in the early hours of the night. He asked 'Umar: When do you observe the *witr*? He replied: At the end of the night. He then said to Abū Bakr: This has followed it with care; and he said

764. The version narrated by al-Nasā'ī indicates that he used to repeat it three times and raise his voice in the third time.

765. This tradition indicates that if one leaves the *witr* due to some excuse, he should pray it later on. It is disputed as to when one should pray it. A view goes that he should pray it before sunrise after the morning prayer. The third view says that one should pray after sunrise (*'Awn al-Ma'būd*, I, 539).

766. The Prophet (may peace be upon him) might have commanded him to observe the *witr* before going to sleep for he was not confident that he would awake before the morning prayer.

to 'Umar: He has followed it with strength.[767]

Chapter 494

ON THE TIME OF *WITR* PRAYER

(1430) Masrūq said: I asked 'Ā'ishah: When would the Apostle of Allah (may peace be upon him) observe the *witr* prayer? She replied: Any time he observed the *witr*, sometimes in the early hours of the night, sometimes at midnight and sometimes towards the end of it. But he used to observe the *witr* just before the dawn when he died.[768]

(1431) Ibn 'Umar reported the Prophet (may peace be upon him) as saying: Make haste to observe the *witr* prayer before morning.

(1432) 'Abd Allah b. Abū Qais said: I asked 'Ā'ishah about the *witr* observed by the Apostle of Allah (may peace be upon him). She replied: Sometimes he observed the *witr* prayer in the early hours of the night, sometimes he observed it at the end of it. I asked: How did he recite the Qur'ān? Did he recite the Qur'ān quietly or loudly? She replied: He did it in any way. Sometimes he recited quietly and sometimes loudly; sometimes he took a bath and then slept and sometimes he performed ablution and then slept.

Abū Dāwūd said: The narrators other than Qutaibah said: This refers to his bath due to sexual defilement.

(1433) Ibn 'Umar reported the Prophet (may peace be upon him) as saying: Make the last of your prayer at night a *witr*.[769]

Chapter 495

THE *WITR* PRAYER IS NOT TO BE REPEATED

(1434) Qais b. Ṭalq said: Ṭalq b. 'Alī visited us on a certain day during Ramaḍān. He remained with us till evening and broke fast with us. He then stood up and

767. It is better to observe the *witr* after the night prayer in the early hours of the night if a man is not confident to awake towards the end of the night. But if one can awake regularly towards the end of the night, he may observe the *witr* along with the *tahajjud* prayer in the end of the night.

768. The time of the *witr* is after the night prayer. But when the dawn breaks, there remains no time for observing *witr*. The commendable time for its observance is the end of the night.

769. The Prophet (may peace be upon him) sometimes prayed two *rak'ahs* sitting after the *witr*. This shows the permissibility of offering the supererogatory prayer after the *witr* prayer Some scholars think that if one observes the *witr* in the early hours of the night, one may offer two *rak'ahs* after it. In case a person observes the *witr* towards the end of the night, he may make the *witr* the last of his prayer.

led us in the *witr* prayer. He then went to his mosque and led them in prayer. When the *witr* remained, he put forward another man and said: Lead your companions in the *witr* prayer, for I heard the Apostle of Allah (may peace be upon him) as saying: There are no two *witrs* during one night.[770]

Chapter 496

ON RECITING SUPPLICATION[771] IN PRAYER

(1435) Abū Hurairah said: By Allah, I shall offer prayer like that of the Apostle of Allah (may peace be upon him). The narrator said: Abū Hurairah used to recite the supplication in the last *rak'ah* of the noon, night and dawn prayers. He would supplicate Allah for the believers and curse the unbelievers.

(1436) Al-Barā' said: The Prophet (may peace be upon him) used to recite the supplication in the dawn prayer [772] The version of Ibn Mu'ādh has the words: "sunset prayer"

(1437) Abū Hurairah said: The Apostle of Allah (may peace be upon him) recited the supplication in the night prayer for a month. He said (in his supplication): O Allah, rescue al-Walīd b. al-Walīd; rescue Salamah b. Hishām,[773] rescue the weak believers; O Allah, trample severely on Muḍar; O Allah, cause them a famine like that of Joseph.[774] Abū Hurairah said: One morning the Apostle of Allah (may peace be upon him) did not make supplication for them. So I told him about it. He said: You do not see that they have come (back).[775]

770. If a man observes the *witr* and then offers supererogatory prayer, he need not repeat the *witr* prayer. This tradition shows that one should not offer the *witr* prayer twice during one night. This is the view of the majority of the Companions and the scholars But al-Tirmidhī has narrated from a group of Companions that the *witr* prayer should be repeated at the end of the supererogatory prayers. This is held by Isḥāq (*'Awn al-Ma'būd*, I, 540).

771. The Arabic is *qunūt* which means being obedient. It is used of certain supplications in the *witr* or in other prayers.

772. Al-Nawawī says that it is commendable to recite the supplication in all prayers when some calamity befalls Muslims. According to al-Shāfi'ī the supplication should always be recited in the dawn prayer. Abū Ḥanīfah and Aḥmad maintain that there is no supplication in the dawn prayer except when some calamity befalls. Mālik holds that the supplication should be recited before bowing. The rest of the jurists are of view that it should be recited after bowing. Further, it is commendable to recite the supplication recited by the Prophet (may peace be upon him) as established by the traditions (*'Awn al-Ma'būd*, I, 540).

773. These were men who were detained by the unbelievers at Mecca. They were persecuted for their faith and held prisoners.

774. There was a severe famine in the time of Joseph. It lasted for seven years.

775. The Prophet (may peace be upon him) recited supplication only for one month and gave it up when they came back.

(1438) Ibn 'Abbās said: The Apostle of Allah (may peace be upon him) recited the supplication daily for a month at the noon, afternoon, sunset, night and morning prayers. When he said: "Allah listens to him who praises Him" in the last *rak'ah*, invoking a curse on some clans of Banū Sulaim, Ri'l, Dhakwān and 'Uṣayyah, and those who were standing behind him said: Amen.

(1439) Muḥammad reported: Anas b. Mālik was asked whether the Apostle of Allah (may peace be upon him) had recited supplication in the dawn prayer. He replied: Yes. He was again asked whether before bowing or after bowing. He said: After bowing.

The version of Musaddad adds the words: "For a short period."

(1440) Anas b. Mālik said: The Prophet (may peace be upon him) recited the supplication for a month (in prayer) and then gave it up.[776]

(1441) Muḥammad b. Sīrīn said that someone who prayed the morning prayer along with the Prophet (may peace be upon him) narrated to me: When he raised his head after the second *rak'ah*, he remained standing for a short while.[777]

Chapter 497

EXCELLENCE OF OFFERING SUPEREROGATORY PRAYER IN ONE'S HOUSE

(1442) Zaid b. Thābit said: The Apostle of Allah (may peace be upon him) built a chamber in the mosque. He used to come out at night and pray there. They (the people) also prayed along with him. They would come (to prayer) every night. If on any night the Apostle of Allah (may peace be upon him) did not come out, they would cough, raise their voices and throw pebbles and sand on his door. The Apostle of Allah (may peace be upon him) came out to them in anger and said: O people, you kept on doing this till I thought that it will be prescribed for you. Offer your prayers in your houses, for a man's prayer is better in his house except obligatory prayer.

(1443) Ibn 'Umar reported the Apostle of Allah (may peace be upon him) as saying: Offer some prayer in your houses; do not make them graves.[778]

776. This means that the Prophet (may peace be upon him) gave up invoking curse on the tribes mentioned in the aforesaid tradition. He also gave up reciting the supplication in all the prayers except morning prayer, as some other traditions indicate. Hence Mālik, al-Shāfi'ī and Aḥmad maintain that the supplication should be recited in the morning prayer and after bowing in the second *rak'ah*. According to Abū Ḥanīfah, there is no supplication in the dawn prayer (*'Awn al-Ma'būd* I, 542)

777. This shows that he recited the supplication in the morning prayer.

778. This shows that supererogatory prayers should be offered in the houses. In the lifetime of the Prophet (may peace be upon him) the Companions used to offer *Sunan* prayers in their houses.

Chapter 498

[ON STANDING FOR A LONG TIME IN PRAYER AT NIGHT]

(1444) 'Abd Allah b. Ḥabshī al-Khath'amī said : The Prophet (may peace be upon him) was asked : Which of the actions is better ? He replied : Standing for long time (in prayer).[779] He was again asked : Which alms is better? He replied : The alms given by a man possessing small property acquired by his labour.

Chapter 499

ENCOURAGEMENT TO GET UP DURING THE NIGHT

(1445) Abū Hurairah reported the Apostle of Allah (may peace be upon him) as saying: May Allah show mercy to a man who gets up during the night and prays, who wakens his wife and she prays; if she refuses, he sprinkles water on her face. May Allah show mercy to a woman who gets up during the night and prays, who wakens her husband and he prays; if he refuses she sprinkles water on his face.[780]

(1446) Abu Sa'īd and Abū Hurairah reported the Apostle of Allah (may peace be upon him) as saying: When a man himself wakes at night and wakens his wife and they pray two *rak'ahs* together, they are recorded among the men and women who make much mention of Allah.

Chapter 500

ON THE REWARD OF RECITING THE QUR'ĀN

(1447) 'Uthmān reported the Prophet (may peace be upon him) as saying: The best among you is he who learns and teaches the Qur'ān.[781]

(1448) Mu'ādh al-Juhanī reported the Apostle of Allah (may peace be upon him)

779. This refers to the prayer at night when a person has much time and he can recite the long *sūrahs* in *tahajjud* prayer. But it should be noted that the *imām* should not prolong the prayer by reciting long *sūrahs* or by lengthening bowing and prostration, for women, sick and needy people stand behind him.

780. The prayer at night (in midnight or in the last hours of night called *tahajjud* prayer) is the most excellent one after the obligatory prayers. This prayer was earlier obligatory on Muslims. As everyone could not offer it regularly, it was later on declared optional. Those who offer it are generally most pious people and get much reward. The supplication is accepted by Allah at this time. Hence the Prophet (may peace be upon him) exhorted people to offer it.

781. The Qur'ān is the Word of Allah. Those who learn or teach it have their link with Allah through this sacred Book. As this Divine Book contains the basic teachings of Islam, its dissemination makes a man distinguished among the people.

as saying: If anyone recites the Qur'ān and acts according to its contents, on the Day of Judgment his parents will be given to wear a crown whose light is better than the light of the sun in the dwellings of this world if it were among you. So what do you think of him who acts according to this?[782]

(1449) 'Ā'ishah reported the Prophet (may peace be upon him) as saying: One who is skilled in the Qur'ān is associated with the noble, upright recording angels,[783] and he who falters when he recites the Qur'ān and finds it difficult for him will have a double reward.[784]

(1450) Abū Hurairah reported the Prophet (may peace be upon him) as saying: No people get together in a house of the houses of Allah (i.e. a mosque), reciting the Book of Allah, and learning it together among themselves, but calmness[785] (*sakīnah*) comes down to them, (Divine) mercy covers them (from above), and the angels surround them, and Allah makes a mention of them among those who are with Him.[786]

(1451) 'Uqbah b. 'Āmir al-Juhanī said: When we were in the *Ṣuffah*, the Apostle of Allah (may peace be upon him) asked: Which of you would like to go out every morning to Buṭḥān or al-'Aqīq[787] and bring two large humped and fat she-camels without being guilty of sin and severing ties of relationship? They (the people) said: Apostle of Allah, we would all like that. He said: If one of you goes out in the morning to the mosque and learns two verses of the Book of Allah, the Exalted, it is better for him than two she-camels, and three verses are better for him than three she-camels, and so on than their numbers in camels.[788]

782. This shows the abundance of reward to the person who learns the Qur'ān and acts upon its teachings. His parents will be given to wear a crown because they stood as a means for providing facilities for their son to learn the Qur'ān.

783. Dexterity in the Qur'ān will raise the rank of a person on the Day of Judgment. Such a person will be associated with the angels of high rank due to his skill in and association with Divine revelation.

784. The reason of double reward is that, instead of his faltering in the recitation, he labours hard and recites, though he cannot recite it easily. He gets the double reward for his recitation and for his labour.

785. Literally, *sakīnah* means tranquillity and calmness. When one recites the Qur'ān, one feels calm and cool at heart and mind.

786. This may refer to angels.

787. The names of two valleys near Medina where camels were sold.

788. The utility and value of camels are shortlived and temporary, while the reward a person gets by reciting the Qur'ān is eternal. Hence recitation of a few verses of the Qur'ān is better than the costly camels.

Chapter 501

ON RECITING SŪRAH AL-FĀTIHAH

(1452) Abū Hurairah reported the Apostle of Allah (may peace be upon him) as saying: All praise be to Allah, the Lord of the Universe'' (Qur'ān, i.) is the epitome or basis of the Qur'ān, the epitome or basis of the Book, and the seven oft-repeated verses.[789]

(1453) Abū Sa'īd b. al-Mu'allā said that when he was praying the Prophet (may peace be upon him) passed by him and he called him. He said: I prayed and then I came to him. He asked: What prevented you from answering me? He replied: I was praying. He said: Has not Allah said: "O you who believe, respond to Allah and the Apostle when he calls you to that which gives you life?"[790] Let me teach you the greatest *sūrah* from the Qur'ān or in the Qur'ān (the narrator Khālid doubted) before I leave the mosque. I said: (I shall memorise) your saying. He said: It is: "Praise be to Allah, the Lord of the Universe,"[791] which is the seven oft-repeated verses, and the mighty Qur'ān.

Chapter 502

A VIEW THAT SŪRAH AL-FĀTIḤAH IS ONE OF THE LONG *SURAHS*

(1454) Ibn 'Abbās said· The Apostle of Allah (may peace be upon him) was given seven repeated long *surahs*,[792] while Moses was given six. When he threw the tablets, two of them were withdrawn and four remained.

Chapter 503

ON THE GREATNESS OF *ĀYAT AL-KURSI*[793] —THRONE VERSE

(1455) Ubayy b. Ka'b said: The Apostle of Allah (may peace be upon him) said:

789. Sūrah al-Fātiḥah is called *Umm al-Qur'ān* and *Umm al-Kitāb* (the epitome or basis of the Qur'ān or of the Book) because it contains in a nutshell all the themes discussed in the whole Qur'ān in detail. It is called *al-sab' al-mathānī* (the seven oft-repeated verses) for it is repeated in prayer or this *sūrah* was revealed twice, in Medina and Mecca.

790. Qur'ān, viii. 24

791. Qur'ān, i.

792. It is difficult to reckon Sūrah al-Fātiḥah from the seven long *sūrahs* of the Qur'ān. A tradition recorded by al-Nasā'ī contradicts it. The tradition is not clear.

793. By the greatness of the Throne verse is meant that it has more words in it as compared to other verses, or it ranks higher as it describes the greatness of Allah and His attributes.

Abū al-Mundhir,[794] which verse of Allah's Book that you have is greatest? I replied: Allah and His Apostle know best. He said: Abū al-Mundhir, which verse of Allah's Book that you have is greatest? I said: Allah, there is no god but He, the Living, the Eternal.[795] Thereupon he struck me on the breast and said: May knowledge be pleasant for you, Abū al-Mundhir.[796]

Chapter 504

ON SŪRAH AL-IKHLĀṢ[797]—UNITY OF ALLAH

(1456) Abū Sa'īd al-Khudrī said: A man heard another man reciting "Say, He is Allah, One."[798] He was repeating it. When the next morning came, he went to the Apostle of Allah (may peace be upon him) and mentioned that to him. The man took it (this *sūrah*) as a small one. The Prophet (may peace be upon him) said: By Him in Whose Hand is my life, it is equivalent to a third of the Qur'ān.[799]

Chapter 505

ON SŪRAH AL-FALAQ[800] AND SURAH AL-NĀS[801]

(1457) 'Uqbah b. 'Āmir said: I was driving the she-camel of the Apostle of Allah (may peace be upon him) during a journey. He said to me: 'Uqbah, should I not teach you two best *sūrahs* ever recited? He then taught me: "Say, I seek refuge in the Lord of the dawn," and "Say, I seek refuge in the Lord of men."[802] He did not see me much pleased (by these two *sūrahs*). When he alighted for prayer, he led the people in the morning prayer and recited them in prayer. When the Apostle of Allah (may peace be upon him) finished his prayer, he turned to me and said: O 'Uqbah, how did you see?[803]

(1458) 'Uqbah b. 'Āmir said: While I was travelling with the Apostle of Allah

794. *Kunyah* of Ubayy b. Ka'b.

795. Qur'ān, ii, 255.

796. This refers to the greatest reward that one gets by reciting this verse.

797. Qur'an, cxii.

798. Ibid.

799. The Qur'ān contains history, law and attributes of Allah. This *sūrah*, though small in words, contains the basic epithets of Allah. Or this means that by reciting this *sūrah* one gets the reward of reciting one-third of the Qur'ān.

800. Qur'ān, cxiii

801. Qur'ān, cxiv.

802. Sūrah al-Falaq and Sūrah al-Nas.

803. These are the most useful *sūrahs* to protect one from magic, evil eye and possession by the evil spirits.

(may peace be upon him) between al-Juḥfah[804] and al-Abwā',[805] a wind and intense darkness enveloped us, whereupon the Apostle of Allah (may peace be upon him) began to seek refuge in Allah, reciting: "I seek refuge in the Lord of the dawn," and "I seek refuge in the Lord of men." He then said: 'Uqbah, use them when seeking refuge in Allah, for no one can use anything to compare with them for the purpose. He said: I heard him reciting them when he led the people in prayer.

Chapter 506

ON THE DESIRABILITY OF RECITING THE QUR'ĀN CAREFULLY

(1459) 'Abd Allah b. 'Amr reported the Apostle of Allah (may peace be upon him) as saying: One who was devoted to the Qur'ān will be told to recite, ascend and recite carefully as he recited carefully when he was in the world, for he will reach his abode when he comes to the last verse he recites.[806]

(1460) Qatādah said: I asked Anas about the recitation of the Qur'ān by the Prophet (may peace be upon him). He said: He used to express all the long accents clearly.[807]

(1461) Ya'la b. Mumallak said that he asked Umm Salamah about the recitation and prayer of the Apostle of Allah (may peace be upon him). She said: What have you to do with his prayer? He would pray, then sleep as long as he had prayed, till morning. She then described his recitation and did so with an exposition word by word.[808]

(1462) 'Abd Allah b. Mughaffal said: On the day of the Conquest of Mecca I saw the Apostle of Allah (may peace be upon him) riding his she-camel reciting Sūrah al-Fatḥ repeating each verse several times.

(1463) Al-Barā' b. 'Āzib reported the Apostle of Allah (may peace be upon him) as saying: Beautify the Qur'ān with your voices.[809]

804. A village about eighty-two miles from Mecca. This is known as Rābigh in modern times.

805. A village between twenty and thirty miles nearer Medina than al-Juḥfah.

806. The other traditions indicate that the ranks or degrees of Paradise are equivalent to the number of the verses of the Qur'ān. Those who recite the complete Qur'ān will get the highest rank. Others will get the ranks according to the verses they memorised and could recite. This is the reward of the Qur'ān-readers, in particular of those who memorise the Qur'ān by heart.

807. It is necessary to recite the Qur'ān very clearly and carefully. All the long and short accents should be pronounced with care.

808. This shows that the Prophet (may peace be upon him) used to recite the Qur'ān so clearly that one could count the words and memorise them.

809. Al-Khaṭṭābī has said that the meaning of this tradition is reverse. This means: "Beautify your voices with the Qur'ān." This implies that one should keep one's tongue engaged in the recitation of the Qur'ān as much as possible (*'Awn al-Ma'būd*, I, 548).

(1464) Sa'd b. Abī Waqqāṣ reported: (The narrator Qutaibah said: This tradition has been narrated by Sa'īd b. Abī Sa'īd in my collection):[810] The Apostle of Allah (may peace be upon him) said: He who does not chant the Qur'ān is not one of us.[811]

(1465) This tradition has also been transmitted by Sa'd (b. Abī Waqqāṣ) from the Prophet (may peace be upon him) in a similar manner through a different chain of narrators.

(1466) 'Ubaid Allah b. Yazīd said: Abū Lubābah passed us and we followed him till he entered his house, and we also entered it. There was a man in a rusty house and in shabby condition. I heard him say: I heard the Apostle of Allah (may peace be upon him) say: He is not one of us who does not chant the Qur'ān. I (the narrator 'Abd al-Jabbār) said to Ibn Abū Mulaikah: Abū Muḥammad, what do you think if a person does not have pleasant voice? He said: He should recite with pleasant voice as much as possible.[812]

(1467) Wakī' and Ibn 'Uyainah said (explaining the meaning of *taghannī*): This means that the Qur'ān makes a man neglect all other things, and be content with it.

(1468) Abū Hurairah reported the Apostle of Allah (may peace be upon him) as saying: Allah has not listened to anything as He does to a prophet chanting the Qur'ān with a loud voice.[813]

Chapter 507

STRICTNESS ABOUT A PERSON WHO MEMORISES THE QUR'ĀN AND THEN FORGETS IT

(1469) Sa'd b. 'Ubādah reported the Apostle of Allah (may peace be upon him) as saying: No man recites [814] the Qur'ān, then forgets it, but will meet Allah on the

810. The narrator Yazīd and Qutaibah transmitted this tradition from Ibn Abī Mulaikah, from Sa'īd b. Abī Sa'īd from Sa'd b. Abī Waqqāṣ. The other (Abū al-Walīd) transmitted it from Ibn Abī Mulaikah from 'Ubād Allah b. Abī Nahīk from Sa'd b. Abī Waqqāṣ.

811. This tradition has been interpreted variantly. First, this means the recitation with pleasant sound giving careful consideration to the long and short accents; second, this means that after recitation of the Qur'ān one should neglect this world or recitation of poems; third, this means that, instead of enjoying any other music, one should recite the Qur'ān. In pre-Islamic days the Arabs used to sing in their meetings and while travelling. With the advent of Islam all this singing was replaced by the Qur'ān (*'Awn al-Ma'būd*, I, 548).

812. This shows that one should recite the Qur'ān in a pleasant tone as far as possible.

813. This is the fourth interpretation of *taghannī* which might also mean recitation of the Qur'ān loudly. The word *taghannī* has two roots, namely, *ghinā'* (chanting) and *ghanā'* (content). If it is taken to have been derived from the former, it means chanting and pleasant tone. In case it has been derived from the latter, it means content, i.e. that one neglects all sorts of music except the Qur'ān.

814. This might mean reading of the Qur'ān by looking at the codex, or memorising it or learn-

Day of Judgment in a maimed condition (or empty-handed, or with no excuse).[815]

Chapter 508

THE QUR'ĀN WAS SENT DOWN IN SEVEN MODES OF READING

(1470) 'Umar b. al-Khaṭṭāb said : I heard Hishām b. Ḥakīm (b. Ḥizām) reciting Sūrah al-Furqān[816] in a different manner from my way of reciting, and the Apostle of Allah (may peace be upon him) had taught me to recite it. I nearly spoke sharply to him, but I delayed till he had finished. Then I caught his cloak at the neck, and I brought him to the Apostle of Allah (may peace be upon him). I said : Apostle of Allah, I heard this man reciting Sūrah al-Furqān in a manner different from that in which you taught me to recite it. The Apostle of Allah (may peace be upon him) then told him to recite. He then recited in the manner I heard him recite. The Apostle of Allah (may peace be upon him) said : Thus was it sent down. He then said to me : Recite. I recited (it). He then said : Thus was it sent down. He said : The Qur'ān was sent down in seven modes of reading,[817] so recite according to what comes most easily.

(1471) Al-Zuhrī said : These modes of reading aimed at the same point, not differing in respect of lawful and unlawful.[818]

ing the meaning of the Qur'ān. In all these cases if one forgets the Qur'ān, one shall have to face this threat. One should not neglect the Qur'ān.

815. Literally, *ajdham* means a person whose hands have fallen off due to leprosy. Here this can be interpreted variantly.

This is a weak tradition. The narrator Yazīd b. Abī Ziyād is not reliable. Moreover, the narrator 'Īsā b. Fā'id did not hear directly from Sa'd b. 'Ubādah. There is a missing link in the chain. Hence the tradition is *munqaṭi'* (*'Awn al-Ma'būd*, I, 459).

816. Qur'ān, xxv.

817. There is a great difference of opinion amongst the scholars about the meaning of *ḥarf*. It is generally held that this refers to the seven dialects of the Arabs. These are : Ḥijāz, Hudhail, Yemen, Hawāzin, Ṭayy, Thaqīf and Banū Tamīm The different tribes of Arabs had their own dialects. Hence a word was pronounced in one way by one tribe, but the same word was pronounced in a different way by another. These different dialects were prevalent in Arabia, and it was not wrong to recite the Qur'ān in one's dialect. It is worthy of remark that "seven" does not refer to a definite number, but points to many dialects.

It is also said that seven *ḥarf* means seven modes of recitation as came down to us from the early generations through continuous chain. (*'Awn al-Ma'būd*, I, 550).

818. This means that the variance of the modes of reading does not change the legal value of an injunction. If one reading, for instance, makes an injunction lawful, another reading does not make it unlawful. The difference of dialect or that of mode of reading is minor and it does not affect the injunction. The injunction is not changed. Hence there is permission of reading a word in one way or the other.

(1472) Ubayy b. Ka'b reported: The Prophet (may peace be upon him) said: Ubayy, I was asked to recite the Qur'ān. I was asked: In one mode or two modes? The angel that accompanied me said: Say, in two modes, I said: In two modes, I was again asked: In two modes or three? The angel that was in my company said: Say, in three modes. So I said: In three modes. The matter reached up to seven modes. He then said: Each mode is sufficiently health-giving, whether you utter "all-hearing and all-knowing" or instead "all-powerful and all-wise". This is valid until you finish the verse indicating punishment on mercy and finish the verse indicating mercy on punishment.[819]

(1473) Ubayy b. Ka'b said: The Prophet (may peace be upon him) was present at the pool of Banū Ghifār, Gabriel came to him and said: Allah has commanded you to make your community read (the Qur'ān) in one mode. He (the Prophet) said: I beg Allah His pardon and forgiveness; my community has no strength to do so. He then came for the second time and told him the same thing till he reached up to seven modes. Finally, he said: Allah has commanded you to make your community read (the Qur'ān) in seven modes; in whichever mode they read, that will be correct.[820]

Chapter 509

SUPPLICATIONS

(1474) Al-Nu'mān b. Bashīr reported the Prophet (may peace be upon him) as saying: Supplication is worship.[821] (He then recited:) "And your Lord said: Call on Me, I will answer you" (xl. 60).

(1475) Ibn Sa'd said: My father (Sa'd b. Abī Waqqāṣ) heard me say: O Allah, I ask Thee for Paradise, its blessings, its pleasure and such-and-such, and such-and-such; I seek refuge in Thee from Hell, from its chains, from its collars, and from such-and-such, and from such-and-such. He said: I heard the Apostle of Allah (may

819. The Prophet (may peace be upon him) was allowed to make a minor change in the names of Allah at the end of the verses. But ordinary persons cannot be allowed to do so (*'Awn al-Ma'būd*, I, 551).

820. It is permissible to read the Qur'ān in any mode of the seven modes of reading agreed upon by the community. If one deviates from these seven approved modes, that will not be recognised as correct.

821. Another tradition goes: Supplication is pith of worship. Allah is almighty and mankind is weak and helpless. Worship indicates the omnipotence of Allah and submissiveness of man. At the end of worship, man begs Allah all his needs. Hence supplication is the pith of worship. The weakness of man is more reflected in his supplication to Allah We find that the whole life of the Prophet (may peace be upon him) was full of supplications to Allah. He taught a large number of supplications for different timings.

peace be upon him) say : There will be people who will exaggerate in supplication. You should not be one of them. If you are granted Paradise, you will be granted all what is good therein ; if you are protected from Hell, you will be protected from what is evil therein.[822]

(1476) Fuḍālah b. 'Ubaid, a Companion of the Apostle of Allah (may peace be upon him), said : The Apostle of Allah (may peace be upon him) heard a person supplicating during prayer. He did not mention the greatness of Allah, nor did he invoke blessings on the Prophet (may peace be upon him). The Apostle of Allah (may peace be upon him) said : He made haste. He then called him and said either to him or to any other person : If any of you prays, he should mention the exaltation of his Lord in the beginning and praise Him ; he should then invoke blessings on the Prophet (may peace be upon him) ; thereafter he should supplicate Allah for anything he wishes.[823]

(1477) 'Ā'ishah said : The Apostle of Allah (may peace be upon him) liked comprehensive supplications and abandoned other kinds.[824]

(1478) Abū Hurairah reported the Apostle of Allah (may peace be upon him) as saying : One of you should not say (in his supplication) : O Allah, forgive me if Thou wilt, show mercy to me if Thou wilt, but there is no one to impose compulsion on Him.[825]

(1479) Abū Hurairah reported the Apostle of Allah (may peace be upon him) as saying : One of you is granted an answer (to his supplication) provided he does not say : I prayed but I was not granted an answer.[826]

(1480) Ibn 'Abbās reported the Apostle of Allah (may peace be upon him) as saying : Do not cover the walls.[827] He who sees the letter of his brother without his

822. This means that one should ask for Paradise and seek refuge in Allah from Hell. This is sufficient.

823. As a formality one should praise Allah in the beginning and then invoke blessings on the Prophet (may peace be upon him) before supplication.

824. A comprehensive supplication is one which is concise in words, profound in meaning, covering the good of this world and of the Hereafter. It is difficult for a common man to compose such supplications. It is, therefore, better to recite supplications mentioned in the Qur'ān or in *Ḥadith*. There are a large number of supplications made by the Prophet (may peace be upon him) for different occasions. His supplications are concise and comprehensive.

825. Allah does all actions in accordance with His will. Hence it is futile to mention His will in supplication. Rather one should firmly believe, while one supplicates, that the supplication will be accepted by Him.

826. Man is to supplicate and Allah is to grant. Sometimes the answer is delayed and a man grows weary and begins to say : I prayed and prayed, but the answer has not been granted. Then he gives up supplication. In fact, Allah better knows whether the object one is demanding is beneficial for him or not. A tradition says that the supplication of a Muslim does not go waste. The answer is granted either in this world or in the Hereafter.

827. The Prophet (may peace be upon him) prohibited to cover the walls, for this is a sign of pride and vanity.

permission, sees Hell-fire.[828] Supplicate Allah with the palms of your hands; do not supplicate Him with their backs upwards. When you finish supplication, wipe your faces with them.[829]

Abū Dāwūd said: This tradition has been transmitted through different chains by Muḥammad b. Ka'b; all of them are weak. The chain I have narrated is best of them; but it is also weak.

(1481) Mālik b. Yasār al-Sakūnī, and then al-'Awfī, reported the Apostle of Allah (may peace be upon him) as saying: When you make requests to Allah, do so with the palms of your hands, and not backs, upwards.

Abū Dāwūd said: The narrator Sulaimān b. 'Abd al-Ḥamīd said: According to us Mālik b. Yasār was a Companion of the Prophet (may peace be upon him).

(1482) Anas b. Mālik said: I saw the Apostle of Allah (may peace be upon him) supplicating Allah in this manner with the palms of his hands and also with their backs upwards.[830]

(1483) Salmān reported the Apostle of Allah (may peace be upon him) as saying: Your Lord is munificent and generous, and is ashamed to turn away empty the hands of His servant when he raises them to Him.

(1484) 'Ikrimah quoted Ibn 'Abbās as saying: When asking for something you should raise your hands opposite to your shoulders; when asking for forgiveness you should point with one finger; and when making an earnest supplication you should spread out both your hands.

(1485) In another version Ibn 'Abbās said: Earnest supplication should be made thus: raising hands and putting their backs next to one's face.

(1486) The above-mentioned tradition has also been transmitted in a similar manner by Ibn 'Abbās from the Apostle of Allah (may peace be upon him).

(1487) Al-Sā'ib b. Yazīd reported on the authority of his father: When the Prophet (may peace be upon him) made supplication (to Allah) he would raise his hands and wipe his face with his hands.

(1488) Buraidah said: The Apostle of Allah (may peace be upon him) heard a man saying: O Allah, I ask Thee, I bear witness that there is no god but Thou, the One, He to Whom men repair, Who has not begotten, and has not been begotten, and to Whom no one is equal, and he said: You have supplicated Allah using His

828. This is a threat for one who reads the private letter of a person without his permission.

829. The recognised mode of supplication is to raise one's hands before one's face, keeping the inner side of the palms upwards and their backs downwards. After finishing the supplication one should wipe one's face with hands. This is commendable and *sunnah* of the Prophet (may peace be upon him).

830. Ordinarily, the Prophet (may peace be upon him) used to supplicate with the palms of his hands upwards. But when he prayed for rain he made the reverse, i.e. the backs of his hands upwards and the palms downwards.

Greatest Name,[831] when asked with this name He gives, and when supplicated by this name He answers.

(1489) The aforesaid tradition has also been transmitted through a different chain of narrators by Mālik b. Mighwal. This version adds : "He has asked Allah using His Greatest Name."

(1490) Anas reported that he was sitting with the Apostle of Allah (may peace be upon him) and a man was offering prayer. He then made supplication : O Allah, I ask Thee by virtue of the fact that praise is due to Thee, there is no deity but Thou, Who showest favour and beneficence, the Originator of the Heavens and the earth, O Lord of Majesty and Splendour, O Living One, O Eternal One. The Prophet (may peace be upon him) then said : He has supplicated Allah using His Greatest Name, when supplicated by this name, He answers, and when asked by this name He gives.

(1491) Asmā' daughter of Yazīd reported the Prophet (may peace be upon him) as saying : Allah's Greatest Name is in these two verses : "And your deity is one deity ; there is no deity but He, the Compassionate the Merciful,"[832] and the beginning of Sūrah Āl 'Imrān, "A.L.M. Allah, there is no deity but He, the Living, the Eternal."[833]

(1492) 'Aṭā' said : The quilt of 'Ā'ishah was stolen. She began to curse the person who had stolen it. The Prophet (may peace be upon him) began to tell her : Do not lighten him.[834]

Abū Dāwūd said : The meaning of the Arabic words *lā tasbikhī 'anhu* means "do

831. Some scholars are of opinion that all names of Allah are great. One is not greater than the other. In this tradition there is no comparison between His names. But this refers only to the greatness and grandeur of all His names.

Anothar group of scholars hold that there are certain particular names of Allah. When He is asked by them He gives and answers one's supplication. But there is a great difference of opinion about the Greatest Name of Allah. Different traditions of the Prophet (may peace be upon him) indicate different names. They are in the following Qur'ānic verses ;

(1) "And your deity is one deity, there is no deity but He, the Compassionate, the Merciful" (ii. 163).

(2) "A.L.M. Allah, there is no deity but He, the Living, the Eternal" (iii. 1).

(3) "There is no deity but Thee, to Whom be the glory. I was indeed a wrongdoer" (xxi. 87).

(4) "And faces shall be humbled before the Living, the Eternal" (xx. 111).

The name mentioned in this tradition is also said to be the Greatest Name. The name "Allah" is said to be the Greatest Name. There are many other opinions about this Name. But the most reliable and correct are those names which have been mentioned by the Prophet (may peace be upon him) in his traditions.

832. Qur'ān, ii. 163.

833. Qur'ān, iii. 1.

834. This means that if 'Ā'ishah went on cursing him, the sin and punishment of the criminal would be lessened or lightened.

not lessen him or lighten him".

(1493) 'Umar said : I sought permission from the Prophet (may peace be upon him) to perform *'Umrah.*[835] He gave me permission and said : My younger brother, do not forget me in your supplication. He ('Umar) said : He told me a word that pleased me so much so that I would not have been pleased if I were given the whole world.

The narrator Shu'bah said : I then met 'Āṣim at Medina. He narrated to me this tradition and reported the wordings: "My younger brother, share me in your supplication."[836]

(1494) Sa'Id b. AbI Waqqāṣ said : The Prophet (may peace be upon him) passed by me while I was supplicating by pointing with two fingers of mine. He said : Point with one finger; point with one finger. He then himself pointed with the fore-finger.[837]

Chapter 510

THE COUNTING OF PRAISE AND GLORIFICATION OF ALLAH ON PEBBLES

(1495) Sa'd b. AbI Waqqāṣ said that along with the Apostle of Allah (may peace be upon him), he once visited a woman in front of whom were some date-stones or pebbles[838] which she was using as a rosary to glorify Allah. He (the Prophet) said : I tell you something which would be easier (or more excellent)[839] for you than that. He said (it consisted of saying) "Glory be to Allah" as many times as the number of what He has created in the heaven ; "Glory be to Allah" as many times as the number of what He has created in the earth ; "Glory be to Allah" as many times as the number of what He has crtated between them ? "Glory be to Allah" as many times as the number of what He is creating ; "Allah is most great" a similar number of times ; "Praise (be to Allah)" a similar number of times ; "There is no god but Allah" a similar number of times ; "There is no might and no power except in Allah" a similar

835. 'Umar had taken a vow to perform *'Umrah* in pre-Islamic days. He went to Mecca to fulfil this vow. It should be noted that one can perform *'Umrah* at any time. There is no time fixed for its performance. The actions of *'Umrah* are *iḥram*, seven circuits around the Ka'bah and to run seven times between Ṣafā' and Marwah, the two hills at Minā.

836. By this the Prophet (may peace be upon him) intended to teach the Muslims that they should supplicate Allah for other Muslims too. They should not confine their supplications to themselves alone. The supplications made in particular moments and in sacred places should be made for all Muslims. The Prophet (may peace be upon him) did not need any supplication for him by 'Umar This was, however, a teaching for the community.

837. Pointing with a single finger refers to the unity of Allah.

838. The narrator doubted whether "date-stones" or "pebbles" was used.

839. The transmitter was not sure whether the word "easier" or "more excellent" was used.

number of times.[840]

(1496) Yusairah[841] said that the Prophet (may peace be upon him) commanded them (the women emigrants) to be regular (in remembering Allah by saying): "Allah is most great"; "Glory be to the King, the Holy"; "There is no god but Allah"; and that they should count them on fingers, for they (the fingers) will be questioned and asked to speak.[842]

(1497) 'Abd Allah b. 'Amr said: I saw the Apostle of Allah (may peace be upon him) counting the glorification of Allah on fingers.

Ibn Qudāmah said (in his version): "with his right hand".

(1498) Ibn 'Abbās said: The Apostle of Allah (may peace be upon him) went out from Juwairyīyah (wife of the Prophet). Earlier her name was Barrah, and he changed it. When he went out she was in her place of worship, and when he returned she was in her place of worship. He asked: Have you been in your place of worship continuously? She said: Yes. He then said: Since leaving you I have three times said four phrases which, if weighed against all of which you have said (during this period), would prove to be heavier. "Glory be to Allah", and I begin with praise of Him to the number of His creatures, in accordance with His good pleasure, to the weight of His throne and to the ink (extent) of his words.

(1499) Abū Hurairah reported: Abū Dharr said: Prophet of Allah, the wealthy persons have gone with all the rewards; they pray as we pray; they fast as we fast; and they have surplus wealth which they give in charity; but we have no wealth which we may give in charity. The Apostle of Allah (may peace be upon him) said: Abū Dharr, should I not teach you phrases by which you get the rank of those who excel you, and no one can get the rank of yours except one who acts like you. He said: Why not, Apostle of Allah? He said: Exalt Allah (say: Allah is most great) after each prayer thirty-three times; and praise Him (say, Praise be to Allah) thirty-three times; and glorify Him (say, Glory be to Allah) thirty-three times, and end it by saying, "There is no god but Allah alone, there is no partner, to Him belongs the Kingdom, to Him praise is due and He has power over everything", his sins will be forgiven, even if

840. The counting of date-stones or pebbles for the glorification of Allah is the origin of rosary in vogue in modern times. It is not correct to hold that the use of rosary is an innovation in religion (*bid'ah*) for the Companions used to count on pebbles or date-stones. The same purpose is also served by the rosary.

841. She was Umm Yāsir, a woman from the Helpers (*Anṣāriyāt*) or from the Emigrants (*Muhājirāt*). It is also said that her name was Usairah (*'Awn al-Ma'būd*, I, 556).

842. According to the Qur'ān, all the organs of a man will be questioned about their actions and will be asked to speak and give evidence. If a man counts the names or praise of Allah on fingers, they will bear witness on the Day of Judgment about this good action of glorifying on the fingers.

This also shows the validity of the use of rosary. It is reported that Abū Hurairah had a knotted thread with him and counted the names of Allah on its knots.

they are like the foam of the sea.

Chapter 511

WHAT A MAN SHOULD RECITE AFTER GIVING THE SALUTATION IN PRAYER

(1500) Al-Mughīrah b. Shu'bah reported: Mu'āwiyah wrote to al-Mughīrah b. Shu'bah: What would the Apostle of Allah (may peace be upon him) recite when he gave the salutation in the prayer? Al-Mughīrah dictated and wrote to Mu'āwiyah: The Apostle of Allah (may peace be upon him) used to say (at the end of the prayer after salutation): "There is no god but Allah, Alone, Who has no partner, to Him belongs the dominion, to Him praise is due, and He is Omnipotent. O Allah no one can withhold what Thou givest, or give what Thou withholdest, and riches cannot avail a wealthy person with Thee."

(1501) Abū al-Zubair said: I heard 'Abd Allah b. al-Zubair saying on the pulpit: When the Prophet (may peace be upon him) finished the prayer, he used to say (at the end of the prayer): "There is no god but Allah, Alone, Who has no partner; to Him belongs the Kingdom, to Him praise is due, and He is Omnipotent. There is no god but Allah to Whom we are sincere in devotion, even though the infidels should disapprove.[843] To Him belongs wealth, to Him belongs grace and to Him is worthy praise accorded. There is no god but Allah to Whom we are sincere in devotion, even though the infidels should disapprove."

(1502) Abū al-Zubair said: 'Abd Allah b. al-Zubair used to recite this supplication after each (prescribed) prayer. He then narrated a similar supplication and added to it: "There is no might and no power except in Allah; there is no god but Allah Whom alone we worship. To Him belongs wealth". The narrator then transmitted the rest of the tradition.

(1503) Zaid b. Arqam said: I heard the Apostle of Allah (may peace be upon him) say (the version of Sulaimān has): The Apostle of Allah (may peace be upon him) used to say after his prayer: "O Allah, our Lord and Lord of everything, I bear witness that Thou art the Lord alone Who hast no partner; O Allah, Our Lord and Lord of everything, I bear witness that Muḥammad is Thy servant and Thy apostle; O Allah, our Lord and Lord of everything, I bear witness that all the servants are brethren; O Allah, our Lord and Lord of everything, make me sincere to Thee, and my family too at every moment, in this world and in the world hereafter, O Possessor of glory and honour, listen to me and answer. Allah is incomparably great. O Allah, Light of the heavens and of the earth".

843. Both these phrases refer to the Qur'ānic verse, xl. 14.

The narrator Sulaimān b. Dāwūd said: "Lord of the heavens and of the earth, Allah is incomparably great. Allah is sufficient for me; and the excellent guardian is He; Allah is incomparably great.

(1504) 'Alī b. Abī Ṭālib said: When the Prophet (may peace be upon him) uttered the salutation at the end of the prayer, he used to say: "O Allah, forgive me my former and latter sins, what I have kept secret and what I have done openly, and what I have done extravagance; and what Thou knowest better than I do. Thou art the Advancer, the Delayer,[844] there is no god but Thou"

(1505) Ibn 'Abbās said: The Prophet (may peace be upon him) used to supplicate Allah: "My Lord, help me and do not give help against me; grant me victory, and do not grant victory over me; plan on my behalf and do not plan against me; guide me, and make my right guidance easy for me; grant me victory over those who act wrongfully towards me; O Allah, make me grateful to Thee, mindful of Thee, full of fear towards Thee, devoted to Thy obedience, humble before Thee, or penitent.[845] My Lord, accept my repentance, wash away my sin, answer my supplication, clearly establish my evidence, guide my heart, make true my tongue and draw out malice in my breast."

(1506) The aforesaid tradition has also been transmitted by 'Amr b. Murrah through a different chain of narrators to the same effect. This version adds: "And make right guidance easy for me." The narrator did not say: "my right guidance".

(1507) 'Ā'ishah (Allah be pleased with her) said: When the Prophet (may peace be upon him) uttered the salutation, he used to say: "O Allah, Thou art peace, and peace comes from Thee, Blessed art Thou, O Possessor of glory and honour".

Abū Dāwūd said: Sufyān heard eighteen traditious from 'Amr b. Murrah.

(1508) Thawbān, the client of the Apostle of Allah (may peace be upon him) said: When the Prophet (may peace be upon him) finished the prayer, he asked forgiveness three times and said: "O Allah. . . . " The narrator then narrated the tradition like that of 'Ā'ishah.[846]

Chapter 512

ON SEEKING PARDON AND REPENTANCE

(1509) Abū Bakr al-Ṣiddīq reported the Apostle of Allah (may peace be upon him)

844. Allah advances anyone He will and delays anyone He wills. There is none to question Him.

845. The narrator doubted which of these two words was used in the tradition.

846. The Prophet (may peace be upon him) used to sit for a short while at the end of the prescribed prayers and recite the supplications mentioned in this chapter. It is commendable to recite these supplications after prayers.

as saying: He who asks pardon is not a confirmed sinner, even if he returns to his sin seventy times a day.[847]

(1510) Al-Agharr al-Muzanī[848] said (Musaddad in his version of this tradition said that he was a Companion of the Prophet): The Apostle of Allah (may peace be upon him) said: My heart is invaded by unmindfulness, and I ask Allah's pardon a hundred times in the day.[844]

(1511) Ibn 'Umar said: We counted that the Apostle of Allah (may peace be upon him) would say a hundred times during a meeting: "My Lord, forgive me and pardon me; Thou art the Pardoning and Forgiving One".

(1512) Bilāl b. Yasār b. Zaid, the client of the Prophet (may peace be upon him), told on his father's authority that his grandfather said that he had heard the Prophet (may peace be upon him) say: If anyone says: "I ask pardon of Allah than Whom there is no deity, the Living, the Eternal, and I turn to Him in repentance," he will be pardoned, even if he has fled in time of battle.[850]

(1513) Ibn 'Abbās reported the Apostle of Allah (may peace be upon him) as saying: If anyone continually asks pardon, Allah will appoint for him a way out of every distress, and a relief from every anxiety, and will provide for him from where he did not reckon.[851]

(1514) Qatādah asked Anas: Which supplication would the Prophet (may peace be upon him) often make? He replied: The supplication he would usually recite was: "O Allah, give us in this world what is good and in the next what is good, and protect us from the punishment of Hell-fire".

The version of Ziyād adds: When Anas wished to supplicate, he uttered this supplication. When he uttered some other supplication, he combined it with this supplication.

847. If a man commits a sin continuously, it becomes major though it is minor in the beginning. Similarly, if a man commits major sin persistently without asking pardon and making repentance, he reaches near unbelief. It is, therefore, necessary to beg pardon of Allah after the commission of a sin, whether minor or major. If one commits a sin repeatedly, but repents sincerely each time, Allah forgives him and he is not recorded as a confirmed sinner.

848. He is sometimes called al-Juhanī instead of al-Muzanī. Moreover, it is to be noted that no tradition other than this has been recorded in the well-known six collections of Tradition (*'Awn al-Ma'būd*, I, 559).

849. This shows the human aspect of the Prophet (may peace be upon him). Sometimes he was engaged in worldly affair and sbecame slightly unmindful of Allah. He reckoned a slight unmindfulness too much for him and sought pardon of Allah. Moreover, by this he wanted to teach the Muslims to seek pardon abundantly.

850. When the infidels invade Muslims, it is necessary for every Muslim to fight them. It is a major sin to run away from the battlefield. But if a man utters this prayer, such a major sin will be forgiven by Allah, let alone minor sins.

851. This shows the significance of asking pardon of Allah constantly.

(1515) Suhail b. Ḥunaif reported on the authority of his father: The Apostle of Allah (may peace be upon him) said: If anyone asks Allah for martyrdom sincerely, Allah will make him reach the ranks of martyrs, though he may die on his bed.[852]

(1516) Asmā' b. al-Ḥakam said: I heard 'Alī (may Allah be pleased with him) say: I was a man; when I heard a tradition from the Apostle of Allah (may peace be upon him), Allah benefited me with it as much as He willed. But when some one of his Companions narrated a tradition to me I adjured him. When he took an oath, I testified him. Abū Bakr narrated to me a tradition, and Abū Bakr narrated truthfully. He said: I heard the Apostle of Allah (may peace be upon him) saying: When a servant (of Allah) commits a sin, and he performs ablution well, and then stands and prays two *rak'ahs*, and asks pardon of Allah, Allah pardons him. He then recited this verse: "And those who, when they commit indecency or wrong their souls, remember Allah" (iii. 134).

(1517) Mu'ādh b. Jabal reported that the Apostle of Allah (may peace be upon him) caught his hand and said: By Allah, I love you, Mu'ādh. I give some instruction to you. Never leave to recite this supplication after every (prescribed) prayer: "O Allah, help me in remembering Thee, in giving Thee thanks, and worshipping Thee well."

Mu'ādh willed this supplication to the narrator al-Ṣunābiḥī and al-Ṣunābiḥi to Abū 'Abd al-Raḥmān.

(1518) 'Uqbah b. 'Āmir said: The Apostle of Allah (may peace be upon him) commanded me to recite *mu'awwadhatain*[853] (the last two *sūrahs* of the Qur'ān) after every prayer.

(1519) 'Abd Allah (b. Mas'ūd) said: The Apostle of Allah (may peace be upon him) liked to supplicate three times and to ask pardon (of Allah) three times.

(1520) Asmā' daughter of 'Umais said: The Apostle of Allah (may peace be upon him) said to me: May I not teach you phrases which you utter in distress? (These are:) "Allah, Allah is my Lord, I do not associate anything as partner with Him."

Abū Dāwūd said: The narrator Hilāl is a client of 'Umar b. 'Abd al-'Azīz. The name of Ibn Ja'far, a narrator, is 'Abd Allah b. Ja'far.

(1521) Abū Mūsā al-Ash'arī said: Once we accompanied the Apostle of Allah (may peace be upon him) on a journey. When we reached near Medina, the people began to say aloud: "Allah is most great," and they raised their voice. The Apostle of Allah (may peace be upon him) said: O people, you are not supplicating one who

852. This shows the significance and excellence of supplication to Allah and sincerity of heart. A man is granted the reward of an action on account of his supplication and prayer and longing, though he does not do it actually. One who supplicates Allah and asks Him for martyrdom, one is granted the reward of martyrs.

853. Qur'ān, cxiii., cxiv.

is deaf and absent, but you are supplicating One Who is nearer to you than the neck of your riding beast.[854] The Apostle of Allah (may peace be upon him) then said: Abū Mūsā, should I not point out to you one of the treasures of Paradise? I asked: What is that? He replied: "There is no might and there is no power except in Allah"

(1522) Abū Mūsā al-Asha'rī said: They (the Companions) accompanied the Prophet (may peace be upon him) while they were climbing the turning of a hill. A man uttered loudly: "There is no god but Allah, and Allah is most great," when he ascended the hill. The Prophet of Allah (may peace be upon him) said: You are not supplicating one who is deaf or absent. He then said: 'Abd Allah b. Qais.[855] The narrator then transmitted the tradition to the same effect.

(1523) The aforesaid tradition has also been transmitted by Abū Mūsā al-Ash'arī through a different chain of narrators. This version adds: Be lenient to yourselves, O people.

(1524) Abū Sa'īd al-Khudrī reported the Apostle of Allah (may peace be upon him) as saying: If anyone says "I am pleased with Allah as Lord, with Islam as religion and with Muḥammad (may peace be upon him) as Apostle," Paradise will be his due.

(1525) Abū Hurairah reported the Apostle of Allah (may peace be upon him) as saying: If anyone invokes blessing on me once, Allah will bless him ten times.[856]

(1526) Aws b. Aws reported the Apostle of Allah (may peace be upon him) as saying: Among the most excellent of your days is Friday; so invoke many blessings on me on that day, for your blessing will be submitted to me. They (the Companions) asked: Apostle of Allah, how can our blessing be submitted to you, when your body is decayed? He said: Allah has prohibited the earth from consuming the bodies of the Prophets.[857]

Chapter 513

PROHIBITION OF CURSING ONE'S FAMILY AND PROPERTY

(1527) Jābir b. 'Abd Allah reported the Apostle of Allah (may peace be upon him) as saying: Do not invoke curse on yourselves, and do not invoke curse on your

854. Literally, "between you and the neck of your beast".

855. This is Abū Mūsā's name and his father's name.

856. This shows the excellence of invoking blessing on the Prophet (may peace be upon him).

857. This shows that the bodies of the Prophets are not decayed in their graves. The Prophets remain alive after their death, but this life of theirs is entirely different from the life in this world. One cannot understand the nature of this life bestowed by Allah on the Prophets.

children, and do not invoke curse on your servants, and do not invoke curse on your property, lest you happen to do it at a time when Allah is asked for something and grants your request.[858]

Chapter 514

ON THE INVOKING OF BLESSING ON A PERSON OTHER THAN THE PROPHET (MAY PEACE BE UPON HIM)

(1528) Jābir b. 'Abd Allah said: A woman said to the Prophet (may peace be upon him): Invoke blessing on me as well as on my husband. The Prophet (may peace be upon him) said: May Allah send blessing on you and your husband.[859]

Chapter 515

SUPPLICATION OF A MUSLIM FOR HIS ABSENT BROTHER

(1529) Abū al-Dardā' said: I heard the Apostle of Allah (may peace be upon him) say: When a Muslim supplicates for his absent brother the angels say: *Āmīn*, and may you receive the like.[860]

(1530) 'Abd Allah b. 'Amr b. al-'Āṣ reported the Apostle of Allah (may peace be upon him) as saying: The supplication which gets the quickest answer is that made by one distant Muslim for another.

(1531) Abū Hurairah reported the Apostle of Allah (may peace be upon him) as saying: Three supplications are answered, there being no doubt about them; that of a father, that of a traveller, and that of one who has been wronged.[861]

858. This shows that invoking curse on anything is not appreciable. One is not aware of the moment when Allah grants one's requests Hence the Prophet (may peace be upon him) prohibited to invoke curse at any moment. He rather exhorted to ask Allah for health, security and peace at all moments.

859. It is disputed amongst the scholars whether invoking blessing on a person other than the Prophet (may peace be upon him) is permissible. According to some, it is permissible unconditionally. Another view goes that it is permissible only for a prophet and not for others. A third view says that one can invoke blessing on others along with the Prophet (may peace be upon him) and not separately. A fourth view says that it is not permissible at all.

860. This shows the significance of a Muslim's supplication for his absent brother. Hence the Prophet exhorted Muslims to supplicate for others.

861. It is not necessary that a person oppressed or wronged is a pious Muslim. He may be a profligate or rather unbeliever.

Chapter 516

WHAT IS SAID WHEN ONE FEARS THE PEOPLE

(1532) Abū Burdah b. 'Abd Allah reported on the authority of his father: When the Prophet (may peace be upon him) feared the people, he would say: "O Allah, we make Thee our shield[862] against them, and take refuge in Thee from their evils."

Chapter 517

SEEKING WHAT IS GOOD FROM ALLAH —*ISTIKHĀRAH*[863]

(1533) Jābir b. 'Abd Allah said: The Apostle of Allah (may peace be upon him) used to teach us the supplication for *istikhārah* (seeking what is beneficial from Allah) as he would teach us a *sūrah* (chapter) from the Qur'ān. He would tell us: When one of you intends to do a work, he should offer two supererogatory *rak'ahs* of prayer, and then say (at the end of the prayer): "O Allah, I seek what is good from Thee by Thy knowledge, and I seek power from Thee by Thy power, and I ask Thee for Thy vast grace, for Thou hast power, and I have no power, and Thou knowest and I do not know, and Thou best knowest the unseen. O Allah, if Thou knowest that this work (one should name the work one is intending to do) is good for me, for my religion and for my livelihood, for my next world, and for the consequence of this work of mine, then appoint it for me, make easy for me, and give blessing to me in it. O Allah, if Thou knowest that it is evil for me and for all those things mentioned formerly, then turn me away from it, and turn it away from me, and appoint for me what is good, wherever it is, and make me pleased with it." A version goes: "If the work is good immediately or subsequently."

Ibn Maslamah and Ibn 'Īsā reported from Muḥammad b. al-Munkadir on the authority of Jābir.

862. Literally, "we make Thee in their necks"

863. A man does not know what will be the result of a work he is intending to do, and whether it will be beneficial or harmful for him. Therefore the Prophet (may peace be upon him) taught Muslims to recite a supplication before starting any work, e.g. journey, service, marriage, etc., and seek help from Allah in its achievement. After reciting this supplication as indicated in the tradition, one should start one's work intending to do it. If that work is beneficial for him, Allah will help him ; in case it is harmful, Allah will create such causes as will prevent him from doing that work.

Chapter 518

SEEKING REFUGE IN ALLAH

(1534) 'Umar b. al-Khaṭṭāb said: The Prophet (may peace be upon him) used to seek refuge in Allah from five things; cowardliness, niggardliness, the evils of old age,[864] evil thoughts,[865] and punishment in the grave.

(1535) Anas b. Mālik said: The Apostle of Allah (may peace be upon him) used to say: "O Allah, I seek refuge in Thee from incapacity, slackness, cowardliness, niggardliness, decreptitude; and I seek refuge in Thee from the punishment in the grave; and I seek refuge in Thee from the trial of life and death."

(1536) Anas b. Mālik said: I used to serve the Prophet (may peace be upon him) and often hear him say: "O Allah, I seek refuge in Thee from care, grief, burden of debt and being overpowered by men." The narrator then narrated some more things which the narrator al-Taimī (in the previous tradition) reported.

(1537) 'Abd Allah b. 'Abbās said: The Apostle of Allah (may peace be upon him) used to teach us this supplication as he taught us the *sūrah* from the Qur'ān. He would say: "O Allah, I seek refuge in Thee from the punishment in Hell, I seek refuge in Thee from the punishment in the grave, I seek refuge in Thee from the testing of the Antichrist,[866] and I seek refuge in Thee from the trial of life and death."[867]

(1538) 'Ā'ishah said: The Prophet (may peace be upon him) used to supplicate with these words: "O Allah, I seek refuge in Thee from the trial of Hell-fire, from the punishment in the Hell-fire, and from the evil of riches and poverty."[868]

864. This means that a man becomes too old that he loses his common sense, incapable of doing any work. In such an advanced age a man becomes burden on others. Hence the Prophet (may peace be upon him) sought refuge from such an age in Allah.

865. Literally, trial of the breast (*fitanat al-ṣadr*). According to the commentators, this means either death without repentance, or merely spiritual death, or this means malice, grudge and immortality (*'Awn al-Ma'būd*, I, 565).

866. This refers to the false Christ (Dajjāl) who will appear in the last days. Muslims will be put to a severe test by the appearance of the Antichrist. He will call to disbelief by temptation. Hence the Prophet (may peace be upon him) sought refuge in Allah from his trial.

867. Riches and opulence are the trial of life. Allah gives man wealth and property to test him whether he obeys Him or not. The trial of death is its agony. One cannot conceive of the pain one feels at the time of death.

868. We should not be unmindful of Allah if He gives us riches, nor should We disobey Him, or be ungrateful to Him if we are poor. In all circumstances Allah wants man to obey His commandments, and to be thankful if he is rich, and show patience and content if he is poor. Riches and poverty are meant for trial of man. They do not count in the eyes of Allah ; what counts is His obedience.

(1539) Abū Hurairah said that the Prophet (may peace be upon him) used to say: "O Allah, I seek refuge in Thee from poverty",[869] lack[870] and abasement, and I seek refuge in Thee lest I cause or suffer wrong."

(1540) 'Abd Allah b. 'Umar said that one of the supplications of the Apostle of Allah (may peace be upon him) was: "O Allah, I seek refuge in Thee from the decline of Thy favour, change in Thy granting well-being, sudden vengeance from Thee, and all Thy displeasure."

(1541) Abū Hurairah said: The Apostle of Allah (may peace be upon him) used to supplicate by saying: "O Allah, I seek refuge in Thee from divisiveness,[871] hypocrisy, and evil character."

(1542) Abū Hurairah said: The Apostle of Allah (may peace be upon him) used to say: "O Allah, I seek refuge in Thee from hunger,[872] for it is an evil bed-fellow; and I seek refuge in Thee from treachery,[873] for it is an evil hidden trait."

(1543) Abū Hurairah said: The Apostle of Allah (may peace be upon him) used to say: "O Allah, I seek refuge in Thee from four things: Knowledge which does not profit, a heart which is not submissive, a soul which has an insatiable appetite, and a supplication which is not heard."

(1544) Anas b. Mālik said: The Prophet (may peace be upon him) used to say: "O Allah, I seek refuge in Thee from a prayer which does not profit." He also mentioned another supplication.

(1545) Farwah b. Nawfal al-Ashja'ī said: I asked 'Ā'ishah, mother of the believers: What did the Apostle of Allah (may peace be upon him) supplicate? She replied: He used to say: "O Allah, I seek refuge in Thee from the evil of what I have done, and from the evil of what I have not done."

(1546) Shutair b. Shakl (b. Ḥumaid) said: I said: Apostle of Allah, teach me a supplication. He said: Say: "O Allah, I seek refuge in Thee from the evil of what I hear, from the evil of what I see, from the evil of what I speak, from the evil of what

869. Some traditions indicate that the Prophet (may peace be upon him) asked for poverty, but some other traditions show that he sought refuge in Allah from poverty. The poverty in which a man has a generous heart, though he lacks property, and he has no temptation for riches, but remains contented with the property given to him, is appreciated. But the poverty in which a man becomes discontented and which embraces his temptation of wealth is condemned.

870. This refers to the lack of virtues to the lack of wealth.

871. This means the opposition of truth. If a man considers a thing to be true, he should not oppose it, but accept it.

872. Hunger makes a man weak and incapable of worshipping Allah and of doing any service to Him. One cannot maintain peace of mind while one feels hungry.

873. Treachery is opposite of honesty. Honesty is a root virtue and treachery is a trait of character which impels a man to do all kinds of evil. It is more serious, for one cannot feel it easily as it is a latent quality (*'Awn al-Ma'būd*, I, 567).

I think, and from the evil of my semen" (i.e. sexual passion).[874]

(1547) Abū al-Yusr said : The Apostle of Allah (may peace be upon him) used to supplicate : "O Allah, I seek refuge in Thee from my house falling on me, I seek refuge in Thee from falling into an abyss, I seek refuge in Thee from drowning, burning and decrepitude. I seek refuge in Thee from the devil harming me at the time of my death, I seek refuge in Thee from dying in Thy path while retreating, and I seek refuge in Thee from dying of the sting of a poisonous creature."

(1548) The aforesaid tradition has also been transmitted by Abū al-Yusr through a different chain of narrators. This version adds : "and from sorrow".

(1549) Anas said : The Prophet (may peace be upon him) used to say : "O Allah, I seek refuge in Thee from leprosy, madness, elephantiasis, and evil diseases."

(1550) Abū Sa'īd al-Khudrī said : One day the Apostle of Allah (may peace be upon him) entered the mosque. He saw there a man from the *Anṣār* called Abū Umāmah. He said : What is the matter that I am seeing you sitting in the mosque when there is no time of prayer ? He said : I am entangled in cares and debts, Apostle or Allah. He replied : Shall I not teach you words by which, when you say them, Allah will remove your care, and settle your debt ? He said : Why not, Apostle of Allah ? He said : Say in the morning and evening : "O Allah, I seek refuge in Thee from care and grief, I seek refuge in Thee from incapacity and slackness, I seek refuge in Thee from cowardice and niggardliness, and I seek refuge in Thee from being overcome by debt and being put in subjection by men." He said : When I did that Allah removed my care and settled my debt.[875]

874. This is the most comprehensive supplication in which the Prophet (may peace be upon him) sought refuge in Allah from all sorts of evil possibly found in man. The evil of the ear means hearing forbidden things such as backbiting, falsehood and music. The evil of the eye refers to looking at a woman with evil passions, and to seeing the prohibited game and play. The evil of the tongue is to tell a lie, to backbite, and to abuse others. The evil of the heart covers all sorts of immoral qualities such as grudge, pride, hypocrisy and niggardliness. The evil of the semen means unlawful intercourse and sodomy.

875. Man is sometimes overcome by debt and entangled in cares and sorrows. He remains grieved all the time and finds no way out of it. The Prophet (may peace be upon him) taught him such a brief and comprehensive supplication by which Allah removes all his cares and settles his debts. A Muslim should memorise this supplication as well as all other supplications taught by the Prophet (may peace be upon him) and recite them at various times.